"This edition of *Sex Crimes: Research and* current body of sex offender and offending of undergraduate or graduate students, pract the contrasts between what is believed to be true about sex offending and what empirical data reveal. The addition of a discussion regarding the nuanced approach taken when investigating sex crimes and interacting with victims is one that is needed and not often found in other texts. I highly recommend this book to anyone teaching courses on sex offenders or offending, conducting research on this topic, and/or working with policy makers to examine and refine our sex offender management tools and laws."

Lisa L. Sample, PhD, *University of Nebraska at Omaha, School of Criminology and Criminal Justice*

"In the updated second edition, Vandiver and Braithwaite provide an engaging, theoretically-anchored, and research-driven exploration of the essential questions pertaining to sexual violence. This book engages readers with both the current state of knowledge about sex crimes and the central questions that remain unanswered, and it does so with rigor and compassion."

Ryan T. Shields, PhD, *University of Massachusetts Lowell, School of Criminology and Justice Studies*

Sex Crimes

Sex Crimes: Research and Realities, 2nd edition, provides succinct overviews and details of the research regarding sex crimes and the persons who commit them, dispelling common myths related to sex crimes that have been contradicted in the scientific literature in recent decades. Throughout the book, survivors of sexual violence are highlighted, including those who have engaged in activism leading to positive changes for victims of sexual violence or came forward with their stories of sexual victimization despite being told "nothing can be done."

The book begins with a broad overview of the number and types of sex crimes that occur annually, then outlines several theories developed to explain sex crimes specifically, along with descriptions of popular criminological theories that have been applied to persons who have committed a sex crime. The next several chapters provide details regarding different types of sex crimes. Subsequently, the authors provide an overview of juveniles and females who commit sex crimes, and of sex crimes that occur within an institution, such as college campuses and sports or youth organizations. New to this edition is a chapter that focuses on victims of sex crimes and the victimology of sexual violence. Attention is given to the nuances of investigating sex crimes and policies (such as registration and civil commitment laws) affecting persons who have committed a sex crime. The conclusion provides an overview of the myths regarding sex crimes and the persons who commit them, again with a summary of what research has unveiled while highlighting areas of recommended future research.

This book is suitable for an undergraduate or graduate-level course for a variety of social science fields. It is invaluable for treatment providers, law enforcement officers, detectives, or policy makers.

Donna Vandiver, PhD, is a Professor at Texas State University. Her research is strongly centered on sex crimes and the persons who commit them. She has co-authored nearly two dozen articles on the topic, and co-authored a book on juveniles who have committed a sex crime. Her research informed the development of a widely used typology of women who have committed sex crimes. She has also co-authored a longitudinal assessment of recidivism among a large sample of women who had committed a sex crime and engaged in collaborative efforts regarding the effects of sex offender registration laws on juveniles who had committed a sex crime.

Jeremy Braithwaite, PhD, is a Tribal Research Specialist at the Tribal Law and Policy Institute and the owner/co-founder of EvaluACT, a research and evaluation consulting business in Los Angeles. His research focuses on violence against women, particularly the sexual victimization of American Indian/Alaska Native women. He is currently the Principal Investigator of multiple National Institute of Justice grant projects focused on crime and justice issues in Indian Country.

Sex Crimes
Research and Realities

SECOND EDITION

Donna Vandiver
Jeremy Braithwaite

NEW YORK AND LONDON

Second edition published 2022
by Routledge
605 Third Avenue, New York, NY 10158

and by Routledge
4 Park Square, Milton Park, Abingdon, Oxon, OX14 4RN

Routledge is an imprint of the Taylor & Francis Group, an informa business

© 2022 Taylor & Francis

The right of Donna Vandiver and Jeremy Braithwaite to be identified as authors of this work has been asserted in accordance with sections 77 and 78 of the Copyright, Designs and Patents Act 1988.

All rights reserved. No part of this book may be reprinted or reproduced or utilised in any form or by any electronic, mechanical, or other means, now known or hereafter invented, including photocopying and recording, or in any information storage or retrieval system, without permission in writing from the publishers.

Trademark notice: Product or corporate names may be trademarks or registered trademarks, and are used only for identification and explanation without intent to infringe.

First edition published by Routledge 2016

Library of Congress Cataloging-in-Publication Data
A catalog record has been requested for this book

ISBN: 978-0-367-46839-2 (hbk)
ISBN: 978-0-367-45760-0 (pbk)
ISBN: 978-1-003-03144-4 (ebk)

DOI: 10.4324/9781003031444

Typeset in Bembo and Futura
by codeMantra

Access the Support Material: www.routledge.com/9780367457600

Dedicated to the survivors of sexual violence who have found the courage to come forward and to those who are still finding their voice.

Contents

Preface   *xiii*

1   Introduction   1

Moral Panic   2
Defining a Sex Crime   2
Sources and Numbers of Sex Crimes and Offenders   3
A Brief History of Research on Sex Crimes   10
State of Current Research on Sex Crimes   10
Once a "Sex Offender," Always a "Sex Offender"   13
Addressing Sex-Crime Myths   14

2   Theories about Sex Crimes and Persons Who Commit Sex Crimes   21

Essential Components of a Theory   21
Probabilistic Nature of Theories   23
Biological Theories   23
Psychological Theories   25
Sex-Crime-Specific Theories   30
Criminological Theories   34
Common Causes Identified to Explain Sexually Offending   39
Conclusion   40

3   Rape and Sexual Assault   49

Myths about Rape   50
Rape Culture   52
Rape Law in the United States   57
Why Do People Rape?   60
Rape Typologies   63
Criminal Justice Response to Rape   66
Conclusion   70

x Contents

4 Child Sexual Abuse   80

    Myths about Child Sexual Abuse   81
    Historical Trends in Child Sexual-Abuse Laws, Policies, and
        Societal Responses   85
    Child Sexual Abuse Typologies   88
    Grooming   92
    Criminal Justice Response to Child Sexual Abuse   94
    Conclusion   99

5 Child Pornography and Sex Trafficking   107

    Myths about Child Pornography   108
    Defining Child Pornography   110
    The History of Child Pornography Law   111
    Child Pornography Offenders   117
    Criminal Justice Responses to Child Pornography Crimes   123
    Sex Trafficking   128
    Conclusion   133

6 Juveniles and Women Who Have Committed a Sex Crime   140

    Number of Sex Crimes Committed by Juveniles and Girls/Women   140
    Common Characteristics of Juveniles Who Have Committed a Sex Crime
        (JSCs)   141
    Juveniles Who Have Committed a Sex Crime (JSCs) Compared to Juvenile
        (Nonsexual) Offenders   145
    Distinctions and Typologies of Juveniles Who Have Committed a Sex crime
        (JSCs)   145
    Explanations of Juveniles Committing Sex Crimes (JSCs)   146
    Assessment of Juveniles Who Have Committed a Sex Crime (JSCs)   149
    Treatment for Juveniles Who Have Committed a Sex Crime (JSCs)   149
    Recidivism Among Juveniles Who Have Committed a Sex Crime (JSCs)   152
    Women Who Have Committed a Sex Crime (WSC)   153
    Characteristics of Women Who Have Committed a Sex Crime (WSC)   153
    Women Who Have Committed a Sex Crime (WSC) Compared to Men Who Have
        Committed a Sex Crime   155
    Distinctions and Typologies of Women Who Have Committed a Sex Crime
        (WSC)   155
    Explanations of Women Who Have Committed a Sex Crime (WSC)   160
    Assessment of Women Who Have Committed a Sex Crime (WSC)   161
    Treatment for Women Who Have Committed a Sex Crime (WSC)   162
    Recidivism of Women Who Have Committed a Sex Crime (WSC)   163
    Conclusion   164

7 Institutional Abuse   176

   Institutional Abuse Characteristics 177
   Sexual Assault within Institutions 185
   *Organizations Facing Both Child Sexual Abuse and Sexual Assault
      Allegations 188*
   *Suggestions for Policies and Procedures to Respond
      to Institutional Abuse 193*
   Conclusion 195

8 The Victimology of Sexual Violence   203

   Victimology and Early Theories of Victimization 204
   Victims of Sexual Violence 205
   Special Populations 206
   Victim Responses to Sexual Violence 210
   False Allegations of Sexual Violence 217
   Sexual Violence Victim Advocacy 220

9 Investigations of Sex Crimes   234

   Failure to Report a Sex Crime 235
   Crime-Scene Profiling and Crime-Scene Basics 235
   Paraphilias and Fantasies 237
   First Responders 239
   Medical Examinations of Rape Victims 240
   Medical Exams of Child Victims 241
   *Interviewing Victims, Suspected Offenders, and Witnesses: The Phased
      Approach 243*
   Sex Crimes with Unique Investigational Obstacles 247
   Common Investigational Failures 250
   Conclusion 252

10 Assessment Tools and Treatment Issues Related to Sex Crimes   261

   Obstacles in Accessing Treatment for Victims of Sex Crimes 261
   *Empirically-Based Approaches of Assessing and Treating Persons Who Have
      Committed a Sex Crime 262*
   Overview of Assessments 264
   Sex-Offender Assessment Tools 266
   Effectiveness of Sex-Offender Assessment Tools 273
   Psychopathy 273
   Treatment of Persons Who Have Committed a Sex Crime 275
   Treatment Effectiveness 282
   Conclusion 283

11 Registration Laws and Civil Commitment of Persons Who Have Committed a Sex Crime — 293

Perceptions of People Who Commit Sex Offenses 294
Sex-Offender Registration and Notification Laws 295
Assumptions of Sex-Offender Registration and Notification Laws 306
Effects of Sex-Offender Registration and Notification Laws 307
Additional Requirements for Registered Sex Offenders (RSOs) 308
Civil Commitment Laws for Sexually Violent Predators 310
State-Level Laws: Erin's Law 313
Conclusion 314

12 Conclusion — 320

Bringing It All Together: All Persons Who Have Committed a Sex Offense Are (Not) the Same 320
Myths Regarding the Number of Sex Crimes, Persons Who Commit a Sex Crime, and Associated Trends 321
Myths Regarding Why Persons Commit Sex Crimes 321
Myths Regarding Rapists, Rape, and Rape Victims 322
Myths Regarding Child Sexual Abuse, Child Molestation, and Child Victims 323
Myths Regarding Child Pornography and Sex Trafficking 323
Myths Regarding Juveniles and Women Who Have Committed a Sex Crime 325
Myths Regarding Institutional Abuse 326
Myths Regarding Victims of Sex Crimes 326
Myths Regarding Investigating Abuse 327
Myths Regarding Assessment and Treatment of Sex Offenders 328
Myths Regarding Which Community Sanctions Should Exist for Sex Offenders 328
The Effects of Sex-Crime and Sex-Offender Myths 329

Index 331

Preface

When we first taught a course on sex crimes, we cobbled resources together, from journal articles to newspaper articles, and sections of books written on narrow topics. Although several books existed, they were highly specialized, just on rape, or just on child sexual, or treatment. After repeating this exercise too many times, we opted to write a textbook. We first had to consider the common stereotypes, misconceptions, and other biases about sex crimes and the persons who commit them. Our students brought them to our attention, as they often asked questions that reflected them (e.g., once a sex offender, always a sex offender, right?), which they had discerned from the media and their own "common-sense" perspectives. This became the foundation of the textbook: identifying common myths and subsequently addressing them with the most recent and best research available.

After several semesters of teaching the course, we realized that the core themes must involve discussion of theories about sex crimes and different types of sex crimes (e.g., rape, child molestation, sex trafficking, and child pornography), identification of salient groups of offenders and the contexts in which they commonly commit their crimes (e.g., juveniles, females, and those who offend in the context of an institution), and providing information about the identification, control, and treatment of those who commit sex crimes. This subsequently became an outline of chapter topics that we believed would provide a comprehensive perspective.

This textbook was written with students in mind, as it considers what is often thought about persons who commit sex crimes by people who have not studied the topic closely. It is appropriate for use in any undergraduate- or graduate-level course that is geared specifically toward the crime itself and the persons who commit them. Also, it can be used in a course that is more broadly oriented toward criminal behavior and/or deviant sexual behavior. It should be useful for instructors not just in criminal justice but also public policy, social work, and sociology.

This textbook differs from competing textbooks in several ways. First, it focuses on sex crimes in a comprehensive way. There are many trade books on narrow aspects of the topic such as juveniles who have committed a sex crime, investigation of sex crimes, and the treatment of persons who have committed a sex crime. There are also many textbooks about crime and criminals in general, but this textbook provides an in-depth discussion of sex crimes and offenders specifically. Second, this book incorporates several broad themes related to criminology (why people commit crimes), policy-related issues (e.g., sex-crime and sex-offender-based laws), and the assessment and treatment of sex offenders—yet this is done with sex crimes and the persons who commit sex crimes in mind. Thus, this textbook integrates many core themes from psychology, sociology, criminology, and law.

ON THE "HOLLYWOOD COUCH" ART ON THE COVER

The artwork on the cover of this textbook represents the interaction of multiple recent sociological phenomena regarding sex crimes, including the #MeToo movement, the culmination of sexual harassment into sexual assault, and the spotlight on powerful individuals such as organization leaders, doctors, religious leaders, and Hollywood producers who have been accused of sexual assault. This dispelled a common myth that child sexual abuse, rape, human trafficking, and pornography is a lower-class problem and led to the acknowledgment that sexual abuse is pervasive and affects a large number of people with diverse backgrounds. The portrayal of a couch in Hollywood was created as a piece of art by Erika Rothenberg's "Road to Hollywood" sculpture, as a place for tourists to have their picture taken. It was a gold chaise couch made out of fiberglass with a mosaic on the ground in front of it reading, "The Road to Hollywood" and the words "how some of us get here" below that. The couch was removed in 2017 in response to a scandal involving a famous movie producer who was accused of offering roles in exchange for sex (Lloyd, 2017).

In 2018, street artists known as "Plastic Jesus and Joshua 'Ginger' Moore," installed a version of the Hollywood casting couch at corner of La Brea Avenue and Hollywood Boulevard. This occurred shortly before the Academy Awards. The gold statue portrayed Harvey Weinstein sitting on a couch in just his bathrobe holding an Oscar trophy in his hand. The artist Ginger Moore, recognizing the position of power and authority of the producer, said the artwork represents " . . . .the practices and methods that are used in Hollywood with these big powerful people . . . They have money and power to give jobs and they use that for their own sexual gratification and there's no better way to visualize this than we did with the casting couch" (McCluskey, 2018).

REFERENCES

Lloyd, A. (2017). https://laist.com/news/removed-couch-sculpture.
McCluskey, M. (2018). Harvey Weinstein 'Casting Couch' Pops Up in Hollywood. *Time*. https://time.com/5183007/harvey-weinstein-casting-couch-statue/.

CHAPTER 1

Introduction

CHAPTER OBJECTIVES

- Assess the relevance of the concept of moral panic for sex crimes and the persons who commit them
- Define a sex crime
- Assess multiple sources for estimating how many sex crimes occur
- Provide a brief history of the research on sex crimes
- Describe the state of current research on sex crimes
- Assess sexual recidivism rates of persons known to have committed a sex crime
- Provide an overview of the research and realities of sex-crime myths

Tune in to your favorite podcast, visit your favorite social media site, or check out the daily newsfeed, and you are likely to come across a story about someone famous who is accused or convicted of a sex crime. Many of us find it hard to look away. It is like a car crash. We don't want to see it, but there seems to be some innate fascination pulling us toward gruesome sights. The same is true of information about a new sex crime. Many celebrities, politicians, and sports figures have been accused or convicted of serious sex crimes, further attracting our attention. Who would have thought the famous comedian, actor, and educator, Bill Cosby, who portrayed a wholesome persona, would spend two years incarcerated for rape? The bottom line is that the list of people who have been accused or convicted of sex crimes now includes people we know. We also know people, famous and not so famous, who have come forward as survivors of sex crimes.

Virtually everywhere, it seems, we are bombarded with real and fictional accounts of sex crimes, making it difficult to distinguish fact from fiction. One goal of this textbook is to debunk many sex-crime fictions—what we call "sex-crime myths"—by examining what research reveals about them. In some instances, the research is definitive, while in other instances, the research is murky. We will examine both types.

In this chapter, we first consider the relevance of the concept of *moral panic* for sex crimes and people who commit them. We also examine several sources of data on how many sex crimes occur and trends in sex-crime rates over time. A brief history of sex-crimes research is presented, and we provide an overview of the state of current research. Last, several sex-crime myths are assessed; they provide guideposts for this book. Each chapter examines some aspect of an overarching myth that all persons who commit sex crimes are the same. This myth is presented alongside research to contradict it.

MORAL PANIC

It has been well documented that many of the public's perceptions of sex crimes and the people who commit them are inaccurate (Stafford & Vandiver, 2016). In 1972, Cohen introduced the term *moral panic,* which can be defined as a collective response to a perceived threat from an individual or group. The response often exceeds the actual threat and is manifested through an us-versus-them, do-something-about-them sentiment. Although the term has relevance for many phenomena, it is clearly reflected in today's hyperbolic media portrayals and punitive U.S. laws regarding people who commit sex crimes.

In his book, *Moral Panic: Changing Concepts of the Child Molester in Modern America,* Jenkins (1998) has attributed many of the public's perceptions of persons who have molested children to a moral panic. He detailed how media portrayals, laws, and public perceptions of children and child molestation have changed over time. For example, he described how children in the 1960s were viewed as seducers, whereas children in the 1940s and 1950s were viewed as potential victims of sex crimes who needed protection. He also described perceptions regarding persons who have committed a sex crime as cyclical, with the current moral panic being a swing in the pendulum toward perceiving offenders as "monsters." The result of the moral panic has been largely ill-conceived and ineffective laws (Klein & Cooper, 2019; Lytle, 2019), which are discussed in Chapter 11.

A noteworthy point made throughout this textbook is that current reactions to people who have committed a sex crime are largely limited to the Americas, especially the United States and Canada. For example, you will learn in Chapter 11 that the United States leads the way in developing sex-crime laws. Many of the assessment tools and treatment programs were developed in the United States and Canada. Much of the research is also done in these countries.

DEFINING A SEX CRIME

Current U.S. federal law defines a sex crime as "a criminal offense that has an element involving a sexual act or sexual contact with another" (42 U.S. Code § 16911 [5][a][1]). This broad and nonspecific definition is reflective of the extensive range of sexual acts that have been criminalized.

Some sex crimes are violent such as rape, other sexual assaults, and sexual abuse of children. Sex crimes also include child pornography production, engaging children in prostitution, and sex trafficking. Still other sex crimes involve social taboos, including exhibitionism (i.e., indecent exposure), voyeurism (i.e., peeping), bestiality (i.e., sexual activity with animals), necrophilia (i.e., sexual activity with bodies of dead persons), and many others.

As you will learn throughout this textbook, the definition of a sex crime is largely time variant, meaning that definitions change over time as a result of social, legal, moral, and even technological changes. Later in this chapter and in Chapter 3, we discuss how the Federal Bureau of Investigation's (FBI's) definition of rape has changed. Also, as noted in Focus Box 1.1, how we refer to persons who have committed a sex crime has changed. With regard to defining rape, it was not so long ago that the FBI limited rape to acts involving

> **Focus Box 1.1** Managing the Terminology—Sex Offender Versus Person Who Committed a Sex Crime
>
> Recently, organizations such as the Association for the Treatment of Sexual Abusers (ATSA) and the American Psychiatric Association (2013) have recognized the stigma of the label *sex offender*. The term carries a wide range of negative meanings, and therefore, it has been suggested that a more person-centered language be adopted, which we do. Thus, we rely primarily on the terminology *persons who have committed a sex crime* as opposed to *sex offenders*. Exceptions are made when this changes the original author's intent or becomes too cumbersome. Although this change in language may appear slight, it can have a substantial impact on people's perceptions. For example, a recent study showed that people were substantially more willing to volunteer to work with "persons who had committed a sex offense" as opposed to "sex offenders" (Lowe & Willis, 2020).

forceful penetration of a female victim. The FBI's new definition allows for both male and female victims and requires only a lack of consent, not force. Likewise, in Chapter 5, we examine how the legal definition of child pornography has evolved over the past 40 years, particularly emphasizing how the internet has affected its definition.

Sex-crime definitions are also contingent on place and culture. For example, only rapes involving white female victims were prosecuted under the apartheid system in South Africa that lasted until the 1990s. Rape of black women was socially accepted (Armstrong, 1994). In some parts of rural India, marriage and sexual relationships between adult men and young girls had no legal sanctions (Ouattara et al., 1998). Even within the United States, what constitutes a sex crime varies among states. For example, most, but not all U.S. states, classify indecent exposure as a sex crime and mandate registration for convicted offenders (Levenson et al., 2010). Throughout this textbook, these kinds of jurisdictional differences are discussed.

The point is that there is considerable heterogeneity in definitions of sex crimes. More information regarding the definitions of specific types of sex crimes, such as rape, child molestation, child pornography, and human trafficking, is presented in subsequent chapters.

SOURCES AND NUMBERS OF SEX CRIMES AND OFFENDERS

A need exists for accurate data to determine how many sex crimes occur. Here, we identify several sources of sex-crime data. We also consider the strengths and weaknesses of each source. First, we examine an international source of sexual-violence data and, subsequently, several sources of U.S. data, which are where we get most of our sex-crime and sex-offender estimates.

United Nations Office on Drugs and Crime (UNODC)

The **United Nations Office on Drugs and Crime** (UNODC) is a source for international sexual-violence data. These data come from multiple surveys, including an annual report questionnaire, an annual self-report survey on crime trends and operations of criminal justice systems, and other national surveys administered in member countries of the United Nations (UNODC, 2020). The data, however, are constrained by the fact that countries define sexual violence differently, making between-country comparisons impossible. Also, some countries change their definitions of sexual violence over time, making temporal comparisons difficult. Data for selected regions and countries are presented in Table 1.1. The

TABLE 1.1 Sexual Violence Rates among Countries

Region	Country	Rate Per 100,000	
		2012	2017
	Cabo Verde	52.1	39.8
	Kenya	10.8	10.9
	Morocco	8.8	11.3
	South Africa	Data not available	87.9
Americas	Bahamas	82.2	84.1
	Canada	76.9	95.3
	Costa Rica	133.3	191.2
	Ecuador	26.4	80.5
	Mexico	31.0	30.7
Europe	Denmark	33.3	83.6
	Estonia	30.2	19.6
	Finland	64.8	55.4
	Germany	44.8	42.1
	Greece	4.5	4.3
	Iceland	83.8	142.3
	Italy	7.8	8.4
	Poland	7.3	8.5
	Spain	19.1	20.3
	Sweden	147.7	190.6
Oceania	Australia	84.9	101.5
	New Zealand	75.8	126.0

Introduction 5

data may reveal real differences among countries, or they are more likely due to different definitions and methods of measuring sexual violence among countries.

FBI: Uniform Crime Reports (UCR), National Incident-Based Reporting System (NIBRS), and Crime Data Explorer

Currently, in the United States, the FBI maintains two separate reporting systems, the *Uniform Crime Reports* (UCR) and the *National Incident-Based Reporting System* (NIBRS). In this section, we will discuss each of them in turn.

The FBI began its crime reporting program in 1929, and today more than 18,000 law enforcement agencies at various levels voluntarily report crime data. These law enforcement agencies include city, university/college, county, state, tribal, and federal organizations. The FBI publishes an annual report, *Crime in the United States*, which has information about many crimes and arrests, including rapes known to law enforcement officials, rape arrests, and arrests for other sex offenses.

In 2013, the UCR began using a revised definition of rape: "penetration, no matter how slight, of the vagina or anus with any body part or object, or oral penetration by a sex organ of another person, without the consent of the victim" (FBI, 2012, n.p.) The difference between the new and legacy (old) definition is that the new definition is gender neutral. In the new definition, the victim and offender can be either male or female. Also, the new definition does not require "force"; it requires "lack of consent" instead.

Before looking at UCR rape data, it is helpful to look first at the trend in the rates for all violent crimes, which include murder and nonnegligent manslaughter, rape, robbery, and aggravated assault. As shown in Figure 1.1, UCR violent crime rates generally decreased from 2000 to 2014. After that, there was a slight increase in the rate for several years, followed by a slight decrease.

As shown in Figure 1.2, which displays the trend of rape using both the traditional and legacy definition, reveals a slight decrease in the rate of rapes known to law enforcement

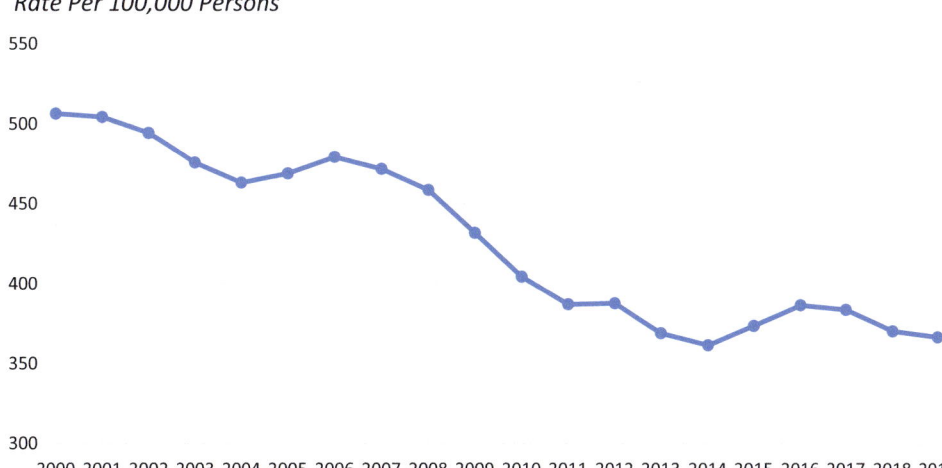

FIGURE 1.1 UCR—All Violent Crimes.

Note: Adapted from FBI (2021).

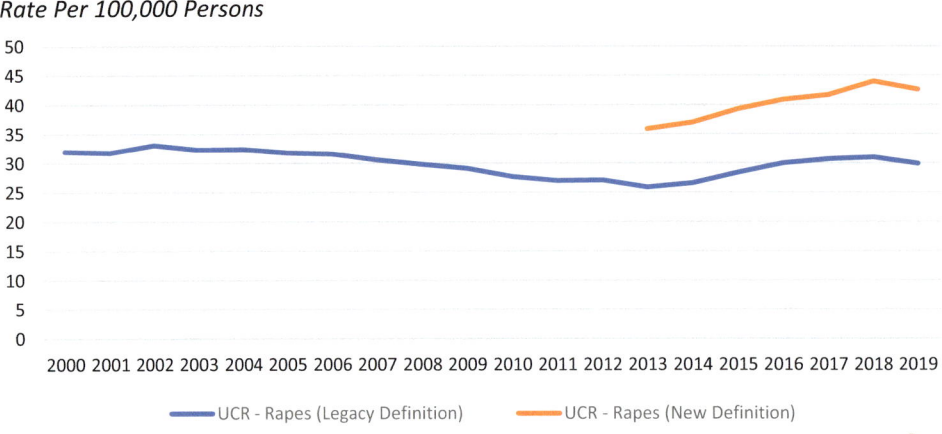

FIGURE 1.2 UCR—Rapes.

Note: Adapted from FBI (2021).

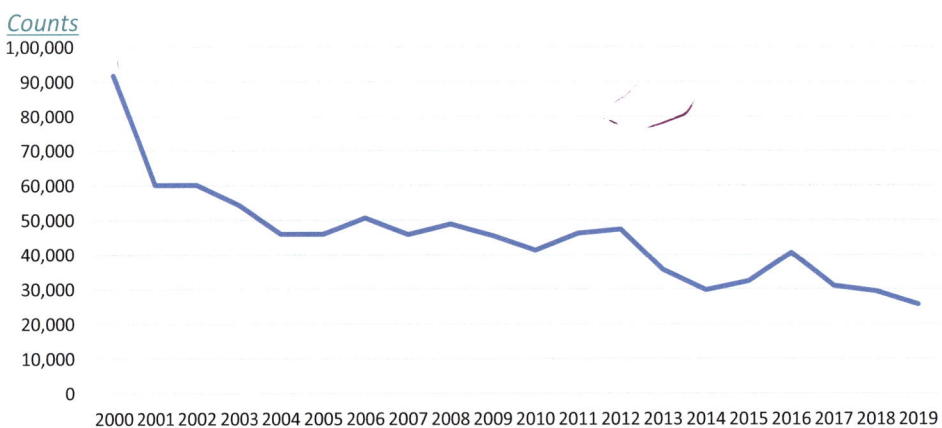

FIGURE 1.3 UCR—Estimated Number of Arrests for Other Sex Offenses (Excludes Rape and Prostitution).

Note: Adapted from FBI (2021).

officials from 2000 to 2013, and this was followed by an increase and a leveling of the rate. Although this pattern generally matches the pattern for all violent crimes in Figure 1.1, the amount of change in the rape rate was much smaller. As a result, the rape rate in 2019 was roughly the same as it was in 2000.

Figure 1.2 also shows the trend in the rape rate with the new definition. The pattern since 2013 is the same as the pattern over the same period with the legacy definition. Using the new definition, however, the rate was higher each year. The reason is the new UCR definition of rape is broader, so more rapes are counted.

In addition to crimes known to law enforcement officials, the UCR also provides arrest data. Figure 1.3 shows the trend in the number of arrests for other sex offenses from 2000 to 2019. Other sex offenses include crimes against chastity, common decency, morals, and the like. Arrests for indecent exposure and prostitution are not included. Rape arrests are reported separately, so they are also not included. Arrests for attempted sex crimes, however, are included. As shown in Figure 1.3, the number of arrests for other sex offenses generally decreased considerably from 2000 to 2019 (72%—from 91,828 in 2000 to 25,684 in 2019), with slight increases and decreases along the way.

A disadvantage of UCR sex-crime data is that they only include crimes known to law enforcement officials and arrests. Crimes unknown to law enforcement officials and crimes not resulting in arrest are not included. Sex crimes are one of the offenses least likely to be reported to law enforcement officials (BJS, 2020). The reasons vary. They include, but are not limited to, embarrassment, fear of not being believed, fear of retribution, and/or fear of the criminal justice system. The victim can hold to myths about sex crimes as well and believe they did something wrong (e.g., drank alcohol or did not fight back hard enough) or believe that it was not rape because the victim knew the offender.

An advantage of UCR data on sex crimes is that they provide consistent estimates of how many sex crimes occur and arrests for sex crimes. The data are presented in an easy-to-read format and can be compared across multiple years, even decades. The UCR also includes a breakdown by states and regions of the United States.

The FBI developed the National Incident-Based Reporting System (NIBRS) to improve crime data. Planning began in the 1980s, with formal implementation taking place in 1991 (FBI, n.d.-b). There was a need for more information about crime than was reported in UCR. For example, instead of simply reporting rapes known to law enforcement officials, there was a need to know more offender and victim information and circumstances associated with rape.

More than one crime may occur at a time; for example, a burglary and a rape may be committed in a criminal incident. There also can be multiple offenders and victims in a single incident. The FBI counts only the most serious crime in a criminal incident in UCR. If both a burglary and a rape occur in a criminal incident, the FBI counts only the rape. An advantage of NIBRS over UCR is that it provides information about all crimes, offenders, and victims in a criminal incident. Another advantage is that NIBRS measures a broader range of crimes than UCR. A disadvantage of NIBRS is that it is still relatively new and developing, and not all states contribute information. By 2020, 37 U.S. states contributed to NIBRS. With regard to sex crimes, NIBRS collects information on incidents that involve: (1) kidnapping/abduction; (2) pornography/obscene material; (3) prostitution offenses, including prostituting, assisting, or promoting prostitution; (4) forcible sex offenses, including forcible rape, forcible sodomy, sexual assault with an object, and forcible fondling; (5) nonforcible sex offenses, including incest and statutory rape; and (6) Peeping Tom (FBI, n.d.-a).

The *Crime Data Explorer* (Figure 1.4) combines data from both the UCR and NIBRS and provides online tools to examine crime rates across the United States: https://crime-data-explorer.fr.cloud.gov. Users can access information about their own state and all of the states combined.

National Crime Victimization Survey (NCVS)

The *National Crime Victimization Survey* (NCVS) collects information about the number of victimizations in the United States for different types of crime regardless of whether they are known to law enforcement officials. A goal of the NCVS is to uncover at least some of the "dark figure of crime" comprising crimes unknown to law enforcement officials. Each

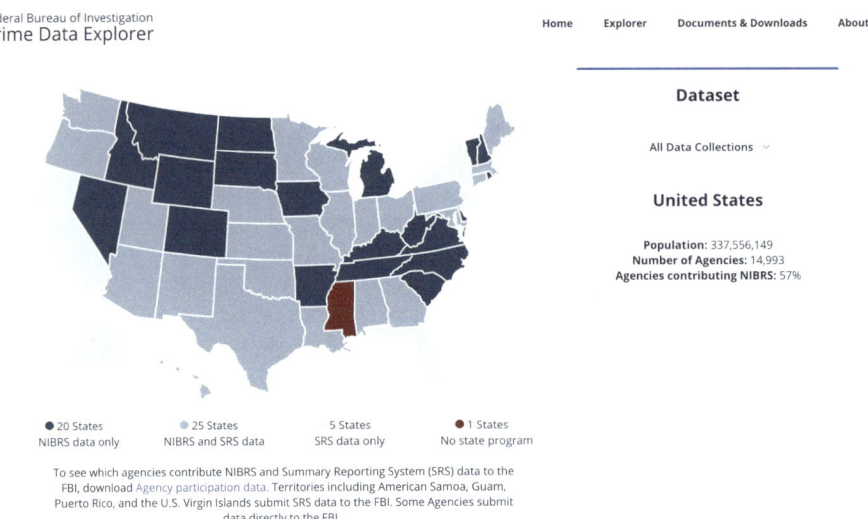

FIGURE 1.4 Crime Data Explorer.

Note: Image from FBI (n.d.).

year, the NCVS samples a large number of U.S. households and interviews each household member age 12 and older. The people in each sampled household are re-interviewed twice a year for three years. The NCVS assesses a wide range of crime victimizations—property and personal crimes—including sex crimes. The NCVS assesses both rape and sexual assault. Rape involves penetration, and sexual assault involves grabbing/fondling and any unwanted sexual contact.

Figure 1.5 shows the rape/sexual assault victimization rate from NCVS since 2000 (FBI, 2021). The trend in rape/sexual assault victimization rates looks different from the trend in UCR rape rates over the same period (Figure 1.2). Recall that the UCR rape rate in 2019 was roughly the same as it was in 2000 with little change in between. In contrast, the NCVS rape/sexual assault rate decreased from 2005 to 2009 and then tended to increase after that. The NCVS rape/sexual assault victimization rate was more than 50% higher in 2019 than it was in 2000.

Some of the differences in the trends in Figures 1.2 and 1.4 may be because the NCVS includes sexual assaults with rapes, whereas the UCR considers rape only. Additionally, the NCVS is based on a self-report survey method and captures rapes and sexual assaults both known and unknown to law enforcement officials. The NCVS reveals that approximately 30% of rapes and sexual assaults captured in their survey are crimes *not* reported to law enforcement officials and, hence, are unknown to them. Victims gave the following reasons for not reporting: fear of reprisal or getting offender into trouble (28%), dealt with in another way/personal matter (20%), police would not or could not help (13%), not important enough to report (6%), or other reason (33%) (Langton et al., 2012).

A limitation of NCVS is that it includes only crimes with victims who are at least 12 years old. Rapes and sexual assaults of younger children are not included. Also, there is underreporting of crimes in the NCVS, just as in UCR. Although an interviewee in the NCVS could have been a sex-crime victim, they may choose not to report it to an NCVS interviewer for a variety of reasons such as embarrassment or shame.

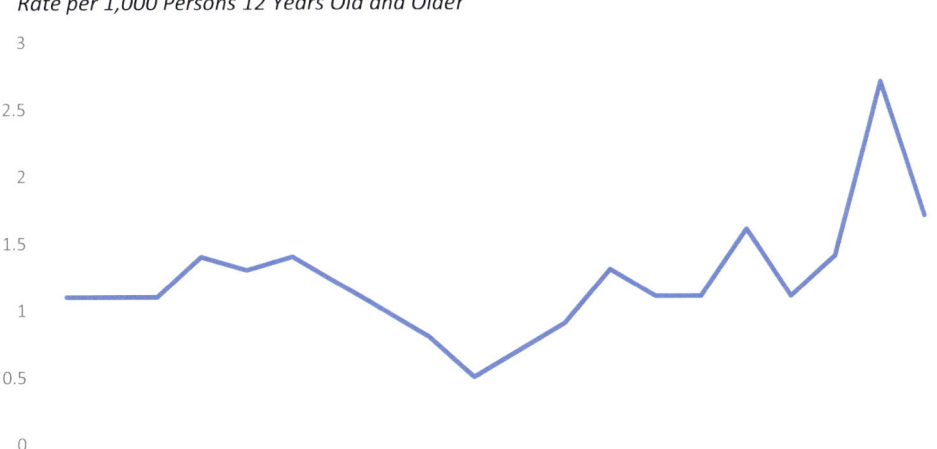

FIGURE 1.5 NCVS—Rape/Sexual Assaults.
Note: Adapted from FBI (2021).

National Child Abuse and Neglect Data System (NCANDS)

In 1988, the Child Abuse Prevention and Treatment Act was passed. This led to the creation of the **National Child Abuse and Neglect Data System** (NCANDS), which includes data from all U.S. states for child abuse and neglect. Thus, the data are not limited to sex crimes. The data-collection process is based on voluntary reporting to child protective service agencies, and data are reported annually (Administration on Children Youth and Families, 2018).

NCANDS data indicate that in 2018, there were 676,000 known child victims of abuse or neglect in the United States. This translates into a rate of 9.1 victims per 1,000 children, which is a 3% increase over the previous five years. Of the 676,000 children, 8.5% were sexually abused (Administration on Children Youth and Families, 2018).

An advantage of NCANDS is that it provides information about child sexual victimizations that may not have been reported to law enforcement officials. The data, however, are limited in that they focus broadly on abuse and neglect and do not provide detailed information about victims. They are also limited in that many instances of child abuse and neglect go unreported to child protective service agencies.

National Intimate Partner and Sexual Violence Survey (NIPSVS)

In 2010, the Centers for Disease Control and Prevention (CDC) began the **National Intimate Partner and Sexual Violence Survey** (NIPSVS). It was conducted in 2010 and again in 2015. The survey is administered over the phone and uses a complex design to yield a nationally representative sample. The most recent survey, conducted in 2015, revealed that approximately one out of four women and one in ten men experienced at least one of the following by an intimate partner in their lifetime: sexual violence, physical violence, and/or stalking. For women, an estimated 517,000 experienced completed forced penetration within the 12 months prior to the survey.

An advantage of NIPSVS is that it counts sexual violence among both women and men. It is also nationally representative and includes current estimates, as well as lifetime estimates, of sexual violence. It also provides many details regarding attempted and completed sexually violent acts. Additionally, with regard to forced sexual activity, there is information about whether drugs and/or alcohol were used for compliance. A disadvantage of the survey is that it is relatively new and has been conducted only twice.

A BRIEF HISTORY OF RESEARCH ON SEX CRIMES

Early research on sex, sexuality, and deviant sexual acts, including sex crimes, occurred under an umbrella of taboo. Early researchers in this area were viewed as both pioneers and villains. One of the first well-known psychologists to assess sexual abuse was Sigmund Freud, who posited in the 1800s that the cause of adults' emotional problems was a suppression of childhood sexual abuse. He termed this the "seduction theory of childhood sexuality." This term would later be recognized as unfortunately worded because it implies some sort of willingness by the child, which is far from what Freud intended in his initial writings (Mason, 1984). The response to his theory was icy; one colleague responded by saying, "It sounds like a scientific fairy tale" (Mason, 1984, n.p.). Freud was generally discredited by many of his peers. He eventually recanted his seduction theory, although the connection between experiencing child sexual abuse and subsequent emotional problems later came to be widely accepted.

Another substantive development in the study of sex, sexuality, and deviant sexual acts was Alfred Kinsey's efforts in the 1940s to show the broad range of sexual behavior among Americans. This resulted in two books, *Sexual Behaviour in the Human Male* (Kinsey, 1948) and *Sexual Behavior in the Human Female* (Kinsey, 1953). Kinsey proposed that "heterosexual" and "homosexual" were ends of a continuum, with many people falling somewhere between the two. He proposed a scale that ranged from zero (exclusively heterosexual) to six (exclusively homosexual) with a separate category for people who were ***asexual*** and had no sexual or romantic attraction to others. This became known as the Kinsey Scale. He also identified many widespread sexual behaviors that were considered deviant at the time such as masturbation and extramarital sexual intercourse. Like Freud, Kinsey received backlash from his peers because of the taboo nature of his research. Of particular interest to this textbook, he was faulted for relying on a source who provided him with detailed accounts of sexually abusing young boys, bringing to orgasm one who was only two months old (Crain, 2004).

STATE OF CURRENT RESEARCH ON SEX CRIMES

The state of current research on sex crimes and persons who commit sex crimes is strong and yet still developing. Our knowledge has increased substantially over the last few decades. So why the "strong and yet still developing" designation? Several factors are discussed here: creation and growth of the Association of the Treatment of Sexual Abusers (ATSA), limitations with nonexperimental research on sex crimes, and a need for more research on diverse groups of people.

Creation and Growth of the Association for the Treatment of Sexual Abusers (ATSA)

The ATSA began with a small gathering of treatment providers, researchers, and practitioners in the 1980s and, since then, has become a large organization that promotes sex-crimes research. Its peer-reviewed journal is *Sexual Abuse: A Journal of Research and Treatment*, which provides information about the causes and consequences of sex crimes and informs the public regarding effective policies, including prevention policies. ATSA's mission advocates "no more victims" of sexual abuse (ATSA, 2012). In addition to ATSA's journal, there are many others, some of which include the following: *Journal of Child Sexual Abuse; Violence and Aggression; Trauma, Violence and Abuse; Child Abuse and Neglect; Journal of Interpersonal Violence; Violence and Victims;* and *Criminal Justice and Behavior*.

Limitations with Nonexperimental Research on Sex Crimes

Sex-crime researchers often work with what they have and use imperfect methodologies. Although most researchers consider a ***classic experimental design*** to be the gold standard, a classic experimental design is used infrequently in research on sex crimes and people who commit sex crimes. As illustrated in Figure 1.6, the classic experimental design minimizes many of the problems with alternative, nonexperimental designs by randomly assigning people to two (or sometimes more than two) groups: (1) an experimental group that receives some stimulus, say offender treatment, and (2) a control group that does not receive the stimulus. Researchers then observe if the experimental group differs significantly from the control group on some predetermined outcome such as *recidivism*. Random assignment allows researchers to conclude that any observed between-group difference in the outcome is caused by the stimulus and nothing else.

Even as a novice researcher, you probably have identified problems with randomly assigning people who commit sex crimes to two groups, for example, one that receives treatment and another that does not. Most persons who are convicted of a sex crime are legally required to participate in a treatment program. Randomly deciding that only some offenders will receive treatment, while others will not, can pose a threat to the community and is unethical. Hence, most sex-crimes studies rely on nonexperimental methods that rely on statistical controls to make causal inferences. Limitations of nonexperimental studies will be considered periodically in this textbook. The bottom line here is that we are still learning

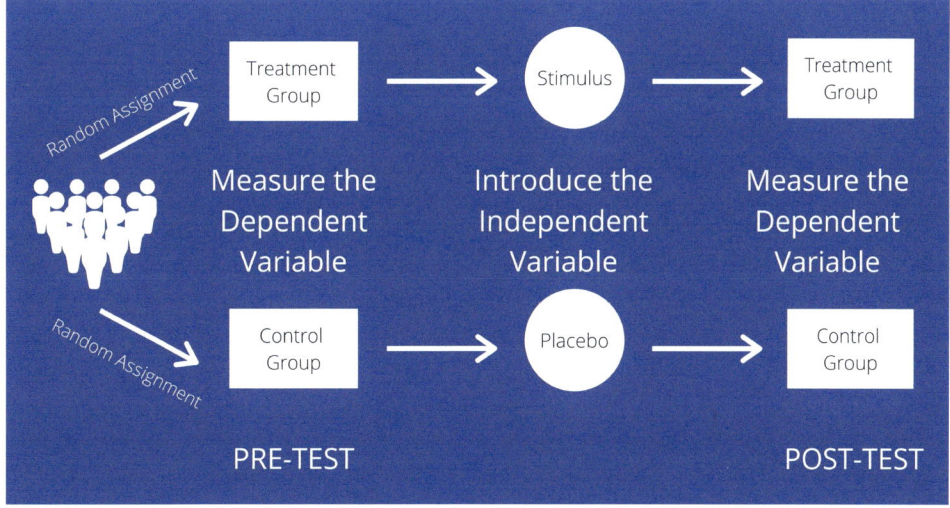

FIGURE 1.6 Classical Experimental Design.

a great deal about sex crimes and the persons who commit them albeit with imperfect methods.

Sex-Crimes Research and Diversity

Over the past decade, one of the more important developments in sex-crimes research has been its widening reach to include more diverse populations of people. What we have known about persons who have committed a sex crime has come largely from studies of white, adult male offenders who live in the United States or Canada and have minor (i.e., child/children) and/or female victims. Recently, there have been movements led by victim advocacy groups and heroes who have paved the way for more victims being encouraged to come forward. As noted in Focus Box 1.2, Tarana Burke led a worldwide movement that fueled sexual assault victims and gave them a voice.

Recently, there have been more studies of previously ignored groups such as nonwhites, juveniles, female offenders, male victims, and offenders and victims outside the United States. Some of this can be attributed to social media efforts that raised the awareness of the diverse persons who are affected by sexual assault. More information on this can be found in Focus Box 1.2. For example, a recent study found that prison-treatment programs for Nigerians who had sexually offended significantly reduced their likelihood of recidivism (Nwokeoma et al., 2019), which corroborates research in the United States.

More research is also being conducted on victims who identify as **LGBTQIA+**: *lesbian*: women who are sexually/romantically attracted to other women; *gay*: persons who are homosexual, sexually/romantically attracted to those of the same sex; *bisexual*: persons who

Focus Box 1.2 Meet a Hero: Tarana Burke

PHOTO 1.1 Tarana Burke: A Hero Fighting for Women's Rights.

Photo Credit: Heather Sten//The New York Times/Redux.

Tarana Burke, a woman's right activist, began the Me Too movement, as she encouraged the use of hashtag with the "MeToo" phrase (#MeToo) on social media to draw attention to the sexual harassment and sexual violence problem that exists (Mendes et al., 2018). Tarana Burke began her activist career early. For example, when she was a teenager, she began initiatives regarding economic injustice, including housing inequality and racial discrimination. Later, she met with other young women who had experienced sexual abuse just as she had. She is now recognized as a global leader in the initiatives combatting sexual violence. Tarana Burke is a book author (*Unbound: My Story of Liberation and the Birth of the Me Too Movement*), book co-editor (*You are Your Best Thing: Vulnerability, Shame Resilience, and the Black Experience*), and author of numerous articles in various popular media sources (Times, The Root, Think, Variety, Elle, ESPN, and many others) regarding sexual violence (TaranaBurke.com) (Photo 1.1).

are sexually/romantically attracted to both men and women; ***transexual***: persons who identify with a sex (male or female) that is in an opposite direction of what sex they were assigned at birth; ***queer:*** persons who do not identify as heterosexual and can include persons who are lesbian, gay, and transgendered; ***questioning***: persons who are questioning their own sexual identity and/or sexual orientation; ***intersexual***: persons who have ambiguous sex organs and/or an unusual combination of sex chromosomes; asexual: persons who are not sexually attracted to others regardless of their sex and/or gender identity; and +: those who are heterosexual, yet identify as an ally (i.e., are supportive of) to those who are LGBTQIA. These groups have been largely ignored by sex-crime researchers until recently.

ONCE A "SEX OFFENDER," ALWAYS A "SEX OFFENDER"

Throughout this textbook, we will examine myths about sex crimes and the people who commit them. One myth permeates many of the others. Many believe that all persons who have committed a sex crime will recidivate and commit more sex crimes one after another. This is the myth that "once a 'sex offender,' always a 'sex offender.'" In addressing this myth, it is important to first examine a few methodological challenges to measuring recidivism, which broadly defined, simply refers to committing a crime again. Most researchers acknowledge that it is impossible to measure "true" recidivism. Researchers often rely on indicators that someone has committed a crime, usually including arrest, conviction, incarceration, or self-reports. Each of these indicators has limitations; primarily they do not capture all sex crimes. Many persons who commit a sexual offense go undetected by law enforcement officials, are never convicted or incarcerated, and if asked in a self-report survey, will underestimate the number of sex crimes they have committed. Thus, as researchers, we rely on imperfect indicators of recidivism.

Numerous studies have been conducted on the recidivism rates of persons who have committed a sex crime. Many of the studies, however, are limited by small, localized samples and do not follow offenders for an extended time. The best way to learn about the recidivism of persons who have committed sex crimes is to examine *meta-analyses* that cover multiple studies. A meta-analysis is a study of studies, where a researcher gathers all relevant studies on a particular topic and analyzes the results to gain a more comprehensive answer to the research question posed. Its advantage is that it creates a large sample of studies.

Two meta-analyses of persons who have committed a sex crime stand out as being the most comprehensive. The first was published in 1998 and included 61 studies in its analyses. A total of 23,393 persons who had committed a sex crime were included. The majority (84%) of the studies relied on reconviction to measure recidivism. Studies also relied on arrests (54%), self-reports (25%), and parole violations (16%). Given that some of the studies relied on multiple measures, the percentages here exceed 100%. The only included studies were those deemed to have strong methods. The known offenders were followed for an average of 4–5 years (Hanson & Bussière, 1998).

The results indicated that, on average, 13.4% of the persons who had committed a sex crime sexually recidivated (i.e., committed another sex crime) (Hanson & Bussière, 1998). The rate of sexual recidivism, however, varied for subgroups of offenders. Rapists recidivated at a higher rate (18.9%) than child molesters (12.7%). Again, it is important to note that although these rates are low, many sex crimes go undetected. The evidence, however, suggests that not all persons who have committed a sex crime recidivate, and their sexual recidivism rates are lower than expected. This study also found that criminal lifestyle, sexual deviance, and psychological maladjustment were predictors of sexual recidivism. More factors associated with predicting recidivism are reported in Chapter 10.

Another meta-analysis was conducted in 2005. It was based on 82 studies and 29,450 known persons who had committed a sex crime. Although the majority of offenders were from the United States, these studies also included offenders from Canada, the United Kingdom, Austria, Sweden, Australia, France, Netherlands, and Denmark. Most of the studies incorporated multiple indicators of recidivism (arrest, parole violations, and other reports), but some relied solely on either arrests or convictions. The offenders were followed for an average of 5–6 years (Hanson & Morton-Bourgon, 2005). The best predictors of sexual recidivism included sexual deviancy and antisocial orientation.

The results of this meta-analysis, like the previous meta-analysis, revealed a 13.7% sexual recidivism rate. The researchers noted that these "should be considered underestimates because not all offenses are detected" (Hanson & Morton-Bourgon, 2005, p. 1157). It should be noted that only persons who were "known" to have committed a sex crime were included in any of the studies.

Although these studies use imperfect indicators of recidivism, other studies may yield further insights. Albeit controversial, much has been learned by using polygraph testing to estimate sexual recidivism. In one study, 147 offenders were polygraphed, all of whom were on probation or parole for sex crimes. "Of the 147 . . . offenders . . . 14 percent (21 out of 147) reported sexually abusing victims while under community supervision through the . . . polygraph process" (English et al., 2000, p. 37). Some of the 21 recidivists received additional legal punishments for these new crimes, but "only one was arrested for sexual recidivism because of information obtained outside the . . . polygraph process" (p. 37). A reliance on arrests, then, would have produced a gross underestimate of sexual recidivism, and polygraph testing may reveal higher sexual recidivism rates than reported in many studies.

ADDRESSING SEX-CRIME MYTHS

Although there are many myths regarding sex crimes and the persons who commit them, one of the most common is that *all persons who have committed a sex crime are the same*. Throughout subsequent chapters, we present evidence that offenders who commit sex crimes are heterogeneous (i.e., vary in their characteristics and behaviors). They vary a great deal in their demographic and social characteristics, from young to old and having no job skills to having highly trained positions such as teacher, coach, or professional sports figure. They vary in their victim choice; for example, a child versus an adult or someone they know versus someone they have never met. They vary in the types of sex crimes they commit, from nonviolent sex crimes, such as exhibitionism, to violent sex crimes such as rape. Many offenders commit more than one type of sex crime rather than specializing in only one. They also vary in how they approach their victims, from years of slowly eroding boundaries (grooming) to a spontaneous attack. This textbook is organized by addressing various sex-crime myths like this one.

Myths Regarding Why Persons Commit Sex Crimes

Many wrongly believe that someone must be mentally ill to commit a sex crime (Center for Sex Offender Management, n.d.), and rape, in particular, is caused by offenders with uncontrollable sexual urges (Michigan State University, 2015). There are various reasons why people commit sex crimes. Chapter 2 presents different theories to explain why someone would commit a sex crime. It should be noted, however, that these theories have only moderate empirical support, so there is still much to learn about why people commit sex crimes.

Myths Regarding Rape and Rape Victims

It has been proposed that women should be careful when walking alone at night for fear that a stranger may rape them (Koester, 2015). The research shows that most rape victims know their rapists (Planty et al., 2013). It also has been proposed that rape is (always) about sex, female victims are often at fault, and there is a "right" way to respond in a rape (University of Minnesota Duluth, 2001). An entire set of rape myths has been identified in the literature and affects the way many people perceive rape. All of these myths are refuted by research and are discussed in Chapter 3.

Myths Regarding Child Sexual Abuse

There are many myths about people who sexually abuse children, the process of an offender eroding boundaries to abuse a child, and the characteristics of child sexual abuse victims. For example, many wrongly believe that child sexual abusers are "boogeymen" who don't appear to be normal (One With Courage, n.d.). Chapter 4 discusses research regarding the characteristics of those who commit child sexual abuse. You will learn that those who commit this crime are a diverse group of offenders. Some people choose employment based on the extent to which it gives them access to children. Also, characteristics of the child-molestation process vary, and there is a wide range of victims.

Myths Regarding Child Pornography and Sex Trafficking

Some persons wrongly believe that the child-pornography industry is small and that the victims of child pornography are not harmed to the same degree as victims of hands-on sex crimes (Pulido, 2013). Neither of these myths is true. In Chapter 5, you will learn that child pornography is a multibillion dollar industry. Victims are harmed through sharing of pornographic images, and offender characteristics vary considerably. Also, we will discuss the myth that only women from economically depressed areas are victims of sex trafficking.

Myths Regarding Juveniles and Women Who Commit a Sex Crime

Many of the myths associated with adults who commit a sex crime apply to juveniles who commit a sex crime. For example, the myth that "once a sex offender always a sex offender" has been applied to juveniles. A version is that they always grow into adults who will commit sex crimes. There are additional myths about juveniles who have committed a sex crime such as they sexually abuse because they have been sexually abused themselves and they are all pedophiles (Fagundes, 2014). The research, discussed in Chapter 6, does not support these myths.

It is often assumed that all persons who commit a sex crime are male (Office of the Attorney General, 2001). Although women comprise a small percentage of persons who commit sex crimes, their numbers are large enough to warrant concern. Although female schoolteachers who have molested male students have been covered extensively in the media, Chapter 7 shows this is only one type of woman who commits a sex crime. Chapter 7 reveals the diverse range of women who have committed a sex crime. Also, victims of women offenders are diverse with regard to their gender and age.

Myths Regarding Institutional Abuse

It has been wrongly assumed that persons who commit a sex crime have no job and hang out in public places looking for potential victims. The reality, however, is that many incidents of child molestation and rape are committed by someone who is in a trusted position (e.g., daycare provider) and knows the victim. Sexual abuse can occur at church by a clergy member, at school by a teacher, at sports practice by a coach, or by a volunteer at a civic organization. Such instances are discussed in Chapter 7.

Myths Regarding Victims of Sex Crimes

A long-held myth about sex crimes generally is that they happen only to certain people (e.g., rape only happens to young, white, sexually desirable women, or rape only happens to "bad" girls). Chapter 8 problematizes this myth by exploring the spectrum of sexual violence victims who do not fit the rape victim stereotype, including the elderly, men, individuals with disabilities, and American Indian/Alaska Native people. The ways in which sexual violence affects victims, both in the short- and long-term, are also wrought with myth and misunderstanding. This chapter discusses victim response to sexual violence with particular emphasis on the neurobiology of sexual trauma, physical and mental/emotional health impacts, and secondary victims of sexual violence.

Myths Regarding Investigations of Sex Crimes

Many of the myths already discussed permeate the investigation process. For example, it is not uncommon for someone to believe that women will claim to be raped when they regret having sex (University of Minnesota Duluth, 2001). This, along with other rape myths, can affect the investigation of sex crimes—from the 911 operator to the lead detective in an investigation. The investigation process is discussed in depth in Chapter 9.

Myths Regarding Treatment of Persons Who Have Committed a Sex Crime

A common sex-offender myth is that treatment is ineffective for persons who have committed a sex crime (Center for Sex Offender Management, 2000). Chapter 10 provides an overview of treatment methods, along with their effectiveness. Research reveals that treatment results in lower sexual recidivism rates (Lösel & Schmucker, 2005).

Myths Regarding Appropriate Responses to Persons Who Have Committed a Sex Crime

It is often wrongly assumed that most persons who have committed a sex crime are caught, convicted, and imprisoned (Center for Sex Offender Management, 2000). Sixty percent of persons convicted of a sex crime are serving probation and live in the community (Greenfeld, 1997). They are, however, often subjected to registration laws and other restrictions such as not living within 500 feet of a school or other area where children congregate. Many of the laws, unfortunately, are based on some of the common misperceptions regarding persons who have committed a sex crime. These laws, and their effectiveness, are discussed in Chapter 11.

REVIEW POINTS

- The current (over)emphasis on the dangerousness of persons who have committed a sex crime is embedded in a moral panic culture.
- A sex crime is broadly defined in the United States as a crime that involves a sexual act or sexual contact. Much of what is considered a sex crime changes over time and is highly dependent on culture.
- There are various sources of data of the number of sex crimes and persons who have committed a sex crime: UNODC, UCR, NIBRS, NCVS, NCANDS, and the National Violence Against Women Survey.
- The UCR rape rate in 2019 was roughly the same as it was in 2000. Each year since 2013, the rape rate using the FBI's new definition of rape was higher than the rate using the legacy definition. Unlike the trend in the UCR rape rate, the NCVS rape/sexual assault rate decreased from 2005 to 2009 and then increased after that. The number of arrests for other sex offenses generally decreased since 2000, according to the UCR.
- Some of the first researchers who studied sex (Sigmund Freud and Alfred Kinsey) were not well received by their peers due to the topic being taboo.
- The state of current research on persons who have committed a sex crime is strong and still developing. This is supported by the growing amount of research conducted on this population, including more diverse and less-studied populations in current research efforts. There are still methodological limitations, however, such as a reliance on nonexperimental methods.
- Meta-analyses conducted on persons who have committed a sex crime reveal a relatively low rate of sexual recidivism contrary to popular belief that all persons who have committed a sex crime go on to sexually recidivate.
- Many myths exist regarding sex crimes and persons who have committed a sex crime, which are dispelled throughout each chapter by examining the research and realities.

REFERENCES

42 U.S. Code § 16911 (5)(a)(1).

Administration on Children Youth and Families. (2018). Child maltreatment, 2016. *U.S. Department of Health and Human Services*. https://www.acf.hhs.gov/sites/default/files/documents/cb/cm2018.pdf

American Psychiatric Association. (2013). *Diagnostic and statistical manual of mental disorders* (5th ed.). Author.

Armstrong, S. (1994). Rape in South Africa: An invisible part of apartheid's legacy. *Gender and Development, 2*(2), 35–39. https://www.doi.org/10.1080/09682869308520009

Association for the Treatment of Sexual Abusers (ATSA). (2012). Adolescents who have engaged in sexually abusive behavior: Effective policies and practices. https://www.atsa.com/pdfs/Policy/AdolescentsEngagedSexuallyAbusiveBehavior.pdf

Bureau of Justice Statistics (BJS). (2020). National Crime Victimization Survey, 2015–2019. https://bjs.ojp.gov/data-collection/ncvs

Center for Sex Offender Management. (2000). Myths and facts about sex offenders. *U.S. Department of Justice, Office of Justice Programs.* https://ccoso.org/sites/default/files/import/mythsfacts.pdf

Center for Sex Offender Management. (n.d.). Section 3: Characteristics of sex offenders. http://www.csom.org/train/etiology/3/3_1.htm

Cohen, S. (1972). *Folk devils and moral panics: The creation of the mods and rockers.* Martin Robertson.

Crain, C. (2004). Alfred Kinsey: Liberator or pervert? *The New York Times.* https://www.nytimes.com/2004/10/03/movies/alfred-kinsey-liberator-or-pervert.html

English, K., Jones, L., Pasini-Hill, D., Patrick, D., & Cooley-Towell, S. (2000). The value of polygraph testing in sex offender management. *U.S. Department of Justice, National Institute of Justice.* https://www.ojp.gov/library/publications/value-polygraph-testing-sex-offender-management

Fagundes, M. (2014). Dangerous myths about juvenile sex offenders: Meghan Fagundes at TEDx AustinWomen. https://www.youtube.com/watch?v=81hy3AZjkr4

Federal Bureau of Investigation (FBI). (2012). UCR program changes definition of rape: Includes all victims and omits requirement of physical force. *Criminal Justice Information Services, 14*(1). https://www.fbi.gov/services/cjis/cjis-link/ucr-program-changes-definition-of-rape

Federal Bureau of Investigation (FBI). (2021). Crime in the United States: 2000–19. *U.S. Department of Justice.* https://www.fbi.gov/services/cjis/ucr/publications

Federal Bureau of Investigation (FBI). (n.d.-a). National incident-based reporting system: General information. *U.S. Department of Justice.* https://www.fbi.gov/about-us/cjis/ucr/nibrs-overviewFederal Bureau of Investigation (FBI). (n.d.-b). NIBRS. *U.S. Department of Justice.* https://www.fbi.gov/about-us/cjis/ucr/nibrs-overview

Federal Bureau of Investigation. (n.d.). Crime data explorer. *U.S. Department of Justice.* https://-crime-data-explorer.fr.cloud.gov/explorer/national/united-states/crime

Greenfeld, L. (1997). Sex offenses and offenders: An analysis of data on rape and sexual assault. *U.S. Department of Justice, Office of Justice Programs, Bureau of Justice Statistics.* https://bjs.ojp.gov/library/publications/sex-offenses-and-offenders-analysis-data-rape-and-sexual-assault

Hanson, R. K., & Bussière, M. T. (1998). Predicting relapse: A meta-analysis of sexual offender recidivism studies. *Journal of Consulting and Clinical Psychology, 66*(2), 348–362. https://www.doi.org/10.1037//0022-006x.66.2.348

Hanson, R. K., & Morton-Bourgon, K. E. (2005). The characteristics of persistent sexual offenders: A meta-analysis of recidivism studies. *Journal of Consulting and Clinical Psychology, 73*(6), 1154–1163. https://www.doi.org/10.1037/0022-006X.73.6.1154

Jenkins, P. (1998). *Moral panic: Changing concepts of the child molester in modern America.* Yale University Press.

Kinsey, A. C., Pomeroy, W. B., & Martin, C. E. (1948). *Sexual behavior in the human male.* Saunders.

Kinsey, A., Pomeroy, W. B., Martin, C., & Gebhard, P. (1953). *Sexual behavior in the human female.* Saunders.

Klein, J. L., & Cooper, D. T. (2019). Punitive attitudes toward sex offenders: Do moral panics cause community members to be more punitive? *Criminal Justice Policy Review, 30*(6), 948–968. https://www.doi.org/10.1177/0887403418767251

Koester, M. (2015). On safety, fear, and walking home alone at night as a woman. *Vice.* http://www.vice.com/read/i-was-assaulted-on-the-street-but-i-still-walk-home-alone-at-night-408

Langton, L., Berzofsky, M., Krebs, C., & Smiley-McDonald, H. (2012). *Victimizations not reported to the police, 2006–2010* [NCJ 238536]. Government Printing Office.

Levenson, J., Letourneau, E. J., Armstrong, K., & Zgoba, K. (2010). Failure to register as a sex offender: Is it associated with recidivism? *Justice Quarterly, 27*(3), 305–331. https://www.doi.org/10.1080/07418820902972399

Lösel, F., & Schmucker, M. (2005). The effectiveness of treatment for sexual offenders: A comprehensive meta-analysis. *Journal of Experimental Criminology, 1*(1), 117–146. https://www.doi.org/10.1007/s11292-004-6466-7

Lowe, G., & Willis, G. (2020). "Sex offender" versus "person": The influence of labels on willingness to volunteer with people who have sexually abused. *Sexual Abuse: A Journal of Research and Treatment, 32*(5), 591–613. https://www.doi.org/10.1177/1079063219841904

Lytle, R. (2019). Beyond panic: Variation in the legislative activity for sex offender registration and notification laws across states over time. *Criminal Justice Policy Review, 30*(3), 451–476. https://www.doi.org/10.1177/0887403416678287

Mason, J. (1984). Freud and the seduction theory: A challenge to the foundations of psychoanalysis. *The Atlantic.* https://www.theatlantic.com/magazine/archive/1984/02/freud-and-the-seduction-theory/376313/

Mendes, K., Ringrose, J., & Keller, J. (2018). #MeToo and the promise and pitfalls of challenging rape culture through digital feminist activism. *European Journal of Women's Studies, 25*(2), 236–246.

Michigan State University. (2015). Sexual assault prevention and awareness center: Myths and facts. https://sapac.umich.edu/article/52

Nwokeoma, B. N., Ede, M. O., Ugwuanyi, C., Mezieobi, D., Ugwoezuonu, A. U., Amoke, C., Egenti, N. T., Nwosu N., Oforka, T. O., Victor-Aigbodion, V., Offordile, E. E., Ezeh, N. E., Eze, C. O., Eluu, P. E., Ugwuanyi, B. E., Uzoagba, N. C., Ugwonna, G. O., Chukwu, C. L., Amadi, K. C., & Eseadi, C. (2019). Efficacy of prison-based cognitive behavioral rehabilitation intervention on violent sexual behaviors among sex offenders in Nigerian prisons. *Medicine, 98*(29). https://www.doi.org/10.1097/MD.0000000000016103

Office of the Attorney General, S. o. C. (2001). Megan's Law—Facts about sex offenders. *State of California Department of Justice.* http://meganslaw.ca.gov/facts.htm

One With Courage. (n.d.). Myths about child sexual abuse. *National Children's Alliance.* http://www.onewithcourage.org/wp-content/uploads/2011/09/myths-about-abuse1.pdf

Ouattara, M., Sen, P., & Thomson, M. (1998). Forced marriage, forced sex: The perils of childhood for girls. *Gender and Development, 6*(3), 27–33. https://www.doi.org/10.1080/741922829

Planty, M., Langston, L., Krebs, C., & Smiley-McDonald, H. (2013). *Female victims of sexual violence, 1994–2010* [NCJ 240655]. Government Printing Office.

Pulido, M. L. (2013). Child pornography: Basic facts about a horrific crime. *The Huffington Post.* http://www.huffingtonpost.com/mary-l-pulido-phd/child-pornography-basic-f_b_4094430.html

Stafford, M. C., & Vandiver, D. M. (2016). Public perceptions of sex crimes and sex offenders. In B. Francis & T. Sanders (Eds.), *Oxford Handbook of Sex Offences and Sex Offenders* (pp. 463–480). Oxford University Press.

United Nations Office on Drugs and Crime (UNODC). (2020). Sexual violence statistics on tableau. https://public.tableau.com/profile/unodc.rab#!/vizhome/Sexualviolence/SexualViolence_

University of Minnesota Duluth. (2001). List of rape myths: Sociology of rape. http://www.d.umn.edu/cla/faculty/jhamlin/3925/myths.html

DEFINITIONS

+: Part of the LGBTQIA+ acronym that refers to those who are heterosexual yet identify as an ally (i.e., are supportive of) to those who are LGBTQIA

Asexual: Persons who are not sexually attracted to others, regardless of their sex and/or gender identity

Bisexual: Persons who are sexually/romantically attracted to both men and women

Classic Experimental Design: Also referred to as a "true experiment," a research method that involves randomly assigning research participants either to an experimental group or a control group—the experimental group is exposed to a stimulus that is being studied and the control group is not exposed to this stimulus

Crime Data Explorer: A tool created by the FBI that combines crime data from two sources, the UCR and the NIBRS

Gay: Persons who are homosexual, sexually/romantically attracted to those of the same sex

Intersexual: Persons who have ambiguous sex organs and/or an unusual combination of sex chromosomes

Lesbian: Women who are sexually/romantically attracted to other women

LGBTQIA+: A commonly used acronym that describes persons who are lesbian, gay, bisexual, transgendered, queer/questioning, intersexual, asexual, and/or a member of the ally community

Meta-analysis: A type of study that involves gathering all relevant studies on a particular topic and analyzing all of the results to gain a more comprehensive answer to the research question posed

Moral Panic: A collective response to a perceived threat from an individual or group, which often exceeds the actual threat and is manifested through an us-versus-them, do-something-about-them sentiment

National Child Abuse and Neglect Data System (NCANDS): A data source based on data from all U.S. states regarding child abuse and neglect claims each year

National Crime Victimization Survey (NCVS): A data source including the number and type of victimizations that occur in the United States each year

National Incident-Based Reporting System (NIBRS): A detailed reporting of crimes that have occurred in the United States published by the FBI

National Intimate Partner and Sexual Violence Survey (NIPSVS): A survey conducted in 2010 and 2015 by the CDC that assesses the extent of intimate partner violence and sexual violence experienced among a representative sample of men and women in the United States

Queer: Persons who do not identify as heterosexual and can include persons who are lesbian, gay, and/or transgendered

Questioning: Persons who are questioning their own sexual identity and/or sexual orientation

Recidivism: An individual's return or relapse into criminal behavior, often after having received treatment for previous criminal behavior

Transexual: Persons who identify with a sex (male or female) that is in an opposite direction of what sex they were assigned at birth

Uniform Crime Reports (UCR): An annual report of crimes and arrests that have occurred in the United State, published by the FBI

United Nations Office on Drugs and Crime (UNODC): An international source of crime statistics, including sexual violence, that is developed from an annual survey on crime trends and operations of criminal justice systems and other national surveys administered in member countries of the United Nations.

CHAPTER 2

Theories about Sex Crimes and Persons Who Commit Sex Crimes

CHAPTER OBJECTIVES

- Identify the essential components of a theory, including their probabilistic nature
- Provide an overview of biological theories, including how hormones/neurotransmitters, the structure of the brain, genetics and sex chromosomes, and intelligence have been applied to explain the commission of sex crimes
- Provide an overview of psychological theories with specific attention to psychoanalytical theory, attachment theory, behaviorism, cognitive-based theories, and distinguishing personality traits among persons who sexually offend
- Describe sex-crime-specific theories, including a self-regulation model of relapse among offenders who have committed a sex crime, precondition theory, and quadripartite theory
- Provide an overview of several criminological theories that have been relied upon to explain persons who sexually offend: social control (bonding) theory, self-control theory, routine activity theory, and social learning theory
- Identify common causes among theories to explain sexual offending

Criminological theories provide an explanation of why someone would commit an offense. Having a sound, reliable, and valid theory can guide the development of assessment tools, identify successful treatment strategies, and develop empirically-based policies. In this chapter, we will broadly discuss some of the theories that have been applied to explain sexually offending. This will include biological, psychological, sex-crime specific and criminological theories. We will conclude by providing an overview of the key components among all of the theories that explain sexually offending.

ESSENTIAL COMPONENTS OF A THEORY

What causes people to commit sex crimes, and how do these people differ from those who do not commit a sex crime? There is no single, universally accepted answer. Instead, there are different answers linked to different theories explaining why persons sexually offend. This begs the question: What is a theory? A theory is more than a mere hunch, and it is more than someone's personal ideas about the causes of something. A conventional definition is that

DOI: 10.4324/9781003031444-2

22 Theories about Sex Crimes

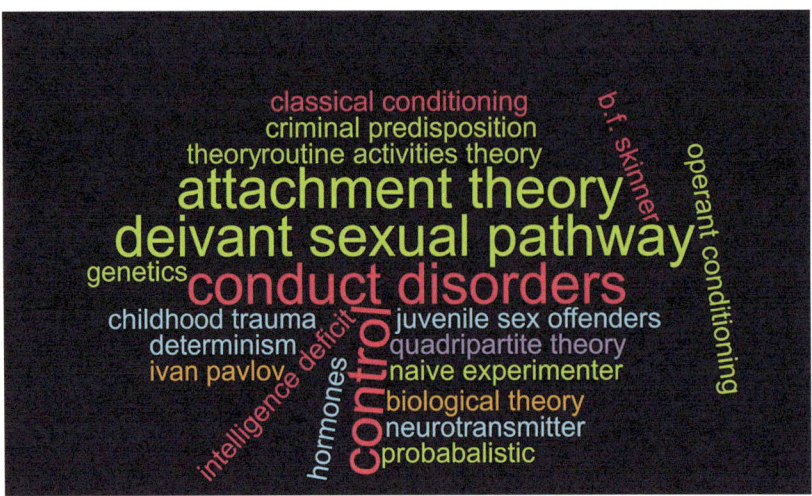

a theory is a "set of logically interrelated statements in the form of empirical assertions about properties of infinite classes of events or things" (Gibbs, 1972, p. 5). As the definition indicates, a theory is first a set of logically interrelated statements. A theory might claim that certain types of brain abnormalities cause people to commit sex crimes and then add that certain types of brain abnormalities cause people to have low-impulse control and low-impulse control is the proximate cause of sex crimes. There are three interrelated statements here. One statement is that certain types of brain abnormalities cause low-impulse control. A second statement is that low-impulse control causes sex crimes. A third statement is that certain types of brain abnormalities cause sex crimes indirectly through (or because of) low-impulse control.

If these interrelated statements comprise a theory that explains sexually offending, they must be in the form of empirical assertions (the second part of Gibbs's definition). That is, at least some of the statements, in theory, must be testable. Thus, there must be a possibility of bringing evidence to bear on the theory's statements about the extent to which they are true or false. This is what primarily distinguishes theories from mere hunches.

Theories are also about "properties of infinite classes of events or things" (the third part of Gibbs's definition). A theory cannot be about why a particular person has committed (or will commit) sex crimes. There might be an identifiable answer, and the answer might be different from why another person has committed sex crimes. But theories are not about particular people. Instead, they are generalizations about classes of people, and the generalizations must not be limited to a particular time and place. For example, it would not be a theory if someone proposed to explain why young males were more likely than other people to have committed sex crimes in the United States last March. If someone proposed a theory to explain why young males are more likely than other people to commit sex crimes, the theory should apply to all young males, preferably in all places and at all times and not just in the United States at a particular time.

Theories about sexually offending help us make sense of what we know about them and their motives. Using the young male example again, in the preceding chapter, there is considerable evidence from sources that young males are more likely than other groups to commit a sex crime. A theory can help us understand why this is the case; for example, it might be due to hormone levels, or it might be learned behavior.

Theories about sexually offending are important not only because they provide understanding but also because they are essential for identifying effective policies about control and treatment. For example, behavioral theories (to be discussed subsequently) are the foundation of many sex-offender treatment programs today. Without accurate theories about the causes of sex crimes and the persons who commit them, we would not know how to respond to them effectively. Theories can be seen as guides to developing good assessments, successful treatment, and empirically-based policies.

PROBABILISTIC NATURE OF THEORIES

Whether the theories are about sexually offending or crime in general, it is important to emphasize that both types of theory propose **probabilistic causes** (i.e., a cause may result in a specified outcome) rather than **deterministic causes** (i.e., a cause *always* results in a specified outcome). A theory might identify some particular factor (e.g., some biological abnormality) always causes one to commit a sex crime, which is to say the theory would propose the factor is a deterministic cause. Neither the version of the psychological theory described above nor **self-control theory** (or any theory we will consider) proposes deterministic causes. Self-control theory does not propose that low self-control *always* causes crime. Instead, it says that low self-control *increases the likelihood* of committing crimes, including sex crimes.

Probabilistic theories are not inferior to deterministic theories; they are different. Today, few deny that cigarette smoking causes lung cancer. Cigarette smoking, however, does not always cause lung cancer, and it is also the case that lung cancer is not always caused by cigarette smoking. Some cigarette smokers never get lung cancer, and some people with lung cancer never smoked cigarettes or were never around cigarette smokers. Cigarette smoking only increases the likelihood of lung cancer, and the more cigarettes people smoke (or the longer the period they smoke), the greater their likelihood of lung cancer. That cigarette smoking is a probabilistic cause of lung cancer does not make it any less of a cause. This is also true of probabilistic causes of sex crimes and the persons who commit them.

BIOLOGICAL THEORIES

As scientific discoveries are made about biological processes, it is not surprising that they are being linked to particular behaviors, including sex crimes. An examination of a broad range of studies revealed that 33%–100% of persons who committed a sex crime had brain abnormalities. For those who had not committed a sex crime, such brain abnormalities were present in 0%–17% of individuals (see Stinson et al., 2008, for discussion). Other abnormalities have also been identified as potential causal factors of sexually offending such as hormones/neurotransmitters, brain structure, sex chromosomes/genetic traits, and intelligence deficits (i.e., developmental disabilities) (Stinson et al., 2008).

Hormones and Neurotransmitters

It is widely accepted that **hormones** (chemical secretions) affect a wide range of bodily functions (Stinson et al., 2008). With regard to hormones, testosterone is most closely associated with the sexual arousal of boys and men. It has been speculated that sexual violence is the result of high levels of testosterone, yet research has produced mixed results (Bain et al., 1987). Moreover, it has been proposed that those who are exposed to high amounts of testosterone or other factors affecting their androgen system (a group of hormones that affect the male reproductive system) while they are in utero are more likely to sexually offend

(Kruger et al., 2019). For example, some support was found between prenatal exposure to testosterone and subsequent child sexually offending (Kruger et al., 2019). The research in this area, however, is scant and relies on relatively small samples.

Also, **neurotransmitters** (chemicals in the brain) affect brain function, mood, and autonomic reactions (heart rate, breathing, and other bodily functions that respond to anxiety-provoking situations) (Stinson et al., 2008). Neurotransmitters, such as serotonin, have been assessed for their link to violent behavior, including sex crimes. Few studies have been conducted in this area, but among them, there is little support for this (see Jakubczyk et al., 2017).

Brain Structural Differences

Some researchers have hypothesized that structural brain differences may exist between persons who have committed a sex crime and persons who have not committed a sex crime (Savopoulos & Lindell, 2018). Much of the evidence from this is based on small samples or even anecdotal evidence. As noted in Focus Box 2.1, cases of sexually offending caused by brain function have been reported.

Recently, one group of researchers systematically reviewed 15 studies that involved brain imaging of persons who have committed a sex crime and those who had not (Kirk-Provencher et al., 2020). These studies assessed a variety of possible brain structural differences between the two groups, including brain size, gray matter volume, cortical thickness, white matter connectivity, and structural and functional differences among regions in the brain. Most of these studies are limited methodologically, using small samples and relied on only male samples. After reviewing the studies, the authors stated that there is not enough evidence to conclude these two groups vary substantially with regard to brain differences (Kirk-Provencher et al., 2020).

Focus Box 2.1 Brain Tumor and Pedophilia Link

Although rare, reports of a brain tumor causing pedophilia have been made. In one instance, a 40-year-old teacher began to exhibit hypersexual behavior, including pedophilic interests. The man, who previously had not engaged in sexually deviant behavior, began viewing child pornography on the internet and soliciting prostitutes. The man's wife reported his sexual advances toward children. He was found guilty of these sex crimes and sentenced to prison. The man recognized that the behavior was problematic and wrong but indicated he did not have the restraint to overcome these feelings. The night before his prison sentence began, he complained of a headache and balance problems, along with the urge to rape his landlady. After going to the hospital, he was diagnosed with a brain tumor. It was removed, and the symptoms disappeared. The man, seven months later, again reported headaches and began collecting child pornography. The tumor had returned. It was removed, and the symptoms disappeared again. A neurologist commented on the case, wondering if the tumor caused hormonal changes, which in turn caused abnormal sexual behavior.

Note. Adapted from Choi (2002).

Genetics and Sex Chromosome Abnormalities

Research has found that genetics (i.e., inheriting certain characteristics) alone does not explain sexually offending (Stinson et al., 2008). Recently, a controversial theory of rape was proposed by Thornhill and Palmer (2000), claiming rape is the product of evolution and that under certain conditions, all men have the capacity to rape. This theory, however, has been highly criticized for lack of systematic evidence (Zion, 2000).

With regard to chromosome abnormalities, males typically have an X and a Y chromosome (XY), whereas females have two X chromosomes (XX). Occasionally, rare combinations of chromosomes occur (e.g., XXY, XXXY, XYY), and it has been suggested these may be linked to the commission of sex crimes (Harrison et al., 2001). Among a sample of men who had committed a sex crime, chromosomal abnormalities occurred at a slightly higher rate (4%) than among persons who had not sexually offended (0.1%) (Harrison et al., 2001). Chromosomal abnormalities may be associated with behavior problems, including impulsive behaviors, which can cause sex crimes. More research, however, is needed.

Intelligence Deficits and Persons with Developmental Disabilities

Some researchers have proposed that persons who commit a sex crime may have lower intelligence overall than persons who do not commit a sex crime. First, it is theorized that there are four common characteristics of persons with a developmental disability that could cause them to act out sexually: (1) impulsive behavior, (2) aggression/acting out, (3) poor interpersonal skills, and (4) poor coping skills and self-esteem issues (Stinson et al., 2008).

Additionally, it is also theorized that there is a link between having developmental disabilities and sexually offending due to the mental age of the offenders. For example, it has been proposed that people with intellectual deficits molest children because the actual age of the victim matches the mental age of the offender (O'Callaghan, 1998). The exact causal mechanism warrants further research (Stinson et al., 2008). Research, however, has not conclusively supported a link between low intelligence and committing a sex crime (see Falligant et al., 2017).

In summary, biological theories identify many possible causes of sex crimes (e.g., excessive testosterone, genetic defect, and developmental disability), yet there is little to moderate support for such theories. Most of the support is anecdotal or based on relatively small samples.

PSYCHOLOGICAL THEORIES

Psychological theories are relied upon as well to explain a broad range of abnormal behavior, including deviant sexual behavior. Psychological theories are deeply rooted in concepts developed by Sigmund Freud, who proposed sexual development as a key construct to explain human behavior. Freud's theories led the way to the emphasis on childhood development, especially the importance of attaching to a caregiver. This led the way to John Bowlby's development of **attachment theory**. Moreover, Ivan Pavlov and B. F. Skinner developed the components of behaviorism, which is still a key element in many treatment programs today for persons who sexually offend. Subsequently, the focus was placed on the thought processes and specific personality traits of those who engage in deviant behaviors. Thus, all of these psychological theories and concepts are discussed in this section.

Freud's Psychoanalytical Theory

Freud identified several psychological concepts that he would later rely upon in his explanation of the development of sexually deviant behavior. First, he proposed that there are five stages of ***psychosexual development:*** (1) oral (focus on the mouth, sucking behavior), (2) anal (focus on the anus, controlling bodily functions), (3) phallic (focus on genitals), (4) latency (relatively calm period with no specific focus), and (5) genital (focus on sexual attraction to others).

Freud proposed that individuals prone to deviant sexual behavior fixate on certain stages—they get "stuck" during development—or they successfully progress through each stage and possibly, later, regress to a particular stage. Thus, ***fixation*** and ***regression*** can result in sexually deviant behavior. Additionally, he proposed that problems can occur during the phallic stage. ***Castration anxiety*** can occur, where boys are fearful of losing or having damage done to their penis. Girls may experience ***penis envy***, which is a feeling of anxiety that occurs when they realize they do not have a penis. This occurs around the ages of three to five years (Freud, 1962).

Freud also proposed three parts to one's personality: (1) ***id***, (2) ***ego***, and (3) ***superego***. The id is responsible for seeking self-pleasure. The ego acts as a mediator between the id and superego. The superego is associated with one's moral principles, acting as one's conscience. These aspects are often in a state of struggle yet eventually determine one's sexual behaviors. For someone who engages in sexual deviance, it is the result of the id not being regulated by the ego and the superego. With regard to child molestation, Freud speculated that the individual's childhood must have involved trauma and the sexual attraction to children results from their attempt to compensate for their own childhood (Freud, 1962).

Bowlby's Attachment Theory

John Bowlby was influenced by Konrad Lorenz's research. Lorenz proposed that attachments were an evolutionary behavior and innate. He raised a group of goslings from eggs and found they would imprint to him. Bowlby assessed this application to humans, noting how important it was for babies to attach to someone when they were young. Bowlby (1958, 1988) proposed that the relationship children have with their primary caretaker affects adulthood functioning, especially with regard to their relationships with others. Children develop a perception of the world and how to process information, which he proposed remains relatively stable throughout life (Bowlby, 1977).

In a summary of Bowlby's research, the Health Research Funding Research Organization (2021, n.p.) identified five main points of the attachment theory. First, "children have an innate need to attach to at least one primary figure." It is also OK for a child to have multiple persons they attach to, but not having anyone to attach to can be devastating for healthy social development. Second, children should receive continuous care for the first two years of their lives from their primary caregiver. Disruption in a caregiver can be traumatic for the child and can have a lasting negative impact. Third, children who do not develop a healthy attachment to their primary caregiver in their first two years of life are at a higher risk of experiencing problems later such as aggression, depression, delinquency, lower intelligence, and difficulty forming an affectionate relationship with others. Fourth, when a child is separated from their primary caregiver during that critical bonding time, the child will experience immediate stress. This can result in the child initially protesting, followed by experiencing despair and, subsequently, detachment. And fifth, every child relies upon the attachment they formed during the first two years of their lives as a model for subsequent relationships.

It is easy to see where attachment theory can be applied to persons who have committed a sex crime. Concerning modern research on the application to explaining sex crimes, persons who have committed a sex crime disproportionately had poor parental attachment and high levels of parental rejection (Marshall, 1989; Marshall et al., 1995). Furthermore, as discussed in the "theories specific to sex-crimes" section, we present an attachment theory developed specifically to explain sexually offending.

Pavlov and Skinner's Behaviorism

Behavioral theories have been relied upon to explain diverse behaviors (Montrenes & Matson, 2021), including the deviant sexual arousal of those who have committed a sex crime. Behavioral theories rely exclusively on the association between giving a stimulus and eliciting a known and predictable response. That is, it takes into account a stimulus (e.g., give a dog food) and the response (e.g., salivate). It does not consider the cognitive processes that occur from the time a stimulus is given to when a response occurs.

The foundations of behavioral theories are rooted in ***classical conditioning*** and ***operant conditioning***. Classical conditioning was developed by Ivan Pavlov and is illustrated in Figure 2.1. Classical conditioning involves eliciting a conditioned response (e.g., a dog salivating at the sight of food) from a neutral stimulus (e.g., the sound of a bell) after successively pairing the two (e.g., sound of a bell resulting in dog salivating). Normally, the neutral stimulus (e.g., sound of a bell) does not instantly elicit a response (e.g., a dog salivating), but eventually the neutral stimulus by itself will elicit a conditioned response (Pavlov, 1927).

Operant conditioning was developed by B. F. Skinner and explains the acquisition and maintenance of behaviors through a process of reinforcement and punishment. Reinforcement results in an increase in the likelihood of a certain behavior, whereas punishment decreases the probability of the behavior. Reinforcement refers to anything that is rewarding (e.g., money, sexual arousal). Punishment refers to anything that is noxious (e.g., a negative feeling, pain; Skinner, 1932). These key concepts are summarized in Figure 2.2.

Cognitive-Based Theories

A variety of cognitive processes (interpretation of emotions, cue perception, and information processing—including learning) affects behaviors and has been relied upon to explain dysfunctional behaviors, including sexually offending (Stinson et al., 2008). Cognitive theories focus on explaining both the development of sexually offending and the maintenance of such behaviors. Cognitive theories are broad, but for the purpose of explaining sexually offending, several concepts are essential: ***cognitive schemas, cognitive distortions, cognitive biases, experiential learning, and vicarious learning***.

Cognitive schemas help us organize information and make sense of the world. They involve creating organized patterns of previous experiences, which we rely upon to interpret new information (Fiske & Taylor, 1991). With regard to persons who have committed a sex crime and cognitive schemas, two related areas of research have emerged: (1) cognitive distortions and (2) causal and blame attributions (Stinson et al., 2008).

Cognitive distortions are a type of automatic thought process that develops and assists in minimizing the seriousness of the offense (Ward, 2000). Child molesters may believe they are "educating" children. Rapists may believe that women secretly desire to be raped. We discuss these cognitive distortions more in-depth in Chapters 3 and 4.

28 Theories about Sex Crimes

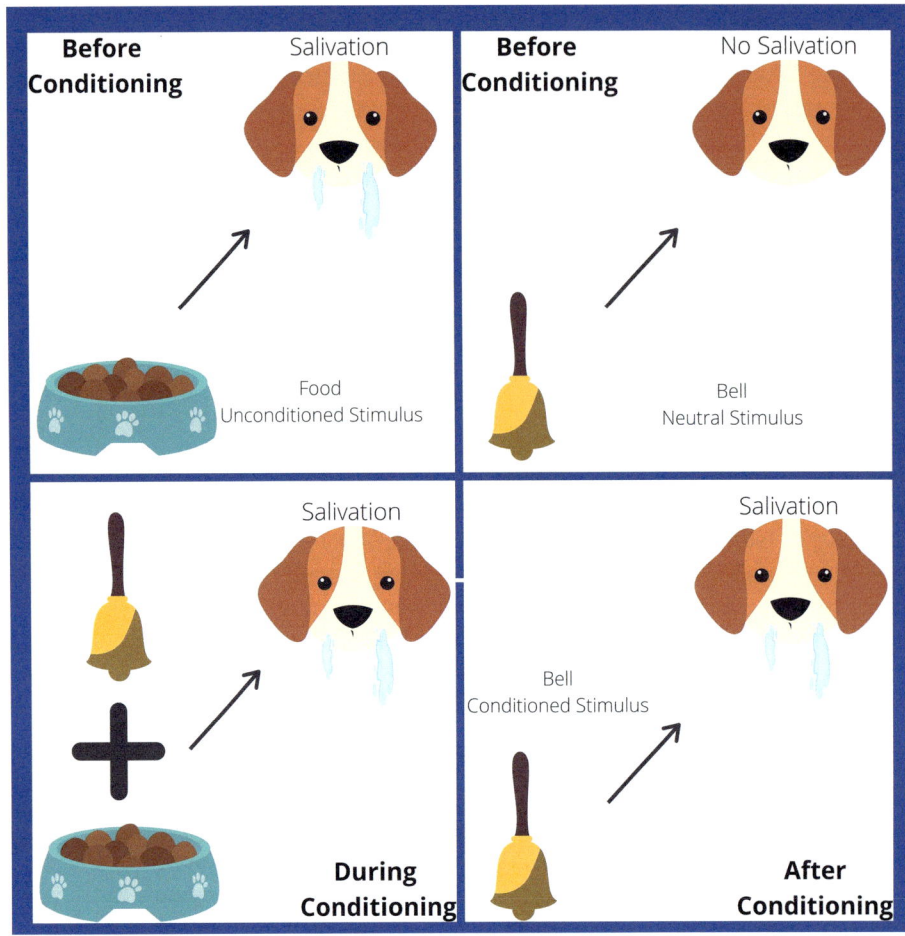

FIGURE 2.1 Pavlov's Classical Conditioning.

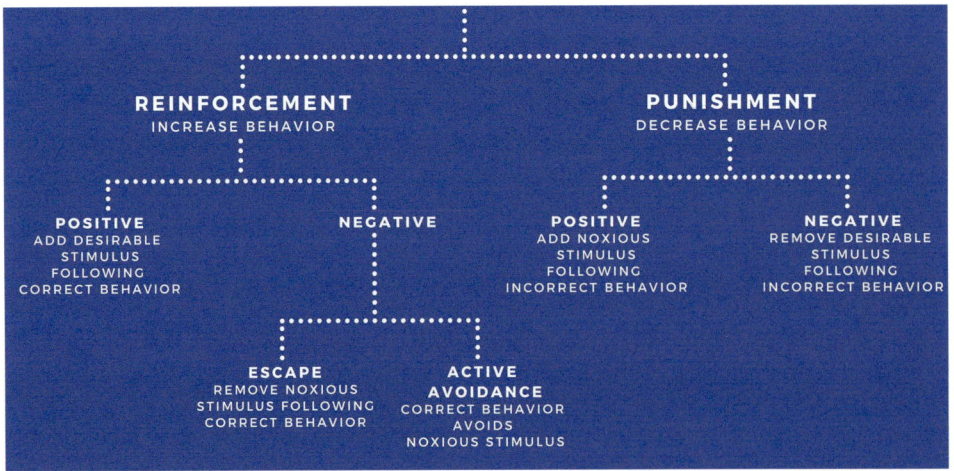

FIGURE 2.2 B. F. Skinner's Operant Conditioning.

Also, explanations of sexually offending have been linked to causal and blame attributions (Stinson et al., 2008). Causal attributions involve offenders' perceptions of the world and how they evaluate their own behaviors. Blame attributions refer to how much offenders blame themselves and others for their own behavior. This becomes a critical factor when considering a treatment approach, as it can dictate different treatment approaches. In one study, for example, those who committed a non-contact offense or an offense against a child placed less blame on external factors than rapists (McAnena et al., 2016).

Cognitive biases refer to illogical thoughts that skew one's perception of the world. Researchers have identified many biases that contribute to sexually offending. For example, some have theorized that persons who commit a sex crime engage in self-serving and self-protective biases due to low self-esteem and a lack of attachment to others (Marshall et al., 1997). Researchers have also speculated that persons who have committed a sex crime possess a sense of sexual entitlement—that is, their needs are greater than their victims' (Hanson et al., 1994).

Many sex-crime-specific and criminological theories rely on two essential learning principles, experiential learning and vicarious learning, to explain the commission of deviant and sexually offending behaviors. Experiential learning involves learning through direct personal experience. In this way, a victim of physical abuse may engage in the same behavior later because they have learned this is a means to achieve an intended goal. Vicarious learning refers to a person learning from what they observe has happened to others. Thus, someone who has been exposed to violence as a means to obtain what they want will learn this can be a viable behavior for them to gain what they want.

Personality Development

Personality development is deeply rooted in psychological theory; Freud proposed that early childhood experiences determine one's personality. More modern research has identified particular personality traits that may combine with biological, cognitive, and social factors to cause sexually offending (Stinson et al., 2008). We discuss the traits that have been identified (**impulsivity**, **callousness** and **lack of empathy**, **narcissism**, **sadism**, and **personality pathology**) below.

Impulsivity is a common characteristic identified among persons who have committed a sex crime and refers to a need for instant gratification and an inability to control impulses (Stinson et al., 2008). For example, impulsivity was found to be prevalent among a sample of male college students who committed rape but not among those who had not committed rape (Mouilso et al., 2013).

Callousness refers to a blunted emotional response to others, whereas a lack of empathy refers to an inability to respond to someone else with appropriate emotions. Researchers have speculated that both of these affect those who commit sex crimes (Barnett & Mann, 2013; Porter et al., 2001). More specifically, they have proposed that child abuse causes one to develop callousness and lack of empathy, increasing the likelihood of engaging in a sex crime (Porter et al., 2001).

Narcissism refers to self-love, grandiose perceptions of one's self, and a sense of entitlement. Narcissistic traits do exist at high rates among rapists who attack women perceived to be unattainable (Baumeister et al., 2002). Researchers have identified sadism, achieving sexual arousal from inflicting pain or humiliation on another person, as a trait that exists among persons who have committed a sex crime. More specifically, it is found among those who commit sexual murder and those who commit violent sex crimes (Berger et al., 1999).

The American Psychiatric Association (2013) has identified many personality disorders that have a host of common traits: impulsivity, egocentricity, mood problems, self-identity issues, harm to self and others, and unpredictable behaviors. Personality pathologies involve a set of emotional and behavioral characteristics that cause maladaptive behaviors, including committing sex crimes. Persons who have committed a sex crime, in general, exhibit problems with interpersonal relationships (Stinson et al., 2008).

Freud's psychoanalytical theory gave way to subsequent psychological theories, and those constructs are still relied upon today. They provide a structure for more modern theories to explain sexually offending. Several sex-crime-specific theories have been developed, and we discuss those next.

SEX-CRIME-SPECIFIC THEORIES

Several researchers have developed unique theories to explain sex crimes and the persons who commit them. These sex-crime- and sex-offender-specific theories are often rooted in other broader theories. For example, biological theories are relied upon to account for diseases that may contribute to people committing sex crimes. Researchers have developed theories to explain deviant sexual arousal, paraphilias, child molestation, rape, and/or accessing child pornography. Some of these theories explain sex crimes broadly, whereas others focus on only one type (e.g., rape). In this section, we highlight a few of the theories developed to explain sex crimes and sexually offending.

A Self-Regulation Model of the Relapse Process in Sexual Offenders (Ward & Hudson, 1998)

Building on the key concepts of behavioral theories, Ward and Hudson (1998) proposed a ***self-regulation model of relapse in sexual offenders***. This model proposes that people behave in a way that is goal directed. They act in certain ways to achieve the desired state or to avoid an undesired state. That is, they seek pleasure and/or avoid pain. Ward and Hudson identified eight paths people can take, with four of them resulting in committing a sex crime against a child. Here, we will focus on the four paths that result in a sex crime.

First, the avoidant-passive pathway involves those who have a desire to commit a sex crime, yet they fail to prevent this from occurring. They try not to offend but are under-regulated or disinhibited. They either lack the ability or refuse to cease a behavioral pattern that has developed. Second, the avoidant-active pathway, also referred to as the misregulation pathway, involves active attempts to avoid deviant thoughts and behavior associated with sexually offending. The active strategies, however, are unsuitable ones such as the use of alcohol or drugs to suppress deviant thoughts. These strategies ultimately lead to relapsing.

The third pathway identified is the approach-automatic pathway. These persons do have a goal of committing a sex crime. Here, cognitive and behavioral patterns have been well established that lead to committing a sex crime. They are affected by situational factors and do not have sophisticated details of planning. The fourth pathway identified is the approach-explicit pathway. These persons have a childhood history that led to sexual aggression cognitions. This type of individual engages in planning, including detailed ***grooming*** behaviors. They have an established goal of committing a sex crime (Ward & Hudson, 1998).

This theory provides a way to classify persons who have committed child sexual abuse in a way that identifies precursors and suggests potential targets for treatment. In a test of this classification system, one study found that this model "could be reliably employed in the classification of child molesters" (Bickley & Beech, 2002, p. 384). Others have written extensively on how this theory can quickly be adapted to treatment approaches successfully (Lindsay et al., 2007) and even combined with other treatment modalities (see Yates & Ward, 2008).

Attachment Theory Specific to Sex Crimes (Ward et al., 1995)

Although we have discussed Bowlby's attachment theory, which applies broadly to the mechanisms and importance of a child forming secure attachments to a caregiver, we summarize a theory that builds on it to specifically explain sexually offending. Ward et al. (1995) specifically identified two attachment styles in explaining deviant sexual behavior: (1) anxious-ambivalent attachment style and (2) avoidant attachment style. Those who develop an anxious-ambivalent attachment style have low self-esteem and poor self-confidence, are dependent on others for approval, and are easily frustrated by interpersonal relationships (Ward et al., 1995). Sexual abuse is the result of engaging in self-serving behavior based on feelings toward others (Marshall, 1993). Typically, the offender assumes the victim is deserving of the abuse (Marshall, 1993). This explanation, therefore, has been relied upon by researchers to explain child molestation (Marshall & Mazzucco, 1995).

Those who develop avoidant attachment styles often devalue relationships. Also, they have low empathy and demonstrate hostility toward others (Ward et al., 1995). This type of attachment style *may* lead to sexually offending. For example, if combined with sexual and aggressive urges, a sense of entitlement and desire for power can lead to a person committing a sex crime (Marshall, 1993). Such behaviors are maintained by the offender to reduce frustration and isolate one's self from intimate relationships (Marshall, 1993). Alternatively, researchers have hypothesized that someone with an avoidant attachment style may commit sex crimes because of an interaction of no or low empathy skills, which is caused by the lack of attachment formed in early childhood, and feelings of hostility (Ward et al., 1995). This person would not be likely to invest in the work associated with forming an intimate relationship, which can lead to committing rape or other sex crimes.

A substantial amount of research supports the existence of these attachment styles (Gunst et al., 2017). Others have built upon these concepts to identify how persons with these different attachment styles are affected by previous trauma (Yoder et al., 2020) and treatment (Miller & Klockner, 2019). Overall, this theory had been widely applied to understand more of the etiology of offending and subsequently points to particular treatment targets for those who are treating persons who have committed a sex crime.

Precondition Theory (Finkelhor, 1984)

Finkelhor's (1984) precondition theory seeks to explain men who commit child sexual abuse. Researchers describe this theory as multifaceted, including explanations of men's sexual arousal with consideration given to situational and contextual variables (Ward & Hudson, 2001). This theory also incorporates several cognitive and behavioral concepts to provide an explanation of committing child sexual abuse. The overall premise of the theory is that for someone to sexually offend, they must have some sort of motivation to commit child sexual abuse, overcome any internal and external inhibitions, and overcome any possible resistance from the child. These preconditions are illustrated in Figure 2.3 and discussed below in more detail.

32 Theories about Sex Crimes

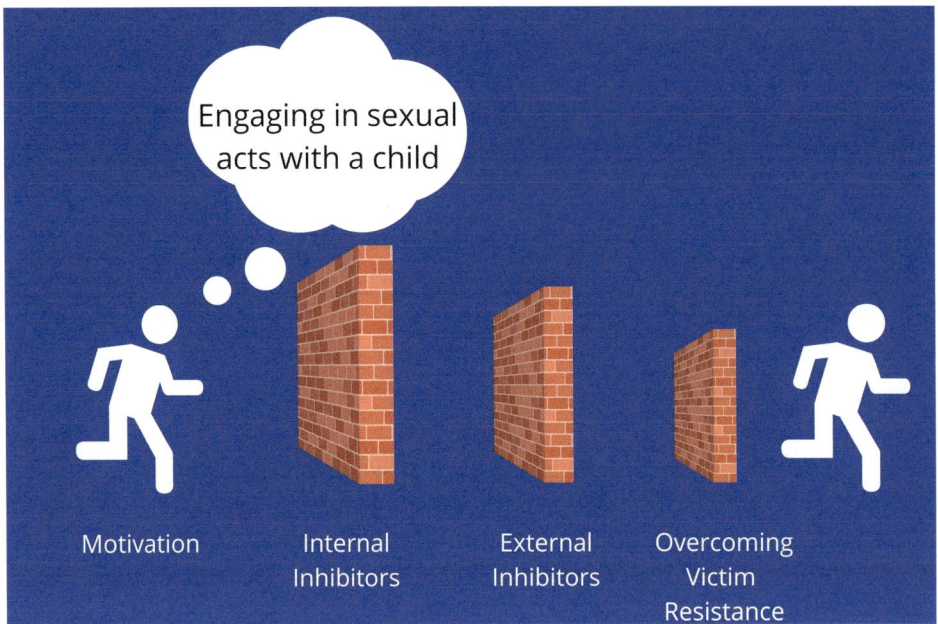

FIGURE 2.3 Finkelhor's Precondition Theory.

The first precondition is that *there must be an offender with the motivation to sexually abuse children* (Finkelhor, 1984). With the exception of reflexive behaviors, such as sneezing and blinking, human behavior is preceded by thought or premeditation. Child sexual abuse is no exception. Men sexually abuse children because they desire to—they are motivated. Their motivation can be manifested in three ways: (1) offenders are aroused by sex with children (*sexual arousal*); (2) child sexual abuse satisfies some emotional need such as intimacy (*emotional congruence*); and (3) there is no other viable source of sexual gratification or nothing as satisfying as sexual abuse of children (*emotional congruence*). This theory, therefore, suggests that child sexual abuse does not "just happen." There are several possible underlying issues that must exist before child sexual abuse occurs.

The second precondition is that *the offender must overcome internal inhibitions against child sexual abuse* (Finkelhor, 1984). In deciding whether to sexually abuse children, people might consider its illegality, the consequences if caught (e.g., imprisonment), its immorality, and the harm to victims. To overcome such inhibitions, motivated offenders often subscribe to cognitive distortions that weaken or even eliminate such obstacles, thus granting themselves "permission" to sexually abuse children. Cognitive distortions minimize or deny the dangerousness of the behavior, justify it, and relieve the offender of responsibility. Cognitive distortions such as "children need to be taught about sex," "children are very seductive," and "the child is too young to know what is happening" can cause child sexual abusers to believe they are doing nothing wrong. Impulse disorder, senility, psychosis, severe stress, alcoholism, and strong patriarchal beliefs that women and children are inferior also weaken internal inhibitions (Beech & Ward, 2004).

The third precondition is that *the offender must overcome external obstacles to the abuse* (Finkelhor, 1984). This involves creating opportunities to sexually abuse children so that the victim is alone (vulnerable) and the offender is unlikely to be caught. Offenders may create opportunities for child sexual abuse by grooming potential victims, which as discussed in more detail in Chapter 4, involves manipulating children into situations where they can be more easily sexually abused and there is less of a chance to be detected.

The fourth precondition is that *the offender must overcome resistance by the child* (Finkelhor, 1984). In some instances, sexually violent offenders use physical violence, weapons, bindings, or verbal intimidation to overcome resistance. Sometimes, they use alcohol and other drugs. More often, they overcome resistance by manipulating the child into giving trust, loyalty, and affection. This can also be part of grooming a potential victim.

Overall, there is moderate to strong empirical support for the precondition theory (see Finkelhor et al., 2006, for a discussion). One of the goals of this theory is to identify "domains that [are] useful targets for prevention and treatment" (Finkelhor et al., 2016, p. 36). To that end, this theory has successfully identified multiple treatment targets such as addressing emotional functioning, low self-esteem, lack of empathy, childhood trauma, narcissism, deviant sexual arousal, relationship skills, alcohol and substance abuse, cognitive distortions/thinking errors, impulsivity, stress management, use of pornography, and recognition of engaging on grooming behaviors (Finkelhor et al., 2016). The clinical application of preconditions theory, however, is limited in its ability to address highly antisocial or psychopathic individuals or those who have severe mental illness (Finkelhor et al., 2016).

Quadripartite Theory (Hall & Hirschman, 1991)

This theory seeks to explain sexual aggression against women. "The [theory's] components . . . —physiological sexual arousal, cognitions that justify sexual aggression, affective dyscontrol, and personality problems—function as motivational precursors that increase the probability of sexually aggressive behavior" (Hall & Hirschman, 1991, p. 662). The authors acknowledge a probabilistic nature component to their theory by stating that each of the precursors can increase a person's chance of committing sexual abuse against women, and this can occur at varying levels depending on the strength of that precursor. We discuss each of the four precursors below. This theory later was expanded as an explanation of child sexual abuse (Ward, 2000).

The first precursor is physiological sexual arousal (Hall & Hirschman, 1991). Although child sexual abuse might result from deviant sexual arousal, sex crimes against adults can result from nondeviant sexual arousal. "Similar psychological processes may underlie sexual arousal that results in appropriate sexual behavior as well as sexual arousal that results in sexual aggression" (Hall & Hirschman, 1991, p. 664). As such, sexual arousal alone does not cause sexual aggression against women.

Cognitions that justify sexual aggression are the second precursor identified by Hall and Hirschman (1991). Physiological sexual arousal must be cognitively assessed before it is acted upon. These cognitions can include justifications and myths suggesting that sexual aggression against women is acceptable and perhaps even appropriate in some situations. For example, a person might support **rape myths** (see Chapter 3) that any sex act, regardless of coercion, is enjoyable for the victim, resulting in the belief that rape is acceptable. When physiological arousal is coupled with this kind of cognitive appraisal, there is an increased probability of sexual aggression.

The third precursor is affective dyscontrol (i.e., difficulty controlling one's emotions). According to Hall and Hirschman (1991), negative emotions often precede cognitive appraisals about committing a sex crime. Anger might be an important negative emotion for rape, whereas, for child molesting, it might be depression. Most people control their negative emotions so that they express their sexual behavior appropriately (e.g., among consenting adults). Sexual aggression, however, may occur "when these affective states become so compelling and powerful that they overcome inhibitions (e.g., guilt, moral conviction, anxiety, empathy for the victim)" (Hall & Hirschman, 1991, p. 664).

Personality problems are the fourth identified precursor (Hall & Hirschman, 1991). Personality problems are more enduring than physiological sexual arousal, cognitions that justify sexual aggression, and affective dyscontrol. Negative childhood and adolescent experiences (e.g., parental neglect or divorce and physical or sexual abuse) and developmental limitations (e.g., limited education and poor social skills) cause enduring personality problems. Sexual aggressors against women may be selfish, exploitative of others, remorseless, and antisocial, with a history of committing other, nonsexual crimes.

This theory has been described as an "extremely influential ... theory," yet a critical analysis was initially lacking (Ward, 2000). In Ward's (2000) systematic evaluation, he noted that some weaknesses exist such as ambiguity and lack of clarity (see Ward, 2000, for a complete discussion). Overall, however, the theory has served and guided research efforts and clinical application and identified multiple pathways to sexually offending.

Integrated Theory (Marshall & Barbaree, 1990)

Like Hall and Hirschman (1991), Marshall and Barbaree (1990) proposed that early, negative childhood experiences can be a precursor to committing a sex crime. Early childhood physical or sexual abuse, neglect, and inconsistent discipline can cause children to see their caregivers as emotionally absent and view themselves as unworthy of being loved. They later become adolescents and adults who are hostile and insensitive to others and use aggression as a way to solve problems. They also have low self-esteem and poor interpersonal and coping skills. A man who considers himself socially inadequate and unworthy of love might develop fantasies of power over and contempt for women.

An important part of the theory is a biological connection between sexual impulses and aggression. Males have a "biologically endowed propensity for self-interest associated with a tendency to fuse sex and aggression" (Marshall & Barbaree, 1990, p. 257). Both types of impulses come from the same part of the brain, which makes it difficult for young boys to distinguish between anger and sexual arousal. They must learn to use inhibitory controls to constrain their sexual and aggressive self-interested behavior in socially acceptable ways. Together with increasing hormone levels that occur during puberty, male adolescents and young men are vulnerable to commit sex crimes. Many sex crimes provide a release of sexual tension, a sense of control over others, interpersonal intimacy, self-esteem, and feelings of masculinity.

In summary, psychological theories include a broad range of constructs, including psychoanalytical theory, attachment theory, behaviorism, cognitive theories, and the identification of distinguishing personality traits. These theories, overall, have received moderate to strong empirical support, often guiding assessment, treatment, and policies. In the next section, we discuss several criminological theories that have been applied to explain sexually offending.

CRIMINOLOGICAL THEORIES

Many criminological theories purport to explain a broad range of crimes (e.g., theft, robbery, murder), including sex crimes (e.g., rape, child molestation, child pornography). To the extent that persons who have committed a sex crime also commit nonsex crimes, broad-based criminological theories are valuable, pointing to causes that are common to all offenders. In this section, we identify a few criminological theories that have been applied to sex crimes. They are **social control ("bonding") theory**, self-control theory, **routine activity theory**, and social learning theory.

Social Control ("Bonding") Theory (Hirschi, 1969)

Hirschi's (1969) social control theory is often referred to as "social bonding theory" because of the emphasis on the strength of people's bonds to society, including bonds to other people. There are four principal types of bonds: (1) **attachment**, (2) **commitment**, (3) **involvement**, and (4) **belief**. Also, probabilistic in nature is that the stronger people's bonds, the less likely they are to commit a crime. The weaker the bonds, the more likely it is they will violate the law. Hirschi (1969) saw the bonds as strongly interrelated. For example, if a person had a weak attachment, then they usually would have weak commitment, involvement, and belief.

Attachment involves the extent to which people have strong affectional ties to other people (Hirschi, 1969). Individuals will refrain from committing a crime if they admire other people and care what others think of them. Crime could jeopardize these affectional ties. Hence, a strong attachment should be a barrier to crime. Commitment refers to the extent to which individuals have an investment (a "stake in conformity") in conventional goals such as education and employment. The cost of losing these investments will prevent people from committing a crime. Involvement pertains to the amount of time spent in conventional activities. The greater the amount of time spent in conventional activities, the less time there is to commit a crime. Belief is the fourth bond, and it is an endorsement of conventional norms, including laws. A belief in the moral validity of law should act as a strong barrier to committing a crime, according to Hirschi.

Tests of social control theory have examined all of the types of bonds and a wide range of offenses, including juvenile delinquency and alcohol and other drug abuse (for a review, see Akers & Sellers, 2012; Loeber, 1990). Research on sex crimes and persons who have committed a sex crime, however, has mainly examined attachment. Recall that attachment is an important factor in some of the sexual-offending-specific theories that we considered earlier in this chapter, so it is hardly surprising that many researchers have focused on sex offenders' attachment to other people. For example, several studies found that a large percentage of juveniles who have committed a sex crime came from dysfunctional families, and they were loners with superficial friendships (Awad et al., 1984; Saunders et al., 1986). Furthermore, Tingle et al. (1986) revealed that child molesters had weak relationships with their fathers. They were frequently abandoned by their parents, and they had problems relating to other students in school.

Self-control Theory (Gottfredson & Hirschi, 1990)

Hirschi later seemed to move away from his social control (bonding) theory and collaborated with Gottfredson on a self-control theory (Gottfredson & Hirschi, 1990). Self-control theory is a general theory in that it purports to explain all deviance and criminal behavior committed by people of all ages. The cause of sex crimes, therefore, is the same as the cause of all other crimes.

According to Gottfredson and Hirschi (1990), people with low self-control are impulsive, self-centered, and hot-tempered, and they are risk-takers who prefer easy gratification, simple tasks, and physical rather than mental activities. They commit crimes when opportunities are available. Speaking specifically about rape, they say several conditions must be met:

> First, there must be a victim who is attractive to an offender, available to the offender, unwilling to engage in sexual activity, and unable to resist the offender's advances. Second, there must be an offender who is insufficiently restrained.
> (Gottfredson & Hirschi, 1990, p. 39)

Reduction of opportunities to commit rape can help prevent it. The rape of women in public places by strangers can be prevented by increasing women's ability to resist—for example, by traveling with companions or carrying pepper spray. Women who live alone can reduce their risk of rape by locking their doors and windows.

Low self-control originates in early childhood from ineffective child-rearing. Children with low self-control have parents who do not closely monitor their behavior and sanction deviance when it occurs (e.g., a young boy shoving his sister to get to toys). It is primarily the family, then, that shapes a child's self-control. According to the theory, self-control is stable throughout one's life. This means that children with lower self-control than other children will continue to have lower self-control throughout their lives. And they will have a greater likelihood of committing crime and deviance.

Gottfredson and Hirschi (1990) propose there is considerable versatility in the types of crime committed by people with low self-control. Criminal offenders are generalists, not specialists. That is, they commit different types of crime rather than specializing in one. Moreover, they are likely to engage in diverse deviant behaviors that are analogous to crime such as smoking, drinking, gambling, and illicit sex. There is considerable evidence that most criminal offenders do not limit themselves to one type of crime; that is, they are generalists rather than specialists. Researchers, however, have shown that many criminal offenders are both generalists and specialists (Sullivan et al., 2006). There is considerable specialization by offenders in the short term (say, over a period of a few months), but they tend to be crime generalists over the long term.

Consistent with self-control theory, there is considerable evidence that persons who have committed a sex crime do not limit themselves to sex crimes (e.g., Lussier, 2005; Miethe et al., 2006; Sample & Bray, 2003; Simon, 1997; Smallbone et al., 2003). Their offending is often characterized by versatility. They might be generalists; however, as far as crime in general is concerned, they still might be specialists with regard to sex crimes (Soothill et al., 2000). They might limit their sex offending to a particular type of sex crime (e.g., child molesting), and they might specialize in their choice of a victim (e.g., young rather than old, female rather than male, and a family member rather than a stranger). The evidence, however, is mixed.

Researchers have assessed convicted persons who have committed a sex crime by using information gained from polygraph examinations (English et al., 2003). Although most of the persons who have committed a sex crime had been convicted of offenses against children, the polygraph results revealed that 39% had previously sexually assaulted adults. Approximately one-third (31%) had sexually assaulted both male and female victims. Two-thirds of the offenders who had committed incest also had sexually assaulted victims outside the family. Hence, there was considerable evidence of **crossover** (versatility) in their offending (see also Abel & Rouleau, 1990). Other researchers, however, say crossover is more characteristic of some persons who have committed a sex crime (Lussier et al., 2008). Persistent persons who have committed a sex crime are not as likely to switch from male to female victims (and the opposite) or change the level of violence in their sex crimes. Moreover, only about

25% of a sample of incarcerated persons who have committed a sex crime was versatile with regard to victim age and gender as well as victim–offender relationships (Cann et al., 2007).

One of the themes in this textbook is that persons who have committed a sex crime are heterogeneous. There are important differences among them, and one difference is the rate at which they recidivate by committing another sex crime. In a review of follow-up studies of persons who have committed a sex crime, researchers concluded that male rapists have a higher sexual recidivism rate than male child molesters (Quinsey et al., 1995). Among child molesters, those with male victims have the highest recidivism rate, followed by men who have molested unrelated females and then incest offenders. Moreover, whereas sex crimes account for only about 4–14% of the criminal behavior of rapists, it is about 40% for child molesters (Lussier et al., 2005). Hanson and Bussière (1998), however, found that when persons who have committed a sex crime recidivate, they are most likely to commit nonsex crimes—a recidivism rate of 36% for general crimes, 12% for violent crimes, and 13% for sex crimes. Moreover, Zimring et al. (2007, p. 507) found that "the best predictor . . . for adult sex offending was the frequency of offending [for any crime] as a juvenile rather than whether a boy committed a sexual offense" (see also Harris et al., 2009).

There are surprisingly few studies of the relationship between self-control and sex crimes. However, one study found that male undergraduate students who self-reported sexual assault had lower self-control than those who did not report sexual assault (Franklin et al.-b, 2012). Low self-control increased acceptance of a non-egalitarian gender-role ideology and alcohol consumption, which are two "abuse-facilitating variables" that increase the likelihood of sexual assault (Franklin et al.-a, 2012, p. 1470). Other researchers have revealed that low self-control increases the likelihood of sexual assault victimization (Franklin et al., 2012b). This is consistent with other research that has found low self-control is related to stalking victimization among women (Fox et al., 2009).

Routine Activity Theory (Cohen & Felson, 1979)

Routine activity theory directs attention away from offenders to other parts of a crime, including victims and one's environment (Cohen & Felson, 1979). According to routine activity theory, three elements must come together for a crime to occur: (1) a motivated offender, (2) a suitable target, and (3) the absence of a capable guardian (anything or anyone whose presence could prevent commission of a crime). People's routine activities affect where, when, and how these elements come together, creating situational opportunities for crime. For example, in discussing sex crimes, Felson and Eckert (2015, p. 53) note "how easy it is for stepparents to gain [sexual] access to stepchildren, priests to choirboys, and child care workers to young children. Offenses usually occur in settings with guardians absent and unable to intervene." Children can also be vulnerable to parents or other family members when there is no one to protect them.

Sometimes, the commission of a nonsex crime produces an opportunity for a sex crime such as when a burglar breaks into a home and finds a woman there alone. He might rape her even though that was not his original intent (Warr, 1988). A rape might be an "added bonus" for a burglar who breaks into a home for material gain and finds a woman there alone. This is indicative of an opportunistic rapist identified in some typologies (e.g., Knight & Prentky, 1990). A study by Pedneault et al. (2015), although not rejecting such a scenario, suggests that this is usually not the case—sexual and "regular" burglars respond to different situational opportunities. Comparing cases of burglaries of residences by persons who have committed a sex crime with regular residential burglaries, they found differences that seemed to disconfirm the "opportunistic sexual burglary" (Pedneault et al., 2015,

p. 391). Sexual burglars were more likely to break into occupied residences, which regular burglars tended to avoid. Moreover, sexual burglaries more often occurred at times when people were more likely to be at home—midnight to 3 a.m. Sexual burglars also were more likely than regular burglars to carry weapons, as if prepared to find someone at home. These findings suggest that there may be more to understanding sex crimes and persons who have committed a sex crime than situational opportunities alone. Sexual and regular burglars may have different motivations, even different expertise.

Moreover, a few related studies offer evidence for the importance of situational opportunities for sex crimes. For example, Wortley and Smallbone (2006) examined child sexual abuse by priests in Queensland. Most (70%) of the abuse occurred in the priest's residence. About 20% occurred in the victim's home. Twenty percent of the priests also took children on overnight trips to be alone with them. A related study of child sexual abuse by priests in the United States, modeled after the Queensland study, found that a relatively high proportion (41%) of it occurred in a parish residence or cleric's home (Terry & Ackerman, 2008). "Living alone in the parish residence or with only one pastor or associate pastor . . . allows for the priest to have the opportunity to abuse" (Terry & Ackerman, 2008, p. 651). Approximately 16% of abuse occurred in a church, 12% in the victim's home, 10% in a vacation home, and 10% in school. About 18% of the abusers said it occurred on planned overnight trips with children so the children would be more vulnerable (with fewer capable guardians to prevent the abuse).

Planning overnight trips to be alone with children is an example of how persons who have committed a sex crime create opportunities for sex crimes. Sullivan and Beech (2004) studied men who admitted to sexually abusing children in the course of their work and found that 15% had chosen the work to provide them with access to children. Another 42% said that access to children was not the only reason for their work, but it was part of the reason. Similarly, other researchers found in a study of a small sample of child sexual abusers in the United Kingdom that they were drawn to particular educational and voluntary organizations that provided them with easy access to potential victims (Colton et al., 2010).

Routine activity theory emphasizes situational crime prevention to reduce opportunities to commit crimes (Felson & Clarke, 1988). This may involve increasing the effort required to commit a crime (e.g., electronic access to garages), increasing the risk of detection (e.g., surveillance cameras), decreasing the anticipated rewards for crime (e.g., access to women's shelters), and removing excuses for crime (e.g., debunking rape myths).

Social Learning Theory (Akers, 1985)

As mentioned before, learning either through one's own experiences or by witnessing other events is instrumental in adopting any deviant behavior such as sexually offending. Social learning theory (Akers, 1985) has been relied upon in a variety of studies to account for sex crimes and persons who have committed a sex crime. Like the other theories discussed in this section of the chapter, social learning theory is about crime in general. In comparison to other general-crime theories, however, social learning theory allows for more offender specialization. The reason is that one of the principal themes in social learning theory is imitation. According to social learning theory, people learn behavior, in part, by observing the behavior of other people and subsequently imitating (or modeling) it (Bandura, 1978).

Through vicarious learning, people can learn from what they observe has happened to others. Also, they can learn through experiential learning, which involves learning through direct personal experience. In this way, a victim of child abuse can become a child abuser. As Felson and Lane (2009) indicate, imitation need not be behavior-specific. "There may be stimulus generalization whereby the model's response to one type of stimulus leads the observer to imitate that response to similar stimuli" (Felson & Lane, 2009, p. 489). It is possible, then, that people can observe a particular type of violence (e.g., physical violence) and generalize it to other (sexual) violence. "Still, a social learning perspective implies that modeling [imitation] of specific behaviors should be strongest as it is the most direct lesson learned from the model" (Felson & Lane, 2009, p. 490).

Child sexual abuse, as discussed in Chapter 4, examines the literature on the abused–abuser hypothesis that sexual abuse during childhood can cause people to later commit child sexual abuse themselves. It is clear that childhood sexual victimization is not a deterministic cause of adult–child sexual abuse. That is, if someone is sexually abused as a child, it does *not* mean that the child will inevitably become a sexual abuser. It is a myth that experiencing child sexual abuse always leads to that victim becoming a child sexual abuser as an adult. Most sexually abused children do not grow up to become adults who sexually abuse children. Moreover, most adults convicted of child sexual abuse do not repeat their offense.

Social learning theory, however, suggests that childhood abuse victimization (of any kind) will increase the likelihood that a child victim will later become an adult who commits sex crimes. The evidence is mixed. In a large study of state and federal prisons, Felson and Lane (2009) tested two hypotheses: (1) sexual abuse during childhood is associated with adult sexually offending, and particularly sex offenses against children, and (2) physical abuse during childhood is associated with adult violent offending.

Suggestive of imitation, they found that offenders who had experienced sexual abuse as a child were much more likely to commit sex offenses, particularly against children (Felson & Lane, 2009). Moreover, offenders who had experienced childhood physical abuse were more likely to commit violent offenses than nonviolent offenses as adults. Other studies, however, have not found an association between childhood sexual victimization and adult sex offending. For example, Widom (1995) found that childhood physical abuse, not sexual abuse, was related to later arrest for sodomy or rape.

COMMON CAUSES IDENTIFIED TO EXPLAIN SEXUALLY OFFENDING

Although many different theories have been proposed about sex crimes and persons who have committed a sex crime, several common characteristics exist such as negative childhood experiences—especially during a critical stage of development—poorly formed attachments to others, deviant sexual pathways, empathy deficits, negative personality features, poor self-management/low self-control, cognitive distortions, and a criminal predisposition. Although not all persons who have committed a sex crime exhibit all of the characteristics, typically, a cluster of several factors are present for any person who commits a sex crime. When these factors exist, they do not always lead to the commission of a sex crime—they simply increase the probability that an individual commits a sex crime. Also, many of the proposed theories vary in their explanation of how these characteristics develop. Most indicate the foundation is laid during childhood, culminating in poor adaptation, interpersonal difficulties, and subsequent behaviors that involve sex crimes: rape, child molestation, human trafficking, and/or viewing child pornography. The next chapters discuss each of these sex crimes.

CONCLUSION

Many theories have been proposed to explain criminal behavior and, more specifically, sex crimes. These theories help us develop sound assessment tools, treatment approaches, and policy, including legal responses to sex crimes and persons who have committed a sex crime. Throughout this chapter, you should have noticed that many factors that lead to committing a crime also pertain to committing sex crimes. We have also noted that persons who have committed a sex crime often commit nonsex crimes as well, leading to murky conclusions about persons who have committed a sex crime as "unique" offenders.

Theories that specifically focus on persons who have committed a sex crime often are narrowly focused on explaining a particular type of sex crime (e.g., child sexual abuse or rape), and the research is relatively mixed with regard to identifying specific characteristics or traits that distinguish persons who have committed a sex crime from persons who have not committed a sex crime. Instead, research has largely identified factors that are common to persons who have committed a sex crime yet, in and of themselves do not necessarily equate to the commission of subsequent sex crimes. Thus, we cannot at the current time distinguish persons who have committed a sex crime from persons who have not committed a sex crime based on a given set of existing characteristics. Nevertheless, theories assist in providing a structure for understanding the offenses they commit and provide better prevention and response strategies.

REVIEW POINTS

- Theories provide a logical set of statements that explain some sort of phenomenon, which help provide a framework for understanding sex crimes.
- Theories are probabilistic in nature, meaning when factors have been identified as a cause of crime, they simply increase the likelihood of crime occurring. By no means does it indicate that when the cause is present, crime will result every time.
- Biological theories propose that sex crimes are caused by abnormalities among hormones, neurotransmitters, brain structures, sex chromosomes/genetic traits, or intelligence deficits. Support for biological theories is quite limited in scope.
- Psychological theories have broad application to explaining sex crimes. This broad classification of theories include psychoanalytical theory, attachment theories, behaviorism, cognitive-based theories, and the identification of personality traits salient to persons who have committed a sex crime (compared to those who have not committed a sex crime).
- Several broad-based criminological theories such as social control (bonding) theory, self-control theory, routine activity theory, and social learning theory have been applied to explain sex crimes and persons who have committed a sex crime. These also have received moderate support.
- Common causes among all of the theories explaining sexually offending include negative childhood experiences—especially during a critical stage of development—poorly formed attachments to others, deviant sexual pathways, empathy deficits, poor self-management/low self-control, cognitive distortions, and a criminal predisposition.

REFERENCES

Abel, G. G., & Rouleau, J. L. (1990). The nature and extent of sexual assault. In W. L. Marshall, Laws, D. R., & H. E. Barbaree (Eds.), *Handbook of sexual assault* (pp. 9–21). https://www.doi.org/10.1007/978-1-4899-0915-2_2

Akers, R., & Sellers, C. S. (2012). *Criminological theories: Introduction, evaluation, and application* (6th ed.). Oxford University Press.

Akers, R. L. (1985). *Deviant behavior: A social learning approach*. Wadsworth.

American Psychiatric Association. (2013). *Diagnostic and statistical manual of mental disorders* (5th ed.). Author.

Awad, G., Saunders, E., & Levene, J. (1984). A clinical study of male sex offenders. *International Journal of Offender Therapy and Comparative Criminology, 28*(2), 105–115.

Bain, J., Langevin, R., Dickey, R., & Ben-Aron, M. (1987). Sex hormones in murderers and assaulters. *Behavioral Sciences and the Law, 5*(1), 95–101. https://www.doi.org/10.1002/bsl.2370050109

Bandura, A. (1978). Social learning theory of aggression. *Journal of Communication, 28*(3), 12–29. https://www.doi.org/10.1111/j.1460-2466.1978.tb01621.x

Barnett, G. D., & Mann, R. E. (2013). Cognition, empathy, and sexual offending. *Trauma, Violence & Abuse, 14*(1), 22–33. https://www.doi.org/10.1177/1524838012467857

Baumeister, R. F., Catanese, K. R., & Wallace, H. M. (2002). Conquest by force: A narcissistic reactance theory of rape and sexual coercion. *Review of General Psychology, 6*(1), 92–135. https://www.doi.org/10.1037/1089-2680.6.1.92

Beech, A., & Ward, T. (2004). The integration of etiology and risk in sexual offenders: A theoretical framework. *Aggression and Violent Behavior, 10*(1), 31–63. https://www.doi.org/10.1016/j.avb.2003.08.002

Berger, P., Berner, W., Bolterauer, J., Gutierrez, K., & Berger, K. (1999). Sadistic personality disorders in sex offenders: Relationship to antisocial personality disorder and sexual sadism. *Journal of Personality Disorders, 13*(2), 175–186. https://www.doi.org/10.1521/pedi.1999.13.2.175

Bickley, J. A., & Beech, & Anthony, R. (2002). An investigation of the Ward and Hudson Pathways model of the sexual offense process with child abusers. *Journal of Interpersonal Violence, 17*(4), 371–393. https://www.doi.org/10.1177/0886260502017004002

Bowlby, J. (1958). The nature of the child's tie to his mother. *International Journal of PsychoAnalysis, 39*(5), 350–373.

Bowlby, J. (1977). The making and breaking of affectional bonds: I. Aetiology and psychopathology in light of attachment theory. *British Journal of Psychiatry, 130*(3), 201–210. https://www.doi.org/10.1192/bjp.130.3.201

Bowlby, J. (1988). Developmental psychiatry comes of age. *American Journal of Psychiatry, 145*(1), 1–10. https://www.doi.org/10.1176/ajp.145.1.1

Cann, J., Friendship, C., & Gonzna, L. (2007). Assessing crossover in a sample of sexual offenders with multiple victims. *Legal and Criminological Psychology, 12*(1), 149–163. https://www.doi.org/10.1348/135532506X112439

Choi, C. (2002, October 21). Brain tumour causes uncontrollable paedophilia. *New Scientist*. https://www.newscientist.com/article/dn2943-brain-tumour-causes-uncontrollable-paedophilia/

Cohen, L. E., & Felson, M. (1979). Social change and crime rate trends: A routine activity approach. *American Sociological Review, 44*(4), 588–608. https://www.doi.org/10.2307/2094589

Colton, M., Roberts, S., & Vanston, M. (2010). Sexual abuse by men who work with children. *Journal of Child Sexual Abuse, 19*(3), 345–364. https://www.doi.org/10.1080/10538711003775824

English, K., Jones, L., Patrick, D., & Pasini-Hill, D. (2003). Sexual offender containment. *Annals of the New York Academy of Sciences, 989*(1), 411–427. https://www.doi.org/10.1111/j.1749-6632.2003.tb07322.x

Falligant, J. M., Alexander, A. A., & Burkhart, B. R. (2017). Offence characteristics and cognitive functioning in juveniles adjudicated for illegal sexual behaviour. *Journal of Sexual Aggression, 23*(3), 291–299. https://www.doi.org/10.1080/13552600.2017.1362271

Felson, M., & Clarke, R. V. (1988). *Opportunity makes the thief*. Policing and Reducing Crime Unit, Home Office Research, Development and Statistics Directorate.

Felson, M., & Eckert, M. (2015). *Crime and everyday life*. Sage.

Felson, R. B., & Lane, K. J. (2009). Social learning, sexual and physical abuse, and adult crime. *Aggressive Behavior, 35*(6), 489–501. https://www.doi.org/10.1002/ab.20322

Finkelhor, D. (1984). *Child sexual abuse: New theory and research*. Free Press.

Finkelhor, D., Cuevas, C. A., & Drawbridge, D. (2016). The four preconditions model: An assessment. In D. P. Boer, A. R. Beech, T. Ward, A. Craig, M. Rettenberger, L. E. Marshall, & W. L. Marchall (Eds.), *The Wiley handbook on the theories, assessment and treatment of sexual offending* (pp. 25–51). Wiley Blackwell.

Fiske, S. T., & Taylor, S. E. (1991). *Social cognition* (2nd ed.). McGraw-Hill.

Fox, K. A., Gover, A. R., & Kaukinen, C. (2009). The effects of low self-control and childhood maltreatment on stalking victimization among men and women. *American Journal of Criminal Justice, 34*(3–4), 181–197. https://www.doi.org/10.1007/s12103-009-9064-4

Franklin, C. A., Bouffard, L. A., & Pratt, T. C. (2012a). Sexual assault on the college campus: Fraternity affiliation, male peer support, and low self-control. *Criminal Justice and Behavior, 39*(11), 1457–1480. https://www.doi.org/10.1177/0093854812456527

Franklin, C. A., Franklin, T. W., Nobles, M. R., & Kercher, G. (2012b). Assessing the effect of routine activity theory and self-control on property, personal, and sexual assault victimization. *Criminal Justice and Behavior, 39*(10), 1296–1315. https://www.doi.org/10.1177/0093854812453673

Freud, S. (1962). *Three essays on the theory of sexuality*. Basic Books.

Gibbs, J. P. (1972). *Sociological theory construction*. Dryden Press.

Gottfredson, M. R., & Hirschi, T. (1990). *A general theory of crime*. Stanford University Press.

Gunst, E., Watson, J. C., Desmet, M., & Willemsen, J. (2017). Affect regulation as a factor in sex offenders. *Aggression and Violent Behavior, 37*, 210–219. https://www.doi.org/10.1016/j.avb.2017.10.007

Hall, G. C. N., & Hirschman, R. (1991). Toward a theory of sexual aggression: A quadripartite model. *Journal of Consulting and Clinical Psychology, 19*(5), 8–23. https://www.doi.org/10.1037/0022-006X.59.5.662

Hanson, R. K., & Bussière, M. T. (1998). Predicting relapse: A meta-analysis of sexual offender recidivism studies. *Journal of Consulting and Clinical Psychology, 66*(2), 348–362. https://www.doi.org/10.1037//0022-006x.66.2.348

Hanson, R. K., Gizzarelli, R., & Scott, H. (1994). The attitudes of incest offenders: Sexual entitlement and acceptance of sex with children. *Criminal Justice and Behavior, 21*(2), 187–202. https://www.doi.org/10.1177/0093854894021002001

Harris, D. A., Mazzerolle, P., & Knight, R. A. (2009). Understanding male sexual offending: A comparison of general and specialist theories. *Criminal Justice and Behavior, 36*(10), 1051–1069. https://www.doi.org/10.1177/0093854809342242

Harrison, L. E., Clayton-Smith, J., & Bailey, S. (2001). Exploring the complex relationship between adolescent sexual offending and sex chromosome abnormality. *Psychiatric Genetics, 11*(1), 5–10. https://www.doi.org/10.1097/00041444-200103000-00002

Health Research Funding Organization. (2021). *John Bowlby's attachment theory explained*. https://healthresearchfunding.org/john-bowlbys-attachment-theory-explained/

Hirschi, T. (1969). A control theory of delinquency. In T. Hirschi (Ed.), *Causes of delinquency* (pp. 289–305). University of California Press.

Jakubczyk, A., Krasowska, A., Bugaj, M., Kopera, M., Klimkiewicz, A., Łoczewska, A., Michalska, A., Majewska, A., Szejko, N., Podgórska, A., Sołowiej, M., Markuszewski, L., Jakima, S., Płoski, R., Brower, K., & Wojnar, M. (2017). *Journal of Sexual Medicine, 14*(1), 125–133. https://www.doi.org/10.1016/j.jsxm.2016.11.309

Kirk-Provencher, K. T., Nelson-Aguiar, R. J., & Spillane, N. S. (2020). Neuroanatomical differences among sexual offenders: A targeted review with limitations and implications for future directions. *Violence and Gender, 7*(3), 86–97. https://www.doi.org/10.1089/vio.2019.0051

Knight, R. A., & Prentky, R. A. (1990). Classifying sex offenders: Issues, theories and treatment of the offender. In W. L. Marshall, D. R. Laws, H. E. Barbaree (Eds.), *Handbook of sexual assault*. Springer US. https://www.doi.org/10.1007/978-1-4899-0915-2_3

Kruger, T. H. C., Sinke, C., Kneer, J., Tenbergen, G., Khan, A. Q., Burkert, A., Müller-Engling, L., Engler, H., Gerwinn, H., von Wurmb-Schwark, N., Pohl, A., Weiß, Amelung, T., Mohnke, S., Massau, C., Kärgel, C., Walter, M., Schiltz, K., Beier, K. M., Ponseti, J., Schiffer, B., Walter, H., Jahn, K., & Frieling, H. (2019). Child sexual offenders show prenatal and epigenetic alterations of the androgen system. *Translational Psychiatry, 9*(1), 1–11. https://www.doi.org/10.1038/s41398-018-0326-0

Lindsay, W. R., Ward, T., Morgan, T., & Wilson, I. (2007). Self-regulation of sex offending, future pathways and the Good Lives Model: Applications and problems. *Journal of Sexual Aggression, 13*(1), 37–50. https://www.doi.org/10.1080/13552600701365613

Loeber, R. (1990). Development and risk factors of juvenile antisocial behavior and delinquency. *Clinical Psychology Review, 10*(1), 1–41. https://www.doi.org/10.1016/0272-7358(90)90105-J

Lussier, P. (2005). The criminal activity of sexual offenders in adulthood: Revisiting the specialization debate. *Sexual Abuse: A Journal of Research and Treatment, 17*(3), 269–292. https://www.doi.org/10.1007/s11194-005-5057-0

Lussier, P., LeBlanc, M., & Proulx, J. (2005). The generality of criminal behavior: A confirmatory factor analysis of the criminal activity of sex offenders in adulthood. *Journal of Criminal Justice, 33*(2), 177–189. https://www.doi.org/10.1016/j.jcrimjus.2004.12.009

Lussier, P., Leclerc, B., Healey, J., & Proulx, J. (2008). Generality of deviance and predation: Crime-switching and specialization patterns in persistent sexual offenders. In M. DeLisi & P. J. Conis (Eds.), *Violent offenders: Theory, public policy and practice* (pp. 97–140). Jones and Bartlett.

Marshall, W. (1989). Intimacy, loneliness, and sexual offenders. *Behavior Research and Therapy, 27*(5), 491–503. https://www.doi.org/10.1016/0005-7967(89)90083-1

Marshall, W. L. (1993). The role of attachments, intimacy, and loneliness in the etiology and maintenance of sex offending. *Sexual and Marital Therapy, 8*(1), 109–121. https://www.doi.org/10.1080/02674659308408187

Marshall, W. L., Anderson, D., & Champagne, F. (1997). Self-esteem and its relationship to sexual offending. *Psychology, Crime & Law, 3*(3), 161–186. https://www.doi.org/10.1080/10683169708410811

Marshall, W. L., & Barbaree, H. E. (1990). Outcome of comprehensive cognitive-behavioral treatment programs. In W. L. Marshall, D. R. Laws & H. E. Barbaree (Eds.), *Handbook of sexual assault: Issues, theories, and treatment of the offender* (pp. 363–385). Plenum Press.

Marshall, W. L., Hudson, S. M., Jones, R., & Fernandez, Y. M. (1995). Empathy in sex offenders. *Clinical Psychology Review, 15*(2), 99–113. https://www.doi.org/10.1016/0272-7358(95)00002-7

Marshall, W. L., & Mazzucco, A. (1995). Self-esteem and parental attachments in child molesters. *Sexual Abuse: A Journal of Research and Treatment, 7*(4), 249–252.

McAnena, C., Craissati, J., & Southgate, K. (2016). Exploring the role of locus of control in sex offender treatment. *Journal of Sexual Aggression, 22*(1), 95–106. https://doi.org/10.1080/13552600.2015.1023374

McKay, M. M., Chapman, J. W., & Long, N. R. (1996). Causal attributions for criminal offending and sexual arousal: Comparison of child sex offenders with other offenders. *British Journal of Criminology, 35*(1), 63–75. https://www.doi.org/1 0.1111/j.2044-8260.1996.tb01162.x

Miethe, T. D., Olson, J., & Mitchell, O. (2006). Specialization and persistence in the arrest histories of sex offenders: A comparative analysis of alternative measures and offense types. *Journal of Research in Crime and Delinquency, 43*(3), 204–229. https://www.doi.org/10.1177/0022427806286564

Miller, S., & Klockner, K. (2019). Attachment styles and attachment based change in offenders in a prison therapeutic community. *Journal of Forensic Psychology Research and Practice, 19*(3), 260–277. https://www.doi.org/10.1080/24732850.2019.1603956

Montrenes, J. J., & Matson, J. L. (2021). Treatments associated with mental health disorders and functional assessment. In J. L. Matson (Ed.), *Functional assessment for challenging behaviors and mental health disorders* (pp. 385–406). Springer. https://www.doi.org/10.1007/978-3-030-66270-7_14

Mouilso, E., Calhoun, K. S., & Rosenbloom, T. (2013). Impulsivity and sexual assault in college men. *Violence and Victims, 28*(3), 429–442. https://www.doi.org/10.1891/0886-6708.vv-d-12-00025

O'Callaghan, D. (1998). Practice issues in working with young abusers who have learning disabilities. *Child Abuse Review, 7*(6), 435–448. https://www.doi.org/10.1002/(SICI)1099-0852(199811/12)7:6<435::AID-CAR517>3.0.CO;2-F

Pavlov, I. (1927). *Conditioned reflexes*. Clarendon Press.

Pedneault, A., Beauregard, E., Harris, D. A., & Knight, R. A. (2015). Rationally irrational: The case of sexual burglary. *Sexual Abuse: A Journal of Research and Treatment, 27*(4), 376–397. https://www.doi.org/10.1177/1079063213511669

Porter, S., Campbell, M. A. W. M., & Birth, A. R. (2001). A new psychological conceptualization of the sexual psychopath. In F. Columbus (Ed.), *Advances in psychology research* (pp. 21–36). Nova Science.

Quinsey, V. L., Lalumière, M. L., Rice, M. E., & Harris, G. T. (1995). Predicting sexual offenses. In J. C. Campbell (Ed.), *Assessing dangerousness: Violence by sexual offenders, batterers, and child abusers* (pp. 114–137). Sage.

Sample, L. L., & Bray, T. M. (2003). Are sex offenders dangerous? *Criminology & Public Policy, 3*(1), 59–82. https://www.doi.org/10.1111/j.1745-9133.2003.tb00024.x

Saunders, E., Awad, G. A., & White, G. (1986). Male adolescent sexual offenders: The offender and the offense. *Canadian Journal of Psychiatry, 31*(6), 542–549. https://www.doi.org/10.1177/070674378603100612

Savopoulos, P., & Lindell, A. K. (2018). Born criminal? Differences in structural, functional and behavioural lateralization between criminals and noncriminals. *Laterality: Asymmetries of Body, Brain and Cognition, 23*(6), 738–760. https://www.doi.org/10.1080/1357650X.2018.1432631

Simon, L. M. J. (1997). Do criminal offenders specialize in crime types? *Applied and Preventative Psychology, 6*(1), 35–53. https://www.doi.org/10.1007/s11194-005-5057-0

Skinner, B. F. (1932). On the rate of formation of a conditioned reflex. *Journal of General Psychology, 7*(2), 274–286. https://www.doi.org/10.1080/00221309.1932.9918467

Smallbone, S. W., Wheaton, J., & Hourigan, D. (2003). Trait empathy and criminal versatility in sexual offenders. *Sexual Abuse: A Journal of Research and Treatment, 15*(1), 49–60. https://www.doi.org/ 10.1177/107906320301500104

Soothill, K. L., Francis, B., Sanderson, B., & Ackerly, E. (2000). Sex offenders: Specialists, generalists—or both? *British Journal of Criminology, 40*(1), 56–67. https://www.doi.org/10.1093/bjc/40.1.56

Stinson, J. D., Sales, B. D., & Becker, J. V. (2008). *Sex offending: Causal theories to inform research, prevention, and treatment.* American Psychological Association. https://www.doi.org/10.1037/11708-000

Sullivan, C. J., Mcgloin, J. M., Pratt, T. C., & Piquero, A. (2006). Rethinking the "norm" of offender generality: Investigating specialization in the short-term. *Criminology, 44*(1), 199–233. https://www.doi.org/10.1111/j.1745-9125.2006.00047.x

Sullivan, J., & Beech, A. (2004). A comparative study of demographic data relating to intra- and extra-familial child sexual abusers and professional perpetrators. *Journal of Sexual Aggression, 10*(1), 39–50. https://www.doi.org/10.1080/13552600410001667788

Terry, K. J., & Ackerman, A. (2008). Child sexual abuse in the Catholic Church: How situational crime prevention strategies can help create safe environments. *Criminal Justice and Behavior, 35*(5), 643–657. https://www.doi.org/10.1177/0093854808314469

Thornhill, R., & Palmer, C. T. (2000). *A natural history of rape: Biological bases of sexual coercion.* The MIT Press.

Tingle, D., Barnard, G. W., Robbins, L., Newman, G., & Hutchinson, D. (1986). Childhood and adolescent characteristics of pedophiles and rapists. *International Journal of Law and Psychiatry, 9*(1), 103–116. https://www.doi.org/10.1016/0160-2527(86)90020-8

Ward, T. (2000). Sexual offenders' cognitive distortions as implicit theories. *Aggression and Violent Behavior, 5*(5), 491–507. https://www.doi.org/10.1016/S1359-1789(98)00036-6

Ward, T. (2001). A critique of Hall and Hirschman's quadripartite model of child sexual abuse. *Psychology, Crime & Law, 7*(4), 333–350. https://doi.org/10.1080/10683160108401801

Ward, T., & Hudson, S. M. (1998). A model of relapse process in sexual offenders. *Journal of Interpersonal Violence, 13*(6), 700–725. https://www.doi.org/10.1177/088626098013006003

Ward, T., & Hudson, S. M. (2001). Finkelhor's precondition model of child sexual abuse. A critique, *Psychology, Crime & Law, 4*, 291–307. https://www.doi.org/10.1080/10683160108401799.

Ward, T., Polaschek, D. L. L., & Beech, A. R. (1995). Attachment style and intimacy deficits in sexual offenders: A theoretical framework. *Sexual Abuse: A Journal of Research and Treatment, 7*(4), 317–335. https://www.doi.org/10.1007/BF02256835

Warr, M. (1988). Rape, burglary, and opportunity. *Journal of Quantitative Criminology, 4*(3), 275–288. https://www.doi.org/10.1007/BF01072454

Widom, C. S. (1995). *Victims of childhood sexual abuse: Later criminal consequences.* National Institute of Justice: Research in Brief.

Wortley, R. K., & Smallbone, S. W. (2006). Applying situational principles to sexual offending against children. In R. Wortley & S. Smallbone (Eds.), *Situational prevention of child sexual abuse. Crime prevention studies* (pp. 7–35). Criminal Justice Press.

Yates, P., & Ward, T. (2008). Good lives, self-regulation, and risk management: An integrated model of sexual offender assessment and treatment. *Sexual Abuse in Australia and New Zealand, 1*(1), 2–19. http://hdl.handle.net/10536/DRO/DU:30034253

Yoder, J., Grady, M. D., Brown, A., & Dillard, R. (2020). Criminogenic needs as intervening factors in the relation between insecure attachments and youth sexual violence. *Sexual Abuse: A Journal of Research and Treatment, 32*(3), 247–272. https://www.doi.org/10.1177/1079063218821108

Zimring, F. E., Piquero, A. R., & Jennings, W. G. (2007). Sexual delinquency in Racine: Does early sex offending predict later sex offending in youth and young adulthood. *Criminology and Public Policy, 6*(3), 507–534. https://www.doi.org/10.1111/j.1745-9133.2007.00451.x

Zion, D. (2000, April 3). To put the ape back into rape. *The Age*. http://www.theage.com.au

DEFINITIONS

Attachment: One of four principal types of bonds identified in Hirschi's (1969) social control theory—attachment involves the extent to which people have strong affectional ties to other people (see, Belief, Commitment, and Involvement)

Attachment Theory: An explanation of dysfunctional adulthood behavior proposed by Bowlby that has been relied upon to explain sexually offending

Belief: One of four principal types of bonds identified in Hirschi's (1969) social control theory—belief refers to an endorsement of conventional norms, including laws (see Commitment, Attachment, and Involvement)

Callousness: A personality trait that involves blunted emotional response to others

Castration Anxiety: A concept identified by Freud that refers to boys around the ages of three to five years becoming fearful of losing or having damage done to their penis

Classical Conditioning: A learning principle identified by Ivan Pavlov in which a neutral stimulus (bell ringing) is successively paired with a potent stimulus (dog food) to eventually cause a known and predictable response (dog salivating) with only the neutral stimulus (bell ringing)

Cognitive Biases: Illogical thoughts that skew one's perception of the world

Cognitive Distortions: Minimizing or denying the dangerousness of a behavior, justifying it, and relieving the offender of responsibility (e.g., children need to be taught about sex; children are seductive; the child is too young to know what is happening)

Cognitive Schemas: Basic building blocks that help individuals organize information and make sense of the world—they involve organized patterns of previous experiences, which are relied upon to interpret new information

Commitment: One of four principal types of bonds identified in Hirschi's (1969) social control theory—commitment refers to the extent to which individuals have an investment (a "stake in conformity") in conventional goals such as education and employment (see Attachment, Belief, and Involvement)

Crossover: Describes sex-offender behavior that involves a variety of victims who vary in their characteristics (e.g., male and female victims, old and young, commit rape and child molestation)

Deterministic Cause: The relationship between a stated cause and effect in which the cause *always* leads to a specified effect (see Probabilistic Cause)

Ego: A concept identified by Freud—the ego acts as a mediator between the id and superego (see Id and Superego)

Experiential Learning: A type of learning that occurs through personal direct experience (see Vicarious Learning)

Fixation: A concept proposed by Freud in which individuals prone to sexually deviant behavior become stuck on a particular developmental stage instead of progressing through them normally

Grooming: The process of befriending and establishing an emotional connection with a child victim for the purpose of sexually abusing them

Hormones: Chemical secretions in the body that affect a wide range of bodily functions

Id: A concept identified by Freud—the id is one of three parts of one's personality that is responsible for pleasure seeking (see Ego and Superego)

Impulsivity: A personality trait that involves a need for instant gratification and an inability to control impulses

Involvement: One of four principal types of bonds identified in Hirschi's (1969) social control theory—involvement pertains to the amount of time spent in conventional activities (see Attachment, Belief, and Commitment)

Lack of Empathy: A personality trait that involves an inability to respond to someone else with appropriate emotions

Narcissism: A personality trait that involves an overwhelming sense of self-love, grandiose perceptions of one's self, and a sense of entitlement

Neurotransmitters: Chemicals in the brain that affect brain function, mood, and autonomic reactions (heart rate, breathing, and other bodily functions that respond in anxiety-provoking situations)

Operant Conditioning: A learning principle identified by B. F. Skinner that explains acquiring and maintaining new behaviors through a process of reinforcement and punishment

Penis Envy: A concept identified by Freud that refers to a feeling of anxiety experienced by girls between the ages of three and five years that occurs when they realize they do not have a penis

Personality Pathology: A set of personality disorders that have been identified by the American Psychiatric Association that involve a set of emotional and behavioral characteristics that cause maladaptive behaviors

Probabilistic Cause: The relationship between a stated cause and effect in which the cause increases the chances that a specified effect will occur (see Deterministic Cause)

Psychosexual Development: Five stages of human development identified by Freud that occur from birth to adulthood: (1) oral, (2) anal, (3) phallic, (4) latency, and (5) genital

Rape Myths: Falsely held beliefs regarding rape (e.g., all women secretly desire to be raped)

Regression: A concept proposed by Freud in which individuals prone to sexually deviant behavior go through developmental stages yet later regress to an earlier developmental stage

Routine Activity Theory: A criminological theory developed by Cohen & Felson that posits crimes occur when three elements converge in space and time: (1) a motivated offender, (2) a suitable target, and (3) the absence of a capable guardian

Sadism: A personality trait that is associated with deriving sexual pleasure from inflicting pain or humiliation on another person

Self-control Theory: A criminological theory developed by Gottfredson and Hirschi that posits children who lack parental supervision later become adults who commit crimes due to low self-control, as they are impulsive, self-centered, and hot-tempered

Self-regulation Model of Relapse in Sexual Offenders: A theory developed by Ward and Hudson explaining sexually offending that is based on concepts from behavioral theory—they proposed that people behave in goal-directed ways and there are four paths that can lead to sexually offending

Social Control ("Bonding") Theory: A criminological theory developed by Hirschi that posits a person will commit a crime when they have weakened or broken bonds (see Attachment, Commitment, Involvement, and Belief)

Superego: A concept identified by Freud—the superego is associated with one's moral principles and acts as one's conscience (see Id and Ego)

Vicarious Learning: A type of learning in which people learn from what they observe has happened to others (see Experiential Learning)

CHAPTER 3

Rape and Sexual Assault

CHAPTER OBJECTIVES

- Identify myths associated with rape and sexual assault
- Describe aspects of the rape culture
- Describe the legal and social evolution of rape as a crime
- Define and identify the common characteristics of those who commit rape
- Summarize rape typologies
- Describe the criminal justice response to rape from police reporting to court adjudication

"*Rape*" and "*sexual assault*" are often used synonymously and interchangeably. The two terms can describe the same act in some instances, but there are important differences in how the two terms are historically and legally defined. The word "rape" dates back to late 14th-century France, where it meant "to seize property, abduct, or take by force." Prior to this, the Latin word *rapere* was infused with a similar meaning and defined as "to seize, carry off by force, or abduct" (Burgess-Jackson, 1999, p. 16). Sexual violation rarely entered into historical connotations of rape, which focused more on issues of force and power. Under ancient Roman law, *raptus* referred primarily to acts of kidnapping and abduction, with sexual violation as a peripheral issue (Moses, 1993).

Today, *rape* refers to any sexual penetration (vaginal, anal, or oral) of a person without their **consent** (Federal Bureau of Investigation, 2016). Prior to recent changes in the legal definition, the crime of rape was much more limited in scope—this is discussed later. *Sexual assault* is a much broader term that encompasses a variety of behaviors that can be considered sex crimes, including voyeurism, exhibitionism, and even sexual harassment in some cases. To put it concisely, all rapes are considered sexual assault, but not all sexual assaults are considered rape. The differences between defining rape versus defining sexual assault can become quite complex, particularly when charging and prosecuting offenders—an idea to which we will return later. Apart from definitional differences, the terms "rape" and "sexual assault" are used interchangeably in this chapter.

The number of reported rapes has decreased since the early 1990s, but it is important to remember from Chapter 1 that the majority of sex crimes go unreported, especially reports of rape. Current estimates show that about one in five women and one in 38 men in the United States have been a victim of a completed or attempted rape at some point in their lifetime (Smith et al., 2018).

MYTHS ABOUT RAPE

There are many misconceptions about the crime of rape, including who commits it, its victims, and when and where it happens. These myths are borne primarily out of biased media coverage of rape, inaccurate reporting, and record keeping of rape statistics. These myths are summarized in Table 3.1.

Rape Happens Only to Young, Attractive Women

Although it is true that about 80% of rape victims are under the age of 30 and that nine out of ten rape victims are female (Rape, Abuse, and Incest National Network [RAINN], 2009), rape is not exclusively limited to this population. Anyone can be raped, including men, the elderly, people with disabilities, LGBTQIA+ populations, and people from every racial, ethnic, religious, and socioeconomic group are susceptible to rape.

Rape Happens Only to "Bad Women"

The belief that we live in a fair world where good things happen to good people and bad things happen to bad people (*just world hypothesis*) is prevalent (Strömwall et al., 2013) and proposes that victims of crime are, therefore, responsible for their own fate. This belief pins the blame on rape victims for not adhering to society's rules (Belknap, 2015) and suggests

TABLE 3.1 Myths about Rape

Myth	Reality
Rape happens only to young and attractive women.	All segments of the population can be and are raped. Rape has less to do with physical and sexual attraction and more to do with power.
Rape happens only to "bad women."	Anyone can be a victim of rape. Certain segments of the population are more vulnerable to rape than others, but it is not exclusive to these segments.
Most rape claims are false.	False rape allegations are rare. It is also important to differentiate between false allegations (which provides substantial evidence that the event did not happen) and unsubstantiated allegations (which fail to prove the event happened). Unsubstantiated allegations are more common than false allegations.
People who rape are mentally ill or psychotic.	The majority of rapes are committed by men who do not suffer from a severe mental illness.
Only men can rape, and only women can be victims.	The most common rape scenario involves a male offender and a female victim, but females can be offenders, and men can be victims of rape.
Unsafe, unmonitored places are breeding grounds for rape and sexual assault.	Most rapes occur at a residence or behind closed doors and are committed by people known to the victim.

that only certain kinds of women are vulnerable to rape and sexual assault. Women seen as promiscuous, having prior sexual experiences, drinking alcohol, or engaging in activities at inappropriate places and/or times are labeled as deviant. Sex workers (or prostitutes) are an example.

This myth is most likely perpetuated by evidence that certain groups are more vulnerable to rape and sexual assault. Female street prostitutes experience high rates of violence. In one study, approximately 40% of Chicago street prostitutes had been raped at some point, and 22% had been raped more than 10 times (Raphael & Shapiro, 2002). Because street prostitutes violate gender norms by selling sex, they are viewed as "loose," "immoral," or "of low moral character." Because of these labels, the violence perpetrated against them has become normalized. Some male customers (or "Johns") believe raping a prostitute does not constitute rape (Oselin & Blasyak, 2013).

Most Rape Claims Are False

In 1680, Sir Matthew Hale, an influential English judge, observed that "rape . . . is an accusation easily to be made and hard to be proved, and harder to be defended by the party accused, though never so innocent" (Hale, 1734, pp. 635–636). Hale's critique of the justice system regarding rape victims under English common law—where the victim is on trial, not the defendant—reflects a common view that female rape victims routinely make false allegations of rape. This view implies that women claim rape as an act of revenge, fantasy, or deceit to hide their own sexual appetites or deviance. Early research to determine the extent of false rape allegations concluded the following:

> False accusations of . . . rape in particular are generally believed to be much more frequent than untrue charges of other [types of] crimes. A woman may accuse an innocent man of raping her because she is mentally sick or given to delusions . . . or because, having consented to intercourse, she is ashamed of herself and bitter at her partner; or because she is pregnant and prefers a false explanation to a true one.
> (Corroborating Charges of Rape, 1967, as cited in Cuklanz, 1996, p. 22)

In a summary of other studies, Rumney (2006) reports false rape allegations account for as little as 2% of reported rape allegations, but as many as 90%. This wide variation in estimates indicates the measurement problems. Studies have either failed to explicitly define what constitutes a false rape allegation, relied on different criteria to identify an allegation as false, or included cases outside the parameters of acceptable definitions. Intentionally false, fabricated reports of rape victimization are actually quite rare, which is further discussed in Chapter 8.

People Who Rape Are Mentally Ill or Psychotic

A commonly accepted myth that has been accepted for decades is that all people who commit rape are psychotic, insane, or otherwise mentally ill. Similar to the myth that only "bad women" are raped, the belief that those who rape are mentally ill provides a false sense of security that "normal" people cannot commit such atrocious crimes. The vast majority of rapes are committed by people who do not suffer from a severe mental illness. In one of the most comprehensive studies analyzing psychiatric diagnoses of 535 individuals convicted of rape from a Swedish prison, only 2.6% suffered a personality disorder, and only 1.7% were deemed clinically psychotic (Långström et al., 2004).

Despite these findings, there is a tendency, especially in the United States among forensic mental-health specialists, to use the residual, paraphilia-not-otherwise-specified diagnosis in assessing and recommending treatment for those convicted of rape. Given that a psychiatric diagnosis is required for civil commitment, such residual diagnoses have been used to detain those who commit rape beyond their sentences (Frances et al., 2008). A great deal of controversy surrounds the notion of "inventing diagnoses" as a basis for further confining people who commit rape when the research does not support it (Zander, 2008).

Only Men Can Rape, and Only Women Can Be Victims

The belief that only men can rape and only women can be raped reflects a broader and more engrained belief that men are aggressive and women are passive. It bears repeating that *anyone* can be a victim of rape. Men not only experience rape and sexual assault victimization at nontrivial rates, but it is also believed that men are significantly less likely to report rape, due to a number of barriers, including lack of social services and support mechanisms. Additionally, the potential stigma of being perceived as weak and having one's sexual identity or orientation questioned is another reason for underreporting among men.

Similarly, there is a widely held belief that women cannot commit rape. Statements such as "women don't do such things" (Wijkman et al., 2010) or "what harm can be done without a penis" (Hislop, 2001) serve to minimize the impact of women who commit rape and sexual assault. Characteristics of this population are further explored in Chapter 6.

Unsafe, Unmonitored Places Are Breeding Grounds for Rape and Sexual Assault

By and large, current sex-crime policies, educational efforts, and primary prevention strategies portray rape and sexual assault as "stranger-danger" offenses that occur in public places such as parks, bus stops, and dark alleys. Only a small percentage of sex crimes occur in such places, however, with the vast majority occurring in the home and between acquaintances or family members (Colombino et al., 2011).

There has been little effort to identify ways that public-education campaigns and community strategies can deter or prevent rapes in nonpublic places. As a result, sex-crime policy has been largely criticized for implementing little more than "feel-good" measures that address a small percentage of rapes and sexual assaults committed each year. Consequently, policies that embrace the "stranger-danger, dark-alley" scenario do little to prevent rape and sexual assault (Ewing, 2011) and may even increase the risk of recidivism by undermining offender reentry and stability (Calkins et al., 2015).

RAPE CULTURE

Think about a recent story you have heard on the news about rape. It might have been a story about a high-profile scandal in the entertainment industry, date rape on a college campus, or the pervasiveness of rape and sexual assault in the military. Chances are that you heard the term "***rape culture***." The basic idea of *rape culture* links the act of rape

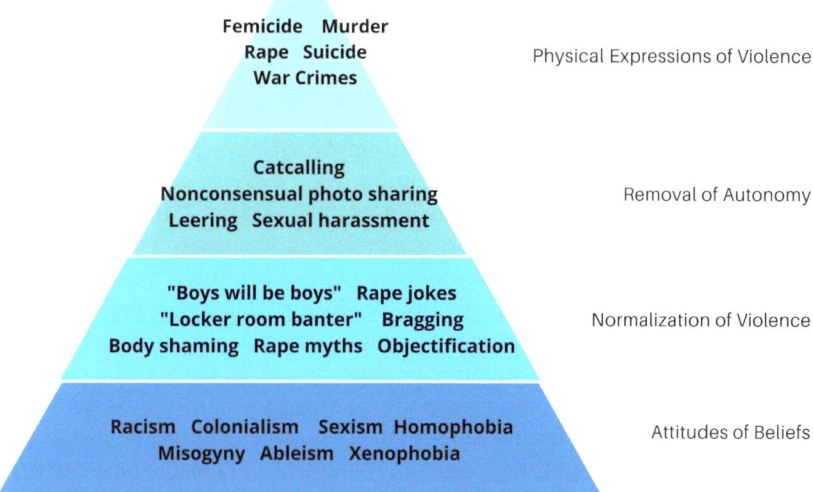

FIGURE 3.1 The Sexual Violence Pyramid.

Note: Adapted from Sexual Assault Centre, University of Alberta (2021).

with the social, political, and cultural fabric of overall society. Scholars have studied this concept for decades, and there is no single definition of this phenomenon. Early scholars described rape culture as "a complex of beliefs that encourages male sexual aggression and supports violence against women . . . a society where violence is seen as sexy and sexuality as violent" (Buchwald et al., 1993, p. v). Simpler definitions position rape culture as "one in which rape, or sexual assault, is an expected, normal occurrence, found worldwide" (Burnett, 2016, p. 1). Regardless of which definition is accepted, rape culture is an environment in which sexual violence is normalized and excused. Viewed through this lens, sexual violence (and other forms of gendered violence) is a predictable outcome of attitudes and belief systems that promote normalization of violence, victim blaming, and offender impunity. The sexual violence pyramid (Figure 3.1) depicts the elements of rape culture.

Attitudes and Belief Systems

Attitudes and belief systems form the base of the sexual violence pyramid. Scholars have long argued that the attitudes that underpin physical and sexual violence are the same belief systems that reinforce male dominance, discrimination, sexual objectification, and heteronormativity. In other words, rape culture is not just concerned with attitudes and beliefs about rape—issues of racism, xenophobia (i.e., fear of those from another culture), homophobia, colonialism (i.e., the policy/practice of acquiring partial or full political control over territory and exploiting it economically), misogyny (i.e., prejudice toward women), and any other belief system that reinforces the dominance of one group over another all intersect in rape culture. This can help us understand why certain populations, including LGBTQ+ people, individuals with disabilities, and Indigenous women, are at particular risk for sexual violence in the United States and beyond (this is explored further in Chapter 8).

Normalization of Violence

The next level of the sexual violence pyramid interrogates the processes that normalize violence (and particularly violence against women). As people are socialized into a culture that promotes attitudes and belief systems encouraging (predominantly) male power and aggression, violent and aggressive behaviors are seen as customary, as are victims' submission to it (Stanko, 2013). These aggressive behaviors are reduced simply to "boys being boys" (Connell, 2013; French, 2003; Messerschmidt, 2012). Sexist humor (e.g., "locker room banter," rape jokes) also creates a norm of tolerance for sexual discrimination and sexism (Ford et al., 2013). Further, men exposed to sexist humor have reported a greater propensity to commit sexual violence against women, including rape (Romero-Sánchez et al., 2017). Subscription to *attitudinal rape myths* is also a major part of the normalization of violence that shapes rape culture.

Attitudinal rape myths explain incorrectly why rapes occur. At their core, attitudinal rape myths are stereotypical, false beliefs about rape, rape victims, and those who commit rape that create a hostile social climate toward rape victims, are sympathetic of those who rape, and are somewhat forgiving of rape. Several rape-myth scales have been developed to gauge these beliefs. Table 3.2 presents one of the most comprehensive and reliable rape-myth acceptance scales, known as the Bumby RAPE Scale (Bumby, 1996), a self-report tool comprising 36 statements reflective of attitudinal rape myths. There are two broad categories of rape myths: excusing rape (beliefs that minimize responsibility or guilt of rape through questioning victim credibility or deficits on the offender's part) and justifying rape (beliefs that minimize the wrongfulness and harmfulness of rape).

For the past 40 years, researchers have sought to determine how rape myths are connected to the commission of rape. It is argued that acceptance of attitudinal rape myths has two different effects. First, it promotes aggressive behavior. Studies have shown that rape-supportive cognition, together with other factors, such as sexual arousal to rape depictions, the inability to control emotions, and personality problems, is related to negative attitudes toward women, gender-role norms, and sexual aggression (Aronowitz et al., 2012; Debowska et al., 2015; Edwards et al., 2011; Fansher & Zedaker, 2020; Hall & Hirschman, 1991). Rape-supportive cognitions have been associated with future sexual aggression (Thompson et al., 2011); likewise, research has shown that decreases in rape-supportive cognitions lead to reductions in aggressive sexual behavior (Lanier, 2001).

The second effect of acceptance of attitudinal rape myths is that it promotes tolerance of sexual abuse. Those who accept these myths perceive rape as something positive compared to those who do not accept such myths. Morry and Winkler (2001) showed that acceptance of rape myths increases acceptance of coercive behavior. Rape-supportive cognitions have also been implicated in leniency being shown toward the perpetrators of sexual aggression. For example, the endorsement of certain rape myths (e.g., if a woman gets drunk at a party, it is her own fault if someone takes advantage of her sexually, or when women wear tight clothes, short skirts, and no bras or underwear, they are asking for sex) is associated with higher levels of victim blaming and lesser perceptions of perpetrator responsibility (Gerger et al., 2007; Suarez & Gadalla, 2010; Süssenbach, 2016; Temkin & Krahé, 2008).

Research also reveals a strong correlation between rape-myth acceptance and endorsement of racism, classism, ageism, homophobia, and religious intolerance (Aosved & Long, 2006; Burt, 1980). One study found that endorsement of the just world hypothesis is correlated with rape-myth acceptance (Hayes et al., 2013). Finally, numerous studies have shown that these beliefs are highly correlated with hostile attitudes toward women in addition to heterosexism, ageism, racism, and classism (Aosved & Long, 2006; Locke & Mahalik, 2005; Suarez & Gadalla, 2010).

TABLE 3.2 Bumby RAPE Scale

Excusing Rape	Justifying Rape
Women generally want sex no matter how they can get it.	Women who get raped probably deserve it.
If a woman does not resist strongly to sexual advances, she is probably willing to have sex.	Because prostitutes sell their bodies for sexual purposes, it is not as bad if someone forces them into sex.
Women often falsely accuse men of rape.	If women did not sleep around so much, they would be less likely to get raped.
A lot of women who get raped had "bad reputations" in the first place.	If a man has had sex with a women before, then he should be able to have sex with her any time he wants.
If a women gets drunk at a party, it is her own fault if someone takes advantage of her sexually.	Fantasizing about forcing someone to have sex isn't all that bad because no one is being hurt.
When women wear tight clothes, short skirts, and no bras or underwear, they are asking for sex.	A lot of times, when women say "no," they are playing hard to get and mean "yes."
A lot of women claim they were raped because they want attention.	Part of a wife's duty is to satisfy her husband sexually whenever he wants it, whether or not she is in the mood.
Victims of rape are usually a little bit to blame for what happens.	As long as a man does not slap or punch a woman in the process, forcing her to have sex is not as bad.
Women who go to bars a lot are mainly looking to have sex.	When a woman gets raped more than once, she is probably doing something to cause it.
Often a woman reports a rape long after the fact because she gets mad at the man she had sex with and is trying to get back at him.	Women who get raped will eventually forget about it and move on with their lives.
Before the police investigate a woman's claim of rape, it is a good idea to find out what she was wearing, if she had been drinking, and what kind of person she is.	On a date, when a man spends a lot of money on a woman, the woman ought to at least give the man something in return sexually.
Generally, rape is not planned—a lot of times it just happens.	If a woman lets a man kiss her and touch her sexually, she should be willing to go all the way.
If a person tells himself he will never rape again, then he probably won't.	When women act like they are too good for men, most men probably think about raping the women to put them in their place.
A lot of men who rape do so because they are deprived of sex.	Society and the courts are too tough on rapists.

(Continued)

TABLE 3.2 Continued

Excusing Rape	Justifying Rape
The reason a lot of women say "no" to sex is because they don't want to seem loose.	Most women are sluts and get what they deserve.
If a woman goes to the home of a man on the first date, she probably wants to have sex with him.	Any woman can prevent herself from being raped if she wants to.
Many women have a secret desire to be forced into having sex.	
Most of the men who rape have stronger sexual urges than other men.	
Most of the time, the only reason a man commits rape is because he was sexually assaulted as a child.	
Men who commit rape are probably responding to a lot of stress in their lives, and raping helps reduce that stress.	

Removal of Autonomy

As violence is normalized and an invalid sense of sexual entitlement begins to build, women and other historically disempowered groups of people experience diminished autonomy and sexual agency. Stanko (2013) argued that "women learn, often at a very early age, that their sexuality is not their own and that maleness can at any point intrude into it" (p. 73). Thus, at this phase, people with oppressive attitudes and beliefs may begin to treat others as less than human. This can manifest in a number of ways, including sexual harassment (e.g., catcalling, unwelcome sexual advances, requests for sexual favors, and other verbal aggressions) to more overt displays of noncontact sexual aggression, including nonconsensual photo sharing and exposure. Although these behaviors do not fit the definition of rape or sexual assault, they are forms of sexual violence that may escalate to rape and sexual assault (Reilly et al., 1992; Ybarra & Thompson, 2018).

The Peak of the Pyramid

The peak of the pyramid is where rape and sexual assault are located. This is where a sense of sexual entitlement and impunity can begin to manifest as physical expressions of violence. It is important to note that rape culture does not just nurture sexual violence but also other forms of violence, including homicide, suicide, war crimes, and genocide.

By and large, rape does not just happen (this is one of the rape myths that serves to excuse or minimize rape); it is the result of repeated exposure to and reinforcement of dogmatic beliefs that certain types of people simply are not equal to others. Preventing rape involves much more than focusing on individuals who commit these crimes. It requires challenging and changing the core cultural logics (i.e., attitudes and belief systems) that normalize rape and sexual assault and make these crimes permissible and socially acceptable. Most sex crimes and sex offender management policy in the United States, however, is focused solely on the peak of the sexual violence pyramid. Prevention efforts are mostly geared toward preventing known individuals who commit rape and sexual assault from committing these crimes again.

RAPE LAW IN THE UNITED STATES

Rape, or forcible rape, to be more precise, currently stands as one of the eight Part I index crimes of the Uniform Crime Reports (UCR). Along with murder, robbery, and aggravated assault, it is classified as a violent crime. Although rape has been a crime with severe punishments for offenders, it has not always been classified as a violent crime. This section presents a survey of the history of rape law to demonstrate how rape and the attendant social and legal reactions to it have changed over time (Federal Bureau of Investigation, 2016).

Women as Property

Throughout most of recorded human history, women have been treated as property. They were the property of their fathers until marriage, at which point ownership was transferred to their husbands. Because women did not exist as independent beings and carried no status independent of their fathers or husbands, rape of a woman was not predicated on a lack of female consent or refusal to engage in sex nor her right to bodily integrity. Rape, therefore, whether against a man's daughter or a man's wife, was treated as a man-on-man crime; it was a property crime committed by one man against another man's property. These principles dominated from the early codes of ancient Babylon through the early 20th century.

No property was valued more than a betrothed virgin. Rape of virgin women was treated as a capital offense, with offenders facing the death penalty and the victimized girl considered guiltless. Married women who were raped did not fare as well. According to the Code of Hammurabi (approximately 4,000 years ago), a man would be killed if he raped a betrothed virgin; the victim suffered no consequence. A married woman who experienced the same crime, however, had to share the blame equally with her attacker. The crime was labeled "adultery," and both parties were thrown into the river. The remnants of these policies and practices are evident in some of the rape myths discussed earlier.

Rape Reform Movement

Until the early 1970s, little had changed with respect to how rape was handled by criminal justice officials. Rules of evidence required a victim to physically resist her attacker, and the victim's testimony often required corroboration. Evidence of the victim's prior sexual history was admissible during trial proceedings. Traditional rape law made it "easy to commit rape and get away with it" (Rodabaugh & Austin, 1981, p. 17). Critics argued that these rules and laws had serious consequences for both the victims and the criminal justice system. They were partially responsible for the unwillingness of victims to report rape, which accounted for low rates of arrest, prosecution, and conviction for rape. Critics charged that the criminal justice response to rape was predicated on rape myths, and the most serious dispositions were reserved for "real" rapes with "real" victims (Spohn & Horney, 1992).

The feminist movement of the 1960s and 1970s was a major catalyst of change for women's rights. It was in the midst of the feminist movement in 1975 that Susan Brownmiller published *Against Our Will: Men, Women, and Rape*. This seminal book characterized rape as a tool of male dominance over women. Rape is a political act, and Brownmiller emphasized the need to make rape a "speakable crime" that can be openly discussed. This book also led to the much-publicized maxim that rape is a violent crime and not a product of men's natural sexual desires. It was against this backdrop that numerous initiatives were born such as speak-outs, rape crisis centers, self-defense classes, and new rape legislation.

By the 1990s, all 50 U.S. states either revised or repealed traditional rape laws and evidentiary standards. Although the exact nature of reform varied across and within states, there were four common reform themes (Spohn & Horney, 1992):

1. The single crime of rape was replaced with a series of offenses graded by seriousness, including sodomy, sexual assault, sexual abuse, sexual battery, and deviant sexual misconduct. The traditional definition of rape excluded acts committed against male victims, acts other than vaginal intercourse, sexual assaults with an object, and rapes committed by a spouse. The language was written in a gender-neutral fashion.

2. The consent standard was changed. *Consent* refers to a clear, knowing, and voluntary agreement to engage in sexual activity. Prior to the reform movement, traditional rape laws required that a victim resists to the utmost (Schwartz, 1983) to demonstrate a lack of consent. Reformers challenged these standards, arguing that such resistance could lead to serious injury to the victim and that the focus should be placed on the offender, not the victim. Although the resistance standard was lifted, consent requirements still vary from state to state.

3. The corroboration requirement (the rule requiring that the testimony of the rape victim be accompanied by the testimony of other witnesses or some other form of evidence) was eliminated. Given the private nature of most rapes, critics cited the immense difficulty in obtaining evidence to corroborate victim testimony.

4. Most states enacted **rape shield laws** that placed restrictions on introducing evidence of a victim's sexual history during trial proceedings.

The extensive grassroots efforts of the 1970s, 1980s, and the early 1990s led to the passage of the Violence Against Women Act (VAWA) as a federal law in 1994. VAWA provides $1.6 billion toward investigation and prosecution of violent crimes against women (including sexual assault, domestic violence, and most recently, dating violence and stalking), imposes restitution requirements on persons convicted of such crimes, and provides opportunities for civil remedies for criminally unprosecuted cases. VAWA was reauthorized in 2000, 2005, and 2013 and, at the time of this writing, has been referred to the Subcommittee on Oversight and Investigations for reauthorization through 2026. VAWA laws provide numerous programs and services, including community prevention programs, funding for victim-assistance services (e.g., rape crisis centers, shelters, and hotlines), and legal aid for victims.

Rape Law Today

Until recently, the legal definition of rape was limited in scope. The U.S. Department of Justice defined rape as "the carnal knowledge of a female forcibly and against her will." In this fairly abstract definition, there are three necessary components. First, "carnal knowledge" refers to the act of a man having a sexual bodily connection with a woman (i.e., sexual intercourse). Second, force is also a necessary condition and is usually established through threats of physical violence or if the female believes resistance would not prevent the rape. Third, "against her

> **Focus Box 3.1** The New Summary Rape Definition
>
> Penetration, no matter how slight, of the vagina or anus with any body part or object, or oral penetration by a sex organ by another person, without the consent of the victim
> The revised definition includes the following:
>
> - Male and female victims and offenders
> - Instances in which the victim is incapable of giving consent because of a temporary or permanent mental or physical incapacity (e.g., age, intoxication)
> - Forms of sexual penetration understood to be rape
>
> Note. Adapted from Federal Bureau of Investigation (2020).

will" indicates that the female is incapable of giving consent due to a temporary or permanent mental or physical incapacity. This definition of rape effectively excludes other types of sexual violence, including **statutory rape**, incest, forcible sodomy, sexual assault with an object, and forcible fondling. Moreover, any sexual assaults against male victims were not considered rape per this definition, nor were assaults that involved oral or anal penetration of either gender.

In the revised definition (see Focus Box 3.1), many states adopted gender-neutral guidelines for forcible rape (i.e., "carnal knowledge of a *person*" instead of "carnal knowledge of a female"), whereas others defined rape in terms of the seriousness of the offense (penetration vs. other sexual contacts), the amount of coercion used by the offender, and the degree of injury to the victim. Most states redefined "penetration."

In 2012, U.S. Attorney General Eric Holder announced revisions to the UCR's definition of rape, stating,

> These long overdue updates to the definition of rape will help ensure justice for those whose lives have been devastated by sexual violence and reflect the Department of Justice's commitment to standing with rape victims. . . . This new, more inclusive definition will provide us with a more accurate understanding of the scope and volume of these crimes.
>
> (U.S. Department of Justice, 2012)

Rape laws continue to evolve across all 50 states. The minimum age that a person can legally consent to sexual activity varies from state to state (Figure 3.2). In most states, the minimum age to consent is 16; in the remaining states, the age of consent is either 17 or 18 years old. Engaging in sexual activity with anyone below the minimum age of consent, regardless of their willingness to participate, is known as *statutory rape*. However, there are other factors that come into play with this crime, including the age of the defendant and the age differential between the two parties. Some states set age thresholds for defendants below which individuals cannot be prosecuted for engaging in sexual activity with minors. For example, in Arkansas, individuals below the age of 20 cannot be prosecuted for engaging in sexual activity with partners ages 14 and older. Some states also consider the age difference between the two parties. For example, in New Hampshire, sexual contact without penetration is legal between those 13–15 years of age and partners who are no more than five years older.

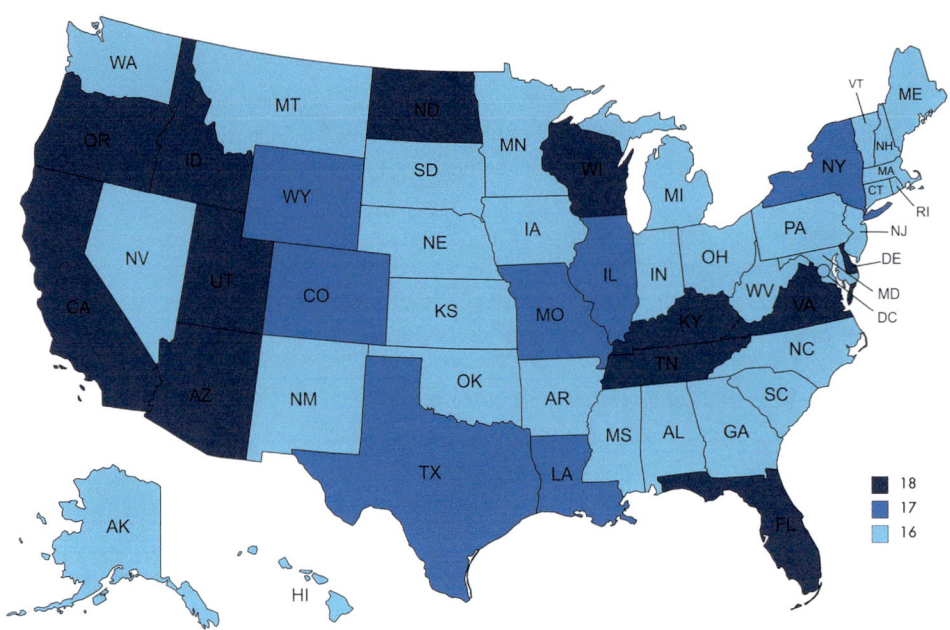

FIGURE 3.2 Minimum Age of Consent in the United States.

Note: Adapted from RAINN (2020).

Rape legislation also varies from state to state. There are two models for defining rape thresholds (i.e., what legally "counts" as rape). The ***consent-based model*** requires that for the act to qualify as rape, there must be a sexual act to which one of the parties did not consent. The ***coercion-based model*** requires that the sexual act was achieved through coercion, violence, physical force or threat of violence, or physical force for the act to qualify as rape. Under the consent-based model, there are basically fewer gray areas—it is still considered rape even if the victim did not clearly say "no," was not threatened or assaulted, or did not fight back. The coercion-based model, conversely, limits the number of scenarios that would qualify as rape. Currently, there are many more states that use the coercion-based model in the legal definition of rape; substantially fewer use the consent-based (Figure 3.3).

WHY DO PEOPLE RAPE?

As discussed earlier, rape seldom fits the stereotype in a fictional book or movie. People who rape are rarely strangers jumping from the bushes or from dark alleys and assaulting females they do not know. Furthermore, rape, contrary to popular opinion, is not motivated solely by sexual desire; people who commit rape are not sex fiends, sex maniacs, or sex psychopaths. We now focus our attention on what types of people commit rape and sexual assault as well as why they do it. There is a wide range of sexually violent and exploitative acts and myriad motivations for committing them; as such, it is impossible to construct a typical profile of someone who rapes. However, fairly consistent characteristics of men who rape women have been documented in clinical and social science literature. They include the following:

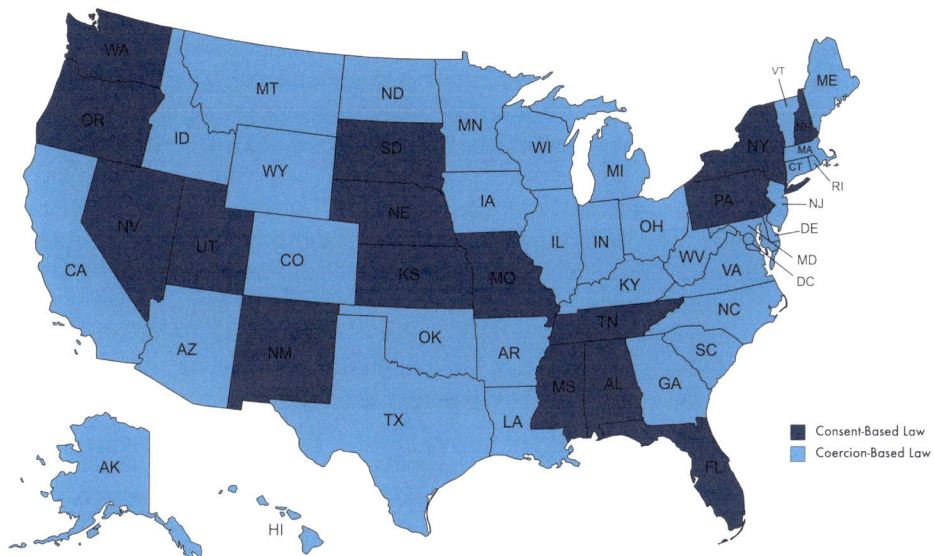

FIGURE 3.3 Rape Legislation in the United States: Consent-Based vs. Coercion-Based Models.
Note: Adapted from Tracy et al. (2012).

1 Hostile masculinity
2 Aggressive sexual beliefs
3 Physical and psychological aggression
4 History of violence
5 Alcohol use and abuse

Hostile Masculinity

Hostile masculinity, referred to as ***hostile masculinity syndrome***, often manifests in individuals who commit rape and sexual assault via two primary sets of attitudes and emotions (Malamuth, 2013). The first consists of hostile, distrustful, insecure feelings toward people, especially women. These feelings are accompanied by misogynous (i.e., woman-hating) attitudes. These attitudes include attitudinal rape myths, including a belief that women secretly desire to be raped. The second set of attitudes and emotions involves a desire to control and dominate women. These desires fuel sexual arousal and sexual gratification. Research has shown that hostile masculinity is strongly associated with sexual assault (e.g., Casey et al., 2017; Russell & King, 2020; Wheeler et al., 2002).

Aggressive Sexual Beliefs

Closely related to hostile masculinity are aggressive sexual beliefs. These include any attitudes supportive of aggression, use of force, coercion, humiliation, or violence and sexuality. Agreeing with statements such as "Get a woman drunk, high, or hot, and she'll let you do whatever you want" are indicative of aggressive sexual beliefs. Aggressive sexual beliefs are often linked to sadism and masochism. Recall that sexual sadism takes place when an individual receives sexual pleasure or excitement from the psychological or physical suffering of another person. Sexual masochism, in contrast, involves sexual pleasure and gratification as a result of *receiving* psychological or physical suffering and pain. Much research has shown that people subscribing to such beliefs are more likely to commit sexual assault (e.g., Abbey et al., 2003a; Bernat et al., 1999).

Some researchers have even argued that viewing adult pornography may be symptomatic of aggressive sexual beliefs. Evidence for this relationship, however, is mixed. Early researchers claimed that pornography predisposes some men to want to rape women or intensifies that predisposition in men already inclined to rape as well as overriding internal and social inhibitions against acting out rape desires (Russell, 1988). A recent meta-analysis, however, found that viewing nonviolent pornography was not associated with sexual aggression (Ferguson & Hartley, 2020). This suggests that the presumed pornography–rape connection is questionable and may be a product of exaggerated claims by politicians, pressure groups, and even some social scientists.

Finally, engaging in frequent casual sex or expectancy of impersonal sex is associated with sexual aggression. One study of college men found that high levels of impersonal sex, as well as hostile masculinity, strongly predict sexual aggression (Wheeler et al., 2002). Another study revealed that sexual assault offenders were more likely than nonoffenders to have high expectations for having sex earlier in a romantic relationship as well as have more positive attitudes about casual sex (Abbey et al., 2007).

Physical and Psychological Aggression

Physical aggression includes behaviors such as grabbing, pushing, slapping, biting, and more serious physical acts that result in serious injury or death. Physical aggression is strongly associated with rape and sexual assault. One study of married couples found that husbands' use of physical aggression strongly predicted forced sex (Marshall & Holtzworth-Munroe, 2002). Another study found that 120 men who reportedly committed rape were also responsible for 1,225 different acts of physical aggression. In this same study, those who committed multiple rapes over time were responsible for 85% of the total acts of physical aggression (Lisak & Miller, 2002).

Psychological aggression is the most common form of aggression in intimate relationships, including dating relationships (Shorey et al., 2008). It encompasses a wide range of verbal and behavioral acts intended to humiliate, criticize, blame, dominate, isolate, intimidate, and threaten one's partner. Some research has concluded that the consequences of psychological aggression are more severe and long-lasting than those of physical aggression (Murphy & Hoover, 1999).

Psychological aggression consists of two highly related components: expressive aggression, such as name-calling, insulting, or humiliating an intimate partner, and coercive control, which includes behaviors intended to monitor and control or threaten an intimate partner (e.g., isolating an intimate partner from family and friends, deciding what clothes an intimate partner should wear, limiting access to money and other financial resources, and threatening to hurt an intimate partner). Psychological aggression has been linked to aggressive sexual beliefs (Marshall & Holtzworth-Munroe, 2002).

History of Violence

Research has revealed that the childhood histories of those who commit rape usually include violent backgrounds. One study found that individuals convicted of rape frequently report experiences of physical abuse, parental violence, emotional abuse, and cruelty to animals (Simons et al., 2008). Researchers contend that physical abuse, parental violence, and emotional abuse result in externalizing behaviors when they occur in combination. For example, one study found that physical and verbal abuse during childhood led to antisocial behavior and callous personality traits, both of which led to aggressive sexual fantasies (Beauregard et al., 2004).

Likewise, research has shown that the combination of physical violence, domestic violence, emotional abuse, and neglect predicts subsequent sex offending. A recent study showed that the risk of completed rape among a sample of adult men was elevated among those who had experienced child sexual abuse, parental physical abuse, exposure to domestic violence, and sibling physical abuse; the risks were even higher among men who experienced multiple forms of child maltreatment (King et al., 2019).

Alcohol Use and Abuse

Alcohol use/abuse and violence are undeniably linked. However, alcohol does not *cause* sexual aggression and rape. Some chemicals and substances (e.g., steroids, phencyclidine/PCP, crack cocaine) can increase one's propensity to engage in violent behaviors (including rape), but alcohol is not one of them. Pharmacologically, alcohol is a depressant and rarely causes aggression. Research has shown the relationship between alcohol use and rape is not a direct one. It has been proposed that alcohol and other substances contribute to rape in multiple ways.

First, mere beliefs about the effects of alcohol will come to fruition. In other words, if one believes that alcohol will make one feel more powerful and more sexually aggressive, it will. In contrast, if one does not connect alcohol to these behaviors, they are unlikely to engage in sexually assaultive behaviors even when heavily under the influence. Several studies have supported this hypothesis (Abbey et al., 1996, 2003b; Presley et al., 1996). Second, alcohol is believed to provide those who rape with an excuse to freely act on those desires. In other words, alcohol may be used to "grease the wheels" for committing rape by people already likely to commit such acts, even without alcohol (Abbey, 2002; Bancroft, 2003; George & Marlatt, 1986). Finally, alcohol may serve to distort perceptions of sexual intent. Alcohol consumption increases the likelihood that misperceptions will occur and escalate to the point where forced sex happens. When intoxicated, people's perceptions are narrowed, making them less able to detect subtle cues and focus only on surface cues. This is known as **alcohol myopia**. Studies have linked alcohol myopia to the increased likelihood of rape and sexual assault (Abbey et al., 1998; Johnson, 2017; Johnson et al., 2000).

RAPE TYPOLOGIES

Typologies—or classification systems—are often utilized to categorize individuals who are alike into distinct categories. Ideally, a typology consists of any number of categories where individuals within each category are similar (or even identical) and each category consists of individuals who are different from the individuals in all other categories (i.e., individuals in Category A are different from individuals in Category B). Typologies have been utilized in criminological research to make distinctions among diverse crimes. Typologies of individuals who commit rape have many practical uses, including aiding the criminal investigation process, informing decisions within the criminal justice system, treatment planning, and understanding the causes of rape. It is important to understand, however, that those who commit rape do not always fit neatly into a single category; they only approximate the characteristics of people in that category. Sometimes, offenders may fit into more than one category, whereas others may not fit into any category. To be considered reliable and accurate, typologies must withstand the test of time. That is, follow-ups must be conducted on a regular basis to see if offenders continue to fall into the categories based on the criteria originally used to develop them.

Caution must be exercised, therefore, in interpreting rape typologies. Rape is a behavior reflecting multidimensional needs. Using typologies to "diagnose" an offender as a certain type can have limiting effects on an investigation. It can ignore other offender motivational patterns and ultimately overlook physical and behavioral evidence. In this section, three of the most common rape typologies are presented. These typologies were constructed using a male offender/female victim dyad. Other typologies representing different dyads (e.g., female offender/male victim) also exist and are covered in Chapter 6.

Most rape typologies organize and classify rapes and the persons who commit them according to the level and intensity of violence involved in the commission of the rape. The first empirically constructed rape typology is **Groth's Typology**, developed by Groth et al. (1977), who interviewed adult male offenders as well as female victims to determine the motivations and goals of those who commit rape. Based on these interviews, four subtypes of individuals who commit rape were identified: power reassurance, power assertive, anger retaliatory, and sadistic (the latter three subtypes involve substantially greater levels of violence compared to the power reassurance rapist, also known as the "gentlemen rapist").

Many typologies have emerged since Groth's initial model. Hazelwood (1987) adapted Groth's Typology to inform profiles of unknown offenders in active law enforcement investigations. **Hazelwood's Typology** separates offenders into two categories based on verbal, sexual, and physical behaviors of the individual committing the rape: pseudo-unselfish offenders (who treat victims as willing participants and do not engage in physical violence in the commission of the rape) and selfish offenders (who utilize physical violence, offensive language, and other degrading behaviors). The Massachusetts Treatment Center (MTC) Rapist Typologies are a series of classification models that have evolved over time and are based on offender motivations for sex and aggression (Knight et al., 1985; Knight & Prentky, 1987, 1990).

The most recent and comprehensive version to date is the **Massachusetts Treatment Center Rapist Typology, Version 3** *(MTC: R3)*, which consists of four main types of offenders (opportunistic, pervasively angry, sexual gratification, and vindictive), which are further broken down into nine subtypes based on offender level of social competence (i.e., the social, emotional, and intellectual skills and behaviors needed to succeed as a member of society) and presence of sadistic tendencies (Knight & Prentky, 1990). A shortcoming of most rape typologies is that they are primarily based on clinical interviews with caught and convicted offenders and/or their victims and are informed primarily by offender-specific factors such as motivation and goals for the assault. This excludes unknown and nonapprehended offenders who do not become involved in the criminal justice system (i.e., the majority of rape offenders).

Perry's Typology (Perry et al., 2018) eliminates the reliance on self-report by offenders and instead examines sexual assault events data from the FBI Violent Criminal Apprehension Program (ViCAP) database. Perry's Typology consists of seven categories of rape based on level of violence, offender approach (i.e., con approach vs. **blitz attack** vs. surprise/impulse attack), and trauma location on the victim's body. A summary of these typologies is provided in Table 3.3.

TABLE 3.3 Summary of Rape Typologies

Typology Summary	Lesser Degree of Violence	Greater Degree of Violence
Groth's Typology is based on self-report interviews of individuals imprisoned for sex crimes (n = 133) and victims of those crimes (n = 92). Offender motivation and the degree of aggression involved in rape informed the classification of offenders. Groth et al. (1977)	*Power reassurance rapists* use as little force or violence as possible; rape serves as a way to compensate for self-perceived inadequacies.	*Power assertive rapists* are impulsive, use moderate levels of force, and seek to prove their masculinity to victims. *Anger retaliatory rapists* commit rape as an expression of hostility that has built over time and usually involves serious physical injury. *Sadistic rapists* display sexual aggression fueled by perverse sexual fantasies and often commit extremely violent and bizarre sexual acts.
Hazelwood's Typology adapts Groth's Typology by separating offenders into two categories based on verbal, sexual, and physical behaviors of the individual committing the rape. Hazelwood (1987)	*Pseudo-unselfish rapists* treat victims as if they are willing participants in the crime and don't use physical violence; they are often reassuring, complimentary, nonprofane, and apologetic.	*Selfish rapists* objectify their victims and are physically abusive, verbally offensive, threatening, demeaning, or degrading.
The Massachusetts Treatment Center Rapist Typology, Version 3 (MTC: R3) categorizes rapes based on offender motivation and is further categorized based on developmental, biological, and environmental factors that result in different degrees of antisocial behavior, sexual aggression, impulsivity, and deviant sexual arousal. Knight and Prentky (1990)	**Opportunistic rapists (type 1 and 2)** usually commit impulsive, unplanned assaults and are seeking immediate sexual gratification; excessive violence/aggression is generally not present (with differentiation by level of social competence). **Sexual gratification–nonsadistic rapists (type 6 and 7)** demonstrate distorted attitudes about women, sexuality, and feelings of inadequacy but do not generally engage in violence (with further differentiation by level of social competence). **Sexual gratification–muted sadists (type 5)** have sadistic fantasies/tendencies but rarely incorporate these into their assaults.	**Pervasively angry rapists (type 3)** are impulsive, primarily driven by hostility toward men and women, and likely to use excessive force resulting in significant bodily harm. **Sexual gratification–overt sadists (type 4)** have sadistic fantasies/tendencies and commit assaults that are characterized by gratuitous violence. **Vindictive rapists (type 8 and 9)** harbor resentment specifically toward women and commit rapes that are humiliating and degrading and involve physical violence (with further differentiation by level of social competence).

(Continued)

TABLE 3.3 Continued		
Typology Summary	Lesser Degree of Violence	Greater Degree of Violence
Perry's Typology categorizes rapes based on situational and behavioral contexts of 4,476 rape incidents extracted from the FBI's ViCAP database, including use of force or restraints, use of a weapon, type of sexual activity, location of physical trauma, and offender approach. Perry et al. (2018)	*Low violence–planful offenders* use low levels of violence and lethal force and employ a con approach to carrying out the assault. *Low violence–impulsive offenders* use low levels of violence and lethal force and employ a blitz approach (i.e., unplanned, spontaneous attacks) to carrying out the assault. *Low violence–socially insecure offenders* use low levels of violence and lethal force and employ a surprise approach to carrying out the assault.	*High violence–planful offenders* employ high levels of aggression and use con approaches to carrying out rape. *High violence–multiple approach offenders* employ high levels of aggression and use surprise and blitz approaches to carrying out rape. *Sadistic sexual offenders* inflict potentially lethal force and unusual assault on the victim, with excessive violence intentionally focused on sexual areas of the victim's body; *sadistic offenders* inflict potentially lethal force and unusual assault on the victim, with the violence inflicted over all areas of the body.

CRIMINAL JUSTICE RESPONSE TO RAPE

Rape and sexual assault laws in the United States have changed significantly over the past 40 years. The scope of these changes varies across jurisdictions, but the legal definition of rape, formerly narrow and restrictive, has been replaced by a series of more inclusive, gender-neutral crimes graded by seriousness. Requirements pertaining to consent, corroboration, resistance, and marital rape exemptions also were relaxed to encourage victim reporting. Rape shield laws were enacted to prevent a victim's sexual history from being introduced as evidence against the victim's credibility during court proceedings. One goal of these changes was to improve the treatment of rape victims and, thus, help them report sexual victimization to the police. Reducing ***case attrition*** (i.e., the failure of a case to advance to the next phase of the criminal justice process) and increasing successful prosecution of offenders were related goals.

Rape is still characterized by underreporting as well as case attrition (Figure 3.4 for the estimated attrition rate of rape cases in the United States). Therefore, it is important to understand the dynamics of police and prosecutorial decision-making and responses to rape. Victims of rape who decide to report their victimization often embark on a long, drawn-out process that involves ongoing interactions with criminal justice officials, including law enforcement officials, medical personnel, social service providers, and prosecuting and defense attorneys. Throughout the process, victims may confront officials who are skeptical about their claims, question their credibility, and sometimes minimize the extent of the harm caused by the offender.

An example of the problems a victim can face during the reporting process became evident when Emma Sulkowicz reported a rape allegation. She later became known for her advocacy as she challenged Columbia University for their lack of response to report of rape victimization. She became known for carrying around a mattress on campus as a protest for the lack of the university's response.

During the reporting process, victims often experience what is known as ***secondary victimization***, which refers to the attitudes and behaviors of criminal justice officials who are blameful,

Out of Every 100 Rapes...

FIGURE 3.4 Attrition of Rape Cases in the United States.

Note: Adapted from RAINN (2009).

PHOTO 3.1 Emma Sulkowicz Protests the University's Lack of Response to Her Report of Rape.

Photo Credit: Jennifer S. Altman//*The New York Times*/Redux.

insensitive, minimizing, and dismissive of the victim. Disregard for victims' needs often so closely mirrors disregard of the victim by their assailant that secondary victimization has also come to be known as "the second rape" or "the second assault" (Campbell & Raja, 1999, p. 261).

Police Reporting and Response

In 2019, about 34% of rape and sexual assault incidents were reported to the police; in 2018, only 25% were reported (Morgan & Truman, 2020). Reasons for nonreporting are many and vary from victim to victim, but research has identified self-blame and guilt, shame and embarrassment, fear of the offender, and lack of faith in the criminal justice system as reasons for most victims (Du Mont et al., 2003). Studies of the factors related to police reporting reveal that victims are more likely to report if they experience what Williams (1984) referred to as the ***classic rape***—when the crime fits within the stereotype of rape (e.g., the victim was assaulted by a stranger, had visible injuries that could corroborate allegations of forced sexual intercourse, the offender used a weapon or physical force). Conversely, victims are less likely to report if they were drinking alcohol or using drugs at the time of the rape or if they knew the offender (Felson & Paré, 2007).

Victims, in other words, report the crime to the police when they believe that the probability of conviction is high. This belief may be arrived at independently or as a result of previous interactions with criminal justice officials who imply that the victim's character, reputation, or behavior at the time of the victimization is questionable. These findings suggest that, despite legal changes that have shifted from victim blaming, rape victims still believe they must conform to stereotypes of "real" rape victims.

For victims who do decide to report their victimization, the process almost always begins with law enforcement officials. They serve an important function in the reporting process and assume many "gatekeeping" roles. They decide whether a crime has occurred, the amount of investigative resources to devote to identifying and apprehending the suspect, whether to make an arrest (and if so, what type of charges to press), and whether to refer the case to the prosecutor's office.

One of the most important and criticized law enforcement decisions is whether to ***unfound*** the case. Unfounding occurs when the responding officer does not believe the victim's story and, therefore, concludes that the rape did not occur. Technically, cases can be unfounded only if it is determined that a crime did not occur. A case with a victim who makes a rape charge and later recants could be unfounded. Unfounded cases are affected by a combination of legal and extralegal factors, including the victim's ability to identify the suspect, the victim's willingness to prosecute, the promptness of the victim's report, whether the victim was assaulted by an acquaintance rather than a stranger, and the suspect's use of a weapon.

In reality, however, law enforcement officials may also unfound a case when they believe the likelihood of arrest or prosecution is low. They are often evaluated in terms of ***clearance rates***, which is the percentage of crimes that are cleared by an arrest. Because of the pressure to perform well in the eyes of management, they may unfound ambiguous or difficult cases. Such cases vary from the victim having a seemingly ulterior motive for pressing a rape charge, such as covering up for infidelity or getting pregnant, to the victim being compromised in some way, such as being under the influence of alcohol or another drug or having a previous consensual sexual relationship with the alleged perpetrator (Martin, 2005). It can also involve the district attorney failing to pursue charges, which is what happened in a New York case. Cammy Duong (pictured below) reported a rape to police along with corroborating evidence (Ransom, 2021). Her case has been described as one where it is credible, but proving it in court would be difficult (Ransom, 2021). Rape typically does not involve any other third-party witnesses (Ransom, 2021). The prosecutor suggested to Cammy Duong that she "go heal" and suing her attacker in a civil court was an option (Ransom, 2021).

An early study by the Law Enforcement Assistance Administration (1977) found that the two most important predictors of whether cases would be founded or unfounded were proof of penetration and the suspect's use of physical force. Despite changes in the definition of rape, these predictors are still relevant today. Law enforcement officials may also unfound a case when the victim fails to strike the correct emotional balance (Venema, 2014). Victims

PHOTO 3.2 Cammy Duong Reports Her Rape but Prosecutors Fail to Pursue.
Photo Credit: Ariana Drehsler//*The New York Times*/Redux.

who provide short answers and are "too matter of fact" are viewed as hiding something or not being completely truthful. In contrast, highly emotional and distraught victims are seen as too unstable and unlikely to provide accurate, logical accounts of the crime. Law enforcement officials may also unfound a case on discriminatory grounds such as socioeconomic status ("she was poor"), race or ethnicity ("she was a Black, Hispanic, or Native American woman"), or previous criminal history ("she was a prostitute" or "she has a record"). These views, reflective of the situational rape myth that rape only happens to "bad" girls, assume that the victim somehow precipitated her attack and that there is no way her story would hold up in court.

Prosecutorial Decision-Making

If a victim has made the decision to report a rape and that charge was cleared by arrest, the next phase involves prosecuting the suspect. Out of all the decision makers in the criminal justice system, the prosecutor has the most discretion. Prosecutors decide who will be charged and who will not, what charge will be filed, who will be offered a ***plea bargain***—an agreement between the prosecutor and defendant where the defendant enters a guilty plea for a particular charge in exchange for some concession from the prosecutor—and what the nature of the plea bargain will be. This is usually a lesser charge, a reduced sentence, or both.

The initial decision of whether to prosecute rape is the most critical phase of the process. As "gatekeepers of justice," prosecutors have considerable discretion, and there are neither legislative nor judicial guidelines that prosecutors must follow in reaching their decisions. These decisions are also not subject to review by the courts. Only 22–25% of all reported rapes are prosecuted (Spohn et al., 2001).

Research on prosecutors' charging decisions reveals they are strongly influenced by legally relevant factors such as the seriousness of the crime, the offender's criminal record, and the strength of the evidence (Frazier & Haney, 1996). A number of studies, however, also point to the powerful influence of victim characteristics (Beichner & Spohn, 2012; Frohmann, 1997). Similar to decision-making by law enforcement officials in unfounding a case, prosecutors may consider the victim's age, occupation, and education; "risk-taking" behavior such as hitchhiking, drinking alcohol, or using other drugs; and the character or reputation of the victim, despite rape shield laws that prohibit consideration of these factors (Kerstetter, 1990).

Case Adjudication

In the event a prosecutor decides to try a case, extralegal characteristics of the offender and the victim often come into play in rape trials. Physical appearance and the attractiveness of both parties are often linked to trial outcomes. In the judicial context, research has shown a ***good-looking effect*** whereby physically attractive defendants, as well as victims, tend to fare more favorably compared to their less attractive counterparts. One experiment by Vrij and Firmin (2001) found that physically attractive victims made a more credible impression and were assigned less responsibility for their victimization than physically unattractive victims. Evidence against the defendant was deemed more powerful when the victim was considered beautiful. Sensitivity to good looks may have been conditioned by acceptance of rape myths. Those who accepted certain attitudinal rape myths were more likely to associate beauty with credibility compared to those who did not accept such myths. These findings underscore the importance of screening potential jurors to assess their rape-myth acceptance.

The relationship between the victim and the offender also affects case outcomes. The ***intimacy effect*** is such that rapes between intimates (e.g., spouses, partners, and friends) are treated as lesser offenses than those between strangers and are less likely to result in guilty verdicts. There is a perception that persons who victimize strangers are predators. Their threats and attacks are perceived as random, thus posing a larger future threat to the community. Those who victimize intimates, conversely, are perceived as inflicting less harm on their victims. The stereotype of marital rape characterizes this crime as involving little actual violence, minimal pain, and less suffering (Finkelhor & Yllo, 1985). People who rape their spouses are viewed as less likely to commit future crimes against random people. Following this stereotype, rape between intimates should be treated as a less serious offense than rape between strangers despite the fact that research has shown that sex forced upon an intimate partner meets, and often surpasses, the harm to victims of stranger rapes (Bennice et al., 2003).

CONCLUSION

Despite the prevalence of rape, as well as considerable research on its causes, numerous myths and stereotypes have clouded our understanding of it. As we have discussed, these misunderstandings lead to ill-informed policy decisions and misdirect intervention and prevention strategies at both the individual and community levels. Research on rape and the individuals who commit it is plentiful. Research has identified risk factors associated with rape such as hostile masculinity, alcohol abuse, and a history of violence and victimization. However, these risk factors are not deterministic; they involve a ***probabilistic cause***. Not everyone who abuses alcohol commits rape, and not all males who experience sexual abuse as children will grow up to commit rape. These factors only increase the likelihood of rape. Many typologies have been developed to identify and categorize people who rape based on motivational and offending patterns. Rapes are largely underreported, and reported cases suffer from a high degree of attrition, resulting in the conviction of a small percentage of people who rape.

REVIEW POINTS

- Rape is a crime involving anger, aggression, and power. Rarely is rape solely motivated by sexual desire.
- Until recently, rape was narrowly defined and included only offenses involving vaginal penetration of a female by a male. Today, the definition of rape allows for any form of penetration (vaginal, oral, or anal). The revised definition also is not gender specific and considers males as potential victims.
- Attitudinal rape myths are beliefs and statements that incorrectly explain or rationalize rape, including beliefs about the offender and the victim. In general, rape myths serve to blame the victim and excuse or minimize the behaviors of the offender. Studies show that people who rape frequently accept rape myths.
- Numerous risk factors have been identified in people who commit rape, including hostile masculinity, aggressive sexual beliefs, physical and psychological aggression, history of violence, and alcohol use and abuse.
- It is estimated that one in five women and one in 38 men experience completed or attempted rape at some point in their lifetime.
- Rape is an underreported crime, with only 26–36% of rapes reported to law enforcement officials each year.
- Few rapes (about 2%) result in a conviction due to underreporting to law enforcement officials, unfounding of rape cases, refusal of prosecutors to accept cases for prosecution, and the influence of extralegal case characteristics.

REFERENCES

Abbey, A. (2002). Alcohol-related sexual assault: A common problem among college students. *Journal of Studies on Alcohol, s14*, 118–128.

Abbey, A., Buck, P. O., Zawacki, T., & Saenz, C. (2003a). Alcohol's effects on perceptions of a potential date rape. *Journal of Studies on Alcohol, 64*(5), 669–677. https://www.doi.org/10.15288/jsa.2003.64.669

Abbey, A., Clinton-Sherrod, A. M., McAuslan, P., Zawacki, T., & Buck, P. O. (2003b). The relationship between the quantity of alcohol consumed and the severity of sexual assaults committed by college men. *Journal of Interpersonal Violence, 18*(7), 813–833. https://www.doi.org/10.1177/0886260503253301

Abbey, A., McAuslan, P., & Ross, L. T. (1998). Sexual assault perpetration by college men: The role of alcohol, misperception of sexual intent, and sexual beliefs and experiences. *Journal of Social and Clinical Psychology, 17*(2), 167–195. https://www.doi.org/10.1521/jscp.1998.17.2.167

Abbey, A., Parkhill, M. R., Clinton-Sherrod, A. M., & Zawacki, T. (2007). A comparison of men who committed different types of sexual assault in a community sample. *Journal of Interpersonal Violence, 22*(12), 1567–1580. https://www.doi.org/10.1177/0886260507306489

Abbey, A., Ross, L. T., McDuffie, D., & McAuslan, P. (1996). Alcohol and dating risk factors for sexual assault among college women. *Psychology of Women Quarterly, 20*(1), 147–169.

Aosved, A. C., & Long, P. J. (2006). Co-occurrence of rape myth acceptance, sexism, racism, homophobia, ageism, classism, and religious intolerance. *Sex Roles, 55*(78), 481–492. https://www.doi.org/10.1007/S11199-006-9101-4

Aronowitz, T., Lambert, C. A., & Davidoff, S. (2012). The role of rape myth acceptance in the social norms regarding sexual behavior among college students. *Journal of Community Health Nursing, 29*(3), 173–182. https://www.doi.org/10.1080/07370016.2012.697852

Bancroft, L. (2003). *Why does he do that?: Inside the minds of angry and controlling men*. Penguin.

Beauregard, E., Lussier, P., & Proulx, J. (2004). An exploration of developmental factors related to deviant sexual preferences among adult rapists. *Sexual Abuse: A Journal of Research and Treatment, 16*(2), 151–161. https://www.doi.org/10.1023/B:SEBU.0000023063.94781.bd

Beichner, D., & Spohn, C. (2012). Modeling the effects of victim behavior and moral character on prosecutors charging decisions in sexual assault cases. *Violence and Victims, 27*(1), 3–24. https://www.doi.org/10.1891/0886-6708.27.1.3

Belknap, J. (2015). *The invisible woman: Gender, crime, and justice* (4th ed.). Cengage Learning.

Bennice, J. A., Resick, P. A., Mechanic, M., & Astin, M. (2003). The relative effects of intimate partner physical and sexual violence on post-traumatic stress disorder symptomatology. *Violence and Victims, 18*(1), 87–94. https://www.doi.org/10.1891/vivi.2003.18.1.87

Bernat, J. A., Wilson, A. E., & Calhoun, K. S. (1999). Sexual coercion history, calloused sexual beliefs and judgments of sexual coercion in a date rape analogue. *Violence and Victims, 14*(2), 147–160.

Brownmiller, S. (1975). *Against our will: Men, women and rape*. Simon and Schuster.

Buchwald, E., Fletcher, P. R., & Roth, M. (Eds.). (1993). *Transforming a rape culture*. Milkweed Editions.

Bumby, K. M. (1996). Assessing the cognitive distortions of child molesters and rapists: Development and validation of the MOLEST and RAPE scales. *Sexual Abuse: A Journal of Research and Treatment, 8*(1), 37–54. https://www.doi.org/10.1177/107906329600800105

Burgess-Jackson, K. (1999). *A most detestable crime: New philosophical essays on rape*. Oxford University Press.

Burnett, A. (2016). Rape culture. *The Wiley Blackwell Encyclopedia of Gender and Sexuality Studies*, 1–5. https://www.doi.org/10.1002/9781118663219.wbegss541

Burt, M. R. (1980). Cultural myths and supports for rape. *Journal of Personality and Social Psychology, 38*(2), 217–230. https://www.doi.org/10.1037/0022-3514.38.2.217

Calkins, C., Colombino, N., Matsuura, T., & Jeglic, E. (2015). Where do sex crimes occur? How an examination of sex offense location can inform policy and prevention. *International Journal of Comparative and Applied Criminal Justice, 39*(2), 99–112. https://www.doi.org/10.1080/01924036.2014.973047

Campbell, R., & Raja, S. (1999). Secondary victimization of rape victims: Insights from mental health professionals who treat survivors of violence. *Violence and Victims, 14*(3), 261–275. https://www.doi.org/10.1891/0886-6708.14.3.261

Casey, E. A., Masters, N. T., Beadnell, B., Hoppe, M. J., Morrison, D. M., & Wells, E. A. (2017). Predicting sexual assault perpetration among heterosexually active young men. *Violence Against Women, 23*(1), 3–27. https://www.doi.org/10.1177/1077801216634467

Colombino, N., Mercado, C. C., Levenson, J., & Jeglic, E. (2011). Preventing sexual violence: Can examination of offense location inform sex crime policy? *International Journal of Law and Psychiatry, 34*(3), 160–167. https://www.doi.org/10.1016/j.ijlp.2011.04.002

Connell, R. (2013). *Gender and power: Society, the person and sexual politics*. John Wiley & Sons.

Cuklanz, L. M. (1996). *Rape on trial: How the mass media construct legal reform and social change*. University of Pennsylvania Press.

Debowska, A., Boduszek, D., Dhingra, K., Kola, S., & Meller-Prunska, A. (2015). The role of psychopathy and exposure to violence in rape myth acceptance. *Journal of Interpersonal Violence, 30*(15), 2751–2770. https://www.doi.org/10.1177/0886260514553635

Du Mont, J., Miller, K. L., & Myhr, T. L. (2003). The role of real rape and real victim stereotypes in the police reporting practices of sexually assaulted women. *Violence Against Women, 9*(4), 466–486. https://www.doi.org/10.1177/1077801202250960

Edwards, K. M., Turchik, J. A., Dardis, C. M., Reynolds, N., & Gidycz, C. A. (2011). Rape myths: History, individual and institutional-level presence, and implications for change. *Sex Roles, 65*(11–12), 761–773. https://www.doi.org/10.1007/s11199-011-9943-2

Ewing, C. P. (2011). *Justice perverted: Sex offense law, psychology, and public policy*. Oxford University Press.

Fansher, A. K., & Zedaker, S. B. (2020). The relationship between rape myth acceptance and sexual behaviors. *Journal of Interpersonal Violence*, 088626052091683. https://www.doi.org/10.1177/0886260520916831

Federal Bureau of Investigation. (2016). *Crime in the United States: 2014*. Government Printing Office. https://www.fbi.gov/about-us/cjis/ucr/crime-in-the-u.s/2014/crime-in-the-u.s.-2014.

Federal Bureau of Investigation. (2020). *Crime in the United States: 2019*. Government Printing Office. https://ucr.fbi.gov/crime-in-the-u.s/2019/crime-in-the-u.s.-2019/topic-pages/rape.pdf

Felson, R. B., & Pare, P. P. (2007). Does the criminal justice system treat domestic violence and sexual assault offenders leniently? *Justice Quarterly, 24*(3), 435–459. https://www.doi.org/10.1080/07418820701485601

Ferguson, C. J., & Hartley, R. D. (2020). Pornography and sexual aggression: Can meta-analysis find a link? *Trauma, Violence, & Abuse*. Advance Online Publication. https://doi.org/10.1177/1524838020942754

Finkelhor, D., & Yllo, K. (1985). *License to rape: Sexual abuse of wives*. Rinehart & Winston Inc.

Ford, T. E., Woodzicka, J. A., Triplett, S. R., & Kochersberger, A. O. (2013). Sexist humor and beliefs that justify societal sexism. *Current Research in Social Psychology, 21*(7), 64–81.

Frances, A., Sreenivasan, S., & Weinberger, L. E. (2008). Defining mental disorder when it really counts: DSM-IV-TR and SVP/SDP statutes. *Journal of the American Academy of Psychiatry and the Law Online, 36*(3), 375–384.

Frazier, P. A., & Haney, B. (1996). Sexual assault cases in the legal system: Police, prosecutor, and victim perspectives. *Law and Human Behavior, 20*(6), 607–628. https://www.doi.org/10.1007/BF01499234

French, S. L. (2003). Reflections on healing: Framing strategies utilized by acquaintance rape survivors. *Journal of Applied Communication Research, 31*(4), 209–319. https://www.doi.org/10.1080/1369681032000132573

Frohmann, L. (1997). Convictability and discordant locales: Reproducing race, class. *Law & Society Review, 31*(3), 531–555. https://www.doi.org/10.2307/3054045

George, W. H., & Marlatt, G. A. (1986). The effects of alcohol and anger on interest in violence, erotica, and deviance. *Journal of Abnormal Psychology, 95*(2), 150–158. https://www.doi.org/10.1037/0021-843X.95.2.150

Gerger, H., Kley, H., Bohner, G., & Siebler, F. (2007). The acceptance of modern myths about sexual aggression scale: Development and validation in German and English. *Aggressive Behavior: Official Journal of the International Society for Research on Aggression, 33*(5), 422–440. https://www.doi.org/10.1002/ab.20195

Groth, A. N., Burgess, A. W., & Holmstrom, L. L. (1977). Rape: Power, anger, and sexuality. *The American Journal of Psychiatry, 134*(11), 1239–1243. https://www.doi.org/10.1176/ajp.134.11.1239

Hale, M. (1734). *Historia placitorum coronae*. Nutt & Gosling.

Hall, G. C. N., & Hirschman, R. (1991). Toward a theory of sexual aggression: A quadripartite model. *Journal of Consulting and Clinical Psychology, 59*(5), 662. https://www.doi.org/10.1037/0022-006X.59.5.662

Hayes, R. M., Lorenz, K., & Bell, K. A. (2013). Victim blaming others: Rape myth acceptance and the just world belief. *Feminist Criminology, 8*(3), 202–220. https://www.doi.org/10.1177/1557085113484788

Hazelwood, R. R. (1987). Analyzing the rape and profiling the offender. In R. R Hazelwood & A. Wolbert Burgess (Eds.), *Practical aspects of rape investigation* (pp. 169–199 [NCJ-105948]). CRC Press.

Hislop, J. (2001). *Female sex offenders: What therapists, law enforcement and child protective services need to know*. Idyll Arbor.

Johnson, J. D., Noel, N. E., & Sutter-Hernandez, J. (2000). Alcohol and male acceptance of sexual aggression: The role of perceptual ambiguity. *Journal of Applied Social Psychology, 30*(6), 1186–1200. https://www.doi.org/10.1111/j.1559-1816.2000.tb02516.x

Johnson, S. A. (2017). Intoxicated perpetrators of sexual assault & rape know what they are doing despite intoxication: What the literature has to say. *Journal of Forensic Sciences & Criminal Investigation, 1*(4), 555–570.

Kerstetter, W. A. (1990). Gateway to justice: Police and prosecutorial response to sexual assaults against women. *Journal of Criminal Law and Criminology, 81*(2), 267–313.

King, A. R., Kuhn, S. K., Strege, C., Russell, T. D., & Kolander, T. (2019). Revisiting the link between childhood sexual abuse and adult sexual aggression. *Child Abuse & Neglect, 94*, 104022. https://www.doi.org/10.1016/j.chiabu.2019.104022

Knight, R. A., & Prentky, R. A. (1987). The developmental antecedents and adult adaptations of rapist subtypes. *Criminal Justice and Behavior, 14*(4), 403–426. https://www.doi.org/10.1177/0093854887014004001

Knight, R. A., & Prentky, R. A. (1990). Classifying sexual offenders. In W. L. Marshall, D. R. Laws, & H. E. Barbaree (Eds.), *Handbook of sexual assault* (pp. 23–52). Springer. https://www.doi.org/10.1007/978-1-4899-0915-2_3

Knight, R. A., Rosenberg, R., & Schneider, B. A. (1985). Classification of sexual offenders: Perspectives, methods, and validation. In A. W. Burgess (Ed.), *Rape and sexual assault: A research handbook* (pp. 222–293). Garland.

Långström, N., Sjöstedt, G., & Grann, M. (2004). Psychiatric disorders and recidivism in sexual offenders. *Sexual Abuse: A Journal of Research and Treatment, 16*(2), 139–150. https://www.doi.org/10.1177/107906320401600204

Lanier, C. A. (2001). Rape-accepting attitudes precursors to or consequences of forced sex. *Violence Against Women, 7*(8), 876–885. https://www.doi.org/10.1177/10778010122182802

Law Enforcement Assistance Administration. (1977). *Forcible rape: A national survey of responses by prosecutors*. U.S. Government Printing Office.

Lisak, D., & Miller, P. M. (2002). Repeat rape and multiple offending among undetected rapists. *Violence and Victims, 17*(1), 73–84. https://www.doi.org/10.1891/vivi.17.1.73.33638

Locke, B. D., & Mahalik, J. R. (2005). Examining masculinity norms, problem drinking, and athletic involvement as predictors of sexual aggression in college men. *Journal of Counseling Psychology, 52*(3), 279–283. https://www.doi.org/10.1037/0022-0167.52.3.279

Malamuth, N. (2013). Hostile masculinity. In R. F. Baumeister & K. K. Vohs (Eds.), *Encyclopedia of Social Psychology* (pp. 447–448). Sage Publications, Inc.

Marshall, A. D., & Holtzworth-Munroe, A. (2002). Varying forms of husband sexual aggression: predictors and subgroup differences. *Journal of Family Psychology, 16*(3), 286. https://www.doi.org/10.1037/0893-3200.16.3.286

Martin, P. Y. (2005). *Rape work: Victims, gender and emotions in organization and community context*. Psychology Press.

Messerschmidt, J. W. (2012). *Gender, heterosexuality, and youth violence: The struggle for recognition*. Rowman & Littlefield.

Morgan, R. E., & Truman, J. L. (2020). *Criminal victimization, 2019 [NCJ 255113]*. Bureau of Justice Statistics.

Morry, M. M., & Winkler, E. (2001). Student acceptance and expectation of sexual assault. *Canadian Journal of Behavioural Science/Revue canadienne des sciences du comportement, 33*(3), 188. https://www.doi.org/10.1037/h0087140

Moses, D. C. (1993). Livys Lucretia and the validity of coerced consent in Roman Law. In A. Laiou (Ed.), *Consent and coercion to sex and marriage in ancient and medieval societies* (p. 3981). Dumbarton Oaks Research Library.

Murphy, C. M., & Hoover, S. A. (1999). Measuring emotional abuse in dating relationships as a multifactorial construct. *Violence and Victims, 14*(1), 39–53. https://www.doi.org/10.1891/0886-6708.14.1.39

Oselin, S. S., & Blasyak, A. (2013). Contending with violence: Female prostitutes strategic responses on the streets. *Deviant Behavior, 34*(4), 274–290. https://www.doi.org/10.1080/01639625.2012.735896

Perry, L. A., Dover, T. J., Lancaster, S. L., Allen, N. E., Keel, T. G., & Eliopulos, L. N. (2018). Development of a sexual assault event typology based on event attributes. *Criminal Justice and Behavior, 45*(11), 1709–1722. https://www.doi.org/10.1177/0093854818784617

Presley, C. A., Meilman, P. W., Cashin, J. R., & Lyerla, R. (1996). *Alcohol and drugs on American college campuses: Use, consequences, and perceptions of the campus environment: Volume III: 1991–93*. Southern Illinois University.

Rape, Abuse, and Incest National Network (RAINN). (2009). *Reporting rates*. http://www.rainn.org/statistics/index.html

Rape, Abuse, and Incest National Network (RAINN). (2020). *Consent laws*. https://apps.rainn.org/policy/compare/consent-laws.cfm

Raphael, J., & Shapiro, D. L. (2002). *Sisters speak out: The lives and needs of prostituted women in Chicago: A research study*. Center for Impact Research.

Reilly, M. E., Lott, B., Caldwell, D., & DeLuca, L. (1992). Tolerance for sexual harassment related to self-reported sexual victimization. *Gender & Society, 6*(1), 122–138. https://www.doi.org/10.1177/089124392006001008

Rodabaugh, B. J., & Austin, M. (1981). *Sexual assault: A guide for community action*. Garland STPM Press.

Romero-Sánchez, M., Carretero-Dios, H., Megías, J. L., Moya, M., & Ford, T. E. (2017). Sexist humor and rape proclivity: The moderating role of joke teller gender and severity of sexual assault. *Violence Against Women, 23*(8), 951–972. https://www.doi.org/10.1177/1077801216654017

Rumney, P. N. (2006). False allegations of rape. *The Cambridge Law Journal, 65*(1), 128–158. https://www.doi.org/10.1017/S0008197306007069

Russell, D. (1988). Pornography and rape: A causal model. *Political Psychology, 9*(1), 41–73. https://www.doi.org/10.2307/3791317

Russell, T. D., & King, A. R. (2020). Distrustful, conventional, entitled, and dysregulated: PID-5 personality facets predict hostile masculinity and sexual violence in community men. *Journal of Interpersonal Violence, 35*(3–4), 707–730. https://www.doi.org/10.1177/0886260517689887

Schwartz, S. (1983). An argument for the elimination of the resistance requirement from the definition of forcible rape. *Loyola of Los Angeles Law Review, 16*(3), 567–602.

Sexual Assault Centre, University of Alberta. (2021). *Create change around sexual violence*. https://www.ualberta.ca/current-students/sexual-assault-centre/create-change.html

Shorey, R. C., Cornelius, T. L., & Bell, K. M. (2008). A critical review of theoretical frameworks for dating violence: Comparing the dating and marital fields. *Aggression and Violent Behavior, 13*(3), 185–194. https://www.doi.org/10.1016/j.avb.2008.03.003

Simons, D. A., Wurtele, S. K., & Durham, R. L. (2008). Developmental experiences of child sexual abusers and rapists. *Child Abuse & Neglect, 32*(5), 549–560. https://www.doi.org/10.1016/j.chiabu.2007.03.027

Smith, S. G., Zhang, X., Basile, K. C., Merrick, M. T., Wang, J., Kresnow, M., & Chen, J. (2018). *The National Intimate Partner and Sexual Violence Survey (NISVS): 2015 data brief—updated release*. National Center for Injury Prevention and Control, Centers for Disease Control and Prevention.

Spohn, C., & Horney, J. (1992). *Rape law reform: A grassroots movement and its impact*. Plenum Press.

Spohn, C., Beichner, D., & Davis-Frenzel, E. (2001). Prosecutorial justifications for sexual assault case rejection: Guarding the gateway to justice. *Social Problems, 48*(2), 206–235. https://www.doi.org/10.1525/sp.2001.48.2.206

Stanko, E. (2013). *Intimate intrusions: Women's experience of male violence*. Routledge.

Strömwall, L. A., Alfredsson, H., & Landström, S. (2013). Rape victim and perpetrator blame and the just world hypothesis: The influence of victim gender and age. *Journal of Sexual Aggression, 19*(2), 207–217. https://www.doi.org/10.1080/13552600.2012.683455

Suarez, E., & Gadalla, T. M. (2010). Stop blaming the victim: A meta-analysis on rape myths. *Journal of Interpersonal Violence, 25*(11), 2010–2035. https://www.doi.org/10.1177/0886260509354503

Süssenbach, P. (2016). Rape myth acceptance and judgments in rape cases—an overview with meta-analysis. *Recht & Psychiatrie, 34*, 35–42. https://www.doi.org/10.1177/1079063219825869

Temkin, J., & Krahé, B. (2008). *Sexual assault and the justice gap: A question of attitude*. Bloomsbury Publishing.

Thompson, M. P., Koss, M. P., Kingree, J. B., Goree, J., & Rice, J. (2011). A prospective mediational model of sexual aggression among college men. *Journal of Interpersonal Violence, 26*(13), 2716–2734. https://www.doi.org/10.1177/0886260510388285

Tracy, C. E., Fromson, T. L., Long, J. G., & Whitman, C. (2012). Rape and sexual assault in the legal system. *National Research Council of the National Academies Panel on Measuring Rape and Sexual Assault in the Bureau of Justice Statistics Household Surveys Committee on National Statistics*.

U.S. Department of Justice. (2012). *Attorney general Eric Holder announces revisions to the uniform crime reports definition of rape* [Press release]. https://www.fbi.gov/news/pressrel/press-releases/attorney-general-eric-holder-announces-revisions-to-the-uniform-crime-reports-definition-of-rape

Venema, R. M. (2014). Police officer schema of sexual assault reports: Real rape, ambiguous cases, and false reports. *Journal of Interpersonal Violence, 31*(5), 872–899. https://www.doi.org/10.1177/0886260514556765

Vrij, A., & Firmin, H. R. (2001). Beautiful thus innocent? The impact of defendants and victims physical attractiveness and participants rape beliefs on impression formation in alleged rape cases. *International Review of Victimology, 8*(3), 245–255. https://www.doi.org/10.1177/026975800100800301

Wheeler, J. G., George, W. H., & Dahl, B. J. (2002). Sexually aggressive college males: Empathy as a moderator in the confluence model of sexual aggression. *Personality and Individual Differences, 33*(5), 759–775. https://www.doi.org/10.1016/S0191-8869(01)00190-8

Wijkman, M., Bijleveld, C., & Hendriks, J. (2010). Women don't do such things! Characteristics of female sex offenders and offender types. *Sexual Abuse: A Journal of Research and Treatment, 22*(2), 135–156. https://www.doi.org/10.1177/1079063210363826

Williams, L. S. (1984). The classic rape: When do victims report? *Social Problems, 31*(4), 459–467. https://www.doi.org/10.1525/sp.1984.31.4.03a00070

Ybarra, M. L., & Thompson, R. E. (2018). Predicting the emergence of sexual violence in adolescence. *Prevention Science, 19*(4), 403–415. https://www.doi.org/10.1007/s11121-017-0810-4

Zander, T. K. (2008). Commentary: Inventing diagnosis for civil commitment of rapists. *Journal of the American Academy of Psychiatry and the Law Online, 36*(4), 459–469.

DEFINITIONS

Alcohol Myopia: Effect of alcohol intoxication whereby people's perceptions are narrowed, making them less able to detect subtle cues and focus only on surface cues

Attitudinal Rape Myths: Faulty explanations of why rape occurs—these explanations operate to excuse rape as well as justify it (also known as rape-supportive cognition)

Blitz Attack: Generally unplanned, spontaneous attacks that occur at any time

Case Attrition: The failure of a criminal case to advance to the next phase of the criminal justice process

Classic Rape: A rape that fits within the stereotypical rape: victim was assaulted by a stranger and had visible injuries that could corroborate allegations of forced sexual intercourse, and the offender used a weapon or physical force

Clearance Rate: Percentage of reported crimes that are cleared by arrest

Consent: Clear, knowing, and voluntary agreement to engage in sexual activity

Coercion-Based Model: Laws that require that sexual acts must be achieved through coercion, violence, physical force or threat of violence, or physical force for the act to qualify as rape

Consent-Based Model: Laws that require that there must be a sexual act to which one of the parties did not consent for the act to qualify as rape

Good-Looking Effect: Courtroom phenomenon whereby physically attractive individuals tend to fare better than their nonattractive counterparts

Groth's Typology: First empirically constructed rape typology that identifies four subtypes of individuals who commit rape: power reassurance, power assertive, anger retaliatory, and sadistic

Hazelwood's Typology: Separates offenders into two categories based on verbal, sexual, and physical behaviors of the offender: pseudo-unselfish offenders (who treat victims as willing participants and do not engage in physical violence in the commission of the rape) and selfish offenders (who utilize physical violence, offensive language, and other degrading behaviors).

Hostile Masculinity Syndrome: A common profile of sexually aggressive men involving (a) a desire to be in control, particularly in relationships with women, and (b) an insecure, defensive, and distrustful reaction to women

Intimacy Effect: Court phenomenon whereby rape and sexual assaults between intimates are viewed as less severe than those occurring between strangers

Just World Hypothesis: The belief that we live in a just and fair world where good things happen to good people and bad things happen to bad people

Massachusetts Treatment Center Rapist Typology, Version 3 (MTC: R3): A typology of rapists developed by Knight and Prentky that includes nine categories of rapists—they are based on the offender's motivation and developmental, biological, and environmental factors (see also Opportunistic Rapists [Type 1 and 2], Pervasively Angry Rapists [Type 3], Sexual Gratification Rapists [Type 4, 5, 6, and 7], and Vindictive Rapists [Type 8 and 9])

Opportunistic Rapists (Type 1 and 2): A category of rapists identified in the MTC: R3 classification of rapists developed by Knight and Prentky—they commit rapes that are typically impulsive, unplanned, and driven by opportunity as a means of seeking immediate gratification and include two subtypes: those who have high social competence (Type 1) and low social competence (Type 2); see also Massachusetts Treatment Center Rapist Typology, Version 3 (MTC: R3); Pervasively Angry Rapists (Type 3); Sexual Gratification Rapists (Type 4, 5, 6, and 7); and Vindictive Rapists (Type 8 and 9)

Perry's Typology: Examines sexual assault events data from the FBI Violent Criminal Apprehension Program (ViCAP) database, yielding seven categories of rape based on level of violence, offender approach (i.e., con approach vs. blitz attack vs. surprise/impulse attack), and trauma location on the victim's body

Pervasively Angry Rapists (Type 3): A category of rapists identified in the MTC: R3 classification of rapists developed by Knight and Prentky—they are rapists who are characterized by impulsive behaviors, low social competence, and long-standing aggression and hostility toward men and women (see also Massachusetts Treatment Center Rapist Typology, Version 3 (MTC: R3); Opportunistic Rapists [Type 1 and 2]; Sexual Gratification Rapists [Type 4, 5, 6, and 7]; and Vindictive Rapists [Type 8 and 9])

Plea Bargain: Agreement between the prosecutor and defendant where the defendant enters a guilty plea in exchange for some concession from the prosecutor

Probabilistic Cause: The relationship between a stated cause in which the cause increases the chances that a specified effect will occur

Rape: Any sexual penetration (vaginal, anal, or oral) of a person without their consent

Rape Culture: An environment in which sexual violence is normalized and excused

Rape Shield Laws: Trial rules that limit a defendant's ability to introduce evidence or cross-examine rape victims about their past sexual behavior

Secondary Victimization: Attitudes and behaviors of criminal justice officials who are blameful, insensitive, minimizing, and dismissive of rape victims

Sexual Assault: Sex crimes involving any unwanted sexual contact

Sexual Gratification Rapists (Type 4, 5, 6, and 7): A category of rapists identified in the MTC: R3 classification of rapists developed by Knight and Prentky—they are rapists who have extensive sexual perversions, many of which are incorporated into the rapes and include four subtypes: (Type 4) overt sadists, who are characterized by high levels of aggression and gratuitous violence; (Type 5) muted sadists, who are less violent and their crimes tend to be more symbolic than injurious; (Type 6) nonsadistic high rapist, who do not exhibit sadistic characteristics and have high social competence; and (Type 7) nonsadistic low rapists, who also do not exhibit sadistic characteristics and have low social competence (see also Massachusetts Treatment Center Rapist Typology, Version 3 (MTC: R3); Opportunistic Rapists [Type 1 and 2]; Pervasively Angry Rapists [Type 3]; and Vindictive Rapists [Type 8 and 9])

Statutory Rape: The crime of engaging in sexual activity with anyone below the minimum age of consent, regardless of their willingness to participate

Typologies: Used to place people into distinct categories—each category includes people who are similar to each other yet different from people in other categories

Unfound: A decision by law enforcement officials to not proceed with formal charging of a crime

Vindictive Rapists (Type 8 and 9): A category of rapists identified in the MTC: R3 classification of rapists developed by Knight and Prentky—they are rapists who direct anger toward women and often humiliate, degrade, and physically harm their victims; they also include two subtypes based on their level of social competence: (Type 8) low social competence and (Type 9) high social competence (see also Massachusetts Treatment Center Rapist Typology, Version 3 (MTC: R3); Opportunistic Rapists [Type 1 and 2]; Pervasively Angry Rapists [Type 3]; and Sexual Gratification Rapists [Type 4, 5, and 6])

CHAPTER 4

Child Sexual Abuse

> **CHAPTER OBJECTIVES**
>
> - Define child sexual abuse and differentiate child sexual abuse from pedophilia
> - Identify myths associated with child sexual abuse
> - Describe societal reactions to child sexual abuse crimes throughout American history
> - Describe child sexual abuse typologies
> - Describe grooming tactics used to sexually abuse children
> - Identify factors affecting criminal trial proceedings in child sexual abuse cases

Child sexual abuse refers to a broad spectrum of behaviors in which an adult (and sometimes an older adolescent) engages in inappropriate sexual acts with a child. All crimes that involve sexually touching a child, as well as noncontact offenses and sexual exploitation, constitute child sexual abuse. Forms of child sexual abuse include child molestation, child rape/sexual assault, incestuous child abuse, child sexual exploitation (including engaging minor children in child prostitution and child pornography), and indecent exposure to a child (see Focus Box 4.1). Similar to rape, the sexual exploitation of children and young people appears to be a universal phenomenon. Evidence shows that *any* child or adolescent can be a victim of child sexual abuse (Lalor & McElvaney, 2010). Child sexual abuse often co-occurs with other forms of child maltreatment, including physical abuse, emotional abuse, and neglect (Vachon et al., 2015).

As we learned in Chapter 3, sex acts between adults do not constitute a crime, provided that both parties have consented (i.e., given sexual permission) to the activity. The sex acts become criminal (as with rape or sexual assault) when at least one of the parties does not consent to it. In contrast, sex acts with children or adolescents are illegal regardless of the minor's seeming consent, compliance, or cooperation. Just as children (in most jurisdictions) are deemed to lack the capacity to make a contract, they also cannot legally consent to sexual acts. An adult who engages in sex acts with a minor who is younger than the legal age of consent (between 16 and 18, depending on the state), therefore, has committed a crime of child sexual abuse (with some exceptions depending on the age of the alleged perpetrator and the difference in age between the two parties, as discussed in Chapter 3).

Thousands of children are victims of child sexual abuse each year. In 2019, 60,927 child sexual abuse incidents were reported in the United States, representing 9.3% of the total number of reported child maltreatment cases that year (U.S. Department of Health and

> **Focus Box 4.1** Summary of Child Sexual Abuse Offenses
>
> Contact sexual offenses against children include the following:
>
> - Fondling a child
> - Making a child touch an adult's sexual organs for sexual pleasure
> - Penetrating a child's mouth, anus, or vagina no matter how slight with any human organ or object that does not serve a valid medical purpose
>
> Noncontact sexual offenses against children include the following:
>
> - Child peeping (voyeurism)
> - Engaging in indecent exposure to a child (exhibitionism)
> - Exposing children to pornographic materials
> - Masturbating in front of a child
>
> Sexual exploitation includes the following:
>
> - Soliciting a child for purposes of prostitution
> - Using a child to photograph, film, or model pornography

Human Services, Administration for Children and Families, 2021). Prevalence estimates of this crime, however, vary. For example, one study estimated that one in nine girls and one in 54 boys experienced contact sexual abuse or assault before the age of 18 (Finkelhor et al., 2014). Research conducted by the Centers for Disease Control and Prevention (CDC) estimated that approximately one in four girls and one in six boys are sexually abused before age 18 (Dube et al., 2005). Approximately 85% of sexual abuse cases occur within the family (UNICEF, 2017).

In this chapter, we begin with a discussion of common myths and misconceptions regarding child sexual abuse. Many of these result from moral panic and misinformation arising from increased attention and heightened concern over sex crimes and the people who commit them in the United States. Next, a brief history of the evolution of social and legal reactions to child sexual abuse in the United States is presented. Situated within this history are a number of public myths and misconceptions that still exist today. We then delve into some of the prominent theories of child sexual abuse and present a sample of the dominant child sexual abuse typologies that describe how and why people commit this crime. Finally, this chapter concludes with an examination of the criminal justice response to child sexual abuse, focusing on investigative procedures and factors that affect criminal trial proceedings.

MYTHS ABOUT CHILD SEXUAL ABUSE

There are many different types of child sexual abuse: contact offenses, noncontact offenses, and sexual exploitation. Each type certainly warrants individualized attention, but it is beyond the scope of this textbook to thoroughly discuss each type. Instead, the focus of this chapter is primarily upon contact sex crimes against children because noncontact sex crimes against children are customarily not accounted for in estimates of incidence and prevalence of sexual abuse against children (Finkelhor, 1984). Throughout the chapter, there is some discussion of certain types of sex crimes when referencing particular studies, but in general, the term "child sexual abuse" is relied upon. Myths regarding child sexual abuse pervade the media, scholarly research, and everyday conversations on the subject. Below, we examine some of the most prevalent myths.

People Who Sexually Abuse Children Target Any and All Children

Those who sexually abuse children do not tend to engage in sexual acts with anyone and everyone. They tend to have sexual tastes and preferences and are aroused by certain types. They also often carefully select their targeted victims. For example, many men who molest children have reported that they often choose children who have family problems, are alone, lack confidence, and are indiscriminate in their trust of others—especially when the child is also perceived as pretty, provocatively dressed, young, or small (Elliott et al., 1995). Sexual abuse against children may not happen instantaneously. It is often the result of an extensive process where the offender psychologically manipulates the child (and sometimes the child's family) into trusting them, thereby diminishing the child's resistance. This process, known as ***grooming***, is discussed later.

Children Who Are Sexually Abused Will Sexually Abuse Others When They Grow Up

There is a widespread belief in the "cycle" of sexual abuse whereby childhood sexual victimization inevitably leads to committing sexual abuse during adulthood. Thus, many assume that if one is sexually abused as a child, they will grow up to become a sex offender. This is a myth, and it is particularly damaging because it assigns the label of "predator" or "sex offender" to an abused child (especially boys) and takes the focus off their needs for help.

The evidence of a link between childhood sexual victimization and later commission of sexual abuse is mixed at best. For example, although a meta-analysis reported a 3.4 times greater likelihood of sexual abuse in childhood in adult who commit sex crimes compared to non-sexually offending adults (Jespersen et al., 2009), other research does not support the ***abused–abuser hypothesis*** (also known as the ***cycle of child sexual abuse***).

Research shows that the majority of child sexual abuse victims do *not* commit sex crimes later in life (Salter et al., 2003; Whitaker et al., 2008). Critics of the abused–abuser hypothesis take issue with its simplicity. Researchers have found that child sexual abuse is a strong predictor of other negative outcomes, such as depression and substance abuse, which are also strongly associated with committing sex crimes in adulthood (Aebi et al., 2015). Moreover, Widom and Maxfield (2001) reported that child physical abuse history better predicts later violent crimes than sex crimes among males. Recall from the introduction to this chapter, however, that sexual abuse in childhood often co-occurs with other types of child abuse. Therefore, in assessing the unique role of child *sexual* victimization in later adult offending, there are several factors that need to be assessed individually and collectively.

Many ***protective factors*** (those that minimize or eliminate risk) are identified that call into question the seemingly strong association between sexual abuse as a child and sex offending later in life. Research has indicated that if children disclose an act of sexual abuse early and are supported by people close to them, they have a much lower likelihood of subsequently committing a sex crime (Alaggia, 2010). Prendergast (1993) identified several factors that safeguard sexually abused male victims from later sexual offending: good self-esteem, availability of emotional support, and a solid knowledge of human sexuality at the onset of their childhood sexual victimization.

Everyone Who Sexually Abuses Children Is a Pedophile

Pedophilia and child sexual abuse/molestation are often used interchangeably; it is important to de-link these two concepts. The growing use of the terms "pedophilia" and "pedophile" has come from expanded publicity and awareness concerning the sexual abuse of children. As we may casually refer to someone as neurotic, paranoid, or delusional without necessarily assuming psychiatric expertise or implying a psychiatric diagnosis, it is increasingly common among laypeople to consider someone who has sexually victimized a child as a pedophile. Labeling all individuals who molest children as pedophiles, however, is incorrect.

Pedophilia consists of a sexual attraction to children that may or may not lead to child sexual abuse, whereas child sexual abuse involves sexual contact with a child that may or may not be due to pedophilia (Camilleri & Quinsey, 2008). Sometimes, there is overlap between pedophilia and child sexual abuse, but in many cases, there is not. According to the ***Diagnostic and Statistical Manual of Mental Disorders, 5th edition (DSM-V)*** (American Psychiatric Association, 2013), a diagnosis of pedophilia requires an individual to meet the following criteria:

1. Have recurrent, intense, and sexually arousing fantasies, urges, or behaviors directed toward a prepubescent child over a period of at least six months
2. Have acted on these urges or to be distressed by them
3. Be at least 16 years old and at least 5 years older than the child victim

Is everyone who sexually abuses a child a pedophile? No. In fact, research overwhelmingly indicates that the majority of individuals who engage in sex acts with children are not pedophiles. One study concisely summarized that "pedophilia is neither a necessary nor a sufficient condition for child sex offenses" (Jahnke & Hoyer, 2013, p. 171). Do all pedophiles sexually abuse children? No. It is true that pedophilia is an important risk factor in child sexual abuse (Baur et al., 2016; Seto, 2018). But remember that pedophilia is clinically defined as a sexual attraction to children. Some pedophiles may elect to view sexually explicit (as well as non-sexually explicit) images of children, an issue we will explore in Chapter 5. Many individuals with pedophilic disorder do not sexually abuse children (Martijn et al., 2020). Some pedophiles may engage in overt strategies to avoid having sexually deviant thoughts. Amelung et al. (2012) suggested that "self-motivated" pedophiles using Androgen Deprivation Therapy may benefit from decreased deviant sexual behaviors and increased empathy for potential victims. The confusion regarding pedophilia is most likely a product of sensationalism in mass media, in which people with pedophilic interests are stereotypically portrayed as violent predators (Kitzinger, 2004).

Increasingly, there is evidence that these two groups differ in a number of important ways. For example, compared to those who molest children (but are non-pedophiles), pedophiles tend to have more victims (Abel & Harlow, 2001), respond more poorly to treatment, and are more likely to re-offend (Hanson & Bussiere, 1998; Seto, 2018). With regard to executive function in the brain, differences have been identified between pedophiles and those who sexually abuse children, with the latter demonstrating greater cognitive deficits compared to the former (Schiffer & Vonlaufen, 2011). In summary, from clinical, legal, and policy perspectives, pedophilia must be carefully distinguished from child sexual abuse. Table 4.1 summarizes these differences.

TABLE 4.1 Characteristics of Pedophiles Versus Child Sexual Abusers

Pedophiles	Child Sexual Abusers
May abuse family members, but the majority of offenses are extrafamilial	Primary sexual attraction/orientation to adults
Have high recidivism rates after incarceration and treatment	More likely to commit intrafamilial abuse
May have hundreds of victims over their lifetimes	Lower number of victims
Are uncomfortable with and reject adult intimacy	Lower rates of recidivism
Involves adult sexual attraction/orientation to children	Abuse of children generally committed to fulfill an emotional need such as powerlessness or loneliness, and not sexual arousal
	More severe cognitive deficits

If We Protect Our Children from Strangers, Child Sexual Abuse Will Not Be a Problem

Most sex-crime legislation and public policy (discussed in greater detail in Chapter 11) are based on the notion of stranger danger. Pinning the problem of child sexual abuse on strangers and formulating strategies to safeguard our children from the "bad guys" provide a sense of security and quell fears that our children could become potential targets. But stranger danger is a red herring (i.e., a fallacy or misdirection). As discussed in this chapter, the overwhelming majority of sex crimes against children are committed not by strangers but by those who are close to them. Often people who commit child sexual abuse are related to their victims. Furthermore, those who are not related become intimately attached to their victims, effectively becoming "like a member of the family."

Child Sexual-Abuse Cases Are Wrought with False Accusations and Exaggerated Accounts

Few prosecutions and convictions of child sexual abuse, however, come from false allegations. There are low rates of false accusations in child sexual abuse cases. Jones and McGraw (1987) found that only 1% of a sample of 576 social service referrals for child sexual abuse was based on fictitious accounts. Likewise, a more recent study found a false allegation rate of 2.5% (Oates et al., 2000).

More often, the opposite holds true. Children are more likely to minimize and/or deny sexual abuse than exaggerate or falsely report it. Studies have repeatedly shown that sexually abused children questioned for the first time are likely to deny the abuse (Lyon, 2007). Moreover, the frequency with which children take back allegations of sexual abuse also confounds this problem. This rate varies from study to study—from 4% at the low end (Bradley & Wood, 1996) up to 23% on the high end (Malloy et al., 2007). Many factors are associated with why a child might take back an allegation of sexual abuse. For example, it is more likely among children abused by a parent or caretaker, and this is made worse when the child's nonoffending caregiver is unsupportive (Malloy et al., 2007). Such cases, therefore, are said to be **unsubstantiated**, meaning that there is insufficient legal evidence to determine that a crime has occurred. Taken together, the evidence suggests that child sexual abuse cases are much more likely to be unsubstantiated than they are to be intentionally false. False allegations of child sexual abuse will be further explored in Chapter 8.

All Child Sexual Abusers Are Monsters

Any mention of someone who abuses children usually elicits images of society's lowest rung. They are creeps, perverts, monsters—and not our family members, neighbors, friends, or coworkers. They lack traditional values, have no work ethic, and have low moral turpitude—they are not upstanding members of our community. They come from neighborhoods and communities with violence, poverty, and inequality. They are not in our communities.

This myth that all child sexual abusers are monsters perpetuates the belief that that abuse is easy for other adults to detect (Ferragut et al., 2020). In one of the most comprehensive studies of child sexual abusers, Abel and Harlow (2001) compared a sample of more than 4,000 admitted child molesters to the general U.S. population on a number of characteristics, including education, employment status, marital status, and religious observance. The results were clear—when compared to the general population of U.S. men, child molesters were no different.

The myths surrounding child sexual abuse did not emerge spontaneously at a specific point in time but rather have been conditioned by social, legal, and political forces that have shaped public opinion on child sex abuse crimes, the people that commit them, and the victims who are targeted. Next, we discuss this history, focusing on the evolution of the societal responses to child sexual abuse.

HISTORICAL TRENDS IN CHILD SEXUAL-ABUSE LAWS, POLICIES, AND SOCIETAL RESPONSES

Sexual abuse of children is far from new. Family historians have discovered that adults in 15th-century elite households sometimes treated children as sexual playthings. In New York, during the late 1700s and through the 1800s, between one-third and one-half of rape victims were younger than 18 years old (Sacco, 2009). Public attention to child sexual abuse has waxed and waned repeatedly throughout U.S. history. Historical research has shown that concern was at its greatest following the Civil War, during the Progressive Era, during and immediately after World War II, and in our own time (Gordon, 1988; Pleck, 1987). Interestingly, this concern did not reflect a sudden spike in reported instances of child sexual abuse but rather evolved from broader social anxieties.

During the Reconstruction Period, after the U.S. Civil War (1865–1877), rapid urbanization, a massive influx of immigrants, and a sharp rise in divorce rates provoked fears about the future of the family. New York City, for example, was flooded with destitute war widows, orphans, crippled veterans, and immigrants, giving visibility to poverty, crime, and disorder. In 1874, the first Society for the Prevention of Cruelty to Children was formed to address child abuse. Within the next 40 years, about 500 such organizations were established throughout the United States. By and large these anti-cruelty organizations acted as moral agents. The focus was on urging women to be diligent mothers and men to be good providers. By 1890, the focus on child abuse shifted to child neglect (Myers, 2008).

The Progressive Era (1890–1920) was marked by anxieties over mass immigration, divorce, child labor, and juvenile delinquency. Similar to reform efforts during Civil War Reconstruction, family professionals and court officials during this era focused on changing the values and behaviors of the poor. Child neglect remained the focus of intervention efforts, and single mothers were disproportionately targeted. Shortly thereafter, Sigmund Freud's *theory of infantile sexuality* (discussed in Chapter 1) posited that children who reported sexual abuse by adults had imagined or fantasized the experience, diffused the moral outrage about child neglect and maltreatment.

From the Progressive Era through the 1950s, concern over child abuse largely retreated from the public conscience. Social service agencies coming across such cases usually classified them as problems of economic strain, family maladjustment, genetic inferiority, or mental pathology. During the Great Depression, child abuse was attributed to economic hardship. During and shortly following World War II, concerns about working mothers, latchkey children, and absent fathers sparked anxieties about child abuse and neglect. Still, however, these were viewed as manifestations of family problems or mental illness and not as a widespread social epidemic (Gordon, 1988).

A focus on family violence in the early 1960s generated interest in the study of child abuse. This is largely credited to the work of pediatric physicians and medical providers. In 1946, pediatric radiologist John Caffey published a case study of six young children with subdural hematomas as well as arm and leg fractures. Although he did not explicitly use the term "child abuse," it was certainly implied in his conclusions (Caffey, 1946). Building on the momentum of this study, physicians and medical providers also began to examine questionable childhood injuries. This culminated in the landmark publication of the **battered child syndrome** by Kempe et al. (1962), which established the duty and responsibility of physicians to fully evaluate injured children and guarantee nonrecurrence of "expected repetition of trauma" (p. 143).

The combined efforts of physicians, medical providers, and others increased interest in the criminalization of child abuse. By 1967, every state had enacted laws requiring physicians to report child abuse to law enforcement officials or social service agencies. In 1974, Congress passed the **Child Abuse Prevention and Treatment Act**, which authorized funds to improve states' investigation and reporting of physical abuse, neglect, and sexual abuse.

Although many sexually abused children were protected prior to the 1970s, recognition of and genuine concern for child sexual abuse lagged behind that of physical abuse. Early scholars noted the virtual absence of literature and discussion of child sexual abuse (Walters, 1975), attributing the void to the taboo nature of it (Sgroi, 1975). The sexual revolution in the United States in the 1960s, typified by a change in beliefs about sex and sexuality, fueled speculation that the taboo of engaging in sexual acts with children would soon dissipate. According to Rush (1980), this sparked a movement in which individuals who molested children claimed sex with children was a civil right and even encouraged practitioners and professionals to defend it. Indeed, the inclination to view child–adult sex as a harmless, victimless crime is a not-too-distant memory in the history of child sexual abuse.

Awareness of the deleterious effects of sexual abuse evolved from the observations of medical providers and pioneering researchers. One surgeon issued the following statement to the National Commission on Pornography and Obscenity in 1970 (p. 611):

> Lately, I've been in gynecology and obstetrics. It's absolutely frightening to see what's going on. The wards and private rooms are filled with young girls. Their insides are torn to pieces. It is impossible to describe the repair jobs we do. These girls suffer from every kind of sexual abuse. It used to be that doctors treated prostitutes in such

condition but now we have to treat young girls from the best of families. Every day we see girls in their teens with disease and infection.

Prior to the 1970s, there was little research on the scope and effects of child sexual abuse. De Francis's (1969) study of 250 sexual abuse cases in Brooklyn underscored the need for systematic inquiries into child sexual abuse issues. De Francis concluded that "the problem of sexual abuse of children is of unknown national dimensions, but the findings strongly point to the probability of an enormous national incidence many times larger than the reported incidence of physical abuse of children" (1969, p. vii). De Francis further concluded that victims of child sexual abuse were the least protected children, emphasizing that communities had, at the time, failed to acknowledge the problem.

Within a decade, much had changed. An explosion in interest was accompanied by an increase in knowledge of child sexual abuse. Research began to reveal its widespread prevalence. One of the most influential studies was Finkelhor's (1979) pioneering work, which estimated that one in four females and one in five males had experienced forced sexual contact before age 18 (Finkelhor, 1979). This burgeoning research, combined with the emergence of strong state-reporting laws, increased the number of cases of suspected child sexual abuse reported to officials and prosecuted (Beckett, 1996). Not surprisingly, media coverage on child sexual abuse increased in the 1970s and 1980s. As newspapers and television news headlined stories of child sexual abuse, moral panic and sex-abuse hysteria followed. Notable during this period was alleged child sexual abuse in daycare centers. Perhaps, the most well-known example of this was the McMartin Preschool Trial, where employees of a family-operated preschool in California were accused of hundreds of acts of child sexual abuse. The abuse allegations were extremely graphic and bizarre, involving torture, Satanism, and witchcraft. After six years of criminal trials, no convictions were obtained, and all of the charges were dropped in 1990. Some of the accusing parties have since come forward to admit the allegations were false. At the cost of approximately $15 million, this case remains one of the most expensive trials in U.S. history.

Such cases undoubtedly contributed to the backlash against rigorously prosecuting child sexual abuse cases in the early 1990s. Some researchers equated the mass hysteria regarding child sexual abuse with the Salem witch trials. In 17th-century Salem, a group of young girls were found to have what medical professionals referred to as hysterical outbursts. Having no medical reasons to explain the causes of these outbursts (that included episodic fits associated with screaming, speechlessness, physical aggression, epileptic-like seizures, and unintelligible utterances), doctors attributed them to demonic possession. Between June and September of 1692 (note the relatively short time frame), many individuals were accused of witchcraft from every stratum of society. By September 1692, 27 were convicted, and 19 were hanged. During the early 1990s, social critics observed an uncanny parallel between 17th-century Salem and the present.

The backlash in the early 1990s was short-lived as Americans began to embrace the "get-tough" criminal justice policies in the late 1990s (Garland, 2001). During this period, concerns about increasing crime rates and failed rehabilitation efforts resulted in broad-sweeping reform to "crack down on crime" by using harsher punishments for convicted individuals (Mauer, 2002). In the early 1990s, the federal and state governments enacted new laws and policies targeting those who commit sex crimes, including registries, residence-restriction laws, and civil commitment and castration statutes (discussed in more detail in Chapter 11). Part of the "get-tough" policy was the revision of death penalty statutes in some states to include convicted child rapists (LaFond, 2005). In 1995, Louisiana became the first state to execute child rapists. Other states soon adopted similar statutes (Bell, 2008).

In 2008, the U.S. Supreme Court ruled in *Kennedy v. Louisiana* (2008), however, that such statutes were unconstitutional under the Eighth and 14th Amendments. The Court also concluded that the execution of child rapists could increase harm to children and may encourage nondisclosure by victims.

Public attention to child sexual abuse has ebbed and flowed throughout U.S. history. Indeed, child sexual abuse law and policy in the United States is a product of political, social, and cultural forces as well as research exploring the underpinnings of this crime. Child sexual abuse is taken seriously today, as evidenced by a potpourri of federal and state legislation aimed at prevention and a burgeoning research agenda focusing on those who commit child sexual abuse, their tactics (most notably, the grooming process), their victims, and the criminal justice response to these crimes. The remainder of this chapter covers these topics.

CHILD SEXUAL ABUSE TYPOLOGIES

The concept of typologies was introduced in Chapter 3. Recall that the purpose of typologies is to classify those who commit sex offenses into distinct categories based on their motivation or proclivity to commit sex crimes, as well as their style or method of carrying them out. This section provides an overview of some of the typologies of people who commit child sexual abuse. Individuals who sexually abuse children are diverse in their motivations to sexually offend and their patterns of offending.

Typologies Based on Level of Sexual Attraction to Children and Modus Operandi

Most child sexual abuse typologies organize and classify these crimes and the persons who commit them according to the extent of the offender's sexual attraction to children as well as the modus operandi of the individual carrying out the abusive act. One of the earliest and most influential typologies is ***Groth's Typology*** (Groth et al., 1982), which identifies two types of offenders who sexually abuse children: fixated and regressed. Groth's Typology characterizes ***fixated abusers*** by a persistent, continuous, and compulsive sexual desire and attraction to children. They are unlikely to have healthy sexual and/or emotional relationships with age-appropriate partners and are often diagnosed with pedophilia. They tend to target young male children who are not related to them, and their actions are often premeditated, as evidenced by lengthy grooming. Fixated offenders are considered to be high risk for sexual recidivism because of their primary deviant sexual interests in children and because they target male victims. They also average the greatest number of victims and offenses, most of which go unreported (Elliot et al., 1995).

Offenders who are categorized as ***regressed abusers*** primarily have "normal" sexual interests toward and relationships with age-appropriate partners. Generally, they tend not to be sexually interested in children, and they may choose sexual contact with children as a means of coping with external stressors such as unemployment, divorce, alcoholism, and substance abuse. Negative emotions, such as loneliness, depression, anxiety, and isolation, may also trigger child sexual abuse.

The ***FBI Typologies***, initially developed by Lanning (1986), expand on Groth's Typology and focus on the need to recognize and evaluate *how* child molesters have sex with children to identify, arrest, and convict them. This typology considers a modus operandi continuum distinguishing between situational and preferential offenders (somewhat resonating with regressed and fixated offenders, respectively). Seven distinct categories of offenders are identified: sadistic, fixated, and seductive (categorized as "preferential offenders") and inadequate, sexually indiscriminate, morally indiscriminate, and regressed (categorized as "situational offenders"). The FBI typology has undergone extensive revision. In the fourth edition (Lanning, 2001), the sexually indiscriminate subtype was dropped from the situational-offender category, and the fixated subtype was dropped from the preferential-offender category. The introverted and diverse categories were added to the latter classification. The latest iteration of the FBI typology (Lanning, 2010) places all individuals who commit sex crimes (not just those who abuse children) along a situational-preferential continuum instead of discrete categories. A summary of these typologies is provided in Table 4.2.

Massachusetts Treatment Center: Child Molester Typology, Version 3 (MTC:CM3)

Knight et al. (1989) used statistical procedures to explore and refine Groth's Typology and FBI Typologies of child sexual abusers. Unlike the previous two typologies, the MTC:CM3 treats child sexual abuse as multidimensional, involving two axes. Axis I addresses the degree to which the offender is fixated on children, which is further broken down to consider the offender's level of social competence. Offenders whose sexual interests are primarily limited to children are considered high fixation. Those with primarily age-appropriate sexual interests are considered low fixation. Social competence refers to the degree of stability and quality of interpersonal relationships with peers, family members, and romantic partners as well as job stability and vocational achievement. Four subtypes comprise Axis I:

1. High fixation/high social competence
2. High fixation/low social competence
3. Low fixation/high social competence
4. Low fixation/low social competence

Axis II evaluates the degree of contact an offender has with a child, the meaning of the contact (e.g., interpersonal and sexual), as well as the presence of threats and/or physical injury involved in the contact. For individuals with high contact with children, two subtypes are identified:

5. High contact/interpersonal: High amount of contact is perceived to be meeting social, emotional, and sexual needs as if they were attempting to have a "relationship."
6. High contact/narcissistic: High amount of contact is considered to be for purely selfish reasons, in that they are attempting to meet their own needs for sexual gratification without consideration for the victim.

For individuals who have low amounts of contact with children (often victims are strangers to the offenders), the extent to which they cause physical injury and whether they are considered to be sadistic or nonsadistic forms the basis for four more Axis II subcategories:

7. Low contact/low physical injury/nonsadistic (exploitative): Physical injury is used only to the extent necessary to gain victim compliance. Generally, the level of planning of the offenses is low.
8. Low contact/low physical injury/sadistic (muted sadistic): Engages in "sham" sadism (i.e., behaviors and fantasies that reflect sadist acts but do not result in serious injury), but again,

TABLE 4.2 Child Sexual Abuse Typologies

Groth's Typology (Groth et al., 1982)

Fixated

- Persistent, compulsive sexual attraction to children
- Unable to form healthy, age-appropriate relationships
- Tend to target young, unrelated male children
- Premeditated crimes with lengthy grooming periods
- High risk for sexual recidivism

Regressed

- Generally not sexually interested in children
- Abuse a means of coping with external stressors (e.g., unemployment, divorce, addiction)
- Tend to target adolescent girls who are related or well-known
- Crimes generally impulsive and unplanned

FBI Typology (Lanning, 1986)

Fixated	Seductive	Inadequate	Sexually Indiscriminate	Sadistic	Morally Indiscriminate	Regressed
Poor psychosexual development, compulsive attraction to children	Groom children and carry on a "relationship" with them through affection, praise, and gifts	Social misfits who see relationships with children as only sexual outlet	Mainly interested in experimentation with children; act out of boredom	Aggressive, sexually excited by violence, targets stranger children; most likely to abduct and/or murder victims	Do not prefer children over adults and use children for own interests (sexual or otherwise)	Abuse children as a substitute for adult relationships; targets victims who are easily accessible (e.g., relatives)

(Continued)

TABLE 4.2 Continued

FBI Typology, Fourth Edition (Lanning, 2001)

Sadistic	Seductive	Introverted	Diverse	Inadequate	Morally Indiscriminate	Regressed
Aggressive, sexually excited by violence, targets stranger children; most likely to abduct and/or murder victims	Groom children and carry on a "relationship" with them through affection, praise, and gifts	Prefers children but lacks the interpersonal skills to seduce them; targets stranger children and very young children	Engages in sexual experimentation with children; may engage in other paraphilic behaviors (e.g., bondage, voyeurism)	Social misfits who see relationships with children as only sexual outlet	Do not prefer children over adults and use children for own interests (sexual or otherwise)	Abuse children as a substitute for adult relationships; targets victims who are easily accessible (e.g., relatives)

FBI Typology Latest Iteration (Lanning, 2010)

Psychosexual/Deviant Sexual Needs ⟷ Biological/Physiological Sexual Needs / Power/Anger Nonsexual Needs

Not one or the other but a continuum

physical injury is used only to the extent necessary to gain victim compliance. Generally, the level of planning of the offenses is moderate.

9. Low contact/high physical injury/nonsadistic (nonsadistic aggressive): Offenders inflict serious injury to their victims but do not show a preference for sadism. Generally, the level of planning of the offenses is low.

10. Low contact/high physical injury/sadistic (sadistic): Engages primarily in sadistic acts with victims, often resulting in a serious physical injury. Sexual acts are often symbolic and, as a result, require a high degree of planning.

GROOMING Put on slicy

Child sexual abuse usually does not occur between strangers. For example, one survey of 182 child sexual abusers found that only 6.5% victimized children they did not know (Smallbone & Wortley, 2001). They become personally and emotionally invested in their victims through a process where trust and confidence are built through emotional manipulation. This process is known as grooming. Grooming generally involves the skillful manipulation of a child into situations where they can be more readily sexually abused and less likely to disclose the incident. This process is quite detailed and lengthy and requires patience on the offender's part to maximize the child's trust. Grooming sometimes is a well-organized, long-term activity. It is carried out in a series of steps that build up to the sexual abuse of a child. In order, these steps are: target selection, befriending the target, desensitizing the target, and maintenance.

Target Selection

Many people who sexually abuse children have acknowledged that they carefully select victims by their perceived vulnerability. Offenders consider many factors in selecting a potential target, including the child's status (e.g., age, physical disability, living in a divorced or broken family, and living in poverty) as well as the child's emotional/psychological state (e.g., a needy child, a depressed child, or a lonely child). One study, for example, found that people who sexually abuse children often target children from dysfunctional families, without supervision, and with physical signs of neglect (Beauregard et al., 2007b). Accordingly, one offender in this study offered the following scenario to illustrate how he selected his child targets (p. 455):

> When I saw a kid that always had a key around his neck and who was badly dressed, I knew that his parents didn't take care of him and that I could easily approach him to offer him things.... I knew that he'd accept because he had nothing.

The work environment may also be used to facilitate the victimization of children. The **sophisticated rape track** comprises those who work with or are involved with children, including teachers, daycare providers, after-school activity leaders, clergy, and others in authoritative positions (Beauregard et al., 2007a). Because of their position and status, they appear nonthreatening to their victims and can easily create situations that allow them to be alone with them (e.g., staying after class/school and camping trips). One study of 41 child molesters who targeted children with whom they worked found that 15% chose their

PHOTO 4.1 Protest at the Vatican.

Photo Credit: Stefano Dal Pozzolo//*The New York Times*/Redux.

profession *solely* on the basis that it provided them access to children. Also, 42% revealed that this arrangement partially motivated their career choice (Sullivan & Beech, 2004).

Beauregard et al. (2007a) also identified ***family infiltrators***—those who become acquainted with families with children (especially single-mother families) and assume a role as surrogate parent or friend to the child.

Befriending the Target

The second step of grooming involves gaining the child's and family's trust and gaining access to the target. The offender may observe the child and assess their vulnerabilities to learn how to approach and interact with the child. They may offer their targets special attention, which may consist of talking with them and offering a sympathetic ear, playing games with them, offering transportation, and giving them gifts and/or treats. Eventually, the offender will begin to play a significant role in the child's life. They sometimes have a remarkable ability to manipulate the relationship so that it appears they are the only one who fully understands the child or meets the child's needs. During the process of befriending the target, the offender will also create opportunities to isolate them. For example, they will babysit the child, take them out of town for weekend getaways, or have the child accompany them on daily errands (Craven et al., 2006).

Desensitizing the Target

Until this point, all behaviors initiated by the offender are "positive" and do not involve any sexually abusive elements. During the desensitization phase, offenders will interweave abuse into their day-to-day interactions with the child to gradually sexualize the relationship (Berliner & Conte, 1990). Abuse does not proceed immediately to a high level but is started at low levels. Slowly, abusive acts progress in a systematic yet subtle fashion. Because the victim does not understand the intention of their new "friend," they become desensitized to seemingly harmless acts that an objective observer might view as danger signals. Offenders might desensitize a child to physical touching by beginning first with nonsexual touching such as tickling or stroking the child's head. Conversations may also become more sexual. The aim is to progress to sexual touching, first on top of clothes and then under or without clothes (van Dam, 2001).

Maintenance

Child sexual abuse is rarely an isolated event. Offenders often take great strides to maintain their relationships with victims. Maintenance activities include reassuring the victim that no harm (physical, emotional, moral, or otherwise) has been done. Statements such as "this is a way we show our love for each other" or "I am trying to teach you" are examples of how offenders mask their behavior.

Those who sexually abuse children rely on secrecy not only to maintain the relationship but also to prevent the child from disclosing the abuse. Offenders will engage in myriad tactics, from instilling shame, blame, or guilt to shifting responsibility to the child. Offenders may also threaten disclosure of the relationship, self-harm, or physical harm to the child or loved ones. The grooming process is not limited to perpetrators from outside the family; grooming also happens in the context of intrafamilial child sexual abuse involving parents, grandparents, siblings, or other immediate family members as perpetrators (Katz & Barnetz, 2016; Katz & Field, 2020).

Online Grooming

Aspects of the grooming process can also be applied to online/virtual environments where interactions between victims and offenders take place via internet communication platforms. O'Connell (2003) identified the following stages of the online sexual grooming process: (a) friendship-forming stage, (b) relationship-forming stage, (c) risk assessment stage, (d) exclusivity stage, (e) sexual stage, and (f) the concluding stage. Generally speaking, these phases align with the grooming phases described above. One important distinction is that online grooming is usually shorter in duration, with sexual intent being introduced much earlier compared to in-person grooming contexts. Whereas the latter usually involves weeks, months, or even years of skillful planning and manipulation, online grooming interactions are usually short-lived in nature, with conversations becoming highly sexualized within minutes (Kloess et al., 2019; Quayle et al., 2014; Whittle et al., 2014).

CRIMINAL JUSTICE RESPONSE TO CHILD SEXUAL ABUSE

Child sexual abuse cases have unique characteristics that make them different from other types of crimes. Victims frequently delay disclosure or only tell part of the story (if they disclose at all), cases are often not isolated incidents but rather transpire over a period of time, conclusive medical evidence is often absent, and children generally are not viewed as credible witnesses by the criminal justice system. In this section, we explore the criminal justice response to child sexual abuse, including investigations, prosecutorial issues, and issues that impact case outcomes.

Reporting Child Sexual Abuse

It is estimated that approximately 60%–70% of adults who experienced child sexual abuse never reported their abuse when they were children. Only a small minority (10%–18%) *ever* reported their abuse to officials (London et al., 2005). Therefore, what is known about the criminal justice response to child sexual abuse, from reporting to investigation to prosecution, is based on a minority of all cases. All U.S. states have statutes identifying persons who are required to report suspected sexual abuse to an appropriate agency such as Child Protective Services (CPS), law enforcement, or a state-operated child abuse reporting hotline. Mandatory reporters are customarily individuals who are in frequent contact with children, including social workers, school personnel, medical examiners, mental health professionals, and law enforcement officials. Other professionals are also identified as mandated reporters in certain states. For example, film processors and developers are mandated to report child sexual abuse in 12 states. Animal control and humane officers have mandated reporters in seven states, and members of the clergy are required to report in 27 states (Child Welfare Information Gateway, 2014). In 18 states, *any person* who suspects child sexual abuse is required to report, regardless of their profession.

The requirement for mandated reporters to report a suspected case of child sexual abuse varies from state to state and depends on a number of factors, including the ages of both parties involved in the sexual act and indications of coercion, bribery, and/or intimidation. For example, in California, if a child is 14–15 years of age and the sexual partner is 13 years old or younger, a report is mandated. If a child is 14–15 years old and the sexual partner is 14–20 years old, *and* there is no indication of abuse, *and* there is no evidence of an exploitative relationship (i.e., coercion, bribery, and/or intimidation has not occurred), this is not a mandatory report, and reporters have the latitude to exercise clinical judgment as to whether they will inform the authorities. Reports of child sexual abuse are generally made to law enforcement officials or CPS. Generally, CPS handles child sexual abuse issues occurring within the home, and law enforcement officials work on extrafamilial cases.

An investigation is conducted once a report has been filed. States, counties, and even cities and townships vary considerably in how investigations are structured. They may involve CPS caseworkers, law enforcement officials, physicians, mental health providers, victim advocates, and other professionals. Many state statutes require a joint CPS–law enforcement investigation for child sexual abuse cases. ***Joint investigations***, which involve inter-agency cooperation and shared information between law enforcement and CPS, have become increasingly common in child sexual abuse investigations. In comparison to independent investigations, which consist of agencies working separately from one another, the benefits of joint investigations are many, including more offender confessions, more victim corroboration, more substantiated reports, more criminal prosecutions, and more guilty pleas (Tjaden & Anhalt, 1994).

Prosecutorial Issues: The Role of Child Testimony

Similar to rape and sexual assault, child sexual abuse mostly occurs behind closed doors and without any eyewitnesses. Because of the secretive nature of child sexual abuse, successful prosecution often rests solely on the testimony of the child victim. The role of the child victim providing testimony in court has become especially important in the past ten years in light of the U.S. Supreme Court case *Crawford v. Washington* (2004), which altered the prosecution of child sexual abuse cases. The decision effectively barred **testimonial hearsay** (evidence that is gathered or collected by state agents for the purpose of prosecution) from entering into criminal trials as evidence. For example, if a law enforcement officer interviews a child sexual abuse victim and that child becomes unavailable for a trial, calling in the officer to court to report to the jury what was said would constitute testimonial hearsay. The *Crawford* decision, therefore, requires the physical presence of child victims in court proceedings, making it difficult, if not impossible, to prosecute cases in which the child witness initially reported the crime but later is afraid or intimidated by the prospect of testifying.

This has led to the reversal of some convictions for sex crimes committed against children. In *Pitts v. State* (2005), the four-year-old victim made consistent statements to a physician, a psychologist, and a forensic interviewer in videotaped interviews revealing sexual abuse. The child also disclosed having seen the defendant sexually abuse the child's cousin, who herself confirmed abuse in a videotaped interview. The state presented both girls at trial, but they appeared too upset and frightened to answer questions and were declared unavailable. The videotaped interviews of both children were admitted, and the conviction was reversed on appeal because the interviews were deemed testimonial hearsay.

Similarly, in *People v. Sharp* (2005), a five-year-old victim was unavailable to testify in court because she suffered enduring trauma from her abuse. The trial court admitted a videotaped statement in which the child disclosed to a forensic interviewer that her father sexually abused her, which was consistent with what she previously told her mother. Again, the appellate court reversed the conviction because the statement was testimonial hearsay. The issue is not that victims are viewed as somehow less credible or believable unless they testify in person. Rather, the issue is procedural in that defendants accused of child sexual abuse are denied their constitutional right to confront and cross-examine witnesses.

Although experienced prosecutors have acknowledged that convictions can be obtained solely on the testimony of child victims (American Prosecutors Research Institute, 2004), the testimony is less persuasive without corroborating evidence such as developmentally unusual sexual behavior by the victim, unusual psychological symptoms (e.g., severe and recurrent nightmares), medical evidence indicative of sexual abuse, eyewitnesses to the alleged crime, offender confessions, or additional complaints against the suspect that confirm the victim's testimony. Nevertheless, research has shown that child sexual abuse cases with no evidence supporting the child's testimony can and do result in the successful prosecution of offenders (Walsh et al., 2010). There are many barriers—legal, social, and cultural—that preclude the acceptance of child testimony in court proceedings. This especially affects very young victims of sexual abuse.

Very Young Victims

Research consistently shows that child sexual abuse victims' first unwanted sexual experiences occur around age ten (Finkelhor, 1979; Godbout et al., 2014). Child sexual abuse, however, involves victims of all ages. Very young children, from infancy to approximately age six, are at a significant disadvantage with respect to successful prosecution and adjudication of suspected sexual abuse. These reports are by far the least likely to be substantiated. One clinician provides the following example to demonstrate the difficulty in substantiating a child sexual abuse case involving a two-year-old female victim:

A two-year-old child was in a domestic violence shelter with her mother. The mother was badly beaten by an alcoholic father. When the mother changed the child's diaper, she grabbed her vulva and cried "Daddy hurt butt! Daddy hurt butt!" The child was also observed to be nervous and anxious around her father and had trouble sleeping after a visit. Law enforcement officers and child protective services conducted a joint investigation but could not substantiate sexual abuse. The child was eventually returned to the father for unsupervised visitation.

(Hewitt, 1999, p. 1)

Scenarios like this are all too common for very young victims of sexual abuse. The difficulties in substantiating sexual abuse of very young victims point to several legal and extralegal factors. First, the likelihood of detecting physical diagnostic evidence in these cases is low (Heger et al., 2002). Many types of sexual abuse do cause injuries, but such injuries can heal completely by the time the child is brought for a medical examination (McCann et al., 2007).

Additionally, very young children may have difficulty communicating in abusive situations. Preverbal children, for example, may use what few verbal skills they have in combination with other gestures and behaviors that are suggestive of abuse (American Prosecutors Research Institute, 2004). There is a low likelihood that such communications will withstand legal scrutiny. Further, it is argued that very young children are unduly suggestive, meaning they may be misled to report inaccurate information. Some earlier critics portrayed the prosecution of child sexual abuse cases as an unethical process led by corrupt professionals on a witch hunt for false allegations (Gardner, 1991). There has never been evidence of such a witch hunt. There is evidence, however, that some well-intentioned therapists, law enforcement officials, attorneys, and social workers have used interview techniques that could distort children's memories. Proper interviewing of vulnerable victims is explored further in Chapter 9.

By and large, successful prosecution, specifically in cases involving the youngest victims, depends on the quality of the verbal evidence and the effectiveness of the child victim's testimony (De Jong & Rose, 1991). It has been established that older children are more likely to disclose sexual abuse, as well as provide more detailed disclosure of it, compared to younger children (London et al., 2005). Before a child can testify in court, the judge must be convinced that the child possesses **testimonial competence**. Testimonial competence requires basic cognitive and moral capacities. The child must be able to understand the difference between a lie and the truth and appreciate the need to tell the truth in court. Moreover, usable testimony also depends on a child's understanding and memory of the abuse, ability to describe what happened, and concerns about the consequences.

In most states, attorneys and judges can inquire about children's understanding of truth and lies (Myers, 2005). For example, in California, witnesses are disqualified from testifying if they are "incapable of understanding the duty of a witness to tell the truth" (California Evidence Code, 2010). As a result, child witnesses are likely to confront questions about their understanding of truth and lies and the importance of telling the truth. Their responses may be used as a prerequisite to allowing their testimony or as a means of evaluating their credibility. For school-age children and adolescents, this is usually not a serious barrier to prosecution. For very young victims with limited verbal communication abilities, however, this can be an insurmountable obstacle.

In the past ten years, the U.S. Supreme Court has increased the significance of oath-taking competency requirements for child witnesses. Under the law in most jurisdictions, children demonstrate oath-taking competency if they understand that "truth" refers to factual statements and that one ought to tell the truth. The ways young children understand abstract concepts such as truth and honesty, often belie some jurisdictions' strict-oath competency requirements. Research has shown that young children conceptually understand notions of "truth" and "lie" despite their inability to articulate them successfully. Researchers had found that maltreated preschool-aged children (ages four to six years) successfully accepted true statements and rejected false statements before they were able to label true and false statements as "truth" and "lie" or as "good" and "bad" (Lyon et al., 2010). This finding is in line with previous research that had found that young children were able to label statements as "truth" or "lie" before they were able to provide a definition or explain the difference between the two (Lyon & Saywitz, 1999). Taken together, this means that children can and do accept true propositions and reject false ones even though they are incapable of articulating their understanding of truth and lies.

If some form of an oath is required, many children who reliably accept true statements and reject false statements will nevertheless be incapable of promising to "tell the truth" because they lack a technical understanding of the kinds of statements to which "the truth" refers. These children appreciate the importance of speaking truthfully but are unable to comment prospectively on whether they would do so and thus would be incapable of promising to tell the truth (Lyon et al., 2010).

Another significant barrier to prosecution of child sexual abuse cases is the common belief that a child will be further traumatized by the legal process, which depending on the nature of the charges, can be a lengthy process, requiring the child to repeatedly face and relive trauma (Walsh et al., 2008). This is intensified when the child victim is related to their abuser and may lack familial support. Although some evidence suggests that longer court processes increase anxiety and distress in child victims, thereby hindering their recovery process (Runyan et al., 1988), the negative effects appear to be short-lived. By the time child sexual abuse cases are resolved, behavioral adjustment of children who testify is similar to that of children who do not testify (Goodman et al., 1992).

Factors Affecting Criminal Trial Proceedings

Child sexual abuse cases have one of the lowest conviction rates of all types of crime (Block & Williams, 2019). There are many factors that can influence whether a prosecutor will accept a case for prosecution, as well as verdict decisions. In this section, we examine the impact of medical and behavioral evidence on prosecutorial and jury decision-making in child sexual abuse cases.

Medical Evidence

Next to an offender's confession, the medical evidence of physical markers of abuse is considered one of the best forms of evidence. Often jurors enter into a sexual abuse criminal trial with the expectation that some form of medical evidence will be presented (Werner & Werner, 2008). Such evidence is not available in most cases (Heger et al., 2002; Smith et al., 2018). When evidence is available, it may not prove whether a child was abused. For example, in a study of 236 sexually abused children, researchers reviewed medical records to determine the frequency of abnormal findings (e.g., absence of hymenal tissue, hymenal lacerations, scarring of anal sphincter tissue) as a result of genital or anal penetration. Examination findings revealed that 28% of cases were rated as normal, 49% were nonspecific, 9% were suspicious, and 14% were rated as abnormal or indicative of abuse/penetration (Adams et al., 1994).

The association between the presence of medical evidence in child sexual abuse cases and the case outcome is disputable, with evidence on both sides. In one of the first studies of decision-making in child sexual abuse cases, researchers concluded that medical evidence nearly doubled the chances of a conviction (Bradshaw & Marks, 1990). Subsequent research has shown that the presence of physical evidence can affect prosecutorial decision-making in that cases with medical evidence of abuse are more likely to be prosecuted than cases without medical evidence (Brewer et al., 1997). In other recent research, physical evidence was found to be neither predictive nor essential for the conviction of 115 child sexual abuse cases that went to criminal trial (De Jong & Rose, 1991). Furthermore, other researchers found that medical evidence was not a significant predictor of whether a prosecutor would accept a child sexual abuse case for the prosecution (Walsh et al., 2008). Unlike medical evidence, behavioral evidence has demonstrated a strong and consistent association with trial outcomes.

Behavioral Evidence

The way victims behave in the courtroom may have a substantial impact on the trial outcome. One study found that too little or too much emotion from the alleged child victim negatively affected credibility in the eyes of the mock jurors (Golding et al., 2003). In this study, the alleged offender was more likely to be convicted when the child was teary eyed versus when the child was calm or hysterical. The age of the victim is important. Research has found that older child victims (12–17) appear to be most emotionally affected by the court process, followed by 7–11-year olds, then 4–6-year olds. In one study of juror perceptions of child sexual abuse victims, 7- to 11-year olds were seen as more sexually naïve and, therefore, more credible, compared to victims ages 12 and older (Bottoms et al., 2004). Taken together, this suggests that mid-adolescent children are likely to be viewed as most credible to jurors provided that they present as emotional but still in control. Certain victim behavioral indicators (such as sleeping difficulties, social withdrawal, depression, and suicidal ideation) also have been found to increase the chances of a guilty verdict (Lewis et al., 2014).

Earlier, the many impacts of sexual abuse on child victims were discussed. Tension-reducing activities, such as self-injury, running away, risky sexual behaviors, and engaging in criminal activity, have been well documented in studies investigating the effects of child sexual abuse. Victims who engage in such activities may be viewed as less credible to jurors. One study found that when child victims showed evidence of destructive behavior or acting in a way that ran counter to social norms, a jury was more likely to discredit their allegations and return a not-guilty verdict (Lewis et al., 2014).

CONCLUSION

Child sexual abuse is a serious social problem that can have serious lifelong consequences. Although concern over the issue has ebbed and flowed, contemporary awareness of widespread sexual abuse of children dates back to the late 1970s. Victims of child sexual abuse vary greatly with respect to the effect these experiences have on them. Some victims do not suffer any immediate or long-term consequences, whereas others suffer a host of short- and long-term negative physical and mental health problems, substance abuse, and possible revictimization later in life. Similar to rape and sexual assault, child sexual abuse is underreported, and many factors affect trial proceedings for cases that are prosecuted.

REVIEW POINTS

- Not all people who sexually abuse children are pedophiles. Child sexual abuse is legally defined as engaging in inappropriate sexual acts with a child, whereas pedophilia is based on clinical diagnosis.
- Most victims of childhood sexual abuse do not go on to sexually abuse children. However, sexual victimization as a child, if accompanied by other factors, such as the co-occurrence of other types of abuse, may contribute to a victim's later emergence as someone who sexually abuses children.
- Often the successful investigation, prosecution, and conviction of perpetrators of child sexual abuse depends on the child's testimony. It is estimated that a small minority of victimizations (10%–18%) are reported to officials.
- Many factors may account for child sexual abuse case dispositions. Behavioral evidence appears to be a better predictor of case outcome compared to medical/physical evidence.

REFERENCES

Abel, G. G., & Harlow, N. (2001). *The stop child molestation book: What ordinary people can do in their everyday lives to save three million children*. Xlibris Corporation.

Adams, J. A., Harper, K., Knudson, S., & Revilla, J. (1994). Examination findings in legally confirmed child sexual abuse: It's normal to be normal. *Pediatrics, 94*(3), 310–317.

Aebi, M., Landolt, M. A., Mueller-Pfeiffer, C., Schnyder, U., Maier, T., & Mohler-Kuo, M. (2015). Testing the "sexually abused-abuser hypothesis" in adolescents: A population-based study. *Archives of Sexual Behavior, 44*(8), 2189–2199. https://www.doi.org/10.1007/s10508-014-0440-x

Alaggia, R. (2010). An ecological analysis of child sexual abuse disclosure: Considerations for child and adolescent mental health. *Journal of the Canadian Academy of Child and Adolescent Psychiatry, 19*(1), 32–39.

Amelung, T., Kuhle, L. F., Konrad, A., Pauls, A., & Beier, K. M. (2012). Androgen deprivation therapy of self-identifying, help-seeking pedophiles in the Dunkelfeld. *International Journal of Law and Psychiatry, 35*(3), 176–184. https://doi.org/10.1016/j.ijlp.2012.02.005

American Prosecutors Research Institute. (2004). *Investigation and prosecution of child abuse*. Sage.

American Psychiatric Association. (2013). *Diagnostic and Statistical Manual of Mental Disorders (DSM-5®)*. Author.

Baur, E., Forsman, M., Santtila, P., Johansson, A., Sandnabba, K., & Långström, N. (2016). Paraphilic sexual interests and sexually coercive behavior: A population-based twin study. *Archives of Sexual Behavior, 45*(5), 1163–1172. https://www.doi.org/10.1007/s10508-015-0674-2

Beauregard, E., Proulx, J., Rossmo, K., Leclerc, B., & Allaire, J. F. (2007a). Script analysis of the hunting process of serial sex offenders. *Criminal Justice and Behavior, 34*(8), 1069–1084. https://www.doi.org/10.1177/0093854807300851

Beauregard, E., Rossmo, D. K., & Proulx, J. (2007b). A descriptive model of the hunting process of serial sex offenders: A rational choice perspective. *Journal of Family Violence, 22*(6), 449–463. https://www.doi.org/10.1007/s10896-007-9101-3

Beckett, K. (1996). Culture and the politics of signification: The case of child sexual abuse. *Social Problems, 43*(1), 57–76. https://www.doi.org/10.1525/sp.1996.43.1.03x0336x

Bell, M. C. (2008). Grassroots death sentences? The social movement for capital child rape laws. *Journal of Criminal Law and Criminology, 98*(1), 1–30.

Berliner, L., & Conte, J. R. (1990). The process of victimization: The victims' perspective. *Child Abuse & Neglect, 14*(1), 29–40. https://www.doi.org/10.1016/0145-2134(90)90078-8

Block, S. D., & Williams, L. M. (2019). *The prosecution of child sexual abuse: A partnership to improve outcomes.* U.S. Department of Justice.

Bottoms, B. L., Davis, S. L., & Epstein, M. A. (2004). Effects of victim and defendant race on jurors' decisions in child-sexual abuse cases. *Journal of Applied Social Psychology, 34*(1), 1–33. https://www.doi.org/10.1111/j.1559-1816.2004.tb02535.x

Bradley, A. R., & Wood, J. M. (1996). How do children tell? The disclosure process in child sexual abuse. *Child Abuse & Neglect, 20*(9), 881–891. https://www.doi.org/10.1016/0145-2134(96)00077-4

Bradshaw, T. L., & Marks, A. E. (1990). Beyond a reasonable doubt: Factors that influence the legal disposition of child sexual-abuse cases. *Crime & Delinquency, 36*(2), 276–285. https://www.doi.org/10.1177/0011128790036002006

Brewer, K. D., Rowe, D. M., & Brewer, D. D. (1997). Factors related to prosecution of child sexual-abuse cases. *Journal of Child Sexual Abuse, 6*(1), 91–111. https://www.doi.org/10.1300/J070v06n01_07

Caffey, J. (1946). Multiple fractures in the long bones of infants suffering from chronic subdural hematoma. *The American Journal of Roentgenology and Radium Therapy, 56*(2), 163–173. https://www.doi.org/ 10.1007/s11999-010-1666-0

California Evidence Code. (2010) § 701, subds. (a)(2).

Camilleri, J. A., & Quinsey, V. L. (2008). Pedophilia: Assessment and treatment. In D. R. Laws & W. O'Donohue (Eds.), *Sexual deviance: Theory, assessment, and treatment*, vol. 2 (pp. 183–212). Guilford Press.

Child Welfare Information Gateway. (2014). *Mandatory reporters of child abuse and neglect.* U.S. Department of Health and Human Services, Children's Bureau.

Craven, S., Brown, S., & Gilchrist, E. (2006). Sexual grooming of children: Review of literature and theoretical considerations. *Journal of Sexual Aggression, 12*(3), 287–299. https://www.doi.org/10.1080/13552600601069414

De Francis, V. (1969). *Protecting the child victim of sex crimes committed by adults: Final report.* The American Humane Association, Children's Division.

De Jong, A. R., & Rose, M. (1991). Legal proof of child sexual abuse in the absence of physical evidence. *Pediatrics, 88*(3), 506–511.

Dube, S. R., Anda, R. F., Whitfield, C. L., Brown, D. W., Felitti, V. J., Dong, M., & Giles, W. H. (2005). Long-term consequences of childhood sexual abuse by gender of victim. *American Journal of Preventive Medicine, 28*(5), 430–438. https://www.doi.org/ 10.1016/j.amepre.2005.01.015

Elliott, M., Browne, K., & Kilcoyne, J. (1995). Child sexual abuse prevention: What offenders tell us. *Child Abuse & Neglect, 19*(5), 579–594. https://www.doi.org/10.1016/0145-2134(95)00017-3

Ferragut, M., Rueda, P., Cerezo, M. V., & Ortiz-Tallo, M. (2020). What do we know about child sexual abuse? Myths and truths in Spain. *Journal of Interpersonal Violence.* https://www.doi.org/10.1177/0886260520918579

Finkelhor, D. (1979). *Sexually victimised children.* Free Press.

Finkelhor, D. (1984). *Child sexual abuse: New theory and research.* Free Press.

Finkelhor, D., Shattuck, A., Turner, H. A., & Hamby, S. L. (2014). The lifetime prevalence of child sexual abuse and sexual assault assessed in late adolescence. *Journal of Adolescent Health, 55*(3), 329–333. https://www.doi.org/ 10.1016/j.jadohealth.2013.12.026

Gardner, R. A. (1991). *Sex abuse hysteria: Salem witch trials revisited*. Creative Therapeutics.
Garland, D. (2001). *The culture of control: Crime and social order in contemporary society*. University of Chicago Press.
Godbout, N., Briere, J., Sabourin, S., & Lussier, Y. (2014). Child sexual abuse and subsequent relational and personal functioning: The role of parental support. *Child Abuse & Neglect, 38*(2), 317–325. https://www.doi.org/ 10.1016/j.chiabu.2013.10.001
Golding, J. M., Fryman, H. M., Marsil, D. F., & Yozwiak, J. A. (2003). Big girls don't cry: The effect of child witness demeanor on juror decisions in a child sexual-abuse trial. *Child Abuse & Neglect, 27*(11), 1311–1321. https://www.doi.org/10.1016/j.chiabu.2003.03.001
Goodman, G. S., Taub, E. P., Jones, D. P. H., England, P., Port, L. K., Rudy, L., Prado, L., Myers, J. E. B., & Melton, G. B. (1992). Testifying in criminal court: Emotional effects on child sexual assault victims. *Monographs of the Society for Research in Child Development, 57*(5), i–159. http://www.doi.org/10.2307/1166127
Gordon, L. (1988). *Heroes of their own lives: The politics and history of family violence: Boston 1880–1960*. Penguin Group USA.
Groth, A. N., Hobson, W. F., & Gary, T. S. (1982). The child molester: Clinical observations. *Journal of Social Work & Human Sexuality, 1*(1–2), 129–144. https://www.doi.org/10.1300/J291v01n01_08
Hanson, R. K., & Bussiere, M. T. (1998). Predicting relapse: A meta-analysis of sexual offender recidivism studies. *Journal of Consulting and Clinical Psychology, 66*(2), 348–362. https://www.doi.org/ 10.1037//0022-006x.66.2.348
Heger, A., Ticson, L., Velasquez, O., & Bernier, R. (2002). Children referred for possible sexual abuse: Medical findings in 2384 children. *Child Abuse & Neglect, 26*(6), 645–659. https://www.doi.org/ 10.1016/s0145-2134(02)00339-3
Hewitt, S. K. (1999). *Assessing allegations of sexual abuse in preschool children: Understanding small voices* (No. 22). Sage.
Jahnke, S., & Hoyer, J. (2013). Stigmatization of people with pedophilia: A blind spot in stigma research. *International Journal of Sexual Health, 25*(3), 169–184. https://www.doi.org/10.1080/19317611.2013.795921
Jespersen, A. F., Lalumière, M. L., & Seto, M. C. (2009). Sexual abuse history among adult sex offenders and non-sex offenders: A meta-analysis. *Child Abuse & Neglect, 33*(3), 179–192. https://www.doi.org/ 10.1016/j.chiabu.2008.07.004
Jones, D. P., & McGraw, J. M. (1987). Reliable and fictitious accounts of sexual abuse to children. *Journal of Interpersonal Violence, 2*(1), 27–45. https://www.doi.org/10.1177/088626087002001002
Katz, C., & Barnetz, Z. (2016). Children's narratives of alleged child sexual abuse offender behaviors and the manipulation process. *Psychology of Violence, 6*(2), 223–232. https://www.doi.org/10.1037/a0039023
Katz, C., & Field, N. (2020). Unspoken: Child–perpetrator dynamic in the context of intrafamilial child sexual abuse. *Journal of Interpersonal Violence*. https://www.doi.org/10.1177/0886260520943723
Kempe, C. H., Silverman, F. N., Steele, B. F., Droegemueller, W., & Silver, M. K. (1962). The battered-child syndrome. *Journal of the American Medical Association, 181*(1), 17–24. https://www.doi.org/ 10.1001/jama.1962.03050270019004
Kitzinger, J. (2004). Media coverage of sexual violence against women and children. In K. Ross & C. M. Byerly (Eds.), *Women and media: International perspectives* (pp. 13–38). Blackwell. https://www.doi.org/ 10.1002/9780470776421

Kloess, J. A., Hamilton-Giachritsis, C. E., & Beech, A. R. (2019). Offense processes of online sexual grooming and abuse of children via internet communication platforms. *Sexual Abuse, 31*(1), 73–96. https://www.doi.org/10.1177/1079063217720927

Knight, R. A., Carter, D. L., & Prentky, R. A. (1989). A system for the classification of child molesters: Reliability and application. *Journal of Interpersonal Violence, 4*(1), 3–23. https://www.doi.org/10.1177/088626089004001001

LaFond, J. Q. (2005). *Preventing sexual violence: How society should cope with sex offenders*. American Psychological Association.

Lalor, K., & McElvaney, R. (2010). Child sexual abuse, links to later sexual exploitation/high-risk sexual behavior, and prevention/treatment programs. *Trauma, Violence, & Abuse, 11*(4), 159–177. https://www.doi.org/10.1177/1524838010378299

Lanning, K. V. (1986). *Child molesters: A behavioral analysis for law enforcement*. U.S. Department of Justice, Federal Bureau of Investigation.

Lanning, K. V. (2001). *Child molesters: A behavioral analysis* (4th ed.). National Center for Missing & Exploited Children.

Lanning, K. V. (2010). *Child molesters: A behavioral analysis for professionals investigating the sexual exploitation of children*. National Center for Missing & Exploited Children with Office of Juvenile Justice and Delinquency Prevention.

Lewis, T. E., Klettke, B., & Day, A. (2014). The influence of medical and behavioral evidence on conviction rates in cases of child sexual abuse. *Journal of Child Sexual Abuse, 23*(4), 431–441. https://www.doi.org/10.1080/10538712.2014.896843

London, K., Bruck, M., Ceci, S. J., & Shuman, D. W. (2005). Disclosure of child sexual abuse: What does the research tell us about the ways that children tell? *Psychology, Public Policy, and Law, 11*(1), 194–226. https://www.doi.org/10.1037/1076-8971.11.1.194

Lyon, T. D. (2007). False denials: Overcoming methodological biases in abuse disclosure research. In M. Pipe, M. Lamb, Y. Orbach, & A. Cederborg (Eds.), *Disclosing abuse: Delays, denials, retractions and incomplete accounts* (pp. 41–62). Erlbaum.

Lyon, T. D., & Saywitz, K. J. (1999). Young maltreated children's competence to take the oath. *Applied Developmental Science, 3*(1), 16–27. https://www.doi.org/10.1207/s1532480xads0301_3

Lyon, T. D., Carrick, N., & Quas, J. A. (2010). Young children's competency to take the oath: Effects of task, maltreatment, and age. *Law and Human Behavior, 34*(2), 141–149. https://www.doi.org/10.1007/s10979-009-9177-9

Malloy, L. C., Lyon, T. D., & Quas, J. A. (2007). Filial dependency and recantation of child sexual abuse allegations. *Journal of the American Academy of Child & Adolescent Psychiatry, 46*(2), 162–170. https://www.doi.org/10.1097/01.chi.0000246067.77953.f7

Martijn, F. M., Babchishin, K. M., Pullman, L. E., & Seto, M. C. (2020). Sexual attraction and falling in love in persons with pedohebephilia. *Archives of Sexual Behavior, 49*(4), 1305–1318. https://www.doi.org/10.1007/s10508-019-01579-9

Mauer, M. (2002). State sentencing reforms: Is the "get tough" era coming to a close? *Federal Sentencing Reporter, 15*(1), 50–52. https://www.doi.org/10.1525/fsr.2002.15.1.50

McCann, J., Miyamoto, S., Boyle, C., & Rogers, K. (2007). Healing of hymenal injuries in prepubertal and adolescent girls: A descriptive study. *Pediatrics, 119*(5), e1094–e1106. https://www.doi.org/10.1542/peds.2006-0964

Myers, J. E. B. (2005). *Myers on evidence in child, domestic, and elder abuse cases*. Aspen Publishers.

Myers, J. E. B. (2008). A short history of child protection in America. *Family Law Quarterly, 42*(3), 449–463.

National Commission on Pornography and Obscenity. (1970). *Technical report of the commission on obscenity and pornography*. U.S. Government Printing Office.

Oates, R. K., Jones, D. P., Denson, D., Sirotnak, A., Gary, N., & Krugman, R. D. (2000). Erroneous concerns about child sexual abuse. *Child Abuse & Neglect, 24*(1), 149–157. https://www.doi.org/ 10.1016/s0145-2134(99)00108-8

O'Connell, R. (2003). *A typology of cyber sexploitation and online grooming practices.* University of Central Lancashire. http://www.image.guardian.co.uk/sysfiles/Society/documents/2003/07/24/Netpaedoreport.pdf

Ogloff, J., Cutajar, M., Mann, E., & Mullen, P. (2012). Child sexual abuse and subsequent offending and victimisation: A 45 year follow-up study. *Trends & Issues in Crime and Criminal Justice [P], 2012*(440), 1–6. https://www.aic.gov.au/publications/tandi/tandi440

Pleck, E. H. (1987). *Domestic tyranny: The making of social policy against family violence from colonial times to the present.* Oxford University Press.

Prendergast, W. E. (1993). *The merry-go-round of sexual abuse: Identifying and treating survivors.* Haworth Press.

Quayle, E., Allegro, S., Hutton, L., Sheath, M., & Lööf, L. (2014). Rapid skill acquisition and online sexual grooming of children. *Computers in Human Behavior, 39*, 368–375. https://www.doi.org/10.1016/j.chb.2014.07.005

Runyan, D. K., Everson, M. D., Edelsohn, G. A., Hunter, W. M., & Coulter, M. L. (1988). Impact of legal intervention on sexually abused children. *The Journal of Pediatrics, 113*(4), 647–653.

Rush, F. (1980). *The best kept secret: Sexual abuse of children.* Prentice-Hall.

Sacco, L. (2009). *Unspeakable: Father-daughter incest in American history.* Johns Hopkins University Press.

Salter, D., McMillan, D., Richards, M., Talbot, T., Hodges, J., Bentovim, A., Hastings, R., Stevenson, J., & Skuse, D. (2003). Development of sexually abusive behaviour in sexually victimised males: A longitudinal study. *The Lancet, 361*, 471–476. https://www.doi.org/10.1016/S0140-6736(03)12466-X

Schiffer, B., & Vonlaufen, C. (2011). Executive dysfunctions in pedophilic and nonpedophilic child molesters. *The Journal of Sexual Medicine, 8*(7), 1975–1984. https://www.doi.org/10.1111/j.1743-6109.2010.02140.x

Seto, M. C. (2018). *Pedophilia and sexual offending against children: Theory, assessment, and intervention.* American Psychological Association.

Sgroi, S. M. (1975). Sexual molestation of children. *Children Today, 4*(3), 18–21.

Smallbone, S. W., & Wortley, R. K. (2001). *Child sexual abuse: Offender characteristics and modus operandi* (Vol. 193). Australian Institute of Criminology. https://www.aic.gov.au/publications/tandi/tandi193

Smith, T. D., Raman, S. R., Madigan, S., Waldman, J., & Shouldice, M. (2018). Anogenital findings in 3569 pediatric examinations for sexual abuse/assault. *Journal of Pediatric and Adolescent Gynecology, 31*(2), 79–83. https://www.doi.org/10.1016/j.jpag.2017.10.006

Sullivan, J., & Beech, A. (2004). A comparative study of demographic data relating to intra- and extra-familial child sexual abusers and professional perpetrators. *Journal of Sexual Aggression, 10*(1), 39–50. https://www.doi.org/10.1080/13552600410001667788

Tjaden, P. G., & Anhalt, J. (1994). *The impact of joint law enforcement-child protective services investigations in child maltreatment cases.* Center for Policy Research.

UNICEF. (2017). *A familiar face: Violence in the lives of children and adolescents.* https://data.unicef.org/resources/a-familiar-face/

U.S. Department of Health and Human Services, Administration for Children and Families, Administration on Children, Youth and Families, Children's Bureau. (2021). *Child maltreatment 2019.* https://www.acf.hhs.gov/cb/research-data-technology/ statistics-research/child-maltreatment

Vachon, D. D., Krueger, R. F., Rogosch, F. A., & Cicchetti, D. (2015). Assessment of the harmful psychiatric and behavioral effects of different forms of child maltreatment. *JAMA Psychiatry, 72*(11), 1135–1142. https://www.doi.org/10.1001/jamapsychiatry.2015.1792

van Dam, C. (2001). *Identifying child molesters: Preventing child sexual abuse by recognizing the patterns of the offenders.* Haworth Maltreatment and Trauma Press/The Haworth Press, Inc.

Walsh, W. A., Lippert, T., Cross, T. P., Maurice, D. M., & Davison, K. S. (2008). How long to prosecute child sexual abuse for a community using a children's advocacy center and two comparison communities? *Child Maltreatment, 13*(1), 3–13. https://www.doi.org/10.1177/1077559507307839

Walsh, W. A., Jones, L. M., Cross, T. P., & Lippert, T. (2010). Prosecuting child sexual abuse: The importance of evidence type. *Crime & Delinquency, 56*(3), 436–454. https://www.doi.org/10.1177/0011128708320484

Walters, D. R. (1975). *Physical and sexual abuse of children: Causes and treatment.* Indiana University Press.

Werner, J., & Werner, M. C. M. (2008). Child sexual abuse in clinical and forensic psychiatry: A review of recent literature. *Current Opinion in Psychiatry, 21*(5), 499–504. https://www.doi.org/10.1097/YCO.0b013e328305e4b0

Whitaker, D. J., Le, B., Hanson, R. K., Baker, C. K., McMahon, P. M., Ryan, G., Klein, A., & Rice, D. D. (2008). Risk factors for the perpetration of child sexual abuse: A review and meta-analysis. *Child Abuse & Neglect, 32*(5), 529–548. https://www.doi.org/10.1016/j.chiabu.2007.08.005

Whittle, H. C., Hamilton-Giachritsis, C. E., & Beech, A. R. (2014). In their own words: Young peoples' vulnerabilities to being groomed and sexually abused online. *Psychology, 5*, 1185–1196. https://www.doi.org/10.4236/psych.2014.510131

Widom, C. S., & Maxfield, M. G. (2001). *An update on the "cycle of violence": Research in brief.* National Institute of Justice.

COURT CASES

Crawford v. Washington, 541 U.S. 36 (2004).
Kennedy v. Louisiana, 554 U.S. 407 (2008).
People v. Sharp, 2005 WL 583755 (111. App. 4 Dist. 2005).
Pitts v. State, 2005 WL 127049 (Ga. App. 2005).

DEFINITIONS

Abused–Abuser Hypothesis: Widespread belief that sexually abused children and adolescents who are sexually abused are at risk of themselves committing sexual abuse (see also Cycle of Child Sexual Abuse)

Battered Child Syndrome: A clinical condition in young children who have received repeated serious physical abuse, including bone fractures, subdural hematomas, failure to thrive, or sudden death, and repetition of that abuse is likely to reoccur without intervention

Child Abuse Prevention and Treatment Act: Key legislation passed in 1974 (and reauthorized by the federal government several times since then) that addressed child abuse and neglect and authorized funds to improve states' investigation, reporting, assessment, prosecution, and treatment of physical abuse, neglect, and sexual abuse of children

Child Sexual Abuse: A broad spectrum of behaviors in which an adult (and sometimes an older adolescent) engages in inappropriate sexual acts with a child

Cycle of Child Sexual Abuse: Widespread belief that sexually abused children and adolescents who are sexually abused are at risk of themselves committing sexual abuse (see also Abused–Abuser Hypothesis)

Diagnostic and Statistical Manual of Mental Disorders, 5th ed.(DSM-5): A publication by the American Psychiatric Association that provides a list and diagnosis criteria of all recognized mental disorders

Family Infiltrators: Those who become acquainted with families with children and assume a role as surrogate parent or friend in order to facilitate child sexual abuse

FBI Typologies: A series of typologies which consider a modus operandi continuum that distinguishes between situational and preferential offenders

Fixated Abusers: Characterized by a persistent, continuous, and compulsive sexual desire and attraction to children

Grooming: The process of befriending and establishing an emotional connection with children for the purpose of sexually abusing them

Groth's Typology: One of the earliest and most influential typologies which identifies two types of broad categories of people who sexually abuse children: fixated and regressed

Joint Investigations: Investigations of child sexual-abuse incidents involving interagency cooperation and shared information between law enforcement officials and CPS

Pedophilia: Psychiatric disorder in which an adult or older adolescent experiences a primary or exclusive sexual attraction to prepubescent children (generally age 11 years or younger)

Protective Factors: Conditions or attributes that, when present, serve to minimize, reduce, or eliminate risk of maladaptive behaviors

Regressed Abusers: Characterized by "normal" sexual interests toward and relationships with age-appropriate partners and may choose sexual contact with children as a means of coping with external stressors

Sophisticated Rape Track: Those who work with or are involved regularly with children, including teachers, daycare providers, after-school activity leaders, clergy, and others in authoritative positions, and use these positions to facilitate child sexual abuse

Testimonial Competence: The mental capacity of individuals to provide testimony in legal proceedings

Testimonial Hearsay: Evidence collected or gathered by state agents (e.g., law enforcement officials, social workers, CPS professionals) for the purpose of a prosecution

Theory of Infantile Sexuality: Theory of sexual development in children (developed by Sigmund Freud) that argues that human sexuality begins at birth—at one point, Freud argued that children who had claimed sexual experiences with adults had imagined the experience

Unsubstantiated: Claims that lack sufficient evidence that a crime has occurred

CHAPTER 5

Child Pornography and Sex Trafficking

CHAPTER OBJECTIVES

- Identify common myths associated with child pornography and child trafficking
- Describe the evolution of U.S. child pornography laws
- Describe the characteristics and offending patterns of child pornography offenders
- Compare and contrast child pornography crimes with other types of sex crimes
- Identify criminal justice responses to child pornography crimes, including response by police and courts
- Identify characteristics of the sex trafficking industry, including its scope, how it operates, and characteristics that can increase one's vulnerability to this type of victimization
- Describe the evolution of U.S. sex trafficking laws over the past two decades

Chapter 4 primarily focused on contact sexual offenses against children. We briefly explored using the internet as a medium through which child sexual abuse is perpetrated, specifically as a grooming tactic to facilitate meeting with a child for sexual purposes. However, this crime represents only the tip of the iceberg in the broad spectrum of crimes that involve the sexual exploitation of children. In this chapter, we widen the aperture to consider a broader range of sexually exploitative crimes. Crimes of ***child pornography*** often involve enticing a child to share sexually explicit images and, in some instances, selling or trading the child's sexual images to others. Often, these crimes create a "permanent record" of a child's sexual exploitation; once images are disseminated and shared in an online environment, their circulation exists in perpetuity. ***Sex trafficking*** involves the use of force, fraud, or coercion to engage children (and sometimes adults) in commercial sex acts, which may include pornography, prostitution, or exchanging a sexual act for items of value, drugs, shelter, food, or clothes. Both child pornography and sex trafficking are global, multibillion-dollar industries.

In this chapter, we begin with a discussion of common myths and misconceptions surrounding child pornography. Next, the evolution of child pornography law and legislation in the United States is discussed with an emphasis on how the interpretation of the Constitution (particularly the First Amendment) shaped these laws over time. Following is a discussion of child pornography offender characteristics and typologies (including possessors, distributors, and producers of child pornography), highlighting the similarities and unique

DOI: 10.4324/9781003031444-5

differences between child pornography offenders and those who commit other types of sex offenses. Next is a summary of the criminal justice response to child pornography crimes with a focus on investigations, prosecution, and sentencing of offenders. Finally, this chapter concludes with a discussion of sex trafficking.

MYTHS ABOUT CHILD PORNOGRAPHY

Similar to other types of sex crimes (rape, sexual assault, child sexual abuse, etc.), crimes of child pornography are also shrouded in myths that incorrectly explain how and why this crime occurs, as well as minimizes the pervasiveness of the crime and the harm done to victims. Below, we explore some common child pornography myths.

Child Pornography Isn't That Big of a Problem

At one point in time, child pornography was fairly well contained and near the brink of eradication. The internet profoundly changed this, and child pornography crimes have been on a continuous rise since the 1990s (Walsh et al., 2013). The National Center for Missing & Exploited Children's CyberTipline is the centralized reporting system for the online exploitation of children. In 2020, CyberTipline received 21.7 *million* reports worldwide of suspected online child pornography from electronic service providers and the broader public—an increase of 28% from the number of reports made in 2019 (National Center for Missing & Exploited Children, 2021). These reports included 31.7 million video files and 33.7 million image files. No corner of the United States or the world is untouched by these crimes; however, many countries do not have laws specifically addressing possession or distribution of child pornography. In a study of child pornography legislation in place in all 187 counties that are members of International Criminal Police Organization (INTERPOL) countries, 93 had no legislation in place addressing child pornography, and only 29 countries had sufficient legislation in place for combating child pornography (ICMEC, 2008). As technology becomes more sophisticated, it becomes exceedingly more difficult to detect child pornography activities. Data on child pornography traffic in peer-to-peer (P2P) computer networks indicate that user numbers greatly exceed the number of individuals identified by arrest (Steel, 2009). Recent research also suggests that content has become progressively more sexually egregious, explicit, and violent over time, with more materials containing sadistic content, bondage, and drug use (Seto et al., 2018). In 2006, expert witnesses at a Congressional hearing estimated that sexual exploitation of children on the internet was a $20 billion industry (Brockman, 2006).

Simply Viewing Child Pornography Is a Victimless Crime

This myth has been used historically as a justification against legislation criminalizing possession of child pornography. Objections to criminalizing possession of child pornography have often been couched in debates as to what is protected by the First Amendment. Only in the past 30 years has accessing and viewing child pornography been a crime. Child pornography is a global, multibillion-dollar industry. As such, the fundamental economic principle of supply and demand belies this myth. Simple access to and possession of child pornography increases the demand for more material. As demand rises, production and distribution of child pornography increase and, thus, the continued predation of child victims.

Viewing Child Pornography Will Prevent Those Viewing It from Committing Actual Sex Offenses against Children

Numerous studies have been connected on the relationship between viewing child pornography and the perpetration of sex crimes against children. Perspectives on the relationship between the two are largely split. One perspective is that child pornography reduces criminal sexual intent. This perspective was borne out of a series of studies that examined the unrestricted availability of pornography generally within certain countries and the incidence of sex crimes. Specifically, these studies concluded that when pornographic and other sexually explicit materials were decriminalized in societies that previously had strict bans on such materials, the rates of rape, sexual assault, and other crimes either decreased or remained stable (Kutchinsky, 1991; Landripet et al., 2006; Ng & Ma, 2001). Although these studies were limited primarily to *adult* pornography, some researchers have theorized that the tempering effect of pornography on sexual violence extends to child pornography as well (Diamond et al., 2011).

The opposing perspective on this topic purports that the consumption of child pornography *promotes* criminal sexual intent. A body of research has found a correlation between traders and purveyors of child pornography and acts of child sexual abuse and child molestation (described later in this chapter). Another perspective in this debate is that there is no correlation whatsoever between viewing child pornography and sexual offending against a child. Impulsive child pornography offenders (also described later) are an illustrative category of child pornography consumers that would align with this perspective in that their engagement with illegal materials neither increases nor decreases their proclivity to engage in criminal sexual acts with children.

In sum, the precise linkage between viewing child pornography and subsequent sexual offending against children is largely unknown. The shortcoming to the vast majority of claims that child pornography either decreases or increases the probability of offending is that they are based primarily on correlational studies, which do not explain cause-and-effect relationships. How child pornography viewing actually shapes and causes offending against children is still largely speculative.

Only Pedophiles View Child Pornography

In Chapter 4, we discussed the myth that only pedophiles sexually abuse children and concluded that labeling all people who commit child sexual abuse as pedophiles is incorrect. Similarly, assuming that only individuals with pedophilia view child pornography is also incorrect. Research has found an *association*, at best, between viewing child pornography and pedophilia in that viewing child pornography can be a predictor of pedophilia *in some cases*. Other researchers have found that pedophiles actually do not construct their erotic fantasies of children using sexually explicit materials but rather through nonsexualized images of children. We will discuss this research in depth later. The bottom line is this: viewing child pornography is not solely limited to pedophiles. An estimated 1%–5% of the male population is believed to have a pedophilic disorder (Ahlers et al., 2011; Bártová et al., 2021; Dombert et al., 2016). It would be naïve to believe that this relatively small population alone could keep a $20 billion industry going.

DEFINING CHILD PORNOGRAPHY

Federal law (18 U.S.C. §2256[8]) defines **child pornography** as the visual depiction (including any photograph, film, video, picture, or computer-generated image or picture as well as undeveloped film or data stored on computer storage devices) of sexually explicit conduct where

- the production of the visual depiction involves the use of a minor engaging in sexually explicit conduct; or
- the visual depiction is a digital image, computer image, or computer-generated image that is, or is indistinguishable from, that of a minor engaging in sexually explicit conduct; or
- the visual depiction has been created, adapted, or modified to appear that an identifiable minor is engaging in sexually explicit conduct.

This definition includes sexually explicit images of real children as well as *virtual child pornography*, which consists of synthesized, manipulated images of children who appear to be engaged in sexual acts. Federal law (18 U.S.C. §1466A) also classifies such images in the forms of drawings, cartoons, sculptures, and paintings as pornographic as well. In recent years, the term *child sexual abuse materials* has emerged as a preferred term for such content because the term *pornography* connotes forms of erotica intended to incite sexual excitement and is, at best, inaccurate for describing sexually explicit content involving children. Both terms are utilized in this chapter. Images themselves (whether actual or virtual) may vary considerably in their sexual content. Researchers have classified pictures of children according to the level of image severity. The COmbating Paedophile Information Networks in Europe (COPINE) scale is one detailed *typology* based on analysis of more than 80,000 publicly available images obtained from websites (Taylor et al., 2001). The scale accounts for a range of content from nonerotic and nonsexualized pictures showing children in their underwear or swimming costumes to pictures showing children engaged in sadistic acts or bestiality (Table 5.1).

Deciding which of these levels actually constitutes child pornography has become difficult, particularly in today's courts. It is arguable that images that are categorized as Levels 1 and 2 (i.e., indicative and nudist) are just as dangerous (if not more dangerous) than those images falling under Levels 9 and 10 (i.e., gross assault and sadism/bestiality). For example, research shows that pedophiles usually construct erotic fantasies *not* through the use of perverse, sexual material but rather through innocuous, nonsexualized images of children such as images from television advertisements, children's clothing catalogs, and even photographs of children at Disneyland (Howitt, 1995). For now, the important takeaway is that the "legitimateness" of material or an image may be irrelevant to an offender, given those sex offenders with interests in children may use perfectly legitimate material to satisfy sexual needs.

Child pornography exists in numerous formats, including printed media, film, CD-ROM, and DVD, to name a few. Today, it is most commonly transmitted on platforms on the internet, including email, websites, internet chat rooms, Instant Messages, File Transfer Protocols, and peer-to-peer (P2P) technology. **Sexting** (i.e., the sending and/or receiving of sexually suggestive images or messages to peers through a cell phone or social media network) by minors is a growing concern, although there is debate as to whether sexting constitutes child pornography (Mitchell et al., 2012). Child pornography is one of the fastest-growing online

TABLE 5.1 Combating Paedophile Information Networks in Europe (COPINE) Scale

Indicative: Non-sexualized pictures collected from legitimate sources (e.g., magazines, catalogs) showing children in undergarments, bathing suits, and so on from either commercial sources or family albums

Nudist: Pictures of naked or semi-naked children in appropriate nudist settings (e.g., baby bathtub photographs)

Erotica: Surreptitiously taken photographs of children in appropriate nudist settings

Posing: Deliberately posed pictures of children fully clothed, partially clothed, or naked

Erotic Posing: Deliberately posed pictures of children fully clothed, partially clothed, or naked in sexualized or provocative positions

Explicit Erotic Posing: Emphasizing genital areas where the child is either naked, partially clothed, or fully clothed

Explicit Sexual Activity: Involves touching, mutual or self-masturbation, oral sex, and intercourse by a child but not involving an adult

Assault: Pictures of children being subject to a sexual assault, involving digital touching, and involving an adult

Gross Assault: Grossly obscene pictures of sexual assault, involving penetrative sex, masturbation, or oral sex involving an adult

Sadism/Bestiality: Pictures showing a child being tied, bound, beaten, whipped, or otherwise subject to something that implies pain; pictures where an animal is involved in some form of sex with a child

Source: Taylor et al. (2001).

businesses, with an estimated 9,550 child sexual abuse web pages hosted by 1,561 individual domains detected in 2012 (Internet Watch Foundation, 2012). A study of arrested child pornography offenders revealed that 83% were in possession of images involving children between the ages of 6 and 12. Also, 39% had images of children between three and five years old. Another 19% had images of infants and toddlers under the age of three (Wolak et al., 2005).

THE HISTORY OF CHILD PORNOGRAPHY LAW

Federal law criminalizes knowingly producing, manufacturing, distributing, or accessing with intent to view child pornography (18 U.S.C. §2252). All 50 U.S. states have enacted laws criminalizing the possession, manufacture, and distribution of child pornography. Violation of these laws may result in both state and federal charges. For the purpose of enforcing the federal law, *minor* is defined as a person under the age of 18 regardless of the legal age of consent (recall from Chapter 3 that this ranges from 16 to 18, depending on the state). The laws that have been developed as a response to child pornography have a unique constitutional history (a summary of key court cases and legislation is provided in Figure 5.1).

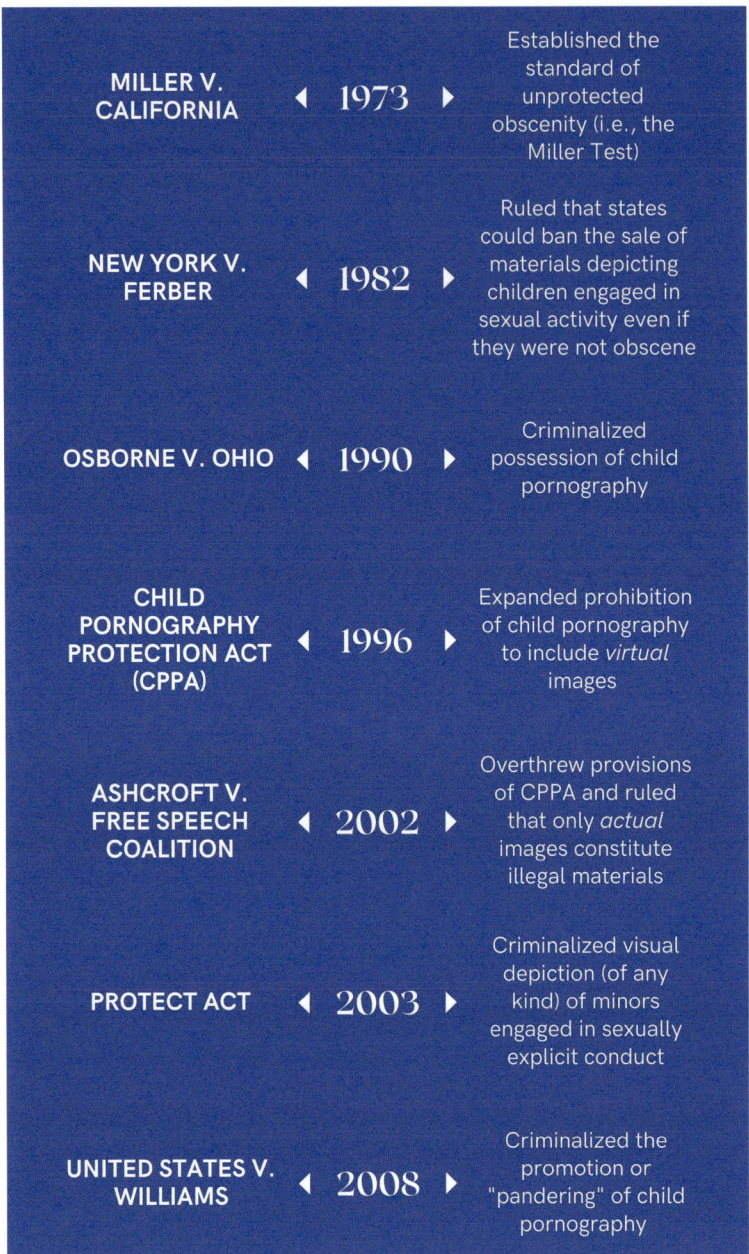

FIGURE 5.1 Timeline of Child Pornography Law in the United States.

History of Obscenity

The concept of **obscenity** laid the groundwork for what would eventually shape the child pornography laws that emerged in the 1970s. Although the term obscenity varies among communities and cultures, it generally refers to what is offensive to decency, filthy, disgusting, or repulsive (Richards, 1974). Obscene materials can include books, photographs, films, paintings, music, press, speech, and even thought. The most common method of regulating obscenity is through censorship. Materials are censored not because of fear that they will incite crimes but rather because they are offensive to others.

Sexual obscenity, therefore, was banned, regulated, or controlled not for fear of inciting sex crimes but because it offended the morals or values of the community. In short, obscenity is immoral, and individuals should not indulge in it, and the community should not tolerate it (Henkin, 1963). Despite the First Amendment protection of freedom of speech in the U.S. Constitution, this moral rule went largely unchallenged for the majority of the 20th century. Also noteworthy, until the mid-1970s, there was no systematic method for determining what constituted obscene material and what was considered protected under the First Amendment.

In 1973, the landmark U.S. Supreme Court case, *Miller v. California*, established the standard of what constitutes unprotected obscenity for First Amendment purposes. In this case, the question before the Court was whether the sale and distribution of obscene material (in this case, sexually explicit illustrated books, labeled "adult material") was protected under the First Amendment's freedom of speech guarantee. The Court ruled that it was not a protected form of speech. The Court, however, also recognized the potential danger in regulating and limiting forms of creative expression. The Court, therefore, created a set of criteria, known as The **Miller Test** (also known as the Three-Prong Obscenity Test), which questionable material must meet to be legitimately regulated by the law. These criteria include the following:

1 Whether the average person, applying contemporary community standards, would find that the work, taken as a whole, appeals to **prurient interests** (i.e., interests in sexual matters)
2 Whether the work depicts or describes, in a patently offensive way, sexual conduct (or excretory functions) specifically defined by the applicable state law
3 Whether the work, taken as a whole, lacks serious literary, artistic, political, or scientific value

This case provided individual states in the United States greater freedom in prosecuting individuals for the production and distribution of obscene materials. It is also important, however, to note that, despite the greater restrictions imposed as to what could be considered obscene material, the law did not specifically target child pornography or child exploitation. A number of major motion pictures released after the ruling featured sexualized images of young children. Many movies, such as *Taxi Driver*, *Pretty Baby*, and *The Blue Lagoon*, featured adult themes involving sexually active children under the age of 18. Films such as these, although featuring child nudity, would have been able to pass the Miller Test because they were produced and distributed for artistic value (see criterion 3). Also, note that at this time period, such laws applied only to *actual images*. Virtual images, including virtual photographs, were not considered under this early legislation.

Growing Awareness of Child Exploitation

As discussed in Chapter 4, by the late 1970s through the early 1980s, awareness of the need to protect children from sexual exploitation was growing in the United States. Even in nations hesitant to tolerate censorship of sexual materials, the use of child subjects crossed a line. It was during this time that fears of child sexual abuse became linked to other social

Focus Box 5.1 *Taxi Driver* (1976)

Jodie Foster was 12 years old when she was cast in the role of a child prostitute in Martin Scorsese's *Taxi Driver*. Foster's older sister stood in as a body double during the more sexually explicit scenes. At the time of the film's release (1976), the laws regulating sexually explicit depictions of children were much less restrictive compared to today. Despite the film's controversial content and subject matter, it was declared "culturally, historically or aesthetically" significant by the United States Library of Congress in 1994 and subsequently selected for preservation in the National Film Registry.

Photo Credit: Alamy

TABLE 5.2 Myths and Realities on Child Pornography Perpetrators

Myths	Reality
The offender is a "dirty old man."	The perpetrator is neither "dirty" nor old.
The offender is a stranger to the child.	Most victims know the perpetrator.
The offender is an alcoholic or drug addict.	Alcohol and other drugs are not critical to the commission of the crime.
The offender is sexually frustrated.	The majority of offenders have normal sexual functioning and relationships with adult partners.
The offender is mentally ill.	Offenders rarely have mental impairments or low intelligence.

ills, including kidnapping, serial homicide, and organized sex trafficking and sex rings. Many myths of the child pornography industry and its associated victims and offenders had been identified. In particular, Groth et al. (1978) exposed a number of misconceptions (presented in Table 5.2) that previously dominated popular thought on the subject. Early attempts to classify and categorize offenders revealed profiles that remarkably mirrored mainstream society—perpetrators were married white males with children, ages 25–45, in the middle class, and with stable community standing (Ayood, 1978; O'Brien, 1983).

This was the backdrop for the unanimous decision of *New York v. Ferber* (1982), which held that states can prohibit the depiction of minors engaged in sexual conduct and that the Miller Test need not be applied in cases of child pornography. *Ferber* essentially separated child pornography from obscene material and labeled it as its own category (Wortley & Smallbone, 2006). This granted states more leeway in regulating material that involved sexual exploitation of children. As important as it was to address the problem of child victims, however, this decision still was limited to the regulation of visual depictions of *actual* minors engaged in sexually explicit conduct (Burke, 1997). Also, this ruling pertained only to individuals who produced, promoted, or distributed such media—possession of these materials was still not criminalized. This would happen in 1990 with the case *Osborne v. Ohio* (1990), which overturned an earlier decision that neither states nor the federal government could prohibit possession of obscene material in the privacy of one's home (*Stanley v. Georgia*, 1969). The state of Ohio's interest in criminalizing possession of child pornography was based on the observation that many child sexual abusers would not merely keep pornographic materials for themselves but also would distribute them to other abusers, thus executing a never-ending cycle of distribution (Ost, 2002, 2009).

As the Supreme Court was rendering decisions that shaped legal responses to child pornography, the U.S. legislature also began to demonstrate a shared interest in the issue. In 1977, Congress passed the Protection of Children Against Sexual Exploitation Act. This act prohibited using children to make pornographic materials for financial gain. Later, in 1984, the Child Protection Act was passed, making it illegal to produce child pornography, regardless of commercial intent. In 1986, Congress also passed the Child Sexual Abuse and Pornography Act, which introduced mandatory sentencing for repeat offenders in addition to civil remedies for victims. Through the mid-1980s and early 1990s, the trafficking of child pornography within the United States continued to decrease and had almost been eradicated because of the tightening of child exploitation laws and successful campaigns by police. Producing such material became difficult and expensive, and reproducing it was equally risky. Purchase, distribution, and receipt of child pornography also became nearly impossible because consumers of such material found it increasingly difficult to find a safe, discreet medium to interact with one another. The improvement of technology, however, has gravely revived it. Today, child pornography has not only resurged as a serious crime in the United States, but it is also a multibillion-dollar business.

How the Internet Changed the Child Pornography Industry and Law

The internet is, at its core, a worldwide network of smaller computer networks connected by cable, telephone lines, or satellite links. It is decentralized, timeless, and spaceless. It is impossible to determine the size of the internet at any moment because it continuously grows. Although the internet has proven invaluable as a communication and educational tool, particularly in the 21st century, this same technological wonder has also proven to be a grave threat to children.

The internet has served as a major catalyst for the accelerated production, distribution, and purchase of child pornography. Today, pornographic images and films of children have flooded the internet and are easily accessible to anyone with access to a computer or cellphone. The internet has allowed the distribution of child pornography to be conducted at an extremely low cost, with virtual anonymity and at extraordinary speed. Additionally, the technology makes constant updating relatively easy (e.g., some distributors claim to update their material biweekly or, in some cases, daily). Furthermore, material that is downloaded from the internet has a unique advantage over other types of media (e.g., film and photographs) in that it does not deteriorate with age or with transfer to other electronic devices. Possessors, distributors, and producers of child pornography also take advantage of sophisticated encryption methods and anonymous networks, collectively known as the **Dark Web** or Darknet, to evade authorities. Approximately 80% of Dark Web traffic is related to access and transfer of child pornography (Kaur & Randhawa, 2020).

Along with easier production and distribution of, and access to, child pornography, the internet has also become a medium through which virtual child pornography (also known as pseudo child pornography) flourishes. Virtual child pornography refers to simulated representations as well as computer-generated or morphed images of children engaged in pornographic, sexual, or other lewd acts. This material takes on two forms: (1) computer-generated images in which a child's head is digitally placed onto the body of an adult who is involved in some form of sexually explicit conduct and (2) depictions of adults over the age of legal sexual consent (18 in the United States) who are portrayed as being a minor.

Prior to the heightened popularity and utility of the internet, the law made no concession for virtual child pornography. Only images of real children engaged in real acts were considered unlawful. As the use of the internet, coupled with advanced imaging software, began to become a staple in the child pornography industry, new fears arose concerning virtual child pornographic images as being equally damaging vis-à-vis their real image counterparts. This called for swift action that prosecuted the production, distribution, and possession of virtual child pornographic images in the same way that real ones were, thereby eliminating any distinction between the two. The first major court decision to arise in response to the internet becoming a mechanism for easier access to child pornography was the Child Pornography Protection Act (1996) (CPPA).

The CPPA expanded the federal prohibition of child pornography to include not only real images involving the sexual abuse of children but also "any visual depiction, including any photograph, film, video, picture, or computer or computer-generated image or picture that is, or appears to be, of a minor engaging in sexually explicit conduct" (18 U.S.C. §2256[8]). Therefore, not only were sexual images involving actual children criminalized but also computer-generated images, namely, the use of adult "body doubles" and sexual images that appeared to be minors or that were advertised as minors, even if minors were not actually involved (Akdeniz, 2013).

CPPA was met with extreme opposition and criticism, namely, by individuals and organizations protesting the act's infringement on constitutional protections. Some opponents, including the American Civil Liberties Union (ACLU), argued that because no actual victim existed in virtual child pornography, and the events in question were not real events with actual child endangerment or harm involved, such images should not be criminalized. The U.S. Judiciary Committee rejected the ACLU's arguments, maintaining that the U.S. government also had a compelling interest in prohibiting computer-generated images due to the potential of future harm to children. Ultimately, the provisions under CPPA were overthrown by the U.S. Supreme Court with *Ashcroft v. Free Speech Coalition* (2002), wherein the Court opined how digitally created images that involved no *real* minor(s) did not have a victim and, therefore, produced no record of the crime.

The *Free Speech Coalition* decision was arguably the most substantial setback for anti-child pornography law in the United States. This decision meant that prosecutors of child pornography cases had to prove, beyond a reasonable doubt, that the sexually explicit material presented as evidence was indeed a *real* image of a minor as opposed to one that was computer generated. In response to this decision, President George W. Bush signed into effect the Prosecutorial Remedies and Other Tools to End the Exploitation of Children Today (PROTECT) Act (Pub.L. 108–21, 117 Stat. 650, S. 151) in 2003. Among many other provisions, the PROTECT Act criminalized the visual depiction (of any kind) of minors engaged in sexually explicit conduct or obscenity, including computer-generated images that appear indistinguishable from that actual images. Drawings, cartoons, paintings, and sculptures were also criminalized provided that they meet the Miller Test standards for obscenity. The PROTECT Act also contained a "pandering provision" that criminalized the advertisement, promotion, and solicitation of materials *intending to cause another person to believe* that those materials contain sexually explicit or obscene depictions of children.

The pandering provision of the PROTECT Act was challenged in *United States v. Williams* (2008). In 2004, Michael Williams was arrested following an illicit photo exchange with an undercover secret service agent during a sting operation. During this photo exchange, Williams bragged that he had sexually explicit pictures of his daughter engaged in sex acts with adult men. He was charged with possession and pandering of child pornography. Williams filed a motion to dismiss the pandering charge on the grounds that the pandering provision of the PROTECT Act was constitutionally overbroad vague and undermined the previous *Free Speech Coalition* decision in that simply stating he was in possession of child pornography to the agent was not the same as actual possession. The U.S. Supreme Court ultimately ruled that offers to provide, promote, or distribute child pornography are *not* protected by the First Amendment, even when the accused is not actually in possession of such materials.

CHILD PORNOGRAPHY OFFENDERS

In the preceding chapters, we have considered individuals who commit certain types of sex crimes and several theoretical explanations for why they occur. As Chapters 3 and 4 have indicated, people who commit sex crimes are sometimes organized by ***typologies***. Whereas typologies have the advantage of allowing us to categorize those who commit sex crimes with similar traits and characteristics, we must also recognize that the categories are not mutually exclusive (i.e., not every offender fits in a typology category, and some offenders may fit in more than one category).

Although several offender typologies exist for rape and child sexual abuse, as discussed in Chapters 3 and 4, fewer exist for child pornography. A major reason for this has to do with an ongoing debate as to whether perpetrators of child pornography crimes constitute a distinct, separate type of offender. In other words, are child pornography offenders the same as other sex offenders (e.g., rapists and child sexual abusers)? Given that the crime of child pornography (as defined today) does not necessarily require direct contact with a victim, questions have arisen as to whether perpetrators of child pornography crimes are a distinct type of sex offender or if they are "typical" sex offenders who simply use technology to execute their crimes.

In a comparison of a group of child pornography offenders to a group of child sexual abusers, Webb et al. (2007) examined psychometric measures to determine risk and personality traits. The results were largely similar for the two groups. Both were similar in terms of ethnicity, child abuse history, education, history of self-harm, and marital status. Child pornography offenders were more likely than child sexual abusers to have previous convictions for a sex crime. Both groups scored similarly on both the Risk Matrix 2000/S and the Stable 2000 (instruments for assessing risk among sex offenders—discussed further in Chapter 10).

Relative to child sexual abusers, child pornography offenders were younger, more likely to have had contact with mental health providers/services during adulthood, and less likely to have healthy intimate relationships, and they had fewer problems with substance abuse (Webb et al., 2007). Child pornographers were also more likely than child sex abusers to complete treatment. Table 5.3 summarizes the differences between child pornographers and child sexual abusers. Although perpetrators of child pornography crimes do share some characteristics with perpetrators of other types of sex crimes, there are important differences.

TABLE 5.3 Differences between Child Pornographers and Child Sexual Abusers

Child Pornographers	Child Sexual Abusers
Offenses more indicative of pedophilia compared to those of child sexual abusers	Offenses less indicative of pedophilia than those of child pornographers
More likely to succeed in treatment	Less likely to succeed in treatment
Less likely to have intimate relationships	More likely to maintain healthy, age-appropriate relationships
Fewer substance abuse problems compared to child sexual abusers	Greater substance abuse problems compared to child pornography users
Greater reported psychological and mental health problems	Fewer reported psychological and mental health problems

Individuals who commit crimes of child pornography can be separated into four categories (Krone, 2004; Lanning, 2001):

1. Those who access child pornography to satisfy curiosity or impulse, without a particular sexual interest in children
2. Those who access child pornography to satisfy sexual fantasies involving children but do not commit actual contact offenses
3. Those who utilize the internet to execute contact sex crimes
4. Those who create and distribute child pornography solely for the purpose of financial gain

In the following sections, we further explore heterogeneity in this population, focusing on these four categories. Although these categories do not constitute a typology, they incorporate categorizations from empirically-validated typologies. Krone's (2004) research of child pornography offenders in Australia yielded a typology comprising nine categories with different degrees of child pornography utility, offending severity, and networking frequency. This typology is presented in Table 5.4.

Impulsive Child Pornography Offenders

Some individuals who access and/or consume child pornography do it to satisfy curiosity or impulse rather than acting from sexual desire or sexual fantasies about children. These offenders are not sexually preoccupied with children, and they do not commit contact offenses against children. These offenders generally act out of impulsivity and carry out this behavior sporadically, sometimes as part of a broader interest in pornography (Elliott & Beech, 2009). According to Krone's typology, browsers may fit this category of child pornography offenders. Browsers access child pornography unintentionally (e.g., receiving a spam email containing a link to child pornography) but knowingly save and keep the material. Research has shown that some child pornography offenders fit this description. For example, one study reported that a sizeable percentage of child pornography offenders scored highly on psychological measures of impulsivity, suggesting that they tended

TABLE 5.4 Krone's (2004) Typology of Child Pornography Offending Behavior

Involvement Type	Features	Networking Level	Nature of Abuse
Browser	Response to spam, accidental hit on suspect site—material knowingly saved	None	Indirect
Private Fantasy	Conscious creation of online text or digital images for private use	None	Indirect
Trawler	Actively seeking child pornography using openly available browsers	Low	Indirect
Nonsecure Collector	Actively seeking material often through P2P networks	High	Indirect
Secure Collector	Actively seeking material but only through secure networks	High	Indirect
Groomer	Cultivating an online relationship with one or more children; pornography may be used to facilitate abuse	Varies—online contact with individual children	Direct
Physical Abuser	Abusing a child who may have been introduced to the offender online; pornography may be used to facilitate abuse	Varies—physical contact with individual children	Direct
Producer	Records own abuse or that of others (or induces children to submit images of themselves)	Varies—may depend on whether individual becomes distributor	Direct
Distributor	May distribute at any one of the above levels	Varies	Indirect

Source: Krone (2004).

to act without thinking and had a lack of regard for future consequences for their crimes (Middleton et al., 2006).

One of the features of the internet is the perceived ease and anonymity with which one can navigate within and across different forums. Some researchers have observed that the perceived anonymity and the playful nature of the online environment can have a powerful disinhibiting effect on some users, and this diminished impulse control has been found to be a factor in problematic use of the internet, including child pornography use (Danet, 1998).

Fulfilling a Sexual Fantasy: The Linkage between Child Pornography Use and Pedophilia

Consumers of child pornography may also be motivated by sexual desires or sexual fantasies involving children. Offender types from Krone's typology fitting this category of child pornography offenders may include private fantasy collectors, nonsecure collectors, and secure collectors. These categories include offenders who may hold sexual interests and attraction to children as well as offenders who engage in high levels of networking (potentially with other like-minded offenders). A common societal reaction to individuals who commit a crime involving child pornography is to label them as a *pedophile*. Recall from Chapter 4 that to be diagnosed as a pedophile, one must meet the diagnostic criteria of pedophilia established by the American Psychiatric Association. To review, to meet the diagnostic criteria of pedophilia, a person must demonstrate the following as specified in the ***Diagnostic and Statistical Manual of Mental Disorders, 5th ed. (DSM-V)*** (American Psychiatric Association, 2013):

- Over a period of at least six months, the person has experienced recurrent, intense sexually arousing fantasies, sexual urges, or behaviors involving sexual activity with a prepubescent child or children (generally age 13 years or younger).
- The person has acted on these sexual urges or the sexual urges, or fantasies caused marked distress or interpersonal difficulty.
- The person is at least 16 years of age and at least five years older than the child or children.

Given this clinical definition, it is still difficult to determine: (1) whether child pornography offenders are also pedophiles and (2) whether child pornography serves to fuel the sexual appetites and desires of these offenders. The vast majority of research on this has indicated that the use of child pornography *in some cases* is a predictor of pedophilia. Riegel (2004) found that 95% of 290 self-identified pedophiles acknowledged using child pornography at some point in their lives, whereas 59% acknowledged using it frequently. In this sample, respondents commonly stated that viewing prepubescent erotica was a useful substitute for actual sexual contact with young boys. Furthermore, recent analyses of actively traded child pornography images involving identified victims indicate that the most common image traded is that of pubescent girls (Seto et al., 2018).

Research has found that viewing child pornography is a better predictor of pedophilia than contact crimes against children because the majority of child pornography offenders demonstrated greater sexual arousal (measured by ***phallometric assessment***—a method of detecting arousal through the change in penile blood volume) in response to images of children compared to images of adults (Seto et al., 2006). In other words, those charged with child pornography offenses were more likely than those charged with sexual abuse or molestation of a child to manifest diagnostic criteria for pedophilia. Seto (2010) offered the following explanation, stating that "some non-pedophilic men commit sexual offenses against children, such as antisocial men who are willing to pursue sexual gratification with girls who show some signs of sexual development but are below the legal age of consent" (p. 592).

Blanchard (2010) recommended that, for diagnostic purposes, digitally engineered, fictitious images of children should be treated the same as real photographs. The rationale is that the sexual arousal experienced by the individual does not discriminate between real and fictitious images. In addition to digitally enhanced or photoshopped sexualized images of children, anime, or Manga cartoon images, therefore, may also serve as relevant indicators of pedophilic interests. Recall that the provisions of the PROTECT Act criminalize this material today.

Although research has established an association between viewing child pornography and a pedophilic diagnosis, this does *not* establish a causal link that the use of such images causes child sexual abuse. As discussed in Chapter 4, not all pedophiles engage in child sexual abuse. Likewise, it is important to exercise caution in equating child pornography offenders with pedophiles. Howitt's (1995) study of pedophiles concluded that they usually construct erotic fantasies *not* through the use of perverse, sexual material but rather through innocuous, non-sexualized images of children such as images from television advertisements, children's clothing catalogs, and even photographs of children at Disneyland. The law, however, obviously does not restrict the availability of these types of materials. This indeed creates a quandary for authorities who attempt to rid communities of child pornography because this material is certainly not the sole source of sexual incitement for offenders targeting children. Individuals wishing to view child pornography may never come in contact with or offend against a living child, whereas active pedophiles who regularly abuse children may be content to view legal and commercially available images of children to incorporate into their fantasies (Miller, 2013).

In summary, the risk of actual offending posed by those in possession of child pornography is largely unknown. It is hypothesized, however, that child pornography offenders with a greater number of collected images, a higher ratio of child to adult images, images depicting younger children, and images including both male and female children are more likely to be at risk for eventually seeking live sexual contact with children (Seto, 2010).

Using Child Pornography to Commit Contact Child Sexual Abuse Crimes

The third grouping of child pornography offenders comprises individuals who concurrently access child pornography and sexually abuse children. Krone's typology, for example, notes the existence of groomers and physical abusers, both of whom inflict abuse on child victims. Online groomers expose their victims to child pornography to desensitize them and lower sexual inhibitions. Physical abusers initiate sex acts with children found online (e.g., chatrooms and social media websites) and may record their encounters with children for personal use after the crime has been committed. A content analysis of newspaper stories revealed there might exist a group of internet offenders, termed **combination trader–travelers**, who trade child pornography as well as travel across state and/or national boundaries to sexually abuse or molest children (Alexy et al., 2005). Examples of such offenders in this study included the following:

- An assistant principal was charged with having sex with a 15-year-old girl with whom he communicated in an internet chatroom; the man also admitted to downloading and distributing child pornography over the internet
- A homeless offender who maintained a child pornography website in a public library; when arrested, it was discovered that the man had been carrying condoms and KY Jelly for an impending sexual encounter with children
- A Scottish university lecturer who sent child pornography, lewd photographs of himself, and traveled to the United States to have sex with a boy he met on the internet (Alexy et al., 2005)

Wolak et al. (2011) also reported the existence of **dual offenders** who committed child pornography and child sexual abuse concurrently. This study found that dual offenders were more likely to live with children under age 18, to have access to children under age 18 through their employment, to have problems with drugs or alcohol, and to have prior arrests for sex crimes against children.

As emphasized throughout this textbook, one of the most problematic issues in sex-crimes research is that the vast majority of studies are limited to official data and reports, capturing only offenders who have been apprehended for their crimes. Largely absent from this research are self-reported data, which include information about crimes, not only those known to formal criminal justice authorities. Bourke and Hernandez (2009) addressed this gap by comparing two groups of child pornography offenders in a voluntary prison treatment program. One group's reported sex-offense history was limited to possession, receipt, and/or distribution of child pornography, whereas the other group, in addition to having similar child pornography criminal histories, also had a history of hands-on crimes. Offenders' self-reported sex-crime histories were assessed at two time points—before and after the completion of an 18-month intensive treatment program. By the end of treatment, 91 of the "Internet-only" offenders admitted to abusing an average of 8.7 child victims, including both pre-and post-pubescent children. This large number of contact sex crimes self-reported by child pornography offenders challenges the notion of the impulsive child pornography offender (someone who consumes out of curiosity or impulsively without a sexual interest in children). This study also demonstrates that child pornographers, like all sex offenders, do not "fit neatly" into the categories discussed in this chapter.

In addition to child pornography offenders who simultaneously commit child sexual abuse, there is also evidence that child pornography use may predict future sexual offending. One of the first studies examining recidivism of child pornography offenders was conducted by Seto and Eke (2005), who examined 201 adult male convicted child pornography offenders. Following release from prison, 17% reoffended *in some* way, and 4% committed a new *contact sexual offense* within 2.5 years. This study was replicated in 2011 to include a larger sample and a lengthier follow-up period (Eke et al., 2011). In this study, 541 child pornography offenders were assessed over a 4.1-year period. The results from this study showed an alarming divergence from the previous study: 32% offended again *in some way*, 4% committed a new *contact sexual offense*, and 7% were charged with a new *child pornography offense* within an average of 4.1 years following release into the community. The results of this study illustrate the importance of longer follow-up periods as well as large samples. They also shed light on important risk factors for recidivism (i.e., criminal history and younger offender age). Other important risk factors for recidivism among child pornographers are lower education, being single, consuming nonInternet child pornography, prior sex-offender treatment, and possessing collections of pornography involving prepubescent children (Faust et al., 2014). Other research suggests, however, that although online offenders may display greater sexual deviancy, they may also exhibit certain psychological characteristics that buffer against sexual recidivism, including greater victim empathy, less emotional identification with children, and fewer cognitive distortions.

Generally speaking, sex offenders rarely reoffend by committing another sex offense. In the majority of cases, those who reoffend commit a wide range of offenses, from writing bad checks to motor vehicle theft to felony homicide. The research on child pornography offenders, specifically, suggests similar reoffending patterns.

Beyond Possession of Child Pornography: Producers, Distributors, and Profiteers

Most of the discussion up to this point has focused on consumers of child pornography. Attention, however, must also be given to the child pornographers who produce and distribute it. This is the final group of child pornographers discussed in this chapter. Krone's typology identifies two examples of offenders in this category: producers and distributors. Research on this final category of offenders is extremely limited due to small sample sizes and challenges accessing this population. Producers of child pornography are involved with the recruitment/solicitation of child victims and the filming and/or photography of sexually explicit material. Research has shown that producers are often members of victims' immediate families or social or educational circles (Estes & Weiner, 2001; Sher, 2007). Distributors are generally not involved with the production of child pornography; rather, their primary role is distributing it across networks of consumers. Both producers and distributors are motivated by profit (hence the term *profiteers*) and do not necessarily have a sexual interest in children, although some studies have found that in some rare instances, profiteers may also consume child pornography (Mitchell & Jones, 2013). Research also shows other distinct differences between producers/distributors and possessors of child pornography. For example, one study showed that producers/distributors are more likely to have drug and alcohol problems, as well as a previous history of violence, compared to possessors of child pornography (Clevenger et al., 2016). Producers/distributors are also more likely to live with a minor child compared to possessors.

CRIMINAL JUSTICE RESPONSES TO CHILD PORNOGRAPHY CRIMES

Over the past 20 years, as awareness and reporting of child pornography crimes have increased, law enforcement agencies and courts have been tasked with identifying, investigating, and prosecuting individuals involved in the child pornography industry—from producers and distributors to collectors and consumers. Criminal justice officials have been forced to adapt to technological innovations that afford offenders greater, easier, faster, and more secretive access to child pornography. As offenders become more tech savvy, law enforcement agencies must continuously fine-tune their investigative practices and procedures. As well, courts must engage in an ongoing review process to ensure the constitutionality of their procedures of search and seizure of evidence, standards of proof, and sentencing of offenders. In this section, we examine the investigation, prosecution, and sentencing of child pornographers more closely.

Investigating Child Pornography

Prior to the advent of the internet, police authorities were able to investigate child pornography crimes similar to the investigation for other types of crime. Traditional search and seizure, sting operations, and child pornography busts were typical methods for managing this type of crime. U.S. Customs special agents were able to seize books and magazines with pornographic child images and prevent them from entering the country via U.S. mail and commercial parcel services. Police even were able to infiltrate offender networks using computers and modems to communicate and exchange information about victims. By the early 1990s, the threat of child pornography was believed to have been successfully contained. As we have learned, the internet has facilitated the return and exponential expansion of child pornography.

Child pornography is now a largely digital and virtual industry both nationally and internationally. Offenders are no longer collecting and transmitting photographs, videotapes, and magazines but rather sending virtual images through complex peer-to-peer (P2P) networks. This crime now falls almost exclusively into the realm of *cybercrime*. The rapid evolution of child pornography crimes has required police to become more technologically savvy and adaptive. Policing child pornography is difficult for three primary reasons: (1) the sheer volume of available illegal material is so vast that it is nearly impossible to determine the full extent of the problem; (2) the lack of reporting limits the number of leads and clues available to initiate an investigation, requiring almost exclusively proactive measures; and (3) the advanced technological expertise necessary to target these crimes usually comes at a high price that is not within the limited resources of many police agencies. It has been found that setting up specialized task forces in police departments is crucial for targeting child pornography crimes (Marcum et al., 2011).

Computer forensics, which involves the assessment of computers and computer-related media for evidence of crimes, has become necessary for detecting child pornography crimes. This is a complex and technical process, so we cover only a brief overview of the procedures employed in criminal investigations of child pornography crimes. Computer-forensic examinations involve three basic steps (Figure 5.2):

1 Acquisition: Investigators must acquire electronic information on a computer or computer media and make an exact physical copy (or "mirror image") of all data on the hard drive to preserve the data exactly as it existed at the time of seizure.

2 Authentication: Investigators must ensure that the mirrored image and the original computer media are identical. This is often accomplished using complex forensics software programs that can verify the precision of the mirrored content.

3 Recovery: Investigators view and analyze the acquired data in addition to hidden files with renamed file extensions, deleted files, and temporary internet files from the computer's cache. Additionally, investigators learn extensive information about a suspect's browsing history, including particular websites visited, the duration of those visits, and any downloading activity.

Prosecuting Child Pornography

The child pornography prosecution rate has increased in recent years, likely as a result of advanced law enforcement detection methods that have brought a greater number of offenders under criminal justice investigation. Charging decisions vary from case to case, and prosecutors often use a mix of complex strategies to try a case. Some prosecutors, for example, may charge one count per image (i.e., if a defendant is caught with 10 illegal images, the prosecutor charges the defendant with 10 counts of child pornography). Other prosecutors have described a saturation point at which there is no reason to go beyond a certain number of images, whereas others have lumped images into categories based on image severity or access date. Some prosecutors base charges not on the number of images but on the number of devices containing illegal images (computer, cell phone, flash drive, and CD-ROM), whereas others charge only for images with an identified victim. Needless to say, there is no single way to prosecute child pornography crimes.

Prosecuting child pornography crimes can be difficult, especially with respect to establishing *mens rea*. It is the duty of the prosecutor to prove that the defendant in question *knowingly* possessed the illegal images. The results of the National Juvenile Online Victimization (N-JOV) Prosecutor Study indicate that a number of defenses are encountered by prosecutors of child pornography (Walsh et al., 2013). Most of these defenses align with

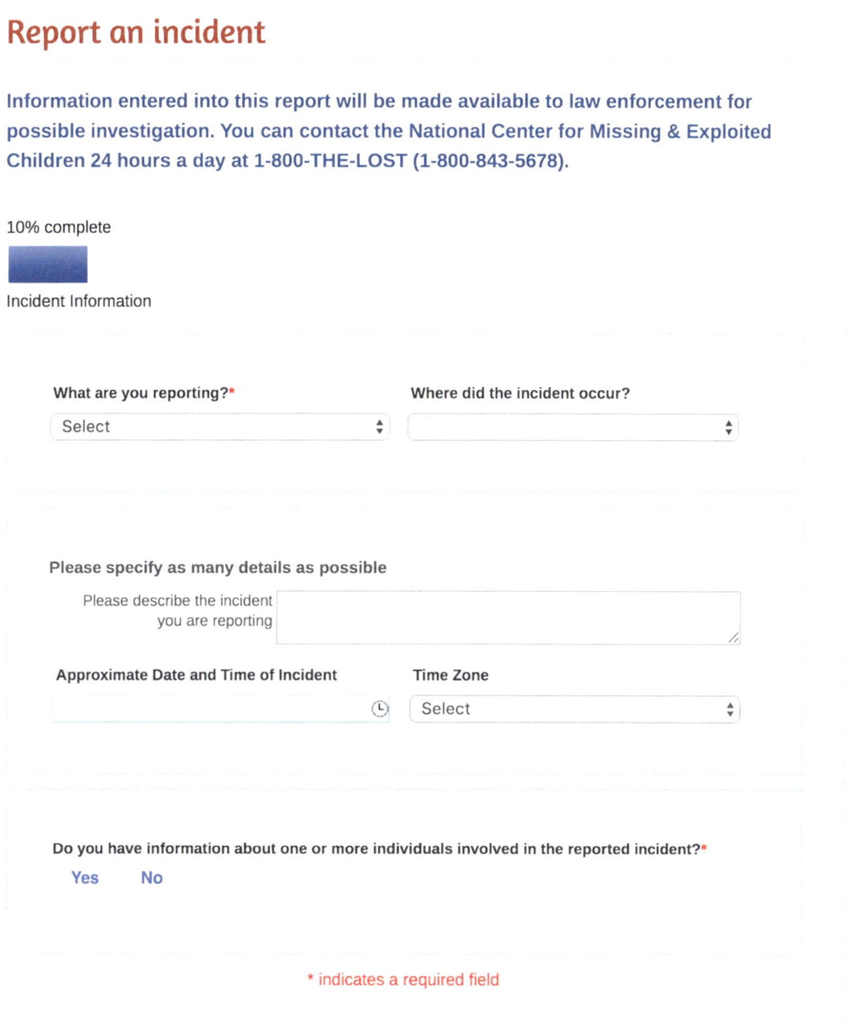

Report an incident

Information entered into this report will be made available to law enforcement for possible investigation. You can contact the National Center for Missing & Exploited Children 24 hours a day at 1-800-THE-LOST (1-800-843-5678).

10% complete

Incident Information

What are you reporting?*

Select

Where did the incident occur?

Please specify as many details as possible

Please describe the incident you are reporting

Approximate Date and Time of Incident

Time Zone

Select

Do you have information about one or more individuals involved in the reported incident?*

Yes No

* indicates a required field

FIGURE 5.2 How to Report Suspected Child Pornography.

Source: Image from National Center for Missing & Exploited Children (2021).

Sykes and Matza's (1957) ***techniques of neutralization***. These defenses (or neutralizations) include the following:

- Unknowing or unintentional download of illegal images
- Someone else with physical access to the defendant's computer who downloaded the illegal images
- Addiction or mental illness
- Downloaded images not construed as child pornography in the eyes of the defendant
- Downloaded images used for research purposes

One way federal and state statutes have construed the knowing possession of child pornography has to do with images found on a defendant's computer cache. A cache is a storage mechanism designed to speed up the loading of internet displays, including pictures and movies. When a person views a web page, the web browser saves a copy of the page in a folder on the computer's hard drive. This folder is known as the cache. The majority of courts take the position that the images or movies on a hard drive are sufficient evidence to demonstrate possession of child pornography.

In the landmark case *United States v. Tucker* (2002), forensic examiners discovered child pornography located on the defendant's browser cache, recycle bin, and C drive. The defendant argued he did not knowingly possess child pornography given that he did not actually download or copy any material and he deleted the content off his computer's cache. Nevertheless, the court rejected Tucker's defense on the basis that he was able to control the viewed images in many ways (e.g., he could enlarge or "zoom in" on particular images, print them, or copy them to other directories). The court affirmed that the mere act of deleting one's cache is evidence enough of possession because one cannot destroy what one does not possess and control.

Prosecutors also face challenges with regard to evidence from police investigations, particularly with computer forensics. In the N-JOV Prosecutor Study, 62% of polled prosecutors noted the following difficulties with computer forensics in child pornography cases:

- Timeliness of the forensics examination: This concerns the amount of time it takes for forensic investigators to provide computer-related evidence that is reliable and comprehensive. The amount of digital evidence submitted for analysis varies from one request to another. One investigation may result in the seizure of a single computer, whereas another may involve multiple computers. As such, cases are often backlogged.
- Chain-of-custody issues: In some instances there are charges of evidence tampering during transportation of evidence among multiple parties.
- Peer-to-peer (P2P) investigations issues: P2P networks have become a common medium for the transfer and sharing of child pornography. Given that these networks do not operate on a centralized server, no one person is responsible for the content of what is shared on them. This creates technical and legal difficulties for prosecutors, especially when deciding whether to try a defendant for dissemination/sharing of child pornography and not only mere possession.
- Credentials of the forensic examiner or the forensic laboratory: Defense attorneys can question the credentials and qualifications of forensic investigators. In some cases, forensic investigators have been found to falsify their certifications, résumés, and professional references.

Penalties and Sentencing for Child Pornographers

Child pornography images are not protected under the First Amendment and are, therefore, considered illegal contraband under federal law. The vast majority of child pornography offenses are committed using the internet to view or transmit images. For these reasons, federal jurisdiction almost always applies to child pornography. Violations of federal child pornography laws are considered serious crimes, and convicted offenders face severe punishments. These punishments are largely dictated by the **Federal Sentencing Guidelines**, which determine sentences based on two factors: (1) the seriousness of the offense and (2) the defendant's criminal history. Depending on the seriousness of the offense and the prior criminal history of the offender, these guidelines specify a sentencing range within which the court may sentence the defendant.

From the inception of the sentencing guidelines in 1987 until now, there have been significant revisions to make the penalties substantially more severe. Prior to 1990, simple child pornography possession was not a federal crime. When Congress criminalized possession of child pornography and possession with intent to sell child pornography, the guidelines were amended to impose harsher punishments. After the PROTECT Act was signed into effect, Congress directed the U.S. Sentencing Commission (USSC) to reduce the frequency of ***downward departures*** (sentences issued by judges, which are less severe than the recommended sentence under Federal Sentencing Guidelines) as well as add enhancements for crimes with aggravated situations such as (a) the images are violent, sadistic, or masochistic in nature; (b) the minor was sexually abused; or (c) the offender has prior convictions for child sexual exploitation. There was a significant impact on punishments for offenders convicted of child pornography. From 1997 to 2007, the mean imprisonment sentence of child pornographers increased from 20.6 months to 91.3 months. The sentencing guidelines currently adhere to the following principles:

1. Harsher punishment for trafficking (distribution, receipt, and production) than for mere possession
2. Harsher punishments if the material involves prepubescent children or sadomasochistic/violent material
3. Harsher punishments if the material was distributed for financial gain
4. Harsher punishments for sending the material to minors or using the material to entice minors into sexual activity
5. Harsher punishments for the use of a computer for activity
6. Harsher punishments for large numbers of images
7. Minimum sentence of 20 years to maximum sentence of life imprisonment for exploitation of an actual child

The USSC received reports of 1,414 cases involving child pornography in 2018 (USSC, 2018a), and 99.1% of offenders in these cases were sentenced to prison. Offenders convicted of trafficking received lengthier sentences on average (136 months) compared to offenders convicted of possession (70 months). Offenders convicted of production received the lengthiest average sentences (262 months). Compared to other sexual offenses reported to the USSC in 2018, child pornography offenses carried a higher sentence than statutory rape (average sentence of 30 months) and abusive sexual contact (average sentence of 27 months) but a lower average sentence compared to rape, which carried a longer average sentence of 178 months (USSC, 2018b). Much controversy surrounds the sentencing of child pornographers. In a survey of federal trial court judges, 70% deemed the guidelines as "too high" as they applied to those in possession of child pornography (USSC, 2010). The Second Circuit Court noted that the guidelines do not do a good job of distinguishing between commercial distributors of child pornography and those merely in possession. As Steiker (2013, p. 42) has shown:

> The guidelines for child pornography are so high that they treat an offender who never had any contact with a child more severely than the Guideline sentences for repeated sex with a child or for aggravated assault with a firearm that results in bodily injury.

As a result, many judges have not adhered to these in sentencing child pornographers. In 2018, 37.2% of child pornography offenders were sentenced under the Sentencing

Guidelines Manual; the remaining 61.2% received a below-range sentencing variance with an average sentencing reduction of 40.1% (USSC, 2018a).

SEX TRAFFICKING

Sex trafficking, often referred to as a form of modern slavery, involves someone who "used force, fraud or coercion" to force a child or adult into "a commercial sex act" (Shared Hope International, 2021). The commercial sex act may include pornography, prostitution, or exchanging a sexual act for money, items of value, drugs, shelter, food, or clothes. Despite the "trafficking" part of the term, victims do not have to be transported to meet the definition of a sex-trafficked person. Some organizations, therefore, refer to it as commercial sexual exploitation (CSE) (Bartol & Bartol, 2021). A pimp or trafficker receives most or all of the money received from the victim's exploitation. The victim is usually isolated, provided with drugs and alcohol, and "broken in" by the pimp or trafficker to ensure compliance and dependency. Young girls and women are the most common victims of sex trafficking, but boys and men can also be targeted.

The number of sex-trafficked individuals is the United States is virtually impossible to estimate for multiple reasons. Few recognize the signs of sex trafficking, and therefore, victims become invisible. Many victims of sex trafficking are viewed as criminals themselves and arrested for prostitution or drug-related offenses. There is virtually no central database for collecting reliable numbers of sex trafficking victims or incidents (Bartol & Bartol, 2021; Franchino-Olsen, 2021). Sex trafficking is a global problem and in many instances involves transporting victims from one country to another.

According to the National Human Trafficking Hotline (n.d.), which is considered one of the more extensive sources of human and sex trafficking information in existence, there were 8,248 cases of sex trafficking reported in 2019 through their tip line. The number of sex trafficking reports increases each year. According to a Bureau of Justice Statistics (BJS, 2021) report, 2,065 cases of sex trafficking and 1,016 cases of child sex trafficking were opened for investigation between 2008 and 2010 (Banks & Kyckelhahn, 2011). This number is likely far less than the number of suspected cases, indicating many reported cases do not result in an investigation.

Sex Trafficking Laws

Sex trafficking is defined specifically as exploiting a person for commercial sex. The Trafficking Victims Protection Act (2000), a federal law, defines sex trafficking as part of human trafficking. Human trafficking includes the following:

a   Sex trafficking in which a commercial sex act is induced by force, fraud, or coercion, or in which the person induced to perform such act has not attained 18 years of age; or
b   The recruitment, harboring, transportation, provision, or obtaining of a person for labor or services, through the use of force, fraud, or coercion for the purpose of subjection to involuntary servitude, peonage, debt bondage, or slavery. (22 U.S.C. § 7102[9])

The laws regarding human trafficking are specifically derived from the 13th Amendment of the U.S. Constitution, which forbids slavery and involuntary servitude (United States Department of Justice, 2017). The 13th Amendment was passed in 1865. Since this time, laws more specific to human trafficking and sex trafficking have been created and passed. These laws, however, only came into existence in the past two decades. As noted in Figure 5.3, a

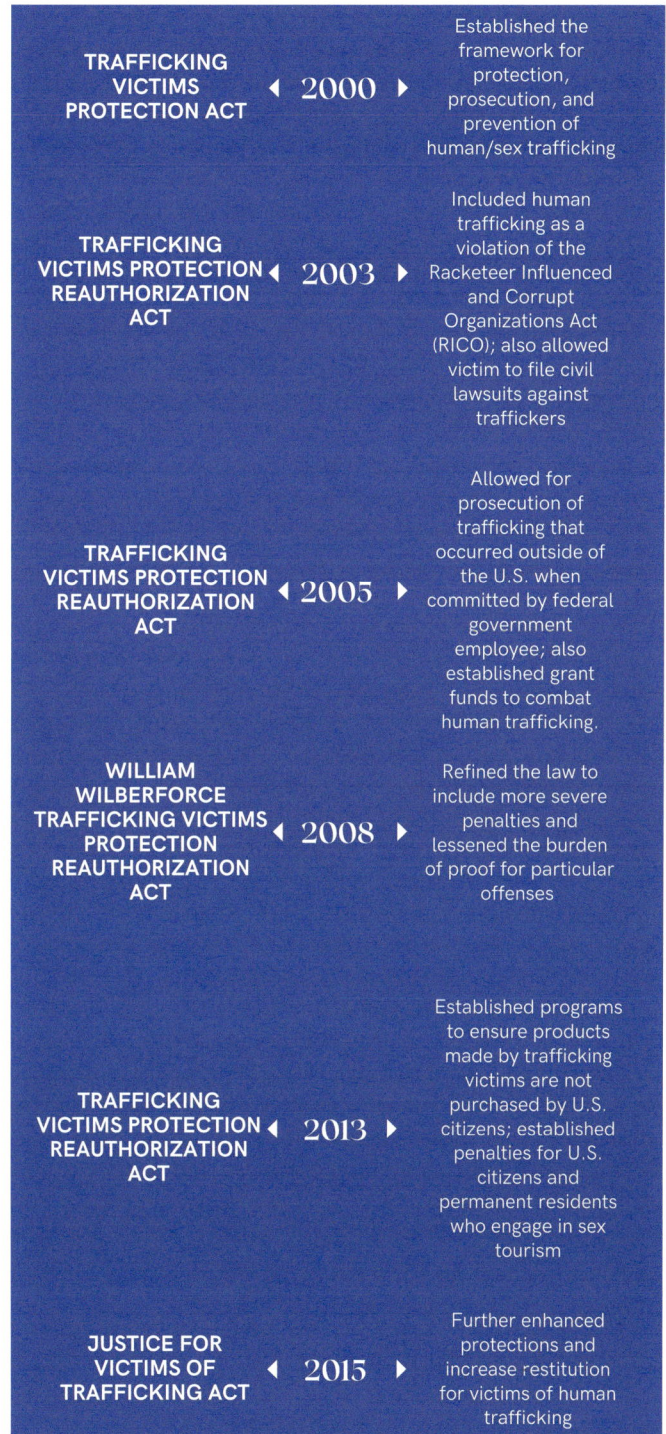

FIGURE 5.3 Timeline of Sex Trafficking Laws in the United States.

timeline shows how these laws have been refined over time to establish targeted approaches to specific issues associated with sex trafficking. For example, U.S. citizens and those with permanent resident status can now be prosecuted for receiving sex from a victim of sex trafficking while they are overseas. This is unique and nuanced in the sense that most U.S. laws focus only on crimes that occur within the U.S. jurisdiction, not in foreign countries. Individual states, in addition to the federal government, have also passed laws against human and sex trafficking, allotting more resources to identifying, investigating, and prosecuting human and sex trafficking cases (BJS, 2021). Between 2015 and 2019, about 500 cases of sex trafficking each year were reported each year among the 46 states that submitted reports (BJS, 2021).

How Sex Trafficking Occurs

A common myth regarding sex trafficking is that it can only happen to women from economically depressed countries. Despite the lack of systematic detection and reporting of sex trafficking incidents, individual research efforts have provided substantial knowledge about how the sex trafficking industry operates, thus defying this myth. This includes information on how recruiters, traffickers, and pimps recruit and traffic the victims, initiate relationships with the victims, and maintain control of the victims.

The victims of sex traffickers include both international and domestic women, men, and children (Raymond et al., 2001). Those who are younger (i.e., younger than 25) are more likely to be trafficked than those who are older. Those who are economically disadvantaged, lack an income, and reside in poverty are more at risk than those who are economically stable. Those who live in economically disadvantaged counties are particularly at risk. In many economically developing countries, girls/women are seen as a liability, and their brothers, fathers, or other male relatives may coerce them or sell them into the sex industry.

Sex trafficking is tied closely to organized businesses such as bars, clubs, brothels, escort services, and the military. Military men who serve overseas will often marry a woman from Korea, Vietnam, Japan, and other countries. After returning to the United States, they will force their wives into prostitution as a source of income. Recruiters, traffickers, and pimps are associated with organized crime networks such as biker gangs and the mafia. Sex trafficking, therefore, often occurs in connection with other criminal activity such as fraud (perhaps creating fraudulent paperwork for international victims), extortion, migrant smuggling, theft, money laundering, and other similar crimes. Such criminal organizations range from small (a few people) to large (more than 50 people). Among the international victims of sex trafficking, boyfriends and husbands typically act as the pimp and initiate the relationship under the guise of a true romantic interest (Raymond et al., 2001).

Recruitment methods are varied, but a common thread in many cases is the promise of security, protection, affection, shelter, economic stability, and a better life (Raymond et al., 2001; SHI, 2021). Victims can be recruited at nightclubs, malls, and other legitimate businesses; they can also be recruited through newspaper ads or the internet. The recruitment method may begin as a promising romantic relationship, even marriage. It can also begin as a financial arrangement such as promising a better job.

Following recruitment, the victim is usually isolated, physically and/or psychologically abused, and forced to participate in sexual activities with others. Victims of sex trafficking are typically exposed to constant and severe abuse as a means of controlling them. Typically, victims are denied any ability to communicate with others, or travel alone, or be without a pimp. They are threatened and intimidated. Often their handler (i.e., trafficker or pimp) will provide them with drugs and alcohol to enforce compliance and ensure dependency on them for more drugs and alcohol. Exposure to physical violence can occur daily along with verbal threats and psychological abuse. Many victims are told they owe a debt to their husband, boyfriend, or a person who agreed to marry them and that they must earn enough money through commercial prostitution to pay that debt, which in reality, is never paid off.

Victims of Sex Trafficking

Victims of sex trafficking experience a multitude of negative consequences that are common among other sexual abuse victims (discussed further in Chapter 8). This includes depression,

---

Focus Box 5.2 Samantha's Story: A Victim of Sex Trafficking

In this testimony, a woman named Samantha (a pseudonym) reports her experience with sex trafficking. As Samantha tells her story, she discusses how she consciously separated herself from the "work" she was doing. She also refers to herself as "you" throughout the story (e.g. "you are doing it because they love you"). Samantha was a high-risk victim with a history of frequently running away as a teenager. Her trafficker pursued her as any other boyfriend–girlfriend relationship. Later, he forced her to engage in prostitution. One of his methods of controlling her was through the use of drugs (heroin) and not allowing her to sleep more than four hours a night.

> [The trafficker] will sweet talk you. . . . They'll make you think that . . . you are doing it because they love you. . . . "If you love me, you'll go sell your body for me," and then they take all your money. They are supposed to take care of you. . . . It's all a form of control. When I first started working, I would have breakdowns in the middle of the session. I couldn't do it till I finally just separated me and who I am when I am working. Otherwise, I'll go crazy of living. You'll numb your mind. The thing about heroin is . . . at a certain point you'll do whatever it takes to get it. You need it. They get you where you are dependent on them for it. . . . I remember one time I was outside smoking, and someone asked me to use my lighter, and [the trafficker] had somebody watching me. I got beat for that later. . . . I was not allowed to talk to anyone . . . and if you messed up in public, then you were gonna get beat as soon as you got back to the room. And he made sure nobody heard, turned up the TV and turn on the shower. And if you cried or screamed or anything, then he'd take you out of the room, and you never knew if death was gonna be an option.
>
> When [people] see an escort or prostitute, all they think is a drug-addicted whore that lives on the street. They don't think about the story behind it. They don't think, 'Is she being forced to do this? Does she have to do this? Is she getting beat if she doesn't do this?'

Note: Adapted from DeliverFund (2021)

132 Child Pornography and Sex Trafficking

higher rates of suicide, posttraumatic stress disorder, and high rates of physical health problems such as the contraction of sexually transmitted infections. Victims of sex trafficking become particularly distrustful of others, including law enforcement or those who work in social service agencies. They may fear retaliation, including death, if their trafficker finds out they are seeking help or working with law enforcement. Providing resources for victims is crucial because they typically lack a formal education or training to support themselves. They typically lack close friends who could provide support. This is a result of the isolation they are often kept in by their trafficker.

The U.S. government has developed public awareness efforts such as the Blue Campaign to prevent and address sex trafficking. This effort was led by the Department of Homeland Security and includes educating the public and law enforcement about indicators of human trafficking. One such effort is presented in the image below. It involved placing posters

PHOTO 5.1 Image of Posters Placed in Airports across the United States

Photo Credit: Donna M. Vandiver.

in areas where human and sex trafficking may occur such as airports. The image below appeared in a women's bathroom stall at the San Antonio airport.

CONCLUSION

Child pornography offenses are sex crimes that involve the visual depiction of children involved in a sexual act. Once on the brink of eradication, the advent of the internet signaled the return and proliferation of child pornography. Like other sex crimes, child pornography is a serious crime with the majority of cases going unreported and unknown to police authorities. The link between possession/consumption of child pornography and actual sexual abuse of children is certainly more suggestive than it is causal, with research showing conflicting evidence as to whether child pornography causes actual abuse against children. Because many child pornography crimes go undetected as a result of sophisticated technologies, it has become imperative for police to adopt advanced methods of cybercrime investigation, including computer forensics examinations. Sex trafficking is a type of sexual victimization that involves forced sexual exploitation that occurs in the United States and globally.

REVIEW POINTS

- There is a range of child pornography crimes, from production and filming to distribution and trafficking to downloads and personal possession.
- Child pornography, once on the brink of eradication, has emerged as one of the fastest-growing online enterprises with an estimated value exceeding $20 billion.
- Because child pornographers have relied on high technology, police, courts, and lawmakers have been required to adapt to apprehend offenders.
- Pedophiles use child pornography to satisfy sexual urges, but not all child pornographers are pedophiles by diagnostic measure. There is evidence that some pedophiles may prefer legal images of children to fuel sexual appetites.
- Similar to other sex offenders, child pornographers demonstrate a low rate of recidivism for the same crime.
- In the majority of cases, child pornography offenses are prosecuted as federal crimes with convicted offenders sentenced under the Federal Sentencing Guidelines.
- The true scope of sex trafficking is unknown, given that it is largely invisible and is misperceived as prostitution.
- Over the past two decades a substantial number of federal and state laws have been passed that has led to more dedicated resources to identifying, investigating, and prosecuting sex trafficking cases and providing victims with resources.
- Sex trafficking preys on vulnerable victims and exposes victims to substantial trauma that prohibits recovery.

REFERENCES

18 U.S.C. §1466A.
18 U.S.C. §2252.
18 U.S.C. §2256[8].
22 U.S.C. § 7102[9].
Ahlers, C. J., Schaefer, G. A., Mundt, I. A., Roll, S., Englert, H., Willich, S. N., & Beier, K. M. (2011). How unusual are the contents of paraphilias? Paraphilia-associated sexual arousal patterns in a community-based sample of men. *Journal of Sexual Medicine, 8*(5), 1362–1370. https://www.doi.org/10.1111/j.1743-6109.2009.01597.x
Akdeniz, Y. (2013). *Internet child pornography and the law: National and international responses*. Ashgate Publishing, Ltd.
Alexy, E. M., Burgess, A. W., & Baker, T. (2005). Internet offenders: Traders, travelers, and combination trader–travelers. *Journal of Interpersonal Violence, 20*(7), 804–812. https://www.doi.org/10.1177/0886260505276091
American Psychiatric Association. (2013). *Diagnostic and statistical manual of mental disorders* (5th ed.). Author.
Ayood, M. F. (1978). The littlest victims. *The Missouri Police Chief* (Winter), 19–22.
Banks, D., & Kyckelhahn, T. (2011). *Characteristics of suspected human trafficking incidents, 2008–2010*. U.S. Department of Justice, Bureau of Justice Statistics.
Bartol, C. R., & Bartol, A. M. (2021). *Criminal behavior: A psychological approach* (12th ed.). Routledge.
Bártová, K., Androvičová, R., Krejčová, L., Weiss, P., & Klapilová, K. (2021). The prevalence of paraphilic interests in the Czech population: Preference, arousal, the use of pornography, fantasy, and behavior. *The Journal of Sex Research, 58*(1), 86–96. https://www.doi.org/ 10.1080/00224499.2019.1707468
Blanchard, R. (2010). The DSM diagnostic criteria for pedophilia. *Archives of Sexual Behavior, 39*(2), 304–316. https://www.doi.org/10.1007/s10508-009-9536-0
Bourke, M. L., & Hernandez, A. E. (2009). The "Butner Study" redux: A report of the incidence of hands-on child victimization by child pornography offenders. *Journal of Family Violence, 24*(3), 183–191. https://www.doi.org/10.1007/s10896-008-9219-y
Brockman, J. (2006). Child sex as internet fare, through eyes of a victim. *The New York Times*. https://www.nytimes.com/2006/04/05/washington/child-sex-as-internet-fare-through-eyes-of-a-victim.html
Bureau of Justice Statistics (BJS). (2021). *Human trafficking data-collection activities: 2020*. U.S. Office of Justice Programs, Bureau of Justice Statistics. https://bjs.ojp.gov/content/pub/pdf/htdca20.pdf
Burke, D. D. (1997). Criminalization of virtual child pornography: A constitutional question. *The Harvard Journal on Legislation, 34*, 439–472.
Child Pornography Prevention Act of 1996 (CPPA), Pub. L. No. 104–208 (1996).
Clevenger, S. L., Navarro, J. N., & Jasinski, J. L. (2016). A matter of low self-control? Exploring differences between child pornography possessors and child pornography producers/distributers using self-control theory. *Sexual Abuse, 28*(6), 555–571. https://www.doi.org/10.1177/1079063214557173
Danet, B. (1998). Text as mask: Gender, play, and performance on the Internet. In S. G. Jones (Ed.), *Cybersociety 2.0: Revisiting computer-mediated communication and community* (pp. 129–158). Sage.
DeliverFund. (2021). Human trafficking stories. https://www.deliverfund.org/the-human-trafficking-problem-in-america/stories-from-survivors/

Diamond, M., Jozifkova, E., & Weiss, P. (2011). Pornography and sex crimes in the Czech Republic. *Archives of Sexual Behavior, 40*(5), 1037–1043. https://www.doi.org/10.1007/s10508-010-9696-y

Dombert, B., Schmidt, A. F., Banse, R., Briken, P., Hoyer, J., Neutze, J., & Osterheider, M. (2016). How common is men's self-reported sexual interest in prepubescent children? *Journal of Sex Research, 53*(2), 214–223. https//doi.org/10.1080/00224499.2015.1020108

Eke, A. W., Seto, M. C., & Williams, J. (2011). Examining the criminal history and future offending of child pornography offenders. *Law and Human Behavior, 35*(6), 466–478. https://www.doi.org/10.1007/s10979-010-9252-2

Elliott, I. A., & Beech, A. R. (2009). Understanding online child pornography use: Applying sexual offense theory to Internet offenders. *Aggression and Violent Behavior, 14*(3), 180–193. https://www.doi.org/10.1016/j.avb.2009.03.002

Estes, R. J., & Weiner, N. A. (2001). *The commercial sexual exploitation of children in the US, Canada and Mexico*. Center for the Study of Youth Policy.

Faust, E., Bickart, W., Renaud, C., & Camp, S. (2014). Child pornography possessors and child contact sex offenders: A multilevel comparison of demographic characteristics and rates of recidivism. *Sexual Abuse: A Journal of Research and Treatment*. https://www.doi.org/10.1177/1079063214521469

Franchino-Olsen, H. (2021). Vulnerabilities relevant for commercial sexual exploitation of children/domestic minor sex trafficking: A systematic review of risk factors. *Trauma, Violence, & Abuse, 22*(11), 99–111.

Groth, A. N., Burgess, A. W., Birnbaum, H. J., & Gary, T. S. (1978). A study of the child molester: Myths and realities. *Journal of the American Criminal Justice Association, 41*(1), 17–22.

Henkin, L. (1963). Morals and the constitution: The sin of obscenity. *Columbia Law Review, 63*(3), 391–414. https://www.doi.org/10.2307/1120595

Howitt, D. (1995). *Paedophiles and sexual offences against children*. Wiley.

International Centre for Missing & Exploited Children (ICMEC). (2008). Child pornography: Model legislation & global review. *International centre for missing & exploited children*. https://www.issuelab-dev.org/resources/3225/3225.pdf

Internet Watch Foundation (IWF). (2012). *Annual and charity report*. https://www.iwf.org.uk/sites/default/files/reports/2016-02/IWF%202012%20Annual%20and%20Charity%20Report%20%28web%29.pdf

Kaur, S., & Randhawa, S. (2020). Dark Web: A web of crimes. *Wireless Personal Communications, 112*(4), 2131–2158. https://www.doi.org/10.1007/s11277-020-07143-2

Krone, T. (2004). *A typology of online child pornography offending*. Australian Institute of Criminology. https://www.aic.gov.au/sites/default/files/2020-05/tandi279.pdf

Kutchinsky, B. (1991). Pornography and rape: Theory and practice? Evidence from crime data in four countries where pornography is easily available. *International Journal of Law and Psychiatry, 14*(1–2), 47–64. https://www.doi.org/10.1016/0160-2527(91)90024-H

Landripet, I., Stulhofer, A., & Diamond, M. (2006). *Assessing the influence of pornography on sexual violence: A cross-cultural perspective*. [Poster presentation]. International Academy of Sex Research, Amsterdam, The Netherlands.

Lanning, K. V. (2001). *Child molesters: A behavioral analysis*. National Center for Missing and Exploited Children.

Marcum, C. D., Higgins, G. E., Ricketts, M. L., & Freiburger, T. L. (2011). An assessment of the training and resources dedicated nationally to investigation of the production of child pornography. *Policing, 5*(1), 23–32. https://www.doi.org/10.1093/police/paq057

Middleton, D., Elliott, I. A., Mandeville-Norden, R., & Beech, A. R. (2006). An investigation into the applicability of the Ward and Siegert Pathways Model of child sexual abuse with Internet offenders. *Psychology, Crime & Law, 12*(6), 589–603. https://www.doi.org/10.1080/10683160600558352

Miller, L. (2013). Sexual offenses against children: Patterns and motives. *Aggression and Violent Behavior, 18*(5), 506–519. https://www.doi.org/10.1016/j.avb.2013.07.006

Mitchell, K. J., Finkelhor, D., Jones, L. M., & Wolak, J. (2012). Prevalence and characteristics of youth sexting: A national study. *Pediatrics, 129*(1), 13–20. https://www.doi.org/10.1542/peds.2011-1730

Mitchell, K. J., & Jones, L. M. (2013). *Internet-facilitated commercial sexual exploitation of children.* Crimes against Children Research Center, University of New Hampshire. https://scholars.unh.edu/cgi/viewcontent.cgi?article=1037&context=ccrc

National Center for Missing & Exploited Children. (2021). National Center for Missing & Exploited Children CybertipLine. https://www.missingkids.org/gethelpnow/cybertipline

National Human Trafficking Hotline. (n.d.). Hotline statistics. https://humantraffickinghotline.org/states

Ng, M. L., & Ma, J. L. C. (2001). Sexuality in Hong Kong special administrative region of the People's Republic of China. In B. Francoeur (Ed.), *The international encyclopedia of human sexuality* (Vol. 4, pp. 217–244). Continuum.

O'Brien, S. (1983). *Child pornography.* Kendall/Hunt Publishing Co.

Ost, S. (2002). Children at risk: Legal and societal perceptions of the potential threat that the possession of child pornography poses to society. *Journal of Law and Society, 29*(3), 436–460.

Ost, S. (2009). *Child pornography and sexual grooming: Legal and societal responses.* Cambridge University Press.

PROTECT Act of 2003 (Pub.L. 108–21, 117 Stat. 650, S. 151).

Raymond, J., Hughes, D., & Gomez, C. (2001). *Sex trafficking of women in the United States: Links between international and domestic sex industries.* Coalition against Trafficking in Women. www.catwinternational.org

Richards, D. A. (1974). Free speech and obscenity law: Toward a moral theory of the First Amendment. *University of Pennsylvania Law Review, 123*(1), 45–91. https://scholarship.law.upenn.edu/cgi/viewcontent.cgi?article=5284&context=penn_law_review

Riegel, D. L. (2004). Letter to the editor: Effects on boy-attracted pedosexual males of viewing boy erotica. *Archives of Sexual Behavior, 33*(4), 321–323. https://www.doi.org/10.1023/B:ASEB.0000029071.89455.53

Seto, M. C. (2010). Child pornography use and Internet solicitation in the diagnosis of pedophilia. *Archives of Sexual Behavior, 39*(3), 591–593. https://www.doi.org/10.1007/s10508-010-9603-6

Seto, M. C., Buckman, C., Dwyer, R. G., & Quayle, E. (2018). Production and active trading of child sexual exploitation images depicting identified victims. http://www.missingkids.org/content/dam/pdfs/ncmec-analysis/Production%20and%20Active%20Trading%20of%20CSAM_FullReport_FINAL.pdf

Seto, M. C., Cantor, J. M., & Blanchard, R. (2006). Child pornography offenses are a valid diagnostic indicator of pedophilia. *Journal of Abnormal Psychology, 115,* 610–615. https://www.doi.org/10.1037/0021-843X.115.3.610

Seto, M. C., & Eke, A. W. (2005). The criminal histories and later offending of child pornography offenders. *Sexual Abuse: A Journal of Research and Treatment, 17*(2), 201–210. https://www./doi.org/10.1007/s11194-005-4605-y

Shared Hope International (SHI). (2021). What is sex trafficking? https://sharedhope.org/the-problem/what-is-sex-trafficking/

Sher, J. (2007). *One child at a time*. Satin Publications Ltd.

Steel, C. M. (2009). Child pornography in peer-to-peer networks. *Child Abuse and Neglect, 33*(8), 560–568. https://www.doi.org/10.1016/j.chiabu.2008.12.011

Steiker, C. S. (2013). Lessons from two failures: Sentencing for cocaine and child pornography under the federal sentencing guidelines in the United States. *Law & Contemporary Problems, 76*, 27–52. https://scholarship.law.duke.edu/cgi/viewcontent.cgi?article=4345&context=lcp

Sykes, G. M., & Matza, D. (1957). Techniques of neutralization: A theory of delinquency. *American Sociological Review, 22*(6), 664–670. https://www.doi.org/10.2307/2089195

Taylor, M., Holland, G., & Quayle, E. (2001). Typology of pedophilic picture collections. *The Police Journal, 74*, 97–107. https://www./doi.org/10.1177/0032258X0107400202

Trafficking Victims Protection Act of 2000 (TVPA), Pub. L. No. 106–386.

United States Department of Justice (USDOJ). (2017). Human trafficking: Key legislation, https://www.justice.gov/humantrafficking/key-legislation

United States Sentencing Commission (USSC). (2018a). Quick facts child pornography offenders. https://www.ussc.gov/sites/default/files/pdf/research-and-publications/quick-facts/Child_Pornography_FY18.pdf

United States Sentencing Commission (USSC). (2018b). Quick facts sexual abuse offenders. https://www.ussc.gov/sites/default/files/pdf/research-and-publications/quick-facts/Sexual_Abuse_FY18.pdf

U.S. Sentencing Commission. (2010). Results of survey of United States district judges: January 2010 through March 2010. *Federal Sentencing Report, 23*, 296. https://www.ussc.gov/sites/default/files/pdf/research-and-publications/research-projects-and-surveys/surveys/20100608_Judge_Survey.pdf

Walsh, W., Wolak, J., & Finkelhor, D. (2013). *Prosecution dilemmas and challenges for child pornography crimes: The Third National Juvenile Online Victimization Study (NJOV-3)*. Crimes against Children Research Center. https://scholars.unh.edu/cgi/viewcontent.cgi?article=1043&context=ccrc

Webb, L., Craissati, J., & Keen, S. (2007). Characteristics of internet child pornography offenders: A comparison with child molesters. *Sexual Abuse: A Journal of Research and Treatment, 19*(4), 449–465. https://www.doi.org/10.1177/107906320701900408

Wolak, J., Finkelhor, D., & Mitchell, K. J. (2005). *Child-pornography possessors arrested in internet-related crimes*. National Center for Missing & Exploited Children. http://www.missingkids.com

Wolak, J., Finkelhor, D., & Mitchell, K. J. (2011). Child pornography possessors: Trends in offender and case characteristics. *Sexual Abuse: A Journal of Research and Treatment, 23*(1), 22–42. https://www.doi.org/ 10.1177/1079063210372143

Wortley, R. K., & Smallbone, S. (2006). *Child pornography on the Internet*. U.S. Department of Justice, Office of Community Oriented Policing Services.

COURT CASES

Ashcroft v. Free Speech Coalition, 535 U.S. 234 (2002)
Free Speech Coalition v. Reno, 98 F.3d 1083 (9th Cir. 1999)
Miller v. California, 413 U.S. 15 (1973)

New York v. Ferber, 458 U.S. 747 (1982)
Osborne v. Ohio, 495 U.S. 103 (1990)
Stanley v. Georgia, 394 U.S. 557 (1969)
United States v. Tucker, 305 F.3d 1193 (2002)
United States v. Williams, 553 U.S. 285 (2008)

DEFINITIONS

Child Pornography: Material visually depicting the sexual exploitation of children and adolescents that can include photographic, film, or other visual representations (see also **Child Sexual Abuse Materials**)

Child Sexual Abuse Materials: Alternative (and in some cases, preferred) term for materials visually depicting the sexual exploitation of children

Combination Trader–Travelers: Child pornographers who trade child pornography as well as travel across state and/or national boundaries to sexually abuse or molest children

Computer Forensics: Assessment of computers and computer-related media for evidence of crimes

Cybercrime: Any criminal act involving computers, networks, or the internet

Dark Web: Part of the internet that isn't visible to search engines and requires the use of sophisticated encryption methods and anonymous networks to access (also known as Darknet)

DSM-5 (Diagnostic and Statistical Manual of Mental Disorders, 5th ed.): A publication by the American Psychiatric Association that provides a list and diagnosis criteria of all recognized mental disorders

Downward Departures: Sentences issued by judges that are less severe than the recommended sentence under Federal Sentencing Guidelines

Dual Offenders: Sex offenders who commit child pornography and child sexual abuse concurrently

Federal Sentencing Guidelines: Rules that set uniform sentencing policy for defendants convicted of serious felonies

Mens Rea: An element of criminal responsibility referring to a guilty mind or wrongful purpose

Miller Test: A set of three criteria for determining whether forms of speech or expression, including visual material, can be labeled obscene and thus not protected by First Amendment rights (also known as the Three-Prong Obscenity Test)

Obscenity: Any statement, act, or material that strongly offends against prevailing moral standards (although not necessarily legal standards) of the time

Pedophilia/Pedophile: A psychiatric disorder in which afflicted individuals exhibit primary or exclusive sexual attraction to prepubescent children (under the age of 12)

Phallometric Assessment: A method of measuring male sexual arousal to both legal and illegal sexual stimuli

Prurient Interests: To have or to encourage excessive interest in sexual matters

Sex Trafficking: A type of sexual victimization that involves enticement, force, fraud, or coercion to commit a sexual act for money—the victim receives none/little of the money; it can involve children or adults, and does not necessarily involve transporting the victim from one location to another, but can; it is also referred to as commercial sexual exploitation and a form of modern slavery

Sexting: The sending and/or receiving of sexually suggestive images or messages to peers through a cell phone or social media network

Techniques of Neutralization: Justifications or rationalizations for violating society's norms and/or committing crimes

Typology: Classification system whereby similar individuals or observations are grouped together—individuals within a group are considered to be similar, whereas groups tend to be distinct

Virtual Child Pornography (also known as pseudo child pornography): Pornographic material that does not include actual images of children but creates the illusion of sexual exploitation

CHAPTER 6

Juveniles and Women Who Have Committed a Sex Crime

> **CHAPTER OBJECTIVES**
>
> - Dispel the myth that all persons who commit a sex crime are older men
> - Identify the number of sex crimes committed by juveniles and girls/women
> - Provide an overview of juveniles who have committed a sex crime, which includes (1) describing their common characteristics, (2) comparing them to juvenile nonsexual offenders, (3) identifying distinctions and typologies, (4) discussing explanations of sexual offending, (5) providing an overview of explanations of sexual offending, (6) describing assessment and treatment efforts, and (7) discussing recidivism rates
> - Identify characteristics of women who have committed a sex crime, which includes (1) describing their common characteristics, (2) comparing them to men who have committed a sex crime, (3) identifying common categories and typologies, (4) discussing explanations of sexual offending, (5) providing an overview of explanations of sexual offending, (6) describing assessment and treatment efforts, and (7) discussing recidivism rates

It is not uncommon for the media to portray only the most serious sex-crime incidents, and these portrayals typically include older, white men. This falsely leads to the impression that only adult men commit sex crimes. In this chapter, we dispel this myth by exploring sex crimes committed by juveniles and girls/women. Although they commit a small portion of all known sex crimes, their crimes still warrant inquiry. It is important to note that although the research on adults who have committed a sex crime has existed for several decades, research on juveniles who have committed a sex crime (JSCs) did not begin until more recently. The research on women who have committed a sex crime (WSC) is even less developed. Nevertheless, the research that does exist sheds light on these special populations of offenders.

NUMBER OF SEX CRIMES COMMITTED BY JUVENILES AND GIRLS/WOMEN

Ample evidence exists that reveals that although the majority of reported sex crimes is committed by adult men, a small yet noteworthy portion of these offenses is committed by juveniles. For example, the Federal Bureau of Investigation (FBI) reported that in 2019, among all arrests

Juveniles and Women 141

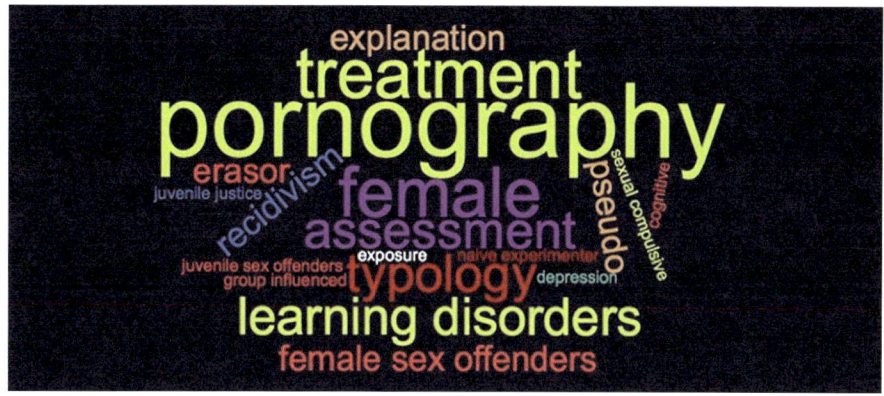

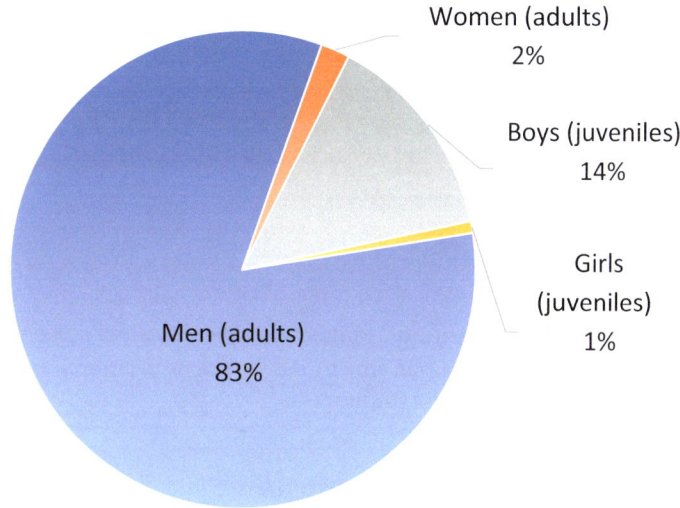

FIGURE 6.1 Arrests for Rapes in 2019.
Note: Adapted from FBI (2021).

for rape (Figure 6.1), juvenile (persons younger than 18 years) males comprised 14% of arrests, whereas juvenile females comprised 1% of arrests. Adult females comprised 2% of all rape arrests, whereas adult males comprised the majority—83%. Also, as noted in Figure 6.2, among arrests for all other sex crimes (excluding prostitution and rape), juvenile males comprised 13%, whereas juvenile females comprised only 1%. Although the majority of other sex crimes have been committed by adult men (80%), adult females committed 6% in 2019. As discussed earlier, official arrest data are limited in estimating true prevalence rates because sex crimes are generally underreported. Further, it is believed that those sexually victimized by girls/women are less likely to report such offenses compared to those victimized by males (Denov, 2004).

COMMON CHARACTERISTICS OF JUVENILES WHO HAVE COMMITTED A SEX CRIME (JSCS)

It should be noted that some researchers define this population as someone who is a juvenile, typically someone who is younger than either 17 or 18 years old (depending on state

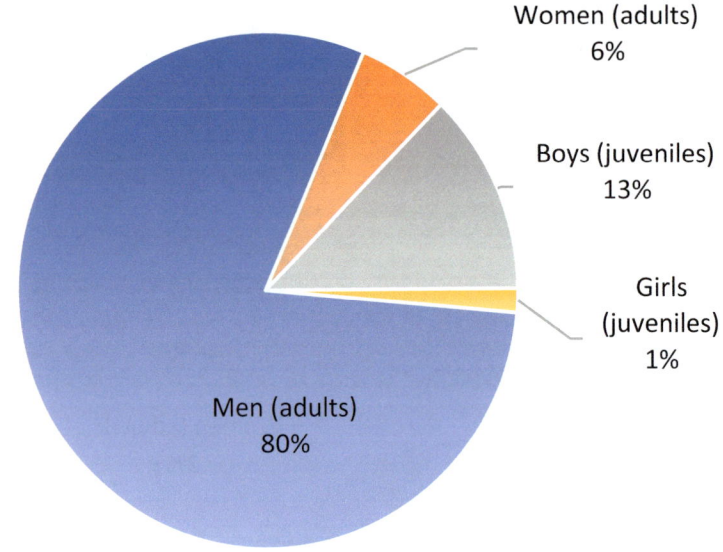

FIGURE 6.2 Arrests for other Sex Crimes in 2019.
Note: Adapted from FBI (2021).

law), whereas others refer to adolescents (those who have entered puberty). Throughout this chapter, we rely on both terms but aim to use the same terminology as the original researcher(s) when referring to specific studies.

Family Dysfunction and Trauma Exposure

JSCs have high rates of family problems (Barra et al., 2018; McCuish & Lussier, 2017; Righthand & Welch, 2004; Ronis & Bourduin, 2007; Yoder et al., 2020). They often grow up in dysfunctional families, which often includes exposure to trauma. Trauma is typically defined as exposure to parental abuse (verbal, physical, and emotional), emotional neglect, witnessing violence in the home, and sexual victimization. JSCs have typically been exposed to multiple types of trauma (Barra et al., 2018; Rasmussen, 2013). Specifically, some studies have demonstrated that JSCs are especially affected by ***Adverse Childhood Experiences*** (ACEs), which include ten categories of adversities experienced during childhood and adolescence that are highly correlated with a wide range of negative physical health, mental health, and behavioral outcomes throughout the life span (Merrick et al., 2019). These categories include (1) physical abuse, (2) emotional abuse, (3) sexual abuse, (4) physical neglect, (5) emotional neglect, (6) growing up with household incarceration, (7) growing up with mental illness within the immediate family, (8) growing up with substance abuse within the immediate family, (9) experiencing parental separation or divorce, and (10) witnessing domestic or intimate partner violence. Studies have generally found that JSCs are more affected by ACEs than the general population. For instance, Levenson et al. (2017) found that the existence of early maltreatment and family problems were more prominent among JSCs compared to youth who committed other types of crimes. The same study also found that female JSCs have substantially higher rates of childhood sexual abuse compared to the general population.

Prior sexual victimization also occurs at high rates among JSCs (Lateef & Jenney, 2020; Veneziano et al., 2000). In a review of more than 50 peer-reviewed articles on the topic, Lateef and Jenney (2020) reported adolescent boys who commit a criminal offense and have a history of child sexual abuse, especially when it occurred over an extended period of time, are more likely to commit a sex crime as compared to committing a nonsex crime.

Academic Performance, Learning Disorders, and Executive Functioning

Many studies show that JSCs exhibit academic impairment and perform poorly in school (Veneziano et al., 2000). For example, one study found that the majority of a sample of JSCs has been suspended previously from school (Ford & Linney, 1995). Other researchers found that almost half of JSCs had diagnosable learning disorders, and 83% had academic difficulties (Awad & Saunders, 1991). Even more alarming, one study found that almost one-third of JSCs had some neurological impairment (Ferrara & McDonald, 1996). Although these studies report high levels of academic problems, poor performance in school, and learning disorders, other subsequent studies have failed to report these problems at such high levels among subsequent samples (see Seto & Lalumière, 2010).

Other studies have also found weaknesses in the executive functioning of JSCs (Butler & Seto, 2002; Veneziano et al., 2004; van Wijk et al., 2006). Executive functioning includes attention, cognitive flexibility, working memory, inhibition, and an ability to self-monitor. Executive function impairment is relevant with regard to treating JSCs. More recently, Yoder et al. (2019) found higher levels of executive dysfunction among JSCs who had experienced sexual abuse themselves. As noted in Chapter 10, the most common type of treatment for offenders who have committed a sex crime is ***cognitive-behavioral treatment***. Such treatment is likely to be ineffective for people with neurological impairments because it relies on the ability to process information.

Emotional Intelligence

Emotional intelligence refers to one's ability to perceive others' emotions and express one's emotions. This includes the ability to process emotional information and respond appropriately to different cues in one's social environment. These characteristics are associated with mental health, leadership skills, and employment performance. In a recent review of 16 studies that assessed the prevalence of low empathy among JSCs, the authors could not conclude enough empirical support exists to make this claim because many of the studies had inherent methodological limitations (Baly & Butler, 2017).

Mental Illness

Much of the literature has identified a high rate of mental illness among JSCs. The types of mental illnesses identified among this population include ***conduct disorders, depression,*** and ***attention deficit (hyperactivity) disorder (ADD/ADHD)*** (Shema, 2019). One may believe that a juvenile who molests another child or sexually assaults an adult must be "sick" or somehow mentally ill. Common types of mental illness among JCS include depression and conduct disorders.

Depression

JSCs have high rates of depression (Briere & Runtz, 1991; Browne & Finkelhor, 1986; Chaffin, 2008; Mash & Barkley, 1996) compared to juveniles who have committed a non-sex crime and nondelinquent juveniles (Katz, 1990), and this is especially true of JSCs who have experienced child abuse and/or neglect (Becker & Stein, 1991). Forty-two percent of the JSCs in one study scored high on a depression inventory scale (Becker & Stein, 1991). It also was found that offenders who reported being sexually abused themselves had a higher rate of depression than those who had not been sexually abused. JSCs often exhibit more withdrawn symptoms compared to those who have not sexually offended (Katz, 1990).

Conduct Disorder and ADD/ADHD

Another distinction between JSCs and juveniles who have committed a nonsex crime is behavior problems, including conduct disorders (Shema, 2019). The American Psychiatric Association (2013) has identified criteria for conduct disorders, as presented in Focus Box 6.1. Although several studies have found it is not uncommon for JSCs to exhibit symptoms of conduct disorders, they do differ significantly on several factors when compared to those with conduct disorders who have not committed a sex crime. For example, families of JSCs committed a sex crime, told more lies, and were more likely to engage in taboo behavior (Baker et al., 2004). Thus, the development of sex crimes appears to have a different etiology (i.e., causality) than the development of conduct-disorder behaviors.

Focus Box 6.1 Conduct Disorder/Antisocial Personality Disorder

The American Psychiatric Association (2013) defined the criteria for a conduct disorder in the DSM-5. A conduct disorder involves a host of behaviors that occur consistently over an extended period of time (with at least three behaviors discussed here occurring during the previous year and with at least one symptom occurring within the previous six months). The problematic behaviors include four broad categories: (1) aggression to people or animals, (2) destruction of property, (3) deceitfulness or theft, and (4) serious violations of rules. Several examples are provided for each category (refer to DSM-5 for a complete list). Examples of aggression to people or animals include bullying, engaging in physical fights, cruelty to animals, and cruelty to people. Destruction of property includes physical damage and damage caused by intentional fire setting. Deceitfulness or theft involves breaking into someone else's property (e.g., house or car), shoplifting, and forgery. Serious violations of rules include violating a curfew, running away, and school truancy. This host of behaviors must cause impairment in one's work, school, or social functioning. This disorder can range in severity from "mild" to "severe." For those who are at least 18 years old, the disorder is referred to as antisocial personality disorder.

Note: Adapted from American Psychiatric Association (2013).

Offense and Victim Characteristics

JSCs commit a wide range of offenses. Approximately two-thirds of the sample in one study engaged in either penetration or oral-genital contact or both (Ryan et al., 1996). Approximately 70% of the victims were female in another study (Righthand & Welch, 2001). When the victim is male, he is typically young (Davis & Leitenberg, 1987). Victims of JSCs are often young—more than 60% were younger than 12; 63% were younger than 9; and 40% were younger than 6 (Ryan et al., 1996). Also, younger victims were more likely than older victims to be related to their offenders (Worling, 1995). The majority of victims are known to their offenders (i.e., acquaintance or relative) (Johnson, 1988). One study reported that 39% of JSCs were related to their victims (Ryan et al., 1996), whereas another study found that 46% of the victims were related to their offenders (Johnson, 1988). Thus, overall, we know that JSCs can commit serious offenses. They typically have younger victims who are either known or related to them.

JUVENILES WHO HAVE COMMITTED A SEX CRIME (JSCS) COMPARED TO JUVENILE (NONSEXUAL) OFFENDERS

In the previous sections, we have highlighted research showing JSCs, as a group, exhibit many problems. These include high rates of family dysfunction, exposure to trauma, poor academic performance, learning disorders, impaired executive functioning, emotional intelligence deficits, and high rates of mental illness, including depression and conduct disorder. However, many of these characteristics are commonplace among the overall juvenile offending population (including juvenile offenders who *do not* commit sex crimes), thus raising the question: How truly unique are those juveniles who commit sexual offenses from juveniles who engaged in other types of criminal behavior?

To address that question, we turn to the results of a ***meta-analysis*** that included 59 studies for a total of 3,855 juvenile males who had committed a sex crime. In their study, Seto and Lalumière (2010) found only a few factors that possibly distinguish JSCs from juvenile offenders who committed a crime but a nonsexual one (i.e., juvenile nonsexual offenders). They found JSCs, compared to juvenile (nonsexual) offenders, had more atypical sexual interests and more extensive sexual abuse histories. These findings have been confirmed by subsequent research as well (see DeLisi et al., 2014). Furthermore, according to the Seto and Lalumière (2010) study, JSCs had *less* extensive criminal histories, fewer antisocial peers, and fewer substance abuse problems when compared to juvenile (nonsexual) offenders. Remarkably, the two groups did not significantly differ with regard to antisocial personality disorder, early conduct problems, intelligence, social problems, and mental illness (i.e., psychopathology). It should be noted, however, the studies that compare JSCs to juveniles with no criminal history or substantial mental health problems are virtually nonexistent.

DISTINCTIONS AND TYPOLOGIES OF JUVENILES WHO HAVE COMMITTED A SEX CRIME (JSCS)

Identifying distinguishing characteristics and typologies serve as a way to organize heterogeneous offenders into homogeneous categories. Typologies can assist in identifying the profile for a specific sex crime. Characteristics of a crime scene, for example, can reveal characteristics about the offender. It should be noted that not all offenders fit into a distinct classification scheme. Hence, multiple typologies have been developed based on various characteristics. Typologies can also be useful for treatment purposes—the motivation or triggers to commit a sex crime may vary among the categories.

Some researchers have identified a distinguishing factor that divides offenders into two categories, whereas others have identified an extensive typology that organizes the offenders into three or more categories. With regard to distinctions that have been made, researchers have argued that JSCs can be distinguished simply by (a) those who molest children, and (b) those who sexually abuse peers or adults (Barbaree & Cortoni, 1993). Other researchers have also made this simple distinction (e.g., Hsu & Starzynski, 1990; Hunter, 2000). Hunter et al. (2003) found those who molested prepubescent victims had greater psychosocial deficits than those who molested pubescent victims.

With regard to typologies, many researchers, individually or with collaborators, have developed at least nine unique typologies (see Becker et al., 1986; Graves et al., 1996; O'Brien & Bera, 1986; Oxnam & Vess, 2006; Prentky et al., 2000; Långström et al., 2000; Richardson et al., 2004; Worling, 2001). Some of these typologies were based on simple observation (rather than any statistical analyses), whereas others were based on only one piece of information such as relying on a score on a common mental health exam or a personality test. Here we describe only one of these typologies, O'Brien and Bera's (1986) typology, which was based on the most factors. These factors include the offender's behaviors, offense motivations, family characteristics, and personality factors. A summary of their typology is presented in Table 6.1.

EXPLANATIONS OF JUVENILES COMMITTING SEX CRIMES (JSCS)

Although many theories have been proposed to explain sexual offending, as presented in Chapter 2, many other possible factors specific to JSCs have been proposed. These explanations include experimentation, exposure to pornography, and the sexual-abuse cycle.

Experimentation

The authors of a *New York Times* e-news article asked, "How can you distinguish a budding pedophile from a kid with real boundary problems?" (Jones, 2007, n.p.). This question illustrates the problem of possible over or underreacting to behaviors that are either within the "normal" range of sexual development or a red flag of future sexual offending. It has aptly noted there are many "in-between" juveniles who are difficult to categorize:

> It's not hard to categorize an act in which a 12-year-old grabs a girl's rear end. And, on the other extreme, it's not difficult to classify a 17-year-old who rapes young children. But many juveniles ***adjudicated*** (a term used in juvenile court to indicate a determination of delinquency) [emphasis added] for sex crimes fall somewhere in between, both in terms of ages and offenses. How, for instance, should we categorize a . . . 14-year-old who was sexually aroused and asked a kindergarten-age girl to lick his penis?
>
> (Jones, 2007, n.p.)

TABLE 6.1 O'Brien and Bera (1986) Typology of Juveniles Who Have Committed a Sex Crime (JSCs)

Categories	Description
Naïve experimenter	- Young (11–14 years old) - Some history of behavior problems - Adequate social skills/peer relationships - Sexually naïve - Most likely to engage in situational abuse such as babysitting abuse or a camping/family outing
Under-socialized child exploiter	- Experiences chronic social isolation - Few friends their own age - Has younger friends (who admire them) - Some history of acting out - Commonly over-involved mother and distant father
Pseudo-socialized	- Older adolescent - Good social skills - Little/no history of behavior problems - May have been victimized when a child - Above-average intelligence - Rationalizes sexual abuse - Shows little guilt/remorse - Views the abuse as nonabusive (intimate, mutually consenting) - Narcissistic
Sexual aggressive	- Abusive/disorganized family - Good social skills with same-age peers - Antisocial or character-disorder personality - Charming/gregarious personality - Uses violence or forced threats - Victimizes peers and/or adults - Uses power, domination, expressions of anger, and humiliation of the victim as motivators - May be a learned sexual arousal response to violence
Sexual compulsive	- Rigid/enmeshed family structure - Emotionally repressive parents - Has difficulty expressing negative emotions - Has paraphilias (that do not involve touch such as voyeurism) - Plans sexual abuse
Disturbed impulsive	- History of psychological problems, learning disorders, and family problems - Impulsive sexual abuse - Usually involves a single act or pattern of odd, ritualistic abuse with children - Impaired inhibitions - Complex motivation for abuse
Group influenced	- Younger teen - No previous contact with the criminal justice system likely - Abuse in the context of a group setting - Victim usually an acquaintance - Places blame on others in the group - Motivation from peer pressure or an attempt to gain approval from peers

Over the past 40 years, perceptions of JSCs have changed substantially. In the past, juveniles who acted out sexually often were perceived as merely "experimenting" (Reiss, 1960). In the 1980s, however, this perception changed (Lussier & Blockland, 2014) because of several findings, including (a) juveniles account for a substantial percentage of sex crimes; (b) this population of juveniles commit up to hundreds of sex crimes during their lifetimes; and (c) some adults began their sex offending during their adolescence (Barbaree & Cortoni, 1993). It was believed that today's JSC is "tomorrow's adult sex offender" (Lussier & Blockland, 2014, p. 153). This belief, however, has been historically rooted in an overreliance on ***retrospective studies,*** which examine the childhood and adolescent histories of adults who had committed a sex crime. Retrospective studies fail to capture those juveniles who desist from sexual offending after they become adults (Abel et al., 1987). Many ***prospective*** and ***longitudinal studies*** have shown little continuation from juvenile to adult sex crime. Overall, a large portion of existing studies have shown that the percentage of JSCs who continue to commit sex crimes into adulthood is low—less than 10% (Kemper & Kistner, 2007; Nisbet et al., 2004; Vandiver, 2006c; Zimring et al., 2009). Some studies that have assessed a sample of JSCs for a long period of time have shown a slightly higher rate of continued offending into adulthood, between 10% and 15% (Lussier et al., 2012). Another study found that 30% JSCs persisted into adulthood (Rubinstein et al., 1993). Still, another study reported that "being a juvenile sex offender did not significantly increase the likelihood for an individual being an adult sex offender, nor did the frequency of sexual offending" (Zimring et al., 2009, p. 58).

Exposure to Pornography

Exposure to pornography, especially at an early age, has been proposed as a possible explanation for JSCs (Huntington et al., 2020; Siria et al., 2020). Among two studies, the rate of exposure to pornography was 70% and 90%, respectively (Becker & Stein, 1991; Siria et al., 2020). In another study, it was found that 41% of JSCs had looked at pornographic magazines compared to only 16% of nonoffenders (Zgourides et al., 1997). It was also found that, for some of the offenders, the use of pornographic material occurred right before the commission of a sex crime. The researchers speculated that the context of the viewing of pornography may be an important factor. JSCs may use pornography as a precursor to a sex crime, whereas a nonoffender may be viewing it out of curiosity. Thus far, the findings have been relatively consistent: juveniles who committed sex crimes have a higher rate of exposure to pornographic material than nonoffenders (Burton & Miner, 2016).

Sexual-Abuse Cycle

Another researcher has proposed a sex-abuse cycle specific to child abuse. First, the juvenile has a negative self-image, possibly related to upbringing and caused by physical abuse, sexual abuse, and/or other factors such as a chaotic, violent household (Becker, 2007). Subsequently, the juvenile develops low self-esteem and becomes socially isolated. This leads to poor coping strategies—especially when negative situations occur. The juvenile begins to predict negative reactions from others. This leads to more social isolation and fantasies stemming from a lack of power and control. When a triggering event occurs, such as boredom, or a traumatic event, these fantasies can lead to the commission of a sex crime. This reinforces a poor self-image and creates a sex-abuse cycle. ***Cognitive distortions*** often facilitate the offending.

ASSESSMENT OF JUVENILES WHO HAVE COMMITTED A SEX CRIME (JSCS)

In 1993, the National Task Force on Juvenile Sexual Offending stated, "Currently, there are no scientifically validated instruments or criteria to assess risk of re-offense" (p. 29). Since then, however, several assessment tools have been developed for JSCs. These include, but are not limited to, the Juvenile Sex Offender Assessment Protocol-II (J-SOAP-II; Prentky & Righthand, 2003), Estimate of Risk of Adolescent Sexual Offender Recidivism (ERASOR; Worling et al., 2012), and the Juvenile Sex crime Recidivism Risk Assessment Tool-II (JSORRAT-II; Epperson et al., 2005, 2006). Empirical evidence for these assessment tools suggests they are able to accurately predict juvenile sexual recidivism (Viljoen et al., 2009). A summary of each of these assessment tools is presented in Table 6.2.

The scoring sheets for many of these assessment tools are freely available on the internet, whereas some are proprietary, requiring a fee to use. Regardless, training is highly recommended and/or required for administering these. Many of the manuals or guidelines for scoring each item are quite lengthy. For example, the scoring guidelines for JSOAP-II is nearly 30 pages of single-spaced text. Most of the developers of these assessment tools offer training sessions by specially trained trainers and include a fee. It should also be noted that some organizations have their own assessment tools that are not listed here but typically include items that are common to the assessment tools listed in Table 6.2. Administering multiple assessments is typically part of a thorough assessment. Assessment tools are also continuously evaluated for their effectiveness. Research on these tools has shown that these tools are not perfect at predicting future sexual recidivism, but they are significantly better than simply guessing (Schwartz-Mette et al., 2019).

TREATMENT FOR JUVENILES WHO HAVE COMMITTED A SEX CRIME (JSCS)

Treatment for JSCs, by and large, is based upon adult sex-offender treatment (Lambie & Seymour, 2006) despite research indicating JSCs may be different from adults who have committed a sex crime (Gunby & Woodhams, 2010). As described by a well-known therapist, Robert Longo, in a *New York Times Magazine* article, treatment for JSCS has changed substantially in the early 2000s:

> As part of [adolescent boys' sex offender] treatment, the boys had to keep journals—which Longo read—in which they detailed their sexual fantasies and logged how frequently they masturbated to those fantasies. They created "relapse-prevention plans," based on the idea that sex offending is like an addiction and that teenagers need to be watchful of any "triggers" (pornography, anger) that might initiate their "cycle" of re-offending. And at the beginning of each group session, the boys introduced themselves much as an alcoholic begins an Alcoholics Anonymous meeting: "I'm Brian, and I'm a sex offender. I sexually offended against a 10-year-old boy; I made him lick my penis three times." Sex-offender therapy for juveniles was a new field in the 1980s, and Longo, like other therapists was basing his practices on what he knew: the adult sex-offender-treatment models. . . . As it turns out, he went on to say, "Much of it was wrong." There is no proof that . . . using adult sex-offender treatments on juveniles is

TABLE 6.2 Summary of Assessment Tools for Juveniles Who Have Committed a Sex Crime (JSCs)

Assessment Tool	Administered to:	Aimed to Predict:	Summary of Items Included in Tool	Use of Scores
Juvenile Sex Offender Assessment Protocol-II (J-SOAP-II) Prentky and Righthand (2003)	Juvenile males between 12 and 18 years old and have already committed a sex crime or have a history of sexually coercing others	Committing future sexual and nonsex crimes	Checklist of 28 items; two scales that measure static factors and two scales that measure dynamic factors	Each scale is scored with a 0, 1, or 2. The items are totaled for an overall score. Higher scores translate into a higher risk. Subscale scores can be used for decisions (e.g., treatment, level of supervision, progress in treatment). There are no cutoff scores for risk level determination; clinician makes a final decision.
Estimate of Risk of Adolescent Sexual Offender Recidivism (ERASOR), Version 2.0 Worling and Curwen (2001)	Juvenile males between 12 and 18 years who have already committed a sex crime	Short-term risk	25 risk factors in several areas such as sexual attitudes, history of sexual assaults, psychosocial functioning, family/environmental functioning, and treatment	Each item is scored as present, possibly or partially present, not present, or unknown. There are no cutoff scores for risk level determination; clinician makes a final risk level decision as low, moderate, or high.
Juvenile Sex Crime Recidivism Risk Assessment Tool-II (JSORRAT-II) Epperson et al. (2005, 2006)	Juvenile males between 12 and 18 years who have already committed a sex crime	Committing future sex crimes	12 items that are based on seven categories: sexual offending history, offense characteristics, sexual crime treatment history, abuse history, special education history, school discipline history, and nonsexual offending behavior	Some items are scored as either 0 or 1, whereas others are scored as 0, 1, or 2. Scores are totaled. 0 = Low risk 1–3 = Low-moderate risk 4–7 = Moderate risk 8+ = Moderate-high

> effective. Adult models he noted don't account for adolescent development and how family and environment affect children's behavior.
>
> (Jones, 2007, n.p.)

Treatment for JSCs was first developed in 1975, yet it was not until the 1980s when more structured programs were created (Lab et al., 1993). In 1980, there were only 20 treatment programs for JSCs (National Adolescent Perpetrator Network, 1993). Also, at this time, the rate of adjudicated JSCs had increased (Reitzel & Carbonell, 2006). Mandatory treatment was urged by the National Adolescent Perpetrator Network (1993). Researchers reported that by 1992, there were 750 outpatient and residential treatment programs for JSCs (Burton & Smith-Darden, 2000).

JSCs are treated either in a residential or outpatient center. One study showed that of 20,000 JSCs who received sex-offender treatment, half received treatment in a residential center (Center for Sex Offender Management, n.d.). Many factors, many of those identified during the assessment phase, will determine whether a juvenile is treated in an inpatient or outpatient center. The following is an explanation provided by the Center for Sex Offender Management (n.d., p. 3) in a training manual regarding such decisions:

> To illustrate, a youth who evidences considerable behavioral disturbances or aggression, demonstrates longstanding or chronic patterns of sexual deviance, resides in a chaotic home environment, and has considerable treatment needs may be best served in a residential program. And if the youth suffers from significant mental health symptoms that cause him to be a danger to himself or others, an inpatient psychiatric setting may be warranted.
>
> Conversely, a juvenile who seems to be more stable overall, has a supportive and structured home environment, has demonstrated a limited number of sexual behavior problems, and is motivated to change will probably be considered appropriate for treatment in the community.

When treatment programs for JSCs were initially developed in the 1980s and later, they lacked a foundation of empirically-based findings to build effective therapy (Reitzel & Carbonell, 2006). More recently, suggested treatment included **wraparound services, functional family therapy**, cognitive-behavioral approaches (Walker et al., 2004), and **multisystemic therapy** (Center for Sex Offender Management, n.d.).

Wraparound services involve assigning a juvenile to a case manager who is responsible for coordinating services within the community. Thus, there is an attempt to manage the juvenile in the community as opposed to providing services in a residential treatment center. Services are provided for not only the youth but also the family. The case manager takes on many roles, including mentoring, supportive, and supervisory roles. It is also common for wraparound services to include a multidisciplinary team approach. Initial research on wraparound services shows promising results, with reduced recidivism rates among those who have received this type of treatment (Aos et al., 2001; Center for Sex Offender Management, n.d.).

Functional family therapy, as the name suggests, focuses on the structure and dynamics of the family. The focus is to provide parents with the skills necessary to provide appropriate boundaries, discipline, and support for the child. This type of therapy has existed for several decades and has been used for families with and without a juvenile who has committed a sex crime (Aos et al., 2001; Center for Sex Offender Management, n.d.).

Multisystemic therapy focuses on "improving family functioning, enhancing parenting skills, increasing the youth's associations with prosocial peers, improving school performance, and building upon community supports" (Center for Sex Offender Management, n.d., p. 9). It is similar to functional family therapy in that it involves the whole family and addresses multiple factors associated with antisocial behavior. The family is involved in developing a treatment plan. Initial research studies showed that not only were recidivism rates lower for those who participated in the treatment, but other improvements were also made such as family functioning, school performance, peer relationships, and prosocial behaviors (Center for Sex Offender Management, n.d.; Saldana et al., 2006).

Cognitive-behavioral treatment is defined by the National Alliance of the Mentally Ill (n.d.) as a form of treatment that examines the intersection of thoughts, feelings, and behaviors. It involves the identification of thinking patterns that are precursors to problem behaviors such as committing a sex crime. It also involves the client and therapist actively working together and includes the client taking an active role in their own treatment (National Alliance for the Mentally Ill, n.d.). Cognitive-behavioral treatment is the most common type of treatment for JSCs, and positive results have been obtained (Center for Sex Offender Management, n.d.; Righthand & Welch, 2001).

Effectiveness of Treatment

The effectiveness of treatment for JSCs has been assessed through a meta-analysis that included 2,986 JSCs from nine studies who were followed for an average of 59 months. The results showed that 13% sexually recidivated. Also, 25% recidivated for nonsexual violent crimes, 29% for nonsexual nonviolent crimes, and 20% for unspecified nonsex crimes. It also showed that JSCs who received treatment had significantly lower recidivism rates than those who did not receive treatment. Thus, treatment appears to reduce recidivism among JSCs. The type of treatment varied substantially from individual treatment, group therapy, family therapy, cognitive-based treatment, and noncognitive-based treatment to combinations of these (Reitzel & Carbonell, 2006).

RECIDIVISM AMONG JUVENILES WHO HAVE COMMITTED A SEX CRIME (JSCS)

Although research shows that a relatively small number of JSCs is arrested for another sex crime when they reach adulthood, the majority of JSCs do go on to commit a nonsexual crime. Research shows that JSCs are not more likely than juveniles who had committed a nonsex crime to commit a subsequent sex crime. In a comparison of JSCs to juveniles in a correctional treatment facility who had no history of committing a sex crime, 12% of the JSCs had a new sex-crime charge compared to 12% of the nonsex offending juveniles (Caldwell et al., 2008). Other researchers have also noted that once juveniles have committed a sex crime, there will not necessarily be a pattern of continued sexual offending (Becker, 1998).

Research suggests that JSCs with only one sex crime on their record have low rates of recidivism when they are in a community-based treatment program as compared to those in a more restrictive setting (Rasmussen, 1999). The following excerpt is from a *New York Times Magazine* article on JSCs and discusses juvenile sex-offender recidivism:

> When I heard about these juveniles, I wondered ... [w]ould they become adult offenders? I asked Mark Chaffin, one of the country's leading experts and the director of research at the Center on Child Abuse and Neglect at the University of Oklahoma Health Sciences Center. Chaffin notes that while most juveniles who have committed sex crimes are boys around 13 or 14, in other ways they are not a homogeneous population. Though a small percentage—no one knows how many—will become adult rapists or pedophiles, the vast majority, 90% or more, will not, Chaffin says. Most have not

committed violent assaults or abused multiple children repeatedly. Usually they have had sexual contact—from fondling to oral sex to intercourse—with a child who is at least two years younger than they are. Also, many of the juveniles have been sexually abused themselves, and as a consequence, they act out sexually, typically for a transitory period.
(Jones, 2007, n.p.)

A meta-analysis conducted to examine the question "How many juveniles who have committed a sex crime re-offend with another sex crime?" provides some answers. The rate of sexual recidivism among JSCs was examined in 63 studies that included a large sample: 11,219. On average, offenders were followed for approximately five years. Sexual recidivism was measured by using arrest or conviction information, depending on availability. The average sexual-recidivism rate was approximately 7%. Thus, only 7% of 11,219 JSCs were rearrested or reconvicted within an average follow-up period of five years. Recidivism for any offense (sexual or nonsexual) for the sample was 43%. The findings are consistent with those from previous studies: the sexual-recidivism rate of JSCs was relatively low, yet the rate of general recidivism was higher. It was also found that studies of adolescents revealed much higher sexual-recidivism rates than studies that examined only adults in their follow-up period. Thus, it appears that once juveniles reach the threshold of "adult," their chances of sexually recidivating decrease substantially (Caldwell, 2010).

WOMEN WHO HAVE COMMITTED A SEX CRIME (WSC)

Women typically are associated with caring, nurturing behaviors, especially toward children. Committing a violent crime, especially a sex crime, is primarily associated with male offenders, not female ones (Daly, 1989; Shaw et al., 2020). Over the past ten years, the amount of research on WSC surpasses that of the previous 30 years combined (Cortoni et al., 2017). Here, we examine the research that has been done to shed light on this group of offenders.

CHARACTERISTICS OF WOMEN WHO HAVE COMMITTED A SEX CRIME (WSC)

WSC are typically young, in their 20s or 30s, and white. They often report a history of sexual victimization and substance abuse. Although mental illness is evident in many women across studies, many of the samples come from mental health clinics. Thus, mental illness may be reported at higher levels in these studies than occurs in the general population (Vandiver, 2006a). This population of offenders typically experiences prior abuse at high rates (ten Bensel et al., 2019b).

Offense and Victim Characteristics

A myth exists regarding WSC in that the level of harm caused may not be "that serious" or harmful. This is not true because the victims of WSC suffer many negative consequences. Most WSC portrayed in the media, for example, involve young female teachers who molest teenage boys. Although minor boys cannot legally consent, they often engage in sexual activity without coercion. It should be recognized this is only one type of WSC and that the effects of this type of abuse have not been fully explored in the literature. Furthermore, there are other types of WSC who cause obvious harm to their victims. Sex crimes committed by women have been described as "not due to impulsivity/poor response inhibition, cognitive rigidity or attention validity. Rather, the crime is planned, intentional and goal directed" (Pflugradt & Allen, 2010, p. 447).

As noted in Focus Box 6.2, one woman admitted to raping approximately 100 children, including babies. Thus, the seriousness of sex crimes committed by women cannot be overstated.

Focus Box 6.2 A Case of a Woman Who Committed Multiple Violent Sex Crimes

Laura Faye McCollum is one of approximately 300 sex offenders who have been committed to McNeil Island, a secure treatment facility located approximately one hour from Seattle, Washington. She is the only female among the residents. The offenders who reside here are considered the "worst of the worst"—Level 3 offenders. The facility resembles a prison, with razor wire encasing the building. Laura agreed to an interview with journalist Lisa Ling from *Inside Edition* (Ling, 2010). In a five-minute edited clip, Laura provided information that reveals the seriousness of the offenses she committed over a lengthy period of time, along with the predatory features of her behavior. Laura, somewhat disheveled, appeared in a prison cell-like room, wearing a "Jesus" T-shirt, and sheepishly answered questions asked of her. She began by explaining that she has already served a prison sentence for raping a child. Laura acknowledged that she "should be here" (meaning in a secure treatment facility without access to society). She found it difficult to answer whether she would be a danger to children if released to society—noting she still has things to work on. Laura recounted her extensive history of raping children. She indicated 15 are "accounted for," yet she emphasized she had repeatedly admitted to 100 or more victims. Her offenses took place while she was a caretaker for babies and young children. She noted that she was not aroused by *all* children—she didn't want to hurt them all. Interestingly, she did pair sexual molestation with causing harm to children—characteristics of sadism. Laura noted that she bathed and clothed the babies/children and committed her offenses while this occurred. She explained that she tried to kill one of her victims by placing a pillow over the baby's head but was interrupted. Laura noted that she did not groom the victims because they were too young, but she did groom their parents. She often raped children who had parents who were vulnerable—had alcohol/drug problems, low income, showed a low-stress tolerance for their child, and had difficulty caring for their child. Laura has been diagnosed with pedophilia and sexual sadism, among other psychiatric disorders. She expressed some degree of remorse, claiming that she prays for her victims. Laura is the mother of four children and noted that none of them lived with her. She indicated that she was raped when she was seven years old. After serving more than 20 years at McNeil Island, Laura was released in 2019 following a psychologist's report stating that she "made progress in treatment in recent years and . . . no longer met the criteria for civil commitment" (Krell, 2019, n.p.). As part of Laura's release conditions, she was required to register as a sex offender and participate in a treatment program. She must also obtain approval to leave her home and have a chaperone present during approved outings.

With regard to the victims of WSC, they are typically known or related to the offender (ten Bensel et al., 2019a). The victims are typically young, on average, and are slightly more likely to be male than female. Female victims are typically chosen when the WSC are acting in concert with another person.

WOMEN WHO HAVE COMMITTED A SEX CRIME (WSC) COMPARED TO MEN WHO HAVE COMMITTED A SEX CRIME

Explanations of variations in male/female offending rates have included socialization differences, gender inequality, and adherence to traditional gender roles (Bloom et al., 2003). WSC may be more affected than the men who have committed a sex crime by self-esteem issues, depression, and a history of victimization (Hardyman & Van Voorhis, 2004). In one study, approximately one-third had at least one psychiatric hospitalization (West et al., 2011). WSC are more likely than men who have committed a sex crime to have substance abuse and mental health problems (Hardyman & Van Voorhis, 2004) and to have experienced physical and sexual abuse (Bloom et al., 2003). Moreover, WSC report more severe prior abuse when compared to men who have committed a sex crime (Oliver, 2007).

WSC are more likely than men who have committed a sex crime to have come from dysfunctional homes (Mathews et al., 1997), have more psychological problems (Johansson-Love & Fremouw, 2009), and have more suicide attempts (Miccio-Fonseca, 2000). With regard to criminal histories, WSC have significantly fewer prior arrests than men who have committed a sex crime (Freeman & Sandler, 2008). WSC are also less likely to have prior drug-, violent-, and sexual-offense arrests. Also, women are less likely than their counterparts to have a prior incarceration and probation sentence (Freeman & Sandler, 2008). WSC are more likely than men to have a male victim (Freeman & Sandler, 2008).

Similarities between men and women who have committed a sex crime have also been found. Men and women who have committed a sex crime have been found in at least one study to be similar in age, race, ethnicity, education level, and life stressors, including job stressors (Miccio-Fonseca, 2000).

Women and men who have committed a sex crime appear to have different pathways to committing a sex crime (Freeman & Sandler, 2008), which may require different assessment tools and, most importantly, different treatment plans when compared to men who had committed a sex crime. In the next section, we discuss distinctions and typologies that have been identified, which again highlight the heterogeneity among WSC and the need to assess women who have committed a sex crime differently from men who have committed a sex crime.

DISTINCTIONS AND TYPOLOGIES OF WOMEN WHO HAVE COMMITTED A SEX CRIME (WSC)

Recently, many researchers have identified that WSC can be distinguished by whether she committed the offense alone or with another person (see Comartin et al., 2018; Miller & Marshall, 2019; ten Bensel et al., 2019a). Given that this is a common category among various typologies, we will focus on this distinction in the typology discussion.

Typologies for WSC only recently emerged and, unfortunately, are limited in that they are constructed using small sample sizes of offenders (see Table 6.3). With the exception of two studies, the typologies were based on samples of less than 30. Despite this limitation, considerable overlap is found among the categories among different typologies. Thus, we focus instead on the three overarching categories that exist among all of the typologies (Vandiver, 2006b). These categories include (a) **nurturer**, (b) co-offending, and (c) other.

The first category of WSC, the *nurturer*, encompasses multiple categories identified among several typologies (e.g., babysitter abuse, independent offenders of males, teacher/lover, exploration/exploitation, and heterosexual nurturers). These types of women typically abuse someone who is a pre-teen or a teenager. The victim is typically male. The offender is usually in some type of caretaking and/or supervisory role such as a teacher or babysitter. The relationship itself mimics a romantic relationship in the sense that there may be the appearance of mutual feelings yet violate the boundaries of their position of authority. The interaction between the offender and victim may include love letters, text messages, emails, and other secret communication that is shared only between the two individuals. The relationship develops through a process of **grooming**, meaning a slow erosion of boundaries that eventually involve sexual contact. Researchers have found that women in this particular category of offending comprise a large portion of all of the offenders assessed (Mathews et al., 1989; Vandiver & Kercher, 2004). This category of offender is also the most likely to be portrayed in the media when a teacher is arrested for molesting a young male student.

For example, in the late 1990s, the media covered Mary Kay Letourneau at length, and she became one of the first well-publicized cases of a teacher who engaged in a sexual relationship with an underage student. She was a schoolteacher who began a relationship with a 12-year-old male student that turned sexual. Despite being arrested and jailed for this offense, she continued her relationship with the student. She had two children with him by the time he turned 15. She eventually married him after he became an adult (Associated Press, 2005; Victor, 2020).

The second category identified among the typologies is the **co-offender** category. It includes male-coerced molester; triads; male-accompanied, familial; and male-accompanied, nonfamilial (see Table 6.3). This category of WSC includes a broad range of behavior but consistently involves at least one other person. The other person is typically male (Vandiver, 2006b). Also, she is typically romantically involved with this other person. What varies among the different versions of the co-offender description that has been identified is the extent that the woman is coerced or actively participates and whether she simply assists in obtaining access to a young victim (i.e., hands-off offense) or actively participates in the sexual abuse (i.e., hands-on offense) (Comartin et al., 2018). Research, thus far, has found that women who co-offend typically exhibit depression and other personal problems at higher rates than those who offend alone (Williams et al., 2019).

Research suggests that women co-offending with others comprises a fairly large portion of women who sexually offend. For example, the FBI reported 227 known cases of WSC in one year (Vandiver, 2006b). Among those cases, 46% committed the offense with another person. Another study reported 35% of females who committed a sex crime acted as a co-offender (ten Bensel et al., 2019a). In an even more exhaustive study of more than 20 years of NIBRS data, 38% of the women committed a sex crime in conjunction with another person. Thus, it is likely that co-offenders comprise about one-third, but possibly close to one-half, of all sex crimes with a female offender.

TABLE 6.3 Description and Source of Typologies for Women Who Have Committed a Sex Crime (WSC)

Author	Categories
Sarrel and Masters (1982)	- Forced assault - Babysitter abuse - Incestuous abuse - Dominant woman abuse
McCarty (1981, 1986)	- Independent offenders of males (1986) - Independent offenders of females (1986) - Co-offenders and accomplices (1986) - Severely psychologically disturbed abuser (1981)
Mathews et al. (1989)	- Teacher/lover - Predisposed - Male-coerced molester - Exploration/exploitation - Psychologically disturbed
Mayer (1992)	- Female rapist - Female sexual harassment - Mother molester - Triads - Homosexual molestation
Syed and Williams (1996; building on Mathews et al.'s, 1989, categories)	- Teacher/lover (Mathews et al., 1989) - Male-coerced (Mathews et al., 1989) - Angry-impulsive - Male-accompanied, familial - Male-accompanied, nonfamilial
Vandiver and Kercher (2004)	- Heterosexual nurturers - Noncriminal homosexual offenders - Female sexual predators - Young adult child exploiters - Homosexual criminals - Aggressive homosexual offenders

An example of a co-offender includes Mathews et al.'s (1989) description of a husband and wife who molested a pair of 13-year-old twins who lived in the same apartment complex. The details include the following:

> [The woman] lived in an apartment building in an urban area. Her husband was unemployed, and she worked many hours to provide for their needs. [The woman's] husband developed a friendship with a pair of 13-year-old twins. . . . He liked to have them come to the apartment to play video games, watch television, and talk. [The woman] was nervous about her husband's interest in these twins, very insecure and jealous of the attention he was showing them, and suspicious of his motive. . . . At a later date [the woman] returned home early from an outing with her sister. When she entered the living room,

the male twin was watching television. She found his sister and her husband in the bedroom. The girl was on the bed, her husband was sitting on a chair, and both were nude. [The woman] . . . began screaming and crying. . . . She again insisted that the children never come back. . . . [Her husband] blamed her for his actions. . . . [He] "bugged" her about changing her mind and allowing the children to visit again. . . . [She] finally relented, and the sexual abuse occurred almost as soon as the children started frequenting their home again. . . . [The female victim] threatened to tell about her previous sexual contact with [the woman's] husband if [the woman] did not join in. . . . She performed oral sex on [the female victim]. . . . [The woman] and her husband also engaged in sexual behaviors in front of the children. . . . A few days later [her] husband was again involved with the girl. [The woman] reported that she felt sorry for the boy because he was left out, so she performed oral sex on him. The sexual contact was very stressful for her.

(Mathews et al., 1989, pp. 19–20)

Focus Box 6.3 A Case of a Women "Co-Offender": Ghislaine Maxwell

Ghislaine Maxwell, a wealthy socialite, was best known for her relationship with Jeffrey Epstein, an extremely wealthy financier. She was his long-term girlfriend. Both Jeffrey Epstein and Ghislaine Maxwell were arrested for trafficking minors. Jeffrey Epstein committed suicide while in jail custody—a finding that has mystery shrouded around it in that some speculate he did not commit suicide on his own will. The victims also reported that they were trafficked to other locations, including Epstein's private island, and forced to have sex with many other men, including many high-profile politicians. A director of the documentary noted that Epstein was "this rich guy who was charismatic and just got away with things" (Gajanan, 2020, n.p.).

In a recent Netflix documentary, *Jeffrey Epstein: Filthy Rich*, interviews of several alleged victims describe an erringly similar story among each other of Maxwell recruiting massage therapists for Epstein. This later would evolve into the victim being sexually assaulted by Epstein. Maxwell's role appeared to be crucial in the grooming process by ensuring silence from the victims after the sexual abuse. It was alleged that Maxwell used pressure tactics to ensure the victims would be silenced. Maxwell currently denies these allegations. Specifically, one of the alleged victims noted that

> [Maxwell] told me to watch my back, that 'I know you like to go running on the West Side Highway, and that's not going to be a safe place for you anymore, because there are a lot of ways to die on the West Side Highway.'

(Dickson, 2020, n.p.)

Another alleged victim stated that Maxwell told that victim she needed to do the same thing she did for Epstein to another well-known celebrity who was a known associate to Epstein. She states she had no knowledge of Epstein engaging in sex with a minor or trafficking minors, nor did she participate in these activities. Maxwell was found guilty of sex trafficking and related charges (Neumeister, 2022). Her sentencing hearing has been set for June of 2022.

The woman was arrested after the female victim's boyfriend reported the sexual abuse. The woman was described as cooperative with law enforcement. She spent time in jail and participated in a sex-offender treatment program.

Another example of WSC with another person is presented in Focus Box 6.3. This example of Ghislaine Maxwell (Jeffrey Epstein's partner) has become well-known through the media but is presented here as a specific type of WSC. As noted in Chapter 4, the critical stages of the grooming process can involve offering something to a prospective victim (e.g., a potential job) and maintaining silence after the abuse occurs through threats.

The third category of WSC includes an "other" category that includes women who have engaged in various offenses and have various identifying characteristics. This includes those who (a) have serious psychological problems, (b) commit incest (i.e., offend against their own children/relatives), (c) commit some version of sexual harassment and/or rape, or (d) cannot be classified as any of the above but have committed sexual assault.

An example of incest was reported by Mathews et al. (1989) when they identified a mother whose husband had passed away, and the mother began first physically abusing her four-year-old daughter and then sexually abusing her.

> When feeling alone and wanting to be close, "I would go into the bedroom and touch [her daughter]." The abuse consisted of kissing and fondling the child, usually over her pajamas or underwear. Initially the abuse occurred when her daughter was awake. As the child grew older, however, [the mother] would wait for [her daughter] to fall asleep before touching her.
>
> (Mathews et al., 1989, p. 15)

The mother was abused by her own father when she was a child. After the mother entered substance-abuse treatment, she reported the sexual abuse she had with her daughter. She was referred to sexual-abuse treatment (Mathews et al., 1989).

It should also be noted that some offenders may meet the description of more than one of these categories. An example of this is a case study reported by two researchers that noted the victimization of an adult male. The male is described as being fearful, not enjoying the experience. One of the victims was a truck driver who was 27 years old. After meeting a woman he had known previously, he went to a motel with her, and the following occurred:

> [H]e was given another drink and shortly thereafter fell asleep. He awoke to find himself naked, tied hand and foot to a bedstead, gagged, and blindfolded. As he listened to voices in the room, it was evident that several women were present.... He was told that he had to "have sex with all of them." He thinks that during his period of captivity four different women used him sexually, some of them a number [of] times. Initially he was manipulated to erection and mounted.... He believes that the period of forcible restrained and repeated sexual assaults continued for more than 24 hours.
>
> (Sarrel & Masters, 1982, pp. 120–121)

After the incident, the man sought therapy. He never reported the incident to the police. He suffered from psychological distress and was not able to complete sexual intercourse. He married later but still was unable to engage in sexual intercourse. His wife was unaware of the rape he endured (Sarrel & Masters, 1982).

This situation involves multiple offenders. Thus, co-offenders were involved and could be classified as a co-offender category. It also involved a rape scenario where a victim was coerced (in this case with possibly a drug disguised in a drink) and by physically restraining the victim. It, therefore, can also be classified as an "other" category involving rape.

EXPLANATIONS OF WOMEN WHO HAVE COMMITTED A SEX CRIME (WSC)

As seen in the typologies presented above, the dynamics of sex offenses take on many different forms, and their explanations are just as varied. Existing research, specifically, has identified the following motivations for WSC:

- Reenactment of sexual abuse (Mayer, 1992; Saradjian & Hanks, 1996)
- Women acting out feelings, narcissistic women abusing their own daughters (Mayer, 1992)
- Extension of battered woman syndrome, socialization to follow male accomplices and to please male partners (Davin et al., 1999)
- Desire for intimacy (Mayer, 1992)
- Economic gain (Vandiver & Kercher, 2004)
- An interaction among cognitive, behavioral, affective (i.e., emotional), and contextual factors (Gannon et al., 2008)

Reenactment of early sexual abuse has been proposed as an explanation of WSC (Mayer, 1992; Saradjian & Hanks, 1996). It is proposed that the victim experiences displaced anger and, thus, identifies with the aggressor. The victim later becomes an offender and acts out her experiences on another person. Typically, researchers will cite the high rates of abuse that many persons who have sexually offended experienced themselves to support this notion. The extent that one affects the other, however, is questionable (Salter, 2018). Although a strong *correlation* between early abuse and later abusing is cited in many studies (see Knopp, 1984), this does not necessarily translate into *causation*. In fact, as noted by Salter (2018), studies including more objective measures (i.e., polygraph) reported 50% fewer victims-turned-victimizer than studies relying on self-report alone. Many persons who have sexually offended and who report being sexually abused as a child had not actually experienced sexual abuse. Furthermore, any of those who were sexually abused as a child did not go on to commit a sex crime.

Narcissism has also been proposed as a possible cause of female sexual offending (Mayer, 1992). One researcher relied upon an example described by Foward and Buck (1978) of a mother who molested her daughters. She perceived the daughters as simply an extension of herself. The need to be nurtured, coupled with the need to nurture, resulted in a narcissistic mother with poor boundaries. Another researcher described a similar situation of a woman with severe nurture deprivations (Groth, 1982).

Although sexual gratification has been explored as a possible cause of female sexual offending, it does not appear to be a sole motivating factor (Davin et al., 1999). It is proposed that instead of a sexual motivation, a need exists to connect with other persons. A sex crime is one avenue for meeting this need.

Several theories have been explored specifically for women who have co-offenders. For example, battered woman syndrome may lead a woman to sexually abuse (Davin et al., 1999). Many women who were coerced into a sex crime have a history of physical abuse by a male partner (Davin et al., 1999). Many women who are victims of abuse, however, do not sexually offend. Davin et al. (1999) relied on sex-role theories in exploring other possible explanations. The authors noted that these theories describe women as passive. Thus, their male counterparts initiate the sexual abuse, and the women follow. One researcher described the abuse as "an emotional process rooted out of fear, coercion, loneliness, and a perceived societal need to please a male partner" (Crawford, 2012, abstract).

A desire for intimacy has been proposed as a cause for adult women "falling in love" with younger boys (Vandiver & Kercher, 2004). Many of these women describe their actions as the outcome of having feelings of "love" for their victims (see Vandiver, 2003). The behavior is not necessarily associated, in the minds of the offenders, with a crime. Additionally, economic gain has been proposed as a possible motivating factor for women who engage in hands-off offenses such as forcing a child into prostitution or posing for pornographic pictures that are later sold (Vandiver & Kercher, 2004).

A more descriptive explanation of WSC is the **Descriptive Model of Female Sexual Offending**. It includes cognitive, behavioral, affective (i.e., emotional), and contextual factors that lead to women committing sex crimes. More specifically, it identifies three factors that potentially distinguish women from men who have sexually offended. First, physically, sexually, and emotionally abusive childhood experiences occurred more frequently and more severely than has been reported in the literature for men who have committed a sex crime. This is speculated to cause vulnerability factors (low self-esteem, passivity or aggression traits, and early mental health problems) and major life stressors (abusive intimate relationships), which lead to the second factor identified among WSC: abusive relationships (Gannon et al., 2008).

Abusive relationships appear to lead to a further vulnerability that places women in risky situations that could lead to sexual offending (Gannon et al., 2008). Such abusive relationships were associated with social isolation, poor coping strategies, passive or aggressive traits, and mental health problems.

The third factor identified among WSC includes co-offender influences. Co-offenders of women who sexually offend seem to assist in planning, establishing a goal, and offense planning. Some co-offenders engaged in grooming the woman who commits the sex crime—to engage in sexual behavior with children. Thus, this research identified unique factors and suggests unique pathways for females who commit sexual abuse as compared to men who had committed a sex crime.

ASSESSMENT OF WOMEN WHO HAVE COMMITTED A SEX CRIME (WSC)

Establishing empirically-based assessments for WSC is difficult because the research on women engaging in sexual abuse is at least 20 years behind that of men who have committed a sex crime (Gannon & Cortoni, 2010). This makes it difficult to establish assessment and treatment approaches because as research has found some differences between men and women who have committed a sex crime. Thus, the assessment approaches for men likely are not fully applicable to women who commit a sex crime. Currently, there are no standard assessment tools tailored to the specific needs of WSC.

Assessments for women who have committed a sex crime should follow accepted practices that have been established in the research literature aimed at assessing women in general

(Gannon & Cortoni, 2010). Assessments, therefore, should examine the following factors (Craig et al., 2008):

- Dispositional factors (e.g., antisocial personality characteristics)
- Historical factors (e.g., adverse developmental experiences and prior criminal history)
- Contextual elements (e.g., details and circumstances of the offense)
- Available support from social networks
- Personal life circumstances (e.g., marital and parental status, education, work, and social functioning)
- Clinical factors (e.g., mental-health and substance-use issues)

Gannon and Cortoni (2010) have recommended consideration of additional factors, including assessing co-offending, sexuality, cognitive biases, problematic relationships, and victimization. They also emphasized the need to assess general antisocial tendencies. With regard to co-offending, they noted that whether the offender willingly participated or was coerced should be examined. Sexuality assessment should include an evaluation of the presence of deviant sexual interests because these have been found to be significant predictors of recidivism among men who have committed a sex crime. For women, they may be significant predictors as well. A history of sexual development should also be assessed, including any history of sexual abuse. All of these may be related to WSC and should be taken into consideration.

Cognitions also have been correlated with sexual abuse. Pro-offending attitudes are correlated with core beliefs regarding relationships and children (Beech et al., 2009). Denial and minimization-cognitive patterns need to be assessed for WSC because this may be critical to the abusive behavior. Also, intimate deficits and problematic relationships are essential to an assessment of WSC (Cortoni & Gannon, 2016; Gannon & Cortoni, 2010). This is an area that is quite different for women who sexually offend compared to men who sexually offend. For female offenders, abuse in relationships appears to be common. Researchers have found, for example, that women become overly dependent on the men in their lives (Eldridge & Saradjian, 2000). Researchers also have found that women who sexually offend often lack emotional support from friends and family. Thus, the assessment of women should include an assessment of social and family support (Cortoni & Gannon, 2016; Gannon & Cortoni, 2010).

With regard to past victimization, the victimization in and of itself may not be a cause of WSC. Rather, it may be more symptomatic of a dysfunctional pattern that women have developed. Also, antisocial tendencies should be assessed. It should be noted, however, that not all women who sexually offend present with these symptoms. It is not known at this time to what extent antisocial characteristics play a role in female offending (Blanchette & Brown, 2006).

TREATMENT FOR WOMEN WHO HAVE COMMITTED A SEX CRIME (WSC)

Treatment efforts for those who have committed a sex crime have been based primarily on male samples and with a focus on treating men who have committed a sex crime, with little attention given to WSC. As the research regarding treatment efforts for WSC increases, the knowledge to develop treatment efforts specific to WSC also increases.

Treatment programs that have been developed for women include cognitive-based programs. Examples can be found in Canada, where the federal system offers sex-offender therapy to women who are incarcerated and in the community under supervision. The treatment provided is based on a thorough review of the literature and offender files of the woman who has committed a sex crime. The therapy involves five components with up to 70 treatment sessions. The components include (a) self-management; (b) deviant arousal; (c) cognitive distortions; (d) intimacy, relationships, and social functioning; and (e) empathy and victim awareness (Blanchette & Taylor, 2010; Correctional Services Canada, 2001).

The self-management component focuses on each offender's history and identifies alternative ways of coping. It also focuses on understanding offense progression, involving feelings, thoughts, and behaviors that led to the sex crime. The second component, deviant arousal, focuses on reducing deviant sexual interests that may have contributed to the sex offending. The cognitive-distortion component involves addressing cognitive distortions through a cognitive restructuring process. The intimacy, relationships, and social-functioning components take into account that many of the women co-offended with a partner. This component focuses on developing healthy relationships and enhancing self-esteem. The empathy and victim-awareness component focuses on developing generalized empathy skills and also empathy skills specific to understanding the effects of sexual offending on victims (Blanchette & Taylor, 2010; Correctional Services Canada, 2001).

Most recently, Pflugradt et al. (2018) proposed a strength-based model of treatment for WSC. This would include an acknowledgment that the characteristics and vulnerabilities of WSC are different than their male counterparts. Rather than considering factors such as frequency and intensity (as is typical of assessments for men who have committed a sexual offense), instead consider the level of intimacy, relational proximity, social integration, communication skills, and self-efficacy. In addition to the five core treatment areas (cognitive processes, emotional processes, intimacy and relationship areas, sexual dynamics, and psychosocial functioning) proposed by Cortoni and Gannon (2013), Pflugradt et al. (2018) recommended considering how these five core areas interrelate with each other and work with the WSC to develop a plan for developing a healthy lifestyle. Positive social functioning should be an integral part of the treatment, focusing more so on building on positive attributes and resources as opposed to addressing deficiencies. Treatment should be trauma informed, address antisocial thoughts and behavior, and improve coping strategies.

This study assessed only additional violent crimes as the recidivism measurement (for any offense). The 18% sexual recidivism rate is based on criminal histories alone; the 28% rate includes reports from Child Protective Services.

RECIDIVISM OF WOMEN WHO HAVE COMMITTED A SEX CRIME (WSC)

As noted in Table 6.4, only a few studies have been conducted on recidivism rates of WSC. Among those studies, the recidivism rate for *any* offense varies from about 10% up to 50%. With regard to sexual recidivism among WSC, the numbers are relatively low, ranging from none to 18%. It should be noted that all of these studies relied upon arrest as a measure of revidivism, with exception: the Bader et al. study also relied upon reports from Child Protective Services, which led to a substantially higher number of sexual recidivism events (28%).

TABLE 6.4 Summary of Studies Examining Recidivism Among Women Who Have Committed a Sex Crime

Study	Percent Recidivism	Description of Study
Travin, Cullen and Protter, 1990	1%	515 sex offenders in a specialized sex offender treatment program
Finkelhor, Hotaling, Lewis and Smith, 1990 (female respondents)	1%	Telephone survey of 1,481 women about their sexual victimization experiences
Rowan, Rowan and Langelier, 1990	1.5%	600 sex offenders from the New Hampshire judicial system and Vermont social service agencies and courts
Vandiver and Kercher, 2004	1.6%	29,376 registered sex offenders in Texas
Sandler and Freeman, 2007	2%	Total number of registered sex offenders in New York in August 2005 not given
Vandiver and Walker, 2002	2.4%	1,644 registered sex offenders in Arkansas
Sandler and Freeman, 2009	3.2%	168,037 registered sex offenders in New York between 1986 and 2006
Vandiver, 2010	3.1%	7,385 adults arrested for a sex offense; all adults arrested for a sex offense in 2001 (NIBRS data, including 21 states)
Faller, 1987	14%	Child Abuse and Neglect Treatment Center in Michigan
Finkelhor et al., 1990 (male respondents)	17%	Telephone survey of 1,145 men about their sexual victimization experiences
Finkelhor, Williams and Burns, 1988	40%	271 child sexual-abuse cases occurring in daycare, nationwide
Petrovich and Templer, 1984	59%	83 incarcerated rapists report of their childhood sexual victimization

CONCLUSION

JSCs and WSC, like adults who have committed a sex crime, are heterogeneous offenders. Substantive research on WSC did not begin until the 1980s, whereas the research on JSCs began earlier. Research on both groups is constrained by small sample sizes that are often limited to small geographical areas. One must interpret this research with caution. Many of the studies present conflicting findings, leading to unclear conclusions. The research is in its early stages and, at this point, is not as strong as the research on adults. It does, however, show some patterns for JSCs and WSC. These are summarized in the Review Points.

REVIEW POINTS

- JSCs should be examined because (a) many adults begin offending when they are juveniles; (b) juveniles account for many of the sexual crimes; (c) sex-offender treatment may need to be modified to fit juveniles' needs.
- Although many adults who have committed a sex crime report committing sex crimes when they were juveniles, JSCs are unlikely to commit sex crimes in their adulthood.
- JSCs are not that unique when compared to juveniles who have committed a nonsexual crime.
- Several typologies of JSCs have been developed and range from two categories (i.e., simply distinguishing between those who abuse children and those who abuse peers) to seven categories of offenders. They are based on psychological tests, criminal histories, social histories, and personality profiles.
- Explanations of why juveniles commit sex crimes include exposure to pornography, a cycle of sexual abuse based on one's perception of self, and other salient factors not explained by general criminogenic development.
- Many assessment tools have been developed specifically for JSCs.
- Structured treatment programs for JSCs did not begin until the 1980s. Cognitive-behavioral therapy is the most common type of treatment. Research shows treatment effectively reduces the likelihood of recidivism.
- WSC account for approximately less than 10% of all reported sex crimes.
- Three common categories of WSC among several developed typologies include (1) nurturer, (2) co-offenders, and (3) other.
- Explanations for women who sexually abuse include reenactment of abuse, narcissism when sexually abusing one's own child, exposure to previous abuse (extension of battered woman syndrome), desire for intimacy, economic gain, and domestic violence.
- Assessment of WSC typically involves assessing a host of criminal, social, and psychological factors because no formal assessment tools have been created for WSC.
- Cognitive-behavioral treatments have been developed and tailored to meet the needs of WSC.
- The majority of studies show that sexual recidivism rates of WSC are relatively low—usually less than 5%. More recent studies, though, suggest moderate rates of recidivism.

REFERENCES

Abel, G., Becker, J. V., Mittelman, M., Cunningham-Rathner, J., Rouleau, J. L., & Murphy, W. D. (1987). Self-reported sex crimes of nonincarcerated paraphiliacs. *Journal of Interpersonal Violence, 2*(1), 3–25.

American Psychiatric Association. (2013). *Diagnostic and statistical manual of mental disorders* (5th ed.). [DSM-5] Author.

Aos, S., Phipps, P., Barnoski, R., & Lieb, R. (2001). *The comparative cost and benefits of programs to reduce crime*. Washington State Institute for Public Policy.

Associated Press. (2005). Letourneau marries Fualaau amid media circus. *Seattle Post-Intelligencer*. http://www.seattlepi.com/local/article/Letourneau-marries-Fualaau-amid-media-circus-1174066.php

Awad, G. A., & Saunders, E. B. (1991). Male adolescent sexual assaulters: Clinical observations. *Journal of Interpersonal Violence, 6*(4), 446–460. https://www.doi.org/10.1177/088626091006004004

Bader, S. M., Welsh, R., & Scalora, M. J. (2010). Recidivism among female child molesters. *Violence and Victims, 25*(3), 349–362. https://www.doi.org/ 10.1891/0886-6708.25.3.349

Baker, A. J. L., Tabacoff, R., Tornusciolo, G., & Eisenstadt, M. (2004). Family secrecy: A comparative study of juvenile sex offenders and youth with conduct disorders. *Family Process, 42*(1), 105–116. https://www.doi.org/10.1111/j.1545-5300.2003.00105.x

Baly, A., & Butler, S. (2017). Empathy deficits and adolescent sexual offending: A systematic review of the evidence base. *Aggression and Violent Behavior, 36*, 81–97. https://www.doi.org/10.1016/j.avb.2017.07.007

Barbaree, H. E., & Cortoni, F. A. (1993). Treatment of the juvenile sex offender within the criminal justice and mental health systems. In H. E. Barbaree, W. L. Marshall & S. M. Hudson (Eds.), *The juvenile sex offender* (pp. 243–263). Guilford Press.

Barra, S., Bessler, C., Landolt, M. A., & Aebi, M. (2018). Patterns of adverse childhood experiences in juveniles who sexually offended. *Sexual Abuse: A Journal of Research and Treatment, 30*(7), 803–827. https://www.doi.org/10.1177/1079063217697135

Becker, J. V. (1998). What we know about the characteristics and treatment of adolescents who have committed sex crimes. *Child Maltreatment, 3*(4), 317–329. https://www.doi.org/10.1177/1077559598003004004

Becker, J. V. (2007). *A snapshot of sex offenders: Juveniles vs. adults*. [Paper presentation]. National Legislative Briefing Sex Offender Management Policy in the States, Washington, DC. http://www.csg.org/knowledgecenter/docs/pubsafety/Becker.pdf

Becker, J. V., Cunningham-Rathner, J., & Kaplan, M. S. (1986). Adolescent sexual offenders: Demographics, criminal and sexual histories, and recommendations for reducing future offenses. *Journal of Interpersonal Violence, 1*(4), 431–445. https://www.doi.org/10.1177/088626086001004003

Becker, J. V., & Stein, R. M. (1991). Is sexual erotica associated with sexual deviance in adolescent males? *International Journal of Law and Psychiatry, 14*(1–2), 85–95. https://www.doi.org/10.1016/0160-2527(91)90026-J

Beech, A. R., Craig, L., Browne, K. D., & Wiley, J. (Eds.). (2009). *Assessment and treatment of sex offenders: A handbook*. Wiley-Blackwell. https://www.doi.org/10.1002/9780470714362

Blanchette, K., & Brown, S. L. (2006). *The assessment and treatment of women offenders: An integrated perspective*. John Wiley & Sons.

Blanchette, K., & Taylor, K. N. (2010). A review of treatment initiatives for female sexual offenders. In T. Gannon & F. Cortoni (Eds.), *Female sexual offenders: Theory, assessment, and treatment* (pp. 119–142). John Wiley & Sons. https://www.doi.org/10.1002/9780470666715

Bloom, B., Owen, B., & Covington, S. (2003). *Gender-responsive strategies: Research practice, and guiding principles for women offenders*. National Institute of Corrections. https://s3.amazonaws.com/static.nicic.gov/Library/018017.pdf

Briere, J., & Runtz, M. (1991). The long-term effects of sexual abuse: A review and synthesis. *New Directions for Mental Health Services, 51*(3), 3–13. https://www.doi.org/10.1002/yd.23319915103

Broadhurst, R., & Loh, N. (2003). The probabilities of sex offender re-arrest. *Criminal Behaviour and Mental Health, 13*(2), 121–139. https://www.doi.org/10.1002/cbm.535

Browne, A., & Finkelhor, D. (1986). Impact of child sexual abuse: A review of research. *American Psychological Association, 99*(1), 66–77. https://psycnet.apa.org/doi/10.1037/0033-2909.99.1.66

Burton, D., & Miner, M. (2016). Exploring the theories explaining male adolescent perpetration of sexual crimes. In *The Wiley handbook on the theories, assessment and treatment of sexual offending* (pp. 497–518). Wiley-Blackwell. https://www.doi.org/10.1002/9781118574003.wattso024

Burton, D. L. & Smith-Darden, J. (2000). *1996 nationwide survey: A summary of the past ten years of specialized treatment with projections for the coming decade.* Safer Society Program & Press.

Butler, S., & Seto, M. C. (2002). Distinguishing two types of adolescent sex offenders. *Journal of American Child Adolescent Psychiatry, 41*(1), 83–90. https://www.doi.org/10.1097/00004583-200201000-00015

Caldwell, M. F. (2010). Study characteristics and recidivism base rates in juvenile sex offender recidivism. *International Journal of Offender Therapy and Comparative Criminology, 54*(2), 197–212. https://www.doi.org/10.1177%2F0306624X08330016

Caldwell, M. F., Ziemke, M., & Vitacco, M. (2008). An examination of the sex offender registration and notification act as applied to juveniles: Evaluating the ability to predict sexual recidivism. *Psychology, Public Policy, and Law, 14*(2), 89–114. https://psycnet.apa.org/doi/10.1037/a0013241

Center for Sex Offender Management. (n.d.). The effective management of juvenile sex offenders in the community: A training curriculum. http://csom.org/train/juvenile/index.html

Chaffin, M. (2008). Our minds are made up—don't confuse us with the facts: Commentary on policies concerning children with sexual behavior problems and juvenile sex offenders. *Child Maltreatment, 13*(2), 110–121. https://www.doi.org/10.1177%2F1077559508314510

Craig, L. A., Browne, K. D., & Beech, A. R. (2008). *Assessing risk in sex offenders: A practitioner's guide.* John Wiley & Sons.

Comartin, E. B., Burgess-Proctor, A., Kubiak, S., & Kernsmith, P. (2018). Factors related to co-offending and coerced offending among female sex offenders: The role of childhood and adult trauma histories. *Violence and Victims, 33*, 53–74. https://www.doi.org/10.1891/0886-6708.33.1.53

Correctional Services Canada. (2001). *Women who sexually offend: A protocol for assessment and treatment.* Author.

Cortoni, F., Babchishin, K. M., & Rat, C. (2017). The proportion of sexual offenders who are women is higher than thought: A meta-analysis. *Criminal Justice & Behavior, 44*(2), 145–162. https://www.doi.org/10.1177%2F0093854816658923

Cortoni, F., & Gannon, T. A. (2013). What works with female sexual offenders. In L. A. Craig, L. Dixon, & T. A. Gannon (Eds.), *What works in offender rehabilitation: An evidence based approach to assessment and treatment* (pp. 271–284). Wiley-Blackwell. https://kar.kent.ac.uk/35062/1/Cortoni%20%26%20Gannon%20What%20Works%20FSOs%20%282013%29%20.pdf

Crawford, E. (2012). *A grounded theory analysis of the perpetration of child sexual abuse by female sex offenders.* [Unpublished doctoral dissertation]. Walden University.

Daly, K. (1989). Rethinking judicial paternalism: Gender, work–family relations, and sentencing. *Gender and Society, 3*(1), 9–36. https://www.doi.org/10.1177%2F089124389003001002

Davin, P. A., Hislop, J., & Dunbar, T. (1999). *Female sexual abusers: Three views*. Safer Society Press.

Davis, G. E., & Leitenberg, H. (1987). Adolescent sex offenders. *Psychology Bulletin, 101*(3), 417–427. https://www.doi.org/10.1037/0033-2909.101.3.417

DeLisi, M., Kosloski, A. E., Vaughn, M. G., Caudill, J. W., & Trulson, C. R. (2014). Does childhood sexual abuse victimization translate into juvenile sexual offending? New evidence. *Violence and Victims, 29*(4), 620–635. https://www.doi.org/10.1891/0886-6708.VV-D-13-00003

Denov, M. S. (2004). *Perspectives on female sex offending: A culture of denial*. Ashgate Publishing Company.

Dickson, E. (2020). 7 shocking revelations from Netflix's new Jeffrey Epstein documentary. *Salon*. https://www.salon.com/2020/05/30/7-shocking-revelations-from-netflixs-new-jeffrey-epstein-documentary_partner/

Eldridge, H., & Saradjian, J. (2000). Replacing the function of abusive behaviors for the offender: Remaking relapse prevention in working with women who sexually abuse children. In D. R. Laws, S. M. Hudson & T. Ward (Eds.), *Remaking relapse prevention with sex offenders: A sourcebook* (pp. 402–426). Sage.

Epperson, D. L., Ralston, C. A., Fowers, D., & DeWitt, J. (2006). Actuarial risk assessment with juveniles who offend sexually: Development of the Juvenile Sex crime Recidivism Risk Assessment Tool-II (JSORRAT-II). In D. S. Prescott (Ed.), *Risk assessment of youth who have sexually abused: Theory, controversy, and emerging strategies* (pp. 222–236). Wood N' Barnes.

Epperson, D. L., Ralston, C. A., Fowers, D., & DeWitt, J. (2005). Scoring guidelines for the Juvenile Sex Crime Recidivism Risk Assessment Tool–II (JSORRAT–II). http://forensiccounselor.org/images/file/JSORRAT-II.pdf

Federal Bureau of Investigation (FBI). (2021). Crime in the United States: 2000–19. *U.S. Department of Justice*. https://www.fbi.gov/services/cjis/ucr/publications

Ferrara, M. L., & McDonald, S. (1996). *Treatment of the juvenile sex offender: Neurological and Psychiatric Impairments*. Jason Aronson.

Ford, M. E., & Linney, J. A. (1995). Comparative analysis of juvenile sexual offenders, violent nonsexual offenders, and status offenders. *Journal of Interpersonal Violence, 10*, 56–70. https://www.doi.org/10.1177%2F088626095010001004

Foward, S., & Buck, C. (1978). *Betrayal of innocence: Incest and its devastation*. J. P. Teacher.

Freeman, N. J., & Sandler, J. C. (2008). Female and male sex offenders: A comparison of recidivism patterns and risk factors. *Journal of Interpersonal Violence, 23*(10), 1394–1413. https://www.doi.org/10.1177%2F0886260508314304

Gajanan, M. (2020). The story behind the Netflix docuseries Jeffrey Epstein: *Filthy Rich*. *Time*. https://time.com/5839057/jeffrey-epstein-netflix-documentary-filthy-rich/

Gannon, T. A., & Cortoni, F. (2010). Female sexual offenders: Theory, assessment and treatment – an introduction. In T. A. Gannon & F. Cortoni (Eds.), *Female sexual offenders: Theory, assessment, and treatment* (pp. 1–7). John Wiley & Sons. https://kar.kent.ac.uk/53594/1/Cortoni&GannoninpressAssessmentFSOs.pdf

Gannon, T. A., Rose, M. R., & Ward, T. (2008). A descriptive model of the offense process for female sexual offenders. *Sexual Abuse: A Journal of Research and Treatment, 20*(3), 352–374. https://www.doi.org/10.1177%2F1079063208322495

Graves, R., Openshaw, K., Ascoine, F., & Ericksen, S. (1996). Demographic and parental characteristics of youthful sexual offenders. *International Journal of Offender Therapy and Comparative Criminology, 40*(4), 300–317. https://www.doi.org/10.1177%2F0306624X96404006

Groth, A. N. (1982). The incest offender. In S. M. Sgroi (Ed.), *Handbook of clinical intervention in child sexual abuse* (pp. 215–239). D.C. Heath and Co.

Gunby, C., & Woodhams, J. (2010). Sexually deviant juveniles: Comparisons between the offender and offence characteristics of "child abusers" and "peer abusers." *Psychology, Crime & Law, 16*(1–2), 47–64. https://www.doi.org/10.1080/10683160802621966

Hardyman, P. L., & Van Voorhis, P. (2004). *Developing gender-specific classification systems for women offenders*. National Institute of Corrections.

Hsu, L. K. G., & Starzynski, J. (1990). Adolescent rapists and adolescent child sexual assaulters. *International Journal of Offender Therapy and Comparative Criminology, 34*(1), 23–30. https://www.doi.org/10.1177%2F0306624X9003400104

Hunter, J. A. (2000). *Understanding juvenile sex offenders: Research findings and guidelines for effective management and treatment*. Juvenile Justice Fact Sheet. Institute of Law, Psychiatry, and Public Policy.

Hunter, J. A., Figueredo, A. J., Malamuth, N. M., & Becker, J. V. (2003). Juvenile sex offenders: Toward the development of a typology. *Sexual Abuse: A Journal of Research and Treatment, 15*(1), 27–48. https://www.doi.org/10.1023/A:1020663723593

Huntington, C., Pearlman, D. N., & Orchowski, L. (2020). The confluence model of sexual aggression: An application with adolescent males. *Journal of Interpersonal Violence*, Advance online publication. https://www.doi.org/10.1177/0886260520915550

Johansson-Love, J., & Fremouw, W. (2009). Female sex offenders: A controlled comparison of offender and victim/crime characteristics. *Journal of Family Violence, 24*, 367–376. https://www.doi.org/10.1007/s10896-009-9236-5

Johnson, T. C. (1988). Child-perpetrators—Children who molest other children: Preliminary findings. *Child Abuse & Neglect, 12*(2), 219–229. https://www.doi.org/10.1016/0145-2134(88)90030-0

Jones, M. (2007). How can you distinguish a budding pedophile from a kid with real boundary issues? *The New York Times Magazine*. http://www.nytimes.com/2007/07/22/magazine/22juvenile-t.html?pagewanted=all&_r=0

Katz, R. (1990). Psychosocial adjustment in adolescent child molesters. *Child Abuse & Neglect, 14*(4), 567–575. https://www.doi.org/10.1016/0145-2134(90)90104-2

Kemper, T. S., & Kistner, J. A. (2007). Offense history and recidivism in three victim-age based groups of juvenile sex offenders. *Sexual Abuse: A Journal of Research and Treatment, 19*(4), 409–424. https://www.doi.org/10.1007/s11194-007-9061-4

Knopp, F. H. (1984). *Retraining adult sex offenders: Methods and models*. Safer Society Press.

Krell, A. (2019). The only woman sex offender on McNeil Island is released after more than 20 years. *The News Tribune*. https://www.thenewstribune.com/news/local/crime/article231261193.html#storylink=cpy

Lab, S. P., Shields, G., & Schondel, C. (1993). An evaluation of juvenile sexual offender treatment. *Crime and Delinquency, 39*(4), 543–553. https://www.doi.org/10.1177%2F0011128793039004008

Lambie, I., & Seymour, F. (2006). One size does not fit all: Future directions for the treatment of sexually abusive youth in New Zealand. *Journal of Sexual Aggression, 12*(2), 175–187. https://www.doi.org/10.1080/13552600600823647

Långström, N., Grann, M., & Lindblad, F. (2000). A preliminary typology of young sex offenders. *Journal of Adolescence, 23*(3), 319–329. https://www.doi.org/10.1177%2F088626000015008005

Lateef, R., & Jenney, A. (2020). Understanding sexually victimized male adolescents with sexually abusive behaviors: A narrative review and clinical implications. *Trauma, Violence, & Abuse*. Advance online publication. https://www.doi.org/10.1177/1524838020906558

Levenson, J. S., Baglivio, M., Wolff, K. T., Epps, N., Royall, W., Gomez, K. C., & Kaplan, D. (2017). You learn what you live: Prevalence of childhood adversity in the lives of juveniles arrested for sexual offenses. *Advances in Social Work, 18*(1), 313–334. https://www.doi.org/10.18060/21204

Ling, L. (2010). Female sex offender's first TV interview video. *OWN*. http://www.oprah.com/oprahshow/Female-Sex-Offenders-First-TV-Interview-Video

Lussier, P., & Blockland, A. (2014). The adolescence-adulthood transition and Robin's continuity paradox: Criminal career patterns of juvenile and adult sex offenders in a prospective longitudinal birth cohort study. *Journal of Criminal Justice, 42*(2), 153–163. https://www.doi.org/10.1016/j.jcrimjus.2013.07.004

Lussier, P., Van den Berg, C., Bijleveld, C., & Hendriks, J. (2012). A developmental taxonomy of juvenile sex offenders for theory, research and prevention. *Criminal Justice and Behavior, 39*(12), 1559–1581. https://www.doi.org/10.1177%2F0093854812455739

Mash, E. J., & Barkley, R. A. (1996). *Child psychopathology*. Guilford Press.

Mathews, R., Hunter, J. A., Jr., & Vuz, J. (1997). Juvenile female sexual offenders: Clinical characteristics and treatment issues. *Sexual Abuse: A Journal of Research and Treatment, 9*(3), 187–199. https://www.doi.org/10.1007/BF02675064

Mathews, R., Matthews, J. K., & Speltz, K. (1989). *Female sexual offenders: An exploratory study*. Safer Society Press.

Mayer, A. (1992). *Women sex offenders: Treatment and dynamics*. Learning Publications, Inc.

McCarty, L. M. (1981). Investigation of incest: Opportunity to motivate families to seek help. *Child Welfare, 60*(10), 679–689.

McCarty, L. M. (1986). Mother–child incest: Characteristics of the offender. *Child Welfare, 65*(5), 447–458.

McCuish, E. C., & Lussier, P. (2017). Unfinished stories: From juvenile sex offenders to juvenile sex offending through a developmental life course perspective. *Aggression and Violent Behavior, 37*, 71–78. https://www.doi.org/10.1016/j.avb.2017.09.004

Merrick, M. T., Ford, D. C., Ports, K. A., Guinn, A. S., Chen, J., Klevens, J., . . . & Mercy, J. A. (2019). Vital signs: Estimated proportion of adult health problems attributable to adverse childhood experiences and implications for prevention—25 States, 2015–2017. *Morbidity and Mortality Weekly Report, 68*(44), 999–1005. https://www.doi.org/10.15585%2Fmmwr.mm6844e1

Miccio-Fonseca, L. C. (2000). Adult and adolescent female sex offenders: Experiences compared to other female and male sex offenders. *Journal of Psychology and Human Sexuality, 11*(3), 75–88. https://www./doi.org/10.1300/J056v11n03_08

Miller, H. A., & Marshall, E. A. (2019). Comparing solo-and co-offending female sex offenders on variables of pathology, offense characteristics, and recidivism. *Sexual Abuse: A Journal of Research and Treatment, 31*(8), 972–990. https://www.doi.org/10.1177%2F1079063218791179

National Adolescent Perpetrator Network. (1993). The revised report from the National Task Force on Juvenile Sexual Offending. *Juvenile and Family Court Journal, 44*, 5–120.

National Alliance for the Mentally Ill. (n.d.). Cognitive behavioral therapy. http://www.nami.org/Learn-More/Treatment/Psychotherapy

National Task Force on Juvenile Sexual Offending. (1993). Preliminary report. *Juvenile and Family Court Journal, 44*(4), 1–120.

Neumeister, L. (2022, January 14). June sentence set for Ghislaine Maxwell in sex trafficking case. ABC News. https://abcnews.go.com/US/wireStory/june-sentence-set-ghislaine-maxwell-sex-traffic-case-82276216

Nisbet, I. A., Wilson, P. H., & Smallbone, S. W. (2004). A prospective longitudinal study of sexual recidivism among adolescent sex offenders. *Sexual Abuse: A Journal of Research and Treatment, 16*(3), 223–234. https://www.doi.org/10.1023/B:SEBU.0000029134.93758.c5

O'Brien, M., & Bera, W. (1986). Adolescent sexual offenders: A descriptive typology. *National Family Life Education Network, 1*(3), 1–4.

Oliver, B. E. (2007). Preventing female-perpetrated sexual abuse. *Trauma, Violence & Abuse, 8*(1), 19–32. https://www.doi.org/10.1177%2F1524838006296747

Oxnam, P., & Vess, J. (2006). A personality-based typology of adolescent sexual offenders using the Millon adolescent clinical inventory. *New Zealand Journal of Psychology, 35*(1), 36–44.

Peterson, K. D., Colebank, K. D., & Motta, L. L. (2001). Female sexual offender recidivism. [Paper presentation]. *Association for the Treatment of Sexual Abusers*.

Pflugradt, D. M., & Allen, B. P. (2010). An exploratory analysis of executive functioning for female sexual offenders: A comparison of characteristics across offense typologies. *Journal of Child Sexual Abuse, 19*(4), 434–449. https://www.doi.org/10.1080/10538712.2010.495701

Pflugradt, D. M., Allen, B. P., & Marshall, W. L. (2018). A gendered strength-based treatment model for female sexual offenders. *Aggression and Violent Behavior, 40*, 12–18. https://www.doi.org/10.1016/j.avb.2018.02.012

Prentky, R., Harris, B., & Righthand, S. (2000). An actuarial procedure for assessing risk with juvenile sex offenders. *Sexual Abuse: A Journal of Research and Treatment, 12*(2), 71–93. https://www.doi.org/10.1023/A:1009568006487

Prentky, R., & Righthand, S. (2003). *Juvenile Sex Offender Assessment Protocol-II (J-SOAP-II) Manual* [NCJ 202316]. Office of Juvenile Justice and Delinquency Prevention.

Rasmussen, L. A. (1999). Factors related to recidivism among juvenile sexual offenders. *Sexual Abuse: A Journal of Research and Treatment, 11*(1), 69–85. https://www.doi.org/10.1177%2F107906329901100106

Rasmussen, L. A. (2013). Young people who sexually abuse: A historical perspective and future directions. *Journal of Child Sexual Abuse, 22*, 119–141. https://www.doi.org/10.1080/10538712.2013.744646

Reiss, I. L. (1960). *Premarital sexual standards in America*. Free Press.

Reitzel, L. R., & Carbonell, J. L. (2006). The effectiveness of sexual offender treatment as measured by recidivism: A meta-analysis. *Sexual Abuse: A Journal of Research and Treatment, 18*(4), 401–421. https://www.doi.org/10.1007/s11194-006-9031-2

Richardson, G., Kelley, T. P., Graham, F., & Bhate, S. R. (2004). A personality-based taxonomy of sexually abusive adolescents derived from the Millon Adolescent Clinical Inventory (MACI). *British Journal of Clinical Psychology, 43*(3), 285–298. https://www.doi.org/10.1348/0144665031752998

Righthand, S., & Welch, C. (2001). *Juveniles who have sexually offended: A review of the professional literature*. Office of Juvenile Justice and Delinquency Prevention.

Righthand, S., & Welch, C. (2004). Characteristics of youth who sexually offend. *Journal of Child Sexual Abuse, 13*(3/4), 15–32. https://www.doi.org/10.1300/J070v13n03_02

Ronis, S. T., & Borduin, C. M. (2007). Individual, family, peer, and academic characteristics of male juvenile sexual offenders. *Journal of Abnormal Child Psychology, 35*(2), 153–163. https://www.doi.org/10.1007/s10802-006-9058-3

Rubinstein, M., Yeager, C. A. Goodstein, C., & Lewis, D. O. (1993). Sexually assaultive male juveniles: A follow-up. *American Journal of Psychiatry, 150*, 262–265. https://www.doi.org/10.1176/ajp.150.2.262

Ryan, G., Miyoshi, T. J., Metzner, J. L., Krugman, R. D., & Fryer, G. E. (1996). Trends in a national sample of sexually abusive youths. *Journal of the American Academy of Child and Adolescent Psychiatry, 35*(1), 17–25. https://www.doi.org/10.1097/00004583-199601000-00008

Saldana, L., Swenson, C., & Letourneau, E. J. (2006). Multisystemic therapy with juveniles who sexually abuse. In R. E. Longo & D. S. Prescott (Eds.), *Current perspectives: Working with sexually aggressive youth and youth with sexual behavior problems* (pp. 119–141). NEARI Press.

Salter, A. (2018). *Predators: Pedophiles, rapists, and other sex offenders.* Basic Books.

Saradjian, J., & Hanks, H. (1996). *Women who sexually abuse children: From research to practice.* John Wiley.

Sarrel, P. M., & Masters, W. H. (1982). Sexual molestation of men by women. *Archives of Sexual Behavior, 11*(2), 117–131. https://www.doi.org/10.1007/BF01541979

Schwartz-Mette, R. A., Righthand, S., Hecker, J., Dore, G., & Huff, R. (2019). Long-term predictive validity of the juvenile sex offender assessment protocol–II: Research and practice implications. *Sexual Abuse: A Journal of Research and Treatment, 32*(5), 499–520. https://www.doi.org/10.1177%2F1079063219825871

Seto, M. C., & Lalumière, M. L. (2010). What is so special about male adolescent sexual offending? A review and test of explanations through meta-analysis. *Psychological Bulletin, 136*(4), 526–575. https://www.doi.org/10.1037/a0019700

Shaw, C. D., Vaughan, T. J., & Vandiver, M. D. (2020). Reported sexual-offense incidents in the United States: Arrest disparities between women and men. *Journal of Interpersonal Violence.* Advance online publication. https://www.doi.org/10.1177/0886260520958661

Shema, C. R. (2019). Forensic psychiatric analysis of juvenile delinquency and sexual abuse perspective. In *Social issues surrounding harassment and assault: Breakthroughs in research and practice* (pp. 394–409). IGI Global. https://www.doi.org/ 10.4018/978-1-5225-7036-3.ch022

Siria, S., Echeburúa, E., & Amor, P. J. (2020). Characteristics and risk factors in juvenile sexual offenders. *Psicothema, 32*(3), 314–321. https://www.doi.org/10.7334/psicothema 2019.349

Syed, F., & Williams, S. (1996). *Case studies of female sex offenders in the Correctional Service of Canada.* Ottawa: Correctional Service of Canada.

ten Bensel, T., Gibbs, B., & Burkey, C. R. (2019a). Female sex offenders: Is there a difference between solo and co-offenders? *Journal of Interpersonal Violence, 34*(19), 4061–4084. https://www.doi.org/10.1177%2F0886260516674202

ten Bensel, T., Gibbs, B. R., & Raptopoulos, K. (2019b). The role of childhood victimization on the severity of adult offending among female sex offenders. *Victims & Offenders, 14*(6), 758–775. https://www.doi.org/10.1080/15564886.2019.1630044

van Wijk, A., Vermeiren, R., Loeber, R., Hart-Kerkhoffs, L., Doreleijers, T., & Bullens, R. (2006). Juvenile sex offenders compared to non-sex offenders: A review of the literature. *Trauma, Violence & Abuse, 7*(4), 227–243. https://www.doi.org/10.1177%2F1524838006292519

Vandiver, D. M. (2003). *Female sex offenders: A case study approach.* [Paper presentation]. Academy of Criminal Justice Sciences.

Vandiver, D. M. (2006a). Female sex offenders. In R. D. M. Anulty & M. M. Burnette (Eds.), *Sex and sexuality* (Vol. 3, pp. 47–80). Praeger.

Vandiver, D. M. (2006b). Female sex offenders: A comparison of solo offenders and co-offenders. *Violence and Victims, 21*(3), 339–354. https://www.doi.org/10.1891/vivi.21.3.339

Vandiver, D. M. (2006c). A prospective analysis of juvenile male sex offenders: Characteristics and recidivism rates as adults. *Journal of Interpersonal Violence, 21*(5), 673–688. https://www.doi.org/10.1177%2F0886260506287113

Vandiver, D. M., & Kercher, G. (2004). Offender and victim characteristics of registered female sexual offenders in Texas: A proposed typology of female sexual offenders. *Sexual Abuse: A Journal of Research and Treatment, 16*(2), 121–137. https://www.doi.org/10.1023/B:SEBU.0000023061.77061.17

Vandiver, D. M., Braithwaite, J., & Stafford, M. C. (2018). A longitudinal assessment of recidivism rates of female sex offenders: comparing recidivist and non-recidivists. *Sexual Abuse: A Journal of Research and Treatment. American Journal of Criminal Justice, 44,* 211–229. https://www.doi.org/10.1007/s12103-018-9451-9

Veneziano, C., Veneziano, L., & LeGrand, S. (2000). The relationship between adolescent sex offender behaviors and victim characteristics with prior victimization. *Journal of Interpersonal Violence, 15*(4), 363–374. https://www.doi.org/10.1177%2F088626000015004002

Veneziano, C., Veneziano, L., LeGrand, S., & Richards, L. (2004). Neuropsychological executive functions of adolescent sex offenders and nonsex offenders. *Perceptual and Motor Skills, 98*(2), 661–674. https://www.doi.org/10.2466%2Fpms.98.2.661-674

Victor, D. (2020). Mary Kay Letourneau, teacher, who raped student and then married him, dies at 58. *New York Times.* https://www.nytimes.com/2020/07/07/obituaries/mary-kay-letourneau-dead.html

Viljoen, J. L., Elkovitch, N., Scalora, M. J., & Ullman, D. (2009). Assessment of reoffense risk in adolescents who have committed sex crimes: Predictive validity of the ERASOR, PCL: YV, YLS/CMI, and Static-99. *Criminal Justice and Behavior, 36*(10), 981–1000. https://www.doi.org/10.1177%2F0093854809340991

Walker, D. F., McGovern, S. K., Poey, E. L., & Otis, K. E. (2004). Treatment effectiveness for male adolescent sexual offenders: A meta-analysis and review. *Journal of Child Sexual Abuse, 13*(3–4), 281–293. https://www.doi.org/10.1300/J070v13n03_14

West, S. G., Friedman, S. H., & Kim, K. D. (2011). Women accused of sex offenses: A gender-based comparison. *Behavioral Sciences and the Law, 29*(5), 728–740. https://www.doi.org/10.1002/bsl.1007

Williams, R., Gillespie, S. M., Elliott, I. A., & Eldridge, H. J. (2019). Characteristics of female solo and female co-offenders and male solo sexual offenders against children. *Sexual Abuse: A Journal of Research and Treatment, 31*(2), 151–172. https://www.doi.org/10.1177%2F1079063217724767

Worling, J. R. (1995). Adolescent sex offenders against females: Differences based on the age of their victims. *International Journal of Offender Therapy and Comparative Criminology, 39*(3), 276–293. https://www.doi.org/10.1177%2F0306624X9503900308

Worling, J. R. (2001). Personality-based typology of adolescent male sexual offenders: Differences in recidivism rates, victim-selection characteristics, and personal victimization histories. *Sexual Abuse: A Journal of Research and Treatment, 13*(3), 149–166. https://www.doi.org/10.1023/A:1009518532101

Worling, J. R., Bookalam, D., & Littlejohn, A. (2012). Prospective validity of the Estimate of Risk of Adolescent Sex crime Recidivism (ERASOR). *Sexual Abuse: A Journal of Research and Treatment, 24,* 203–223. https://www.doi.org/10.1177%2F1079063211407080

Worling, J., & Curwen, T. (2001). Estimate of risk of adolescent sex crime recidivism (The ERASOR—Version 2.0). In M. C. Calder (Ed.), *Juveniles and children who sexually abuse: Frameworks for assessment* (pp. 372–397). Russell House Publishing.

Yoder, J., Brown, A., Grady, M., Dillard, R., & Kennedy, N. (2020). Positive caregiving styles attenuating effects of cumulative trauma among youth who commit sexual crimes. *International Journal of Offender Therapy and Comparative Criminology.* Advance online publication. https://www.doi.org/10.1177/0306624X20952390

Yoder, J., Grady, M., & Precht, M. (2019). Relationships between early life victimization, antisocial traits, and sexual violence: Executive functioning as a mediator. *Child Sexual Abuse, 28*, 667–689. https://www.doi.org/10.1080/10538712.2019.1588819

Zgourides, G., Monto, M., & Harris, R. (1997). Correlates of adolescent male sex crime: Prior adult sexual contact, sexual attitudes, and use of sexually explicit materials. *International Journal of Offender Therapy and Comparative Criminology, 41*(3), 272–283. https://www.doi.org/10.1177%2F0306624X97413006

Zimring, F., Jennings, W. G., & Piquero, A. (2009). Investigating the continuity of sex offending: Evidence from the second Philadelphia birth cohort. *Justice Quarterly, 26*(1), 58–76. https://www.doi.org/10.1080/07418820801989734

DEFINITIONS

Adjudicated: An analogous term for "convicted" in an adult court proceeding—convicted refers to what occurs in an (adult) criminal court; adjudicated refers to what occurs in a juvenile court

Adverse Childhood Experiences (ACEs): Ten potentially traumatic events that occur in childhood (0–17 years) that are highly correlated with chronic physical, mental, and emotional health issues in adulthood

Attention Deficit (Hyperactivity) Disorder (ADD/ADHD): A childhood disorder characterized by an inability to maintain focus, pay attention, or control behavior and excess activity for a period of time exceeding 6 months

Cognitive-Behavioral Treatment: A type of therapy based on behaviorism and cognitive therapy that focuses on the connections among feelings, thoughts, and actions—It is used for a broad range of psychological disorders, including but not limited to depression, anxiety, posttraumatic stress disorders, and sex crimes and is the most common type of therapy used for sex offenders currently

Cognitive Distortions: Minimizing or denying the dangerousness of behavior, justifying it to relieve the offender of responsibility (e.g., children need to be taught about sex; children are seductive; the child is too young to know what is happening)

Conduct Disorder: A behavioral and emotional disorder affecting children and teenagers, characterized by long-lasting disruptive behavior, violence, and an inability to follow rules—behaviors can include aggressiveness, destructiveness, deceitfulness, and violation of rules and/or laws

Co-offender: A common category of WSC across several typologies—this category of women involves at least one other offender who is usually a romantic male partner; she may be coerced or is an active participant in the abuse

Depression: Also known as major depression or clinical depression, a mental health disorder characterized by long-lasting symptoms of loss of interest in activities that were once pleasurable, low self-esteem, and a pervasive low/depressed mood

Descriptive Model of Female Sexual Offending: A model proposed by Gannon that includes cognitive, behavioral, affective (i.e., emotional), and contextual factors that lead to women committing sex crimes; specifically, it includes three factors that potentially distinguish WSC from men who have committed a sex crime: (1) physical, sexual, and emotionally abusive childhood; (2) abusive relationships; and (3) co-offender influences

Emotional Intelligence: One's ability to perceive others' emotions and express one's emotions, which includes one's ability to process emotional information and respond appropriately to different cues in one's social environment—these characteristics are associated with mental health, leadership skills, and employment performance

Functional Family Therapy: A type of therapy for juveniles who have committed an offense that focuses on the structure and dynamics of the family, providing parents with the skills necessary to provide appropriate boundaries, discipline, and support for the juvenile

Grooming: The process of befriending and establishing an emotional connection with children for the purpose of sexually abusing them

Longitudinal Study: An empirical investigation that follows a sample or defined population over an extended period of time, usually several years or decades

Meta-analysis: A type of study that involves gathering all relevant studies on a particular topic and analyzes all of the results to gain a more comprehensive answer to the research question posed

Multisystemic Therapy: A type of therapy for juveniles who have committed an offense that involves an interdisciplinary approach focusing on family functioning, school performance, peer relationships, and prosocial behaviors

Nurturer: A common category of WSC across several typologies—these women typically sexually abuse someone who is a pre-teen or a teenage male; the offender is usually in some type of caretaking and/or supervisory role such as a teacher or babysitter

Prospective Study: An empirical investigation that begins with a sample or defined population and continues to follow it as subjects age over time

Retrospective Study: An empirical investigation that begins with a sample or defined population and assesses events that occurred previous to that time

Wraparound Services: A type of therapy for juveniles who have committed an offense that involves coordinating services within the community for the juvenile and their family

CHAPTER 7

Institutional Abuse

> **CHAPTER OBJECTIVES**
>
> - Define and identify the characteristics of institutional abuse
> - Describe the prevalence and characteristics of child molestation that occurs within the context of several organizations such as churches, schools, and civic organizations
> - Describe the prevalence and characteristics of sexual assault that occur within the context of several organizations such as higher-education institutions and the military
> - Describe the prevalence and characteristics of organizations (athletic organizations, police departments, prisons, and facilities for delinquent youth) that are affected by both child molestation and sexual assault
> - Provide suggestions for policies and procedures for organizations to respond appropriately to cases of sexual abuse allegations

People who are in positions to provide critical services to children have recently been thrust into the public spotlight by cases of clergy abuse. Other highlighted cases have involved people who serve in the capacity of a caretaker or a mentorship role. Others in the public eye, such as sports figures, have also found themselves in the media spotlight following sexual abuse allegations. In this chapter, we specifically address the myth that sex offenders do not have professional careers. Many persons who have committed a sex crime have successful careers and are in positions of authority. Child molestation occurs in a variety of settings and institutions such as churches, schools, and civic organizations. Sexual assault also occurs in various settings such as higher-education institutions and the military.

Moreover, some organizations face the challenges of responding to both child molestation and sexual assault. What is evident by the end of this chapter is that employees within these organizations, regardless of whether they respond to cases of child molestation or sexual assault, lack proactive policies and procedures to respond effectively to such incidents. In the conclusion of this chapter, we identify suggestions for a path forward to prevent and respond to cases of sexual abuse allegations.

We have discussed in Chapter 3 that rape and sexual assault serves as a way for an offender to exert power over a victim. Extensive research, both on offenders and victims, suggests that issues of power and anger (not just sexual arousal) are essential for understanding sex offenders' behavior, particularly rapists. Although research using both clinical and nonclinical samples has supported the notion of rape as an expression of power, the road less traveled examines offenders in *professions* of power who commit these crimes. In recent years, professionals who use their work or authority as a guise for targeting and sexually abusing people (particularly women and children) have come into public focus (Sullivan & Beech, 2002). In this chapter, we discuss sexual abuse as a tool used by authority figures.

A common theme in this chapter is that many organizations are ill-equipped to respond to sex crimes. Most lack proper employee training and formal policies about how to respond. This chapter, therefore, focuses on organizational systems and how claims of child molestation and sexual assault are responded to by those who are in decision-making positions within the organization. This includes a discussion of sex crimes (child molestation and sexual assault) within an institutional setting and the response to those sex crimes.

INSTITUTIONAL ABUSE CHARACTERISTICS

Institutional abuse is estimated to account for only about 3% of all referrals of child sexual abuse. This includes all sexual abuse of children by persons who come in contact with children in some institutional setting. This can include a formal or informal organization such as a school, Boy Scouts of America, or a local community group that is volunteer based. The offender can be a teacher, a coach, or even a volunteer. Offenders who commit institutional abuse, however, often operate with considerable sophistication in grooming victims and bystanders (Sullivan & Beech, 2002).

Three processes identified as critical to the commission of institutional sexual abuse include (1) gaining access to victims, (2) initiating and maintaining the abuse, and (3) concealing the abuse (Colton et al., 2010). Although the molestation may occur outside of institutional settings, much of the groundwork has occurred there. Researchers have examined how these processes occur in institutional settings by assessing eight men who committed institutional abuse with 35 victims (Colton et al., 2010). Regarding gaining access to victims, there is anecdotal support for the notion that offenders choose employment opportunities that provide them with access to children (Colton et al., 2010). Furthermore, if their job does not provide them with access to children, they will adapt to create such opportunities (Leclerc et al., 2005). This includes providing home-tutoring duties. The institutional setting and context of the job are relied upon to prey on victims (Brannan et al., 1993). For example, one teacher contacted the victim when the victim was referred to him by a coworker (Colton et al., 2010). The offender had become known as someone who could handle troubled youth.

Manipulation is a critical aspect of gaining access to potential victims. The following description illustrates how a volunteer manipulated those around him to gain access to a victim:

> I manipulated the system, changed the timetables and made sure that [the victim] was on my roster, so we saw a lot of each other. . . . I manipulated the system very cleverly and made sure that it was well covered up. . . . I made some very calculated moves.
> (Colton et al., 2010, p. 353)

Child molesters often choose victims who are vulnerable, including those who lack a support system or have emotional problems (Salter, 2003). In the following scenario, an abuser describes targeting a particular victim:

> I targeted boys who were loners or less exuberant or less likely to say anything, or those single parents with usually only . . . [mom] at home who saw me as a father figure. . . .

> I got to know the boy's family and offered to take him home for the weekend to give his ... [mom] a break.... I targeted him at six years old, from when I discovered he was in trouble. He had behavior problems. I was seen as someone who could control him.... If the child was troublesome or a loner, then people were less likely to listen to him.... He was difficult and I preyed on that ... I created a cage for [him]. He'd only talk to me. His ... [mom] would ring me up to ask me to talk to him. I became very pleased with myself that this was an MO that seemed to work.
>
> (Colton et al., 2010, p. 354)

It is clear that the emotional and/or behavioral problems of a child can be used as a way to isolate and victimize them. Those who work in an institution become experts in identifying vulnerabilities and using them to target children (Colton et al., 2010).

The second process is initiating and maintaining the abuse. Child molesters are more likely to use manipulative strategies as opposed to simply relying on physical coercion (Leclerc et al., 2005). The offender's manipulative strategies include giving the victim's family the perception that the offender is "helping" the child. The offender often relies on a position of power and authority, providing rewards to the victim, pairing "treats" (taking the child somewhere they want to go) with offers to help the family and exposing the victim to pornography (Colton et al., 2010). Regarding touch, one offender describes its importance:

> Light, physical contact I would use as well. If I put my arm around them.... I would know straight away, if children backed off ... I wouldn't go near that child again. I would go through a gradual sort of progression.... I would be tactile in various ways outside the clothing, if they didn't object or didn't say anything then I just progressed from that.... I knew it was okay to carry on to an extra stage.... Each child was a potential victim as far as I was concerned.... The [victims] were the children I could get away with it.
>
> (Colton et al., 2010, p. 355)

Thus, this particular offender perceived all children as potential victims and simply would find ones who responded quickly to grooming techniques.

The third process is concealing the abuse. Research has found that disclosing abuse within an institutional setting often results in the offender's coworkers not believing the victim (Green, 2001). Building trust among coworkers is critical (Colton et al., 2010). One researcher described an offender who concealed the child molestation "by being a good teacher, popular" (Colton et al., 2010, p. 356). The offender noted that everyone, including his mother, believed he was innocent until he pled guilty.

Combining an established good reputation with a close relationship to the victim is usually sufficient to dissuade anyone from believing that the person committed a sex crime. For example, one offender noted that he minimized the abuse allegation by stating the victim would always come to him and that her parents knew she was coming over to his house for help with homework. Relying on one's good reputation and the use of implied threats can conceal abuse. One offender who was a home tutor indicated that if the students wanted to pass their exams, they had to seek assistance directly from the home tutor. Creating this type of situation is a type of implied threat. If they did not go to him for assistance (and be victimized), they might not pass their exams. He relied on his reputation as an excellent tutor to lure students. Typically, abusers have unsupervised access to children, which allows for victimization to occur. More importantly, supervised access to children allows for concealing the abuse. Furthermore, they are often in a trusted position.

Several researchers (Sullivan & Beech, 2002; Westcott, 1991) have identified four barriers to reporting sexual abuse within an institution:

1. A lack of policies and procedures that would allow reporting and investigation of sexual allegations
2. A view of the problem as limited to a single person rather than an institutional problem
3. The lack of transparency in the institution
4. The general "belief system" that surrounds the institution

Institutional abuse, therefore, is fraught with inadequate avenues for reporting sexual allegations and a lack of procedures for responding appropriately to such allegations. We now discuss specific institutions with attention to the unique problems each faces regarding reporting and responding to child sexual abuse allegations.

Religious Institutions

The movie/documentary *Spotlight* told the story of the Boston Globe investigative journalists who broke the story of sexual abuse in the Catholic Church. They won the 2003 Pulitzer Prize for Public Service. They detailed the sexual abuse committed by several priests that was systematically swept under the rug for decades. Subsequent to this reporting, the United States Conference of Catholic Bishops (USCCB) developed the Charter for the Protection of Children and Young People in 2002. The charter called for a National Review Board to conduct a study regarding the nature and scope of the problem. The charter and the National Review Board commissioned researchers at John Jay College of Criminal Justice to conduct a study. They conducted two studies, the *Nature and Scope of Sexual Abuse of Minors by Catholic Priests and Deacons: 1950–2002* (Terry & Tallon, 2004) and *The Causes and Context of Sexual Abuse of Minors by the Catholic Priests in the United States: 1950–2010* (Terry et al., 2011). They produced the most comprehensive report to date regarding details of sexual abuse of children within the Catholic Church (Terry et al., 2011).

The report addressed a pressing question: How many priests and victims existed in the Catholic Church? It was found that 4,392 of 109,694 priests who served for at least some time between 1950 and 2002 had allegations of some sex crime against them (Terry et al., 2011). By 2003, the dioceses were aware of 10,667. Thus, approximately 4% of priests were accused of sex crimes. Few allegations occurred from 1950 through the mid-1970s. The majority of the allegations were made in the late 1970s and early 1980s, and they sharply declined after that.

The offending priests at the time of their first sex crime were as young as 25 and as old as 90. Most (69%) were diocesan priests serving as a pastor or associate pastor at the time. Fifty-six percent of the priests had only one victim. Interestingly, however, 4% of the offending priests were responsible for 26% of the victims who had been identified by 2002. The findings suggest the possibility of a few "'rotten apples,' the colloquial term for a deviant individual who may elude even the most sophisticated of the exclusionary criteria for acceptance into the ministry" (Terry et al., 2011, p. 16).

Also noteworthy, less than 5% of the priests accused of child sexual abuse met the criteria for pedophilia (Terry et al., 2011). As noted in Chapter 4, many of those who molest children do not meet the criteria of a pedophile as defined by the DSM-5 (Terry et al., 2011). The priests who were sexually abusing children did not differ from priests who had not abused children on intelligence tests or psychological tests (Terry et al., 2011). Yet, the priests did show intimacy deficits and often lacked close personal relationships before and during seminary (Terry et al., 2011). Most of the victims were male (Terry et al., 2011), and the majority of the incidents (41%) occurred at the priest's home (Puro et al., 1997).

The results of the study identified several causes of the sex crimes, which include the following:

1. *General cultural factors*: including the impact of social changes in the 1960s and 1970s on individual priests' attitudes and behaviors and on organizational life, including social stratification, emphasis on individualism, and social movements
2. *Church-specific factors*: including the aftermath of Vatican II, changes in priestly formation, the impact of resignations from ministry, and changes in diocesan structures and leadership
3. *Environmental factors*: including changes in the patterns of parish activities, youth ministry, and changes in living situations and responsibilities of parish priests
4. *Psychological factors*: including psychological disorders, sexuality, past behavior, developmental issues, and vulnerabilities of individual priests
5. *Structural and legal factors*: including changes in the understanding of the legal status of particular behavior in society (Terry et al., 2011, p. 7)

As with sexual abuse in general, sex crimes within the Catholic Church resulted from a multitude of complex factors rather than a single underlying problem. Thus, they cannot place blame on the demands of celibacy alone or the presence of pedophilic tendencies (Terry et al., 2011).

The majority of the allegations of sexual abuse within the church resulted in having the priests participate in some type of treatment program, which included sex-offender-specific treatment, spiritual counseling, psychotherapy, or general counseling. When a priest had more than one allegation against him, he was more likely to participate in a treatment program. Legal officials were rarely involved in these cases. Only 14% of the offending priests were referred to authorities, and many of those cases involved expired statutes of limitation. Only 3% of priests were convicted, and 2% received a prison sentence (Terry et al., 2011).

Child molestation in the church is not limited to the Catholic Church, nor is it limited to the United States. Although official studies on child molestation in the Catholic Church have been conducted (Terry et al., 2011), such studies are virtually nonexistent in other religions. Many reported cases, however, do exist for a wide range of churches. In the excerpt below, for example, a victim of child molesting notes how the Pentecostal Church failed to respond appropriately to molestation allegations committed by a youth pastor:

> The Royal Commission into the Institutional Responses to Child Sexual Abuse has completed hearings into the way Pentecostal churches managed complaints of child sexual abuse in Victoria, New South Wales, and Queensland.
> On the final day of evidence at the Sydney hearing, Peter O'Brien, the lawyer representing a man who was abused by the youth pastor read a statement from his client, known as ALA, that said the past 10 years had been a "living hell."
> "They failed to detect the abuse. They failed to prevent the abuse. They failed to support us through the criminal trial process," ALA said.
> "It appears to me they were more concerned about the reputation and financial position of the ACC (Australian Christian Churches) above all else."
> (Chettle, 2014, n.p.)

Again, this example shows the lack of an adequate formal response to sex crimes against children. The Australian Christian Churches, however, pledged to pay advisors to develop child-protection policies.

K-12 Schools

Limited research exists concerning sex crimes committed by school employees (Shakeshaft, 2004). In general, there is a lack of systematic data collection on such incidents (Robert & Thompson, 2019). Moreover, the sources of data that do exist lack accuracy and are not complete (Robert & Thompson, 2019). Among the existing data, one researcher who relied upon a study by the American Association of University Women reported that approximately 7% of eighth- to 11th-grade students experienced unwanted sexual contact (Shakeshaft, 2004). Of those, 21% involved unwanted sexual contact from educators. Another study noted that 14% of surveyed high school students reported having sex with a teacher (Wishnietsky, 1991).

Also noteworthy, educator **sexual misconduct** is not limited to the United States —it is a global problem. For example, one study in Israel reported that 8% of secondary school students suffered sexual victimization by educational staff (Khoury-Kassabri, 2006). Likewise, the problem was recognized in Canada when the Ontario College of Teachers defined educator abuse and established a prevention plan (Ontario College of Teachers, 2002). Research conducted in the Netherlands on sexual misconduct committed by teachers shows that teacher–student sexual abuse does not always occur in seclusion (Timmerman, 2003).

Shakeshaft (2004) coined the term **educator misconduct**, which involves someone in a school, such as a teacher or coach, sharing pornography, having conversations with sexual talk, masturbation in the presence of a student, or other sexual behavior. The author noted that some of this behavior is illegal and some are not. All of the behavior, however, is considered inappropriate. Teachers who had jobs that involved time alone with students (e.g., coaches, tutors) were more likely to engage in educator misconduct than those who did not have such jobs.

Sexual crimes against students can also involve management personnel such as a principal or even a school district board member. The following is an example involving a school district board member in Virginia.

> A former Stafford School Board member agreed to a deal Tuesday in which he was convicted of five charges involving child molestation. . . . In exchange for the pleas . . . [the] prosecutor . . . dropped 106 other charges and agreed to seek no more than 4 years in prison when [the defendant] is sentenced. . . . The allegations first surfaced in 1997, when [the defendant], who had a top secret clearance as an employee of the Defense Intelligence Agency, was required to take a polygraph so he could perform work for the Central Intelligence Agency. During that polygraph, [the defendant] admitted having sexual desires for children. . . . [Later, the defendant] again admitted to a lifelong sexual interest in children. He told investigators that he likes children between 4 and 10 and prefers girls, though some of his victims were boys. He detailed in taped interviews and written statements how he would set up circumstances for his sexual gratification in ways in which the children would not recognize what was going on. This included watching them naked in bathtubs and improperly touching them when drying them off. [The defendant's] statements were turned over to the Stafford Sheriff's Office, which identified four victims who are all now adults. . . . [The defendant] served on the Stafford School Board for eight years, serving one term as the

Garrisonville District representative and one as the Hartwood District representative, and he was the chairman in 2005. His other local community involvement included the Boy Scouts and St. William of York Catholic Church.

(Epps, 2014, para. 1–15)

None of the victims in this example reported the incident to the police (Epps, 2014). The defendant also was involved in Boy Scouts and his church, which illustrates how sex offenders often place themselves in a position of authority and a have access to children.

Research has found that other adults often do not report suspected sex crimes given the serious nature of such accusations (Shakeshaft, 2013). Thus, other adults contribute to the problem by not reporting their suspicions. Shakeshaft (2013) identified warning signs for two types of educators that engage in sexual misconduct for the purpose of preventing educator misconduct. First, the ***fixated abuser*** makes up approximately one-third of known educator perpetrators. This type of perpetrator is typically a male elementary- or early middle-school teacher; perceived as an excellent teacher by his peers, students, parents, and administrators; and has received many teaching awards. He typically victimizes a male student he has groomed. The student's parents have also been groomed by offering extra attention by tutoring and taking the student to special events such as camping or fishing.

The second type of educator perpetrator identified is the ***opportunistic offender***, who comprise approximately two-thirds of educator perpetrators (Shakeshaft, 2013). These offenders are the regressed type because they are not exclusively attracted to children. The education has boundary and judgment problems. Such behaviors are relatively easy to identify. The offender will often chat with students and attend the same kinds of events where students are to fit in. This person is perceived as "hip" or "cool" by the students. The offender typically knows more about the personal lives of the students than is appropriate. The opportunistic offender can also be a female teacher who victimizes a student under the guise of romantic pursuit. As noted in Chapter 6, other researchers who developed typologies of women who commit sex crimes identified the teacher/lover (Mathews et al., 1989) and heterosexual female nurturer (Vandiver & Kercher, 2004). The students often perceive they are in love and dating the teacher.

Educators who groom students typically find vulnerable students (e.g., those estranged from their parents). After they are identified, the teacher praises the student, offers additional help and mentoring, and finds opportunities for overnight outings (Knoll, 2010; Robins, 2000). Throughout the process, the teacher increases the level of physical touching until they progress into sex. The teacher may also groom the parents. Parents are typically appreciative of the extra help the teacher is providing to the child. One researcher (Robins, 2000, p. 376), combining several sources of information ("Districts Should Appoint," 2006; Shakeshaft, 2004; Sutton, 2004), created a list of warning signs of educator sexual misconduct:

- Obvious or inappropriate preferential treatment of a student
- Excessive time spent alone with a student
- Excessive time spent with the student outside of class
- Repeated time spent in private spaces with a student
- Driving a student to or from school
- Befriending parents and making visits to their home
- Acting as a particular student's "confidant"
- Giving small gifts, cards, or letters to a student
- Inappropriate calls or emails to a student

- Overly affectionate behavior with a student
- Flirtatious behavior or off-color remarks around a student
- Other students often suspecting and joking about the student and teacher

In the case study below, an educator exhibits many of the warning signs noted above.

> The summer before [the victim] started high school, John met Mr. Ricci. John was an active member in the school sports club when Mr. Ricci requested a student to sit on the school council; John volunteered. At the same time, Mr. Ricci told John's mother that on occasion John could stay at his house to work on student council business and that he could be paid. Mr. Ricci convinced John's mother that such an arrangement would help John cope with his father's illness. John's mother agreed to this. . . . Several times, Mr. Ricci called to say John had fallen asleep on the couch and suggested John just stay overnight. John's grades began to fall and he had no explanation for his mother. . . . Mr. Ricci took John on a trip to New York City. For days after the trip, John['s] behavior markedly changed. He was withdrawn, sarcastic, and isolated himself. . . . John finally told his mother that Mr. Ricci had taken him to a gay bar and that night he awoke to being orally sodomized by the teacher. The mother reported the abuse to police. An investigative interview revealed that the teacher had been sexually abusing John between the ages of 14 and 17 at the teacher's home. In addition, Mr. Ricci would use explicit sexual talk, show pornographic videos, provide alcohol, invite men over for sex parties, tell John he was gay, buy explicit sexual toys, and threaten him with grave consequences should the activity be disclosed.
> (Burgess et al., 2010, pp. 391–392)

Responses to educator sexual misconduct have varied. In one study of 225 cases of educator sexual misconduct, none resulted in a report to legal officials (Shakeshaft & Cohan, 1995). Only 15% were terminated, whereas 20% were formally reprimanded or suspended. One percent lost their license to teach. Disciplinary action against teachers for sex crimes against children is usually lengthy (Knoll, 2010). Typical background checks of teachers usually detect only felonies, and many of these cases do not meet the criteria for a felony offense. Offending teachers typically retain their teaching license because they appeal any decision not in their favor. Teachers are then allowed to move to another state and use their license to get a new teaching position. School districts avoid problems for themselves by agreeing to cease any formal action if the teacher moves and promises not to initiate any civil charges against the school district, a practice known as **"passing the trash"** (Knoll, 2010; Moskowitz, 2001).

There have been efforts to outline prevention strategies. Below is a list of prevention strategies that have been identified by one researcher (Knoll, 2010, p. 382) by combining several sources (Fauske et al., 2006; Shakeshaft, 2004; Sutton, 2004):

- District and school-level policies prohibiting educator sexual misconduct
- Standardized hiring practices
- Standardized screening methods and criminal background checks
- Standardized investigative practices in response to allegations
- Development of a centralized reporting agency and registry
- Reporting all allegations to law enforcement and child protective services
- Regular training on educator sexual misconduct and prevention
- Enacting state statutes on educator sexual misconduct and prevention

Civic Organizations and Child Molestation

Sex crimes in civic organizations have also come to the attention of many through media and other accounts. For example, a series of news articles in the *Washington Times*, along with a book, *Scout's Honor: Sexual Abuse in Americas Most Trusted Institutions*, by Patrick Boyle, resulted in greater public awareness of sex crimes in the Boy Scouts of America (Terry et al., 2011). The majority of the abuse, according to Boyle, occurred during camping trips.

In response to the sex-crime allegations, Boy Scouts of America conducted an extensive training program to raise awareness of scouts and scoutmasters. New requirements included having volunteers pass a background check and a minimum of two adults present at every event. Children were not to be left alone with only one adult at any time (Boyle, 1994). In 2020, Boy Scouts of America filed for bankruptcy, yet they are still operating (Brickley & De Avila, 2021). As of 2021, approximately 84,000 reported child sexual abuse to Boys Scouts of America. Although Boys Scouts of America is working to settle these claims, no clear financial resolution has been reached as of May of 2021.

Big Brothers Big Sisters has also been scrutinized for sex crimes in their organization (Terry et al., 2011). This organization was established to provide mentors to economically disadvantaged youth. As recently as 2011, there were no data on sexual abuse occurring within this organization. However, Terry and Tallon (2004) searched major newspapers to establish the prevalence of sex crimes affecting this organization. There were only six published incidents between 1973 and 2001. In 2002, the president of Big Brothers Big Sisters indicated they received fewer than ten accusations of sex crimes per year. This is extremely small, given that 220,000 children were matched with mentors. One of the allegations of sexual victimization led to a lawsuit. The *Doe v. Big Brothers Big Sisters of America* (2005) ruling found that the organization was not liable for the abuse that occurred given that it had strict hiring and supervision procedures.

Other civic organizations have also been affected by sex crimes. The cover-up of the sexual abuse that occurs within these organizations is typically systematic and large scale (Harris & Terry, 2019). Below is an example of sexual abuse committed by a scout leader in Scouts Canada.

> Scott Stanley always surrounded himself with young teenaged boys because he felt "inadequate" with people his own age. He positioned himself as a City of Ottawa lifeguard and a Scouts Canada leader. And for a year and a half ending in 2013, he groomed and sexually exploited four boys in his Scout troop. They were aged 12 to 15. He preyed on the boys even after Scouts Canada had warned him 22 times to never be alone with any of the boys. On Wednesday, Stanley, 31, was condemned to five years in prison on convictions for sexual exploitation, invitation to sexual interference, and internet child luring. [The judge] took into account Stanley's pre-sentence custody, so he will actually serve three years and 281 days. In . . . sentencing, the judge credited him for immediately pleading guilty, and sparing his young victims from testifying in court. The judge also accepted his remorse as genuine, and she noted his desire to remain in therapy. Though the boys didn't file victim-impact statements, some of their parents did. One father said the boys would be emotionally scarred for life. [The judge] noted: "Clearly, their parents are devastated. They had entrusted their children to your care and supervision and you violated that trust." The judge also said the victims' development might be halted because of the sex crimes against them. Once he's released from prison, Stanley will be forbidden to be anywhere near children under 16 and must stay two kilometres away from his victims. In September, Stanley stood

up in the prisoner's dock and read a brief statement, calling his scheme to molest vulnerable boys as "shameful and monstrous." "Who I am hates who I was and what I've done," Stanley said. He said he has taken full responsibility and acknowledged that "my behaviour was not that of a proper and responsible adult toward my victims.["] "I betrayed their trust. . . . I became a monster."

(Dimmock, 2014, n.p.)

This example highlights how this child molester used his position to gain access to children. Unfortunately, it also shows that many civic organizations do not have adequate formal procedures to handle allegations of sex crimes against children.

SEXUAL ASSAULT WITHIN INSTITUTIONS

In the previous sections, we focused on institutions that face child sexual abuse allegations. In the following sections, we focus on institutions that face sexual assault allegations that typically involve adults accused of sexually assaulting another adult. Here, we distinguish between sexual *misconduct* and sexual *violence*. Whereas the former refers to sex acts that are not typically classified as sex crimes (e.g., flirting while on duty, consensual sex while on duty, or conducting a traffic stop to "get a closer look"), the latter refers to serious sex crimes (e.g., rape, offenses against juveniles, and sexual shakedowns). In this section, we focus on sexual violence. Although such allegations occur at many institutions, we focus on higher-education institutions and the military.

Higher-Education Institutions

Recently, several cases of rape on college campuses have made headlines, warranting attention to the lack of policies, procedures, and actions taken on several college campuses (Mummert & Piatak, 2018). These include the University of Texas (Prindle, 2018), University of Chicago, University of Colorado, Florida State, Vanderbilt, Notre Dame, and Harvard (Newman & Sander, 2014; Wade et al., 2014). As a result, there is increased scrutiny of higher-education institutions (Wade et al., 2014). Additionally, the U.S. Congress passed the **Student Right-to-Know and Campus Security Act** in 1990, which requires higher-education institutions to release information regarding crime rates on campus. This was based, at least partly, on the increased attention on the sexual victimization of women (Fisher et al., 2000). In 1992, the **Campus Sexual Assault Victims' Bill of Rights** was passed, requiring higher-education institutions to release awareness and prevention policies regarding sexual victimization and ensure basic rights of sexual-assault victims. In 1998, the act was amended to **Jeanne Clery Disclosure of Campus Security Policy and Campus Crime Statistics Act,** which included additional reporting obligations, including a daily crime log available to the public. In 2013, the **Campus Sexual Violence Elimination Act** was passed in response to **Title IX** violation complaints at Swarthmore College. The act requires clearer and more publicized policies, students' rights education efforts, and bystander education.

The true scope of the problem of rape on college campuses is difficult to assess because of many obstacles. For example, many of the studies (see Table 7.1) vary widely regarding how they define and measure sexual assault. Also, they vary with regard to whether the numbers are actual number of sexual assault incidents from a sample or whether they are population estimates based on a sample. In Table 7.1, the numbers reported focus on rape or attempted rape.

TABLE 7.1 Research Summary of National Studies on Rape on College Campuses and Universities

Authors:	Study Conducted:	Key Findings:
Koss et al. (1987)	Sexual Experiences Survey ($n = 6,159$)	27% of women surveyed experienced rape or attempted rape within the previous year. <1% of men surveyed experienced rape or attempted rape within the previous year.
Fisher et al. (2000)	National College Women Sexual Victimization Survey (NCWSV) ($n = 4,446$)	3% of women surveyed experienced rape or attempted rape (during a seven-month period).
Kilpatrick et al. (2007)	Rape Among College Students ($n = 5,001$)	11% of women surveyed experienced rape; 5% occurred within the previous year.
Cantor et al. (2015)	American Association for Universities (AAU) Campus Climate Survey on Sexual Assault and Sexual Misconduct ($n = 5,482$)	23% of women surveyed experienced rape; 13% occurred within the previous year. 4% of men surveyed experienced rape or sexual assault; 3% occurred within the previous year.

Women are at their highest risk of being raped in their late teens to early 20s (Fisher et al., 2010). Researchers initially concluded that college women are more at risk of sexual victimization than women of the same age who do not attend college (Fisher et al., 2000). Since this study was published, however, more recent research efforts have shown the opposite: college women are less likely to be raped than the same-age women who do not attend college (Axin et al., 2018). More research is needed in this area to clarify when and where women are more at risk for rape.

Regardless, external factors that exist on college campuses make college women at risk for rape (Fisher et al., 2010). These include co-ed housing with unfamiliar persons (Fisher et al., 2000), availability and frequent use of alcohol, and attending parties (Sampson, 2002). A combination of these factors leads to many potential victims and offenders. The relationship between drinking and rape has been well researched and reveals a high correlation between the two. To clarify, alcohol in and of itself does not cause rape, yet drinking heavily leads to vulnerable potential victims and may disinhibit potential offenders, leading to rape incidents (Wade et al., 2014).

Other factors identified by researchers include psychological factors, the context that facilitates rape, and the presence of a rape culture (Wade et al., 2014). A few men on college campuses are seemingly predisposed to commit sexual assault. Research has shown 6% of college men have admitted to committing sexual assault (Lisak & Miller, 2002). Two-thirds of those admitted to serial rapes, with an average of six rapes. Regarding the context, one researcher noted that rape-prone environments include parties with loud music, dancing, drinking, few places to sit, and flirting (Sanday, 2003). Concerning culture, belief in rape myths, such as date rape is not really rape, contributes to a rape-prone culture (Wade et al., 2014).

The majority of the sexual victimization incidents on college campuses, 97%, involved female victims. Eighty-two percent of the victims were white (Peters, 2012). Ninety-nine percent involved male offenders (Peters, 2012). Alcohol use by the victim was common. For example, one study reported that almost three-fourths of raped students were intoxicated at the time (Mohler-Kuo et al., 2004). Seventy percent of the sexual attacks involved victims and offenders who were acquaintances or friends. Similarly, the National College Women Sexual Victimization Survey (NCWSV) study also found that approximately 90% of the victims and offenders knew each other (Fisher et al., 2000). Most took place over the weekend, with 71% occurring between 12 p.m. and 4 a.m. (Peters, 2012). Similarly, approximately half of the sexual victimizations in the NCWSV study also occurred after midnight. Eighty-one percent of the victimizations occurred in a dormitory (Peters, 2012). Approximately half (46%) chose not to report the incident to law enforcement (Peters, 2012). Even fewer, only 5%, reported the incident to law enforcement in the NCWSV study (Fisher et al., 2000). Reasons given included that the victim had the perception that the incident was not harmful enough to report. Others reported barriers to reporting such as not wanting family (or other people) to know about the incident, lack of proof, fear of reprisal, fear of hostility from police, and fear of not being believed (Fisher et al., 2000).

Military

Common to many of the organizations discussed in this chapter is the difficulty in believing that someone in a position of authority (often a revered position, with honor and dedication) can commit rape. Historically, common law crimes—including rape—were responded to within the civilian judicial system (Carson & Carson, 2018). In the late 1980s, however, updates to the Uniform Military Justice changed the landscape and allowed the military courts to process sexual assault cases (Carson & Carson, 2018). Although this occurred in the 1980s, the majority of the reform has occurred in the past decade. This, however, introduced new challenges by allowing the military itself to respond to sexual assault claims that occur within its own organization. It is unique to the military because one's superior is designated to determine guilt or innocence. As noted by one researcher, "Nowhere in America do we allow a boss to decide if an employee was sexually assaulted or not, except in the U.S. military" (Wade et al., 2014, p. 24). Recent efforts in the U.S. Senate include a push to remove the authority of a few commanding officers who decide whether a case can proceed to a court-martial (i.e., the equivalent to trying a case) (Kime, 2014).

Another obstacle is that the military has a restrictive definition of what constitutes rape (Warner, 2020). It requires either threat of force or actual force that caused "grievous body harm" (Joint Service Committee on Military Justice, 2012: A2/30–31, A27/1–6, A28/1–6). The standard, therefore, sets a relatively high bar for the prosecution to meet.

Many sexual assault victims in the military (men and women) are subject to a unique form of retaliation. Their jobs and livelihood depend on being able to function in the military environment. Recently, the *New York Times* reported the stories of six men who were sexually assaulted in the military and suffered subsequent psychological distress brought on not only by the rape but also their inability to remain in the military afterward (Calvert, 2019). The victims are often discharged for not being able to perform their duties. The majority, an estimated four out of five rape victims in the military, do not officially report the incident (Calvert, 2019). Sixty-two percent of those who have reported sexual assault in the military have experienced retaliation—a number that has remained stable over the past two years (Kime, 2014).

Currently, the United States Department of Defense Sexual Assault Prevention and Response (DoD SAPRO, 2021) gathers and reports data on sexual assault allegations in an annual report. The number of sexual assault allegations has roughly doubled over the past decade from 3,327 to 7,815, according to a recent report. This equates to about five persons per 1,000 in the military who report rape. This increase, however, is likely the result of improvement in the data collection and reporting processes rather than an actual increase in the number of rapes.

The conviction rate of these cases is relatively low, which may be due to the military "prioritz[ing the] mission," and seeking alternatives for addressing the offense outside of the military (Warner, 2020, p. 265). Also, the number of cases that result in conviction is comparable to conviction rates in the civilian court system, which is quite low (see RAINN, 2021).

ORGANIZATIONS FACING BOTH CHILD SEXUAL ABUSE AND SEXUAL ASSAULT ALLEGATIONS

Many organizations' employees have access to both children and adults, complicating the matter. This forces them to respond to both child sexual abuse allegations and rape allegations. Although there are many organizations affected, we focus on athletic organizations, police agencies, and prisons. Recently, media attention has highlighted these organizations, and subsequently more research has occurred on these organizations.

Athletic Organizations

Recent headlines have drawn attention to sexual abuse in athletic organizations that include both child molestation and rape allegations. For example, the Pennsylvania State University football coach, Jerry Sandusky, was recently convicted of 40 criminal counts regarding sex crimes for victimizing eight boys over an eight-year period. He is currently serving a 30- to 60-year sentence in prison (Wieberg & Carey, 2012). Even more recently, Lawrence ("Larry") Nassar, a physician with USA Gymnastics, was convicted of multiple sexual abuse charges against children, resulting in a prison sentence that pretty much guarantees he will spend the rest of his life in prison (Udowitch, 2020). Part of the story includes well-known gymnast, Simone Biles (see Focus Box 7.1).

> #### Focus Box 7.1 Meet a Hero: Simone Biles
>
> Simone Biles was one of many sexual assault victims who spoke out against Larry Nassar, a Team USA doctor who sexually assaulted victims under the guise of performing routine physicals of the athletes representing the United States in the Olympics. Simone Biles recently dropped out of 2020 Olympics in Tokyo due to "twisties" and stress that resulted in an inability to perform at her normal peak levels. Simone tells a journalist, "At the end of the day, I am not representing USA Gymnastics" (n.p.) The report indicates Simone Biles plans to dedicate her performance to sexual assault survivors.
>
> Note: Adapted from Pearl (2021).

PHOTO 7.1 Simone Biles: Speaking Out Against Her Abuser and for Herself.

Photo Credit: Chang W. Lee//*The New York Times*/Redux.

Recently, a large-scale survey of elite child athletes revealed that 3.6% of elite athletes experienced sexual abuse when they were a minor (Hamilton & Timon, 2021). Additionally, 8.4% experienced sexual assault as a minor or as an adult by a sports official or peer athlete. Additional research on this topic has revealed unique details regarding grooming, obstacles in reporting, and the global extent of the problem.

Grooming behavior typically involves socializing with the victim's family (Stirling & Kerr, 2009). This was apparent in Jerry Sandusky's behavior with his alleged victims. For example, reports indicated he gave his victims gifts and promised a "walk-on" for one of the victims (Ganim, 2011). Another common grooming technique is to ask the child to play games with the offender or teach the child a sport (Gallagher, 2000). In the case of Larry Nassar, the parents reportedly witnessed some of the abuse yet did not perceive it as sexual abuse (Udowitch, 2020).

Many obstacles exist in discovering and bringing to light sex crimes within a sports organization. Much of the social science research on sex crimes has not been on male victims (Hartill, 2008). Male victims often do not initially disclose the sex crime (Gallagher, 2000). Many sports organizations often reinforce a patriarchal structure with a dominant heterosexual-male culture (Hargreaves, 1986). Also, these organizations are comprised primarily of men who subscribe to this patriarchal structure (Burstyn, 1999). Thus, the environment is not conducive to reporting unwanted sexual advances and victimization. The culture also involves ensuring the protection of children, despite evidence to the contrary (Hartill, 2008). Also, when the offender is held in high esteem in the community, the problem of disclosure is further compounded (Gallagher, 2000). Those in positions of authority in sports organizations, such as staff and managers, are not likely to follow up on sexual abuse allegations perhaps to protect the organization and due to the lack of procedures in place for handling such allegations (Sullivan & Beech, 2002). Thus, many of these organizations offer a safe haven of sorts for offenders.

Sex crimes in athletic organizations also occur outside the United States, and governments have responded by instituting formal guidelines and practices for prevention and response. For example, in Canada, a documentary reported several female rowers who were sexually assaulted by their coach when they were children (Canadian Broadcasting Corporation Television, 1993). Later, the Canadian Strategy for Ethical Conduct in Sport (2011) expressly prohibited harassment and abuse of any kind. In Australia, the Australian Sports Commission also provides ethical guidelines to prevent sex crimes against children. The Child Protection Sport Unit in the U.K. originated from the efforts and funds from two organizations, Sport England and the National Society for the Prevention of Cruelty to Children. More specifically, the organization was the result of efforts of Celia Brackenridge, who was an advocate for preventing and recognizing sex crimes in sports organizations (Hartill, 2008). In the U.K., sex crimes in sports organizations came to the forefront when Paul Hickson, an Olympic swimming coach, was convicted for the rape of teenage female athletes on his team.

Concerning rape accusations committed by athletes, several studies report that athletes are at a higher risk of committing rape than nonathletes (Beaver, 2019). Researchers have focused attention on the rape culture that can occur within sports as a possible explanation for fueling this behavior. For example, one researcher recognized an existing recipe for sexual assault to occur among male athletes.

> Assemble a group of young men. Promise them glory for violently dominating other groups of young men. Bond the group with aggressive joking about the sexual domination of women. Add public adulation that permeates the group with the scent of entitlement. Provide mentors who thrived as young men in the same system. Allow to simmer.
>
> (Wade et al., 2014, p. 22)

High-profile cases have highlighted some of the unique aspects of allegations of rape committed by athletes. Two such cases involved Kobe Bryant and several Duke lacrosse team members. For example, convictions are difficult to obtain in such cases. Neither of these cases resulted in a conviction due to lack of evidence. Kobe Bryant was accused of raping a 19-year-old hotel employee. He admitted to having sex with the woman but claimed it was consensual. Subsequently, the judge dropped the criminal charges after the accuser refused to testify as a witness. A civil suit was also filed and settled for an undisclosed amount of money (Shapiro & Stevens, 2004).

The Duke lacrosse scandal began when strippers were requested at a party held off campus at a home where the team's captain resided. One of the strippers made rape allegations, which led to the arrest of two of the Duke lacrosse team members. The prosecutor in the case was disbarred for making false allegations during a criminal proceeding. The charges against the defendants were dropped for lack of evidence (Cohan, 2014).

The research on athletes who have committed sex crimes occurs within the broader context of athletes who have committed a broad range of crimes, including murder, assault and battery, weapons charges, and illegal substance abuse (Otto, 2009). Thus, athletes commit not only rape but also other crimes. Regarding athletes' propensity to commit sex crimes, researchers have found in a comparison of athletes and nonathletes that the athletes have higher rates of violent crimes against women (Chandler et al., 1999; Crossett et al., 1996). Fifteen percent of the athletes reported fondling someone against their will, compared to only 5% of nonathletes (Chandler et al., 1999). Eight percent of athletes reported forcing someone to have sex, compared to 2% of nonathletes (Chandler et al., 1999). A more recent study also found that among a group of male nonathletes and athletes, athletes were significantly more likely to have used some form of sexual coercion (54% compared to 38%) (Young et al., 2017).

Moreover, among a group of professional and collegiate athlete convictions from 1991 to 2008, Otto (2009) found 86 athletes had 144 criminal charges. Fifty-nine percent of the charges involved a sex crime or rape. Twenty-five percent of those who were charged with a sex crime had a reduced charge, whereas 89% of those charged with rape also had a reduced charge. Approximately one-third of those charged with a sex crime or rape received a prison sentence. This corroborates other research that has found that sex-crime allegations against an athlete were more likely than those against nonathletes to result in an arrest and indictment but less likely to result in a conviction (Benedict & Klein, 1997).

Researchers also have found that approximately one in five National Football League players have experienced a charge for a serious crime. Fourteen percent of those crimes were sexual assaults. Few of those charges, however, led to a conviction (Benedict & Klein, 1997). According to these studies (Benedict & Klein, 1997; Otto, 2009), sex crimes comprise a substantial portion of crimes committed by athletes. Sports sociologists have proposed that sports are a microcosm of society. That is, athletes' behavior is a reflection of society in general (Coakley, 2007).

The overwhelming majority of athletes do not rape (Wade et al., 2014). Many higher-education institutions have implemented programs, such as Male Athletes Against Rape, which involve peer education and encourages bystanders to respond to factors that can lead to rape. Such programs focus on disrupting layers of protective silence that surround high-status male groups (e.g., college athletes), which serve to facilitate a rape culture (Wade et al., 2014). As discussed in Chapter 8, the bystander approach encourages students who witness situations such as a group of men assisting a drunk woman to an isolated location, to intervene and prevent this from occurring (Moynihan et al., 2010). It is evident that a culture of "silence" can perpetuate sexual assaults, as in the case of Jerry Sandusky, where many bystanders simply did nothing when they witnessed sexual behaviors. Routine values and a culture of silence in higher-education institutions can lead to rape incidents (Wade et al., 2014). This can occur within athletic organizations and in higher-education institutions (Wade et al., 2014).

Law Enforcement Officials Who Commit Child Molestation/Sexual Assault

Existing research has not fully explored police sexual violence. Subsequently, the numbers are difficult to come by because there is no central database kept on this. Recently, however, research was conducted on all arrest incidents that led to a police officer arrest (Stinson et al., 2020a, 2020b). From that, data on police who were arrested for sexual violence were garnered. Google Alerts email update services were used to capture all news reports of police officers arrested from 2005 to 2019. Four hundred and nineteen police officers were arrested for forcible rape. An additional 636 were arrested for forcible fondling and 219 for forcible sodomy. These data are likely not conclusive because not all sexual victimizations are reported to the police, nor are they always reported in the media. As noted in Table 7.2,

TABLE 7.2 Sexual Violence Committed by Law Enforcement Officials (Stinson et al., 2020a)

Circumstance	Description
Driving While Female	Use traffic enforcement authority to pull over women and sexually coerce them
Child Predation	Use their authority to gain access to children and coerce them
Involvement in the Sex Industry	Use authority as a police officer and known victim status as a sex worker to coerce them

three common situations of law enforcement officials who commit sexual violence were identified in this study.

Also problematic are law enforcement officers who commit sexual violence habitually. Police sexual violence can be a **pattern-prone offense**, referring to offenders who commit the same offense successively (Stinson et al., 2014). For example, in 2008, police sergeant Jeffrey Pelo was tried and convicted of raping four women in Bloomington, Illinois—a medium-sized Midwestern town. Authorities discovered that the sergeant had been obsessively tracking women, sneaking into their homes, and sexually assaulting them since 2003. Other research showed that 41% of police sexual violence cases are committed by recidivist officers who averaged four victims each over a three-year span of offending (Rabe-Hemp & Brathwaite, 2013). These results collectively show that cases, such as the Pelo case, are not random aberrations but are part of a consistent pattern of sex offending for a small number of police officers.

In another case of police rape, the victim called 911 to report a brick thrown through her window. The police officer who responded was subsequently convicted of raping the woman. A description of the case is presented below.

> Within minutes, two police officers responded. One took her 15-year-old brother outside to speak to him. The other cop, Police Officer Ladmarald Cates, gave her boyfriend $10 and told him to go the store and get some water.... The cop she had summoned to protect her instead chose this moment to grab the back of her head by her hair and sodomize her. Then he raped her. Her revulsion in the aftermath was so visceral that she vomited as she ran outside.... Cates appeared and grabbed her by the waist, spinning her around. Her swinging feet may or may not have struck the partner. She was handcuffed and taken in, told at the stationhouse that she was being charged with assaulting a police officer. She became more coherent but no less outraged and vocal as she continued cry out from a holding cell that she had been raped. She also continued to vomit. The other cops dismissed her as a liar. After 12 hours, she was interviewed by internal affairs and taken to a hospital, where a rape kit was used to collect evidence. She was then taken to the county jail and held for four days before being released without actually being charged. She took her story to the Milwaukee District Attorney's office.... On January 11, the jury convicted Cates of violating the victim's civil rights by raping her.
>
> (Daly, 2014, n.p.)

Responses and remedies to cases of sexual violence committed by police officers are often contentious. In addition to inflicting physical and emotional harm on the citizens they victimize, sexual-violence offenders who are police officers also jeopardize the reputation of fellow police officers, their police agency, and the broader community. These cases are typically one of the hardest types of cases to prove in criminal court due to the private nature of the events, the "he said; she said" testimony, and fact that a police officer is the defendant. District attorneys often fail to try these cases given the difficulty of attaining a guilty verdict (Du Mont & Myhr, 2000; Spohn et al., 2001).

The failure of criminal justice responses to police sexual violence in many instances has led victims to pursue lawsuits against individual police departments (Puro et al., 1997). Determining liability for police-perpetrated sex crimes usually rests on the offender's prior history of sexual violence as well as disciplinary record. Unfortunately, the threat of lawsuits may be a deterrent against reporting by police administrators who become knowledgeable of sex crimes that occur in their agencies (Puro et al., 1997). Even more problematic is the threat of *officer shuffle*, which involves the transfer of officers across jurisdictions when allegations of police sexual violence and other forms of misconduct occur (Rabe-Hemp & Braithwaite, 2013). "Passing the buck" on this form of sexual violence allows the crime to flourish because accused officers maintain their certification, affording them opportunities for repeat offending.

Juveniles and Adults in Detention Centers, Jails, and Prisons

Rape in jails, prisons, and facilities for delinquent youth led to the U.S. Congress passing the **Prison Rape Elimination Act (PREA)** in 2003. This act focuses on the identification, prevention, prosecution, and response to prison sexual violence. Sexual violence in detention centers, jails, and prisons can involve both staff-on-detainee/inmate and detainee/inmate-on-detainee/inmate sexual violence. Prior to PREA, a U.S. Supreme Court case, *Farmer v. Brennan* (1994), ruled that rape and sexual abuse are "not part of the penalty that criminal offenders pay for their offenses against society." Rape in prisons is problematic because the state or federal government operates the prison (Wolff et al., 2007). The prison has the responsibility to keep the inmates safe and not exposed to preventable harm.

The implementation of PREA has led to the increased systematic collection of sexual violence reports in detention facilities, jails, and prisons. The most recent numbers of sexual victimization indicate that nearly 10% of youth held in detention centers and about 2% of youth in jails/prisons experience victimizations (Beck & Stroop, 2017; Heaton et al., 2016). Among adults in jails and state and federal parsons, approximately 3%–4% experience sexual victimization (Beck, 2014).

Similar to rape in other institutions, environmental factors also play a role in rapes that occur in incarceration facilities. Factors that have been identified include prisons with barrack housing (i.e., one bed on top of another in a bunk-bed style), inadequate security, and overcrowding (Struckman-Johnson et al., 1996). Also, rape supportive attitudes, such as "rape is just part of the prison culture," contribute to prison rape (Man & Cronan, 2001). Although the discussion here has been on inmate-on-inmate prison rape, staff-on-inmate rape also exists (Man & Cronan, 2001). Among youth facilities, sexual violence occurs at higher rates at facilities where the number of written detainee complaints is high, there are not enough staff, and they have a higher reported number of gang fights (Heaton et al., 2016).

SUGGESTIONS FOR POLICIES AND PROCEDURES TO RESPOND TO INSTITUTIONAL ABUSE

Enough empirically-based evidence has accumulated to identify substantial pitfalls in how organizations have failed to respond proactively to claims of sexual abuse, which has led to many organizations developing better policies and procedures to address such allegations (Udowitch, 2020). Most of these strategies have involved three general practices, as summarized in Table 7.3.

A new screening tool has been developed and proposed. It is highlighted in Focus Box 7.1. This tool reveals a potential to have an empirically derived tool that identifies applicants of positions in youth-serving facilities who are hidden child molesters and/or have cognitions that are supportive of child molestation. This tool represents substantial progress toward preventing child sexual abuse.

TABLE 7.3 Strategies to Combat Institutional Abuse

Method	Examples
Prevention strategies	• Using criminal background checks on new employees • Developing centralized databases to share with others in the field to avoid "passing the trash," "officer shuffle," and so on • Instituting no-child-left-alone-with-adult policies
Establish laws, policies, and procedures to respond to claims	• Actively advocate for laws, policies, and procedures to protect victims and their rights • Establish objective reporting authorities who are *not* in the chain of command of the person reporting • Require all to report known cases of alleged sexual abuse • Require more surveillance in areas where children are, including body-cam surveillance for officers • Allow anonymous reporting • Designate resources to ensure compliance with all laws, policies, and procedures in place
Proactively educate	• Educate parents, children, employees, and students on signs of sexual abuse, prevention techniques, and best response procedures • Educate all on consent requirements for sexual interactions between adults.

Focus Box 7.1 The Development of a Child Protection Screening Instrument to Identify Problematic Applicants (Abel et al., 2018).

Although we discuss many assessment tools in Chapter 10 for those who have committed a sexual offense, no tool—until 2018—had been developed to identify potential child molesters and those who have cognitive distortions that encourage and/or tolerate child sexual boundaries of themselves and/or others (Abel et al., 2018). With the purpose of preventing child sexual abuse, Abel et al. (2018) developed a screening instrument to be used for those who are applying to employment positions that allow the employee direct access to children. Their instrument was developed by relying on more than 19,000 participants and resulted in a valid and reliable instrument that would detect men and women who were likely hidden abusers and/or those who tolerate poor sexual boundaries with children.

The instrument itself is based on three components. The first component asks about the person's hobbies and interests, cognition questions, identification with children, adolescent experiences, and number of home relocations over the previous five years. One example of the adolescent-experience questions asks the person if they had a best friend who was at least five years younger than themselves when they were a teenager. This component assesses applicants to a job as either those who sexually abuse and conceal their abuse or those who have not sexually abused a child.

The second component of this tool allows participants to admit to sexually abusing a child. Although common sense may indicate that no one would admit to sexually abusing a child, some do. The third component of this tool assesses cognitions supportive of child sexual molestation such as "A 4-year-old girl has the right to have sex with any adult she wants" and "No child has ever been hurt by having sex with an adult." The impact of developing such an instrument represents great strides toward the goal of preventing and protecting children from sexual abuse.

CONCLUSION

In this chapter, we build on Chapters 3 and 4, which examined child molesting and rape. This chapter extends these topics into organizations and institutions where rape and child molestation have occurred. Overall, known cases of institutional child abuse occur at relatively low rates. That is, within any organization or institution, a small portion are victims of a sex crime. Common among many of these incidents, however, is the lack of response to allegations of child molesting and rape, allowing them to go ignored for long periods of time. Many organizations and institutions have responded by developing specific policies, procedures, educational efforts, and in some cases, laws that assist victims in reporting sexual-assault incidents. It is likely in the future that these responses will continue to be developed to protect victims from sexual assault.

REVIEW POINTS

- Reported cases of institutional sexual abuse account for only 3% of child sexual-abuse allegations.
- Four percent of Catholic priests were accused of sex crimes. Less than 5% of those met the criteria for pedophilia.
- Sexual abuse within athletic organizations has been reported to occur among approximately 9% of athletes in one study.
- Child molestation within civic organizations is estimated to be low. One study reported fewer than ten sexual accusations occur per year. Many civic organizations have responded by requiring a background check and having two adults present with children.
- A few cases of rape by law enforcement officers have been reported. Although these occur rarely, it has been found that those who do rape are often serial rapists, having many victims.
- Rape cases involving athlete offenders often result in an arrest but rarely result in a conviction.
- Several laws have been enacted to protect university students in allegations of rape. Six percent of college men have admitted to committing sexual assault.
- Estimates indicate one out of ten inmates is sexually victimized.
- Estimates indicate 5% of active-duty military women are raped.
- A new screening instrument has been developed by Abel (2018) to identify those applying to youth-service facilities who are hidden child molesters.

REFERENCES

Abel, G. G., Jordan, A., Harlow, N., & Hsu, Y. (2018). Preventing child sexual abuse: Screening for hidden child molesters seeking jobs in organizations that care for children. *Sexual Abuse: A Journal of Research and Treatment, 31*(6), 662–683. https://www.doi.org/10.1177/1079063218793634

Beaver, W. (2019). College athletes and sexual assault. *Society, 56*, 620–624. https://www.doi.org/10.1007/s12115-019-00426-w

Beck, A. J. (2014). *PREA data collection activities, 2014.* U.S. Department of Justice, Office of Justice Programs, Bureau of Justice Statistics. https://bjs.ojp.gov/content/pub/pdf/pdca14.pdf

Beck, A. J., & Stroop, J. (2017). *PREA data collection activities, 2017.* U.S. Department of Justice, Office of Justice Programs, Bureau of Justice Statistics. https://bjs.ojp.gov/content/pub/pdf/pdca17.pdf

Benedict, J., & Klein, A. (1997). Arrest and conviction rates for athletes accused of sexual assault. *Sociology of Sport Journal, 14*(1), 86–94. https://www.doi.org/10.1123/SSJ.14.1.86

Boyle, P. (1994). *Scout's honor: Sexual abuse in America's most trusted institution.* Prima Publishing.

Brannan, C., Jones, R., & Murch, J. (1993). *Castle Hill report.* Shropshire County Council.

Brickley, P., & De Avila, J. (2021, May). Many boy scouts victims find little comfort as bankruptcy nears end. *The Wall Street Journal.* https://www.wsj.com/articles/many-boy-scouts-victims-find-little-comfort-as-bankruptcy-nears-end-11621854003

Burgess, A. W., Welner, M., & Willis, D. G. (2010). Educator sexual abuse: Two case reports. *Journal of Child Sexual Abuse, 19*(4), 387–402. https://www.doi.org/10.1080/10538712.2010.495045

Burstyn, V. (1999). *The rites of men: Manhood, culture and the politics of sport.* University of Toronto Press.

Calvert, M. F. (2019, September). Six men tell their stories of sexual assault. *The New York Times.* https://www.nytimes.com/interactive/2019/09/10/us/men-military-sexual-assault.html

Canadian Broadcasting Corporation Television. (1993). *Crossing the line: Sexual harassment in sport.* The Fifth Estate.

Canadian Strategy for Ethical Conduct in Sport. (2011). *Sport Canada strategy on ethical sport.* https://www.canada.ca/content/dam/pch/documents/services/ethics-sport/canadian-strategy-ethical-conduct-sport-eng.pdf

Cantor, D., Fisher, B., Chibnall, S. H., Bruce, C., Townsend, R., Thomas, G., & Lee, H. (2015). *Report on the AAU campus climate survey on sexual assault and sexual misconduct.* Westat. https://www.aau.edu/sites/default/files/%40%20Files/Climate%20Survey/AAU_Campus_Climate_Survey_12_14_15.pdf

Carson, J. K., & Carson, B. R. (2018). The historical roots and future directions for military law and policies on rape and sexual assault. *Military Psychology, 30*(3), 181–192. https://www.doi.org/10.1037/mil0000180

Chandler, S. B., Johnson, D. J., & Carroll, P. S. (1999). Abusive behaviors of college athletes. *College Student Journal, 33*(4), 638–645.

Chettle, N. (2014). Child sex abuse inquiry: Youth pastor victim says church more concerned with reputation than him. *ABC News.* http://www.abc.net.au/news/2014-10-17/church-abuse-victim-says-last-decade-a-living-hell/5822918

Coakley, J. (2007). *Sports in society: Issues & controversies* (9th ed.). McGraw Hill.

Cohan, W. D. (2014). *The price of silence: The Duke lacrosse scandal, the power of the elite, and the corruption of our great universities*. Scribner.

Colton, M., Roberts, S., & Vanstone, M. (2010). Sexual abuse by men who work with children. *Journal of Child Sexual Abuse, 19*(3), 345–364. https://www.doi.org/10.1080/10538711003775824

Crossett, T. W., Ptacek, J., McDonald, M. A., & Benedict, J. R. (1996). Male student athletes and violence against women. *Violence Against Women, 2*(2), 163–179. https://www.doi.org/10.1177/1077801296002002004

Daly, M. (2014). She dialed 911. The cop who came to help raped her. *The Daily Beast*. http://www.thedailybeast.com/articles/2012/01/29/she-dialed-911-the-cop-who-came-to-help-raped-her.html

Dimmock, G. (2014). Former Ottawa Scout leader Scott Stanley gets 5 years for sexually abusing boys. *Ottawa Citizen*. http://ottawacitizen.com/news/local-news/ottawa-scout-leader-scott-stanley-gets-5-years-for-sexually-abusing-boys

Districts should appoint teacher-led teams to train staff about professional boundaries. (2006). *Educator's Guide to Controlling Sexual Harassment, 14*(2), 2, 5. https://www.doi.org/10.1080/10538712.2010.495047

Du Mont, J., & Myhr, T. L. (2000). So few convictions: The role of client-related characteristics in the legal processing of sexual assaults. *Violence against Women, 6*(10), 1109–1136. https://www.doi.org/10.1177/10778010022183541

Epps, K. (2014). Former Stafford School Board member takes plea deal in child-molestation case. *The Free Lance Star*. https://fredericksburg.com/news/former-stafford-school-board-member-takes-plea-deal-in-child-molestation-case/article_ef744b48-7b25-5174-9671-cde201159099.html

Fauske, J., Mullen, C., & Sutton, L. (2006). *Educator sexual misconduct in schools: Implications for leadership preparation* [Paper presentation]. University Council for Educational Administration Conference Proceedings for Convention, San Antonio, Texas.

Fisher, B. S., Cullen, F. T., & Turner, M. G. (2000). *The sexual victimization of college women*. Government Printing Office. https://www.ojp.gov/pdffiles1/nij/182369.pdf

Fisher, B. S., Daigle, L. E., & Cullen, F. T. (2010). *Unsafe in the ivory tower: The sexual victimization of college women*. Sage Publications, Inc.

Gallagher, B. (2000). The extent and nature of known cases of institutional child sexual abuse. *British Journal of Social Work, 30*(6), 795–817. https://www.doi.org/10.1093/bjsw/30.6.795

Ganim, S. (2011, November 5). The complete details of charges: Allegations against Penn State legend Jerry Sandusky involve eight boys as young as 10 said to have showered and traveled with the coach. *The Patriot-News*. http://www.pennlive.com/midstate/index.ssf/2011/11/readers_digest_indictment.html

Green, L. (2001). Analysing the sexual abuse of children by workers in residential care homes: Characteristics, dynamics and contributory factors. *Journal of Sexual Aggression, 7*(2), 5–24. https://www.doi.org/ 10.1080/13552600108416164

Hamilton, M. A., & Timon, C. (2021). *Report: Five key findings of the Elite Athlete Survey*. Child USA. https://childusa.org/wp-content/uploads/2021/03/Five-Key-Findings-from-the-EAS-Final.pdf

Hargreaves, J. A. (1986). Where's the virtue? Where's the grace? A discussion of the social production of gender relations in and through sport. *Theory, Culture, & Society, 3*(1), 109–121. https://www.doi.org/10.1177/0263276486003001010

Harris, A. J., & Terry, K. J. (2019). Child sexual abuse in organizational settings: A research framework to advance policy and practice. *Sexual Abuse: A Journal of Research and Treatment, 31*(6), 635–642. https://www.doi.org/10.1177/1079063219858144

Hartill, M. (2008). The sexual abuse of boys in organized male sports. *Men and Masculinities, 12*(2), 225–249. https://www.doi.org/10.1177/1097184X07313361

Heaton, L., Cantor, D., Bruce, C, Ren, W., Hartge, J., & Beck, A. J. (2016). *Facility-level and individual-level correlates of sexual victimization in juvenile facilities, 2012.* Bureau of Justice Statistics Working Paper Series. https://bjs.ojp.gov/content/pub/pdf/flilcsvjf12.pdf

Joint Service Committee on Military Justice. (2012). Manual for court-martial United States 2012 edition. *USAPD.* https://www.loc.gov/rr/frd/Military_Law/pdf/MCM-2012.pdf

Khoury-Kassabri, M. (2006). Student victimization by educational staff in Israel. *Child Abuse & Neglect, 30*(6), 691–707. https://www.doi.org/10.1016/j.chiabu.2005.12.003

Kilpatrick, D. G., Resnick, H. S., Ruggiero, K. J., Conoscenti, L. M., & McCauley, J. (2007). *Drug-facilitated, incapacitated, and forcible rape: A national study.* National Criminal Justice Reference Service. https://www.ojp.gov/pdffiles1/nij/grants/219181.pdf

Kime, P. (2014, December 5). Incidents of rape in military much higher than previously reported. *Military Times.* http://www.militarytimes.com/story/military/pentagon/2014/12/04/pentagon-rand-sexual-assault-reports/19883155/

Knoll, J. (2010). Teacher sexual misconduct: Grooming patterns and female offenders. *Journal of Child Sexual Abuse, 19*(4), 371–386. https://www.doi.org/10.1080/10538712.2010.495047

Koss, M. P., Gidycz, C. A., & Wisniewski, N. (1987). The scope of rape: Incidence and prevalence of sexual aggression and victimization in a national sample of higher education students. *Journal of Consulting and Clinical Psychology, 55*(2), 162–170. https://www.doi.org/10.1037/0022-006X.55.2.162

Leclerc, B., Proulx, J., & McKibben, A. (2005). Modus operandi of sexual offenders working or doing voluntary work with children and adolescents. *Journal of Sexual Aggression, 11*(-2), 187–195. https://www.doi.org/10.1080/13552600412331321314

Lisak, D., & Miller, P. M. (2002). Repeat rape and multiple offending among undetected rapists. *Violence and Victims, 17*(1), 73–84. https://www.doi.org/10.1891/vivi.17.1.73.33638

Man, C. D., & Cronan, J. P. (2001). Forecasting sexual abuse in prison: The prison subculture as a backdrop for "deliberate indifference." *The Journal of Criminal Law and Criminology, 92*(1), 127–185. https://core.ac.uk/download/pdf/191055333.pdf

Mathews, R., Matthews, J. K., & Speltz, K. (1989). *Female sexual offenders: An exploratory study.* Safer Society Press.

Mohler-Kuo, M., Dowdall, G., Koss, M. P., & Wechsler, H. (2004). Correlates of rape while intoxicated in a national sample of college women. *Journal of Studies on Alcohol and Drugs, 65*(1), 37–45. https://www.doi.org/10.15288/jsa.2004.65.37

Moskowitz, A. (2001). Assessing suicidality in adults: Integrating childhood trauma as a major risk factor. *Professional Psychology: Research & Practice, 32*(4), 367–372. https://www.doi.org/10.1037/0735-7028.32.4.367

Moynihan, M. M., Banyard, V. L., Arnold, J. S., Eckstein, R. P., & Stapleton, J. G. (2010). Engaging intercollegiate athletes in preventing and intervening in sexual and intimate partner violence. *Journal of American College Health, 59*(3), 197–204. https://www.doi.org/10.1080/07448481.2010.502195

Mummert, S. J., & Piatak, K. A. (2018). Rape and sexual assault on college and university campuses. In C. M. Hilinski-Rosick & D. R. Lee (Eds.), *Contemporary Issues in Victimology: Identifying Patterns and Trends* (pp. 155–173). Lexington Books.

Newman, J., & Sander, L. (2014, April 30). Promise unfulfilled? *The Chronicle of Higher Education*. http://chronicle.com/article/Promise-Unfulfilled-/146299/

Ontario College of Teachers. (2002). *Professional advisory: Professional misconduct related to sexual abuse and sexual misconduct*. http://www.oct.ca/publications/pdf/advisory100802_e.pdf

Otto, K. E. (2009). Criminal athletes: An analysis of charges, reduced charges and sentences. *Journal of Legal Aspects of Sport, 19*(1), 67–102. https://www.doi.org/10.1123/jlas.19.1.67

Pearl, R. (2021, August 23). Doctors can learn more from Simone Biles than mental-health lessons. *Forbes*. https://www.forbes.com/sites/robertpearl/2021/08/23/doctors-can-learn-more-from-simone-biles-than-mental-health-lessons/?sh=5322ae135258

Peters, B. (2012). *Analysis of college campus rape and sexual assault reports, 2000–2011*. Massachusetts Executive Office of Public Safety and Security. https://www.mass.gov/files/2017-08/analysis-of-college-campus-rape-and-sexual-assault-reports-2000-2011.pdf

Prindle, D. F. (2018). The University of Texas "rape survey": A case study of politicized social science. *Academic Questions, 31*(1), 77–83.

Puro, S., Goldman, R., & Smith, W. C. (1997). Police decertification: Changing patterns among the states, 1985–1995. *An International Journal of Police Strategies & Management, 20*(3), 481–496. https://www.doi.org/10.1108/13639519710180097

Rabe-Hemp, C., & Braithwaite, J. (2013). An exploration of recidivism and the officer shuffle in police sexual violence. *Police Quarterly, 19*(2), 127–147. https://www.doi.org/10.1177/1098611112464964

Rape, Abuse, & Incest National Network (RAINN). (2021). *The criminal justice system, statistics*. https://www.rainn.org/statistics/criminal-justice-system

Robert, C. E., & Thompson, D. P. (2019). Educator sexual misconduct and Texas educator discipline database construction. *Journal of Child Sexual Abuse, 28*(1), 7–25. https://www.doi.org/10.1080/10538712.2018.1476999

Robins, S. L. (2000). *Protecting our students*. Ministry of the Attorney General.

Salter, A. C. (2003). *Predators: Pedophiles, rapists, and other sex offenders*. Basic Books.

Sampson, R. J. (2002). *Acquaintance rape of college students*. U.S. Department of Justice, Office of Community Oriented Policing Services. http://www.ncdsv.org/COPS_Acquaintance-Rape-of-College-Students-17_2002.pdf

Sanday, P. R. (2003). Rape-free versus rape-prone: How culture makes a difference. In C. B. Travis (Ed.), *Evolution, gender, and rape* (pp. 337–362). MIT Press.

Shakeshaft, C. (2004). *Educator sexual misconduct: A synthesis of existing literature*. Hofstra University and Interactive, Inc. https://www2.ed.gov/rschstat/research/pubs/misconductreview/report.pdf

Shakeshaft, C. (2013). Know the warning signs of educator sexual misconduct. *Kappan, 94*(5), 8–13. https://www.doi.org/10.1177/003172171309400503

Shakeshaft, C., & Cohan, A. (1995). Sexual abuse of students by school personnel. *Phi Delta Kappan, 76*(7), 513–520.

Shapiro, J. S., & Stevens, J. (2004). *Kobe Bryant: The game of his life*. Revolution Books, LLC.

Spohn, C., Beichner, D., & Davis-Frenzel, E. (2001). Prosecutorial justification for sexual assault case rejection: Guarding the "Gateway to Justice." *Social Problems, 48*(2), 206–235. https://www.doi.org/10.1525/sp.2001.48.2.206

Stinson, P. M., Liederbach, J., Brewer, S. L., & Mathna, B. E. (2014). Police sexual misconduct: A national scale study of arrested officers. *Criminal Justice Policy Review*. https://www.doi.org/10.1177/0887403414526231

Stinson, P. M., Liederbach, J., Taylor, R. W., Wentzlof, C., Wise, N. M., Sager, B., & Bettinelli, M. (2020b). Police sexual violence: A few bad apples or a cultural norm?

Criminal Justice Faculty Publications, 106. https://scholarworks.bgsu.edu/cgi/viewcontent.cgi?article=1105&context=crim_just_pub

Stinson, P. M., Taylor, R. W., & Liederbach, J. (2020a). The situational context of police sexual violence: Data and policy implications. *Criminal Justice Faculty Publications, 117.* https://scholarworks.bgsu.edu/cgi/viewcontent.cgi?article=1117&context=crim_just_pub

Stirling, A. E., & Kerr, G. A. (2009). Abused athletes' perceptions of the coach–athlete relationship. *Sports in Society, 12*(2), 330–335. https://www.doi.org/10.1080/17430430802591019

Struckman-Johnson, C., Struckman-Johnson, D., Rucker, L., Bumby, K., & Donaldson, S. (1996). Sexual coercion reported by men and women in prison. *Journal of Sex Research, 33*(1), 67–76. https://www.doi.org/10.1080/00224499609551816

Sullivan, J., & Beech, A. (2002). Professional perpetrators: Sex offenders who use their employment to target and sexually abuse the children with whom they work. *Child Abuse and Review, 11*(3), 153–167. https://www.doi.org/10.1002/car.737

Sutton, L. (2004). Preventing educator sexual misconduct. *School Business Affairs*, 9–10. http://www.asbointl.org

Terry, K. J., Smith, M. L., Schuth, K., Kelly, J. R., Vollman, B., & Massey, C. (2011). *The causes and context of sexual abuse of minors by Catholic priests in the United States, 1950–2010.* United States Conference of Catholic Bishops. http://archspmresources.s3.amazonaws.com/The-Causes-and-Context-of-Sexual-Abuse-of-Minors-by-Catholic-Priests-in-the-United-States-1950-2010.pdf

Terry, K. J., & Tallon, J. (2004). *The nature and scope of sexual abuse of minors by Catholic priests and deacons in the United States, 1950–2002.* United States Conference of Bishops: John Jay College. https://www.bishop-accountability.org/reports/2004_02_27_JohnJay_revised/2004_02_27_John_Jay_Main_Report_Optimized.pdf

Timmerman, G. (2003). Sexual harassment of adolescents perpetrated by teachers and peers: An exploration of the dynamics of power, culture, and gender in secondary schools. *Sex Roles, 48*(5/6), 231–244. https://www.doi.org/10.1023/A:1022821320739

Udowitch, H. (2020). The Larry Nassar nightmare: Athletic organizational failure to address sexual assault allegations and a call for corrective action. *DePaul Journal of Sports Law, 16*(1), 92–146. https://via.library.depaul.edu/cgi/viewcontent.cgi?article=1184&context=jslcp

United States Department of Defense Sexual Assault Prevention and Response (DoD SAPRO). (2021). *Department of Defense annual report on sexual assault in the military, fiscal year 2020.* https://www.sapr.mil/?q=reports

Vandiver, D. M., & Kercher, G. (2004). Offender and victim characteristics of registered female sexual offenders in Texas: A proposed typology of female sexual offenders. *Sexual Abuse: A Journal of Research and Treatment, 16*(2), 121–137. https://www.doi.org/10.1023/B:SEBU.0000023061.77061.17

Wade, L., Sweeney, B., Derr, A. S., Messner, M. A., & Burke, C. (2014). Ruling out rape. *Contexts, 13*(2), 16–25. https://www.doi.org/10.1177/1536504214533495

Warner, C. M. (2020). The role of military law and systematic issues in the military handling of sexual assault cases. *Law & Society Review, 54*(1), 265–300. https://www.doi.org/10.1111/lasr.12461

Westcott, H. (1991). *Institutional abuse of children—from research to policy: A review.* National Society for the Prevention of Cruelty to Children (NSPCC). https://www.doi.org/10.1080/09687599466780271

Wieberg, S., & Carey, J. (2012). Penn State abuse scandal chilling in details. *USA Today.* http://usatoday30.usatoday.com/sports/college/football/bigten/story/2011-11-06/penn-state-abuse-scandal-chilling/51100830/1

Wishnietsky, D. H. (1991). Reported and unreported teacher-student sexual harassment. *Journal of Education Research, 84*(3), 164–169. https://www.doi.org/10.1080/00220671.1991.10886010

Wolff, N., Shi, J., Blitz, C. L., & Siegel, J. (2007). Understanding sexual victimization inside prisons: Factors that predict. *Criminology and Public Policy, 6*(3), 535–564. https://www.doi.org/10.1111/j.1745-9133.2007.00452.x

Young, B. R., Desmarais, S. L., Baldwin, J. A., & Chandler, R. (2017). Sexual coercion practices among undergraduate male recreational athletes, intercollegiate athletes, and non-athletes. *Violence against Women, 23*(7), 795–812. https://www.doi.org/10.1177/1077801216651339

COURT CASES

Doe v. Big Brothers Big Sisters of America, No 1–04–1985 Ill. App. 3d LEXIS 803 (2005)
Farmer v. Brennan (92–7247), 511 U.S. 825 (1994)

DEFINITIONS

Campus Sexual Assault Victims' Bill of Rights: A federal law passed in 1992 requiring higher-education institutions to release awareness and prevention policies regarding sexual victimization and ensure basic rights of sexual-assault victims

Campus Sexual Violence Elimination Act: A federal law that was passed in 2013 in response to Title IX violation complaints at Swarthmore College and requires clearer and more publicized policies, students' rights education efforts, and bystander education

Educator Misconduct: A term developed by Shakeshaft that describes inappropriate behavior that involves a school employee such as a teacher or coach, sharing pornography, conversations with sexual talk, or masturbation

Fixated Abuser: One of two categories of educator misconduct (identified by Shakeshaft) that involves a male or female educator who grooms a student and sexually abuses them—the most common fixated abuser involves a male teacher and a male student/victim

Institutional Abuse: A term developed by Gallagher that describes the sexual abuse of children by adults who have contact with them within some institution (e.g., organized sports, community center, school)

Jeanne Clery Disclosure of Campus Security Policy and Campus Crime Statistics Act: A federal law passed in 1998 that amended Campus Sexual Assault Victims' Bill of Rights and included additional reporting obligations, including a daily crime log available to the public

Opportunistic Offender: A term developed by Shakeshaft that describes a large portion of educators who molest children—they are the most common type of child molester and are typically regressed offenders with poor boundaries and judgment

Passing the Trash: An informal practice of handling teachers' sexual misconduct by asking the teacher to move out of the district in lieu of facing any charges from their behavior

Pattern-Prone Offense: When offenders are likely to offend multiple times

Prison Rape Elimination Act (PREA): A federal law passed in 2003 that focuses on the identification, prevention, prosecution, and response to prison sexual violence

Sexual Misconduct: Sex acts that are not typically classified as sex crimes (e.g., flirting while on duty, consensual sex while on duty, or conducting a traffic stop to "get a closer look")

Sexual Violence: A term that encompasses a broad range of sexual victimization, including rape, sexual assault, child sexual abuse, sexual exploitation, and other contact and non-contact offenses, as well as acts that are not codified in law as criminal but are nevertheless harmful and traumatic to the victim experiencing them

Student Right-to-Know and Campus Security Act: A federal law passed in 1990 that requires higher-education institutions to release information regarding crime rates on campus

Title IX: A federal law that requires that universities investigate and resolve claims of sexual misconduct

CHAPTER 8

The Victimology of Sexual Violence

CHAPTER OBJECTIVES

- Describe the discipline of victimology and the early history of victimization theories
- Identify the risk factors for rape, sexual assault, and child sexual abuse victimization
- Describe the "real rape" myth, and identify populations of sexual violence victims that refute this myth
- Describe and apply the Defense Cascade Model to sexual violence victimization
- Identify barriers to sexual violence disclosure and seeking support
- Identify the physical, mental/emotional, and other secondary impacts of sexual violence victimization
- Identify the prevalence and etiology of false claims of sexual violence
- Summarize the history of the sexual violence victim advocacy movement in the United States

The first edition of this textbook did not have a specific chapter dedicated to the discussion of victims of sex crimes. Instead, each chapter contained relevant discussions of victims and victimization issues. For example, Chapter 4 (Child Sexual Abuse) previously included a brief section on child sexual abuse victims, wherein we discussed the long-term impacts of victimization and barriers to disclosure. Shortly after the publication of the first edition in late 2016, attention to victims of *sexual violence* victims reached unprecedented heights. Accusations of sexual assault and child molestation against leading figures in the entertainment, political, sport, and clergy sectors sparked the #MeToo movement, a social movement against sexual abuse and violence against women that revealed the widespread prevalence of sexual harassment and violence. As this social activism was unfolding, we quickly realized the need for a more victim-focused approach that would center survivor voices and experiences. Part of this included a chapter dedicated to the examination of sexual victimization.

In this chapter, we begin with a general discussion of *victimology* and theories of victimization with an emphasis on the ways in which early theories served to weaponize and place blame on victims of sexual violence. Following is a comprehensive overview of victimization risk factors, including a thorough discussion of special populations of victims that challenge the "real rape" stereotype. We then delve into the myriad victim responses to sexual violence, including discussions of the neurobiology of sexual trauma and how the brain and body react during sexual victimization, victim disclosure behaviors, short- and long-term physical and mental health impacts, and issues of **secondary victims** and **secondary traumatic stress**. We then turn to issues of false allegations of sexual violence. This chapter concludes with a review of social justice and activist movements that have shaped our present-day understanding of victims of sexual violence victimization.

This chapter relies on the term **sexual violence** as a term that encompasses a broad range of sexual victimization, including rape, sexual assault, child sexual abuse, sexual exploitation, and other contact and noncontact offenses. It also includes acts that are not codified in law as criminal (e.g., sexual harassment, unwanted sexual attention) but are nevertheless harmful and traumatic to the victim experiencing them. Because we did not want to focus a discussion of sex crime victimization to one specific type of victim (e.g., rape victims), we opted for a treatment of the subject that is more inclusive. That being said, references to victims of specific sex crimes are also made where relevant.

VICTIMOLOGY AND EARLY THEORIES OF VICTIMIZATION

Victimology, simply put, is the study of victims of crime and victimization, with a particular emphasis on the causes of victimization, the consequences and impacts of crime on victims, and the relationships among victims, offenders, and the criminal justice system. The discipline emerged in Europe and was stimulated by post-World War II humanitarian efforts to understand the plight of victims of war, violence, famine, poverty, and disease (Elias, 1986). Eventually, the focus of victimology narrowed and became centrally concerned with victims of crime specifically. Early pioneers of victimology were focused on why certain people become victims of crime and others do not, and their theories argued that victimization was partially (if not wholly) attributed to victim attitudes and actions (a concept known as **victim precipitation**). Typologies (as we have discussed previously) were used to isolate the factors that appeared to make some people more prone than others. Work by Benjamin Mendelsohn, for example, focused on the victims, resulting in a sixfold typology of victims based on the extent to which they were responsible their own victimization, ranging from the completely innocent victim to the most guilty victim (Mendelsohn, 1956). Hans von Hentig also was interested in how victims may provoke their own victimization and argued that victims could be grouped into one of 13 categories based on their propensity for victimization (von Hentig, 1948). These victims contribute to their victimization by virtue of their

The concept of victim precipitation should look familiar because many of the attitudinal rape myths discussed in Chapter 3 are predicated on the notion that rape and sexual assault victims are somehow responsible for their victimization. Early empirical studies are partially responsible for perpetuating these myths. Marvin Wolfgang studied homicides in Philadelphia between 1948 and 1952, concluding that approximately 25% were victim precipitated (Wolfgang, 1958). Menachem Amir studied rape incidents that occurred between 1958 and 1960. Similar to his predecessors, Amir examined the extent to which victims provoked or precipitated their own victimization and concluded that almost one in five rapes (particularly those in which the victim was judged to have engaged in seductive behavior, used risqué language, and wore revealing clothing) were victim precipitated (Amir, 1967). Amir's study was controversial and characterized as victim blaming. As we have learned, victims of sexual violence today still face these attitudes and views when coming forward with their experiences of victimization.

VICTIMS OF SEXUAL VIOLENCE

Based on the National Crime Victimization Survey estimates, 459,310 people reported rape/sexual assault victimization in the United States in 2019 (Morgan & Truman, 2020). That same year, 60,927 child sexual abuse incidents were reported (Administration for Children and Families, 2021). Although the accurate reporting of these crimes is a complicated task (due to definitional issues, less-than-perfect data collection strategies, and gross underreporting), it is estimated that one in five women and one in 38 men annually are the victim of a completed or attempted rape and that as many as one in four girls and one in six boys are sexually abused before age 18.

As research continues to address risk factors related to rape perpetration (as discussed in Chapter 3), risk factors for sexual victimization have also been identified. As we have discussed, this is a controversial subject that requires careful and thoughtful framing. Earlier research on the subject, such as that by Amir, has served as a tool to weaponize, discredit, or otherwise blame victims of rape and other crimes of sexual violence. In no way should these risk factors be equated with issues of victimization culpability or responsibility. Understanding risk factors related to victimization is important because it allows for the development of tailored, victim-centered intervention and prevention strategies.

Risk Factors for Rape and Sexual Assault Victimization

Several demographic variables have been identified as highly relevant to rape and sexual assault victimization risk, including gender, age, race, sexual orientation, relationship status, and income/financial situation. By and large women are more at risk for experiencing rape and sexual assault than men (Black et al., 2011, WHO, 2021). Limited studies have found exceptions to this trend. For example, in a study of sexual violence victimization in 10 European Union countries, men reported higher victimization rates compared to women in five countries—Cyprus, Greece, Lithuania, Poland, and Portugal (Krahé et al., 2015). These results are consistent with previous studies on male victimization patterns in Greece and Portugal (Chan et al., 2008; Papadakaki et al., 2012). Younger age is also a marked risk factor with those younger than 25 being more likely to experience rape and sexual assault compared to those older than 25 years old (Breiding, 2014; Elliott et al., 2004). In particular, college students are at particular risk of experiencing rape and sexual assault (De Keseredy & Kelly, 1995, Fisher, 2000) with freshmen and sophomore students and sorority members being among the highest at-risk populations (Krebs et al., 2007). Multiracial and American Indian/Alaska Native people are substantially more likely to experience rape and sexual assault compared to non-Natives (Breiding, 2014; Rosay, 2016; Tjaden & Thoennes, 2000). Other high-risk populations include LGBTQ+ men and women (Drabble et al., 2013; Schapanksy et al., 2020), homeless individuals (Browne & Bussuk, 1997; Stermac & Paradis, 2001; Wenzel et al., 2000), and single/nonmarried people (Schapansky et al., 2020).

Previous victimization history is also correlated with sexual violence victimization risk, including experiencing sexual abuse in childhood and physical assault in adulthood (Acierno et al., 1999; Elliott et al., 2004). Research also suggests that certain lifestyle and behavioral factors may contribute increased odds of sexual violence victimization. For instance, greater numbers of past consensual sexual partners have been correlated with increased odds of sexual victimization (Franklin, 2010), as has earlier age of first sexual experience (Schapansky et al., 2020). Other risky sexual practices such as unprotected sex, indiscriminate sexual conduct, or having sex while under the influence of alcohol or other drugs are also correlated with a higher likelihood of victimization (Combs-Lane & Smith, 2002; Koss, 1985; Koss & Dinero, 1989).

Risk Factors for Child Sexual Abuse Victimization

As discussed in Chapter 2, one of the earliest theories to explain criminal victimization was first posed by Cohen and Felson (1979). To recap, *routine activities theory* suggests that victimization occurs when adequate supervision of a victim's guardian is absent in situations where victims are in close proximity to individuals who are both motivated to commit an offense and view the victim as an attractive target. Within this framework, victims of child sexual abuse are believed to be situated in risky environments that heighten the likelihood of experiencing abuse. What is not accounted for is the reality that many instances of child sexual abuse involve family members and acquaintances and that many children who are abused do not necessarily engage in activities that put them in risky environments.

Subsequent theoretical frameworks considered broader ecological factors such as characteristics of the child, family, and community (Belsky, 1980; Bolan, 2001). Through these theories, scholars have identified risk factors for understanding the risk of child sexual abuse victimization. While some factors pertain to child characteristics (e.g., child gender, the existence of behavioral or physical health problems), others pertain to family-level factors (e.g., substance abuse, parental unemployment, and violence in the household) and characteristics of the broader community (e.g., high rate of crime and violence in the neighborhood, poor social family supports, and societal attitudes/beliefs toward children and maltreatment).

In one of the most extensive meta-analysis conducted to date, researchers examined 765 child sexual abuse risk factors from 72 empirical studies (Assink et al., 2019). The factors most predictive of child sexual abuse included prior child sexual abuse victimization of the child and/or siblings, prior victimization of the child other than child abuse, prior or concurrent forms of child abuse in the child's home environment, a parental history of child abuse victimization, household violence (e.g., intimate partner violence), parenting problems (e.g., low quality of parent–child interactions), and other child problems (e.g., having a chronic mental/physical condition).

SPECIAL POPULATIONS

Historically, there has been a long-held belief that sexual violence happens to only certain types of people. The concept of "real rape" was introduced by Estrich (1987) to demonstrate the dominant stereotype of rape as a crime exclusively involving a white, young, and sexually desirable victim who is attacked at night by a stranger who is motivated by sexual gratification. We explored this myth in Chapter 3. We know empirical-based evidence that *anyone* (regardless of gender, race, sexual orientation, religious beliefs, or socioeconomic status) can be a victim of rape. As Brownmiller (1975) reminds us, sexual violence is a tool of power, an agent of fear, and a weapon of force against women and people with less power. Therefore, it stands to reason that those at a particular power disadvantage are more likely to experience victimization. Here, we explore different populations of sexual violence victims that challenge the accuracy of the "real rape" stereotype.

Elderly Victims

Elder abuse is an ever-growing crime because people are living longer and the world population is rapidly aging. Limited research has explored the intersection of elder abuse and sexual violence, meaning that our knowledge and understanding of prevalence, crime characteristics, risk factors, and impacts on victims is extraordinarily limited. Recent estimates indicate that a little less than 1% of individuals over the age of 60 experience some form of sexual abuse or exploitation (Yon et al., 2017). These crimes generally involve forcing an elderly individual to take part in a sexual act when they either do not or cannot provide consent. Acts of elder sexual abuse are generally more violent compared to sex crimes committed against nonelderly adults, and they are also more likely to occur in the victim's residence (Bows & Westmarland, 2017; Chopin & Beauregard, 2020; Lea et al., 2011).

Within institutional settings specifically (i.e., elder nursing and residential care facilities), the estimated prevalence of elder sexual abuse is believed to be higher than sexual abuse among the general elder population (which is less than 1%) at 1.9% (Yon et al., 2019). Research shows that perpetrators are commonly employees of those facilities, but facility residents and family members are also among the accused perpetrators (Ramsey-Klawsnik et al., 2008). The presence of dementia or other cognitive deficits is a major risk factor for elder sexual abuse (Burgess & Phillips, 2006). In addition, those who sexually abuse elders with dementia are less likely to be arrested and prosecuted compared to those who sexually abuse elders without dementia.

Male Victims

In October 2017, as numerous Hollywood actresses went public with their accounts of sexual victimization at the hands of Hollywood movie producer Harvey Weinstein, former professional football player and actor Terry Crews revealed publicly that he had been groped at a party by a male Hollywood executive. Shortly after, celebrity talk show host Wendy Williams announced that she believed Crews was "just talking" and that this admission may have a negative impact on his career. Further, she compared Crews's disclosure to that of former child star Corey Feldman, who earlier in 2013 revealed that he had been a victim of child sexual abuse at the hands of Hollywood talent agents and other celebrities. Williams stated "the difference is that [Feldman] doesn't have the same credibility as a present day person that we know . . . who's a grown man." Williams was immediately lambasted on Twitter and other social media platforms for making light of male sexual assault.

According to the 2015 National Intimate Partner and Sexual Violence Survey, almost 25% of men in the United States (approximately 27.6 million) experienced some form of contact sexual violence (which includes rape, being made to penetrate someone else, sexual coercion, and/or unwanted sexual contact) in their lifetime, with 2.6% (about 2.8 million) having experienced an attempted or completed rape (Smith et al., 2018). Unlike female victims of sexual violence whose perpetrators are overwhelmingly male, the sex of perpetrators of sexual violence committed against males vary by the type of offense committed. According to Breiding (2014), male rape victims predominantly have male perpetrators, but other forms of sexual violence experienced by men were either perpetrated predominantly by women (e.g., forced penetration and sexual coercion) or split more evenly among male and female perpetrators (e.g., unwanted sexual contact).

Scientific research on the prevalence, scope, and impact of rape involving male victims has received increased attention in recent years but is estimated to be roughly 20 years behind research on female rape (Pearson & Barker, 2018). Despite the importance of understanding male rape, the subject remains largely overlooked, dismissed, or ignored. This is largely due to the perpetuation of rape myths. In Chapter 3, we introduced the Bumby RAPE Scale, which comprises 36 statements reflective of rape myths (e.g., "women who get raped probably deserve it," "a lot of women claim they were raped just because they want attention"). Most of these myths pertain to female rape victims. However, recent research has focused on rape myths related specifically to male victims. These are summarized in Table 8.1. Similar

TABLE 8.1 Male Rape Myths
Men cannot be raped.
"Real" men can defend themselves against rape.
Only gay men are victims and/or perpetrators of rape.
Men are not affected by rape (or not as much as women).
A woman cannot sexually assault a man.
Male rape happens only in prisons.
Sexual assault by someone of the same sex causes homosexuality.
Homosexual and bisexual individuals deserve to be sexually assaulted because they are immoral and deviant.
If a victim physically responds to an assault, he must have wanted it.

Source: Turchik and Edwards (2012).

to female rape myths, rape myths concerning males serve to further marginalize and silence men who experience these crimes by either minimizing victims' rape or blaming the victim for their rape.

Research on the factors associated with male rape and sexual assault victimization is also underdeveloped, but some studies have shown that certain populations report higher rates of rape and sexual assault than the general population. For example, studies show male rape and sexual assault rates as high as 17% among gay or bisexual men (Heidt et al., 2005). Other forms of sexual violence (excluding rape and sexual assault) as high as 47% in gay and bisexual men (Walters et al., 2013). Recent research also suggests that college men, particularly those living in fraternity settings, are at heightened risk of sexual assault victimization compared to nonfraternity men because fraternity settings are often conductive to a constellation of sexual assault risk factors such as hazing, large parties, heavy drinking, and high endorsement/belief in rape myths (McCabe et al., 2005; Murnen & Kohlman, 2007). Because the research on this specific population is still very much in its infancy, estimates of how widespread this problem is are unreliable. However, one study showed that greater than 25% of fraternity men admitted to experiencing either a penetrative sexual assault or attempted penetrative sexual assault since entering college (Luetke et al., 2020).

Incarcerated men are also believed to be a high-risk population. Estimates of prison rape in the existing research range from less than 1% to 21% (Neal & Clements, 2010). A realistic estimate of prison rape is one out of 10 inmates experience rape victimization (Struckman-Johnson et al., 1996). One factor that has been identified as unique to prison rape is the resulting physical injury that occurs (beyond that caused by the rape itself). Researchers have found that more than half of all rapes in prison involve other physical injuries such as bruises, cuts, scratches, or physical injury to the anus and throat (Wolff et al., 2007). Medical attention was required for almost one-third of rape victims. Some inmates are more at risk of being sexually victimized than others. These include inmates who are white (Hensley et al., 2003), young (Wolff et al., 2007), middle- or upper-class, first-time inmates (Man & Cronan, 2001), or perceived as weak (Chonco, 1989). Also if they have feminine characteristics, small stature (Man & Cronan, 2001), or have a nonheterosexual orientation (Struckman-Johnson et al., 1996), they are more at risk for sexual victimization. Inmates who have a history of depression, anxiety, posttraumatic stress disorder (PTSD), schizophrenia, and bipolar disorder are also at risk for sexual victimization while behind bars (Wolff et al., 2007).

Victims with Disabilities

A great body of evidence suggests that people with disabilities (a broad term encompassing physical, intellectual, developmental, and sensory impairments) are at greater risk of sexual victimization across the life span compared to those without a disability (e.g., Basile et al., 2016; Krnjacki et al., 2016; Nixon et al., 2017). A recent meta-analysis estimated that the risk of sexual victimization of those with disabilities is twice that of their nondisabled counterparts (Mailhot Amborski et al., 2021). There is variation in the estimated prevalence of this crime depending on the nature of the victim's disability. For example, another meta-analysis concluded that about one in three adults with an intellectual or developmental disability are victims of sexual abuse as adults and that the probability of victimization increases as the severity of the disability increases (Tomsa et al., 2021). The highest risk of sexual victimization is associated with sensory impairment (such as blindness or deafness), with individuals experiencing sexual violence victimization at a rate four times that of other impairments, including intellectual, developmental, and physical disabilities (Mailhot Amborski et al., 2021). Other studies suggest that women and young children with disabilities are at particular risk for victimization (Byrne, 2018; Curry et al., 2011). As well, living in congregate settings magnifies the chances of victimization (Fisher et al., 2016).

Indigenous Victims

American Indian/Alaska Native (AI/AN) women are at the greatest risk for rape and sexual assault compared to any other racial group in the United States. According to the 2010 National Intimate Partner and Sexual Violence Survey, 35% of AI/AN women have experienced sexual violence with penetration or attempted penetration in their lifetime compared to 20% of white, non-Hispanic women (Rosay, 2016). This is consistent with estimates in prior decades that found that 34% of AI/AN women will be raped in their lifetime, compared to 19% of African American women, 18% of white women, and 7% of Asian and Pacific Islander women (Tjaden & Thoennes, 2000).

Historically, sexual violence was used as a colonial tool for domination and dehumanization of Native people. Forced removals of Native people from their ancestral lands (e.g., Trail of Tears) were wrought with the sexual exploitation of Native women by white settler men (Deer, 2004). The lingering impacts of these colonial legacies (collectively referred to as **historical trauma**) are believed to persist for Native families over generations and shape the overall health and wellness of Native people today (Walters et al., 2013). Indigenous scholars have linked the high rates of sexual violence experienced by AI/AN people today to the progressive loss of ancestral land, language, culture, and traditional lifeways. These cumulative losses have had an eroding effect on traditional Indigenous value systems, including heavy disruption to traditional gender roles and relationships among Native people (Braithwaite et al., 2019). This, in turn, is what conditions the vulnerability of AI/AN people to alcoholism, drug abuse, suicide, domestic violence, and rape and sexual assault.

Also unique to Indigenous victims is the complex configurations of criminal justice systems in Indian Country that make rape almost impossible to prosecute. Research has shown

> **Focus Box 8.1** Desa Jacobsson: Sexual Abuse Survivor and Crusader for Women's and Children's Rights in Alaska
>
>
>
> Desa Jacobsson (Yup'ik/G'wichin) was an Alaska Native artist, educator, victim advocate, and social justice activist. She was born in Hooper Bay (a coastal village of the Yukon-Kuskokwim Delta region of Alaska) in 1947; soon after, her family relocated to the village of Marshall. At the age of 10, she was sexually abused by a family friend. The abuse went on for several years. She never disclosed the abuse to anyone until she entered treatment for alcoholism and addiction in her adult years. Desa dedicated her life to bringing awareness to Alaska Native women's and children's rights, as well as broader political issues impacting Alaska Native people (including subsistence rights and environmental protection). She worked as a trainer for numerous organizations that assist victims of sexual assault and domestic violence. At the time of her cancer diagnosis, she was mounting a political campaign to address state budget cuts that left victims of sexual violence without much needed protection against their perpetrators. Desa passed away at the age of 69 on September 21, 2017.
>
> Photo Credit: Teresa Jacobsson

that Native women are especially targeted for rape because of the impunity enjoyed among perpetrators; this is especially true of non-Tribal members who commit sex crimes within Tribal Reservation borders (Lisak & Miller, 2002).

VICTIM RESPONSES TO SEXUAL VIOLENCE

The impact of sexual violence has been extensively studied for decades. Hundreds (perhaps thousands) of studies have examined the impact of rape, sexual assault, and child sexual abuse on victims' physical, mental, emotional, and spiritual health—both during the immediate aftermath of victimization as well as years later. Research has examined outcomes at multiple levels from the physiological and neurobiological response to violence to the impact of sexual violence on entire economic and geopolitical systems. Research has examined outcomes not only of primary victims (i.e., those that directly experienced sexual violence) but also those of secondary victims (e.g., romantic partners/significant others, family members, friends, and colleagues). Research methods have ranged from individual case studies to multiyear national studies of victim outcomes. Opinions on how and why sexual violence affects victims are widely varied, but the common denominator across decades of scholarly research is this: "[sexual violence] is one of the most severe of all traumas, causing multiple, long-term negative outcomes" (Campbell et al., 2009, p. 225).

The Neurobiology of Sexual Trauma

Marie, a 25-year-old woman, reports to her local emergency room to receive care following a sexual assault. Marie is placed a private examination room, and a sexual assault nurse examiner (SANE) nurse and an attending physician gather details about the assault. Marie is unable to make eye contact with the doctor and nurse, speaks softly with little emotion, and provides details about the incident that seem to be contradictory at times. She states that she was unable to speak, shout, or even move and reports having felt disconnected from her body during the assault. Her memory of the incident also appears incomplete, and Marie states that she "blacked out" at one point during the assault.

In the immediate aftermath of rape, sexual assault, or other form of sexual trauma, victims experience a flood of emotions, including shock, fear, anger, guilt, shame, and confusion. The way a victim reacts (or does not react) during the commission of the sex offense and immediately afterward can factor heavily in the decision to report victimization to the authorities and seek medical attention. Victim behavior during and after the offense also shapes professional perceptions of the victim. Victims of sexual violence often encounter remarks made by police, forensic nurse examiners, social workers, and other victim service providers such as "What they said makes no sense," "No one would have acted like that in that situation," and "Why would they have just laid there and taken it?" Such remarks reflect the prevalent lack of awareness of ways in which the brain operates while experiencing victimization. To understand victims' immediate responses and reactions to sexual violence, we must understand the neurobiological response to threat. Doing so allows us to see that experiences like Marie's (including immobility, memory fragmentation, and dissociation) are actually *predictable* reactions to life-threatening events such as sexual victimization.

There are many bodily systems involved in the biological response to threat and stress, including the nervous, endocrine, and immune systems. For most of the 20th century, explanations centered around the **fight or flight response to threat**. Put simply, this is a survival mechanism that prepares the body to respond to an imminent threat by either fighting or, if that is not possible, physically running from the threat. When presented with a threat of a stressor, both the sympathetic nervous system and adrenal glands are activated, which results in increases in heart rate and blood pressure as well as producing a surge in adrenaline. Automatic reactions include an ability to think and make decisions quickly and an attentional focus on the source of the threat and potential avenues for escape. Taken together, this series of bodily changes mounts defense for either fighting the impending threat or running away. The fight or flight response to threat, however, is one dimensional and fails to account for why individuals neither fight nor flee when presented with a threat but instead may freeze.

A more recent understanding of the fight or flight response is reflected in the **defense cascade model** (Schauer & Elbert, 2015), which describes a more comprehensive set of responses that individuals exposed to threat may experience, including freeze, flight, fight, fright, flag, and faint. Figure 8.1 displays the **defense cascade model** as it progresses across the six phases during a life-threatening event such as sexual violence. The six phases are summarized as follows:

1. *Freeze.* At this stage, the victim first freezes and adopts a "stop–look–listen" response. This is typically a short-lived phenomenon often lasting only a few seconds that is characterized by heightened attention, enhanced vigilance to stress cues, body tension, and initial bradycardia (i.e., slower-than-normal heart heart).

2–3. *Flight or Fight:* Shifting out of the freeze response often lands the individual into either a flight or fight response. At this point, the sympathetic nervous system is activated, and this

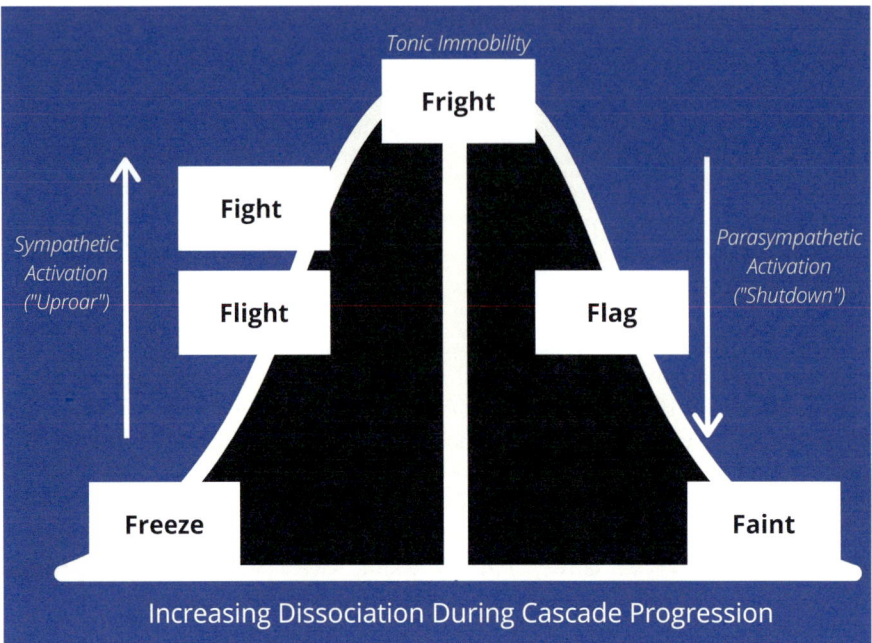

FIGURE 8.1 The Defense Cascade Model.

Note: Adapted from Schauer and Elbert (2015).

is characterized by sharp increases in heart rate, blood pressure, and muscle tension, as well as a release of the hormone **cortisol**, which regulates blood glucose levels so the body can have the energy to initiate fight or flight actions.

4   *Fright:* This response signals the peak of arousal and distress. Tachycardia (higher-than-normal heart rate), hyper-alertness, cortisol release, and muscular constriction have all skyrocketed. Because there is no viable strategy for the body to unleash this energy, the body begins to shut down, and sensations, perceptions, and motor abilities are substantially altered. Victims may experience loss of movement, inability to call for help, and insensitivity to pain. This is known as **tonic immobility** (or rape-induced paralysis).

5   *Flag:* At this point, the parasympathetic nervous system is activated as the body's natural defense against the extreme arousal that has built over the previous four responses. Victims may experience bradycardia (slowed heart rate) and numbing. As the trauma is happening, the body releases a flood of natural opiates that attach to the brain's amygdala receptors, which compromise the brain's ability to encode memories. Victims may have reduced or no memory of what is happening to them at this point.

6   *Faint:* This final response in the cascade is the result of compromised cerebral function and decreased oxygen or glucose availability as a result of tonic immobility. At this point, the victim has limited, if any, awareness of what is happening. Memory cannot be consolidated. When the victim comes to, they usually will display a flat emotional affect, which is a result of a surge in natural opiates that that body has released during the trauma.

If we review the scenario of Marie's encounter with medical professionals following her sexual assault, it should be clear that her reports of an inability to shout, yell, or move; memory fragmentation; dissociation/disconnection from her body; and flat emotional affect while reporting the incident are all *predictable* and *common* neurobiological responses initiated by Maria's body to prepare and protect her as she endured the traumatic event. In a recent study on 1,874 rape cases, it was found that 49% of victims reported loss of consciousness and 33% reported some memory loss (Valentine et al., 2019). The neurobiology of sexual trauma is often not understood by criminal justice professionals; as such, victims often encounter skepticism when they report. This lack of understanding influences decision-making at every phase of the criminal justice system and results in low victim reporting, arrest rates, and prosecution rates (Kelly & Valentine, 2018; Valentine et al., 2016).

Disclosure and Help-Seeking Behaviors

Disclosure of sexual victimization either formally (e.g., to police or other formal support systems) or informally (e.g., to family or friends) is the first step in obtaining help in the wake of sexual violence. However, not all victims disclose their experiences. As discussed in Chapters 3 and 4, crimes of rape, sexual assault, and child sexual abuse often go unreported to police. They also may not disclose these crimes to people close to them, nor do they seek any kind of professional help (Sabina & Ho, 2014). For victims who do disclose their victimization, disclosure can often be a delayed process. The process of disclosure, including barriers and facilitators, is markedly varied for adults versus children.

Disclosure by Adult Victims

Nearly two-thirds of all adult rape and sexual survivors disclose their victimization to at least one person (Fisher et al., 2003). Situational elements of the assault often inform whether victims disclose these crimes to either formal or informal support systems. For instance, assaults by strangers and assaults involving weapons are both more likely to be reported to formal or informal support systems (Starzynski et al., 2005). Research also suggests that greater severity of victimization is associated with higher rates of help-seeking by victims (Fisher et al., 2003; Wolitzky-Taylor et al., 2011). Victims are also more likely to seek help when their victimization persists over a long period of time or when they are experiencing **polyvictimization**, meaning they are experiencing multiple forms of interpersonal violence concurrently (Katz & Rich, 2015; Sabina & Straus, 2008).

Victims who do disclose victimization, either formally or informally, may encounter negative social reactions from significant others and community systems, including victim-blaming responses, skepticism of claims, or responses that encourage secrecy or nondisclosure of the assault (Ahrens, 2006; Davis et al., 1991; Ullman, 2002). Such reactions might deter disclosure of future victimization. For example, findings from one study showed that for victims who disclosed their victimization, 91% felt disappointed, 89% felt violated, 71% felt depressed, and 80% were not likely to seek further help after their encounters with the social services systems (Campbell, 2005).

Disclosure by Child Victims

A range of factors influence disclosure of sexual abuse by child victims, including feeling responsible for the abuse, feeling shame and stigma, fear of being blamed or judged, fear of how they may be perceived sexually (particularly for male victims), fear of skepticism, fear of family disruption (e.g., divorce, separation, or parental rights termination), and concern for the perpetrator who is often a family member (Alaggia et al., 2019; Lemaigre et al., 2017; Morrison et al., 2018; Paine & Hansen, 2002). Summit's (1983) **child sexual abuse accommodation syndrome** provides one explanation for delays in disclosing child sexual abuse, and there are five highly interrelated dynamics:

1 **Secrecy**: The abuse occurs when the victim and offender are alone, and the offender encourages the victim to maintain secrecy.
2 **Helplessness**: Children are obedient to adults and are naturally inclined to obey an offender who insists on secrecy.
3 **Entrapment and Accommodation**: Once the child is helplessly entrenched in an abusive situation, they assume responsibility for the abuse and begins to dissociate (i.e., mentally disconnect or "check out") from it.
4 **Delayed Disclosure**: Due to lengthy periods between initial abuse and disclosure to authorities, many victims' disclosures are subsequently questioned and scrutinized.
5 **Retraction**: Facing disbelief, lack of emotional support, and sometimes disappointment and anger from officials, family members, and peers, victims might retract their disclosures.

It is a common myth that when children disclose sexual abuse, they will provide a clear, detailed account of the incident(s). This is not consistent with research on disclosure. Similar to the grooming process, a victim's disclosure unfolds gradually and may be presented as a series of hints (Canadian Centre for Child Protection, 2014). Children may begin by implying that something *may* have happened to them without directly stating they were sexually abused. This is a method of testing the reaction of the child's confidante. The child is ready, and depending on the initial reaction of the confidante, they might follow up with a larger hint.

Physical Trauma, Injury, and Chronic Health Issues

Sexual violence is a significant public health issue affecting the safety, health, and well-being of millions of people annually. The pernicious effects of sexual violence are both acute and chronic, with some effects being lifelong and costing the health care system more than $100 billion each year (Miller et al., 1996). Physical injury to rape and sexual assault victims occurs at nonnegligible rates with prevalence estimates of physical injury varying by study. Generally, nationally representative studies have found that a slight majority of rape and sexual assault victims do *not* experience acute injury (Cartwright, 1987; Kilpatrick et al., 1992; Tjaden & Thoennes, 2000). However, genital bruising and abrasions are reported by almost two in five victims of rape and sexual assault (Basile et al., 2020). Victims of sexual violence are also more likely to contract a sexually transmitted disease (STD) compared to nonvictims. For instance, research has shown that women experiencing forced sex were more likely than women who did not to be diagnosed with chlamydia, herpes, and genital warts. Recent analysis of the National Intimate Partner and Sexual Violence (NISVS) survey estimated that approximately 12.3% of victims reported a contracted STD as a result of the rape victimization (Basile et al., 2020).

Sexual violence is also highly associated with serious physical health functioning problems that can persist throughout the life course. The odds of experiencing chronic health issues, including asthma, irritable bowel syndrome, frequent headaches, chronic pain, difficulty sleeping, activity limitations, high cholesterol, heart disease, and strokes are significantly higher for victims compared to nonvictims (Basile et al., 2020, Sachs-Ericsson et al., 2014;

Smith & Breiding, 2011). Child sexual abuse can also lead to serious chronic physical health conditions later in life including hypertension and heart disease, thyroid disorders, diabetes, and cancer (Andersen et al., 2014).

Mental and Emotional Health Outcomes

In additional to physical trauma, sexual violence can also lead to serious mental health scarring. Numerous mental health issues have been associated with sexual violence victimization, including depression (McDougall et al., 2019; Santaularia et al., 2014), PTSD symptoms (Basile et al., 2015; Zinzow et al., 2010), anxiety (Choudhary et al., 2012; Iverson et al., 2013; Santaularia et al., 2014), fear (Amstadter & Vernon, 2008), and suicidal ideation (Brabant et al., 2014; Santaularia et al., 2014; Sarkar, 2010) and suicide attempts (Iverson et al., 2013). These outcomes can be lifelong problems for survivors of sexual violence. Campbell et al.'s (2009) meta-analysis on the effects of sexual assault provide the following statistics: 13–51% of women meet diagnostic criteria for depression following sexual assault; 23–44% experience suicidal ideation with 2–19% attempting suicide; dependence on alcohol can be seen in 13–49% of victims, and 28–61% report the use of other illegal substances.

Men who experience sexual violence suffer a number of psychological effects that differ from women. For males, sex-role confusion and fears about sexuality are commonly cited psychological effects of rape. Walker et al. (2005) found that 68% of male rape victims reported long-term effects on their sense of masculinity, and 70% reported long-term problems with sexual identity. Men with untreated sexual trauma have increased alcohol consumption, rape-related phobias, suicidality, sleep disturbances, difficulties in interpersonal relationships, fear of men, and social isolation.

In total, a wide range of reactions can impact victims of sexual violence. Table 8.2 summarizes these outcomes.

Secondary Victims of Sexual Violence

In Chapter 3, we discussed secondary victimization in the context of the retraumatization of victims of sexual violence—for example, through the interactions with insensitive or victim-blaming criminal justice system professionals. Sexual violence does not always only affect the primary victim (i.e., the one directly experiencing the assault); the consequences of this crime can radiate out and exert negative effects on victims' intimate partners, parents, other family members, friends, colleagues, and wider support systems (Ahrens & Campbell, 2000; Burge, 1983; Remer & Elliott, 1988). These are known as **secondary victims**. Understanding the impact of sexual violence on secondary victims is important because of the role they play in supporting the primary victim in coping with their experience following a sexually traumatic incident. If support providers and their relationship to the primary victim are negatively affected, this may contribute to additional emotional turmoil for the primary victim.

Studies on the impact of sexual violence on primary victims' romantic partners, for instance, have found that partners can experience reactions of psychological distress, self-blame, loss of trust, and victim blame, which can result in changes in their relationship with the victim, including changes to the sexual relationship and total relationship dissolution (Brookings et al., 1994; Smith, 2005). Victims' significant others may also experience an emotional toll in supporting the survivor and feel that their own personal needs are left unmet, resulting in a strained relationship with the survivor (O'Callaghan et al., 2021).

TABLE 8.2 Effects of Sexual Violence on Victims

Physical Impacts

- Genital Bruising/Abrasions
- Sexually Transmitted Diseases (STDs)
- Asthma
- Irritable Bowel Syndrome
- Frequent Headaches

- Chronic Pain
- Sleeping Challenges
- Activity Limitations
- High Cholesterol
- Heart Disease/Hypertension
- Strokes

Psychological Reactions

- Nightmares and Flashbacks
- Post-Traumatic Stress Disorder (PTSD)
- Depression
- Panic Disorders

- Substance Abuse and Addiction
- Phobias
- Low Self-Esteem
- Suicidal Ideation
- Sexual Identity Challenges

Emotional Responses

- Guilt
- Shame
- Embarrassment
- Fear
- Social and Physical Isolation
- Anger

- Revenge
- Shock
- Numbness
- Confusion
- Denial
- Betrayal

Children who are sexually abused require the support of parents or other guardians to maximize the possibility of recovery and positive long-term outcomes (Godbout et al., 2014); in particular, maternal (mother) support has been found to provide an especially positive source of emotional support for child sexual abuse victims, leading to beneficial therapeutic outcomes (Corcoran, 2004; Cyr et al., 2002). When children experience sexual victimization, parents can experience a wide range of emotional responses, including guilt, shame, self-blame, anger, and disbelief (Foster, 2014). These responses, in turn, influence the quality of support parents are able to provide for their children. For example, Fuller (2016) found that negative emotional responses often resulted in parents becoming overprotective of their children to the point of physical and social isolation.

Professionals who assist people in recovering from sexual violence can also fall victim to its devastating impacts. These professionals, such as rape crisis center staff, victim advocates, and sexual assault therapists, can enjoy immense personal and professional satisfaction and fulfillment but also experience considerable stress as a result of their work. **Secondary traumatic stress** (STS) occurs as a reaction to indirect exposure to trauma experienced by another person (Bride et al., 2007). Other terms to describe this secondary exposure include vicarious trauma and burnout. All terms refer to the psychological, cognitive, and physiological reactions experienced by providers, which is similar to clients' trauma symptoms (Baird & Jenkins, 2003).

According to the fifth edition of the *Diagnostic and Statistical Manual of Mental Disorders, 5th ed.* (DSM-5), if severe enough, STS is classified as a form of PTSD where providers experience certain symptomatology such as functional impairment, distressing emotions, avoidance, and physiological arousal (American Psychiatric Association, 2013). The reported prevalence of STS among professionals and providers serving victims of sexual violence and abuse is widely varied and depends on how STS is defined and measured and the specific occupation or profession being studied. For example, Choi (2011) estimated STS prevalence rates between 21% and 29% among social workers serving family violence and sexual violence survivors. STS can affect the quality of service and therapeutic care delivered to clients (Bride et al., 2007; Choi, 2011; Salston & Figley, 2003). Robinson-Keilig (2014) reported that higher levels of STS symptoms are significantly associated with less use of constructive communication in favor of passive or avoidant communication styles with clients. Likewise, providers suffering from STS impairment are more likely to miss deadlines, forget appointments, dramatically change work habits, or become extremely critical and abrasive (Emerson & Markos, 1996).

FALSE ALLEGATIONS OF SEXUAL VIOLENCE

Throughout this book, we have frequently revisited the myth that victim reports of rape, sexual assault, child sexual abuse, and other forms of sexual violence are wrought with false allegations. With limited exception, intentional embellishment or complete fabrication of sexual violence victimization is uncommon. More often, reports of sexual violence are (a) not disclosed by victims at all, (b) unfounded or unsubstantiated by police or the courts (meaning there is insufficient evidence for pursuing arrest or prosecution of the crime), or (c) truthfully reported and subsequently recanted by victims. However, false allegations of sexual violence do occur, and they occur at nontrivial levels. Although false allegations comprise an extremely small proportion of all incidents of sexual violence that happen annually, it is important nevertheless to examine how and why they occur.

It may seem strange to include a discussion of false allegations of sexual violence in a chapter focused on victims of sexual violence. However, this issue has important implications for actual victims of sexual violence. As we will see, the prevalence of false allegations has been blown out of proportion by the media, the criminal justice workforce, and researchers alike, posing direct threats to the credibility of a much larger population of victims who actually experience these crimes.

False Rape Allegations

Researching false allegations of rape and sexual assault is a complicated matter. This is evidenced by a comprehensive review of studies published in 2006 that estimated false allegations at rates ranging between 1.5% and 90% (Rumney, 2006). The wide variability in estimated prevalence is an artifact of the lack of a uniform definition of what constitutes a false allegation. The most widely accepted and most technically accurate definition of a false allegation is described in the International Association of Chiefs of Police's (IACP, 2005, pp. 12–13) comprehensive model policy, which states the following:

> The determination that a report of sexual assault is false can be made only if the evidence establishes that no crime was committed or attempted. *This determination can be made only after a thorough investigation.* This should not be confused with an investigation that fails to prove a sexual assault occurred.

Under this definition, evidence of a false allegation may include physical evidence and/or statements from credible witnesses that contradict key aspects of a victim's account. It *does not* include factors such as lack of victim cooperation with investigators, cases where investigators determine there is insufficient evidence, cases where victims make a delayed report, or cases where victims make inaccurate statements. These factors are actually common in rape and sexual assault cases, yet they are frequently misclassified as false allegations (Lisak et al., 2010; Saunders, 2012).

Using the correct definition promulgated by IACP, the rate of false allegations found in the past four decades of empirical studies is consistently low, contradicting the stereotype that false rape allegations are a common occurrence. At the low end, prevalence of false rape allegations has been estimated at 2.1% (Heenan & Murray, 2006), 2.5% (Kelly et al., 2005), 3.0% (McCahill et al., 1979), and 5.9% (Lisak et al., 2010); at the high end, estimates have included 10.3% (Clark & Lewis, 1977) and 10.9% (Harris & Grace, 1999). Motivations for a false rape allegation may include an attempt to conceal infidelity, consensual sex that is later regretted, the breakdown of a relationship, or an attempt to manipulate or provoke sympathy (Kelly et al., 2005; Saunders, 2012; Turvey, 2011). Another researcher identified five overlapping categories of motivation: avoiding trouble or providing an alibi, anger or revenge, attention seeking, mental illness, and guilt or remorse (O'Neal et al., 2014).

False Allegations of Child Sexual Abuse

Similar to allegations of rape and sexual assault, estimates of the frequency of false child sexual abuse (CSA) allegations are varied in the literature. For example, recent Child Protective Services investigations data showed that 0.06% (or approximately 1 in 1,500) allegations of CSA were ruled as intentionally false (Administration for Children and Families, 2014). Other studies estimating the rate of false allegations using child protective agency data have estimated rates ranging from 0.28% to 6% (Administration for Children and Families, 2003; Goodwin et al., 1978; Jones & McGraw, 1987). Researchers have also estimated false allegations through surveying police officers and mental health professionals. For instance, one study revealed that approximately 5% of CSA claims were deemed as fictitious by law enforcement and mental health professionals (Kendall-Tackett & Watson, 1991). Another survey of social services workers revealed an estimated rate of 4.7% of suspected false allegations (Everson & Boat, 1989). Although varied definitions and measurements do not allow for a precise estimate of the true frequency of false accusations of CSA, two broad conclusions can be made: (1) most allegations of CSA are true; however (2) false allegations do occur at a non-negligible rate (Donohue et al., 2018). Research on false allegations of CSA has been primarily conducted in three contexts: (1) research on the accuracy of children's memories of CSA, (2) research examining false allegations or false memories of CSA made in adulthood, and (3) studies examining intentionally false allegations of CSA in the context of custody disputes.

Accuracy of Children's Recollections of CSA

As discussed in Chapter 4, successful prosecution of CSA often requires the physical presence of child victims in court proceedings to provide an account of the alleged incident. The dramatic increase in the number of child victims involved in legal proceedings in the 1980s and 1990s led to fundamental concerns about the reliability of children's testimony and strategies and tactics used to draw information from them. Child victims involved in sexual abuse investigations are often exposed to other events or sources of information that can influence the accuracy of their recollections of their personal victimization. Certain exposures can strengthen the accuracy of memories, whereas other exposures can contaminate memories. Rehearsal through repetition is one strategy that strengthens the accuracy of recollections of CSA. Research has shown that when children are given the opportunity to rehearse memories of an incident, they are more likely to retain accurate memories of the event. This can be accomplished through many mechanisms, including engaging children in a nonsuggestive, open-ended conversation about the alleged incident, having an adult repeat back details consistent with what occurred during an incident, and watching a video of a highly similar incident (Principe et al., 2000; Roberts et al., 1999). There is also evidence suggesting that psychological counseling received by child victims during prosecution may improve memory of sexual abuse incidents (Goodman et al., 2017).

However, other exposures and suggestive influences can induce memory errors (known as *false memory syndrome*) in children. Research has shown that human memory is not a "steel trap" but rather is highly suggestible and malleable (Ceci & Loftus, 1994). In some studies, for example, when children were repeatedly interviewed by police, social workers, or parents about an incident of sexual abuse with questions containing inaccurate descriptions, they later reported those inaccuracies when questioned with nonsuggestive prompts (Bruck & Ceci, 1999; Bruck et al., 1995; Korkman et al., 2014).

CSA Allegations by Adult Survivors

In May 1991, 53-year-old Marilyn Van Derbur, a former Miss America pageant champion, visited the University of Colorado, Denver to make a family donation to the Kempe National Center for the Prevention and Treatment of Child Abuse and Neglect. Addressing a small audience of approximately 150 people, Van Derbur revealed a dark secret: her father had repeatedly raped and abused her from the age of 5 until she was 18. She claimed that she had no conscious memories of what her father had done until she reached the age of 24 and explained that she developed dissociative fugue as a means of coping with the trauma. She had repressed these memories. A reporter happened to be in the audience that evening, and within the next two days, Van Derbur's long-buried secret made national headlines. Van Derbur's story, along with many others that went public during the 1980s and 1990s, was a turning point for CSA survivors. Previously, stories like Van Derbur's would have been summarily dismissed by psychiatrists as hysterical fantasies; now, the power balance had shifted. Adult victims of CSA began to come forward with their stories of survival. News shows and made-for-TV dramatic films about the horrors of CSA proliferated. Books about incest and CSA flooded the market; by 1994, more than 800,000 women had bought a self-help book called *The Courage to Heal*. Legislators passed laws extending the statute of limitations on abuse cases to three years after the victim first remembered the crime. The percentage of American women who were believed to be survivors of childhood sexual trauma skyrocketed, with some studies estimating that as many as 50% of women were CSA survivors (Satter, 2003). However, some researchers were skeptical about the validity and accuracy of all these claims.

Memories of CSA are often recovered by adults in the course of therapy and counseling. In response to the exponential increase in the number of adults coming forward with repressed memories of CSA, researchers began questioning the validity of some of recovered memories and proposing the possibility that some adults are susceptible to acquiring memories of CSA that did not actually occur (Lindsay & Read, 1994; Loftus, 1993; Loftus & Ketcham, 1996). Research has shown that certain therapeutic methods are more conducive to the creation of false memories, which presents a challenge to the credibility of some allegations of CSA. **Recovered-memory therapy** (also known as repressed-memory therapy) is a form of psychotherapy that utilizes controversial interviewing techniques such as hypnosis, guided imagery, and sedative-hypnotic or psychotropic drugs to purportedly help clients recall "repressed" memories. Recovered-memory therapy has been scientifically challenged by many researchers who claim that such memory recovery techniques can distort patients' recollections of CSA or entirely implant fictitious accounts of CSA in patients' minds (Bottoms et al., 1996; Gardner, 2004; Lynn et al., 2003; Rofé, 2008).

At the other end of the spectrum are those who believe that the mind is capable of traumatic memory repression and loss as a result of CSA (Briere & Conte, 1993; Freyd, 1996; Van der Kolk & Fisler, 1995). Some researchers have gone as far to argue that the false memory defense is contrived and often erroneous with the potential of misleading juries (Brown, 2001) as well as reinforcing the silence surrounding CSA by challenging victims' disclosures. In some studies, the authenticity of recovered memories was corroborated by other sources (Brenneis, 2000; Kluft, 1995; Martínez-Taboas, 1996). In Marilyn Van Derbur's case, the validity of her memories of her traumatic past were corroborated (and therefore strengthened) when her elder sister reported having experienced similar CSA victimization at the hands of their father. The debate surrounding the recovery of repressed CSA memories in adulthood remains a contentious and polarized one. Today, it is widely accepted that both true and false memories exist in the recovery of CSA memories by adults later in life (Mann & Naugle, 2019). However, *proving* these memories (as true or false) is next to impossible in most cases.

CSA Allegations during Custody Disputes

In 1985, Columbia University psychiatrist Dr. Richard Gardner coined the term **Parental Alienation Syndrome** to describe what he believed to be a prevalent phenomenon in child custody proceedings of one parent imposing undue influence and psychological manipulation on their children to prevent an ongoing relationship between the child and other family members (Gardner, 1985). Specifically, Gardner blamed vindictive mothers for pressuring their children to make false accusations of sexual abuse against their fathers in an effort to prevent continued contact with them. Gardner's claims have subsequently been largely discredited by numerous studies showing false sexual abuse allegations in the context of parental separation and divorce to be fairly rare (Bruch, 2001; Faller, 1998; Hoult, 2006; Thoennes & Tjaden, 1990). In a large-scale study of child maltreatment allegations that occurred within the context of parental separation, researchers found that 6% of all CSA allegations were intentionally fabricated, compared to 36% that were deemed unsubstantiated but made in good faith (Trocmé & Bala, 2005).

SEXUAL VIOLENCE VICTIM ADVOCACY

The 1960s signaled a marked shift with respect to how victims were viewed by the criminal justice system and the broader public. As the crime rate in the United States began to climb in the 1960s, attention and attitudes toward victims of crimes became more sympathetic as scholars and activists began demonstrating the ways in which crime was a by-product of broader societal beliefs and values. For example, a major focal concern of the women's liberation movement was how crimes such as rape and domestic violence were by-products of sexism, misogyny, traditional gender roles, and the subjugation of women. Likewise, the civil rights movement created awareness of how racial minorities were mistreated (both as offenders and as victims) by the criminal justice system. The ideologies of these social movements coalesced to create the victims' rights movement, which pushed forward an agenda focused on procedural changes to the criminal justice system for the benefit of victims of crime.

The victims' rights movement gave way to the anti-rape movement in the late 1960s and early 1970s, which elevated sexual violence as an important social problem in critical need of attention. As early as 1970, the first rape workshops and conferences were held throughout the country to challenge long-standing assumptions about sexual violence. "Speakouts" featuring public testimony by rape and sexual assault victims also emerged during this period (Connell & Wilson, 1974). The first emergency rape hotline for victims was established in 1972, and by 1977, crisis lines for victims were made available in nearly all major cities and college communities (Rose, 1977). Community programs and rape crisis centers aided victims as they navigated medical, police, and court procedures in the aftermath of victimization. Grassroots activists and prevention groups advocated for more sensitive handling of sexual violence cases by police and medical personnel. Thousands of rape prevention and self-defense classes were held throughout the country on a monthly basis. As discussed in Chapter 3, substantial legislative revision to rape laws were instituted, including the elimination of corroboration requirements and the enactment of rape shield laws.

The 1970s were a time of rapid progress for the anti-rape movement; however, they were also turbulent times as national priorities shifted, resulting in decreased availability of federal dollars to support victim assistance programs and the defunding of the Law Enforcement Assistance Administration, the major source of grant funding for victim-centered services, in 1979. Victim advocates, realizing that state action was crucial for ensuring the sustainability of victim assistance programs, urged state public officials to establish state funding mechanisms; California was the first state to do so in 1980. The Reagan administration breathed new life into the movement in the early 1980s. The first federal allocation of money for sexual violence prevention services was distributed to sexual assault centers in 1982 through the Preventive Health and Health Services Block Grant. Subsequent funds through the Victims of Crime Act in 1984 and the Violence Against Women Act (VAWA) in 1994 (and subsequent reauthorizations in 2000, 2005, 2013, and 2021) have enabled crisis centers and shelters to provide direct services, victim advocacy and education, and community prevention programming. VAWA also established the Rape Prevention and Education Program, which is administered by the Centers for Disease Control and Prevention and supports rape prevention and education programs in all 50 states.

#MeToo Movement

Tarana Burke, a woman's right activist, began the Me Too movement, and she encouraged the use of hashtag with the "MeToo" phrase (#MeToo) on social media to raise awareness of sexual harassment and sexual violence (Mendes et al., 2018). Subsequently in 2017, Hollywood actress Alyssa Milano encouraged the use of #MeToo on Twitter to identify the pervasiveness of sexual harassment and sexual violence (Mendes et al., 2018). During the first day of this prompt, #MeToo was used 12 million times on social media (CBS, 2017). The #MeToo movement provided women all over the world with an opportunity to express their disappointment and anger over their victimization. It also allowed victims to identify with others who had similar experiences. The #MeToo movement was also closely tied to the story of Hollywood movie producer Harvey Weinstein and scores of Hollywood actresses harassed and raped by Weinstein over the past 30 years. More than 100 actresses, including Kate Beckinsale, Cate Blanchett, Heather Graham, Daryl Hannah, Rose McGowen, Annabella Sciorra, and Uma Thurman, have come forward with their own stories of victimization, demonstrating how Weinstein "personified the way powerful men could abuse their status to establish dominance over women" (Kantor & Twohey, 2019, p. 42).

The implications of the #MeToo movement are far-reaching. Beyond the number of girls and women who have shared their stories on social media and the amount of media attention sexual violence has received, research efforts have also identified the critical role of social media in the fight against sexual violence. For example, one group of researchers found that in addition to the use of #MeToo, other hashtags have also appeared such as #BeenRapedNeverReported (Mendes et al., 2018). In a formal study that involved 82 interviews of reactions of sharing sexual violence victimization reports on social media, the researchers recognize a "growing trend of the public's willingness to engage with *resistance* and *challenges* . . . [to sexual violence] via . . . uptake of digital communication" (Mendes et al., 2018, p. 237). Their research told powerful stories that women shared about their reactions after posting details of their sexual violence experiences such as the following (p. 238):

> I got an overwhelming awesome response the night I posted. . . . There was one. . . . All she said was, "We stand with you, friend." And that one made me cry. I'll admit it, that one made me cry. And then there was one that told me I was incredibly strong and brave for doing what I did. . . . There was six or seven comments like that. Which, for me, was overwhelming because I didn't really think that anyone would say these things, you know, it was just I was helping the hashtag understand why things weren't being reported. And I didn't really expect any response at all. And next thing you know, I got likes and favourites and comments, and I was just, like, oh, my gosh, what is going on here.

REVIEW POINTS

- Early theories of criminal victimization relied upon the concept of victim precipitation to identify how victims partially contribute to or wholly cause their own victimization; for victims of sexual violence, the concept of victim precipitation is heavily embedded in beliefs supportive of attitudinal rape myths today.
- Several demographic and background characteristics have been identified as highly relevant to rape and sexual assault victimization risk, including gender, age, race, sexual orientation, relationship status, and income or financial situation.
- The factors most predictive of child sexual abuse included prior CSA victimization of the child and/or siblings, prior victimization of the child other than child abuse, prior or concurrent forms of child abuse in the child's home environment, a parental history of child abuse victimization, household violence, parenting problems, and other child problems.
- The stereotype of the "real rape" victim (i.e., a young, white female) is challenged by several victim populations that don't fit this composite, including the elderly, men, disabled individuals, and Indigenous women.
- The Defense Cascade Model demonstrates why the inability to shout, yell, or move' memory fragmentation; dissociation or disconnection from the body; and flat emotional affect while reporting victimization are all *predictable* and *common* neurobiological responses of the body during rape and sexual assault.
- Sexual violence is one of the most severe of all traumas, causing multiple, long-term negative outcomes at multiple levels.
- False allegations of rape and child sexual abuse occur at nonnegligible rates; however, they are fairly rare occurrences.

REFERENCES

Acierno, R., Resnick, H., Kilpatrick, D. G., Saunders, B., & Best, C. L. (1999). Risk factors for rape, physical assault, and posttraumatic stress disorder in women: Examination of differential multivariate relationships. *Journal of Anxiety Disorders, 13*(6), 541–563. https://doi.org/10.1016/S0887-6185(99)00030-4

Administration for Children and Families. (2003). *Child maltreatment*. US Department of Health & Human Services.

Administration for Children and Families. (2014). *Child maltreatment*. US Department of Health & Human Services.

Administration for Children and Families. (2021). *Child maltreatment*. US Department of Health & Human Services.

Ahrens, C. E. (2006). Being silenced: The impact of negative social reactions on the disclosure of rape. *American Journal of Community Psychology, 38*(3–4), 263–274. https://doi.org/10.1007/s10464-006-9069-9

Ahrens, C. E., & Campbell, R. (2000). Assisting rape victims as they recover from rape: The impact on friends. *Journal of Interpersonal Violence, 15*, 959–986. https://doi.org/10.1177/088626000015009004

Alaggia, R., Collin-Vézina, D., & Lateef, R. (2019). Facilitators and barriers to child sexual abuse (CSA) disclosures: A research update (2000–2016). *Trauma, Violence, & Abuse, 20*(2), 260–283. https://doi.org/10.1177%2F1524838017697312

American Psychiatric Association. (2013). *Diagnostic and statistical manual of mental disorders* (Vol. 5). American Psychiatric Association.

Amir, M. (1967). Victim precipitated forcible rape. *The Journal of Criminal Law, Criminology, and Police Science, 58*(4), 493–502. https://doi.org/10.2307/1141908

Amstadter, A. B., & Vernon, L. L. (2008). Emotional reactions during and after trauma: A comparison of trauma types. *Journal of Aggression, Maltreatment & Trauma, 16*(4), 391–408. https://doi.org/10.1080/10926770801926492

Andersen, J. P., Hughes, T. L., Zou, C., & Wilsnack, S. C. (2014). Lifetime victimization and physical health outcomes among lesbian and heterosexual women. *PLOS ONE, 9*(7), Article e101939. https://www.doi.org/10.1371/journal.pone.0101939

Assink, M., van der Put, C. E., Meeuwsen, M. W. C. M., de Jong, N. M., Oort, F. J., Stams, G. J. J. M., & Hoeve, M. (2019). Risk factors for child sexual abuse victimization: A meta-analytic review. *Psychological Bulletin, 145*(5), 459–489. https://www./doi.org/10.1037/bul0000188

Baird, S., & Jenkins, S. R. (2003). Vicarious traumatization, secondary traumatic stress, and burnout in sexual assault and domestic violence agency staff. *Violence and Victims, 18*(1), 71–86. https://doi.org/10.1891/vivi.2003.18.1.71

Basile, K. C., Breiding, M. J., & Smith, S. G. (2016). Disability and risk of recent sexual violence in the United States. *American Journal of Public Health, 106*(5), 928–933. https://www.doi.org/10.2105/AJPH.2015.303004

Basile, K. C., Smith, S. G., Chen, J., & Zwald, M. (2020). Chronic diseases, health conditions, and other impacts associated with rape victimization of US women. *Journal of Interpersonal Violence*, https://doi.org/10.1177/0886260519900335

Basile, K. C., Smith, S. G., Walters, M. L., Fowler, D. N., Hawk, K., & Hamburger, M. E. (2015). Sexual violence victimization and associations with health in a community sample of Hispanic women. *Journal of Ethnic and Cultural Diversity in Social Work, 24*(1), 1–17. https://doi.org/10.1080/15313204.2014.964441

Belsky, J. (1980). Child maltreatment: An ecological integration. *American Psychologist, 35*, 320–335. http://www.doi.org/10.1037/0003-066X.35.4.320

Black, M. C., Basile, K. C., Breiding, M. J., Smith, S. G., Walters, M. L., Merrick, M. T., Chen, J., & Stevens, M. R. (2011). Sexual violence victimization. In *National intimate partner and sexual violence survey: 2010 summary report* (pp. 15–26). Centers for Disease Control and Prevention.

Bolan, R. M. (2001). *Child sexual abuse: Its scope and our failure.* Kluwer Academic Publishers.

Bottoms, B. L., Shaver, P. R., & Goodman, G. S. (1996). An analysis of ritualistic and religion-related child abuse allegations. *Law and Human Behavior, 20*(1), 1–34. https://doi.org/10.1007/BF01499130

Bows, H., & Westmarland, N. (2017). Rape of older people in the United Kingdom: Challenging the "real-rape" stereotype. *British Journal of Criminology, 57*(1), 1–17. https://doi.org/10.1093/bjc/azv116

Brabant, M. E., Hébert, M., & Chagnon, F. (2014). Predicting suicidal ideations in sexually abused female adolescents: A 12-month prospective study. *Journal of Child Sexual Abuse, 23*(4), 387–397. https://doi.org/10.1080/10538712.2014.896842

Braithwaite, J., Deer, S., & Freedman, H. V. (2019). Barriers to justice for victims of sexual violence in Indian Country. *Family & Intimate Partner Violence Quarterly, 12*(1), 67–74.

Breiding, M. J. (2014). Prevalence and characteristics of sexual violence, stalking, and intimate partner violence victimization—National Intimate Partner and Sexual Violence Survey, United States, 2011. *Morbidity and Mortality Weekly Report. Surveillance Summaries, 63*(8), 1–18.

Brenneis, C. B. (2000). Evaluating the evidence: Can we find authenticated recovered memory? *Psychoanalytic Psychology, 17*(1), 61–77. https://psycnet.apa.org/doi/10.1037/0736-9735.17.1.61

Bride, B. E., Jones, J. L., & MacMaster, S. A. (2007). Correlates of secondary traumatic stress in child protective services workers. *Journal of Evidence-Based Social Work, 4*(3–4), 69–80. https://doi.org/10.1300/J394v04n03_05

Briere, J., & Conte, J. (1993). Self-reported amnesia for abuse in adults molested as children. *Journal of Traumatic Stress, 6*(1), 21–31. https://doi.org/10.1007/BF02093360

Brookings, J. B., McEvoy, A. W., & Reed, M. (1994). Sexual assault recovery and male significant others. *Families in Society, 75*(5), 295–299. https://doi.org/10.1177%2F104438949407500512

Browne, A., & Bassuk, S. S. (1997). Intimate violence in the lives of homeless and poor housed women: Prevalence and patterns in an ethnically diverse sample. *American Journal of Orthopsychiatry, 67*(2), 261–278. https://doi.org/10.1037/h0080230

Brownmiller, S. (1975). *Against our will: Men, women, and rape.* Ballantine Books.

Bruch, C. S. (2001). Parental alienation syndrome and parental alienation: Getting it wrong in child custody cases. *Family Law Quarterly, 35*(3), 527–552. https://doi.org/10.2139/ssrn.298110

Bruck, M., & Ceci, S. J. (1999). The suggestibility of children's memory. *Annual Review of Psychology, 50*(1), 419–439. https://doi.org/10.1146/annurev.psych.50.1.419

Bruck, M., Ceci, S. J., Francoeur, E., & Barr, R. (1995). "I hardly cried when I got my shot!" Influencing children's reports about a visit to their pediatrician. *Child Development, 66*(1), 193–208. https://doi.org/10.1111/j.1467-8624.1995.tb00865.x

Burge, S. K. (1983). Rape: Individual and family reactions. In C. Figley & H. McCubbin (Eds.), *Stress and the family: Coping with catastrophe* (pp. 103–119). Brunner/Mazel.

Burgess, A. W., & Phillips, S. L. (2006). Sexual abuse, trauma and dementia in the elderly: A retrospective study of 284 cases. *Victims and Offenders, 1*(2), 193–204. https://doi.org/10.1080/15564880600663935

Byrne, G. (2018). Prevalence and psychological sequelae of sexual abuse among individuals with an intellectual disability: A review of the recent literature. *Journal of Intellectual Disabilities, 22*(3), 294–310. https://www.doi.org/10.1177/1744629517698844

Campbell, R. (2005). What really happened? A validation study of rape survivors' help-seeking experiences with the legal and medical systems. *Violence and Victims, 20*(1), 55–68. https://doi.org/10.1891/vivi.2005.20.1.55

Campbell, R., Dworkin, E., & Cabral, G. (2009). An ecological model of the impact of sexual assault on women's mental health. *Trauma Violence Abuse, 10*(3), 225–246. https://www.doi.org/10.1177/1524838009334456

Canadian Centre for Child Protection, Inc. (2014). Child sexual abuse: It is your business. Canadian Centre for Child Protection, Inc. https://www.cybertip.ca/pdfs/C3P_ChildSexualAbuse_ItIsYourBusiness_en.pdf

Cartwright, P. S. (1987). Sexual assault study group. Factors that correlate with injury sustained by survivors of sexual assault. *Obstetrics and Gynecology, 7*, 44–46. https://doi.org/10.1016/0020-7292(88)90321-9

CBS. (2017). More than 12M "MeToo" Facebook posts, comments, reactions in 24 hours. https://www.cbsnews.com/news/metoo-more-than-12-million-facebook-posts-comments-reactions-24-hours/

Ceci, S. J., & Loftus, E. F. (1994). "Memory work": A royal road to false memories? *Applied Cognitive Psychology, 8*(4), 351–364. https://doi.org/10.1002/acp.2350080405

Chan, K. L., Straus, M. A., Brownridge, D. A., Tiwari, A., & Leung, W. C. (2008). Prevalence of dating partner violence and suicidal ideation among male and female university students worldwide. *Journal of Midwifery & Women's Health, 53*(6), 529–537. https://doi.org/10.1016/j.jmwh.2008.04.016

Choi, G. Y. (2011). Secondary traumatic stress of service providers who practice with survivors of family or sexual violence: A national survey of social workers. *Smith College Studies in Social Work, 81*(1), 101–119. https://doi.org/10.1080/00377317.2011.543044

Chonco, N. R. (1989). Sexual assaults among male inmates: A descriptive study. *The Prison Journal, 69*(1), 72–82. https://doi.org/10.1177/003288558906900110

Chopin, J., & Beauregard, E. (2020). Elderly sexual abuse: An examination of the criminal event. *Sexual Abuse, 32*(6), 706–726. https://doi.org/10.1177%2F1079063219843899

Choudhary, E., Smith, M., & Bossarte, R. M. (2012). Depression, anxiety, and symptom profiles among female and male victims of sexual violence. *American Journal of Men's Health, 6*(1), 28–36. https://doi.org/10.1177%2F1557988311414045

Clark, L. M., & Lewis, D. J. (1977). *Rape: The price of coercive sexuality*. Women's Press.

Cohen, L. E., & Felson, M. (1979). Social change and crime rate trends: A routine activity approach. *American Sociological Review, 44*, 588–608. https://www.doi.org/10.2307/2094589

Combs-Lane, A. M., & Smith, D. W. (2002). Risk of sexual victimization in college women: The role of behavioral intentions and risk-taking behaviors. *Journal of Interpersonal Violence, 17*(2), 165–183. https://doi.org/10.2307/2094589

Connell, N., & Wilson, C. (1974). *Rape: The first sourcebook for women*. New American Library.

Corcoran, J. (2004). Treatment outcome research with the non-offending parents of sexually abused children: A critical review. *Journal of Child Sexual Abuse, 13*(2), 59–84. https://doi.org/10.1300/J070v13n02_04

Curry, M. A., Renker, P., Robinson-Whelen, S., Hughes, R. B., Swank, P., Oschwald, M., & Powers, L. E. (2011). Facilitators and barriers to disclosing abuse among women with disabilities. *Violence and Victims, 26*(4), 430–444. https://doi.org/10.1891/0886-6708.26.4.430

Cyr, M., Wright, J., Toupin, J., Oxman-Martinez, J., McDuff, P., & Thériault, C. (2002). Predictors of maternal support: The point of view of adolescent victims of sexual abuse and their mothers. *Journal of Child Sexual Abuse, 12*(1), 39–65. https://doi.org/10.1300/J070v12n01_03

Davis, R. C., Brickman, E., & Baker, T. (1991). Supportive and unsupportive responses of others to rape victims: Effects on concurrent victim adjustment. *American Journal of Community Psychology, 19*(3), 443–451. https://doi.org/10.1007/BF00938035

De Keseredy, W. S., & Kelly, K. (1995). Sexual abuse in Canadian university and college dating relationships: The contribution of male peer support. *Journal of Family Violence, 10*(1), 41–53. https://doi.org/10.1007/BF02110536

Deer, S. (2004). Federal Indian law and violent crime: Native women and children at the mercy of the state. *Social Justice, 31*(4), 17–30.

Drabble, L., Trocki, K. F., Hughes, T. L., Korcha, R. A., & Lown, A. E. (2013). Sexual orientation differences in the relationship between victimization and hazardous drinking among women in the National Alcohol Survey. *Psychology of Addictive Behaviors, 27*(3), 639–658. https://www.doi.org/10.1037/a0031486

Elias, R. (1986). *The politics of victimization: Victims, victimology, and human rights.* OUP Catalogue.

Elliott, D. M., Mok, D. S., & Briere, J. (2004). Adult sexual assault: Prevalence, symptomatology, and sex differences in the general population. *Journal of Traumatic Stress: Official Publication of the International Society for Traumatic Stress Studies, 17*(3), 203–211. https://doi.org/10.1023/b:jots.0000029263.11104.23

Emerson, S., & Markos, P. A. (1996). Signs and symptoms of the impaired counselor. *The Journal of Humanistic Education and Development, 34*(3), 108–117. https://doi.org/10.1002/j.2164-4683.1996.tb00335.x

Estrich, S. (1987). *Real rape.* Harvard University Press.

Everson, M. D., & Boat, B. W. (1989). False allegations of sexual abuse by children and adolescents. *Journal of the American Academy of Child & Adolescent Psychiatry, 28*(2), 230–235. https://doi.org/10.1097/00004583-198903000-00014

Faller, K. (1998). The parental alienation syndrome: What is it and what data support it? *Child Maltreatment, 3*(2), 100–115. https://doi.org/10.1177%2F1077559598003002005

Fisher, B. (2000). *The sexual victimization of college women.* National Institute of Justice, U.S. Department of Justice.

Fisher, B. S., Daigle, L. E., Cullen, F. T., & Turner, M. G. (2003). Reporting sexual victimization to the police and others: Results from a national-level study of college women. *Criminal Justice and Behavior, 30*(1), 6–38. https://doi.org/10.1177%2F0093854802239161

Fisher, M. H., Baird, J. V., Currey, A. D., & Hodapp, R. M. (2016). Victimisation and social vulnerability of adults with intellectual disability: A review of research extending beyond Wilson and Brewer. *Australian Psychologist, 51*(2), 114–127. https://doi.org/10.1111/ap.12180

Foster, J. M. (2014). Supporting child victims of sexual abuse: Implementation of a trauma narrative family intervention. *The Family Journal, 22*(3), 332–338. https://doi.org/10.1177%2F1066480714529746

Franklin, C. A. (2010). Physically forced, alcohol-induced, and verbally coerced sexual victimization: Assessing risk factors among university women. *Journal of Criminal Justice, 38*(2), 149–159. https://doi.org/10.1016/j.jcrimjus.2010.02.004

Freyd, J. J. (1996). *Betrayal trauma: The logic of forgetting childhood abuse.* Harvard University Press.

Fuller, G. (2016). Non-offending parents as secondary victims of child sexual assault. *Trends and Issues in Crime and Criminal Justice, 500,* 1–7.

Gardner, R. A. (1985). Recent trends in divorce and custody litigation. *Academy Forum, 29*(-2), 3–7.

Gardner, R. A. (2004). The psychodynamics of patients with false memory syndrome. *Journal of the American Academy of Psychoanalysis and Dynamic Psychiatry, 32*, 77–90. https://doi.org/10.1521/jaap.32.1.77.28336

Godbout, N., Briere, J., Sabourin, S., & Lussier, Y. (2014). Child sexual abuse and subsequent relational and personal functioning: The role of parental support. *Child Abuse & Neglect, 38*(2), 317–325. https://doi.org/10.1016/j.chiabu.2013.10.001

Goodman, G. S., Goldfarb, D., Quas, J. A., & Lyon, A. (2017). Psychological counseling and accuracy of memory for child sexual abuse. *American Psychologist, 72*(9), 920. https://psycnet.apa.org/doi/10.1037/amp0000282

Goodwin, J., Sahd, D., & Rada, R. T. (1978). Incest hoax: false accusations, false denials. *The Bulletin of the American Academy of Psychiatry and the Law, 6*(3), 269–276.

Harris, J., & Grace, S. (1999). *A question of evidence? Investigating and prosecuting rape in the 1990s* [Home Office Research Study 196]. London: Home Office.

Heenan, M., & Murray, S. (2006). *Study of reported rapes in Victoria, 2000–2003*. Office of Women's Policy, Department for Victorian Communities.

Heidt, J. M., Marx, B. P., & Gold, S. D. (2005). Sexual revictimization among sexual minorities: A preliminary study. *Journal of Traumatic Stress, 18*(5), 533–540. https://doi.org/10.1002/jts.20061

Hensley, C., Tewksbury, R., & Castle, T. (2003). Characteristics of prison sexual assault targets in male Oklahoma correctional facilities. *Journal of Interpersonal Violence, 18*(6), 595–606. https://doi.org/10.1177%2F0886260503251132

Hoult, J. (2006). The evidentiary admissibility of parental alienation syndrome: Science, law, and policy. *Children's Legal Rights Journal, 26*(1), 1–61.

International Association of Chiefs of Police (IACP). (2005). *Investigating sexual assaults: Concepts and issues paper.* Author.

Iverson, K. M., Dick, A., McLaughlin, K. A., Smith, B. N., Bell, M. E., Gerber, M. R., . . . & Mitchell, K. S. (2013). Exposure to interpersonal violence and its associations with psychiatric morbidity in a US national sample: A gender comparison. *Psychology of Violence, 3*(3), 273. https://psycnet.apa.org/doi/10.1037/a0030956

Jones, D. P., & McGraw, J. M. (1987). Reliable and fictitious accounts of sexual abuse to children. *Journal of interpersonal Violence, 2*(1), 27–45. https://doi.org/10.1177%2F088626087002001002

Kantor, J., & Twohey, M. (2019). *She said: Breaking the sexual harassment story that helped ignite a movement*. Penguin Books.

Katz, J., & Rich, H. (2015). Partner covictimization and post-breakup stalking, pursuit, and violence: A retrospective study of college women. *Journal of Family Violence, 30*(2), 189–199. https://doi.org/10.1007/s10896-014-9665-7

Kelly, D., & Valentine, J. (2018). The science of neurobiology of sexual assault trauma and the Utah legal system. *Utah Journal of Criminal Law, 3*, 70–86.

Kelly, L., Lovett, J., & Regan, L. (2005). *A gap or a chasm? Attrition in reported rape cases*. Great Britain. Home Office. Research, Development and Statistics Directorate. https://doi.org/10.1037/e669452007-001

Kendall-Tackett, K. A., & Watson, M. W. (1991). Factors that influence professionals' perceptions of behavioral indicators of child sexual abuse. *Journal of Interpersonal Violence, 6*(3), 385–395. https://doi.org/10.1177%2F088626091006003010

Kilpatrick, D. G., Edmunds, C. N., & Seymour, A. K. (1992). *Rape in America: A report to the nation*. National Victim Center & Medical University of South Carolina.

Kluft, R. P. (1995). The confirmation and disconfirmation of memories of abuse in DID patients: A naturalistic clinical study. *Dissociation: Progress in the Dissociative Disorders, 8*(4), 253–258.

Korkman, J., Juulosa, A., & Santtila, P. (2014). Who made the disclosure? Recorded discussions between children and caretakers suspecting child abuse. *Psychology, Crime & Law, 20*(10), 994–1004. https://doi.org/10.1080/1068316X.2014.902455

Koss, M. P. (1985). The hidden rape victim: Personality, attitudinal, and situational characteristics. *Psychology of Women Quarterly, 9*(2), 193–212. https://doi.org/10.1111%2Fj.1471-6402.1985.tb00872.x

Koss, M. P., & Dinero, T. E. (1989). Discriminant analysis of risk factors for sexual victimization among a sample of college women. *Journal of Consulting and Clinical Psychology, 57*(2), 242−250. https://doi.org/10.1037/0022-006x.57.2.242

Krahé, B., Berger, A., Vanwesenbeeck, I., Bianchi, G., Chliaoutakis, J., Fernández-Fuertes, A. A., Fuertes, A., de Matos, M. G., Hadjigeorgiou, E., Haller, B., Hellemans, S., Izdebski, Z., Kouta, C., Meijnckens, D., Murauskiene, L., Papadakaki, M., Ramiro, L., Reis, M., Symons, K., … Zygadło, A. (2015). Prevalence and correlates of young people's sexual aggression perpetration and victimisation in 10 European countries: a multi-level analysis. *Culture, Health and Sexuality, 17*(6), 682–699. https://doi.org/10.1080/13691058.2014.989265

Krebs, C. P., Lindquist, C. H., Warner, T. D., Fisher, B. S., & Martin, S. L. (2007). *The campus sexual assault (CSA) study*. National Institute of Justice, US Department of Justice.

Krnjacki, L., Emerson, E., Llewellyn, G., & Kavanagh, A. M. (2016). Prevalence and risk of violence against people with and without disabilities: Findings from an Australian population-based study. *Australian and New Zealand Journal of Public Health, 40*(1), 16–21. https://www.doi.org/10.1111/1753-6405.12498

Lea, S. J., Hunt, L., & Shaw, S. (2011). Sexual assault of older women by strangers. *Journal of Interpersonal Violence, 26*(11), 2303–2320. https://doi.org/10.1177%2F0886260510383036

Lemaigre, C., Taylor, E. P., & Gittoes, C. (2017). Barriers and facilitators to disclosing sexual abuse in childhood and adolescence: A systematic review. *Child Abuse & Neglect, 70*, 39–52. https://www.doi.org/10.1016/j.chiabu.2017.05.009

Lindsay, D. S., & Read, J. D. (1994). Psychotherapy and memories of childhood sexual abuse: A cognitive perspective. *Applied Cognitive Psychology, 8*(4), 281–338. https://doi.org/10.1002/acp.2350080403

Lisak, D., & Miller, P. M. (2002). Repeat rape and multiple offending among undetected rapists. *Violence and Victims, 17*(1), 73–84. https://doi.org/10.1891/vivi.17.1.73.33638

Lisak, D., Gardinier, L., Nicksa, S. C., & Cote, A. M. (2010). False allegations of sexual assault: An analysis of ten years of reported cases. *Violence against Women, 16*(12), 1318–1334. https://doi.org/10.1177%2F1077801210387747

Loftus, E. F. (1993). The reality of repressed memories. *American Psychologist, 48*(5), 518–537. https://doi.org/10.1037/e500372006-011

Loftus, E., & Ketcham, K. (1996). *The myth of repressed memory: False memories and allegations of sexual abuse*. Macmillan.

Luetke, M., Giroux, S., Herbenick, D., Ludema, C., & Rosenberg, M. (2020). High prevalence of sexual assault victimization experiences among university fraternity men. *Journal of Interpersonal Violence*. https://doi.org/10.1177/0886260519900282

Lynn, S. J., Lock, T., Loftus, E. F., Krackow, E., & Lilienfeld, S. O. (2003). The remembrance of things past: Problematic memory recovery techniques in psychotherapy. In S. O. Lilienfeld & S. J. Lynn (Eds.), *Science and pseudoscience in clinical psychology* (pp. 205–239). Guilford Press.

Mailhot Amborski, A., Bussières, È. L., Vaillancourt-Morel, M. P., & Joyal, C. C. (2021). Sexual violence against persons with disabilities: a meta-analysis. *Trauma Violence and Abuse, 1*, 1–14. https://www.doi.org/10.1177/1524838021995975

Man, C. D., & Cronan, J. P. (2001). Forecasting sexual abuse in prison: The prison subculture of masculinity as a backdrop for deliberate indifference. *Journal of Criminal Law & Criminology, 92*(1), 127–186. https://doi.org/10.2307/1144209

Mann, A., & Naugle, A. E. (2019). Recovered memory and sexual assault. In *Handbook of sexual assault and sexual assault prevention* (pp. 323–335). Springer, Cham. https://doi.org/10.1007/978-3-030-23645-8_19

Martínez-Taboas, A. (1996). Repressed memories: Some clinical data contributing toward its elucidation. *American Journal of Psychotherapy, 50*(2), 217–230. https://doi.org/10.1176/appi.psychotherapy.1996.50.2.217

McCabe, S. E., Hughes, T. L., Bostwick, W., & Boyd, C. J. (2005). Assessment of difference in dimensions of sexual orientation: Implications for substance use research in a college-age population. *Journal of Studies on Alcohol, 66*(5), 620–629. https://doi.org/10.15288/jsa.2005.66.620

McCahill, T. W., Meyer, L. C., & Fischman, A. M. (1979). *The aftermath of rape*. Lexington Books.

McDougall, E. E., Langille, D. B., Steenbeek, A. A., Asbridge, M., & Andreou, P. (2019). The relationship between non-consensual sex and risk of depression in female undergraduates at universities in maritime Canada. *Journal of Interpersonal Violence, 34*(21–22), 4597–4619. https://doi.org/10.1177%2F0886260516675468

Mendelsohn, B. (1956). The victimology. *Etudes Internationales de psycho-sociologie criminelle, 3*, 25–26.

Mendes, K., Ringrose, J., & Keller, J. (2018). # MeToo and the promise and pitfalls of challenging rape culture through digital feminist activism. *European Journal of Women's Studies, 25*(2), 236–246. https://doi.org/10.1177%2F1350506818765318

Miller, T. R., Cohen, M. A., & Wiersema, B. (1996). *Victim costs and consequences: A new look* [NCJ 155282]. National Institute of Justice, U.S. Department of Justice. https://www.ncjrs.gov/pdffiles/victcost.pdf

Morgan, R. E., & Truman, J. L. (2020). *Criminal victimization, 2019* [NCJ 255113]. Bureau of Justice Statistics.

Morrison, S. E., Bruce, C., & Wilson, S. (2018). Children's disclosure of sexual abuse: A systematic review of qualitative research exploring barriers and facilitators. *Journal of Child Sexual Abuse, 27*(2), 176–194. https://www.doi.org/10.1080/10538712.2018.1425943

Murnen, S. K., & Kohlman, M. H. (2007). Athletic participation, fraternity membership, and sexual aggression among college men: A meta-analytic review. *Sex Roles, 57*(1–2), 145–157. https://doi.org/10.1007/s11199-007-9225-1

Neal, T., & Clements, C. B. (2010). Prison rape and psychological sequelae: A call for research. *Psychology, Public Policy, and Law, 16*(3), 284–299. https://doi.org/10.1037/a0019448

Nixon, M., Thomas, S. D. M., Daffern, M., & Ogloff, J. R. P. (2017). Estimating the risk of crime and victimisation in people with intellectual disability: A data-linkage study. *Social Psychiatry and Psychiatric Epidemiology, 52*(5), 617–626. https://www.doi.org/10.1007/s00127-017-1371-3

O'Callaghan, E., Lorenz, K., Ullman, S. E., & Kirkner, A. (2021). A dyadic study of impacts of sexual assault disclosure on survivors' informal support relationships. *Journal of Interpersonal Violence, 36*(9–10), NP5033–NP5059. https://doi.org/10.1177%2F0886260518795506

O'Donohue, W., Cummings, C., & Willis, B. (2018). The frequency of false allegations of child sexual abuse: A critical review. *Journal of Child Sexual Abuse, 27*(5), 459–475. https://doi.org/10.1080/10538712.2018.1477224

O'Neal, E. N., Spohn, C., Tellis, K., & White, C. (2014). The truth behind the lies: The complex motivations for false allegations of sexual assault. *Women & Criminal Justice, 24*(4), 324–340. https://doi.org/10.1080/08974454.2014.890161

Paine, M. L., & Hansen, D. J. (2002). Factors influencing children to self-disclose sexual abuse. *Clinical Psychology Review, 22*(2), 271–295. https://doi.org/10.1016/S0272-7358(01)00091-5

Papadakaki, M., Tsalkanis, A., Aravantinou, A., Eftixidi, R., Iosifidis, J., & Chliaoutakis, J. (2012). Factors that promote sexual aggression in young men. *Psychology: The Journal of the Hellenic Psychological Society, 19*(4), 445–460. https://doi.org/10.12681/psy_hps.23700

Pearson, J., & Barker, D. (2018). Male rape: What we know, don't know and need to find out—a critical review. *Crime Psychology Review, 4*(1), 72–94. https://doi.org/10.1080/23744006.2019.1591757

Principe, G. F., Ornstein, P. A., Baker-Ward, L., & Gordon, B. N. (2000). The effects of intervening experiences on children's memory for a physical examination. *Applied Cognitive Psychology: The Official Journal of the Society for Applied Research in Memory and Cognition, 14*(1), 59–80. https://doi.org/10.1002/(SICI)1099-0720(200001)14:1%3C59::AID-ACP637%3E3.0.CO;2-4

Ramsey-Klawsnik, H., Teaster, P. B., Mendiondo, M. S., Marcum, J. L., & Abner, E. L. (2008). Sexual predators who target elders: Findings from the first national study of sexual abuse in care facilities. *Journal of Elder Abuse & Neglect, 20*(4), 353–376. https://doi.org/10.1080/08946560802359375

Remer, R., & Elliott, J. E. (1988). Characteristics of secondary victims of sexual assault. *International Journal of Family Psychiatry, 9*, 373–387.

Roberts, K. P., Lamb, M. E., & Sternberg, K. J. (1999). Effects of the timing of postevent information on preschoolers' memories of an event. *Applied Cognitive Psychology: The Official Journal of the Society for Applied Research in Memory and Cognition, 13*(6), 541–559. https://doi.org/10.1002/(SICI)1099-0720(199912)13:6%3C541::AID-ACP618%3E3.0.CO;2-5

Robinson-Keilig, R. A. (2014). Secondary traumatic stress and disruptions to interpersonal functioning among mental health therapists. *Journal of Interpersonal Violence, 29*(8), 1477–1496. https://doi.org/10.1177%2F0886260513507135

Rofé, Y. (2008). Does repression exist? Memory, pathogenic, unconscious and clinical evidence. *Review of General Psychology, 12*(1), 63–85. https://doi.org/10.1037%2F1089-2680.12.1.63

Rosay, A. (2016). *Violence against American Indian and Alaska Native women and men*. National Institute of Justice, U.S. Department of Justice.

Rose, V. M. (1977). Rape as a social problem: A byproduct of the feminist movement. *Social Problems, 25*(1), 75–89. https://doi.org/10.2307/800469

Rumney, P. N. (2006). False allegations of rape. *The Cambridge Law Journal, 65*(1), 128–158. https://doi.org/10.1017/S0008197306007069

Sabina, C., & Ho, L. Y. (2014). Campus and college victim responses to sexual assault and dating violence: Disclosure, service utilization, and service provision. *Trauma, Violence, & Abuse, 15*(3), 201–226. https://doi.org/10.1177%2F1524838014521322

Sabina, C., & Straus, M. A. (2008). Polyvictimization by dating partners and mental health among US college students. *Violence and Victims, 23*(6), 667–682. https://doi.org/10.1891/0886-6708.23.6.667

Sachs-Ericsson, N., Kendall-Tacket, K. A., Sheffler, J., Rushing, N. C., & Corsentino, E. (2014). The influence of prior rape on the psychological and physical health functioning of older adults. *Aging & Mental Health, 18*(6), 717–730. https://doi.org/10.1080/13607863.2014.884538

Salston, M., & Figley, C. R. (2003). Secondary traumatic stress effects of working with survivors of criminal victimization. *Journal of Traumatic Stress, 16*(2), 167–174. https://doi.org/10.1023/A:1022899207206

Santaularia, J., Johnson, M., Hart, L., Haskett, L., Welsh, E., & Faseru, B. (2014). Relationships between sexual violence and chronic disease: a cross-sectional study. *BMC Public Health, 14*(1), 1–7. https://doi.org/10.1186/1471-2458-14-1286

Sarkar, N. N. (2010). Childhood sexual abuse and its impact on woman's health. *International Medical Journal, 17*(2), 107–112.

Satter, B. (2003). The sexual abuse paradigm in historical perspective: Passivity and emotion in mid-twentieth-century America. *Journal of the History of Sexuality, 12*(3), 424–464. https://doi.org/10.1353/sex.2004.0014

Saunders, C. L. (2012). The truth, the half-truth, and nothing like the truth: Reconceptualizing false allegations of rape. *British Journal of Criminology, 52*(6), 1152–1171. https://doi.org/10.1093/bjc/azs036

Schapansky, E., Depraetere, J., Keygnaert, I., & Vandeviver, C. (2020). Prevalence and risk factors of sexual victimization: Findings from a national representative sample of Belgian adults aged 16–69. *SocArXiv*. https://doi.org/10.31235/osf.io/t7ue9

Schauer, M., & Elbert, T. (2015). Dissociation following traumatic stress. *Zeitschrift für Psychologie/Journal of Psychology, 218*(2), 109–127. https://doi.org/10.1027/0044-3409/a000018

Smith, M. E. (2005). Female sexual assault: The impact on the male significant other. *Issues in Mental Health Nursing, 26*(2), 149–167. https://doi.org/10.1080/01612840590901617

Smith, S. G., & Breiding, M. J. (2011). Chronic disease and health behaviors linked to experiences of non-consensual sex among women and men. *Public Health, 125*(9), 653–659. https://doi.org/10.1016/j.puhe.2011.06.006

Smith, S. G., Zhang, X., Basile, K. C., Merrick, M. T., Wang, J., Kresnow, M. J., & Chen, J. (2018). *National intimate partner and sexual violence survey (NISVS): 2015 data brief—updated release*. National Center for Injury Prevention and Control, Centers for Disease Control and Prevention.

Starzynski, L. L., Ullman, S. E., Filipas, H. H., & Townsend, S. M. (2005). Correlates of women's sexual assault disclosure to informal and formal support sources. *Violence and Victims, 20*(4), 417–432. https://doi.org/10.1891/0886-6708.20.4.417

Stermac, L., & Paradis, E. K. (2001). Homeless women and victimization: Abuse and mental health history among homeless rape survivors. *Resources for Feminist Research, 28*(3–4), 65–82.

Struckman-Johnson, C., Struckman-Johnson, D., Rucker, L., Bumby, K., & Donaldson, S. (1996). Sexual coercion reported by men and women in prison. *Journal of Sex Research, 33*(1), 67–76. https://doi.org/10.1080/00224499609551816

Summit, R. C. (1983). The child sexual-abuse accommodation syndrome. *Child Abuse & Neglect, 7*(2), 177–193. https://doi.org/10.1016/0145-2134(83)90070-4

Thoennes, N., & Tjaden, P. G. (1990). The extent, nature, and validity of sexual abuse allegations in custody/visitation disputes. *Child Abuse & Neglect, 14*(2), 151–163. https://doi.org/10.1016/0145-2134(90)90026-P

Tjaden, P., & Thoennes, N. (2000). Prevalence and consequences of male-to-female and female-to-male intimate partner violence as measured by the National Violence against Women Survey. *Violence Against Women, 6*(2), 142–161 https://doi.org/10.1177/10778010022181769

Tomsa, R., Gutu, S., Cojocaru, D., Gutiérrez-Bermejo, B., Flores, N., & Jenaro, C. (2021). Prevalence of sexual abuse in adults with intellectual disability: Systematic review and meta-analysis. *International Journal of Environmental Research and Public Health, 18*(4), 1–17. https://www.doi.org/10.3390/ijerph18041980

Trocmé, N., & Bala, N. (2005). False allegations of abuse and neglect when parents separate. *Child Abuse & Neglect, 29*(12), 1333–1345. https://doi.org/10.1016/j.chiabu.2004.06.016

Turchik, J. A., & Edwards, K. M. (2012). Myths about male rape: A literature review. *Psychology of Men & Masculinity, 13*(2), 211–226. https://psycnet.apa.org/doi/10.1037/a0023207

Turvey, B. E. (2011). *Criminal profiling: An introduction to behavioral evidence analysis*. Academic Press. https://doi.org/10.1016/B978-0-12-385243-4.00005-8

Ullman, S. E. (2002). Social reactions to child sexual abuse disclosures: A critical review. *Journal of Child Sexual Abuse, 12*(1), 89–121. https://doi.org/10.1300/J070v12n01_05

Valentine, J. L., Sekula, L. K., Cook, L. J., Campbell, R., Colbert, A., & Weedn, V. W. (2019). Justice denied: Low submission rates of sexual assault kits and the predicting variables. *Journal of Interpersonal Violence, 34*(17), 3547–3573. https://doi.org/10.1177%2F0886260516681881

Valentine, J. L., Shaw, J., Lark, A., & Campbell, R. (2016). Now we know: Assessing sexual assault criminal justice case processing in an urban community using the Sexual Assault Nurse Practitioner Evaluation Toolkit. *Journal of Forensic Nursing, 12*(3), 133–140. https://doi.org/10.1097/jfn.0000000000000115

Van der Kolk, B. A., & Fisler, R. (1995). Dissociation and the fragmentary nature of traumatic memories: Overview and exploratory study. *Journal of Traumatic Stress, 8*(4), 505–525. https://doi.org/10.1007/BF02102887

Von Hentig, H. (1948). *The criminal and his victim: Studies in the sociology of crime.* Yale University Press.

Walker, J., Archer, J., & Davies, M. (2005). Effects of rape on men: A descriptive analysis. *Archives of Sexual Behavior, 34*(1), 69–80.

Walters, M. L., Chen, J., & Breiding, M. J. (2013). *The national intimate partner and sexual violence survey (NISVS): 2010 findings on victimization by sexual orientation.* Centers for Disease Control and Prevention, National Center for Injury Prevention and Control. http://www.cdc.gov/ViolencePrevention/pdf/NISVS_SOfindings.pdf

Wenzel, S. L., Koegel, P., & Gelberg, L. (2000). Antecedents of physical and sexual victimization among homeless women: A comparison to homeless men. *American Journal of Community Psychology, 28*(3), 367–390. https://doi.org/10.1023/A:1005157405618

WHO. (2021, March). *Violence against women prevalence estimates, 2018: Global, regional and national prevalence estimates for intimate partner violence against women and global and regional prevalence estimates for non-partner sexual violence against women.* World Health Organization.

Wolff, N., Blitz, C. L., Shi, J., Siegel, J., & Bachman, R. (2007). Physical violence inside prisons: Rates of victimization. *Criminal Justice and Behavior, 34*(5), 588–599. https://doi.org/10.1177%2F0093854806296830

Wolfgang, M. E. (1958). *Patterns in criminal homicide.* University of Pennsylvania Press.

Wolitzky-Taylor, K. B., Resnick, H. S., Amstadter, A. B., McCauley, J. L., Ruggiero, K. J., & Kilpatrick, D. G. (2011). Reporting rape in a national sample of college women. *Journal of American College Health, 59*(7), 582–587. https://doi.org/10.1080/07448481.2010.515634

Yon, Y., Mikton, C. R., Gassoumis, Z. D., & Wilber, K. H. (2017). Elder abuse prevalence in community settings: A systematic review and meta-analysis. *The Lancet Global Health, 5*(2), e147–e156. https://doi.org/10.1016/S2214-109X(17)30006-2

Yon, Y., Ramiro-Gonzalez, M., Mikton, C. R., Huber, M., & Sethi, D. (2019). The prevalence of elder abuse in institutional settings: a systematic review and meta-analysis. *European Journal of Public Health, 29*(1), 58–67. https://doi.org/10.1093/eurpub/cky093

Zinzow, H. M., Resnick, H. S., McCauley, J. L., Amstadter, A. B., Ruggiero, K. J., & Kilpatrick, D. G. (2010). The role of rape tactics in risk for posttraumatic stress disorder and major depression: Results from a national sample of college women. *Depression and Anxiety, 27*(8), 708–715. https://doi.org/10.1002/da.20719

DEFINITIONS

Child Sexual Abuse Accommodation Syndrome: Theory that describes how children respond to and internally resolve experiences of sexual abuse and also accounts for why children fail to disclose or delay the disclosure of these experiences

Cortisol: A stress hormone released to prepare the body for a fight or flight response when exposed to a threat

Defense Cascade Model: A comprehensive set of responses that individuals exposed to threat may experience, including freeze, flight, fight, fright, flag, and faint

False Memory Syndrome: Pseudomemories that are factually and objectively false but in which the person strongly believes as real memories

Fight or Flight Response to Threat: A survival mechanism that prepares the body to respond to an imminent threat by either fighting or, if that is not possible, physically running from the threat

Historical Trauma: Multigenerational trauma experienced by a specific cultural or ethnic group

Parental Alienation Syndrome: Thought to be a common phenomenon in child custody proceedings where one parent (often the mother) imposes undue influence and psychological manipulation on their children to prevent an ongoing relationship between the child and other family members

Polyvictimization: Experiencing multiple forms of victimization concurrently

Recovered-Memory Therapy: A form of psychotherapy that utilizes controversial interviewing techniques such as hypnosis, guided imagery, and sedative-hypnotic or psychotropic drugs to purportedly help clients recall "repressed" memories

Routine Activities Theory: An early theory of victimization that suggests adequate supervision of a victim's guardian is absent in situations where child victims are in close proximity to individuals who are both motivated to commit an offense and view the victim as an attractive target

Secondary Traumatic Stress: A set of observable reactions to working with people who have been traumatized and mirrors the symptoms of PTSD

Secondary Victims: Individuals who are close to a victim of sexual violence (e.g., romantic partners, parents, other family members, friends, coworkers, and wider support systems) and experience negative physical, psychological, social, and spiritual effects as a result of the primary victim's experience

Sexual Violence: A term that encompasses a broad range of sexual victimization, including rape, sexual assault, child sexual abuse, sexual exploitation, and other contact and noncontact offenses, as well as acts that are not codified in law as criminal but are nevertheless harmful and traumatic to the victim experiencing them

Tonic Immobility: A form of rape-induced paralysis wherein victims may experience loss of movement, inability to call for help, and insensitivity to pain

Victim Precipitation: An early victimological concept that victims contribute (partially or wholly) to the criminal actions that harm them, either through provoking or facilitating the crime

Victimology: The study of victims of crime and victimization with a particular emphasis on the causes of victimization, the consequences and impacts of crime on victims and the relationships among victims, offenders, and the criminal justice system

CHAPTER 9

Investigations of Sex Crimes

> **CHAPTER OBJECTIVES**
>
> - Address failure to report sex crimes
> - Define and identify key concepts related to crime-scene profiling and crime-scene basics, including the identification of paraphilias and the role of fantasies
> - Describe the criteria associated with responding to sex crimes as a first responder and a medical examiner
> - Identify guidelines for interviewing victims and suspects
> - Describe the characteristics of sex crimes with unique investigational challenges, including alcohol- and drug-facilitated rapes
> - Identify three broad categories of types of investigative failures

The goals of any police investigation, including the investigation of a sex crime, are identifying what happened or even if a crime occurred at all, and determining who committed the crime (Hess et al., 2016). Law enforcement officers do this by assessing evidence from the crime scene and interviewing witnesses, suspects, and victims. Furthermore, the goal of any police interview is to obtain accurate, complete, and relevant accounts from the interviewee (McGurk et al., 1993).

This chapter presents information about the investigation of a sex crime, including the problem of failing to report a sex crime, identification of profiling techniques and crime-scene characteristics that law enforcement officers rely upon during their investigations. We also present critical aspects of responding to sex crimes, including crucial information for 911 operators and the role nurses have in collecting evidence, and the process of interviewing victims and suspects. We also discuss the unique challenges of alcohol- and/or drug-facilitated rapes. Common investigation failures are identified to create an awareness of them. This chapter, therefore, is intended to cover some key components and duties of police officers and other officials who are involved in the investigation of a sexually motivated crime. It is not intended to be a how-to manual for those who are part of a sex-crime investigation but rather highlights some of the processes involved in sex-crime investigations to provide a broader perspective of the complexities of responding to sex crimes, victims, and offenders.

Sex crimes pose unique investigational challenges. For example, when someone commits an alcohol- or drug-facilitated rape, the consent of the victim may be difficult to discern. Other scenarios exist that present additional challenges, and we discuss a few of those in

DOI: 10.4324/9781003031444-9

this chapter, including distinguishing accidental deaths (from *autoerotic asphyxiation*) from suicides.

Finally, given the recent media attention on false convictions, we present an overview of commonly identified investigative mistakes with attention given to sex crimes. We also present ways to avoid these common investigative failures.

FAILURE TO REPORT A SEX CRIME

Many sex crimes are doomed from the beginning: no one, including the victim, reports the sex crime. As noted in Chapter 8, many fail to report due to multiple factors such as fear of retribution, not being believed, and not wanting to face the accused—as most victims know their offender. In the Focus Box 9.1, a military veteran tells his story to the *New York Times* about his sexual assault and obstacles in reporting.

CRIME-SCENE PROFILING AND CRIME-SCENE BASICS

Details of a sex-crime scene can provide information critical to solving the crime. Sex-crimes scenes can be complicated by the fact that they have occurred in multiple locations and/or locations that have been subsequently contaminated (public spaces, hotel rooms, etc.). Critical to deconstructing a crime scene are any clues to the offender's *modus operandi* (MO). MO refers to an offender's unique behavioral pattern during the commission of the offense. An offender's MO can change depending on several factors such as a deteriorating mental state, use of drugs and/or alcohol, changes in habits/lifestyle, and learning how to commit the crime more effectively (Bartol & Bartol, 2021; Turvey, 2011). Many offenders do learn how to commit their crimes in a more sophisticated manner over time. For example, many offenders read media accounts of their crimes (Bartol & Bartol, 2021). Such information can provide information about the police investigation and cause the offender to

---

Focus Box 9.1 Meet a Hero: Jack Williams Comes Forward about His Sexual Assault

Jack Williams enrolled in the Air Force and was raped by a sergeant after he was choked and bent him over a desk. He was raped twice by the same person during basic training. His sergeant indicated "no one will believe you" (n.p.) if he reported it. The rapes left him with a torn rectum and kidney damage, which led to him being forced out of the air force due to being medically unfit. Jack Williams later reported the rape, but nothing occurred. Jack Williams currently suffers many signs and symptoms of post-traumatic stress syndrome, including sleepless nights. No resources or prevention programs were in place at the time of rape. Jack Williams is now recognized as a victim of sexual assault by the military, and receives a monthly check, which cannot be equated with fair compensation in his mind.

Note. Adapted from Phillips (2019)

change their MO to improve their strategy (Bartol & Bartol, 2021). For those who molest children, relying on information from the victim's caregiver may also provide information that causes the offender to alter their MO for future crimes.

In the 1980s, much information was gained about crime-scene profiling by the Federal Bureau of Investigation's (FBI's) Behavioral Science Unit (BSU). They interviewed incarcerated sexual murderers to gather information about common motives and behavior patterns. Later in the 1980s, interviews focused on serial rapists. As a result of these interviews and studies, crime scenes were classified as organized, disorganized, or mixed (DeNevi & Campbell, 2011).

Organized crime scenes are indicative of premeditation—an offender planning the sex crime ahead of time. Premeditation is typically present. The offender does not choose a random victim but carefully selects one. The offender typically maintains control throughout the commission of the sex crime. A **disorganized crime scene**, in contrast, appears chaotic and messy. The offender is usually motivated by rage or some other heightened emotional state. Premeditation does not exist in these types of crimes. The victim is generally decided upon by chance—being in the wrong place at the wrong time. More characteristics of the organized offense and disorganized offense are presented in Table 9.1. A **mixed crime scene** includes elements of both. For example, a premeditated sex crime that falls apart while it occurs can lead to a mixed crime scene. For example, an offender may encounter a victim who fights back. Subsequently, the plan falls apart and the offense occurs in a chaotic fashion (DeNevi & Campbell, 2011).

The **signature** of the offender is another earmark of the criminal profile (Bartol & Bartol, 2021). The signature is anything that the offender does that goes beyond what is necessary

TABLE 9.1 Characteristics of Organized and Disorganized Offenders' Crime Scene

Organized Offender	Disorganized Offender
• Above-average Intelligence	• Average intelligence
• Socially competent	• Immature socially
• Plans the offense	• Spontaneous offense
• Targets a stranger victim	• Victim/location known
• Has controlled conversations with the victim	• Depersonalizes the victim
• Control reflected in crime scene	• Has no/little conversation with the victim
• Demands the victim is submissive	• Random/sloppy crime scene
• Uses restraints of the victim	• Sudden violence to the victim
• Engages in aggressive acts before victim's death	• Minimal use of restraints
	• Sexual acts occurring after victim's death
	• Victim's body left in view where the offense occurred
	• Weapon/evidence typically present

Note: Adapted from DeNevi and Campbell (2011).

to carry out the crime. The signature reveals the offender's unique cognitive processes associated with the sex crime. It is relatively consistent when the offender carries out the same crime repeatedly. The signature is typically more consistent than the MO, which changes as the offender learns how to carry out the crime more effectively. Profiling crime scenes of violent serial offenders are arguably easier when the offender exhibits psychopathology. This includes sadistic torture and/or other mutilations (Pinizzotto, 1984). Another example of a signature is a ***trophy***, taking something from the crime scene such as jewelry, a driver's license, or underwear. It is usually a meaningful item that the offender uses to remember the incident.

In the case of serial sex crimes, the offenses often occur within a limited geographical area, revealing a pattern of offender behavior. ***Geographical profiling*** involves analyzing the spatial distribution of a set of offenses committed by a single offender. ***Geographical mapping*** analyzes the spatial patterns of a series of crimes committed over a specified time period by all offenders of known offenses. Thus, ***geographical profiling*** focuses on an individual offender, whereas geographical mapping focuses on a geographical area where crimes have occurred (Bartol & Bartol, 2021).

The media often refer to the occurrence of a "random" crime. Moreover, how a person commits a sex offense, hunts for their victims, and chooses the location is not random. The crime locations of a serial rapist become spatial clues that lead to relevant information for the investigation. Analyzing these patterns is known as geographic profiling. Developed by criminologist and former law enforcement officer Kim Rossmo, geographic profiling involves specialized software to generate color probability maps showing the most likely areas where the offender lives (Rossmo, 2000). The foundation of the software is a criminal-hunting algorithm called ***Criminal Geographic Targeting***.

The main function of geographic profiling is to prioritize suspects and areas of interest. A geo-profile probability is created, which varies by color: dark red areas represent the highest likelihood and gray the lowest. The technique is typically used in conjunction with a psychological profile. These two techniques outline the "who" and "where" of the offender. Neither method can solve a crime on its own, but they can help police prioritize the thousands of suspects and tips that often emerge during a major crime investigation. Geographic profiling is related to but different than crime mapping. Geographic profiling involves focusing only on the crimes of an individual serial offender, whereas crime mapping involves an analysis of locations of all reported crimes committed by all the offenders in a given area over a specific time period (Harries, 1999).

Understanding how criminals hunt—their search for, and attack on a victim—is an essential element of geographic profiling. The criminal-search typology includes ***hunters***, ***poachers***, ***trollers***, and ***trappers*** (Rossmo, 2009a). Hunters purposely set out to look for victims. They tend to stay within a relatively stable geographical area near their home and usually search through familiar places where they may find suitable targets. Poachers (also known as commuters) are more transient; they travel some distance from their homes to search for victims. Trollers are opportunistic offenders who encounter victims while engaged in routine, non-criminal activities. Trappers entice their victims to a location they control by taking in borders, entertaining victims, placing ads in newspapers or on the internet, or offering employment.

PARAPHILIAS AND FANTASIES

Part of profiling a sex crime can involve assessing the presence (or lack thereof) of any ***paraphilias***. The American Psychiatric Association defines paraphilias in the *Diagnostic and*

Statistical Manual of Mental Disorders (DSM)—a sort of "bible of mental disorders." However, the criteria established in their most recent edition (fifth) are not without controversy because what is considered sexually abnormal is often culturally dependent (McManus et al., 2013). That is, what is considered a paraphilia varies between places and over time. For example, up until 1973, the DSM included homosexuality as a paraphilia (McManus et al., 2013). Notably, many **paraphilic disorders** do not constitute a crime. For example, a fetish that involves a sexual attraction to ladies' shoes is not a crime. However, if an individual with a ***fetishistic disorder*** breaks into a house to steal ladies' shoes, a crime has then occurred. Any fetish that lacks consent is also a crime.

A paraphilia is defined as "any intense and persistent sexual interest other than sexual interest in genital stimulation or preparatory fondling with phenotypically normal, physically mature, consenting human partners" (American Psychiatric Association, 2013, p. 685). A paraphilic disorder is defined as a "paraphilia that is currently causing distress or impairment to the individual or a paraphilia whose satisfaction has entailed personal harm, or risk of harm, to others" (American Psychiatric Association, 2013, pp. 685–686). This definition varies from an earlier version in that the newer version requires the presence of distress or impairment by the person who has these thoughts or engages in related behavior. Also, the symptoms of the disorder must exist for at least six months.

The American Psychiatric Association specifies such disorders, along with a residual "other" category:

Exhibitionist Disorder: Deriving sexual pleasure from exposing one's private parts to an unsuspecting person or performing sexual acts that can be watched by others
Frotteuristic Disorder: Deriving sexual pleasure from touching/rubbing against a nonconsenting person
Voyeuristic Disorder: Deriving sexual pleasure from observing an unsuspecting person who is naked, undressing, or engaging in sexual activities or in activities deemed to be of a private nature
Fetishistic Disorder: Deriving sexual pleasure from specific inanimate objects
Pedophilic Disorder: Sexual preference for prepubescent children
Sexual Masochism Disorder: Deriving sexual pleasure from wanting to be humiliated, beaten, bound, or otherwise made to suffer
Sexual Sadism Disorder: Deriving sexual pleasure from inflicting pain or humiliation on another person
Transvestic Fetishism: Deriving sexual pleasure from clothing associated with members of the opposite sex
Other Specified Paraphilic Disorder: These include other paraphilic behaviors not already listed (Brannon, n.d.)

The importance of law enforcement officers having knowledge of paraphilic disorders can be informative to the investigation. More specifically, identification of

> such information may prove useful to police officers responsible for sexual crime investigations. For example, sexual offenders with certain types of . . . paraphilic behaviors may carry out their offense in a certain way (e.g., to use physical restraint against the victim, to mutilate the victim . . .) that is likely to reflect their own personality and other psychology preferences.
>
> (Chan & Beauregard, 2016, p. 2261)

This example reveals that the offender has a sadistic motive.

Also important to the investigation of a sex crime is the identification of the presence of the offender's fantasy. Among police officers, it is known that thought always precedes the action (Napier, 2017). Thus, the action an offender has taken provides clues to what they were thinking, their fantasy. Someone who commits a sex crime has, therefore, typically thought about this activity beforehand. An offender's fantasy can provide key insights into their victim choice and behavior during the offense. A surviving victim can provide details of the offender's behavior and motivation for committing the offense. For example, the victim can provide details about the tone of the conversation: did the offender ask the victim to tell them they were sexy, for example. This could be indicative of the offender's insecurity and need for confirmation. Fantasies should be assessed with regard to the offender's verbal, physical, and sexual behavior (Napier, 2017). An offender who asks or demands the victim do or say certain things reveals their fantasy. It can also reveal clues to the offender's personality, what their insecurities are, and what they perceive to be sexually arousing.

For example, when the serial rapist and murderer, Dennis Radar (also known as the BTK serial rapist and murderer, for bind, torture, kill), was interviewed, he mentioned the importance of his fantasy and how he viewed himself as the director of a movie (Napier, 2017). He referred to his fantasies as having control over him. This captured serial rapist and murderer expressed wanting to carry out his fantasy regardless of whether the victim was dead or alive. He often would pose his victims during and after the commission of the crime just as he had previously fantasized. Thus, identifying what the offender's behavior was during and after the crime can be telling in their psyche and assist in developing a profile.

FIRST RESPONDERS

Typically, a first responder to a report of a sex crime can include emergency (911) operators. They are critical to the process of sex-crime investigation because they are typically the first person to have contact with a victim or witness. The information the 911 operator obtains from the victim or witness can be relevant to the investigation. The interaction between the victim or a witness and the 911 operator becomes a starting point for the investigation. Emergency 911 operators, when receiving a call regarding a potential sex crime, should tell the victim the following:

- Not to wash any clothing
- Not to shower
- Not to destroy any clothing
- To keep any evidence, that is, anything the offender had contact with (Tittle, 2006)

Following such instructions may be difficult for victims because they will want to remove their clothing and shower. The operator should tell the victim that a police officer is on the way and attempt to keep the victim calm (Tittle, 2006). They should ask whether the victim is seriously injured and in need of medical attention (Jetmore, 2006). If so, an ambulance should be dispatched. The victim should also be instructed to go to a safe location until a police officer arrives (Jetmore, 2006).

For the police officers who are the first to arrive at a scene where a sex crime has been reported, several activities should occur:

- Reconstruct what happened, and establish that a crime occurred.
- Identify, document, and collect evidence of what occurred.

- Link the victim and the suspect to the scene of the crime.
- Identify and locate any witnesses.
- Identify and apprehend the person(s) who committed the crime (Jetmore, 2006).

MEDICAL EXAMINATIONS OF RAPE VICTIMS

Part of collecting evidence during a sexual-assault investigation involves a medical examination of the victim. A registered nurse (RN) with additional education and clinical experience in forensic examinations of sexual-assault victims typically conducts these examinations (Littel, 2001). As of 1997, fewer than 100 **Sexual Assault Nurse Examiner (SANE)** programs existed. These programs were developed from a need among nurses to have specialized knowledge and training when conducting forensic examinations. SANE programs provide valuable knowledge to those who administer forensic examinations to sexual-assault victims. The goals include providing victims with prompt, compassionate care while collecting extensive forensic evidence. The Office of Victims of Crime has provided substantial support to increase SANE programs. Their support led to the development of a practical guide to SANE programs. Although there are more than 700 SANE programs in the United States, Canada, and Australia (International Association of Nurses, 2015), there is still a shortage of such nurses, especially in rural areas (Thomas et al., 2020).

Sexual assault victims have been traumatized during the assaults, and in many instances, victims are retraumatized during the investigation (Littel, 2001). This is especially true when an invasive medical examination occurs. Many experts in the field have recognized that collecting medical evidence from a victim shortly after the assault encompasses many problems. For example, victims may have had to wait too long to be examined. It is not uncommon for victims to wait 4–10 hours to be examined. Victims are often denied food, water, and bathroom access while waiting for their examinations because this may destroy evidence.

Most SANE programs rely on a group of SANEs who are available any time of day or night. Most respond to a sexual assault report within a short period of time (usually within 30–60 minutes). After serious injuries are treated, and no immediate medical concerns exist, the SANE begins to assess, treat and collect evidence, which includes the following:

- Obtain information about the victim's pertinent health history and the crime.
- Assess psychological functioning sufficiently to determine whether the victim is suicidal and is oriented to person, place, and time.
- Perform a physical examination to inspect and evaluate the body of the victim (not a routine physical examination).
- Collect and preserve all evidence and document findings.
- Treat and/or refer the victim for medical treatment (a SANE may treat minor injuries, such as minor cuts and abrasions, but further evaluation and care of serious trauma are referred to a designated medical facility or physician).
- Provide the victim with prophylactic medication for the prevention of sexually transmitted diseases and other care needed as a result of the crime.
- Provide the victim with referrals for medical and psychological care and support (Littel, 2001).

Those who examine the victim may lack experience and training, causing additional stress to the victim (Littel, 2001). Many physicians avoid sexual assault examinations because they do not want to testify in court. The staff and doctors at emergency departments often view sexual-assault victims as less of a priority than those with life-threatening injuries (Ledray & Simmelink, 1999). They may also not understand the victimization; this could include holding stereotypes or false assumptions such as the victim may have done something to instigate the sexual assault (Littel, 2001). This can subsequently affect their willingness to collect and document all forensic evidence, especially in nonstranger sexual assaults. In contrast SANE programs attempt to address problems experienced by sexual-assault victims (Littel, 2001).

SANE programs provide many benefits to processing sexual-assault cases and responding to sexual-assault victims (Littel, 2001; Thomas et al., 2020). As one detective in Alexandria, Virginia, noted, SANE programs "have taken response to sexual assault victims at the emergency department out of the dark ages" (Littel, 2001, p. 7). SANE programs provide more thorough forensic evidence and more extensive documentation that adds to the information detectives collect. Local and state prosecutors are typically supportive of SANE programs because they affect the outcome in sexual-assault cases (Littel, 2001). Yet, the stresses associated with these types of jobs means that many people will find other career paths (Iritani, 2016).

Evidence collected during this medical examination is referred to as a "**rape kit**," which can provide crucial DNA evidence (Campbell et al., 2017). Such evidence can identify offenders in previously unsolved crimes, identifying serial rapists and confirming the identify of offenders, and exonerate those wrongly convicted (Campbell et al., 2017). Despite how critical this information is, yet bound to limited funding, many rape kits go untested and sit on shelves in storage for years and, in some cases, decades (Campbell & Fehler-Cabral, 2020). The true extent of the number of untested rape kits is not known, yet city-level reports indicate it is a lot. In New York, for example, approximately 16,000 untested kits were identified (Bashford, 2013). Many advocacy groups have taken up the issue and shed light on the problem, which has led to increasing the number of processed rape kits. For example, many states have enacted laws requiring the testing of rape kits (Davis et al., 2021).

Sex crimes pose an additional challenge because they may have occurred at various locations and many hours, days, or weeks before the incident was reported. In those cases, corroborating evidence should be identified. Sex crimes can involve a **vulnerable victim**, which requires following additional guidelines to obtain information. The next section includes information on this.

MEDICAL EXAMS OF CHILD VICTIMS

Most children who have experienced sexual abuse will not have significant physical findings (e.g., evidence of significant injury, healed trauma, or sexually transmitted infections) on examination (Adams, 2011; Sirotnak et al., 2006). This is because most examinations for signs of sexual abuse are conducted after the most recent abuse incident of occurred. A diagnosis of child sexual abuse is made on the basis of a full medical history, physical exam, and laboratory evidence. The degree of certainty of child sexual abuse from a medical examination depends on the physical examination findings. While some medical findings are highly indicative of sexual abuse (a victim's account who is pre-pubescent in combination with physically supporting evidence), other findings should be interpreted cautiously as they may or may not indicate sexual abuse (Adams et al., 1992, 1994; Bays & Chadwick, 1993; Vidanapathirana, 2014).

As noted in Table 9.2, although there are many physical signs that do indicate sexual abuse, there are many physical signs that are unclear in their association to sexual abuse. Typically, medical findings alone cannot definitively diagnose exposure to child sexual abuse. For example, a "normal" medical exam that yields indeterminate findings or findings that would seem to rule out sexual abuse may still be founded as probable sexual abuse if the child makes a clear statement indicating he or she experienced abuse (e.g., "someone touched my private area"). In short, the absence of physical findings should *never* rule out the possibility of sexual abuse in children.

Diagnosing child abuse generally, and child sexual abuse specifically, requires specialized medical training and board certification. Child abuse is specific sub-specialty within the

TABLE 9.2 Interpretation of Medical Findings in Child Sexual Abuse Diagnosis

Findings Diagnostic of Sexual Trauma

- Fresh/acute trauma to genital or anal area
- Hymenal abnormalities, including a markedly enlarged vaginal opening for the child's age, transections or scars
- Pregnancy
- Recovery of sperm, semen or semen marker (e.g., acid phosphatase) from the body
- Sexually transmitted diseases (e.g., syphilis, gonorrhea, chlamydia, HIV) without history of transmission from birth

Indeterminate Findings of Sexual Abuse (No Expert Consensus)

- Anal dilation
- Anal fissures (i.e., tears)
- Anal scars
- Certain sexually transmitted diseases not acquired at birth (e.g., genital herpes)
- Certain sexually transmitted diseases that may be transmitted non-sexually (e.g., bacterial vaginosis)
- Cracking of posterior fourchette (area between vaginal and anal openings)
- Hymenal abnormalities, including bumps, notches, clefts or asymmetry
- Major adhesions of labia minora in children out of diapers

Findings Where Sexual Abuse is Ruled Out/Findings Often Mistaken as Abuse

- Hymenal and/or labial redness or bumps
- Redness of genital tissues
- Urethral or rectal prolapse
- Yeast infections

Note: Adapted from Adams (2011).

pediatrics specialty and all physicians are required to complete three-year full-time fellowship program and pass a certifying examination in order to specialize in identifying child abuse (Council of Pediatric Subspecialties, 2021). Peer review of medical findings is highly encouraged.

INTERVIEWING VICTIMS, SUSPECTED OFFENDERS, AND WITNESSES: THE PHASED APPROACH

Critical to conducting appropriate interviews of victims, suspected offenders, and witnesses were the development of guidelines based on the results of many psychological studies (Bull, 2010; Read et al., 2009). Oddly, many of the interview techniques used for victims is the same as what is used for suspected offenders and witnesses. Experts in the field and researchers suggest employing the ***phased approach***. This has five phases, with each phase occurring only after the previous phase is complete: (1) establish a good rapport, (2) introduce the topic, (3) obtain as much free narrative as possible, (4) ask questions of the right type and in the right order, and (5) have meaningful closure (Bull, 2010; Read et al., 2009).

The first phase, establishing good rapport, involves discussing topics that are of interest to the witness and are considered neutral. This phase should also include establishing good communication with the witness, making them comfortable. It is critical during this stage to reassure the witness that it is acceptable to answer questions with a "don't understand" or "don't know" or "can't remember" response when that is the case. This is especially critical if, for example, a child has a low IQ or a learning disability, because these victims may give inaccurate information otherwise (Bull, 2010).

The second phase involves introducing the topic. This may occur as part of the first phase, establishing rapport. It can also be a subtle shift from talking about the background of the person being interviewing to the topic of concern. During this stage, it is critical that the interviewer does not share too many details of the offense or become confrontational by indicating what the allegations are. It has been recommended that the interviewer be direct and not assume prior information the interviewer has received is true (Read et al., 2009).

The third phase, obtaining as much free narrative as possible, involves asking the witness to provide as much information about the incident as they remember. This should not involve interruptions from the interviewer, who should make statements such as "Tell me more about that." Some vulnerable witnesses, such as elderly adults or children with a low IQ, will provide less information than others. Thus, for some individuals, the questioning phase becomes critical (Bull, 2010).

The fourth, the questioning phase, should begin with ***open questions***, which are based on information that the witness provided in the narrative stage (Bull, 2010). For example, if a witness states during the narrative that a woman appeared in the window of a nearby apartment after the incident, the interviewer can ask, "What did the woman look like?" After asking open questions, ***specific questions*** are asked. These questions typically seek additional information or clarify information already provided and assist the witness in understanding what is relevant. This typically involves asking what, who, where, and when-type questions.

After specific questions are asked, and only then should ***forced-choice questions*** be asked. These include questions such as "Did the offender cut your necklace off before or after the assault?"

Research has shown that vulnerable interviewees may be yes prone or no prone, which means answering yes always, or no always, regardless of the correct answer (Matikka & Vesala, 1997). Such questions should be asked in an either-or format (Bull, 2010): "Did he touch you under your clothes or on top of your clothes?" Either-or questions are more likely than yes-no questions to yield an accurate response (Heal & Sigelman, 1995).

Relying upon the phased approach of interviewing is critical; research has shown that the first two stages of interviewing (establishing a rapport and obtaining a free narrative) are conducted relatively well and adhere to these established guidelines. Few interviews that were assessed systematically, however, adhered to criteria established in the third phase: open questions followed by specific questions and only afterward using forced-choice questions (Davies et al., 1995; Warren et al., 1996). Research has found that interviewers who encouraged free narrative, followed by open questions, obtained interviews that appeared to reflect actual events (Craig et al., 1999; Wood & Garven, 2000).

The fifth phase, the closure phase, should involve the following: (1) summarize the important information provided by the witness as much as possible in the witness's own words, having told the witness to intervene if any summarizing is incorrect, (2) answer any questions the witness has, (3) thank the witness and try to assist the witness to leave the interview in an as positive a frame of mind as possible (e.g., by returning to the neutral topics discussed in the rapport phase), and (4) provide the witness with the interviewer's contact details (e.g., in case the witness decides to provide more information; Bull, 2010).

Interviewing Victims

Victims of sex crimes can be children or adults, each with unique circumstances that should be taken into consideration. Child victims can pose unique challenges to a sex-crime investigation because they may not have the verbal skills to convey what happened to them. As noted in Chapter 8, several allegations of sexual abuse in daycare settings occurred in the 1980s. A few of those cases are presented in Focus Box 9.1. Most noteworthy, these cases involved poor interviewing techniques and, subsequently, an inability to determine actual guilt or innocence. This brought attention to the lack of guidelines that existed when interviewing vulnerable victims, including children, elderly adults, and those with special needs. Since these cases, many improvements have occurred in establishing guidelines for interviewing children and other vulnerable victims. In this section, we will discuss the interview style that should be adopted, the speed of conducting an interview, and recent developments of investigation strategies that are informed by research on neurobiology and trauma on victims.

The style of the interviewer affects the quality of the information gathered (Bull, 2010). Research has found that a supportive style is superior to a businesslike or authoritative manner (Paterson et al., 2002). A supportive style involves an informal demeanor, smiling, eye contact, and introducing self with a first name. Those who used a supportive style yielded correct free recall, recall to open questions, recall to reflection questions (repeating back to the interviewee what they said), and recall to final prompt for "more information."

Research has also found that the pace of the interview should be much slower for vulnerable witnesses (Milne & Bull, 1999). This includes the interviewer slowing down their speech rate, allowing extra time for witnesses to respond to the questions, providing time for the witness to prepare a response, being patient with slow responses, avoiding rapid-fire questions once the interviewee has responded, and avoiding interruptions (Milne & Bull, 1999). Also, it is critical not to underestimate the ability of vulnerable witnesses to provide accurate information; research has shown that when the proper protocol has been followed, vulnerable witnesses are capable of producing accurate information (Agnew & Powell, 2004).

> **Focus Box 9.1** An Overview of Daycare Abuse Cases
>
> The McMartin Pre-School Case (1986): In Manhattan Beach, California, a criminal case was made against Ray Buckey and his mother for sexually abusing children in a satanic ritual. Neither resulted in a guilty verdict because evidence was lacking (Eberle & Eberle, 1993).
>
> Fells Acres Day School (1986–1987): In Malden, Massachusetts, allegations of sexual abuse were made by one child against Gerald Amirault, the owner's son. Later several other children made allegations against Violet, Gerald, and Cheryl Amirault. Violet had been running the daycare for two decades. Her son, Gerald, also worked at the school as a bus driver and handyman. Violet's daughter, Cheryl, also worked at the school. At trial, the children were allowed to provide testimony in the courtroom; they were placed where the jury could see them but the defendants could not. All defendants were found guilty and sentenced to lengthy prison sentences. After serving eight years in prison, a new trial was granted because of the children's testimony allowed during the trial for Cheryl and Violet, which violated the defendants' right to face their accusers. Gerald's appeal was denied. Two years later, the judge reinstated the conviction and vacated the order for a new trial. In 1997 a rehearing was ordered again; however, Violet died of cancer. The rehearing for Cheryl never occurred. Cheryl agreed not to discuss the case with others and not to profit from it in exchange for the judge agreeing she would not return to prison to complete her sentence ("Fells Acres Sexual Abuse Trials: 1986–87," n.d.)
>
> Wee Care Nursery School (1988): In Maplewood, New Jersey, Kelly Michaels was convicted of 115 counts of sexual abuse against 20 children. She denied all accusations, waived her Miranda rights, and passed a polygraph. The investigation continued. During the trial, the judge questioned the children in his chambers on closed-circuit television. He played ball with them, held them on his lap, and whispered in their ears. Kelly was convicted and received a 47-year sentence. She served five years before she successfully appealed the case because of the way the judge questioned the children. Kelly was released, and the prosecutor dropped all of the charges (Frontline, 1998).

Interviewing Suspects

Part of a police officer's job includes questioning suspected rapists, child molesters, child pornographers, and others who have committed a wide range of sex crimes. Interviewing such offenders is not an easy task. The officer must be able to ask questions with a certain degree of sensitivity (Burns, 1993). Asking questions of suspects is a critical component of the investigation. Police officers encounter many obstacles in obtaining information from a sex-crime suspect. For example, research has found that police officers are often stressed when they interview persons who are suspected of molesting a child (Soukara et al., 2002).

Research also shows that officers fail to show empathy toward such offenders until a confession has been obtained (Soukara et al., 2002). Police officers also have mental obstacles to overcome when they are confronted with a suspect to interview. For example, they often minimize the offense allegedly committed (Ward et al., 1997). Although cognitive distortions, such as false justifications for sexual abuse, are typically associated with the abuser, police officers can also have cognitive distortions regarding the characteristics and severity of the offense.

Given the severe negative perceptions often associated with persons who commit a sex offense, police officers will often deny their involvement in the investigation process to close friends and family members (Thomas, 2000). Police officers, like those in the community, typically hold negative attitudes toward persons who commit a sex offense—sometimes, even more so than toward murderers (Holmberg & Christianson, 2002). Research has, in fact, shown that persons who commit a sexual offense, compared to murderers, were more likely to report negative interviewer behaviors (Holmberg & Christianson, 2002).

The style that police officers adopt during suspect interviews can be categorized as a dominant or humane style. **Dominant (suspect) interviews** are associated with impatience, hostility, aggressiveness, and condemnation. **Humane (suspect) interviews** are associated with friendliness, empathy, cooperation, and a personal approach. Police officers are more likely to obtain an admission of guilt if they use a humane approach (Holmberg & Christianson, 2002; Kebbell et al., 2006). However, in a study that examined the use of empathy alone, no differences were found in the amount of **investigation relevant information (IRI)** obtained, which refers to information that is helpful in determining information about the crime. Quality interviews, in general, will yield IRI, which includes the following key pieces of information: (1) what happened, (2) how the crime was committed, (3) who was involved, (4) when and where the offense occurred, and (5) any objects used to assist in committing the offense.

Research has found, however, that the amount of IRI obtained is significantly improved when **appropriate (or productive interview) questions** are asked by the interviewer as opposed to **inappropriate questions**. Appropriate questions include open questions (e.g., "Can you describe the room to me?"), probing questions (e.g., "What happened next?"), and encouragements and acknowledgments (e.g., "OK, I see."). Inappropriate questions include echo questions (e.g., Suspect says, "I may have . . ."; interviewer says, "You may have . . ."), closed questions (e.g., "Did you leave your house last night?"), leading questions (e.g., "Then you went to the living room, right?"), forced-choice questions (e.g., "The phone is in your name or your wife's?"), multiple questions (e.g., "Did you leave before nine o'clock? Where did you go?"), and opinion-based statements (e.g., "You are trying to protect yourself.") (Oxburgh et al., 2012).

Thus, appropriate questions are useful to the investigation of sex crimes. Research has shown that police officers typically ask, on average, three inappropriate questions for every one appropriate question, indicating a need for additional training concerning interviewing suspects (Oxburgh et al., 2012).

Two methods of interviewing suspects have also been identified. First, the **accusatorial method (of suspect interviewing)**, primarily used in the United States, is confrontational and assumes guilt. This method typically establishes control; uses psychological manipulation (e.g., custody and isolation and confrontation followed by offering sympathy and face-saving excuses); uses closed-ended, confirmatory questions; and focuses on anxiety cues to determine deception (based on the suspect's verbal and nonverbal cues). The primary goal is confession (Meissner et al., 2012).

The second method, **information gathering**, relies on establishing rapport; using direct, positive confrontation; using open-ended, exploratory questions; and focusing on cognitive clues of deception (Meissner et al., 2012). The use of cognitive clues is deeply embedded in empirical research that shows individuals will remember an event more accurately after they have been asked to remember the emotions, perceptions, and sequence of events in the situation of interest. The primary goal of the information-gathering method is to elicit information. The suspects are given the opportunity to explain the circumstances. Only then are they questioned and asked about any inconsistent or contradictory information. The goal is to establish facts as opposed to obtaining a confession (as in the accusatorial method). Relying on this approach has been deemed more acceptable among a sample of participants when compared to other strategies that involve accusatorial methods (Jones & Brimbal, 2017).

Recently, substantial progress has occurred in the science of interviewing suspects that focuses on the effects of the police officer relying on a ***rapport-building method of interviewing*** (Brimbal et al., 2019). This method is in line with an information-gathering approach. The use of the rapport-building method of interviewing is defined differently throughout existing research but generally involves positive interactions between the interviewer and interviewee and a communication style that leads to developing respect and trust; it relies heavily upon open-ended questions, reflective and summary statements (i.e., repeating back key details to ensure accuracy), and affirmations (i.e., providing positive feedback to the interviewee such as "I appreciate your honesty.") (Brimbal et al., 2019; Duke et al., 2018; Miller & Rollnick, 2013; Tickle-Degnen & Rosenthal, 1990). All of these methods often result in obtaining information from the interviewee that may not have been acquired with an accusatorial style of interview (Kelly & Valencia, 2020).

A specific technique, usually associated with the information-gathering method of investigation, is to have the suspect tell the series of events in reverse order. For example, the suspect is asked what happened prior to discovering the crime, and what happened directly before that, and so on. Research has shown that this technique often distinguishes those who are deceptive from truth tellers (Vrij et al., 2008).

A meta-analysis that compared accusatorially and information-gathering interviewing found that the information-gathering style interview is more likely than accusatorial interviews to elicit true confessions and reduce false confessions. These results, however, were based on a small number of studies. More research is needed to determine the outcome of both methods of interviewing a suspect (Meissner et al., 2012).

SEX CRIMES WITH UNIQUE INVESTIGATIONAL OBSTACLES

Sex crimes can create unique problems for the investigator, given the context of the offense. For example, offenders may be the parents of the victim, or the intent may be vengeful (e.g., to expose the victim to a sexually transmitted disease). Also, the victim may be unable to cooperate or understand what happened to them (e.g., a vulnerable victim).

In this section, we investigate a few additional sexual offenses that present unique investigational obstacles. ***Alcohol- and drug-facilitated rapes*** occur after the victim has been exposed to alcohol or drugs, making consent more ambiguous. Autoerotic asphyxiation deaths are often mistaken for suicides, as opposed to accidental deaths. As you read through this section, you will become aware of the difficulties each of these offenses may cause in terms of conducting a successful investigation.

Alcohol- and drug-facilitated rapes occur when victims have either voluntarily or involuntarily consumed a legal or illegal substance, rendering them unable to give consent to have sexual intercourse. The victims and offenders can be strangers or acquaintances, just as with other rapes; however, these offenses often occur during a dating situation. They present unique challenges to an investigator. For example, victims will often delay reporting for a variety of reasons—one being that they voluntarily consumed alcohol or illegal drugs. Also, victims may not want to report for fear of identifying friends who also engaged in illegal drug use. They may fear retaliation from the offender, may not want others to know they were raped, or may believe there is insufficient evidence that they were raped.

Another investigational challenge is presented because victims are not sure of what happened. They may not recall or even have been conscious during the rape. The victim, therefore, may not remember the event at all. It is also rare that force or coercion occurred (Chancellor, 2012).

Alcohol- and drug-facilitated rapes typically occur through one of two strategies. The **proactive approach** involves intentionally getting a victim drunk or giving them a drug without their knowledge. The victim is usually then taken to another location for sexual intercourse. The **opportunistic approach** involves taking advantage of someone who has already been exposed to alcohol or drugs (Chancellor, 2012).

Four important components need to be assessed during an alcohol- and drug-facilitated investigation: (1) actual credibility, (2) ability to perceive at the time of the incident, (3) ability to remember what occurred, and (4) existence of corroborative evidence. First, actual credibility can be established by identifying corroborating evidence such as forensic evidence and witness testimony. It should be noted that victims do not always cooperate because they may feel responsible for the rape occurring. The victim may withhold certain information, which could be perceived as a false rape allegation (Chancellor, 2012; Scalzo & National District Attorneys Association, 2007).

Second, as indicated above, the victim may not be able to perceive what was happening at the time of the incident because the victim may have been unconscious or heavily under the influence of alcohol and/or drugs (Chancellor, 2012; Scalzo & National District Attorneys Association, 2007). An investigator should be aware that the victim may not be able to corroborate what happened and instead rely on forensic and eyewitness accounts.

Third, the ability of the victim to remember the events may also be diminished—again, requiring the investigator to rely on alternative sources of information. Any details the victim can recall, however, can be helpful in building a case (Chancellor, 2012). Finally, as indicated above, the use of corroborative evidence is critical, especially when the victim was unconscious and cannot recall details of the incident (Chancellor, 2012).

The role of alcohol in rape has been well documented—as many as 50% of sexual assaults involve alcohol to some degree (Chancellor, 2012). Alcohol affects cognitive abilities by lowering one's inhibitions and decreasing one's ability to make logical judgments and, therefore, can lead to risk-taking situations, including rape. It also affects motor control.

Below is an example of a typical report of an alcohol-facilitated rape where an offender went to a victim's home to "talk." The victim and offender had not had a previous sexual relationship and were simply coworkers.

> We were both off that day, and James, a guy I know from work, came over to my house for lunch. . . . I think he was looking for someone to talk to about his wife, because I know they were having problems. . . . He asked for a drink so I gave him a small glass and set a bottle of gin on the table and got . . . orange juice out of the refrigerator. We talked for a while longer. . . . He was telling me about his wife and family and some of their personal issues. I only had two weak drinks and was actually starting on my third when I decided it didn't taste very good and actually poured most of it down the sink

while he was using the restroom. . . . I started to feel a little sick and was sitting on the toilet . . . trying to avoid throwing up. . . . James walked into the bathroom and took my hand and tried to make me stand up. I was telling him to stop. . . . I finally was brought to my feet, but my panties and shorts were still around my ankles.

(Chancellor, 2012, p. 297)

The offender forced her into the bedroom and had sexual intercourse with her against her wishes. She threw up several times during the assault. The suspect corroborated almost every aspect of the incident, with the exception that it was consensual and that the victim was actually the aggressor. This case shows that the offender often gets the victim to voluntarily consume alcohol and then takes advantage of her by forcing sex upon her (Chancellor, 2012).

Drug-facilitated rapes have much in common with alcohol-facilitated rapes. There are differences, however, which make rape even more difficult to investigate. For example, victims of drug-facilitated rapes are almost always unconscious during the assault. Although someone may take advantage of a victim who is unconscious, most drug-facilitated rapes are planned well in advance. Drug-facilitated rapes are often characterized by the following:

- Force does not occur.
- Victim is not fearful.
- Victim does not resist.
- Offender is sexually gratified by control over the victim.
- Victim may engage in illegal drug use (knowingly).
- Torture typically is not present.
- It is almost always a planned event.
- Efforts are made by offenders to hide their actions (Littel, 2001).

Four components of a drug-facilitated rape exist: (1) means: offender's access to drugs and knowledge of their effects; (2) opportunity: ability to successfully carry out the rape without detection; (3) plan: have a plan to not only carry out the rape but to avoid detection; and (4) setting: a location that allows the victim to be controlled. These four components are known as the MOPS, an acronym referring to the MO of drug-facilitated rapes (LeBeau et al., 2001).

With regard to investigating drug-facilitated rapes, investigation strategies must be adjusted to take into consideration that information normally obtained from the victim may not be available. Also, offender behavior may not be as relevant. It can be assumed there was a lack of consent, and evidence indicating victim resistance will likely not exist (Chancellor, 2012). It should also be noted that victims sometimes remember events in short spurts, "flashbulb memories," and these can be useful for investigations (LeBeau et al., 2001). Also, a victim should be questioned about the timing of the effects of the drugs because some drugs, such as gamma-hydroxybutyric acid (GHB) or Rohypnol, do not take effect immediately. Other drugs include, but are not limited to, Xanax, Ecstasy, Klonopin, and street drugs (marijuana, cocaine, opiates, etc.).

With regard to a medical examination, which is usually conducted within 72 hours of the assault, examinations after alcohol- and drug-facilitated rapes can take place up to 96 hours after the assault. The investigator should request additional analyses of the urine to test for drugs. The investigation may involve several locations because the event may have involved more than one location (Chancellor, 2012).

COMMON INVESTIGATIONAL FAILURES

Researchers have identified several common investigative failures over the past several decades through the careful analysis of past cases. Rossmo (2009b) has identified those investigative failures in his book *Criminal Investigative Failures*. Investigative failures are organized into three broad categories: (1) **cognitive biases**, (2) organizational traps, and (3) errors in probability. Each of these is discussed here. Although these are found to occur among a wide range of criminal activities, it can be argued that sex crimes are highly susceptible to such investigative failures.

Cognitive Biases

Cognitive biases involve inaccurate perception, inaccurate intuition, and/or **tunnel vision**. With regard to perception, Rossmo has noted, "Perception is based on both awareness and understanding, we often perceive what we expect to perceive" (2009b, p. 9). Humans are limited by their working memory, which has been shown in research studies to only hold five to nine items in conscious memory (Rossmo, 2009b). Thus, although we are bombarded with multiple stimuli at any one time during any one incident, what we remember is quite limited. With regard to sex crimes, it is not uncommon for a victim's perception to vary a great deal from that of the alleged offender and even from the witnesses' accounts, if they exist. For example, an offender may perceive the victim was willing to engage in sex, whereas the victim believes it was rape.

Another cognitive bias involves intuition, or rather one's "gut instinct." Intuition relies on one's perception (usually derived through an automatic process) and reason (usually derived through a deliberate process). Intuition is prone to error because it is influenced by emotion. Police officers often make intuitive decisions under chaotic conditions and do so quickly. Such intuition is susceptible to error. Only under a slow, methodical analysis of reliable information are decisions less prone to error. Humans are prone to taking cognitive shortcuts, especially when presented with incomplete information. This often leads to error (Rossmo, 2009b).

Another cognitive bias that can occur, especially in a criminal investigation, is tunnel vision. This occurs "when there is a narrow focus on a limited range of alternatives" (Rossmo, 2009b, p. 13). With regard to the type of work to which police officers are exposed, they can quickly eliminate the actual offender and/or quickly narrow their focus on an innocent person (Cory, 2001). Tunnel vision can also affect a victim's account as well. The victim may remember the gun that was pointed at them in great detail but not be able to identify the race of the offender.

These cognitive biases (inaccurate perception, inaccurate intuition, and tunnel vision) can lead to problems in evaluating evidence such as ignoring context and misjudging a situation. For example, a police officer can mistakenly shoot someone jogging after a robbery is reported. The police officer fails to recognize the context—the person was in jogging clothing on a jogging trail and not involved in the robbery.

Confirmation bias can also occur, which involves paying attention only to information that corroborates one's theory and ignoring any information that discredits the theory. Additionally, research shows that individuals are more influenced by vivid information as opposed to data and statistics (Heuer, 1999). Thus, eyewitness description (which can be inaccurate) carries a lot of weight. Police officers can also fail to account for a lack of evidence. For example, a missing bottle of the victim's favorite perfume, given by an ex-boyfriend, can easily be overlooked (Rossmo, 2009b).

Organizational Traps

In addition to an individual's susceptibility to error, several organizational traps exist: (1) **groupthink**, (2) rumor, and (3) ego. Each of these traps contributes to **criminal investigative failures** in unique ways. Groupthink involves the unwillingness of a person to question a "dominant" theory or idea among a cohesive group of individuals such as police officers. The result can be disastrous: failing to critically assess ideas and wrongly discarding alternative ideas or theories. Thus, in an investigation, the dominant theory could be that a rape did not occur; the victim is making up the incident. Subsequently, others jump on board, refusing to challenge the status quo (Rossmo, 2009b).

Rumors also can negatively affect a case. These are termed **red herrings**, which refer to tips that misdirect a case. It is particularly problematic in high-profile cases where tip lines are established for anyone to contact. In such cases, certain components, often dramatic in nature, are exaggerated in importance. Information, however, that could be quite valuable is often lost in the process (Rossmo, 2009b).

Correctly identifying offenders often involves being able to question assumptions. Personal ego and organizational ego can negatively affect the outcome of a case. In the following excerpt Rossmo provides an example of this:

> Supervisory Special Agent John Douglas of the FBI's Behavioral Science Unit prepared a psychological profile for the sexual killer of nine-year-old Christine Jessop from Queensville, Ontario. . . . When police later arrested Guy Paul Morin, who closely matched the profile, Douglas touted the case as a success story. . . . DNA testing of semen stains on Jessop's underwear later exonerated Morin.
>
> (2009b, pp. 27–28)

In this case, personal ego and organizational ego (the "power" of the FBI and its employees) led to the assumption that the FBI profile was accurate, when in actuality, it led to the arrest of an innocent individual.

Errors in Probabilities

Probabilities, the likelihood that something will happen/has happened or won't happen/didn't happen, are critical to the investigation of all crimes, including sex crimes. Critical to probabilities are coincidences and how often they can occur during the investigation of a crime, as noted by Rossmo in the following quote:

> Mark Kennedy, a St. Louis sex crimes detective pursuing a serial rapist responsible for numerous crimes in several jurisdictions over many years, once commented to me—half-seriously—that he could have convicted three people if it were not for DNA. What he meant was the task force had looked at so many suspects that some of them, by sheer chance, circumstantially appeared guilty—until they were cleared by DNA testing. A few people will just be in the wrong place at the wrong time.
>
> (2009b, p. 37)

Thus, investigators are exposed to numerous coincidences that can inevitably lead to arresting an innocent person. Police officers must rely on all tools available to them, including DNA, to identify the guilty person.

Although DNA is often used as the ultimate resource for determining guilt, it is important to note that it is a science that is also susceptible to human error. Humans are responsible for collecting material with DNA, a process that is subject to error. In 2003, at the height of relying on DNA in criminal cases, the *New York Times* reported that a laboratory in Houston had a leaky roof, contaminating many DNA samples. This was only the beginning of problems with the laboratory. It was reported that the laboratory, in general, utilized poor methods for processing samples. Calibration and maintenance of equipment were considered to be poor. A lack of safeguards existed for contaminating samples. Poor record keeping was also found. Below is just one of the cases where DNA evidence was linked to the wrong suspect.

Mr. Sutton, serving a 25-year sentence, was convicted of raping a woman in October 1998 after she was taken from her apartment complex by two men and later left in a field. Several days later, he and a companion were arrested, although only Mr. Sutton was charged.

During his trial, a police crime laboratory employee offered evidence to suggest that a DNA sample recovered by investigators was a precise match for Mr. Sutton's. Other DNA experts disagreed (Madigan, 2003). Mr. Sutton was exonerated in 2003, having been arrested in 1999, after serving several years in prison (Flynn, 2015).

The problems with DNA testing have not disappeared over the years despite improvements. As recently as 2015, it was noted that the way DNA was examined when several people were present involved questionable protocol: "In a statement ... Travis County District Attorney ... said her office ... discovered an issue with the database it uses to calculate DNA statistics" (Osborn & Ulloa, 2015, p. A1). It was noted that the state was using an outdated protocol. Prosecutors inevitably overstated the reliability of linking the DNA sample to the suspect. Often this involved stating in court that a specific suspect is accurately linked to the material found at a crime scene (i.e., semen from a rape examination) within "a fraction of a fraction of a percent" (Osborn & Ulloa, 2015, p. A4).

In summary, investigative failures often boil down to one commonality: human error. Humans are limited by their ability to process only limited information at one time. Crime scenes involving sex crimes are often complex in that the victim, offender, and witnesses bring their own biases and distortions to the table. Organizational structures also lead to potential errors, especially given that they comprise humans who often make errors.

CONCLUSION

Investigating sex crimes often involves following guidelines that have been developed as a result of identifying mistakes from past investigations. Much can be gained from examining a crime scene about the offender. In some instances, in particular, when the victim is young or does not remember the sex crime occurring due to alcohol or drugs, the investigators must rely on alternative sources of information. Many of those who investigate sex crimes have received specialist training because working with sex crimes can be psychologically draining. Those who are first responders and those who interview suspects must be aware of the mistakes that can occur during an investigation, potentially damaging the case. Given that people are involved in the process, human error may occur. Special care must therefore be taken to eliminate or at least minimize mistakes.

REVIEW POINTS

- Sexual deviances are defined as paraphilias in the Diagnostic and Statistical Manual of Mental Disorders, 5th ed.
- Profiling a sex crime involves identifying an MO, determining whether a crime scene is organized or disorganized, identifying any signature, and potentially conducting a geographical profile.
- Emergency 911 operators and first responders to a sex crime must take great care to preserve and identify any potential evidence.
- Interviewing vulnerable victims involves taking additional precautions such as allowing a trained advocate to be present and asking questions in a phased approach.
- A medical examination is usually required, which should be conducted by a specially trained nurse, usually through a SANE program.
- Interviewing a sex-crime suspect should be done using a humane interview approach, asking appropriate questions, and using an information-gathering approach.
- Several types of sex crimes involve unique investigational obstacles. These include alcohol- and drug-facilitated rapes and deaths caused by autoerotic asphyxiation.
- Alcohol- and drug-facilitated rapes present unique investigational challenges because the victim often does not remember the incident.
- Many who die accidentally from autoerotic asphyxiation are misidentified as suicides by those who find the victim.
- There are three broad categories of common investigational mistakes that can affect a sex crime investigation: cognitive biases, organizational traps, and errors in probabilities.

REFERENCES

Adams, J. A. (2011). Medical evaluation of suspected child sexual abuse: 2011 update. *Journal of Child Sexual Abuse, 20*(5), 588–605. https://doi.org/10.1080/10538712.2011.606107

Adams, J. A., Harper, K., & Knudson, S. (1992). A proposed system for the classification of anogenital findings in children with suspected sexual abuse. *Adolescent and Pediatric Gynecology, 5*(2), 73–75. https://doi.org/10.1016/S0932-8610(19)80070-1

Adams, J. A., Harper, K., Knudson, S., & Revilla, J. (1994). Examination findings in legally confirmed child sexual abuse: It's normal to be normal. *Pediatrics, 94*(3), 310–317.

Agnew, S., & Powell, M. (2004). The effect of intellectual disability on children's recall of an event across different question types. *Law and Human Behavior, 28*(3). https://www.doi.org/10.1023/B:LAHU.0000029139.38127.61

American Psychiatric Association. (2013). *Diagnostic and statistical manual of mental disorders* (5th ed.). American Psychiatric Publishing.

Bartol, C. R., & Bartol, A. M. (2021). *Criminal behavior: A psychological approach*. Pearson.

Bashford, M. (2013). *How New York city tackled its backlog*. [Webinar] National Center for Victims of Crime, Washington, DC.

Brannon, G. E. (n.d.). Paraphilic disorders. http://emedicine.medscape.com/article/291419-overview

Brimbal, L., Dianiska, R. E., Swanner, J. K., & Meissner, C. A. (2019). Enhancing cooperation and disclosure by manipulating affiliation and developing rapport in investigative interviews. *Psychology, Public Policy, and Law, 25*(2), 107–115. https://www.doi.org/10.1037/law0000193

Bull, R. (2010). The investigative interviewing of children and other vulnerable witnesses. Psychological research and working/professional practice. *Legal and Criminological Psychology, 15*(1), 5–23. https://www.doi.org/10.1348/014466509X440160

Burns, I. M. (1993). Foreword to McGurk, B., Carr, M. J., & McGurk, D. In *Investigative interviewing courses for police officers: An evaluation*. Home Office Police Department. http://citeseerx.ist.psu.edu/viewdoc/download?doi=10.1.1.603.4361&rep=rep1&type=pdf

Campbell, R., & Fehler-Cabral, G. (2020). "Just bring us the real ones": The role of forensic crime laboratories in guarding the gateway to justice for sexual assault victims. *Journal of Interpersonal Violence*. Advance online publication. https://www.doi.org/10.1177/0886260520951303

Campbell, R., Feeney, H., Fehler-Cabral, G., Shaw, J., & Horsford, S. (2017). The national problem of untested Sexual Assault Kits (SAKs): Scope, causes, and future directions for research, policy, and practice. *Trauma, Violence, & Abuse, 18*(4), 363–376. https://www.doi.org/10.1177/1524838015622436

Chan, H. C., & Beauregard, E. (2016). Non-homicidal and homicidal sexual offenders: Prevalence of maladaptive personality traits and paraphilic behaviors. *Journal of Interpersonal Violence, 31*(13), 2250–2290. https://www.doi.org/10.1177/0886260515575606

Chancellor, A. S. (2012). *Investigating sexual assault cases*. Jones & Bartlett Publishers.

Cory, P. (2001). *The injury regarding Thomas Sophonow*. Government of Manitoba.

Council of Pediatric Subspecialties. (2021). *Child abuse pediatrics*. https://www.pedsubs.org/about-cops/subspecialty-descriptions/child-abuse/

Craig, R., Scheibe, R., Raskin, D., Kircher, R., & Dodd, D. (1999). Interviewer questions and content analysis of children's statements of sexual abuse. *Applied Developmental Science, 3*(2), 77–85. https://www.doi.org/ 10.1207/S1532480XADS0302_2

Davies, G., Wilson, C., Mitchell, R., & Milsom, J. (1995). *Videotaping children's evidence: An evaluation*. Home Office.

Davis, R. C., Jurek, A., Wells, W., & Shadwick, J. (2021). Investigative outcomes of CODIS matches in previously untested sexual assault kits. *Criminal Justice Policy Review*. Advance online publication. https://www.doi.org/10.1177/0887403421990723

DeNevi, D., & Campbell, J. H. (2011). *Into the minds of madmen: How the FBI's Behavioral Science Unit revolutionized crime investigation*. Prometheus Books.

Duke, M. C., Wood, J. M., Bollin, B., Scullin, M., & LaBianca, J. (2018). Development of the Rapport scales for investigative interviews and interrogations (RS3i), interviewee version. *Psychology, Public Policy, and Law, 24*, 64–79. https://www.doi.org/10.1037/law0000147

Eberle, P., & Eberley S. (1993). *The abuse of innocence: The McMartin Preschool trial*. Prometheus Books.

"Fells Acres Sexual Abuse Trials: 1986–87." (n.d.). Great American Trials, Encyclopedia.com. https://www.encyclopedia.com/law/law-magazines/fells-acres-sexual-abuse-trials-1986-87

Flynn, M. (2015). Advances in DNA testing could put thousands of Texas cases in legal limbo. *Houston Press*. http://www.houstonpress.com/news/advances-in-dna-testing-could-put-thousands-of-texas-cases-in-legal-limbo-7816089

Frontline, P. (1998). Innocence lost: The plea. *Frontline*. http://www.pbs.org/wgbh/pages/frontline/shows/innocence/etc/other.html

Harries, K. (1999). *Mapping crime: Principle and practice* [NCJ 178919]. National Institute of Justice.

Heal, L., & Sigelman, C. (1995). Response bias in interviews of individuals with limited mental ability. *Journal of Intellectual Disability Research, 39*(4), 331–340. https://www.doi.org/10.1111/j.1365-2788.1995.tb00525.x

Hess, K. M., Orthmann, C. H., & Cho, H. L. (2016). *Criminal investigations* (11th ed.). Delmar Cengage Learning.

Heuer, R. J., Jr. (1999). *Psychology of intelligence analysis*. Center for the Study of Intelligence, Central Intelligence Agency.

Holmberg, U., & Christianson, S. Å. (2002). Murderers' and sexual offenders' experiences of police interviews and their inclination to admit or deny crimes. *Behavioral Sciences and the Law, 20*(1–2), 31–45. https://www.doi.org/10.1002/bsl.470

International Association of Nurses. (2015). SANE Program Listing. http://www.forensicnurses.org/?page=a5

Iritani, K. (2016). Sexual Assault: Information on Training, Funding, and the Availability of Forensic Examiners [Report]. https://scholar.google.com/scholar_lookup?title=Sexual%20assault%3A%20information%20on%20training%2C%20funding%2C%20and%20the%20availability%20of%20forensic%20examiners&publication_year=2016&author=U.S.%20Government%20Accountability%20Office#d=gs_cit&u=%2Fscholar%3Fq%3Dinfo%3AEDzh6u3YNQQJ%3Ascholar.google.com%2F%26output%3Dcite%26scirp%3D0%26hl%3Den

Jetmore, L. (2006). Investigating rape crimes, part 1: Guidelines for first responders. *Police One*. https://www.policeone.com/police-products/investigation/evidence-management/articles/509858-Investigating-Rape-Crimes-Part-1-Guidelines-for-first-responders/

Jones, A. M., & Brimbal, L. (2017). Lay perceptions of interrogation techniques: Identifying the role of Belief in a Just World and Right Wing Authoritarianism. *Journal of Investigative Psychology and Offender Profiling, 14*(3), 260–280. https://www.doi.org/10.1002/jip.1476

Kebbell, M. R., Hurren, E. J., & Roberts, S. (2006). Mock suspects' decisions to confess: Accuracy of eyewitness evidence is crucial. *Applied Cognitive Psychology, 20*(4), 477–486. https://www.doi.org/10.1002/acp.1197

Kelly, C. E., & Valencia, E. J. (2020). You ask and do not receive, because you ask wrongly. *International Journal of Police Science & Management*. Advance online publication. https://www.doi.org/10.1177/1461355720955077

LeBeau, M. A., Mozayani, A., & Assault, D. F. S. (2001). *A forensic handbook*. John Wiley & Sons, Ltd.

Ledray, L. E., & Simmelink, K. (1999). Sexual assault: Clinical issues, efficacy of SANE evidence collection, a Minnesota study. *Journal of Emergency Nursing, 23*(1), 75–77. https://www.doi.org/10.1016/s0099-1767(97)90070-2

Littel, K. (2001). *Sexual assault nurse examiner (SANE) programs: Improving the community response to sexual assault victims*. GPO. http://www.vawnet.org/Assoc_Files_VAWnet/OVC_SANE0401–186366.pdf

Madigan, N. (2003). Houston's troubled DNA crime lab faces growing scrutiny. *The New York Times*. http://www.nytimes.com/2003/02/09/us/houston-s-troubled-dna-crime-lab-faces-growing-scrutiny.html

Matikka, L., & Vesala, H. (1997). Acquiescence in quality of life interviews with adults who have mental retardation. *Mental Retardation, 35*(2), 75–82. https://www.doi.org/10.1352/0047-6765(1997)035<0075:AIQIWA>2.0.CO;2

McGurk, B., Carr, J., & McGurk, D. (1993). *Investigative interviewing courses for police officers: An evaluation* [Police Research Series: Paper No. 4]. Home Office.

McManus, M. A., Hargreaves, P., Rainbow, L., & Alison, L. J. (2013). Paraphilias: Definition, diagnosis and treatment. *F1000 Prime Reports, 5*(36), 36–41.

Meissner, C. A., Redlich, A. D., Bhatt, S., & Brandon, S. (2012). Interview and interrogation methods and their effects on true and false. *Campbell Systematic Reviews, 13*(1), 1–52. https://www.doi.org/10.4073/csr.2012.13

Miller, W. R., & Rollnick, S. (2013). *Motivational interviewing: Helping people change* (3rd ed.). Guilford Press.

Milne, R., & Bull, R. (1999). *Investigative interviewing: Psychology and practice*. Wiley.

Napier, M. R. (2017). *Behavior, truth and deception: Applying profiling and analysis to the interview process* (2nd ed). CRC Press.

Osborn, C., & Ulloa, J. (2015). Hundreds of local criminal cases to be reviewed. DNA lab issues affect Texas cases. *Austin American-Statesman*, A1.

Oxburgh, G., Ost, J., & Cherryman, J. (2012). Police interviews with suspected sex offenders: Does use of empathy and question type influence the amount of investigation relevant information obtained? *Psychology, Crime & Law, 18*(3), 259–273. https://www.doi.org/10.1080/1068316X.2010.481624

Paterson, B., Bull, R., & Vrij, A. (2002). *The effects of interviewer style on children's event recall.* [Paper presentation]. 25th Congress of Applied Psychology, Singapore.

Phillips, D. (2019, September 10). Six men are speaking out to break the silence. *New York Times*. https://www.nytimes.com/interactive/2019/09/10/us/men-military-sexual-assault.html

Pinizzotto, A. J. (1984). Forensic psychology: Criminal personality profiling. *Journal of Police Science and Administration, 12*(1), 32–40. https://www.doi.org/10.1007/BF01352750

Possley, M. (n.d.). *The National Registry of Exonerations: Violet Amirault*. http://www.law.umich.edu/special/exoneration/pages/casedetail.aspx?caseid=3863

Read, J. M., Powell, M. B., Kebbell, M. R., Milne, R. (2009). Investigative interviewing of suspected sex offenders: A review of what constitutes best practices. *International Journal of Police Science & Management, 11*(4), 442–459. https://www.doi.org/10.1350/ijps.2009.11.4.143

Ressler, R. K., Burgess, A. W., & Douglas, J. E. (1988). *Sexual homicide: Patterns and motives*. Simon and Schuster.

Rossmo, D. K. (2000). *Geographic profiling*. CRC Press.

Rossmo, D. K. (2009a). Geographic profiling in serial rape investigations. In R. R. Hazelwood & A. W. Burgess (Eds.), *Practical aspects of rape investigation: A multidisciplinary approach* (4th ed., pp. 139–169). CRC Press.

Rossmo, D. K. (2009b). *Criminal investigative failures*. CRC Press, Taylor & Frances Group, LLC.

Scalzo, T. P., & National District Attorneys Association. (2007). *Prosecuting alcohol-facilitated sexual assault*. American Prosecutors Research Institute.

Sirotnak, A. P., Moore, J. K., & Smith, J. C. (2006). Child sexual abuse. In C. Brittain's (Ed.), *Understanding the medical diagnosis of child maltreatment: A guide for nonmedical professionals* (pp. 105–147). Oxford University Press.

Soukara, S., Bull, R., & Vrij, A. (2002). Police detectives' aims regarding their interviews with suspects: Any change at the turn of the millennium? *International Journal of Police Science and Management, 4*(2), 101–114. https://www.doi.org/10.1177/146135570200400202

Thomas, T. (2000). *Sex crime: Sex offending and society*. Wiley.

Thomas, T. L., Nobrega, J. C., & Britton-Susino, S. (2020). Rural health, forensic science and justice: A perspective of planning and implementation of a sexual assault nurse examiner training program to support victims of sexual assault in rural underserved areas. *Forensic Science International: Reports*, Advance online publication. http://www.doi.org/10.1016/j.fsir.2019.1000053

Tickle-Degnen, L., & Rosenthal, R. (1990). The nature of rapport and its nonverbal correlates. *Psychological Inquiry, 1*, 285–293. https://www.doi.org/10.1207/s15327965pli0104_1

Tittle, T. (2006). *Rape and sexual assault investigation*. [Paper presentation]. Police training session, Normal, IL.

Turvey, B. E. (2011). *Criminal profiling: An introduction to behavioral evidence analysis*. Academic Press.

Vidanapathirana, M. (2014). Child sexual abuse: A medico-legal analysis. *International Journal of Medical Toxicology and Forensic Medicine, 4*(3), 91–97. https://doi.org/10.22037/ijmtfm.v4i3(Summer).5885

Vrij, A., Mann, S. A., Fisher, R. P., Leal, S., Milne, R., & Bull, R. (2008). Increasing cognitive load to facilitate lie detection: The benefit of recalling an event in reverse order. *Law and Human Behavior, 32*(3), 253–265. https://www.doi.org/10.1007/s10979-007-9103-y

Ward, T., Hudson, S. M., Johnston, L. H., & Marshall, W. L. (1997). Cognitive distortions in sexual offenders: An integrative review. *Clinical Psychology Review, 17*(5), 1–29. https://www.doi.org/10.1016/s0272-7358(97)81034-3

Warren, A., Woodall, C., Hunt, J., & Perry, N. (1996). "It sounds good in theory, but . . .": Do investigative interviewers follow guidelines based on memory research? *Child Maltreatment, 1*(3), 231–245. https://www.doi.org/ 10.1177/1077559596001003006

Wood, J. L., & Garven, S. (2000). How sexual abuse interviewers go astray: Implications for prosecutors, police and child protection services. *Child Maltreatment, 5*(2), 109–118. https://www.doi.org/10.1177/1077559500005002003

DEFINITIONS

Accusatorial Method (of Suspect Interviewing): A style of interviewing suspects used primarily in the United States, which is confrontational and assumes guilt—this method typically establishes control, uses psychological manipulation (e.g., custody and isolation and confrontation followed by offering sympathy and face-saving excuses); uses closed-ended, confirmatory questions; and focuses on anxiety cues to determine deception (based on the suspect's verbal and nonverbal cues), and the primary goal is confession

Alcohol- and Drug-Facilitated Rape: A rape that occurs when a victim has either voluntarily or involuntarily consumed a legal or illegal substance, rendering them unable to give consent to have sexual intercourse

Appropriate (or Productive Interview) Questions: A type of question asked during a criminal investigation that includes open questions (e.g., "Can you describe the room to me?"), probing questions (e.g., "What happened next?"), encouragements and acknowledgments (e.g., "OK, I see.") (see Inappropriate [Interview] Questions)

Autoerotic Asphyxiation: Restricting oxygen while sexually aroused for the purpose of enhancing orgasm intensity

Cognitive Biases: Involve inaccurate perception, inaccurate intuition, and/or tunnel vision

Confirmation Bias: Paying attention only to information that corroborates one's theory and ignoring any information that discredits the theory

Criminal Geographic Targeting: An investigative method developed by criminologist Kim Rossmo, used in conjunction with criminal profiling, that analyzes spatial characteristics of a specified offender's crime patterns—the program creates a topographical map that identifies probabilities that a specific area falls within the offender's territory (see *Geographical Profiling*)

Diagnostic and Statistical Manual of Mental Disorders, 5th ed. (DSM-5): A publication by the American Psychiatric Association that provides a list and diagnosis criteria of all recognized mental disorders

Disorganized Crime Scene: A chaotic and messy crime scene indicative of a lack of planning and/or rage associated with the offender (see Organized Crime Scene and Mixed Crime Scene)

Dominant (Suspect) Interview: A type of suspect interview associated with impatience, hostility, aggressiveness, and condemnation; police officers are less likely to obtain an admission of guilt if they use a humane approach (see Humane [Suspect] Interview)

Exhibitionist Disorder: A paraphilic disorder that involves deriving sexual pleasure from exposing one's private parts to an unsuspecting person or performing sexual acts that can be watched by others

Fetishistic Disorder: A paraphilic disorder that involves deriving sexual pleasure from specific inanimate objects

Forced-Choice Questions: A type of interview question in which the answer has only limited options, including questions such as this: Did the offender cut your necklace off before or after the assault?

Frotteuristic Disorder: A paraphilic disorder that involves deriving sexual pleasure from touching or rubbing against a nonconsenting person

Geographical Mapping: Analysis of the spatial patterns of a series of crimes committed over a period of time by all offenders of known offenses—the focus is on a specific geographical area

Geographical Profiling: Analysis of the spatial distribution of a set of offenses committed by a single offender—the focus is on the individual offender

Groupthink: The unwillingness of a person to question a "dominant" theory or idea among a cohesive group of individuals such as police officers

Humane (Suspect) Interview: A type of suspect interview, associated with friendliness and empathy, that is cooperative and personal; police officers are more likely to obtain an admission of guilt if they use a humane approach (see Dominant [Suspect] Interview.)

Hunters: A type of criminal who seeks victims as they set out from their home base to places they are familiar with and believe suitable targets can be found; hunters tend to stay within a relatively stable geographical area that is near their own homes (See Trollers, Trappers, and Poachers)

Inappropriate Questions: Types of questions that are used during an investigation that include echo questions (e.g., Suspect says, "I may have . . ."; interviewer says, "You may have . . ."), closed questions (e.g., "Did you leave your house last night?"), leading questions (e.g., "Then you went to the living room, right?"), forced-choice questions (e.g., "The phone is in your name or your wife's?"), multiple questions (e.g., "Did you leave before nine o'clock? Where did you go?"), and opinion-based statements (e.g., "You are just trying to protect yourself") (see Appropriate Questions)

Information Gathering: Relies on establishing rapport; using open-ended, exploratory questions; and focusing on cognitive clues to deception; the use of cognitive clues is deeply embedded in empirical research that shows individuals will remember an event more accurately after they have been asked to remember the emotions, perceptions, and sequence of events in the situation of interest—the primary goal of the information-gathering method, associated with Great Britain, is to elicit information; the suspects are given the opportunity to provide explanations and explain the circumstances, and only then are they questioned and asked about any inconsistent or contradictory information, with the goal to establish facts as opposed to obtaining a confession (as in the accusatorial method)

Investigation Relevant Information (IRI): Information that is helpful in determining information about the crime; quality interviews, in general, will yield IRI, which includes the following key pieces of information: (1) what happened, (2) how the crime was committed, (3) who was involved, (4) when and where the offense occurred, and (5) any objects used to assist in committing the offense

Mixed Crime Scene: A crime scene that includes elements of both and organized and disorganized crime scene (see Organized Crime Scene and Disorganized Crime Scene)

Modus Operandi (MO): An offender's unique behavioral pattern during the commission of the offense

Open Questions: Questions that are based on information that the witness provided in the narrative and are open ended (e.g., What did the offender look like?)

Opportunistic Approach: A type of approach that occurs during an alcohol- and drug-facilitated rape that involves taking advantage of someone who has already been exposed to alcohol or drugs

Organized Crime Scene: A crime scene that reveals planning on the part of the offender; the crime scene appears in order (see Disorganized Crime Scene and Mixed Crime Scene)

Other Specified Paraphilic Disorder: These include a variety of other paraphilic behaviors not already listed in the DSM-5

Paraphilia: Any intense and persistent sexual interest in anything other than genital stimulation or preparatory fondling with physically mature, phenotypically normal, consenting human partners

Paraphilic Disorder: The presence of a paraphilia that causes distress or impairment to the individual or has led to personal harm or risk of harm to others

Phased Approach: An approach that is suggested to be used when working with vulnerable victims that includes four phases: (1) establish a good rapport, (2) obtain as much free narrative as possible, (3) ask questions of the right type and in the right order, and (4) then have meaningful closure

Pedophilic Disorder: A paraphilic disorder that involves having a sexual preference for prepubescent children

Poachers: A type of offender who is usually more transient—they will travel some distance from their residence to search for victims (see Hunters, Trollers, and Trappers)

Proactive Approach: Involves an offender who commits rape—the offender intentionally gets a victim drunk or gives them a drug without their knowledge; the victim is usually then taken to another location for sexual intercourse

Rape Kit: Evidence collected during a medical examination, usually conducted at a hospital, after someone reports being raped—the information included in the rape kit can contain crucial DNA evidence that identifies the offender

Rapport-Building Method of Interviewing: An interviewing technique that involves positive interactions between the interviewer and interviewee and a communication style that leads to developing respect and trust; it relies heavily upon open-ended questions, reflective and summary statements (i.e., repeating back key details to ensure accuracy), and affirmations (i.e., providing positive feedback to the interviewee such as "I appreciate your honesty")

Red Herrings: Tips received in a crime investigation, usually a high-profile case, that misdirects a case

Sexual Assault Nurse Examiner (SANE): Nurses who have specialized knowledge and training to conduct forensic examinations of sexual assault victims

Sexual Masochism Disorder: A paraphilic disorder that involves deriving sexual pleasure from wanting to be humiliated, beaten, bound, or otherwise made to suffer

Sexual Sadism Disorder: A paraphilic disorder that involves deriving sexual pleasure from inflicting pain or humiliation on another person

Signature: Anything that the offender does that goes beyond what is necessary to carry out the crime—it reveals the offender's unique cognitive processes associated with the sex crime and is relatively consistent when the offender carries out the crime repeatedly

Specific Questions: Questions that typically seek additional information or clarify information already provided and assist the witness to understand what is relevant—this usually involves asking what, who, where, and when-type questions

Transvestic Fetishism: A paraphilic disorder that involves deriving sexual pleasure from clothing associated with members of the opposite sex

Trappers: A type of offender who places their victims in a position of opportunity by taking on borders, entertaining victims, placing ads, or assuming an employment position that brings victims to them (see Hunters, Poachers, and Trollers)

Trollers: Often encounter their victims randomly and do not specifically search out victims—they locate their victims while engaging in some other activity (See Hunters, Poachers, and Trappers)

Trophy: An item taken by the offender from the crime scene such as jewelry, a driver's license, or underwear—it is usually a meaningful item that the offender uses to remember the incident

Tunnel Vision: When one has a narrow focus on a limited range of alternatives

Voyeuristic Disorder: A paraphilic disorder that involves deriving sexual pleasure from observing an unsuspecting person who is naked, undressing, or engaging in sexual activities or in activities deemed to be of a private nature

Vulnerable Victims: A type of victim who may have difficulty communicating events such as children, elderly adults, and those with special needs

CHAPTER 10

Assessment Tools and Treatment Issues Related to Sex Crimes

CHAPTER OBJECTIVES

- Assess key issues related to treating victims of sex crimes
- Define empirically-based approaches with regard to the development of assessments and treatment approaches for persons who have committed a sex crime
- Identify the key components of the Risk, Need, and Responsivity (RNR) Model as applied to treatment for persons who have committed a sex crime
- Describe the purpose and goals of the assessment process in evaluating persons who have committed a sex crime
- Define and describe three categories of assessment tools: (1) nonactuarial assessment tools, (2) assessment tools that rely on objective measures yet do not provide cutoff scores for risk levels, and (3) actuarial assessment tools that provide cutoff scores for levels of risk and are based on empirical findings from systematic research
- Define psychopathy and how it affects sex-offender assessments
- Discuss and identify treatment approaches throughout modern history with regard to hormones and castration, behavioral therapy, use of the polygraph, cognitive-behavioral therapy, and trauma-informed care
- Provide an overview on how effective treatment is for persons who have committed a sex crime

Assessment and treatment issues related to sex crimes pertain to both those who have been victimized and those who commit sex crimes. We begin this discussion by discussing key issues related to victims off sex crimes. Next, we focus on persons who have committed a sex crime. Critical to assessing persons who have committed a sex crime are **empirically-based approaches** and the use of a **Risk, Need, and Responsivity Model**, which are crucial to the assessment processes and developing the best treatment approach.

OBSTACLES IN ACCESSING TREATMENT FOR VICTIMS OF SEX CRIMES

As discussed in Chapter 8, the need to treat victims is critical, yet victims must overcome many barriers to receive treatment. These barriers include, but are not limited to, myths surrounding that the victim deserved the offense, they should have fought back, they must have wanted it. Victims often fear being portrayed as weak (Holland et al., 2016). As pictured below, Keith Smith, a survivor of kidnapping and rape faced many obstacles in coming to terms with being a male victim of rape, despite the fact his victimization occurred when he was only 14 years old. As an adult, Keith sought treatment and noted that he was fearful of coming forward as he assumed most would believe he should have fought back more. Keith Smith is a rape survivors advocate and is affiliated with Rape, Abuse & Incest National Network (RAINN).

These barriers are even more pronounced for those who are in special categories, such as same-sex victimizations, inmates in a jail or prison, male victims, and those who are raped in the context of their job, such as the military. In one assessment of military personnel, the barriers included fear of their leaders perceiving the victim differently (i.e., negatively), and their peers losing confidence in them (Holland et al., 2016). Military personnel also felt unsafe in reporting the sexual abuse (Holland et al., 2016).

More specifically, many men who experienced sexual violence in the military are left without any mental health treatment and experienced post-traumatic stress disorder (PTSD). In a *New York Times* investigation, one of six men who came forward to report his story of rape in the military was Paul Lloyd, a 30-year-old who had enlisted in the Army National Guard when he was 17 years old (Philipps, 2019). He "earned top scores in marksmanship and physical fitness, and wanted a career in the military, but he said a sense of betrayal and disgust at being raped started to gnaw at him" (n.p). He did not tell anyone about the sexual assault that occurred in a small shower area that resulted in an emergency room visit with a torn rectum and internal injuries. He refused to tell anyone what happened until five years after. The attack left him with difficulty coping with daily life. He left for Christmas, went home, and failed to return. The military forced him to return and he was discharged eventually for misconduct. Paul Lloyd's story highlights the barriers victims of sexual assault experience, especially those who are male, and experience the abuse in the military. In the adjoining photograph, Mr. Lloyd was experiencing symptoms of PTSD, as the smell of shampoo reminded him of the assault that occurred in the showers of his military barracks.

EMPIRICALLY-BASED APPROACHES OF ASSESSING AND TREATING PERSONS WHO HAVE COMMITTED A SEX CRIME

A large amount of research over the past several decades has been conducted on treating persons who have committed a sex crime and has carved a path toward better assessment and treatment. To describe what empirically-based assessments and treatment are, it may be best to begin with what it is not. If someone were treated based simply on logic, that would not be an empirically-based approach. For example, some of the initial treatment approaches that involved **castration** of persons who had committed a sex crime were based on logic: treat a sex problem with a sex approach (i.e., remove the person's capacity to have sex). Most initial treatment attempts for any issue, physical or mental, usually are logic based. Sometimes that can work, but relying on an empirically-based approach is more effective. An empirically-based approach means that it has been shown to be effective through an experimental approach that implements the highest scientific standards and is vetted by one's peers.

An experimental approach involves gathering a large number of persons who are suffering from the ailment of interest (i.e., persons who have committed a sex crime). Next, the large sample is randomly divided into two groups, and one of the groups (i.e., the control group) is provided either the standard treatment approach or is not treated at all, whereas the

PHOTO 10.1 Keith Smith: Overcoming the Obstacles of Rape as a Male Victim.

Photo Credit: Michael Nagle//*The New York Times*/Redux.

other group (i.e., the experimental group) is provided the new treatment approach. If the experimental group performs better (i.e., reduction in sexual recidivism) than the control group, those results are typically vetted by experts in the field and subsequently validated with other groups of offenders. If the new treatment produces the desired effect, it then becomes an empirically-based treatment approach.

A problem, however, with developing an empirically-based treatment approach for persons who have committed a sex crime is because few of those persons will go on to commit another sexual offense, regardless of any treatment. As you'll recall from earlier research reviewed, only about 10%–15% of sex offenders sexually reoffend (Hanson & Bussière, 1998). Thus, it becomes difficult to identify an approach that substantially and significantly reduces one's likelihood of reoffending when the differences between that control group and experimental group are so small—this is known as the ***low base-rate problem***: few are going to reoffend regardless of the treatment (or complete lack thereof) that the treatment they have.

Nevertheless, many studies have been conducted that have shown some factors to occur significantly more among persons who have committed a sex crime compared to those who have not committed a sex crime, lending credence to including those factors in empirically-based assessment tools. Furthermore, some treatment approaches have also received empirically-based support in reducing sexual recidivism more so than those who received either no treatment or other treatment models without empirical support. Before we discuss assessment and treatment approaches, we will discuss the RNR Model, which provides guiding principles relevant to assessments and treatments.

Risk, Need, and Responsivity (RNR) Model

The RNR Model is critical to both assessing an offender and identifying a treatment approach. This is based on the assumption that supervision and treatment are most effective when more resources are geared toward high-risk offenders, and also low-risk offenders are provided with fewer resources. Assessment predictions can assist decision-making to appropriately direct and conserve resources while at the same time increasing public safety (Gottfredson & Moriarty, 2006). Research has shown that providing a low-risk offender with high levels of treatment can actually lead to increased recidivism (Bonta & Andrews, 2007).

Within the RNR Model, *criminogenic needs* (i.e., crime-causing factors) are targeted for treatment (Andrews & Bonta, 2006). The RNR Model also recognizes that treatment should take into account individual learning styles, motivation level, and level of functioning (Bonta & Andrews, 2007). Also, this model includes a strength-based approach, where not only are the offender's available resources and skills assessed for the purpose of identifying ones that are deficient, but consideration and focus are given to where the person's strengths lie.

Although the RNR Model has been applied to offenders in general, recent research has shown that it has been effectively applied to persons who have committed a sex crime (Hanson, 2006). Assessments enhance the RNR Model by utilizing resources most effectively (Center for Sex Offender Management, 2007), which includes conducting a thorough assessment to appropriately and effectively target people with the correct amount of treatment (Smid et al., 2014).

OVERVIEW OF ASSESSMENTS

Assessments assist in the criminal justice processing of a person who has committed a sex crime and typically determine the amount and type of treatment and punishment. Assessment results can lead to a requirement that the community is notified of an offender's presence (Lanterman et al., 2014). Assessments can be conducted during sentencing and in determining prison and probation conditions. They can also be conducted when the offender is being released from prison in deciding reentry plans. Additionally, assessments can also be conducted to determine progress and compliance with treatment (Center for Sex Offender Management, 2007).

Assessments are critical to the criminal justice process, but we should emphasize that they are not used to determine guilt or innocence. There is no assessment tool that unequivocally determines whether a person has committed a sex crime. Rather, assessments are used to provide objective information for judges in determining the most appropriate judicial response to those who have already committed a sex crime (Center for Sex Offender Management, 2007).

Many factors affect whether an offender will commit a future sex crime. Assessments assist in determining what the risk level is with regard to committing a future sex crime. Sexual recidivism rates of persons who have committed a sex crime, overall, are relatively low, typically between 10% and 15% (Hanson & Bussière, 1998), making predictions difficult. No assessment is perfect. They can, however, provide an informed prediction, based on known factors, whether a person is at a low, moderate, or high risk of recidivating. Two false outcomes are possible (Craig et al., 2004). First, the outcome of an assessment can place someone at a high level of risk and the person does not recidivate. This is known as a false positive. Second, someone can be assessed at low risk but does recidivate, which is a false negative and a more serious problem. The goal is to correctly predict the level of risk and provide the appropriate level of supervision.

We discuss three broad categories of assessments in this chapter: (1) ***nonactuarial***, which are based solely on a clinician's judgment, (2) assessment tools that rely on objective measures yet do not provide cutoff scores for risk levels, and (3) ***actuarial***, which involve assessment tools that provide cutoffs for levels of risk and are based on empirical findings from systematic research. Also, static and ***dynamic factors*** are critical to the assessments. ***Static factors*** refer to unchangeable or "fixed" factors related to an offender. They include factors that will not change in the future. For example, age at first sexual experience does not change over time—it is, therefore, a static factor. ***Dynamic factors*** can and do change over time. This can include a person's attitude toward treatment, for example, or employment status. Some assessment tools include either static factors or dynamic factors, whereas others include both. This chapter provides a summary of several types of assessment tools. These are a few of the more widely used assessments and are not intended to comprise an exhaustive list. Also, to conduct an assessment, specialized training and education are required.

Assessing persons who have committed a sex crime is not new, yet it was not until the 1980s and 1990s that many assessment tools were developed. This section provides a history of the development of sex-offender assessment tools. The goals of the assessments are also provided, with an acknowledgment that this is still a developing area. Also noteworthy, we discuss methods for utilizing sex-offender assessments.

Goals and Purpose of Assessments

Many of the actuarial risk assessments discussed in this chapter provide a score that relates to a risk level, usually low, moderate, or high. Much information is needed, however, to assess someone (Hanson, 2009). Decision makers, for example, want not only an estimate of risk but an estimate of the potential consequences of committing a sex crime and possible mitigating factors (Hanson, 2009). An example of the use of assessments is presented below in a summary of a bail hearing of an alleged offender accused of molesting a nine-year-old girl:

> The judge was provided a document, called a superform, which generally spells out why police believe there is probable cause to hold someone in jail. . . . As a district court judge, [she] is asked to determine if police have proven that enough probable cause exists for the arrest. She is also asked to decide if bail is warranted. She is expected to consider whether the defendant poses a danger to the community and is likely to commit a violent offense, or if the defendant is likely to interfere with the administration of justice. . . . [The judge] declined to discuss [the defendant's] case specifically, saying it wouldn't be appropriate for her to talk about a case now pending. . . . In general, she said that she considers what information the police have provided in the superform. She also considers the static adult risk assessment, which uses a person's age, gender, and criminal history to predict future behavior. She also may hear from alleged victims or from people who support the accused. "These are difficult decisions. We take them very seriously. We're talking about a person's freedom and also the potential effects on the alleged victims and the effects on the public," [the judge] said. "We do the best we can with the information we have. We don't have the benefit of hindsight or a crystal ball."
>
> (Hefley, 2014, n.p.)

TABLE 10.1 Goals of Assessments for Persons Who Have Committed a Sex Crime

- Assess risk factors to commit a subsequent sexual offenses
- Identify reliable and valid assessments of causal factors that can assist in the best response
- Provide estimates of recidivism risk
- Inform treatment and risk management strategies
- Allow the assessment of both long-term and short-term changes in risk
- Assess protective factors as well as risk factors
- Facilitate engaging the patient or offender in the assessment process
- Identify a treatment response that is easy to implement in a broad range of settings

Note: Adapted from Hanson (2009).

In this case, the accused was released from jail without bail. This, however, is not always the case because the judge may order a specific bail amount for the defendant to be released. Also, the judge can deny bail altogether, requiring the defendant to remain in jail until trial. The assessments discussed in this chapter are often used for similar purposes portrayed in the above scenario.

The goals and purposes of assessments for persons who have committed a sex crime are presented in Table 10.1. It should be noted that the goals and purposes cover a broad range of issues that directly affect criminal justice responses and treatment approaches.

Common Risk Factors among Assessments

Research has identified several risk factors correlated with sexual recidivism among persons known to have already committed a sex crime (Hanson et al., 2010). These factors include demographics, prior offense history, and several psychosocial factors. In order from least to most correlated, these factors include personal distress or mood disorder, psychosis, violence used in the index offense, substance abuse, prior violent offense, low intelligence, a juvenile criminal record, a prior adult criminal record, age, negative or criminal companions, antisocial personality disorder or ***psychopathy***, and deviant sexual interests (Hanson & Bussière, 1998; Hanson & Morton-Bourgon, 2005; Mann et al., 2010).

SEX-OFFENDER ASSESSMENT TOOLS

There are essentially three broad categories of sex-offender assessment tools. First, ***nonactuarial assessments*** rely exclusively on clinical judgments. Typically, nonactuarial assessments are combined with other assessment types (Tully et al., 2013). Second, a sort of hybrid type of assessment includes clinical judgment along with some objective measurement. These types of assessments, however, do not provide a cutoff score for risk levels. Third, ***actuarial assessments*** include empirically derived scales that have been validated (Monahan, 1996) and usually provide some sort of cutoff score for levels of risk. A summary of assessment tools is presented in Table 10.2, followed by a brief discussion of at least one from each category.

TABLE 10.2 Summary of Assessment Tools

Category of Assessment:	Assessment Tool	Developed by:	Description of Items
(1) Nonactuarial Assessment, No Cutoff Scores	Clinical Judgment	N/A	Relies on clinician judgment.
(2) Assessment Tools With Objective Measures, No Cutoff Scores	Phallometric Tests	Freund (1963)	Measures penile reaction to images.
	ABEL Assessment for Sexual Interest-3™ **(AASI-3)**	Abel et al. (1998)	Measures visual reaction time to images. Measures sexual interest in children, cognitive distortions, social desirability, sexual victimization, and past child sexual abuse by assessing visual reaction time and includes ten self-report items (i.e., admitted sexual history of behavior, fantasy, alcohol and drug use).
	Sexual Violence Risk-20 (SVR-20), Version 1 and 2	Boer et al. (1997); Hart and Boer (2020)	Includes 20 items (yes or no) based on three areas: (1) *psychosocial adjustment*: sexual deviancy, victim of abuse, mental illness, substance use, suicidal/homicidal thoughts, relationships, employment issues, and prior criminal history; (2) *sexual offenses*: prior sex offense characteristics, denial of offenses, and attitude in support of sex offenses; and (3) *future plans*: presence or lack of realistic future plans, and attitude toward intervention.
(3) Actuarial Assessments, Cutoff Scores	**Structured Anchored Clinical Judgment (SACJ-Min)**	Thornton[1]	Conducted in three steps: (1) determine current conviction history; (2) assess aggravating factors (i.e., stranger victim, male victims, never married, convictions for noncontact sex offenses, substance abuse, placement in residential care as a child, deviant sexual arousal and psychopathy); and (3) assessing current behavior (dynamic factors).
	Rapid Risk Assessment of Sex Offender Recidivism (RRASOR)	Hanson (1997)	Includes four items: prior sex offenses, male victim, unrelated victim, ages between 18 and 25.
	Static-99R	Hanson and Thornton (2000) and revised subsequently	Includes ten items based on a combination of the SACJ-Min and RRASOR.

(Continued)

TABLE 10.2 Continued

Category of Assessment:	Assessment Tool	Developed by:	Description of Items
	Static-2002	Hanson and Thornton (2003)	Includes 14 items based on five concepts: age at offense, persistence of offending, deviant sexual interest, relationship to victim, and general criminality.
	Sex Offender Risk Appraisal Guide (SORAG)	Quinsey et al. (2006)	Includes 14 items to measure violent recidivism among sex offenders: lived with biological parents, adjustment problems, alcohol abuse history, marital status, criminal history, victim characteristics, age, mental health history, deviant sexual interest, and psychopathy.
	Violence Risk Appraisal Guide (VRAG)	Quinsey et al. (2006)	Includes 12 items to determine violent recidivism among sex offenders and to be used in conjunction with SORAG when the offender has a sex offense.
	Risk Matrix 2000/S (RM2000/S)	Thornton (2007)	Includes seven concepts measured that predict future sex offenses and is based on the SACJ-Min and empirical factors associated with sexual recidivism.
	Minnesota Sex Offending Screening Tool (MnSOST)	Minnesota Department of Corrections (2012)	Includes nine items to determine sexual recidivism based on criminal history, age, type of release from the criminal justice system, completion of sex offender and substance abuse treatment, and a male victim.

[1] As noted in Beech et al. (2003), the SACJ-Min "was developed by David Thornton," yet the validation of it occurred through subsequent published studies with different authors.

Assessment Tools with Objective Measures but Without Cutoff Scores

Assessment tools with objective measures but without cutoff scores include the phallometric assessment. The first phallometric assessment, a penile *plethysmograph*, was developed in 1957 by Kurt Freund (1963). The purpose was to measure penile engorgement while erotic visual material was presented. Later, several others introduced a phallometric test that measured change in the circumference of the penis (Bancroft et al., 1966). By measuring sexual arousal to stimuli, it was believed that a person's true sexual deviance could be identified, given that his physiological response was involuntary. It can also be used in conjunction with *behavioral therapy* approaches to modify one's sexual deviance (Marshall & Laws, 2003). A similar apparatus has also been developed for women, called a vaginal plethysmograph (Pras et al., 2003). An example of current-day usage of the plethysmograph is described below:

> Massil Benbouriche, a professor at the University of Montreal's school of criminology, invented the system to assess whether sex offenders are likely to re-offend. The system incorporates . . . [the] "penile plethysmography," which involves outfitting a patient's penis with a sensor-equipped "ring" and presenting him with visual and auditory stimuli . . . to assess their state of arousal. . . . Benbouriche took the technique one step further by administering it in a cube-shaped "vault," creating an all-immersive virtual reality experience. Because sex offenders often try to throw the results of penile plethysmographs by averting their eyes from the contents onscreen, Benbouriche's virtual reality system uses "eye-tracking" technology to ensure that the person inside the booth is keeping his eyes fixed on the images onscreen. . . . Many experts on pedophilia believe that sexual attraction to children is a fixed and immutable sexual orientation. . . . It's unlikely that a self-avowed pedophile would be able to control his biological response to the stimuli onscreen.
>
> (Dickson, 2014, n.p.)

Research regarding the penile plethysmograph is contradictory (Laws & Marshall, 2003). Many methodological problems exist in the research that has examined its use. No current standards exist for implementing its use (Marshall & Fernandez, 2000; Marshall & Laws, 2003). The information gained from a plethysmograph is not admissible in court (Dickson, 2014). Also, it is speculated that many pedophiles never act on their sexual arousal (Dickson, 2014). Thus, despite sexual arousal to children, one may never sexually abuse a child. The plethysmograph, however, is still widely used today despite the existing problems (Laws & Marshall, 2003) and can be used for treatment purposes (Dickson, 2014).

ABEL Assessment for Sexual Interest-3™ (AASI-3)

The *ABEL Assessment for Sexual Interest-3™ (AASI-3)* assesses not only sexual deviancy but also a broad range of sexual problems. This assessment is unique in that it can be used for male and female clients. It has been validated through several research studies. "It is specifically designed to measure a client's sexual interest and to obtain information regarding involvement in a number of abusive or problematic or sexual behaviors" (Abel Screening, n.d.). The assessment is taken on a computer and subsequently sent to Abel Screening, where a detailed report is provided.

Critical to the AASI assessment tool is the level of arousal toward a person. Research has shown that an individual will act in a sexual manner toward a person when they are sexually aroused by that person (Hanson & Bussière, 1996, 1998). The assessment involves showing a series of 160 photographs of people with diverse characteristics (young, old, male, female, etc.). The subject is asked to rate the attractiveness of the person they are viewing. This assessment, however, considers the visual reaction time, that is, how long the subject examines the photograph. The visual reaction time is used as a measure of who the subject is most attracted to (Tong, 2007). The AASI test is seen as a replacement for the plethysmograph, which as mentioned previously, is an instrument that measures genital blood flow (Tong, 2007).

An advantage of this assessment is that it can be used with offenders who deny their attraction to children. Below is a description of the problem and how this assessment is useful:

> It may be inevitable that some deniers will be ordered into community based treatment. Frequently these individuals are persons released from prison, or who are involved in child protective services cases where there is insufficient case information to generate a charge. . . . This raises the question of how can clinicians break through denial in these clients, so as to enable moving on with the formalized sexual offender specific treatment. . . . [Blasingame] directed a pilot project involving paroled sexual offenders. . . . Two of the original twelve parolees were in complete denial when they presented for the intake interview, and two admitted only that they had been charged for molestation (but made no real admissions). After completion of their Abel Assessments, review of the victim information in their charges was found to be congruent with the sexual interest categories identified by the Abel Assessment. Three of the four admitted to their offenses when confronted with this information and the reminder that there would be a polygraph examination soon. The fourth client was returned to prison for a parole violation. . . . The three had been charged with a total of three victims and while their original admissions after the intake were at one (1) victim/charge, their final admissions totalled nineteen (19) victims with approximately two-hundred and fifty acts committed against those victims, all in the age and gender categories on the Abel Assessment for Sexual Interest.
>
> (Blasingame, 2014, n.p.)

Sexual Violence Risk-20 (SVR-20)

Mental health professionals use the **Sexual Violence Risk-20 (SVR-20)** for the purpose of evaluating an individual's sexual violence risk. This instrument includes structured professional judgment guidelines. Thus, mental health professionals must still rely on their own assessment, yet this tool provides general guidelines. The SVR-20 is based on six activities: (1) gather information about the examinee's personal, social, occupational, mental health, illegal, and other relevant behavior; (2) gather information by using a variety of sources and methods, including (but not limited to) record reviews, interviews, and psychological, physiological, and medical techniques; (3) gather information from the offender, relatives and acquaintances, the victim(s), professionals who have interacted with the examinee, and any other persons likely to yield useful information; (4) consider the offender's history and future exposure to risk factors; (5) critically weigh the accuracy, credibility, and applicability of the data that have been gathered; and (6) conduct ongoing risk assessment, with regular reassessments for many examinees (Boer et al., 1997).

The results of the SVR-20 yield low-, moderate-, or high-risk levels of offenders. The developers of the risk assessment suggest a final report that addresses the following questions:

(a) what is the likelihood that the person will engage in sexual violence if no efforts are made to manage the risk; (b) what is the probable nature, frequency, and severity of any future sexual violence; (c) who are the likely victims of any future sexual violence; (d) what steps could be taken to manage the person's risk for sexual violence; and (e) what circumstances might exacerbate the person's risk for sexual violence (Boer et al., 1997)?

Actuarial Assessments

Actuarial models are relied upon more often than clinical judgments alone because actuarial models are based on empirically derived scales that have been validated (Monahan, 1996), and during the past two decades, a large number of them have been developed. They also include a cutoff score for risk levels. Actuarial models have outperformed clinical judgments by accurately predicting outcomes (i.e., sexual recidivism) in more cases than clinical judgment (Goggin, 1994). As noted in Table 10.3, the number of such assessment tools has increased substantially in the past several decades. Due to the large number of them, we will focus on the **Static-99R** and **Static-2002** because they are the most commonly used assessment tools used today (Kelley et al., 2020).

Static-99R and Static-2002

Those who have completed a Static-99R training session can use this assessment tool. It is the most widely used sex-offender assessment scale in the world (National Institute of Corrections, n.d.). A copy of the questions and how they are scored is presented in Table 10.3.

The questions, although simple on their face, can be complicated to score accurately. The authors provide an 80-page manual explaining how to score each item. For example, the second item may be difficult to score if the offender has lived with someone for two years, but it was a same-sex relationship. The authors clarify situations such as this by noting that same-sex relationships should be counted in this category. Other situations are also clarified such as the offender being incarcerated for much of their adult life. This is scored as not having lived with a lover for at least two years. Also, if the offender lived with a lover for two years, but with different persons, this item is scored as not living with a lover for two consecutive years. Clarifications are made for each item in this manual (Harris et al., 2003).

Each of the items is based on empirical findings showing that each factor is associated with the risk of recidivism. For example, the first item is based on a correlation between offender age and the likelihood of recidivism. The younger the offender is at the time of the risk evaluation, the more likely they are to recidivate. It should be noted that the Static-99R is intended for male adults at least 18 years old (Beck & Harrison, 2008). Furthermore, research regarding the use of Static-99 for those who are white, Black, and Hispanic has yielded similar accuracy among these different race and ethnicity groups, including Native Americans (Myer, 2019), Latinos, and Blacks (Lee & Hanson, 2017), and also among those who have low intellectual functioning. This tool is also versatile in that it has been recommended for global use (Sandbukt et al., 2020).

The Static-2002 is based on similar items to the Static-99R and was developed to increase conceptual cohesion and clarification (Hanson & Thornton, 2003). A weighted score is calculated for each of the five sets of questions. Those scores are then totaled to yield one of five possible risk levels: low, low moderate, moderate, moderate high, and high. This assessment predicts sexual recidivism slightly better than the Static-99R (Phenix et al., 2008), yet both are still widely used today.

TABLE 10.3 Static-99R Assessment Tool

Item #	Risk Factor	Codes		Score
1	Age at release from index sex offense	Age 18–34.9		1
		Age 35–39.0		0
		Age 40–59.9		−1
		Age 60+		−3
2	Ever lived with a lover or significant other	Ever lived with lover for at least two years?		
		Yes		0
		No		1
3	Index nonsexual violence	No		0
	Any convictions	Yes		1
4	Prior nonsexual violence	No		0
	Any convictions	Yes		1
5	Prior sex offenses	Charges	Convictions	
		0	0	0
		1–2	1	1
		3–5	2–3	2
		6+	4+	3
6	Four or more prior sentencing dates (excluding index offense sentencing)	No		0
		Yes		1
7	Any convictions for noncontact sex offense	No		0
		Yes		1
8	Any unrelated victims	No		0
		Yes		1
9	Any stranger victims	No		0
		Yes		1
10	Any male victims	No		0
		Yes		1
	TOTAL SCORE	Add up scores from each individual risk item.		

(Continued)

TABLE 10.3 Continued

Interpretation of Total Score From Above

Nominal Risk Levels 2016 Version	Total Score	Risk Level
	−3 or −2	I. Very Low Risk
	−1 or 0	II. Below Average Risk
	1, 2, 3	III. Average Risk
	4, 5	IVa. Above Average Risk
	6+	IVb. Well Above Average Risk

Note: Adapted from Phenix et al. (2016).

EFFECTIVENESS OF SEX-OFFENDER ASSESSMENT TOOLS

A common method of assessing the effectiveness of predicting sexual recidivism is to test the tool with a sample of persons who have committed a sex crime. The assessment is scored for each person. Subsequently, the level of risk is compared to whether the offender actually recidivated. A statistical test is conducted, and the results are expressed as "area under the curve" (AUC). That number indicates the accuracy of the test in predicting sexual recidivism. For example, if a test places all those who do not actually recidivate in a low-risk category and places all those who do actually recidivate in a high-risk category, the measure is considered perfect. As indicated earlier, no test is perfect. Many of the tests have exceedingly high accuracy, as high as 0.9 AUC, where 1 corresponds to a perfect measure. The lowest AUC is 0, and any test that yields 0.5 or less is considered a failed test or, rather, no better than guessing. Thus, it does not accurately predict enough cases to warrant its use. Table 10.4 contains a summary of the results of a meta-analysis that assessed several sex-offender assessments (Tully et al., 2013). As noted in Table 10.4, most of the scales, on average, fall in the moderate range of predicting recidivism (Rice & Harris, 2005).

PSYCHOPATHY

Psychopathy is a critical factor for many assessment processes; some have regarded it as the most important clinical factor in forensic psychology and the criminal justice system (Larsen et al., 2020). Psychopathy refers to a personality disorder that includes antisocial behavior, callousness, lack of empathy toward others, a lack of remorse for harming others, and a lack of a conscience. It has been posited as a stable trait, one not subject to change, and some have even questioned whether those with psychopathy are amenable to treatment. In a systematic review, Larsen et al. (2020) did find those with high levels of psychopathy (as measured by the **Hare Psychopathy Checklist Revised**) were significantly more likely to commit subsequent criminal offenses, yet it did not have any bearing on treatment outcomes or predict a lack of conscience. The **Hare Psychopathy Checklist Revised (PCL-R)** and **Levenson Self-Report Scale of Psychopathy** are discussed next.

A clinician administers the PCL-R. The clinician conducts a semi-structured interview with the individual and relies on a checklist of 20 items. The clinician provides a score of 0, 1,

TABLE 10.4 Summary of Actuarial Assessment Tools' Effectiveness

Assessment	Number of Studies Conducted	AUC Range	AUC Average
Static-99	30	0.57–0.92	0.69
RRASOR	13	0.42–0.77	0.69
SORAG	9	0.67–0.77	0.68
RM2000/S	8	0.58–0.76	0.67
Static-2002	7	0.67–0.76	0.70
SVR-20	5	0.59–0.83	0.70
MnSOST-R	5	0.59–0.71	0.64
SACJ-Min	1	0.67	0.67

Note: This chart was developed and based on several sources, including Tully et al. (2013) and Hanson and Thornton (2000).

or 2 to each item, depending on the interviewee's response. Given that the clinician chooses which score to assign to responses, the clinician should be well trained with appropriate credentials for performing psychological examinations (Hare, 1991).

The first factor measures personality characteristics of psychopathy and includes an interpersonal facet and an affective facet. "Interpersonal" refers to a person's ability to communicate with others. This includes the following components: glibness (i.e., superficial charm), grandiose sense of self-worth, pathological lying, and cunningness or manipulativeness. The second facet, "affect," refers to a person's display of emotional states. This includes lack of remorse or guilt, emotional shallowness, callousness or lack of empathy, and failure to accept responsibility for one's own actions (Hare, 1991).

The second factor measures antisocial behavior and includes the third and fourth facets. The third facet includes lifestyle. The lifestyle facet includes a need for stimulation or a proneness to boredom, a parasitic lifestyle (living off of someone else's work, wealth, etc.), lack of realistic or long-term goals, irresponsibility, and impulsivity. The fourth facet reflects antisocial factors and includes poor behavioral control, early behavioral problems, juvenile delinquency, revocation of conditional release, and criminal versatility (Hare, 1991).

In addition to the four facets, a few other items are also included in the checklist: successive, short-term marital relationships and promiscuous sexual behavior. All of these items are relied upon for a clinician to assess the degree of psychopathy (Hare, 1991).

The Levenson Self-Report Scale of Psychopathy was developed in 1995 by Michael Levenson. The scale includes 26 items in a self-report survey (Levenson et al., 1995). For each item, an individual responds to what extent they agrees with the item, from agree to disagree, on a five-point scale with a "neutral" option in the middle. A sample of some of the items is presented in Table 10.5.

The scores are totaled for a final score between one and five on primary and secondary psychopathy, where primary refers to the emotional aspects of psychopathy and secondary refers to antisocial aspects of psychopathy.

An example of a person who has committed a sex crime who exhibited psychopathic traits is described in excerpts from a news article below:

TABLE 10.5 Sample Items From the Levenson Self-Report Scale of Psychopathy

- Success is based on survival of the fittest; I am not concerned about the losers.
- My main purpose in life is getting as many goodies as I can.
- I let others worry about higher values; my main concern is with the bottom line.
- People who are stupid enough to get ripped off usually deserve it.
- When I get frustrated, I often let off steam by blowing my top.
- In today's world, I feel justified in doing anything I can get away with to succeed.
- I don't plan anything far in advance.
- Making a lot of money is my most important goal.
- I quickly lose interest in tasks I start.
- Looking out for myself is my top priority.
- I often admire a clever scam.

Note: Adapted from Levenson (1995).

> Serial sex offender and convicted killer William Chandler Shrubsall is still too dangerous to be released from prison, the Parole Board of Canada decided ... "You are noted to be able to camouflage your deviant behaviours," the parole board wrote ... Mr. Shrubsall used a bat to attack a clerk in a Halifax waterfront store during a robbery ... Mr. Shrubsall beat, robbed and sexually assaulted a 21-year-old student in a Tower Road driveway. He repeatedly smashed her face on the asphalt. That woman's injuries were so severe that she required surgery to have her contact lens removed ... He was also found guilty of aggravated sexual assault—choking and confining a 26-year-old woman he'd met at a Halifax nightclub in June 1998 ... "You admit to being extremely sensitive to slights, especially slights by females with whom you have a romantic interest," the parole documents said. "You admit to low self-esteem and take criticism as a personal attack ... It was noted that you lacked empathy with your primary focus tending to be your own victimization. Of note, you indicated you were willing to forgive your mother and 'didn't know how.'"
>
> (The Chronicle Herald, 2014, n.p.)

The offender in this description adheres to many of the criteria of psychopathy: lack of empathy, impulsivity, low self-esteem, and extensive criminal behavior.

TREATMENT OF PERSONS WHO HAVE COMMITTED A SEX CRIME

The treatment of persons who have committed a sex crime has changed over time; emphasis has been placed on different theories during the past several decades. Here, we will discuss several types of treatment that have existed over time. Currently, ***cognitive-behavioral therapy*** is the most common type of treatment (Moster et al., 2008). Here, we discuss developments that led to cognitive-behavioral therapy to provide an understanding of the many elements that comprise it.

History of Treatment Developments

It should be noted that although those who have committed a sex crime are different and various theoretical models have been applied to various groups (e.g., rapists vs. child molesters), many of the treatment efforts involve one broad type of treatment. Cognitive-behavioral treatment is a broad type of treatment that allows for variation among sex-offender clients. For example, ***cognitive distortions*** are found to exist among all types of persons who have committed a sex crime, but the kinds of distortions vary among such offenders. For rapists, cognitive distortions include rape myths. These include: "no" means "yes," or if a girl dresses a certain way, she must want sex. For child molesters, however, the cognitive distortion may be that the child was acting sexually and wants to have sex. Cognitive-behavioral therapy allows a therapist to focus on cognitive distortions, in general, as well as on specific ones as they arise in the context of therapy sessions.

A brief overview of the assessments and treatment developments is presented in Figure 10.1. It should be noted that all of the developments, with the exception of treatment based on medical procedures (hormonal response and castration), comprise today's cognitive-behavioral therapy. Phallometric tests, specifically, are used primarily for assessment purposes. Each of the remaining treatment developments is discussed below along with the elements that make up today's cognitive-behavioral treatment approach.

Responses to persons who have committed a sex crime in the 1940s were based on a medical model (Terry, 2013). It was assumed that disease, rather than the choice made by a person (i.e., free will), was the root cause of committing a sex crime (Terry, 2013). The first hormonal-response treatment (chemical castration) was used in 1940 when one incarcerated person who had committed a sex crime was given stilboestrol, a type of estrogen (Dunn, 1940). These types of medications are known as anti-androgens, testosterone-reducing medications. It was considered relatively successful but was not widely implemented due to the negative side effects, which included feminization (Bowden, 1991). Later, other drugs (e.g., cyproterone acetate and medroxyprogesterone acetate) were used to reduce libido and are still used today.

Whether chemical castration is effective for persons who have committed a sex crime is difficult to determine. Based on a thorough review of the literature, several researchers acknowledge that such treatment likely reduces sexual desire and sexual behavior (Rice &

1940s & 1950s	1960s	1970s	1980s	1990s	2000s +
• Hormonal responses • Behavioral therapy	• Surgical castration • Phallometric tests	• Focus on cognitive processes • Social skills training • Addressing cognitive distortions	• Relapse training • Social-learning skills • Cognitive restructuring • Victim empathy	• Polygraph • Cognitive-behavioral therapy	• Risk–need–responsivity model • Trauma-informed care

FIGURE 10.1 History of Treatment of Persons Who Have Committed a Sex Offense.

Harris, 2011). What is not known, however, is whether this treatment reduces recidivism among persons who have committed a sex crime. As noted by these researchers, "Good evidence is sorely lacking. . . . Much more research is needed before . . . [chemical castration] has a sufficient scientific basis to be relied upon as a principal component of sex offender treatment" (p. 315).

Castration can involve either chemical castration (as discussed earlier) or surgical castration. This type of treatment is based on a biological premise that if a person cannot maintain an erection, he will not be able to commit a sex crime that involves penetration (Mancini, 2014). It is also based on the logic that a reduction in sexual urges will lead to reduced recidivism among known offenders (Mancini, 2014). It is based on several assumptions that do not have complete empirical support.

First, it is assumed that only adult men commit sex crimes. As noted in Chapter 7, women and juveniles comprise a small yet noteworthy portion of persons who have committed a sex crime. Second, it is assumed that forcible rape is the most common type of sex crime (Mancini, 2014). Statistics, however, show that other offenses make up a substantial portion of sex crimes (Federal Bureau of Investigation, 2014). These include child-pornography offenses and other types of victimization, including fondling (Terry, 2006). Third, it is assumed that sex crimes are motivated by sexual desire (Mancini, 2014). It has been documented in the literature that those who sexually offend do so for reasons other than sexual desire. As noted in Chapter 3, several categories of rapists offend for reasons of power (Prentky et al., 1985). For such reasons, many organizations formally oppose the use of castration for persons who have committed a sex crime, including the Association for the Treatment of Sexual Abusers and the American Civil Liberties Union.

Surgical and chemical castrations are rare types of treatments or punishments for persons who have committed a sex crime. In the United States, as of 2019, six states allowed chemical castration: California, Florida, Iowa, Louisiana, Montana, and Wisconsin (Hignite, 2019). Subsequently, Alabama implemented a castration law, yet no offenders were castrated two years after it was enacted (Beck, 2021). Thus, as of 2021, seven states have a law allowing castration of sex offenders. News sources have reported that at least 15 persons who had committed a sex crime in California have undergone surgical castration as a way to avoid civil commitment, which requires incapacitation of persons who have committed a sex crime indefinitely (Sealy, 2014). Among other states, it is difficult to assess the actual number of offenders who have been castrated because there is no central database.

Several research studies have indicated that such offenders who have been castrated recidivate at lower levels than those who refused castration (Heim & Hursch, 1979; Stūrup, 1972). It is important to note, however, that being castrated does not eliminate sexual recidivism. One of the study participants sought and obtained testosterone, for example, and subsequently recidivated (Stūrup, 1972). This type of research is criticized on methodological grounds in that those who volunteer to be castrated may have more desire to cease sex offending than those who refuse, thus affecting the results of the study (Rice & Harris, 2005).

Behavioral Therapy

Behavioral psychologists' approach for persons who had committed a sex crime was largely based on Pavlov's conditioning model or Skinner's operant-conditioning model (Marshall & Laws, 2003), as discussed in Chapter 2. It was a popular form of treatment for a variety of psychological maladies from 1920 to 1960 (Marshall & Laws, 2003). An assumption during this time was that persons who have committed a sex crime were acting on their deviant sexual thoughts. An example of a behaviorist treatment for persons who had committed a sex crime would involve pairing an undesirable stimulus (noxious smell, induced vomiting, mild shock, etc.) with the deviant sexual act. This is known as **aversion therapy**. This type of therapy, however, has not ever been observed to lead to permanent changes in sexual behavior (Quinsey & Earls, 1990; Quinsey & Marshall, 1983).

Cognitive Processes

In the 1970s, cognitive processes began to make their way into sex-offender treatment that was once solely based on behaviorism (Marshall & Laws, 2003). An example of this is the modification of sexual fantasies (Abel & Blanchard, 1974). This could involve encouraging people to have sexual fantasies that involve age-appropriate partners and consensual, non-deviant thoughts. Other cognitive processes that emerged included social skills training and ways to address cognitive distortions (Terry, 2013), a **relapse prevention** plan, increased social learning skills that include **cognitive restructuring** (Beck & Weishaar, 1995), and development of victim empathy (Marshall & Laws, 2003). Many of these are used in today's cognitive-behavioral treatment and are discussed below.

Polygraph

A **polygraph** test, also known as a "lie detector test," does not directly detect lies necessarily but rather is a physiological measure of blood pressure, respiration patterns, and skin conductance (i.e., perspiration) to determine truthfulness (Rosenfeld, 1995). The ability of a polygraph test to accurately assess truthfulness has been questioned and is debated in the field (Rosky, 2012). Discussions of polygraph use among criminal justice professionals usually involve the possibility of "fooling" the machine (i.e., countermeasures) and also the inability to use the results in court proceedings (Committee to Review the Scientific Evidence on the Polygraph: National Research Council U.S., 2003; English et al., 2000).

In 2003, the National Academy of Sciences provided an executive summary of the usefulness of the polygraph exam (Committee to Review the Scientific Evidence on the Polygraph: National Research Council U.S., 2003). They noted there are many limitations of assessing the ability of the polygraph because many studies are based on mock situations and may not apply to real-world situations. For example, a mock situation is contrived such as asking someone to steal one of three items (paper clip, scissors, or pencil) and then asking them to lie when asked about which item they stole. The response to a contrived situation may not be the same as lying about a real-world situation. The National Academy of Sciences, however, concluded that "polygraph tests can discriminate lying from truth telling at rates well above chance, though well below perfection" (National Research Council, 2003, p. 4) They limit this conclusion to those who have not been trained to "fool the machine" (i.e., countermeasures) and to specific-incident polygraph exams.

The effectiveness of a polygraph exam depends on the examiner's experience level, verbal and nonverbal communication style, and style of engagement (Blasingame, 1998; Jensen et al., 2015). Other factors, such as the examinee's mental disorders, mental retardation, drug and alcohol use, and refusal to cooperate, can also affect the results of a polygraph exam (Jensen et al., 2015).

Although there are limits to the use of the polygraph, it can still be a valuable tool for criminal justice professionals working with persons who have committed a sex crime. An example of the usefulness of a polygraph test was seen in the abduction and murder of nine-year-old Jessica Lunsford in Florida. During the investigation, a person of interest and a registered sex offender, John Evander Couey, confessed *after* he had submitted to a polygraph test (Candiotti & Courson, 2005). Couey stated, "You don't need to tell me the results, I already know what they are, could I have the investigators come back in?" (Hawke, 2005, n.p.). He apologized to the investigators for wasting their time. The results of the polygraph were not reported in the news. This shows how simply having someone submit to a polygraph can gain truthful information.

Furthermore, the process of exposing someone to a polygraph test yields substantial information that would not have been gathered otherwise. Research has found that those exposed to a polygraph test are more likely to disclose information and more likely to cooperate with treatment (Gannon et al., 2014). The preparation for an exam also produces substantial information from the offenders. Research has found that as an individual prepares for a polygraph test by answering a series of questions, that person is more likely to disclose information to avoid deceit (Blasingame, 1998).

Polygraph testing is used for assessment, management (English, 2005), and as noted earlier, investigative purposes for persons who have committed a sex crime. One researcher identified five types of polygraph uses with persons who have committed a sex crime, and those are identified in Table 10.6.

Although the results of polygraph examinations are not generally admissible in a court of law, they can still be a valuable tool for criminal justice and treatment providers who work with persons who have committed a sex crime (English, 2005). Such offenders have honed their skills to deceive others (Salter, 2003). Gaining truthful information from them can prove to be a difficult task, and polygraph examinations can be an effective tool to help with this.

More recently, alternatives to the polygraph test have been recommended. Rather than measuring a physiological response during a structured question-and-answer session, measuring an individual's brain waves has been proposed as a superior method (Bashore & Rapp, 1993). Measuring brain waves, however, is not without criticism; it may not be superior to the traditional polygraph test (Rosenfeld, 1995). More research is needed to fully assess these two methods.

TABLE 10.6 Types of Polygraph Tests for Persons Who Have Committed a Sex Crime

1	Initial Sexual Offense Examination: Assess the type and extent of offenses committed. It can be used to resolve discrepancies in the information.
2	Sexual History Examination: Confirm an offender's report of their sexual history such as any victimizations and sexual experiences.
3	Compliance Examination: Determine compliance with treatment and/or probation or parole restrictions. It can be administered every 4 to 6 months or more frequently if needed. It can identify and deter high-risk behavior.
4	Parental Risk Assessment Polygraph Examination: Determine offender's risk to sexually offend against their own children.

Note: Adapted from English (2005).

Cognitive-Behavioral Therapy

Cognitive-behavioral therapy is typically a structured, short-term type of treatment (Beck, 1995). It is deeply rooted in behaviorism, cognitive therapy, and a combination of the two (Beck, 1995; González-Prendes & Resco, 2012). This type of therapy is used for a broad range of psychological disorders, including but not limited to depression, anxiety, and post-traumatic stress disorders. Additionally, it began to emerge in the late 1960s and is presently the most common type of treatment for persons who have committed a sex crime (Laws & Marshall, 2003).

Cognitive-behavioral therapy has been described by the National Alliance for the Mentally Ill (2012, n.p.) as "a form of treatment that focuses on examining the relationships between thoughts, feelings and behaviors." Individuals are encouraged to explore patterns of thinking that have led to self-destructive behavior, including committing sex crimes. The objective is for them to change their current thought patterns to reduce or eliminate undesirable behavior. The client and therapists actively work together (National Alliance for the Mentally Ill, 2012). The therapist is "problem-focused, and goal-directed in addressing the challenging symptoms" (n.p.). Thus, the therapist and client address specific problems (e.g., commission of sex crimes), and the therapist assists the client in selecting specific strategies for countering the thought process that leads to the behavior. Cognitive-behavioral therapy is an active intervention, and the client can expect to do homework outside of sessions with the therapist (National Alliance for the Mentally Ill, 2012).

Cognitive-behavioral therapy is based on three assumptions. First, it is assumed the client can access and be aware of cognitive processes that occur. This may require training and practice because the client may not be immediately able to access such information. Second, it is assumed that one's reaction to events is highly dependent upon one's thinking. Thus, if someone has had a negative experience with a given event or person in the past, they may avoid a similar situation, given the history. Third, it is assumed that the way one thinks and feels about a certain situation, event, or person can be identified. Those thoughts and feelings can then be modified and changed (Dobson & Dobson, 2009).

An example of these assumptions can be found easily in cognitive-behavior treatment for persons who have committed a sex crime. For example, an offender may have the belief that it is acceptable to view children as sexual objects. This can lead to perceiving a certain situation (e.g., children in bathing suits playing at a local swimming pool) as a cue to commit a sex crime. This type of thought may be formed from a person's past experiences with children. This type of thought is a cognitive distortion and can be targeted for change through a myriad of processes. For example, it can involve group therapy, where others confront the person with information to the contrary—children are not sexual objects and should not be targeted for a sex crime.

Cognitive-behavioral therapy programs vary widely in how they treat persons who have committed a sex crime (Terry, 2013). Many commonalities, however, also exist among them. Terry (2013) identified nine goals of cognitive-behavioral programs for persons who have committed a sex crime.

It is also critical when providing cognitive-behavioral therapy to persons known to have committed a sex crime that not only are the needs of the offender addressed but that the community is protected as well (Moster et al., 2008).

Cognitive-behavioral therapy for persons who have committed a sex crime can involve several areas of focus, including addressing cognitive distortions, learning to manage emotions, increasing interpersonal skills, addressing empathy deficits, reducing deviant sexual behavior, and ensuring **relapse prevention**, along with learning self-management skills (Moster et al., 2008). Cognitive distortions are false beliefs that support offending behaviors (Marshall et al., 1999). The rape myths discussed in Chapter 3 are cognitive distortions. An example of this includes the following: if a woman is dressed provocatively, she must want to have sex. Research has found that persons who have committed a sex crime often have cognitive distortions that justify or minimize their sex crimes (Blumenthal et al., 1999).

Through a process of cognitive restructuring, the therapist explains the role of the falsely held belief and provides the offender with information regarding how to correct it (Marshall et al., 1999). Subsequently, the offender distinguishes cognitive distortions from reality, paving the way for the offender to no longer have the cognitive distortion (Murphy, 1990). Group therapy also can be used during this process. Members of a group can evaluate an offender's false beliefs as they describe the sex crime in detail (Marshall et al., 1999).

Managing emotion is also a critical component of cognitive-behavioral therapy with persons who have committed a sex crime. Psychological well-being is positively related to how well one can cope with negative emotions and events (Endler & Parker, 1990). Offenders are asked to identify emotions that can lead to committing a sex crime. For some offenders, it may not be just negative emotions, but positive ones as well, that can lead to offending. For example, a positive event can lead to a sense of entitlement and subsequently lead to the commission of a sex crime (Howells et al., 2004). The therapist can draw a diagram of the offense cycle for the offender to identify the chain of events. Offenders are asked to be aware when they experience such emotions and be mindful of these as they occur (Moster et al., 2008).

With regard to interpersonal skills and persons who have committed a sex crime, areas such as intimacy, loneliness, attachment deficits, self-esteem, and relationships have been identified as of critical importance (Marshall et al., 1999; Moster et al., 2008). Researchers have theorized that interpersonal skills are directly affected by inadequate attachments formed in childhood (Marshall, 1989). Thus, communication skills are necessary to create and maintain intimate relationships with appropriate partners (Correctional Services of Canada, 1995). Topics addressed should include intimacy along with developing and maintaining appropriate relationships (Moster et al., 2008).

Empathy deficits should also be addressed in cognitive-behavioral therapy (Moster et al., 2008). Empathy refers to the ability to recognize another person's perspective by recognizing their emotions and having compassion for that person's feelings (Pithers, 1999). Researchers have hypothesized that when persons who have committed a sex crime empathize with their victims, future sex crimes are prevented (Fernandez & Marshall, 2003). Techniques to increase empathy include the use of videos, victim impact statements, and letter writing (to or from victim and offender; Moster et al., 2008). Videos can involve documentaries in which a victim has detailed their struggle with a sex crime. Victim impact statements are often provided during the criminal justice process and involve victims detailing how the offender's action affected their lives. Occasionally, victims write letters directly to the offender about their experience. The offender can share with group members and discuss their reactions to this letter.

Cognitive-behavioral therapy for persons who have committed a sex crime often involves addressing **deviant sexual behavior**, which is sexual behavior that involves children and/or violent sexual activities (Dougher, 1996). This is usually measured during the assessment process by using a plethysmograph or the AASI-3. Several techniques are available to reduce deviant sexual behavior. One example involves covert sensitization, which involves introducing a negative stimulus (e.g., noxious smell, electrical impulse, or simply imagining a negative feeling such as nausea) while engaging in deviant sexual behavior (Dougher, 1996).

A critical component to many cognitive-behavioral programs includes relapse prevention and self-management. The goal is to assist the offenders in maintaining behavioral changes through anticipation and use of coping strategies (Center for Sex Offender Management, 2000). Relapse prevention involves the development of a plan that identifies triggers and dangerous situations. Strategies are developed to avoid high-risk situations and to cope with them when they occur. For example, a child molester may be asked to babysit a friend's child. This is a high-risk situation for them, as they are sexually attracted to children. They can develop strategies for responses they may have to this type of situation, which may include telling the friend that they are not able to watch the child because they are not good with children or have a prior engagement.

Trauma-Informed Care

Relatively recently, there has been a shift toward incorporating ***trauma-informed care*** for treating persons who have committed a sex crime (Levenson et al., 2020). Trauma-informed care recognizes the complex causalities of why one would commit a sexual offense while squarely focusing on the recognition that most persons who commit a sexual offense were exposed to multiple ***Adverse Childhood Experiences (ACEs)*** such as exposure to violence, child maltreatment, and multiple forms of family dysfunction (Felitti et al., 1998; Levenson et al., 2020). Such childhood experiences affect those children throughout their entire lives. This includes their psychosocial functioning, ability to trust others, ability to form meaningful relationships, and their physical health.

Trauma-informed care recognizes the relationship between these Adverse Childhood Experiences and their subsequent maladaptive behaviors (e.g., committing a sexual offense) and assessing their treatment through this trauma-based lens (Levenson et al., 2020). Trauma-informed care is typically combined with a cognitive-behavioral lens, and such therapists work with their clients to assess their thoughts, feelings, and behaviors with the consideration of their early negative life events that shape who they are today. The clients, with the guidance of their therapists, help identify patterns of thinking that led to their abusive behavior and work to identify strategies for developing new skills to cope with stress as they occur in the clients' lives.

TREATMENT EFFECTIVENESS

A typical question one may ask about persons who have committed a sex crime and treatment is this: can persons who have committed a sex crime be "cured?" In general, those who treat persons who have committed a sex crime do not discuss them in terms of whether they can be "cured"—rather, they discuss treatment in terms of *management*. Similar to an alcoholic, who is not cured but rather can control their urges to consume alcohol, persons who have committed a sex crime are taught to resist the urges to commit a sex crime and place focus on developing and maintaining healthy relationships.

Assessing effectiveness is difficult, given the necessary methodological criteria needed (e.g., lengthy follow-ups and control groups are required). Studies to assess treatment are often constrained by those who drop out of treatment along with the problem that few persons who have committed a sex crime recidivate. Measuring recidivism is difficult because many sex crimes go undetected. Despite these constraints, researchers have conducted several meta-analyses to determine the effectiveness of treatment for persons who have committed a sex crime.

It is no surprise that many may believe that persons who have committed a sex crime cannot be effectively treated—as the research in the 1990s reported just that. One meta-analysis conducted in 1995 (Hall, 1995) reported that those in the treatment had higher sexual recidivism rates than those not treated. Just a few years later, in 1999, another meta-analysis found that those treated were slightly less likely than those not treated to sexually recidivate (Alexander, 1999). Hanson et al. (2002), in a meta-analysis of 43 studies, found those treated recidivated less compared to those not treated. More specifically, 17.5% of those who did not receive treatment sexually recidivated, whereas 11.1% of those treated sexually recidivated. Thus, the treatment led to an average of a 6% reduction in sexual recidivism.

More recently, Lösel and Schmucker (2005) in their meta-analysis concluded that "the last decade has shown a strong increase and more positive outcomes in evaluations of sex offender treatment" (p. 119). In their meta-analysis involving 22,181 subjects, the treated offenders sexually recidivated 6% less than those not treated. Although this may not seem like much of a difference, it translates into substantially less recidivism. A problem with sexual recidivism research is that so few of the offenders recidivate, often referred to as a low base-rate problem. Given that, one may ask what is the difference between 11.1% and 17.5%? The answer is that it means more than a third (37%) fewer individuals in the treatment group committed a further sexual offense compared to the nontreatment group, a significant difference. With regard to sex-offender treatment, cognitive-behavioral programs currently have the best outcome.

CONCLUSION

Given the heterogeneous nature of persons who have committed a sex crime, there is a need to determine their risk for sexual recidivism. A variety of assessment tools have been developed over the past several decades. One may ask whether there is a need for so many different types of assessment tools. One researcher recently noted that by relying on more than one assessment tool, prediction of risk is incrementally increased (Eher et al., 2011; Hanson & Thornton, 2000). Thus, sex-offender treatment providers often use a variety of assessment tools. Most of the treatment programs for persons who have committed a sex crime today are based on cognitive-behavioral therapy. More recently, this has been combined with trauma-informed care, which acknowledges that many persons who have committed a sex crime were exposed to multiple ACEs that affect their thoughts, feelings, and behaviors. The more recent assessments of cognitive-behavioral treatment for persons who have committed a sex crime reveal lower recidivism rates when compared to persons who have committed a sex crime who have not received such treatment.

REVIEW POINTS

- Risk factors for sexual recidivism among persons who have committed a sex crime are examined through the use of assessments, which typically rely on static (unchanging) and dynamic (changing) factors.
- The RNR Model is often applied to persons who have committed a sex crime and suggests applying the appropriate level of criminal justice and treatment response based on the person's level of need. It also focuses on criminogenic needs, that is, crime-causing factors that led to the commission of the sex crime.
- Common risk factors for assessments include demographics, prior offense history, and several psychosocial factors.
- Commonly used assessment tools for persons who have committed a sex crime include nonactuarial assessments (clinician judgment), assessments that include some objective measurement but do not provide cutoff scores (phallometric tests, AASI-3, SVR-20), and actuarial assessments (SACJ-Min, RRASOR, Static-99R, Static-2002, SORAG, VRAG, and MnSOST).
- Assessment tools do not perfectly predict recidivism, but most are in the moderate range of predicting recidivism.
- Psychopathy refers to a personality disorder that includes antisocial behavior, callousness, lack of empathy toward others, a lack of remorse for harming others, and a lack of a conscience.
- Many treatment developments (hormonal response, behavioral therapy, surgical castration, phallometric tests, focus on cognitive processes, social skills training, addressing cognitive distortions, relapse training, social learning skills, victim empathy, and the polygraph) were emphasized prior to today's use of cognitive-behavioral treatment.
- Cognitive-behavioral therapy is the most common type of treatment for persons who have committed a sex crime.
- Recently, there has been an acknowledgment of the high number of Adverse Childhood Experiences that persons who have committed a sex crime experienced; this had led to trauma-informed care.
- Persons who have committed a sex crime are not "cured" but rather managed to control their impulses. Those treated with cognitive-behavioral therapy recidivate at a lower rate than those not treated.

REFERENCES

Abel, G. G., & Blanchard, E. B. (1974). The role of fantasy in the treatment of sexual deviation. *Archives of General Psychiatry, 30*(4), 467–475. https://www.oi.org/10.1001/archpsyc.1974.01760100035007

Abel, G. G., Huffman, J., Warberg, B., & Holland, C. L. (1998). Visual reaction time and plethysmography as measures of sexual interest in child molesters. *Sexual Abuse: A Journal of Research and Treatment, 10*(2), 81–95. http://www.doi.org/1079-0632/98/0400

AbelScreening.(n.d.) AbelScreening. http://abelscreening.com/products/evaluation-treatment-planning/aasi-3/

Alexander, M. A. (1999). Sexual offender treatment efficacy revisited. *Sexual Abuse: A Journal of Research and Treatment, 11*(2), 101–116. https://www.doi.org/10.1177/107906329901100202

Andrews, D. A., & Bonta, J. (2006). *The psychology of criminal conduct* (4th ed.). Lexis/Nexis.

Bancroft, J. H. J., Jones, H. G., & Pullan, B. R. (1966). A simple transducer for measuring penile erection, with comments on its use in the treatment of sexual disorders. *Behaviour Research and Therapy, 4*(3), 239–241. https://www.doi.org/10.1016/0005-7967(66)90015-5

Bashore, T. T., & Rapp, P. E. (1993). Are there alternatives to traditional polygraph procedures. *Psychological Bulletin, 113*(1), 3–22. https://www.doi.org/10.1037/0033-2909.113.1.3

Beck, C. (2021). Chemical castration law hasn't been used since 2019 enactment. *Alabama Daily News*. https://www.annistonstar.com/news/state/chemical-castration-law-hasnt-been-used-since-2019-enactment/article_bb07d0b4-cef6-11eb-ab55-1346251959d3.html

Beck, J. (1995). *Cognitive therapy: Basics and beyond*. Guilford.

Beck, A., & Harrison, P. M. (2008). *Sexual victimization in state and federal prisons reported by inmates, 2007* [Special report]. Bureau of Justice Statistics. http://www.bjs.gov/content/pub/pdf/svsfpri07.pdf

Beck, A. T., & Weishaar, M. E. (1995). Cognitive therapy. In R. J. Corsoni & D. Wedding (Eds.), *Current psychotherapies* (5th ed., pp. 229–261). F. E. Peacock Publishers.

Beech, A. R., Fisher, D. D., & Thornton, D. (2003). Risk assessment of sex offenders. *Professional Psychology: Research and Practice, 34*(4), 339. https://www.doi.org/10.1037/0735-7028.34.4.339

Blasingame, G. D. (1998). Suggested clinical uses of polygraphy in community-based sexual offender treatment programs. *Sexual Abuse: A Journal of Research and Treatment, 10*(1), 37–45. https://www.doi.org/10.1023/A:1022154614885

Blasingame, G. D. (2014). Overcoming denial among sexual offenders with the use of the Abel assessment for sexual interest and polygraph examinations. https://ccoso.org/newsletter/overcoming-denial-among-sexual-offenders-use-abel-assessment-sexual-interest-and

Blumental, S., Gudjonsson, G., & Burns, J. (1999). Cognitive distortions and blame attribution in sex offenders against adults and children. *Child Abuse and Neglect, 23*(2), 129–143. https://www.doi.org/10.1016/S0145-2134(98)00117-3

Boer, D. S., Hart, P., Kropp, P., & Webster, C. (1997). *Manual for the Sexual Violence Risk-20*. The British Columbia Institute Against Family Violence and Mental Health, Law, and Policy Institute at Simon Fraser University.

Bonta, J., & Andrews, D. A. (2007). *Risk-Need-Responsivity Model for offender assessment and treatment* [User Report No. 2007–06]. Public Safety Canada.

Bowden, P. (1991). Treatment: Use, abuse and consent. *Criminal Behaviour and Mental Health, 1*(2), 130–136.

Candiotti, S., & Courson, P. (2005, March 20). Suspect in 9-year-old's death booked into Florida jail. *CNN*. http://www.cnn.com/2005/US/03/19/missing.girl/

Center for Sex Offender Management. (2000). *Myths and facts about sex offenders*. U.S. Department of Justice, Office of Justice Programs.

Center for Sex Offender Management. (2007). *The importance of assessment in sex offender management: An overview of key principles and practices*. Government Printing Office.

Committee to Review the Scientific Evidence on the Polygraph: National Research Council U.S. (2003). *The polygraph and lie detection—Evaluation*. The National Academic Press.

Correctional Services of Canada. (1995). *Sex offenders and programs in CSC*. http://www.csc-scc.gc.ca/text/pa/cop-prog/cp-eval-eng.shtml

Craig, L. A., Browne, K. D., & Stringer, I. (2004). Comparing sex offender risk assessment measures on a UK sample. *International Journal of Offender Therapy and Comparative Criminology, 48*(1), 7–27. https://www.doi.org/10.1177/0306624X03257243

Dickson, E. J. (2014, November 4). "Virtual reality penis sensors" are being used to monitor sex offenders. *Daily Dot*. http://www.dailydot.com/technology/virtual-reality-penis-ring/

Dobson, D., & Dobson, K. S. (2009). *Evidence-based practice of cognitive-behavioral therapy*. Guilford Press.

Dougher, M. J. (1996). In S. H. R. Cellini (Ed.), *The sex offender: Corrections, treatment and legal practice* (pp. 15.11–15.18). Civic Research Institute.

Dunn, C. W. (1940). Stilbestrol-induced gynecomastia in the male. *Journal of the American Medical Association, 115*(26), 2263–2264. https://www.doi.org/10.1001/jama.1940.02810520025006

Eher, R., Schilling, F., Haubner-Maclean, T., & Rettenberger, M. (2011). Dynamic risk assessment in sexual offenders using STABLE-2000 and the STABLE-2007: An investigation of predictive and incremental validity. *Sexual Abuse: A Journal of Research and Treatment, 24*(1), 5–28. https://www.doi.org/10.1177/1079063211403164

Endler, N. S., & Parker, D. A. (1990). Multidimensional assessment of coping: A critical evaluation. *Journal of Personality and Social Psychology, 58*(5), 844–854. https://www.doi.org/10.1037//0022-3514.58.5.844

English, K. (2005). To tell the truth: The latest in polygraph research. [Paper presentation]. Illinois Association for the Treatment of Sexual Abuse, Normal, IL.

English, K., Jones, L., Pasini-Hill, D., Patrick, D., & Cooley-Towell, S. (2000). *The value of polygraph testing in sex offender management*. U.S. Department of Justice, National Institute of Justice.

Federal Bureau of Investigation. (2014). *National Incident-Based Reporting System: 2012*. Government Printing Office. https://www.fbi.gov/about-us/cjis/ucr/nibrs/2012/data-tables.

Felitti, V. J., Anda, R. F., Nordenberg, D., Williamson, D. F., Spitz, A. M., Edwards, V., & Marks, J. S. (1998). Relationship of childhood abuse and household dysfunction to many of the leading causes of death in adults: The Adverse Childhood Experiences (ACE) Study. *American Journal of Preventive Medicine, 14*(4), 245–258. https://www.doi.org/10.1016/S0749-3797(98)00017-8

Fernandez, Y. M., & Marshall, W. L. (2003). Victim empathy, social self-esteem, and psychopathy in rapists. *Sexual Abuse: A Journal of Research and Treatment, 15*(1), 11–26. https://www.doi.org/10.1177/107906320301500102

Freund, K. (1963). A laboratory method for diagnosing predominance of homo- or heteroerotic interest in the male. *Behaviour Research and Therapy, 1*(1), 85–93. https://www.doi.org/10.1016/0005-7967(63)90012-3

Gannon, T. A., Wood, J. L., Pina, A., Tyler, N., Barnoux, M. F., & Vasquez, E. A. (2014). An evaluation of mandatory polygraph testing for sexual offenders in the United Kingdom. *Sexual Abuse: A Journal of Research and Treatment, 26*(2), 178–203. https://www.doi.org/10.1177/1079063213486836

Goggin, C. E. (1994). *Clinical versus actuarial prediction: A meta-analysis*. University of New Brunswick.

González-Prendes, A. A., & Resco, S. M. (2012). Cognitive-behavioral therapy. In S. Ringel & J. Brandell (Eds.), *Trauma: Contemporary directions in theory, practice, and research* (pp. 14–40). Sage Publications, Inc.

Gottfredson, S. D., & Moriarty, L. J. (2006). Clinical versus actuarial judgments in criminal justice decisions: Should one replace the other. *Federal Probation, 15*(2), 15–18.

Hall, G. C. N. (1995). Sexual offender recidivism revisited: A meta-analysis of recent treatment studies. *Journal of Consulting and Clinical Psychology, 63*(5), 802–809. https://www.doi.org/10.1037//0022-006x.63.5.802

Hanson, R. K. (1997). The development of a brief actuarial risk scale for sexual offense recidivism [User Report No. 1997-04]. Department of the Solicitor General of Canada.

Hanson, R. K. (2006). Long-term follow-up studies are difficult: Comment on Langevin et al. (2004). *Canadian Journal of Criminology and Criminal Justice, 48*(1), 103–105.

Hanson, R. K. (2009). The psychological assessment of risk for crime and violence. *Canadian Psychology, 50*(3), 172–182. https://www.doi.org/10.1037/a0015726

Hanson, K., & Bussière, M. T. (1996). *Predictors of sexual offender recidivism: A meta-analysis* (1996–04). Department of the Solicitor General of Canada.

Hanson, R. K., & Bussière, M. T. (1998). Predicting relapse: A meta-analysis of sexual offender recidivism studies. *Journal of Consulting and Clinical Psychology, 66*(2), 348–362. https://www.doi.org/10.1037//0022-006x.66.2.348

Hanson, R. K., Gordon, A., Harris, A. J. R., Marques, J. K., Murphy, W. D., Quinsey, V. L., & Seto, M. C. (2002). First report of the collaborative outcome data project on the effectiveness of psychological treatment for sex offenders. *Sexual Abuse: A Journal of Research and Treatment, 14*(2), 169–194. https://www.doi.org/10.1177/107906320201400207

Hanson, R. K., Helmus, L., & Thornton, D. (2010). Predicting recidivism amongst sexual offenders: A multi-site study of Static-2002. *Law and Human Behavior, 34*(3), 198–211. https://www.doi.org/10.1007/s10979–009–9180–1

Hanson, R. K., & Morton-Bourgon, K. E. (2005). The characteristics of persistent sexual offenders: A meta-analysis of recidivism studies. *Journal of Consulting and Clinical Psychology, 73*(6), 1154–1163. https://www.doi.org/10.1037/0022-006X.73.6.1154

Hanson, R. K., & Thornton, D. (2000). Improving risk assessments for sex offenders: A comparison of three actuarial scales. *Law and Human Behavior, 24*(1), 119–136. https://www.doi.org/10.1023/A:1005482921333

Hanson, R. K., & Thornton, D. (2003). *Notes on the development of Static-2002* [User Report No. 2003–01]. Department of the Solicitor General of Canada. https://www.publicsafety.gc.ca/cnt/rsrcs/pblctns/nts-dvlpmnt-sttc/nts-dvlpmnt-sttc-eng.pdf

Hare, R. (1991). *The Hare psychopathy checklist-revised*. Multi-Health Systems.

Hart, S. D., & Boer, D. P. (2020). Structured professional judgment guidelines for sexual violence risk assessment: The sexual violence risk-20 (SVR-20) versions 1 and 2 and risk for sexual violence protocol (RSVP). In K. S. Douglas & R. K. Otto (Eds.), *Handbook of violence risk assessment* (pp. 322–358). Routledge.

Harris, A., Phenix, A., Hanson, K., & Thornton, D. (2003). *STATIC-99 coding rules revised—2003*. http://www.static99.org/pdfdocs/static-99-coding-rules_e.pdf

Hawke, C. (2005, March 18). Cops: Man admits killing Fla. girl. *CBS News*. http://www.cbsnews.com/news/cops-man-admits-killing-fla-girl/

Hefley, D. (2014, June 6). Man released from jail without bail again a molestation suspect. *Herald Net*. http://www.heraldnet.com/article/20140606/NEWS01/140609502

Heim, N., & Hursch, C. J. (1979). Castration for sex offenders: Treatment or punishment? A review and critique of recent European literature. *Archives of Sexual Behavior, 8*(3), 281–304. https://www.doi.org/10.1007/BF01541244

Hignite, L. R. (2019). Chemical castration. *The Encyclopedia of Women and Crime*, 1–3. https://www./doi.org/10.1002/9781118929803.ewac0047

Holland, K. J., Rabelo, V. C., & Cortina, L. M. (2016). Collateral damage: Military sexual trauma and help-seeking barriers. *Psychology of Violence, 6*(2), 253. http://dx.doi.org/10.1037/a0039467

Howells, K., Day, A., & Wright, S. (2004). Affect, emotions and sex offending. *Psychology, Crime & Law, 10*(2), 179–195. https://www.doi.org/10.1080/10683160310001609988

Jensen, T. M., Shafer, K., Roby, C. Y., & Roby, J. L. (2015). Sexual history disclosure polygraph outcomes do juvenile and adult sex offenders differ? *Journal of Interpersonal Violence, 30*(6), 928–944. https://www.doi.org/10.1177/0886260514539766

Kelley, S. M., Ambroziak, G., Thornton, D., & Barahal, R. M. (2020). How do professionals assess sexual recidivism risk? An updated survey of practices. *Sexual Abuse: A Journal of Research and Treatment, 32*(1), 3–29. https://www.doi.org/10.1177/1079063218800474

Lanterman, J. L., Boyle, D. J., & Ragusa-Salerno, L. M. (2014). Sex offender risk assessment, sources of variation, and the implications of misuse. *Criminal Justice and Behavior, 41*(7), 822–843. https://www.doi.org/10.1177/0093854813515237

Larsen, R. R., Jalava, J., & Griffiths, S. (2020). Are Psychopathy Checklist (PCL) psychopaths dangerous, untreatable, and without conscience? A systematic review of the empirical evidence. *Psychology, Public Policy, and Law, 26*(3), 297–311. https://www.doi.org/10.1037/law0000239

Laws, D. R., & Marshall, W. L. (2003). A brief history of behavioral and cognitive behavioral approaches to sexual offenders: Part 1. Early developments. *Sexual Abuse: A Journal of Research and Treatment, 15*(2), 75–92. https://www.doi.org/10.1177/107906320301500201

Lee, S. C., & Hanson, R. K. (2017). Similar predictive accuracy of the Static-99R risk tool for white, Black, and Hispanic sex offenders in California. *Criminal Justice and Behavior, 44*(9), 1125–1140. https://www.doi.org/10.1177/0093854817711477

Levenson, J. S., Willis, G. M., & Prescott, D. S. (2020). Evidence-based practice and the role of trauma-informed care in sex offending treatment. In H. Swaby, B. Winder, R. Lievesley, K. Hocken, N. Blagden, & P. Banyard (Eds.), *Sexual Crime and Trauma*. https://www.doi.org/10.1007/978-3-030-49068-3_8

Levenson, M. (1995). Levenson Self-Report Scale of Psychopathy. http://personality-testing.info/tests/LSRP.php

Levenson, M., Kiehl, K., & Fitzpatrick, C. (1995). Assessing psychopathic attributes in a non-institutionalized population. *Journal of Personality and Social Psychology, 68*(1), 151–158. https://www.doi.org/ 10.1037//0022-3514.68.1.151

Lösel, F., & Schmucker, M. (2005). The effectiveness of treatment for sexual offenders: A comprehensive meta-analysis. *Journal of Experimental Criminology, 1*(1), 117–146. https://www.doi.org/10.1007/s11292-004-6466-7

Mancini, C. (2014). *Sex crime, offenders, and society: A critical look at sexual offending and policy*. Carolina Academic Press.

Mann, R., Hanson, R. K., & Thornton, D. (2010). Assessing risk for sexual recidivism: Some proposals on the nature of psychologically meaningful risk factors. *Sexual Abuse: A Journal of Research and Treatment, 22*(2), 191–217. https://www.doi.org/10.1177/1079063210366039

Marshall, W. (1989). Intimacy, loneliness, and sexual offenders. *Behavior Research and Therapy, 27*(5), 491–503. https://www.doi.org/ 10.1016/0005-7967(89)90083-1

Marshall, W. L. (2018). A brief history of psychological theory, research, and treatment with adult male sex offenders. *Current Psychiatry Reports, 20*(8), 1–8. https://www.doi.org/10.1007/s11920-018-0920-0

Marshall, W. L., Anderson, D., & Fernandez, Y. (1999). *Cognitive behavioural treatment for sexual offenders*. Wiley.

Marshall, W. L., & Fernandez, Y. M. (2000). Phallometric testing with sexual offenders: Limits to its value. *Clinical Psychology Review, 20*(7), 807–822. https://www.doi.org/10.1016/S0272-7358(99)00013-6

Marshall, W. L., & Laws, D. R. (2003). A brief history of behavioral and cognitive behavioral approaches to sexual offender treatment: Part 2. The modern era. *Sexual Abuse: A Journal of Research and Treatment, 15*(2), 93–120. https://www.doi.org/10.1177/107906320301500202

Minnesota Department of Corrections. (2012). *The Minnesota Sex Offender Screening Tool-3.1 (MNSOST-3.1): An update to the MnSOST-3*. Minnesota Department of Corrections.

Monahan, J. (1996). Violence prediction: The past twenty and the next twenty years. *Criminal Justice and Behavior, 23*(1), 107–120. https://www.doi.org/10.1177/0093854896023001008

Moster, A., Wnuck, D. W., & Jeglic, E. L. (2008). Cognitive behavioral therapy interventions with sex offenders. *Journal of Correctional Health Care, 14*(2), 109–121. https://www.doi.org/10.1177/1078345807313874

Murphy, W. D. (1990). Assessment and modification of cognitive distortions in sex offenders. In W. L. Marshall, D. R. Laws, & H. E. Barbaree (Eds.), *Handbook of sexual assault: Issues, theories, and treatment of the offender* (pp. 331–342). Plenum Press.

Myer, A. J. (2019). Examining the predictive validity of the Static-99R on Native American sex offenders. *Justice Evaluation Journal, 2*(2), 181–195. https://www.doi.org/10.1080/24751979.2019.1636614

National Alliance for the Mentally Ill. (2012, July). *Cognitive behavioral therapy?* http://www.nami.org/Content/NavigationMenu/Inform_Yourself/About_Mental_Illness/About_Treatments_and_Supports/Cognitive_Behavioral_Therapy1.htm

National Institute of Corrections. (n.d.). Offender assessment/screening: Static-99/Static-99R. *The United States Department of Justice*. http://nicic.gov/library/027582

National Research Council. (2003). The polygraph and lie detection. https://www.nap.edu/read/10420/chapter/1

Phenix, A., Doren, D., Helmus, L., Hanson, R. K., & Thornton, D. (2008). *Coding rules for Static-2002*. Public Safety Canada.

Phenix, A., Hernandez, Y., Harrison, A. J. R., Helmus, L., Hanson, R. K., & Thornton, D. (2016). *Static-99R coding rules revised 2016*. Public Safety Canada. http://www.static99.org/pdfdocs/Coding_manual_2016_v2.pdf

Phillips, D. (2019, September 10). Six men are speaking out to break the silence. *New York Times*. https://www.nytimes.com/interactive/2019/09/10/us/men-military-sexual-assault.html

Pithers, W. D. (1999). Empathy: Definition, enhancement, and relevance to the treatment of sexual abusers. *Journal of Interpersonal Violence, 14*(3), 257–284. https://www.doi.org/10.1177/088626099014003004

Pras, E., Wouda, J., Willemse, P. H., Zwart, M., de Vries, E. G., & Schultz, W. C. (2003). Pilot study of vaginal plethysmography in women treated with radiotherapy for gynecological cancer. *Gynecology Oncology, 91*(3), 540–546. https://www.doi.org/10.1016/j.ygyno.2003.08.002

Prentky, R. A., Cohen, M., & Segnorn, T. (1985). Development of a rational taxonomy for the classification of rapists: The Massachusetts treatment center system. *Bulletin of the American Academy of Psychiatry and the Law, 18*(1), 79–83. http://www.ncbi.nlm.nih.gov/pubmed/3995189

Quinsey, V. L., & Earls, C. M. (1990). The modification of sexual preferences. In W. L. Marshall, D. R. Laws, & H. E. Barbaree (Eds.), *Handbook of sexual assault: Issues, theories and treatment of the offender* (pp. 279–295). Plenum Press.

Quinsey, V. L., Harris, G. T., Rice, M. E., & Cormier, C. A. (2006). *Violent offenders: Appraising and managing risk* (2nd ed.). American Psychological Association.

Quinsey, V. L., & Marshall, W. L. (1983). Procedures for reducing inappropriate sexual arousal: An evaluation review. In J. G. Greer & I. R. Stuart (Eds.), *The sexual aggressor: Current perspectives on treatment* (pp. 267–289). Van Nostrand Reinhold.

Rice, M. E., & Harris, G. T. (2005). Comparing effect sizes in follow-up studies: ROC area, Cohen's d, and r. *Law and Human Behavior, 29*(5), 615–620. https://www.doi.org/10.1007/s10979-005-6832-7

Rice, M. E., & Harris, G. T. (2011). Is androgen deprivation therapy effective in the treatment of sex offenders? *Psychology, Public Policy and Law, 17*(2), 315–332. https://www.doi.org/10.1037/a0022318

Rosenfeld, J. P. (1995). Alternative views of Bashore and Rapp's (1993) alternatives to traditional polygraphy: A critique. *Psychological Bulletin, 117*(1), 59–166.

Rosky, J. W. (2012). The (f)utility of post-conviction polygraph testing. *Sexual Abuse: A Journal of Research and Treatment, 25*(3), 259–281. https://www.doi.org/10.1177/1079063212455668

Salter, A. C. (2003). *Predators: Pedophiles, rapists, and other sex offenders*. Basic Books.

Sandbukt, I. J., Skardhamar, T., Kristoffersen, R., & Friestad, C. (2020). Testing the Static-99R as a global screen for risk of sex crime recidivism in a Norwegian routine sample. *Sexual Abuse: A Journal of Research and Treatment*. Advance online publication. https://www.doi.org/10.1177/1079063220951194

Sealy, G. (2014, March 2). Some sex offenders opt for castration. *ABC News* http://abcnews.go.com/US/story?id=93947

Smid, W. J., Kamphuis, J. H., Wever, E. C., & Van Beek, D. J. (2014). A comparison of the predictive properties of nine sex offender risk assessment instruments. *Psychological Assessment*. Advance online publication. https://www.doi.org/10.1037/a0036616

Stūrup, G. K. (1972). Castration: The total treatment. In H. L. P. Resnick & M. E. Wolfgang (Eds.), *Sexual behaviors: Social, clinical, and legal aspects* (pp. 361–382). Little, Brown and Company.

Terry, K. J. (2006). *Sexual offenses and offenders: Theory, practice, and policy*. Wadsworth.

Terry, K. J. (2013). *Sexual offenses and offenders: Theory, practice and policy*, 2nd ed. Wadsworth Cengage Learning.

The Chronicle Herald. (2014, November 18). Sex offender, killer William Shrubsall denied parole again. http://www.thechronicleherald.ca/metro/1251813-sex-offender-william-shrubsall-denied-parole-again

Thornton, D. (2007). *Scoring guide for risk matrix 2000.9/SVC*. http://www.birmingham.ac.uk/Documents/college-les/psych/RM2000scoringinstructions.pdf

Tong, D. (2007). The penile plethysmograph, Abel Assessment for Sexual Interest, and MSI-II: Are they speaking the same language? *The American Journal of Family Therapy, 35*(3), 187–2007. https://www.doi.org/ 10.1080/01926180701226762

Tully, R. J., Chou, S., & Browne, K. D. (2013). A systematic review on the effectiveness of sex offender risk assessment tools in predicting sexual recidivism of adult male sex offenders. *Clinical Psychology Review, 33*(2), 287–316. https://www.doi.org/10.1016/j.cpr.2012.12.002

DEFINITIONS

ABEL Assessment for Sexual Interest-3™ (AASI-3): An assessment tool for persons who have committed a sex crime that measures visual reaction time to pictures for the purpose of determining a person's deviant sexual interests

Actuarial Assessments: A method for determining whether an event (i.e., recidivism) will occur based on known factors that relies on the statistical analysis of an objective measure

Adverse Childhood Experiences (ACEs): Ten potentially traumatic events that occur in childhood (0–17 years) that are highly correlated with chronic physical, mental, and emotional health issues in adulthood

Aversion Therapy: A type of behavioral therapy that involves pairing an undesirable stimulus with undesirable behavior (deviant sexual act) for the purpose of eliminating the undesirable behavior

Behavioral Therapy: A type of therapy based on Pavlov's conditioning model or Skinner's operant-conditioning model that focuses on stimuli present and the responses produced

Castration: The physical removal of the testes (physical castration) or providing a medication that reduces testosterone (chemical castration) for the purpose of reducing sexual recidivism

Cognitive-Behavioral Therapy: A type of therapy based on behaviorism and cognitive therapy that focuses on the connections among feelings, thoughts, and actions that is used for a broad range of psychological disorders, including but not limited to depression, anxiety, posttraumatic stress disorders, and sex crimes—the most common type of therapy used for persons who have committed a sex crime

Cognitive Distortions: Minimizing or denying the dangerousness of a behavior, justifying it, and relieving the offender of responsibility (e.g., children need to be taught about sex; children are seductive; the child is too young to know what is happening)

Cognitive Restructuring: A key component of cognitive-behavioral therapy that involves a therapist explaining the role of a falsely held belief and provides the offender with information regarding how to correct it

Criminogenic Needs: Factors that cause crime such as young age, sex, antisocial attitudes and behaviors, delinquent peers, and so on

Deviant Sexual Behavior: Sexual behavior that involves children and/or violent behaviors.

Dynamic Factors: Factors that will change throughout one's life depending on one's situation, including attitude toward work and employment status

Empirically-Based Approaches: Approaches used for assessment tool development and treatment approaches that have implemented the highest scientific standards of conducting research, which typically involves a control group and experimental group to determine differences between the two groups

Levenson Self-Report Scale of Psychopathy: A 26-item self-report survey that assesses a person's level of psychopathy

Low Base-Rate Problem: A recognized problem in conducting empirically-based approaches when few persons reoffend, making it statistically difficult to identify a difference between an experimental group and a control group

Minnesota Sex Offender Screening Tool-3.1 (MnSOST-3.1): A nine-item actuarial assessment used to predict future sex crimes that is based on criminal history, age, type of release from the criminal justice system, completion of sex-offender and substance abuse treatment, and male victim

Nonactuarial Assessments: A method for determining whether an event (i.e., recidivism) will occur based on known factors that relies exclusively on the judgment of a clinician

Plethysmograph: An instrument developed to measure penile engorgement while erotic visual material is presented

Polygraph: Also known as a lie detector test, a physiological measure of blood pressure, respiration patterns, and skin conductance (i.e., perspiration) to determine truthfulness

Psychopathy: A personality disorder that includes antisocial behavior, callousness, lack of empathy toward others, a lack of remorse for harming others, and lack of consciousness

Hare Psychopathy Checklist Revised: An assessment involving a semi-structured interview to determine one's level of psychopathy

Rapid Risk Assessment of Sex Offender Recidivism (RRASOR): An actuarial test based on four static questions used to predict future risk for sexual recidivism

Relapse Prevention: A key component of cognitive-behavioral therapy that involves identifying and preventing high-risk situations that can lead to sex crimes

Risk, Need, and Responsivity (RNR) Model: A guiding principle in the criminal justice system that subscribes to applying the appropriate level of response based on the person's level of need

Risk Matrix 2000/S (RM2000/S): An actuarial assessment used to predict future sex crimes that was developed from an existing scale, the Structured Anchored Clinical Judgment (SACJ), in addition to combining empirical factors in the literature

Sex Offender Risk Appraisal Guide (SORAG): A 14-item actuarial assessment used to measure violent recidivism among persons who have committed a sex crime

Sexual Violence Risk-20 (SVR-20): A nonactuarial assessment tool comprising 20 yes-or-no questions used to measure one's risk level for committing future sexual crimes

Static Factors: Factors that will remain stable throughout one's life and include factors such as age at the first sexual experience and whether one has been victimized as a child

Static-99R: A 10-item actuarial assessment of persons who have committed a sex crime based on static factors used for the purpose of predicting sexual recidivism

Static-2002: A revised version of the Static-99R assessment of persons who have committed a sex crime used for the purpose of predicting sexual recidivism

Structured Anchored Clinical Judgment (SACJ-Min): An actuarial risk assessment tool used to predict future sex crimes that is conducted in three stages: (1) determine current conviction history, (2) assess aggravating factors, and (3) assess current behavior (dynamic factors)

Trauma-informed Care: A type of treatment that recognizes the complex causalities of behaviors, with attention placed on the role that exposure to multiple Adverse Childhood Experiences such as exposure to violence, child maltreatment, and multiple forms of family dysfunction has had a person

Violence Risk Appraisal Guide (VRAG): A 12-item actuarial assessment used to determine violent recidivism among persons who have committed a sex crime—it is to be used in conjunction with SORAG when the offender has committed a sex offense

CHAPTER 11

Registration Laws and Civil Commitment of Persons Who Have Committed a Sex Crime

CHAPTER OBJECTIVES

- Describe the relationship between fear of and misinformation regarding sex crimes and sex-crime and sex-offender management policies
- Describe the development of U.S. sex-offender registration laws; identify the key components of federal laws regarding sex-offender registration
- Identify the role of the Office of Sex Offending Sentencing, Monitoring, Apprehending, Registering, and Tracking (SMART)
- Discuss the assumptions and effects of sex-offender registration laws
- Summarize civil commitment laws for sexual violent predators
- Describe Erin's Law

In the 1990s and through the 2000s, several U.S. high-profile cases that involved abduction, sexual assault, and murder of children or young adults led to a public outcry to take preventive action. State legislatures, and subsequently the federal government, responded with laws that required persons who were convicted of a sex crime to register with their local law enforcement officials. This was later expanded to require notification of where registered sex offenders (RSOs) live along with details of their offenses. More restrictive laws followed and gave local jurisdictions minimum standards to implement and, to a large extent, license to develop additional restrictive guidelines such as prohibiting RSOs from living within a certain distance from places where children congregate.

This textbook considers many myths about sex crimes and persons who commit a sex crime and how they are refuted by existing research. Many false assumptions have fueled recent laws. For example, many people assume identifying such offenders on a public website will cause people to act more cautiously (e.g., supervise their children more closely) and that this will lead to a decrease in sexual victimizations. These assumptions, along with several others, are closely examined in this chapter.

This chapter provides an overview of sex-crimes prevention strategies associated with sex-offender registration and notification laws. We identify sex-offender registration and notification laws in countries with emphasis on U.S. laws. This includes discussion of the ***Jacob Wetterling Crimes Against Children and Sexually Violent Offender Registration Act (the Wetterling Act)***, the first law that required persons convicted of a sex crime to register with law enforcement officials. After this, ***Megan's Law*** was enacted, requiring personal information to be publicly posted about the offender. The **Pam Lychner Sex Offender Tracking and Identification Act** required a **national sex-offender registry.** Given differences among states in how they implemented these laws, a federal law was passed, the **Adam Walsh Act**, to create minimum guidelines for sex-offender registration and notification. Each of these laws and acts was enacted in response to high-profile cases, followed by highly emotional public reactions. We examine the assumptions underlying these laws.

In addition to the enactment of laws about sex-offender registration and notification, the courts have shaped sex-offender policy by allowing sex offenders released from prison to be further detained through a process of civil commitment. The key U.S. Supreme Court case was **Kansas v. Hendricks (1997)**, which we examine in this chapter, along with the current state of civil commitment policies among U.S. states. Finally, **Erin's Law** is discussed as a primary prevention effort.

PERCEPTIONS OF PEOPLE WHO COMMIT SEX OFFENSES

Historically, society's view of people who commit sex crimes has been one of extreme fear, hatred, and disgust. To put it succinctly, "They are generally perceived as the worst of the worst" (Stafford & Vandiver, 2017, p. 463). Social stigma and media attention have reinforced the archetype of those who commit sex crimes as sexually violent predators who suffer extreme mental illness and addiction and attack without warning. As discussed in previous chapters, these stereotypes are wrought with myth and divert the focus from the real dangers and places where potential victims are at greater risk (Fuselier et al., 2002).

Sex crimes and the persons who commit them generate considerable worry and fear among the public. Greater than 90% of respondents in a national telephone survey agreed that sex crimes should be a "top priority for state and federal policy makers" (Mears et al., 2008, p. 545). Kernsmith et al. (2009) found that the highest level of fear is usually directed toward those who offend against children, specifically. Another study found that individuals report that they would feel more outraged with a known child molester living in their neighborhood compared to a convicted murderer (Redlich, 2001). As discussed in Chapter 1, conversations about sex crimes and the people who commit them are fertile issues for the development of **moral panic**. To recap, moral panic refers to an intense, emotional reaction to an issue that is a gross violation of social order (like a sex crime) and is characterized by exaggerated or misdirected fear of the issue (Cohen, 1972).

Public fear and moral panic contribute to misperceptions, overgeneralizations, and erroneous statements concerning sex crimes and those who commit them. The Center for Sex Offender Management (2000) has observed a great deal of misinformation regarding sex crimes, particularly as it pertains to issues related to offenders, the relationship between victims and offenders, treatment issues, recidivism, and sex offender management practices. We've discussed many of these misperceptions and overgeneralizations in previous chapters, including *all persons who commit a sex crime are male, all sex offenders are adults, alcohol causes rape, childhood victimization causes future offending behavior, strangers are the greatest threat to our children's safety, once a sex offender, always a sex offender*, and *sex crimes are on the rise in the United States.*

We know these statements are inaccurate and a by-product of the culture of fear and moral panic. These inaccuracies have been consistently debunked by scholarly research; yet, this misinformation has and continues to shape criminal justice law and policy around sex crimes and sex offender management. Many studies have suggested that fear and misinformation are particularly important influencers of support for management policies regarding persons who commit sex crimes (Comartin et al., 2009; Kernsmith et al., 2016; Pickett et al., 2013; Rosselli & Jeglic, 2017). For instance, one study showed that greater fear of people who commit sex offenses coupled with acceptance of misinformation was predictive of greater levels of support for harsh management policies, particularly with severe sanctions such as chemical castration and life imprisonment (Kernsmith et al., 2016).

Beginning in the mid-1990s, there has been a surge of federal, state, and local policies concerning the management of persons who commit a sex crime, including issues of registration and notification, residency restrictions, electronic monitoring, civil commitment, and chemical castration. The ultimate goal of these policies is to reduce the sexual recidivism of convicted offenders and deter potential offenders. The impetus for many of these policies has been highly publicized, particularly heinous sex crimes committed by strangers against young children—usually resulting in the abduction and death of the child. Understandably, such cases spurred widespread fear, outrage, and demand for laws and policies that keep children and the broader public safe. At the same time, however, these types of cases do not represent the norm; they were significant exceptions to the norm that would become a poster child for the urgency regarding awareness and prevention. Many of the policies that would be developed have been criticized for doing more harm than good. In the next section, we explore these laws and policies, as well as their impact, in depth.

SEX-OFFENDER REGISTRATION AND NOTIFICATION LAWS

A great deal of sex-crime and sex-offender management policy is focused on registration and notification laws. Registration and notification laws are known as **tertiary prevention strategies** in that they do not attempt to prevent sex crimes before they occur, nor do they involve an immediate reaction to a sex crime. Instead, they attempt to manage the impact of such crimes (Association for the Treatment of Sexual Abusers, n.d.). The goal of tertiary strategies is to prevent further harm caused by the persons who have been apprehended and convicted of a sex crime.

The United States is not the only country to require those convicted of a sex crime to register and notify the public where they live. Table 11.1 presents information about registration and notification laws in diverse countries. The table shows that the United States was the first country to require sex-offender registration. Many other countries followed suit by enacting their own sex-offender registration laws. Also noteworthy, a few countries (Bermuda, Kenya, Maldives, South Korea, parts of the United Kingdom, and the United States) require some form of notification about where the offenders live. In most countries, there would not be postcard mailings notifying people of RSOs living in their neighborhood, as in the United States. The United States is the only country that requires a *public* registry. This means that the information is maintained by a registering authority (usually local law enforcement officials), and the public can access a database (via the internet). Most countries listed in Table 11.1 do not require RSOs to notify law enforcement officials when traveling to them. The offenses considered registerable and the length of registration vary among countries.

TABLE 11.1 Sex-Offender Registration Laws across the Globe

Country	Sex-Offender Registration Law Enacted	Public Notification System	Public Registry Website	International Travel Notice Required	Scope of Registerable Offenses	Duration and Frequency of Registration
Argentina	2013	None	None	No	Sexual abuse of minors, forcible sexual abuse of any person	Indefinite duty to update address
Australia	2004 (national database)	None (at the national level)	None (at the national level)	Varies across states/territories	Varies across states/territories	Varies across states/territories
Bermuda	2001	2009[1]	None	No	Carnal knowledge, sexual exploitation, indecent acts, sexual assault	10 years, must update name changes or residence changes
Canada	2004 (national)	None (at the national level)	None (at the national level)[2]	No[3]	Nearly all sexually related offenses	Ranges from 10 years to lifetime registration, depending on maximum incarceration term
France	2004	None	None	No	Serious sexual assaults, corruption of a minor under 15, certain other offenses at the discretion of the court/prosecutor	10–20 years (depends on severity of offense) Verification every 6 months or annually, address change within 15 days
Germany	No national system	None	None	No	N/A	N/A
Republic of Ireland	2001	None	None	Yes	All (on listed schedule)	5 years– lifetime (depends on severity of offense), any changes to registration information must be reported

TABLE 11.1 Continued

Country	Sex-Offender Registration Law Enacted	Public Notification System	Public Registry Website	International Travel Notice Required	Scope of Registerable Offenses	Duration and Frequency of Registration
Jamaica	2009	None	None	Yes	Most serious sex offenses	Indefinite, after 10 years offender can petition to be removed, must verify annually and verify name/address changes within 14 days
Jersey	2001	None	None	Discretionary	Most serious sex offenses	Specified by sentencing court, suggested minimum is 5 years, address/name changes made within 24 hours
Kenya	2006	Anyone with reasonable interest	None	Yes	Unclear from legislation, any sex offense can potentially be included	Lifetime; address, employment/school, any other changes must be made in advance, where feasible
Maldives	2009	Enacted law provides for public website disclosure	Authorized, but not yet established	No	Most serious sexual offenses involving children	Unclear
Malta	2012	None	None	Yes	Most serious sex offenses	2 years–lifetime, depends on severity, must update any information changes within 3 days
Pitcairn Islands	2010	None	None	Yes	Most serious sex offenses	2 years–lifetime, depends on severity, must update any information changes within 3 days
South Africa	2007	None	None	No	Any sex offense against a child	5 years–lifetime, depends on severity, updating information requirements not developed

(Continued)

TABLE 11.1 Continued

Country	Sex-Offender Registration Law Enacted	Public Notification System	Public Registry Website	International Travel Notice Required	Scope of Registerable Offenses	Duration and Frequency of Registration
South Korea	2000	Yes	Yes[4]	No	Any sex offense against a child	20 years, changes in information must be reported within 30 days, verify information required annually
Taiwan	2005	None	None	No	Rape and indecent acts	5–7 years, depending on severity, changed information must be made within 7 days
Trinidad and Tobago	2000	None	None	No	Any sex offense	5 years–lifetime, depending on severity, name and address changes must be made within 14 days of any change
United Kingdom	1997	Varies	None	Yes	Nearly all sex offenses	2 years–lifetime, depending on severity, any changes must be made within 3 days
United States	1994 (federal)	Yes	Yes	Yes	Most sex offenses	15 years, 25 years, or lifetime, depending on severity; annual, semi-annual, or quarterly verification required

Note: Adapted from U.S. Department of Justice (2014).

[1] A risk assessment is required for disclosure of information. It can vary from limited disclosure to specific persons but can include broadcasting or publishing information about the offender.
[2] Alberta and Manitoba have limited public-registry websites.
[3] Those who are in Canada for more than 7 days, but convicted outside of Canada, are required to register.
[4] Offender information is posted for 5–10 years, depending on sentence received.

Jacob Wetterling Crimes against Children and Sexually Violent Offender Registration Act

Background

Jacob Wetterling was 9 years old in 1989 (Farley, 2008). Jacob, his younger brother, and a friend rode their bikes to rent a movie at a local store. They were riding back on a country road in St. Joseph, Minnesota, when a man approached them, brandished a gun, and ordered them off their bikes. The man took Jacob and ordered the others to ride away without looking back. No one saw Jacob after that. Although no direct evidence indicated a "sex offender" took Jacob, it was speculated that is what occurred. It was not known to local police at the time but discovered later that halfway houses in the city housed persons convicted of a sex crime after release from incarceration (Pennsylvania State Police, n.d.). Jacob's mother, Patty, became an advocate for missing children. She was subsequently appointed to a governor's task force, which led to tougher laws, including the Wetterling Act, which was part of the Federal Violent Crime Control and Law Enforcement Act of 1994. (As this textbook went to press, a person convicted of a sex crime admitted to molesting and killing Jacob, and the killer led law enforcement officials to Jacob's remains.)

Enactment

The Wetterling Act established guidelines for states to track RSOs. Each state would track them for 10 years after their release into the community. The offenders would have their place of residence confirmed once a year for 10 years. If they committed a violent sex crime, their place of residence would be confirmed four times a year for the rest of their lives. RSOs also were required to update their addresses when there was a change. Information was released to the public only when there was an interest to do so—for public safety reasons (SMART, n.d.). Thus, information was rarely released to the public. This, however, would change with Megan's Law.

Megan's Law

Background

Megan Kanka was 7 years old in 1994 when she was abducted and killed by a neighbor in Hamilton Township, New Jersey. The neighbor, a twice-convicted child molester, lured Megan by asking if she wanted to see a puppy. Megan was raped, killed, and dumped in a nearby park. Her parents, devastated, indicated they would never have left Megan unsupervised in their neighborhood if they had known a person convicted of a sex crime lived nearby. This led to Megan's Law, requiring public notification of RSOs (Farley, 2008; Pennsylvania State Police, n.d.).

Enactment

Although the Wetterling Act had substantial consequences for persons convicted of a sex crime, the federal Megan's Law, enacted in 1996, required that information regarding such offenders' registration be made public. The law was an amendment to the Violent

Crime Control Act of 1994. Prior to Megan's Law, the focus was to inform law enforcement officials of sex offenders. This law broadened the focus to include community notification.

Pam Lychner Sex Offender Tracking and Identification Act of 1996

Background

Pam Lychner was a real estate agent in the Houston area. The following describes the harrowing incident that she survived:

> One day in 1990 [Pam Lychner] received a telephone call at home from a man who expressed an interest in looking at a house. Pam asked her husband, Joe, to come along for the showing. Pam stayed in the kitchen, and Joe went to another part of the house. A laborer who worked for the company Pam had hired to clean the house entered the house at the time of the appointment, claiming he had returned to finish the job. Police later theorized that it was he who had called to make the appointment. When Pam turned her back, the laborer—apparently unaware that someone else was in the house—grabbed her from behind, put his hand over her mouth, and attempted to rape her.
>
> Hearing noises, Joe rushed to help his wife. While Joe struggled with the assailant, Pam ran to a neighbor's house for assistance. The suspect was arrested, convicted, and eventually sent to prison for 20 years. The suspect turned out to be a convicted rapist and child molester who had been released from state prison under a mandatory early release policy designed to ease prison overcrowding.
>
> (Albro, 1997, n.p.)

Pam Lychner's ordeal led to her becoming an activist for victims. This eventually led to the Pam Lychner Sex Offender Tracking and Identification Act of 1996 (Albro, 1997).

Enactment

The Pam Lychner Sex Offender Tracking and Identification Act of 1996 led to the establishment of the **National Sex Offender Registry**. It allowed the Federal Bureau of Investigation (FBI) to require sex offenders who lived in states with only minimal sex-offender registry programs to register on this national registry. It also required the FBI to periodically verify the addresses of the registered sex offenders. As needed, information could be released to the public. The Act also established guidelines for RSOs to notify the registering authority when they moved to other states.

Adam Walsh Act

Background

In July 1981, Adam Walsh and his mother went to a department store in Hollywood, Florida. Adam saw a small group of other children playing a video game in the store.

His mother left him with the other children and shopped in another part of the store, approximately 75 feet away. When she returned, Adam was gone. A security guard said there had been a small skirmish, and the children were told to leave. It was speculated Adam was taken by Ottis Toole, a serial killer, who confessed but was never convicted (CNN, 2008; Pennsylvania State Police, n.d.). Toole was associated with another serial killer, Henry Lee Lucas.

Adam Walsh's father, John Walsh, became an advocate for abducted children. He later became the star of the television show *America's Most Wanted*. This show highlighted heinous crimes and asked the public to contact the police with any information that could lead to the capture of the offenders. The show last aired in 2011 and claimed responsibility for the arrest of more than 1,000 offenders.

Enactment

The Adam Walsh Act, also known as the Sex Offender Registration and Notification Act (SORNA), became law on July 27, 2006. It replaced the requirements of the Wetterling Act and its amendments. In addition to creating a new federal felony offense for failing to register as a sex offender, it established minimum guidelines for sex-offender registration.

It is noteworthy that once these minimum guidelines are established, state legislatures and local governments can enact stricter guidelines. For example, if SORNA requires a minimum of 10 years of registration for a particular offense, a state can require more than that, such as 15 years or even lifetime registration (McPherson, 2007).

SORNA establishes three tiers of RSOs, and each tier has specific registration guidelines. Tier III includes the most serious offenders based on the offense committed. These offenders are required to register for life. They are required to renew their registration every three months. Additionally, any person who was a Tier II sex offender, a less serious tier, and commits a subsequent felony sex offense will become a Tier III sex offender, regardless of the tier level of the subsequent felony sex offense. The sex offenses that qualify a person as Tier III are punishable by at least one year of incarceration. They include the following:

- Sex acts with another by force or threat
- A sex act with another who has been rendered unconscious or involuntarily drugged or who is otherwise incapable of appraising the nature of the conduct or declining to participate
- Sex acts with a child under age 12
- Nonparental kidnapping of a minor (McPherson, 2007, p. 2)

Next, Tier II offenses are less serious than Tier III offenses yet are considered more serious than Tier I offenses. Tier II offenders are required to register for 25 years. Again, anyone who was a Tier I offender and commits a subsequent felony sex offense will become a Tier II sex offender, regardless of the tier level of the subsequent felony sex offense. Tier II sex offenses include the following:

- Offenses involving the use of minors in prostitution
- Offenses against minors involving sexual contact
- Offenses involving the use of a minor in a sexual performance
- Offenses involving the production or distribution of child pornography (McPherson, 2007)

Next, Tier I sex offenders are considered the least serious. They are required to register for 15 years. They renew their registration once a year. This tier of sex offenders is a catch-all tier for sex offenders who are not Tier II or Tier III. It includes people who have committed a misdemeanor and felony sex offenses that meet the criteria of a sex offense as defined in federal law (see § 42 U.S.C. 16911 [5]) (McPherson, 2007).

In addition to establishing a tier system, seven key requirements/policies were established for all tier levels: (1) the information required, (2) location of registration, (3) forensic information kept on file, (4) public notification requirements, (5) guidelines for removal from the sex-offender registry, (6) application of retroactivity, and (7) application to juveniles.

All RSOs are required to submit *at least* the following information to law enforcement officials:

- Name (including nicknames, pseudonyms)
- Social security number (actual and purported)
- Home, work, and school addresses
- License plate number
- Description of any vehicle they own or drive
- Date of birth (actual and purported)
- Email addresses
- Pseudonyms used for instant messaging programs
- Passport numbers
- Phone numbers (cell phones and landlines) (McPherson, 2007)

Additionally, when RSOs travel for more than seven days, they are required to notify their local law enforcement officials for the purpose of notifying officials in the destined location (McPherson, 2007).

With regard to the location, RSOs are required to register where they live, work, and attend school. For their initial registration, they are required to register where they were convicted prior to release from prison if they served a prison sentence. Typically, the offenders begin registering when they are released from prison or after they are sentenced to probation. They are required to register within three days when not serving a prison sentence. If they did serve a prison sentence, they are required to register upon release (McPherson, 2007).

RSOs are required to submit forensic information to law enforcement officials including DNA, fingerprints, and palm prints. Additionally, officials maintain a copy of the violated law that led to the registration and the offender's criminal history (McPherson, 2007).

The information RSOs are required to submit to law enforcement is released to the public—with a few exceptions. For example, the victim's identity, offender's social security number, passport or immigration documents, and arrests other than the one that led to the registration requirement are not released to the public. Law enforcement officials may also opt to exclude the offender's employer and/or school.

There is a process for persons convicted of a sex crime to request exemption from the registration requirements. This request can be made, however, only after the offender has been registered for an extensive period of time. For example, Tier III offenders, which include those convicted of the most serious sex crime, must wait 25 years to apply for exemption. Tier I offenders must wait 10 years (McPherson, 2007). RSOs can make the request that their registered time be reduced only if they have no other subsequent arrests (U.S. Department of Justice, 2008).

SORNA specifically allows for retroactive application of the law for some. For example, offenders who are in prison or criminal justice supervision (i.e., probation or parole) for the registerable offense or for another crime are required to register under SORNA. Also, those who were already subject to a former registration requirement (i.e., the Wetterling Act) and those who are re-arrested for another crime (any crime) are required to register. These offenders are required to register in accordance with SORNA within three months to one year, depending on their tier level (Tier III: three months; Tier II: six months; and Tier I: one year) (McPherson, 2007).

Juveniles are not exempt from SORNA's registration requirements. Juveniles adjudicated in juvenile court and who are at least 14 years old and commit an offense that is similar to, or more serious than, the federal aggravated sexual assault statute are also required to register. This includes any type of forcible rape or any crime that involves the sexual penetration of a victim who is younger than 12. A "*Romeo and Juliet*" *clause* also exists, which allows for an exemption of registration for those who have engaged in consensual sex with a victim at least 13 years old and involves an offender who is no more than four years older than the victim (McPherson, 2007).

In 2000, the **Campus Sex Crimes Prevention Act** supplemented the Wetterling Act's standards. This required that institutions of higher education maintain and disseminate information about known RSOs (U.S. Department of Education, 2002). Most universities and colleges report known sex offenders who work at or attend their institutions on a website.

In summary, SORNA represents an attempt to "level the playing field" by establishing minimum guidelines that all states are required to enact. Although it was passed with overwhelming support, it is still considered controversial by some. Perhaps the most debated aspects of SORNA are its retroactive application of the law and inclusion of juveniles, who are often seen as more amenable to treatment and exempt from many of the punishments of the adult criminal court system.

Office of Sex Offending Sentencing, Monitoring, Apprehending, Registering, and Tracking (SMART)

SORNA also established the *Office of Sex Offending Sentencing, Monitoring, Apprehending, Registering, and Tracking (SMART)* to assist states, U.S. territories, and American Indian/Alaska Native Tribes with the implementation of SORNA's requirements and assess jurisdictions' compliance with SORNA. It also tracks important legal developments regarding SORNA. Currently, 18 states (Figure 11.1), four U.S. territories (American Samoa, Guam, Commonwealth of the Northern Mariana Islands, and U.S. Virgin Islands), and 136 Tribal jurisdictions (across 28 states) have fully implemented SORNA's requirements.

SORNA implementation comes with high costs, including additional personnel, new hardware, software installation and maintenance, increased jail and prison space, and administrative costs. The program is also severely underfunded at the federal level; in 2020, approximately $19 million in Department of Justice grant funds were made available to U.S. states, territories, and Tribes to implement SORNA, with a maximum funding ceiling of $400,000. States that do not comply face losing a reduction of their annual Edward Byrne Memorial Justice Assistance Grant, which provides funds for crime control and criminal justice reform

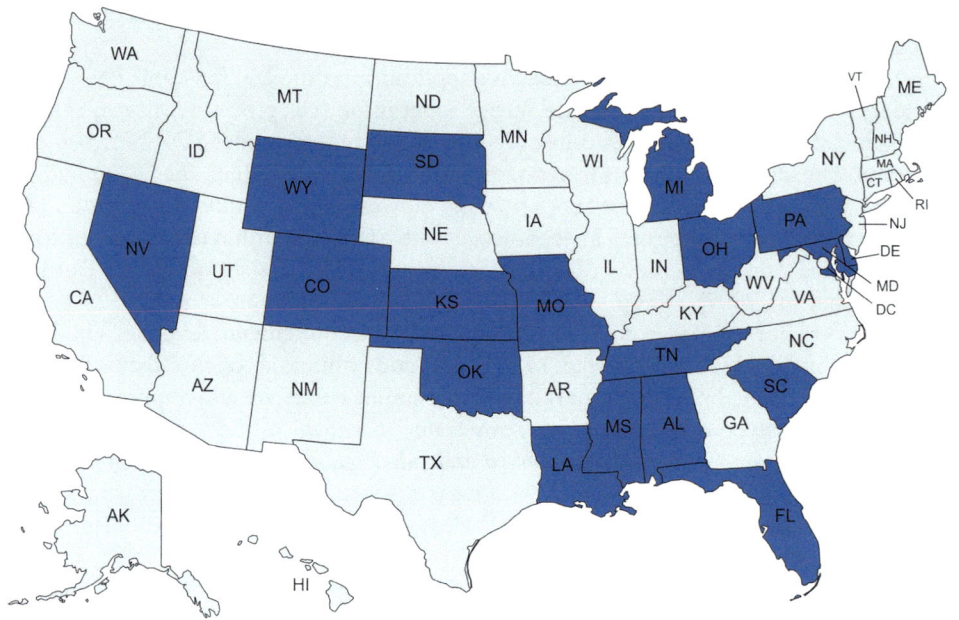

FIGURE 11.1 SORNA Implementation by U.S. States

Note: The states in blue are in compliance and those in gray are not in compliance. Adapted from U.S. Department of Justice (2021).

activities. Officials from several states (Arizona, Arkansas, California, Texas, and Nebraska) have indicated it is too expensive to implement and have refused (Prison Legal News, 2015). As an example, a study by the Texas Senate Criminal Justice Commission estimated that it would cost $38.7 million annually to substantially implement SORNA but the state would stand to lose only $1.4 million in Byrne funds as a penalty for noncompliance (Lyons, 2011). As sovereign governments, federally recognized American Indian/Alaska Native Tribes could elect whether to implement SORNA on lands subject to Tribal jurisdiction. Tribes are subject to the same registration and notification requirements as states and U.S. territories. If the SMART Office determines that a Tribe is unable or unwilling to implement SORNA within a reasonable amount of time, the Tribe's registration and notification duties can be delegated to the state(s) in which the territory of the Tribe is located.

National Sex Offender Public Registry

Background

Dru Sjodin, a college student at the University of North Dakota in Grand Forks, went missing in 2003. She was on her way home from work. The investigation led to the arrest of Alfonso Rodriguez, Jr., who was a RSO in Minnesota and had recently been released from a 23-year prison sentence. Five months after the arrest, Dru Sjodin's body was found. Rodriguez was sentenced to death for the crime; he had crossed state lines to commit it,

> **Focus Box 11.1** McGirt v. Oklahoma and the Impact on Tribal Implementation of SORNA
>
> In 1997, Jimmy McGirt was tried and convicted of the crimes of first-degree rape, lewd molestation, and forcible sodomy of a four-year-old girl. While serving two consecutive life sentences in the Oklahoma Department of Corrections, McGirt challenged his conviction on the basis that his crimes were committed on the Muscogee Creek Reservation in Eastern Oklahoma and that the state of Oklahoma lacked any jurisdiction to prosecute him. The state of Oklahoma and the U.S. government argued that since Oklahoma statehood in 1907, the Muscogee Creek Reservation had been formally disestablished, a process by which Tribal lands are taken "out of trust" by the federal government, effectively divesting Tribes of the special legal status and autonomy to manage those lands. In 2020, the Supreme Court ruled that the Muscogee Creek Reservation had never been disestablished and was still reservation land for jurisdictional purposes. Further, the Court ruled that the State of Oklahoma was not the appropriate entity to prosecute McGirt.
>
> *McGirt v. Oklahoma* is a significant case because it set a precedent for the prosecution of crimes by Native Americans on the Tribal lands of Eastern Oklahoma (Cherokee Nation, Chickasaw Nation, Choctaw Nation, Muscogee Creek Nation, and Seminole Nation). Criminal justice jurisdiction for these crimes now falls under the jurisdiction of the Tribal Courts and federal judiciary rather than Oklahoma State Courts. This has had major implications for SORNA implementation on Tribal lands. Within the Cherokee nation, for example, the jurisdictional land base has expanded from the smaller area of fee and trust land that Tribe currently maintains a registry for to a much larger land area comprising the full reservation. Instead of being responsible for registering sex offenders who reside, work, or go to school on the minimal area of fee and trust land, it has now increased exponentially to all offenders residing in the land area for which the Tribe is responsible (14 counties total). In total, the Tribe has gone from being responsible for maintaining registration for less than ten offenders to more than 1,000, with dual registration anticipated for many offenders.

making it an aggravated homicide. This case put a spotlight on identifying information on RSOs, regardless of their resident state (SMART, n.d.).

Enactment

SORNA included Dru Sjodin's law. It changed the name of the National Sex Offender Public Registry to the ***Dru Sjodin National Sex Offender Public Registry***. This website (https://www.nsopw.gov, see Figure 11.2) provides information about registered sex offenders across all states.

Summary of Registration/Notification Laws

The sex-offender registration and notification laws in the United States were enacted in the 1990s and 2000s, and they led to strict requirements for persons convicted of a sex crime to

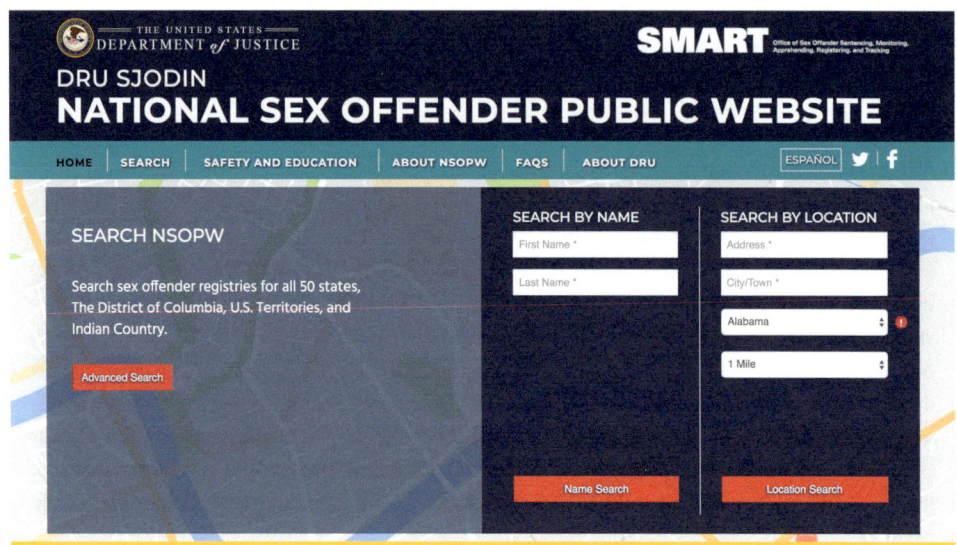

FIGURE 11.2 Dru Sjodin National Sex Offender Public Website (https://www.nsopw.gov).

register with law enforcement officials. Registration (the Wetterling Act) then led to public notification (Megan's Law), and these laws were largely overhauled by the Adam Walsh Act (SORNA), which established minimum guidelines for the control of sex offenders. Many states and local governments have established more restrictive guidelines, including posting of yard signs to identify that a sex offender lives there and establishing "safe zones" to bar sex offenders from living within so many feet (500, 1,000, or even 2,500 feet) of places where children are known to congregate. SORNA co-occurred with the development of a national sex-offender registry (Dru Sjodin National Sex Offender Public Registry).

You may have noticed that each of the laws occurred in response to an assault, usually of a child or young adult. The loved ones of the victim often led the way to a new law in hopes of preventing more sex crimes. There is an untestable assumption that if Megan's parents knew about a RSO in their neighborhood, she would not have been unsupervised and would not have been abducted. The same is true of the other victims. If a national registry existed, would Dru Sjodin have been abducted? Although these assumptions cannot be tested, we can review research on the observed effects of public registration/notification laws.

ASSUMPTIONS OF SEX-OFFENDER REGISTRATION AND NOTIFICATION LAWS

The purpose of the sex-offender registration and notification laws has been to "provide . . . the public with information about known sex offenders in an effort to assist parents and potential victims to protect themselves from dangerous predators" (Levenson et al., 2007, p. 587). An obvious assumption is that registration and notification will make community members and the police more aware of the whereabouts of such offenders. This, however, may not be the case. A Gallup poll revealed that only 23% of adults have actually checked the registry (Saad, 2005). This was true of only 36% of adults with children.

Also, research has consistently shown that sex-offender registries are often inaccurate. One study found that the location of nearly half (49%) of all RSOs in Massachusetts was unknown (Mullvihill et al., 2003). Similarly, more than half of RSOs who were assessed in Florida were either deceased, incarcerated, or not living at the address in the registry (Payne, 2005). As many as 25% of the addresses of registered sex offenders in Kentucky were wrong (Tewksbury, 2002). Although the offenders are required to register their addresses, it cannot be assumed that this is always done.

It was assumed that registration laws would prevent child molestation and rapes. This, however, begs the question: have registration laws actually led to decreases in such crimes? Several studies have examined this question. One study of rape concluded "that the sex offender legislation seems to have no uniform and observable influence on the number of rapes reported in the [10] states analyzed" (Vásquez et al., 2008, p. 188). But does registration decrease the likelihood of recidivism by sex offenders? Maddan (2005) found that RSOs recidivated at approximately the same rate (about 10%) as offenders who were not required to register. Later research also found no differences in sex-offender recidivism among those required to register and those not required to register (Zgoba et al., 2010). Still another study, using different samples and study designs, also found that registration had no effect on recidivism rates of these offenders (Letourneau et al., 2010).

It is also assumed that persons convicted of a sex crime have a high recidivism rate. As noted in Chapter 1, recidivism rates of convicted sex offenders are relatively low. The overwhelming majority of persons convicted of a sex crime are not re-arrested for another sex offense. Thus, many of the underlying assumptions of sex-offender registration laws have not been supported by existing evidence.

EFFECTS OF SEX-OFFENDER REGISTRATION AND NOTIFICATION LAWS

Many RSOs have reported that registration decreases the chances they will reenter their communities successfully (Levenson et al., 2007), which poses a greater risk of re-offending. For example, one study reported that a majority of RSOs suffer negative consequences from registration such as depression, shame, and hopelessness (Levenson et al., 2007). Additionally, a majority of RSOs reported job loss as a result of registration (Levenson et al., 2007). Thus, sex-offender registration laws can lead to limited access to education, housing, and employment (Bonnar-Kidd, 2010).

Many RSOs also report being harassed. This includes threats of harassment and property damage (Levenson et al., 2007). As noted in Focus Box 11.2, many of these incidents involve serious physical harm, even sometimes death. Some people who commit vigilante acts against RSOs view themselves as heroes.

In addition to the offender being harassed, family members of RSOs have also reported harassment (Farkas & Miller, 2007; Levenson & Tewskbury, 2009). Research has shown that relatives of RSOs also experience depression, frustration, and targeted hostility from other family members who chose not to stay in contact with the registered sex offender (Farkas & Miller, 2007). This often leads to relatives distancing themselves from RSOs, creating further isolation (Levenson & Tewskbury, 2009). Thus, it is clear that sex-offender registration laws can result in negative, collateral consequences that affect relatives of RSOs.

There is a clearly documented perception that many community members believe sex-offender registration laws are useful in that they (1) create better public awareness, (2) increase

> **Focus Box 11.2** Cases of Vigilantism
>
> A gunman was given a life sentence, without the chance of parole, in Washington for gunning down two registered sex offenders. The gunman left behind a note taking credit for the murders and for "taking care of some problems." He was described as unremorseful and apologized only for the collateral damage he caused, not for gunning down the registered sex offenders. When he was captured, he admitted to a plan to continue killing registered sex offenders until he was captured by the police (Bartkewicz, 2012).
>
> A 20-year-old gunman turned a gun on himself in Boston, committing suicide as he was about to be captured by police. The gunman-turned-suicide victim had previously killed two registered sex offenders. He identified the sex offenders by going online to a public registry (Adams, 2006).
>
> Jack King from the National Association of Criminal Defense Lawyers in Washington described a case of vigilantism that occurred shortly after the sex-offender registry became public in the early 1990s. He described an incident where the brother of a registered sex offender was mistaken for a registered sex offender and was beaten nearly to death using a baseball bat (Adams, 2006).

community surveillance, (3) deter recidivism by known sex offenders, and (4) promote child safety (Matson & Lieb, 1996). Thus, sex-offender registration laws, which were developed in response to several high-profile cases, have assuaged the public's fear by providing public information about known sex offenders.

The Center for Sex Offender Management, a reputable resource of sex-offender information, summarizes laws regarding persons convicted of a sex crime:

> [M]yths about sex offenders and victims, inflated recidivism rates, claims that sex-offender treatment is ineffective, and highly publicized cases involving predatory offenders fuel negative public sentiment and exacerbate concerns by policymakers and the public alike about the return of sex offenders to local communities. Furthermore, the proliferation of legislation that specifically targets the sex offender population—including longer minimum mandatory sentences for certain sex crimes, expanded registration and community notification policies, and the creation of "sex offender free" zones that restrict residency, employment, or travel within prescribed areas in many communities—can inadvertently but significantly hamper reintegration efforts.
>
> (2007, p. 1)

ADDITIONAL REQUIREMENTS FOR REGISTERED SEX OFFENDERS (RSOs)

As noted earlier, SORNA established minimum guidelines (McPherson, 2007). State and local governments could pass additional requirements and limitations affecting RSOs. These vary a great deal. Below are just a few of the requirements in different jurisdictions:

- Several counties in Southern California passed ordinances forbidding registrants to decorate their houses or keep any lights on Halloween night. They are required to post a sign, "No candy or treats at this residence" (Silver, 2012).
- Those in Louisiana are required to include their status as a sex offender in large red type on their driver's licenses (Silver, 2012).
- Some states require GPS devices so the police know the whereabouts of RSOs (Silver, 2012).
- A law in Gonzales, Texas, requires RSOs to post a sign in their yard indicating a "sex offender" lives there (KMOV, 2015).
- Manitowoc, Wisconsin, forbids RSOs from living anywhere in the city. Exceptions exist, for example, offenders who lived in the city for at least five years prior to the law's passage (Nesemann, 2015).

These are just a few of the restrictions placed on RSOs. One of the most common restrictions, however, is a residence restriction, which is discussed next in greater detail.

Residence Restrictions

Residence restrictions typically forbid RSOs to live and sometimes just be within so many feet (500–2,500 feet) of areas where children congregate such as schools, daycare centers, and parks (Mustaine, 2014). Such restrictions are based on unsupported assumptions. For example, it is assumed that these restrictions effectively prevent RSOs from living near areas where children congregate. Support for this has not been found (Birchfield, 2011). These restrictions also are based on the assumption that offenders encounter their victims by going to places where children congregate (Mustaine, 2014). Instead, such offenders typically choose victims who are acquaintances or relatives (Colombino et al., 2009).

Although there are many negative consequences of sex-offender laws, one positive consequence is that such laws make the public feel good (Mustaine, 2014). Beyond this, documented benefits are difficult to find. In contrast, there are many negative consequences reported in the existing literature. RSOs subjected to residence restrictions report a high degree of frustration and stress (Tewksbury & Mustaine, 2009). One of the most serious negative consequences involves housing. Nearly one-third of surveyed RSOs in one study reported having to move because of residence restrictions (Tewksbury & Mustaine, 2009). Another one-fifth were forced to move because of either social pressure from the community or financial problems. Many RSOs have no choice but to live in high-crime neighborhoods (Mustaine & Tewksbury, 2011).

Another serious consequence of residence restrictions is homelessness. Reporters in Miami, Florida, highlighted the problem of homelessness among RSOs. Pictured in many newspapers was a series of tents underneath the Julia Tuttle Causeway occupied by RSOs who believed they had no choice but to live there. This was described as a consequence of a "patchwork of laws" that prohibited RSOs from living anywhere else. This included a 2,500-foot residence restriction preventing RSOs from living near schools. Many organizations legally had their status changed to "school," which eliminated much of the city as a possible place to live. In 2014, the Florida American Civil Liberties Union filed a lawsuit challenging these laws. The lawsuit alleged that criminal justice officials were aware of the problem and actually directed sex offenders to the tent cities (Flatow, 2014).

Some state and local officials have recognized the negative consequences of these laws. For example, in December 2015, California reversed previous laws forbidding RSOS from living near parks, schools, or other places where children congregate. The current law only forbids those who had molested children from living near such areas. Thus, more than 4,200 of the nearly 6,000 RSOs will not be subjected to residence restrictions (Associated Press, 2015). Perhaps this is a sign of what is to come: a serious reconsideration of laws that were developed on a weak empirical foundation.

CIVIL COMMITMENT LAWS FOR SEXUAL VIOLENT PREDATORS

Civil commitment laws have been used in the United States for approximately two decades. They allow for persons who meet certain criteria to be involuntarily institutionalized—typically in psychiatric institutions. Civil commitment laws vary from state to state. These laws typically have been used for people with mental illnesses who were in need of treatment. Beginning in the 1960s, emphasis was placed on community-based treatment as opposed to institutionalization (Brooks, 2007). Therefore, many civil commitments resulted in a mandate to community-based treatment as opposed to in-patient psychiatric care. Most states require that there is an imminent danger that a mentally ill person will kill themselves or someone else to be civilly committed (Szabo, 2013).

Only recently were civil commitments used for persons convicted of a sex crime. This allows for persons who have already served a prison sentence for a sex crime to be civilly committed and their institutionalization to continue. The offender can be continuously committed and, therefore, indefinitely institutionalized. We will discuss the background of civil commitment laws for sex offenders, along with their current implementation.

Leroy Hendricks

Leroy Hendricks had a lengthy history of sex offending, and it was his case that led to civil commitments for sex offenders. Hendricks began his career of sex offending in 1955 when he exposed himself to two young girls. He was caught and pled guilty to two charges of indecent exposure. Later, in 1957, he was convicted of lewdness. This case involved a young girl. He received a short jail sentence for that offense.

Three years later, in 1960, he was working at a carnival when he molested two young boys. He served two years of the sentence when he was paroled. He was again arrested for molesting a young girl who was only seven. He received treatment in a state psychiatric institution and was released. Not too long after that, in 1967, however, he performed oral sex on an eight-year-old girl and fondled an 11-year-old boy. He was imprisoned and refused to participate in sex-offender treatment. Despite this, he was paroled in 1972. He was diagnosed as a pedophile and entered a treatment program, which he did not complete. Soon after his parole in 1972, he abused two more victims—his stepdaughter and stepson. He continued to abuse them for four years. He also attempted to fondle two teenage boys. He was arrested, convicted, and remained in prison until 1994.

The Kansas Sexually Violent Predator Act

In 1994, the Kansas legislature approved the Sexually Violent Predator Act, allowing "sexually violent predators" to be civilly committed after they completed their criminal sentences. A sexually violent predator included:

> [A]ny person who has been convicted of or charged with a sexually violent offense and who suffers from a mental abnormality or personality disorder which makes the person likely to engage in the predatory acts of sexual violence, if not confined in a secure facility.
>
> (Kan. Stat. Ann. § 59–29a02(a)(Supp. 1996))

Sexually violent offenses included rape, indecent liberties with a child, sodomy, aggravated sodomy, indecent solicitation of a child, sexual exploitation of a child, aggravated sexual battery, and aggravated incest. It also included all of the offenses listed previously that were attempted or committed prior to the enactment of the law. It even included a broad range of offenses that are considered "sexually motivated."

The civil commitment process in Kansas requires the agency in charge of the inmate's release (i.e., the State Department of Corrections) to notify the Attorney General, along with a multidisciplinary team, of the inmate's imminent release. This affects inmates who may meet the sexually violent predator criteria. The multidisciplinary team, providing guidance to the prosecutor, decides whether to file a petition to commit the inmate civilly. The judge decides whether probable cause exists. The inmate is given the right to legal counsel, to present evidence, and to cross-examine witnesses. If probable cause exists, the inmate is transferred to a secure facility for a professional mental evaluation.

The last stage involves a trial that determines whether the inmate is a sexually violent predator. In addition to the rights given at the probable cause hearing, the inmate is also provided the right to elect for a jury trial (which requires a unanimous jury decision), a mental evaluation by a professional, and a standard of proof that involves "beyond a reasonable doubt." Probable cause refers to a standard that involves an adequate amount of evidence, whereas "beyond a reasonable doubt" refers to a stricter standard, requiring more evidence. If it is found that the inmate is a sexually violent predator, he or she is transferred to a secure facility "until such time as the person's mental abnormality or personality has so changed that the person is safe to be at large" (Kan. Stat. Ann. § 59–29a02[a][Supp. 1996]).

The U.S. Supreme Court and the Sexually Violent Predator Act

The jury unanimously decided that Leroy Hendricks was a sexually violent predator and civilly committed him (*Kansas v. Hendricks*, 1997). The case was appealed to the U.S. Supreme Court.

The following excerpt is from the U.S. Supreme Court decision:

> Hendricks admitted that he had repeatedly abused children whenever he was not confined. He explained that when he "get[s] stressed out," he "can't control the urge" to molest children.... Although Hendricks recognized that his behavior harms children, and he hoped he would not sexually molest children again, he stated that the only sure way he could keep from sexually abusing children in the future was "to die."
>
> (*Kansas v. Hendricks*, 1997, p. 355)

The U.S. Supreme Court established that civil commitments could be used for sexually violent predators. The Court specifically examined the constitutionality of civilly committing a sexually violent offender on the basis of (1) due process and (2) double jeopardy. With regard to due process, it was specifically questioned whether a law could be created *ex-post facto* (after the fact). Second, with regard to double jeopardy, the U.S. Constitution prohibits more than one prosecution of the same defendant for the same crime in the same jurisdiction. Hendricks argued that this applied to him; he had completed his sentence for the crime he committed and could not be punished again. The U.S. Supreme Court, however, found that the Sexually Violent Predator Act is constitutional on the grounds that it is a civil proceeding, not criminal. This was a five-to-four decision among the Justices, indicating considerable disagreement.

Civil commitments are generally thought of as rehabilitative and protecting people from harm to themselves and/or others. This is as opposed to criminal proceedings, which are deemed punitive in nature. In 2010, the U.S. Supreme Court expanded the civil commitment of sexually violent predators to those with federal charges (not just state charges) in *U.S. v. Comstock* (2009).

Civil Commitment Laws in the United States

Given that the U.S. Supreme Court has found that the Kansas and federal-level Sexually Violent Predator Act do not violate any constitutional rights, states are allowed to develop similar laws. Twenty states plus the District of Columbia have enacted such laws (Figure 11.3). Recent estimates reveal that approximately 6,300 people are detained in state and federal civil commitment programs (Hoppe et al., 2020). Although the states vary in how civil commitments are carried out, many have been condemned for the few who are rehabilitated through treatment and subsequently released from detention. As noted in Focus Box 11.3, Minnesota is fighting this battle; they have the largest number of civilly committed sex offenders.

Focus Box 11.3 An Overview of Minnesota

Minnesota has the highest rate, per capita, of civilly committed sex offenders. One source indicates that more than 700 sex offenders are civilly committed (Bakst, 2015). Not a single sex offender who has been civilly committed in Minnesota has been released (Bakst, 2015). It costs approximately $120,000 each year to detain a sex offender in Minnesota. The facility resembles something akin to a prison: razor wire, locked metal doors, and regular head counts conducted by the staff (Davey, 2015). The controversy is deeply political. For example, the democrat governor, Mark Dayton, proposed a plan—later abandoned—to release a rapist who admitted to sexually assaulting over 60 women. He faced intense criticism. Attempts to provide psychiatric services, such as risk evaluations for sex offenders, have also met criticism (Davey, 2015). Recently, a federal judge, noting that none of the offenders were being "treated," ordered risk assessment of all of the sex offenders who were civilly committed (Bakst, 2015). The focus of conducting risk assessments is to develop a plan to rehabilitate the offenders so they can be released. The judge noted that indefinite commitments were unconstitutional. Sweeping reform measures were laid out, but a legal battle ensued and is still being dealt with in the courts.

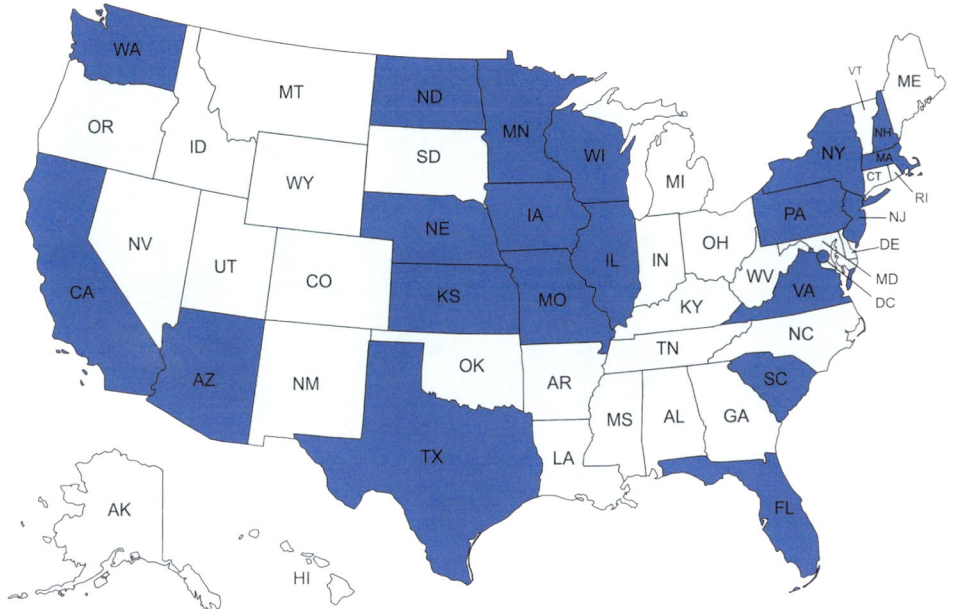

FIGURE 11.3 Civil Commitment Laws in the United States.

Note: The states in dark blue indicate they have civil commitment laws for persons convicted of a sex crime. Adapted from DeMatteo et al. (2015).

STATE-LEVEL LAWS: ERIN'S LAW

Erin's Law, unlike the federal laws covered thus far, is a state law. Also, unlike the laws discussed thus far, it is a primary prevention effort, meaning it is aimed at preventing sex crimes from occurring in the first place rather than responding after they have already occurred (Townsend, 2008). ***Primary prevention strategies*** usually involve teaching people about healthy relationships, how to identify potentially abusive situations, and changing social structures and social norms that allow sex crimes to occur.

Erin's Law was championed by author, activist, and childhood sex-assault survivor Erin Merryn. She introduced the legislation in her home state of Illinois. Merryn was a victim of child rape by an uncle from ages 6 to 8 years as well as incest by an older cousin from ages 11 to 13. Erin's Law (Public Act 096–1524) was drafted and introduced in the Illinois Senate in early 2010 to amend the school code within the education law of Illinois.

There are two main components of the law: (1) creation of a task force to gather information about evidence-based sex abuse prevention programs and (2) implementation of sex abuse prevention programs in Illinois public schools based on task-force findings. The law requires all public schools to adopt a prevention-oriented child sex-abuse program that teaches children pre-Kindergarten through 12th-grade age-appropriate techniques to recognize sex abuse as well as educate school personnel and parents on child sex abuse, including warning signs and referral and resource information to support child victims.

After the successful passage of Erin's Law in Illinois, Merryn continued her advocacy efforts in other states. Many states have since passed Erin's Law, requiring schools to adopt sex-abuse education programs (e.g., personal body safety, signs of abuse, and how to respond).

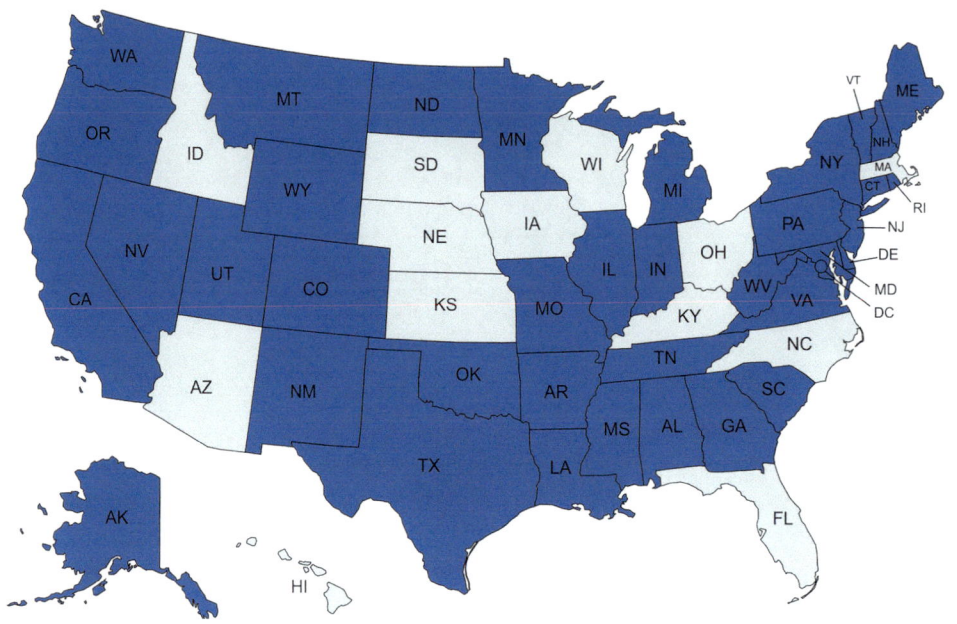

FIGURE 11.4 Passage of Erin's Law in the United States.

Note: The states in dark blue indicate they have passed a version of Erin's Law. Adapted from Erin's Law (2021).

Currently, 37 states have passed Erin's Law (Figure 11.4), compared to 26 states by year-end 2015. It is too early to ascertain the long-term impacts of the law, given that primary prevention efforts are predicated on changing social structures and social norms that allow sex crimes to occur. However, preliminary evidence of Erin's Law's impact demonstrates promise. One study concluded that with Erin's Law in place, teachers are likely more comfortable with the subject of child sexual abuse and have a better understanding of their role in preventing it (Fowler & Vallett, 2021). Adoption of Erin's Law across the U.S. may signal substantial progress.

CONCLUSION

As noted throughout this textbook and this chapter, there are many myths about persons who have committed a sex crime. More specifically, in this chapter, there are many myths in the form of assumptions about sex crimes and the persons who have committed them that have culminated in what some have deemed "feel-good" laws (Freeman-Longo, 1996). Thus far, there is little empirical evidence that such restrictive laws lead to fewer sex crimes.

Nevertheless, a series of U.S. laws have paved the way for other countries to implement laws to require sex offenders to register with law enforcement officials. In the United States, this information is made public, and several states have enacted additional laws, including restrictions on where sex offenders can live. Only recently have there been hints of reconsidering such laws. For the time being, however, it appears these laws will probably stay in place for a considerable time.

REVIEW POINTS

- Many countries have enacted sex-offender registration laws; however, the United States was the first to have these laws and currently has the strictest laws.
- The Wetterling Act, passed in 1994, was the first U.S. law to require persons convicted of a sex crime to register with law enforcement officials.
- The federal Megan's Law, passed in 1996, required that the public have access to information about RSOs.
- The Pam Lychner Sex Offender Tracking and Identification Act of 1996 led to a national sex-offender registry.
- The Adam Walsh Act, also known as the Sex Offender Registration and Notification Act (SORNA), became law in 2006. It amended previous laws, establishing national guidelines, including a three-tier system of registration requirements.
- The Office of Sex Offending Sentencing, Monitoring, Apprehending, Registering, and Tracking (SMART) is responsible for assisting with the implementation of SORNA laws.
- State and local governments are allowed to implement more restrictive laws than the minimum guidelines established by SORNA. This includes, but is not limited to, posting yard signs to notify others that a sex offender lives there, requiring sex-offender notification on driver's licenses, and restricting where a sex offender can live.
- Twenty states allow persons convicted of a sex offense and have completed a prison sentence to be civilly committed to an institution after they have completed their criminal sentences.

REFERENCES

Adam Walsh Child Protection and Safety Act of 2006, 42 U.S.C. § 16911(5) (2006).

Adams, G. (2006, April 18). Maine killings raise vigilantism fears (two sex offenders killed). *Free Public.* http://www.freerepublic.com/focus/news/1617207/posts

Albro, W. (1997). She refused to give up. *National Association of Realtors.* http://realtormag.realtor.org/news-and-commentary/feature/article/1997/04/she-refused-give-up

Associated Press. (2015, December 14). California's sex offenders free to live near parks and schools. *New York Post.* http://nypost.com/2015/12/14/californias-sex-offenders-free-to-live-near-parks-and-schools/

Association for the Treatment of Sexual Abusers. (n.d.). Sexual violence prevention fact sheet. *ATSA Making Society Safer.* http://www.atsa.com/sexual-violence-prevention-fact-sheet

Bakst, B. (2015, October 29). Judge orders review of all Minnesota sex offenders in civil commitment. *Fox 9 KMSP.* http://www.fox9.com/news/40851395-story

Bartkewicz, A. (2012, September 19). Unrepentant Washington vigilante who killed two registered sex offenders gets life in prison. *Daily News.* http://www.nydailynews.com/news/national/unrepentant-washington-vigilante-killed-registered-sex-offenders-life-prison-article-1.1162753

Birchfield, K. B. (2011). Residence restrictions. *Criminology and Public Policy, 10*(2), 411–419. https://doi.org/10.1111/j.1745-9133.2011.00716.x

Bonnar-Kidd, K. K. (2010). Sexual offender laws and prevention of sexual violence. *American Journal of Public Health, 100*(3), 412–419. https://www.doi.org/10.2105/AJPH.2008.153254

Brooks, R. (2007). Psychiatrists' opinions about involuntary civil commitments: Results of a national survey. *Journal of American Academy of Psychiatry and the Law, 35*(2), 219–228.

Center for Sex Offender Management. (2000). *Myths and facts about sex offenders.* Office of Justice Programs: U.S. Department of Justice. http://www.csom.org/pubs/mythsfacts.html

Center for Sex Offender Management. (2007). *Managing the challenges of sex offender reentry.* http://www.csom.org/pubs/reentry_brief.pdf

CNN. (2008, December 16). Police: Drifter killed Adam Walsh in 1981. http://www.cnn.com/2008/CRIME/12/16/walsh.case.closed/index.html

Cohen, S. (1972). *Folk devils and moral panics: The creation of the mods and the rockers.* MacGibbon and Kee Ltd.

Colombino, N., Mercado, C. C., & Jeglic, E. L. (2009). Situational aspects of sexual offending: Implications for residence restriction laws. *Justice Research and Policy, 11*(1), 27–44. https://doi.org/10.3818/JRP.11.2009.27

Comartin, E., Kernsmith, P., & Kernsmith, R. (2009). Sanctions for sex offenders: Fear and public policy. *Journal of Offender Rehabilitation, 48*(2), 605–619. https://doi.org/10.1080/10509670903196066

Davey, M. (2015). States struggle with what to do with sex offenders after prison. *The New York Times.* http://www.nytimes.com/2015/10/30/us/states-struggle-with-what-to-do-with-sex-offenders-after-prison.html

DeMatteo, D., Murphy, M., Galloway, M., & Krauss, D. A. (2015). A national survey of United States sexually violent person legislation: Policy, procedures, and practice. *International Journal of Forensic Mental Health, 14*(4), 245–266. https://doi.org/10.1080/14999013.2015.1110847

Erin's Law. (2021). *What is Erin's Law?* http://www.erinslaw.org/erins-law/

Farkas, M. A., & Miller, G. (2007). Reentry and reintegration: Challenges faced by the families of convicted sex offense recidivism. *Criminal Justice and Behavior, 35*(4), 484–504. https://www.doi.org/10.1525/FSR.2007.20.2.88

Farley, L. G. (2008). The Adam Walsh Act: The scarlet letter of the twenty-first century. *Washburn Law Journal, 47*(1), 471–503.

Flatow, N. (2014, October 23). *Inside Miami's hidden tent city for 'sex offenders'.* http://thinkprogress.org/justice/2014/10/23/3583307/in-miami-dade-sex-offenders-are-relegated-to-outdoor-encampments/

Fowler, L., & Vallett, J. (2021). Conditional nature of policy as a stabilizing force: Erin's Law and teacher child abuse reporting practices. *Administration & Society.* https://www.doi.org/10.1177/0095399720976534

Freeman-Longo, R. E. (1996). Feel good legislation: Prevention or calamity. *Child Abuse & Neglect, 20*(2), 95–101. https://www.doi.org/10.1016/0145-2134(95)00126-3

Fuselier, D., Durham, R., & Wurtele, S. (2002). The child sexual abuser: Perceptions of college students and professionals. *Sexual Abuse: A Journal of Research and Treatment, 14*(3), 271–280. https://doi.org/10.1177/107906320201400306

Hoppe, T., Meyer, I. H., De Orio, S., Vogler, S., & Armstrong, M. (2020). *Civil commitment of people convicted of sex offenses in the United States.* UCLA School of Law Williams Institute. https://williamsinstitute.law.ucla.edu/publications/civil-commitment-us/

Kan. Stat. Ann. § 59–29a02(a)(Supp. 1996).

Kernsmith, P., Comartin, E., & Kernsmith, R. (2016). Fear and misinformation as predictors of support for sex offender management policies. *Journal of Sociology & Social Welfare, 43*(2), 39–66. https://scholarworks.wmich.edu/jssw

Kernsmith, P. D., Craun, S. W., & Foster, J. (2009). Public attitudes toward sexual offenders and sex offender registration. *Journal of Child Sexual Abuse, 18*(3), 290–301. https://www.doi.org/10.1080/10538710902901663

KMOV. (2015). Sex offenders required to put identifying signs in yard. *KMOV4*. http://www.kmov.com/story/30706993/sex-offenders-required-to-put-identifying-signs-in-yard

Letourneau, E. J., Levenson, J. S., Bandyopadhyay, D., Sinha, D., & Armstrong, K. (2010). Effects of South Carolina's sex offender registration and notification policy on adult recidivism. *Criminal Justice Policy Review, 21*(4), 435–458. https://www.doi.org/10.1177/0887403409353148

Levenson, J., D'Amora, D. A., & Hern, A. L. (2007). Megan's Law and its impact on community re-entry for sex offenders. *Behavioral Sciences and the Law, 25*(4), 587–602. https://www.doi.org/ 10.1002/bsl.770

Levenson, J., & Tewskbury, R. (2009). Collateral damage: Family members of registered sex offenders. *American Journal of Criminal Justice, 34*(1), 54–68. https://www.doi.org/10.1007/s12103-008-9055-x

Lyons, D. (2011). Sex offender law: Down to the wire. *National Conference of State Legislatures*. https://www.ncsl.org/research/civil-and-criminal-justice/sex-offender-law-down-to-the-wire.aspx

Maddan, S. (2005). *Sex offenders as outsiders: A reexamination of the labeling perspective utilizing current sex offender registration and notification policies* [Unpublished doctoral dissertation]. University of Nebraska at Omaha.

Matson, S., & Lieb, R. (1996). *Community notification in Washington State: 1996 survey of law enforcement*. http://wsipp.wa.gov/ReportFile/1242

McPherson, L. (2007). Practitioner's guide to the Adam Walsh Act. *National Center for Prosecution of Child Abuse, 20*(9 & 10), 1–7.

Mears, D. P., Mancini, C., Gertz, M., & Bratton, J. (2008). Sex crimes, children, and pornography: Public views and public policy. *Crime & Delinquency, 54*(4), 532–559. https://doi.org/10.1177/0011128707308160

Mullvihill, M., Wisniewski, K., Meyers, J., & Wells, J. (2003, November). *Monster next door: State losing track of sex offenders*. Boston Herald.

Mustaine, E. E. (2014). Sex offender residency restrictions: Successful integration or exclusion? *Criminology and Public Policy, 13*(1), 169–177. https://www.doi.org/10.1111/1745-9133.12076

Mustaine, E. E., & Tewksbury, R. (2011). Assessing the informal social control against the highly stigmatized: An exploratory study of differential experiences and resulting stress of registered sex offenders. *Deviant Behavior, 32*(10), 944–960. https://www.doi.org/10.1080/01639625.2010.538361

Nesemann, M. (2015, December 22). Manitowoc sex offender ordinance approved. *Herald Times Reporter*. http://www.htrnews.com/story/news/2015/12/22/manitowoc-sex-offender-ordinance-approved/77755062/

Payne, M. (2005). *Sex offender site criticized*. Southwest Florida News-Press.

Pennsylvania State Police. (n.d.). *Megan's Law website*. http://www.pameganslaw.state.pa.us

Pickett, J., Mancini, C., & Mears, D. (2013). Vulnerable victims, monstrous offenders, and unmanageable risk: Explaining public opinion on the social control of crime. *Criminology, 51*(3), 729–759. https://www.doi.org/10.1111/1745-9125.12018

Prison Legal News. (2015, September 19). Some states refuse to implement SORNA, lose federal grants. *Prison Legal News*. https://www.prisonlegalnews.org/news/2014/sep/19/some-states-refuse-implement-sorna-lose-federal-grants/

Public Act 096–1524 (2011).

Redlich, A. D. (2001). Community notification: Perceptions of its effectiveness in preventing child sexual abuse. *Journal of Child Sexual Abuse: Research, Treatment, & Program Innovations for Victims, Survivors, & Offenders, 10*(3), 91–116. https://www.doi.org/10.1300/J070v10n03_06

Rosselli, M. K., & Jeglic, E. L. (2017). Factors impacting upon attitudes toward sex offenders: The role of conservatism and knowledge. *Psychiatry, Psychology and Law, 24*(4), 496–515. https://www.doi.org/10.1080/13218719.2016.1254562

Saad, L. (2005, June 9). Sex offender registries are underutilized by the public. *Gallup*. http://www.gallup.com/poll/16705/sex-offender-registries-underutilized-public.aspx

Silver, C. (2012). Pariahs among us: Sex offender laws in the 21st century. *Aljazeera*. http://www.aljazeera.com/indepth/opinion/2012/10/2012101474052331874.html

SMART. (n.d.). *Learn more about the functionality and capabilities of NSOPW: About NSOPW*. http://www.nsopw.gov

Stafford, M. C., & Vandiver, D. M. (2017). Public perceptions of sex crimes and sex offenders. In T. Sanders (Ed.), *The Oxford handbook of sex offences and sex offenders* (pp. 463–481). Oxford University Press.

Szabo, L. (2013, January 7). Committing a mentally ill adult is complex. *USA Today*. http://www.usatoday.com/story/news/nation/2013/01/07/mental-illness-civil-commitment/1814301/

Tewksbury, R. (2002). Validity and utility of the Kentucky sex offender registry. *Federal Probation, 66*(1), 21–26.

Tewksbury, R., & Mustaine, E. E. (2009). Stress and collateral consequences for registered sex offenders. *Journal of Public Management and Social Policy, 15*(2), 215–239. https://www./doi.org/10.1177/0306624X16653978

Townsend, S. M. (2008). *Primary prevention of sexual violence: A technical assistance guide for planning and evaluation*. Pennsylvania Coalition against Rape.

U.S. Department of Education. (2002, October 24). *Disclosure of education records concerning registered sex offenders*. http://www2.ed.gov/policy/gen/guid/fpco/hottopics/ht10-24-02.html

U.S. Department of Justice. (2008). *Frequently asked questions: The Sex Offender Registration and Notification Act (SORNA) final guidelines*. http://ojp.gov/smart/pdfs/faq_sorna_guidelines.pdf

U.S. Department of Justice. (2014). *Global overview of sex offender registration and notification systems*. https://www.icmec.org/wp-content/uploads/2015/10/US-Global-Overview-of-Sex-Offender-Systems.pdf

U.S. Department of Justice. (2021). *SORNA implementation status*. https://smart.ojp.gov/sorna/sorna-implementation-status

Vásquez, B. E., Maddan, S., & Walker, J. T. (2008). The influence of sex offender registration and notification laws in the United States. *Crime and Delinquency, 54*(2), 175–192. https://www.doi.org/10.1177/0011128707311641

Zgoba, K., Veysey, B. M., & Dalessandro, M. (2010). An analysis of the effectiveness of community notification and registration: Do the best intentions predict the best practices? *Justice Quarterly, 27*(5), 667–691. https://www.doi.org/10.1080/07418820903357673

COURT CASES

Kansas v. Hendricks, 521 U.S. 346 (1997)
McGirt v. Oklahoma, 591 U.S. ___ (2020)
U.S. v. Comstock, 551 F.3d 274 (4th Cir. 2009)

DEFINITIONS

Adam Walsh Act (SORNA): A federal law enacted in 2006, replacing the requirements of the Jacob Wetterling Act and its amendments, that established a three-tier system of registration requiring that sex offenders register for 10 years, 15 years, or life, depending on the type of offense committed

Campus Sex Crimes Prevention Act: A federal-level law passed in 2000 that required that institutions of higher education maintain and disseminate information about known registered sex offenders

Dru Sjodin National Sex Offender Public Registry: Formerly named the National Sex Offender Registry and renamed after Dru Sjodin and includes sex offenders' registration information, regardless of where they live

Erin's Law: A state law adopted in Illinois and several other states that creates a task force for sex-abuse prevention programs and implements a sex-abuse prevention program in public schools—it is a primary prevention strategy

Jacob Wetterling Crimes against Children and Sexually Violent Offender Registration Act: Known as the Wetterling Act, a federal level law passed in 1994 that requires sex offenders to register with law enforcement officials, usually the local police

Megan's Law: A federal law that passed in 1996 that requires that information regarding sex offenders' registration be made public—the law is an amendment to the Violent Crime Control Act of 1994

Moral Panic: An intense, emotional reaction to an issue that is a gross violation of social order (like a sex crime) and is characterized by exaggerated or misdirected fear of the issue

National Sex Offender Registry: Established by the Pam Lychner Sex Offender Tracking and Identification Act of 1996, it requires a national registry be established for the purpose of maintaining all sex offenders' information, regardless of the state where they live—it was subsequently named the Dru Sjodin National Sex Offender Public Registry

Office of Sex Offending Sentencing, Monitoring, Apprehending, Registering, and Tracking (SMART): This office was established to assist states with the implementation of SORNA's requirements—it also provides information about the implementation of SORNA

Pam Lychner Sex Offender Tracking and Identification Act of 1996: Established a national registry for sex offenders (National Sex Offender Registry)

Primary Prevention Strategies: Action taken before a sex crime has occurred for the purpose of preventing victimization and re-victimization

"Romeo and Juliet" Clause: A clause in the SORNA guidelines that allows for exemption of registration for those who have engaged in consensual sex with a victim who is at least 13 years old and involves an offender who is no more than 4 years older

Tertiary Prevention Strategies: Action taken after a sex crime has occurred for the purpose of managing its impact

CHAPTER 12

Conclusion

> **CHAPTER OBJECTIVES**
>
> - Discuss the myth, "All those who commit a sex offense are the same"
> - Assess unanswered questions and potential future directions of sex-offender research
> - Identify the effects of myths regarding sex crimes and persons who commit a sex crime

As noted in the beginning of this textbook, a great deal of sex-crime research has been conducted over the past several decades, leading to substantial strides in what we know now. While we know much more about persons who have committed a sex crime today than we knew in the past, there are still many unanswered questions. Furthermore, throughout history, there has been a pendulum swing from indifference toward persons who commit a sex crime to a moral panic about them. This has shaped many of the myths that surround sex crimes and the persons who have committed a sex crime, which has affected sex-offender identification, treatment and punishment, research, and policy development. In this chapter, we provide a summary of many of the myths that surround sex crimes and persons who have committed a sex crime with attention to potential future directions for research.

BRINGING IT ALL TOGETHER: ALL PERSONS WHO HAVE COMMITTED A SEX OFFENSE ARE (NOT) THE SAME

One particular myth, *all those who have committed a sex offense are the same*, is embedded in many of the other myths that have been highlighted throughout this textbook. It has been said that although many persons who committed a sex offense have common characteristics (intimacy deficits, poor self-control, antisocial tendencies, etc.), their criminal behaviors vary (they commit rape, child molestation, sex trafficking, and/or child pornography, etc.).

Persons who have committed a sex offense also have diverse backgrounds. For example, some are female and some are very young (Chapter 6). Also, some persons who commit a sex crime are in a position of authority, such as clergy, teachers, and law enforcement officials (Chapter 7). Most persons who have committed a sex offense know their victim and, therefore, are not strangers, dispelling the myth that a person who has committed a sex offense is someone who attacks a victim on the street, late at night, while the victim is alone. Victims of sex crimes also vary from very young to very old. They include both males and females, although young women are at a particular risk for rape (Chapter 3).

MYTHS REGARDING THE NUMBER OF SEX CRIMES, PERSONS WHO COMMIT A SEX CRIME, AND ASSOCIATED TRENDS

It has been emphasized in this textbook that it is (wrongly) believed by many that the number of sex crimes and offenders has recently increased. This is mired in an emerging culture of "panic," resulting in policies that may or may not decrease sex crimes. Evidence from several sources indicates that the number of sex crimes has actually decreased over the past several years.

There are many unanswered questions surrounding this myth, however. For example, much of the research covered in Chapter 1 is limited to just a few data sources. Most of those data sources require that a crime be reported to law enforcement officials. What we do not know is the true number of sex crimes that occur. We know, for example, that:

- Many victims do not report sex crimes for a variety of reasons.
- Sex crimes have additional investigational obstacles to successful prosecution.
- Victims of sex crimes are often "groomed" and not forced by gunpoint.
- Most persons who have committed a sex crime know their victims.
- Some persons who commit a sex crime are in a position of authority to the victim (e.g., teacher or relative).

All of these lead to low reporting of sex crimes. More accurate measures of sex crimes and the persons who commit them are needed. Research that involves more than one measure of sex crimes, for example, can yield more accurate results. As noted in Chapter 10, the use of polygraph examinations for persons convicted of a sex crime has resulted in increased knowledge about the range of sex crimes they commit. There are opportunities to capture more accurate information about sex crimes and the persons who commit them.

Another unanswered question is why those who have committed a sex crime have low recidivism rates. More research is needed to address this question through carefully designed studies that accurately measure recidivism. For example, are persons who commit a sex crime more likely to recidivate than others who commit a non-sex offense crime, such as burglars? As noted by Bader et al. (2010), using multiple indicators of recidivism (such as arrest records and reports to child protective service agencies) has revealed higher rates of recidivism than relying only on one measure, such as arrest records. Currently, our knowledge is based on those we know have committed sex crimes because they have been caught, but we do not know about those who have not been caught.

MYTHS REGARDING WHY PERSONS COMMIT SEX CRIMES

Although many may (wrongly) believe that one must be "sick" or "mentally ill" to commit a sex crime, researchers have examined a much broader range of theoretical explanations. There is still too little research, however, about why people commit sex crimes. Much of the research regarding sex-offender specific theories (Chapter 2) has simply identified correlates rather than providing a coherent theoretical explanation. Despite a large number of studies showing that persons who have committed a sex crime commit other types of non-sex crimes too—that is, they are generalists—relatively little research has been conducted applying general crime theories to persons who have committed a sex crime.

MYTHS REGARDING RAPISTS, RAPE, AND RAPE VICTIMS

There is also a great deal of misunderstanding regarding the context in which rape occurs. A widespread belief is that rapes are spontaneous, violent attacks involving strangers. Research has consistently shown that scenarios like this are the exception, rather than the norm. By and large, rapes are committed against a victim by someone who is known to her or him. A very small percentage of rapes involve strangers. Rapists are usually not impulsive; most rapes are acts of premeditated violence.

The idea that once a rapist begins to engage in sex, he (or she) can be provoked to "a point of no return" reinforces the stereotype that rape is an act of uncontrollable passion and symptomatic of high sexual energy. Focus Box 12.1 presents a criminal case involving a police officer who committed numerous rapes against victims whose reputations were questionable (reflecting the myth that certain women are "unrapeable").

Focus Box 12.1 Former Oklahoma City Police Officer Targets "Bad Women" for Rape and Sexual Assault

In December 2015, former Oklahoma City police officer Daniel Holtzclaw was found guilty of 18 counts of rape and sexual assault against over a dozen women between December 2013 and June 2014. By design, Holtzclaw methodically targeted Black/African American teenagers and elderly women with criminal records and histories of drug abuse and sex work. Holtzclaw used his authority to run background checks and outstanding arrest warrants on the women as a means to coerce sex, offering reprieve from warrants and jail time in exchange for sex. Holtzclaw's defense attorney, Scott Adams, acknowledged that the accusers in the case waited months to report his crimes to authorities because they were not "perfect victims" or "perfect accusers." In fact, Adams went so far as to claim that while Holtzclaw was "naïve and very gullible," his victims possessed "street smarts like you can't imagine," effectively portraying Holtzclaw's targets as the predators and responsible for the trauma that they endured. Holtzclaw was sentenced to 263 years in prison for his crimes in January 2016. Critics and commentators have observed that this verdict illustrates the budding momentum of the "Black Lives Matter" campaign, an activist social movement that protests violence against those who are Black/African American and broader issues of police brutality, racial profiling, and abuse of authority. As discussed throughout this textbook, legal decisions regarding sex crimes and the persons who commit them are often the result of shifting social and political climates, and scientific research plays a major role in shaping some of these shifts (Helsel, 2015).

MYTHS REGARDING CHILD SEXUAL ABUSE, CHILD MOLESTATION, AND CHILD VICTIMS

It is estimated that approximately 1 in 5 girls and 1 in 20 boys is a victim of child sexual abuse. The actual prevalence of this crime is difficult to determine, as child sexual abuse is not uniformly defined and, similar to crimes of rape, suffers from under-reporting. As such, the general consensus among experts is that the prevalence rate is higher than official statistics suggest.

There is a great deal of mythology and public denial regarding child sexual abuse with regards to offenders and victims. For example, it is widely assumed that people who look and act "normal" cannot sexually abuse children. Closely related is the belief that all offenders who sexually abuse children are pedophiles. Both myths distort the true image of child sexual abusers. On the whole, offenders who commit sex crimes against children are very similar to their non-offending counterparts. Many maintain employment, are active in their communities, are well-educated, and engage in age-appropriate sexual relationships. They are knowledgeable about the importance of securing a "good-guy" image and appear charming, socially responsible, and sincere. Maintaining this image is a component of the grooming process, where offenders establish trust with potential victims and their caregivers.

Many laws and prevention strategies that have been developed in response to child sexual abuse are predicated on the notion of "stranger danger" (i.e., children are taught early on to avoid contact with strangers, presumably to eliminate the risk of victimization). However, very few crimes of child sexual abuse involve offenders that are unknown to the child. As part of the grooming process, child molesters and other child sexual abusers engage in long-term relationships with potential targets and their families. It may be weeks, months, or even years until abusive acts against the child begin.

Further, the majority of child sexual abusers *do not* fit the diagnostic criteria for pedophilia, yet many confuse child molestation and pedophilia. Someone can molest a child and have no sexual attraction to children. This person would be considered a child molester and not a pedophile. Alternatively, someone can have a strong sexual attraction to children, yet not behave sexually toward a child. This person would be considered a pedophile who does not violate any laws. As noted in Focus Box 12.2, two self-proclaimed pedophiles (who also claim not to molest children) founded an organization, **Virtuous Pedophiles**, allowing people similarly inclined toward pedophilia, but wishing to abstain from pedophilic behaviors and actions, to connect with others in a supportive environment. This website, and in particular the statement from one of the founders set out in Focus Box 12.2, provides an example of someone who is a pedophile, yet is not, reportedly, a child molester.

Similar to rape, claims of child sexual abuse are sometimes met with skepticism, and many victims are accused of making false accusations. It is important to note that although many claims of child sexual abuse are unsubstantiated (meaning there is insufficient legal evidence to determine whether a crime has occurred), very few claims are intentionally fabricated.

MYTHS REGARDING CHILD PORNOGRAPHY AND SEX TRAFFICKING

In general, the rate of sex crimes has been decreasing over the past 20 years. For example, as learned in Chapter 1, official statistics show that there was a 35% reduction in the number of arrests for rape between 2005 and 2014. Likewise, victimization surveys (which are

> **Focus Box 12.2** Pedophiles Are Not Necessarily Child Molesters
>
> Nick Devin and Ethan Edwards founded a website, Virtuous Pedophiles, that provides a forum for those who have a sexual attraction to children (i.e., pedophilia), yet have not molested any child. Below Nick Devin provides his background:
>
> I'm in my mid-60s and married, with four adult children. I have advanced degrees from prestigious universities, a very good job, a lot of friends and am well respected in my community.
>
> I am also a pedophile. I am sexually attracted to boys in the early stages of puberty (typically ages 12–14).
>
> I've never touched a child in any way that could be considered remotely sexual, and am confident I never will. I've resisted my sex drive for more than 50 years, and I'm long past the age where acting on it is even a remote possibility. I know that many children have been harmed by pedophiles, and I refuse to do anything that could harm a child.
>
> On various occasions, I've suffered from low self-esteem and even self-hatred as a result of my pedophilia, feeling that I was somehow immoral as a result of being attracted to kids, even though I never acted on that attraction. With the help of a supportive psychologist, I came to understand that there's nothing morally wrong with being attracted to children as long as I don't have sexual contact with them. I did not choose my sexual orientation, and there is nothing I can do to change it. I cannot be evil simply because I have sexual feelings that I didn't choose and can't change, so long as I don't act on those feelings. In hindsight this strikes me as obvious, but it wasn't at all obvious at the time, and the realization that I am not evil was enormously helpful. . . To those of you who are reading this, I realize that the concept of someone being sexually attracted to children is extremely distasteful to you, but I'll leave you with this. If you had a child who was unfortunate enough to be sexually attracted to children, would you want him to be alone, to feel dirty and evil, to suffer from depression and self-hatred, to possibly even become suicidal? Or would you instead want him to have access to a place like Virtuous Pedophiles, a place where he could receive support in his efforts to resist his pedophilia, where he could have the example of decent, well-adjusted men who have successfully done so?
>
> Note. Adapted from VirPed (n.d.).

able to capture incidents not reported to law enforcement officials) estimate that rape rates have decreased 58% from 1995 to 2010. The trend for child sexual abuse is similar, with studies showing that rates are about half of what they were 20–30 years ago (Finkelhor & Jones, 2006).

Sex crimes involving child pornography, however, have *increased* over the past 20 years. Though child pornography was approaching near-eradication in the 1980s, the internet dramatically changed the scale and nature of the child-pornography problem. From 2000 to 2009, the total number of arrests for child-pornography production more than doubled (Wolak et al., 2012). From an entrepreneurial perspective, child pornography is one of the fastest growing online businesses, generating billions of dollars in annual revenue.

It is widely believed that all individuals who view child pornography will inevitably go on to commit contact offenses against children. However, this is only one of several hypothesized relationships between consumption of child pornography and hands-on offending. For example, some research has indicated that instead of propelling an individual to commit contact offenses against children, viewing child pornography may provide a substitute for actual contact offending (Taylor & Quayle, 2003). Other research has shown that offenders who sexually abuse children may seek out child pornography as an additional form of sexual gratification (Marshall, 2000). In this light, the offender's sexual interest in children drives child pornography consumption, and not the other way around.

It is also assumed that any adult who views child pornography is a pedophile. Although child pornography is a diagnostic indicator of pedophilia (perhaps even more than contact offenses against children), many child pornography offenders do not fit the diagnostic criteria for pedophilia. For example, some may be recreational users (i.e., those who seek out material out of impulse or curiosity). Others may maintain collections or libraries of images, yet do not maintain exclusive sexual interest in children (i.e., they may maintain age-appropriate relationships in addition to viewing child pornography).

Though adult males are the most likely to commit crimes involving child pornography, there has been an increase in the number of youth participating in these crimes. In fact, between 2000 and 2009, the number of arrests for illegal images produced, distributed, and downloaded for youth increased from 22 to 1,198 (an approximate 5,500% increase) (Wolak et al., 2012).

Some of these crimes involve "sexting" incidents, which have been sensationalized in the media as being widespread among youth, but the majority involve youth-produced images that were created as a result of adult solicitation (i.e., cases involving adult offenders who entice adolescent or child victims to produce images).

With regard to sex trafficking, it can affect anyone, but primarily affects young women/girl and some men/boys. Research regarding sex trafficking is still relatively new, but reveals it can affect not only persons from economically-developing countries, but those in the United States as well. Sex trafficking is usually tied to organized crime or another business that serves as a front for the trafficking. Victims of sex trafficking are typically introduced to alcohol and drugs, relying on their handler for their addictions. The victims are isolated and often suffer physical and verbal abuse as well, instilling a sense of fear and avoiding contact with others who could help them.

MYTHS REGARDING JUVENILES AND WOMEN WHO HAVE COMMITTED A SEX CRIME

Although many assume persons who have commit a sex crime are usually adults, a substantial proportion of sex crimes are committed by juveniles. A prevalent myth regarding juveniles who have commit sex crimes is that they continue to offend as adults. The research shows that very few juveniles who sexually offend go on to commit sex crimes as adults. Many of the questions surrounding concern how to respond to them. Should they be treated, given their low recidivism rates? There is no consensus regarding whether juveniles should be required to register, and if so for how long and for what offenses?

Over the past decade, many women who have committed a sex crime have been portrayed in the media. It has become common to hear about a teacher who has molested a pre-teen or teenage boy. This leaves the impression that such women are young, pretty, and "fall in love" with a young, male student. It is often couched in terms of a consenting victim.

By law, children cannot consent to sexual relationships with adults. Such relationships are abusive. Also, the existing research on girls/women who commit sex crimes has identified many who are not teacher-lovers. Thus, there is a broad range of sex crimes committed by girls/women. It has also been documented that such offenders do in fact inflict harm on their victims. Many questions still exist regarding girls/women who commit sex crimes. It is not known, for example, whether they exhibit pedophilia. No assessment tool has been designed specifically for women. Does the same type of treatment relied upon for boys/men work for girls/women It is not clear whether girls/women who have committed a sex crime recidivate at the same rate as their male counterparts.

MYTHS REGARDING INSTITUTIONAL ABUSE

Although there has been considerable effort to eradicate the myth of "stranger danger" (i.e., sex offenders choosing stranger victims), it is still difficult for many people to accept that a person who has committed a sex crime could be someone who is in a trusted position, such as a teacher, daycare provider, or clergy member. Many organizations are ill-equipped to respond to sexual-assault allegations. Future research should identify obstacles in responding appropriately to sexual-assault allegations.

MYTHS REGARDING VICTIMS OF SEX CRIMES

Although some people are at higher risk to become a victim of a sex crime, anyone can become a sex crime victim. As noted in Focus Box 12.3, Andrea Constand does not represent someone who would be vulnerable to a sexual assault. She was confident, athletic, and

PHOTO 12.1 Andrea Constand Testifies Against her Sexual Assault Abuser.

Photo Credit: Matt Rourke//*The New York Times*/Redux.

> **Focus Box 12.3** Meet a Hero: Andrea Constand
>
> Although most victims of sexual assault fail to make a formal report about the sexual violence they endured, Andrea Constand had the courage to come forward and name her abuser: Bill Cosby. She considered him a mentor, and reports he gave her a sedative and proceeded to touch her breasts. He then penetrated her vagina with his fingers without her consent, as she was too incapacitated to speak or move (Truesdell, 2021).
>
> Andrea Constand met her offender when she was only 29 years old. She worked for Temple University as the Director of the women's basketball team. A mutual friend introduced her to her offender, who was 35 years older than her. This was in 2002. After the two met on several occasions to discuss her career and generally became friends. On their fourth meeting, he provided her with a pill to help her relax and then a he-said, she-said sexual encounter occurred (Truesdell, 2021).
>
> She shared the experience with her mother in 2005 after she suffered a flashback of the incident. She subsequently reported the incident to police. The district attorney failed to pursue any charges at that time due to lack of evidence. More than 60 women came forward making similar allegations against Bill Cosby. In 2018, finally, the accused faced a trial in which he was found guilty of three counts of aggravated indecent assault. He served nearly three years before the decision was overturned on a legal technicality. Despite this disappointing setback, she "urge[d] all victims [of sexual assault] to have their voices heard" (Truesdell, 2021, n.p.).

held a prestigious coach position at Temple University. Thus, anyone can be a victim of a sex crime. Their gender, sexuality, strength, prestige, or socio-economic status are no guarantee against a sexual assault.

MYTHS REGARDING INVESTIGATING ABUSE

A critical component of controlling sex crimes is the arrest of known sex offenders. Law enforcement officials, however, are subject to the same biases everyone else has. That means they are subject to the same moral panic that persists in the United States. To guard against biases, whether they are in response to the moral panic regarding sex offenders or the many myths regarding the number, characteristics, and recidivism rates of sex crimes and sex offenders, law enforcement officials must conduct investigations in a thorough manner. Although much has been learned about improved strategies for investigating sex crimes, there is considerable room for improvement. Techniques have been developed, such as distinguishing between an organized offender and a disorganized offender (based on crime-scene characteristics), which allow for narrowing potential suspects. This process can also exclude potential suspects, but does not decisively indicate who the offender is. Similarly, geographical mapping and geographical profiling can narrow the scope of an investigation, but it will not indicate that "John Smith" committed the sex crime.

Much of what we know about investigating sex crimes is based on known errors that have occurred during past investigations. For example, it was found that strict guidelines must be in place when interviewing vulnerable victims, as they are highly suggestible (Bull, 2010). Children, for example, must be allowed to provide as much information about the sex crime as possible prior to asking forced-choice questions (e.g., Was the rapist Black or white?). Research is needed that clearly assesses best practices for interviewing victims, witnesses, and suspects.

MYTHS REGARDING ASSESSMENT AND TREATMENT OF SEX OFFENDERS

There are two myths that relate to assessment and treatment. First, it is (wrongly) believed that persons who have committed a sex crime have a high rate of recidivism—once a sex offender, always a sex offender. Research has consistently shown that sexual recidivism rates among persons who have committed a sex crime are relatively low. Second, it is often believed that persons who have committed a sex crime cannot be treated. Although research in the 1990s reported virtually no positive effects of treatment (Hall, 1995), subsequent research has revealed that successful completion of treatment leads to lower sexual recidivism rates among persons convicted of a sex crime.

With regard to treatment, cognitive-behavioral treatment programs have yielded positive results (Lösel & Schmucker, 2005). Cognitive-behavioral treatment programs encompass a wide variety of components (such as addressing cognitive distortions, learning to manage emotions, increasing interpersonal skills, addressing empathy deficits, reducing deviant sexual behavior, ensuring relapse prevention, and learning self-management skills), but it has not been determined which factors are the most beneficial and for whom. There are unanswered questions regarding the length of treatment. When should treatment of a person who has committed a sex crime be ended, if ever?

There are still sizeable gaps in assessment tools. For example, although it has been shown that using more than one actuarial assessment increases predictive accuracy, no one has assessed which combination of available assessment tools yields the most valid and reliable risk predictions.

MYTHS REGARDING WHICH COMMUNITY SANCTIONS SHOULD EXIST FOR SEX OFFENDERS

Given the heinous nature of sex offenses, many may believe that all offenders are given lengthy prison sentences. While some persons who have committed a sex crime do receive lengthy prison sentences, most (60%) live in the community under some form of supervision (Greenfeld, 1997). Due to several high-profile cases of children (and young adults) who were abducted, sexually assaulted, and murdered, registration and community notification laws have been enacted. These laws, however, are based on assumptions that are difficult, if not impossible, to support with existing evidence. It is assumed that if the public is more aware of persons known to have committed a sex crime, preventive action will be taken and, therefore, lead to fewer sex crimes.

Beyond sex-offender registration requirements, it is not known what other types of restrictions should exist for persons who have committed a sex crime. Should there be restrictions on where such offenders can live, work, or engage in recreation? It is not known whether publicly identifying persons convicted of a sex crime (e.g., sex-offender notification on drivers' licenses, signs in yards, flyers distributed to neighbors) leads to a reduction in recidivism.

While it is clear that sex crimes are not unique to the United States, the strictest registration and community-notification laws exist in the United States. Due to substantial differences in reporting standards across countries, comparisons among different countries are difficult, if not impossible.

THE EFFECTS OF SEX-CRIME AND SEX-OFFENDER MYTHS

As noted throughout this textbook, there are many myths regarding sex crimes and the persons who commit them. The effects of these cannot be ignored, as they affect every effort to minimize the number of sexual-abuse victims. For example, as noted in Chapter 1, a taboo has always existed regarding any research that involves "sex," including sex crimes and sex-offender research. It is a relatively small group of people who conduct sex-offender research, especially when compared to those in the broader fields of psychology, sociology, social work, and criminology who study other types of crime. We have learned a great deal about sex crimes and the persons who commit them over the past few decades; however, much of what we know can still be refined and expanded upon.

The myths regarding sex crimes and the persons who commit them have negatively affected victims. Victims of sexual abuse are reluctant to report for a variety of reasons, including the shame associated with being a victim. Victims receive blame not only from others, but also from themselves. This blame negatively impacts research. For example, research has revealed that positive reactions from others in response to sexual-assault disclosure can lessen the severity of posttraumatic stress disorder (PTSD) symptoms (Ullman & Peter-Hagene, 2014). Critical to understanding persons who commit sex crimes is to gain information from victims. Without reports of sexual victimization, new knowledge cannot be garnered.

For those who do report, a culmination of myths comes into play. Investigations are hampered by false assumptions about sex crimes, the persons who commit sex crimes, victims, and how to best find out what happened. Typically sexual assault victims are questioned about what they did to cause the assault, and even questioned whether it occurred. For other crimes, a car theft for example, it is likely no one questions the car owner like this: "Are you sure your car was stolen? Did you leave it unlocked? Why did you park your car there?," etc. In other words, it would be unusual if a police officer asked the victim what he or she did that led to car theft. For a rape victim, an altogether different story occurs, unfortunately.

The myths regarding persons who commit sex crimes have fueled a moral panic. This, in turn, has led to laws that have lacked empirical support for reducing sex crimes. We have yet to identify effective ways of treating and managing persons who have committed a sex crime. As additional research is conducted, more of these myths can be dispelled, and more effective strategies for managing such offenders can be developed.

REFERENCES

Bader, S. M., Welsh, R., & Scalora, M. J. (2010). Recidivism among female child molesters. *Violence and Victims, 25*(3), 349–362.

Bull, R. (2010). The investigative interviewing of children and other vulnerable witnesses, psychological research and working/professional practice. *Legal and Criminological Psychology, 15*(1), 5–23.

Finkelhor, D., & Jones, L. (2006). Why have child maltreatment and child victimization declined? *Journal of Social Issues, 62*(4), 685–716.

Greenfeld, L. (1997). *Sex offenses and offenders: An analysis of data on rape and sexual assault.* U.S. Department of Justice, Office of Justice Programs, Bureau of Justice Statistics.

Hall, G. C. N. (1995). Sexual offender recidivism revisited: A meta-analysis of recent treatment studies. *Journal of Consulting and Clinical Psychology, 63*(5), 802–809.

Helsel, P. (2015, December 11). *Ex-Oklahoma City cop Daniel Holtzclaw found guilty of multiple on-duty rapes.* Washington Post. https://www.washingtonpost.com/news/morning-mix/wp/2015/12/08/ex-cop-on-trial-for-rape-used-power-to-prey-on-women-prosecutor-says/

Letourneau, E. J., Levenson, J., Bandyopadhyay, D., Sinha, D., & Armstrong, K. (2010). Effects of South Carolina's sex offender registration and notification policy on adult recidivism. *Criminal Justice Policy Review, 21*(4), 435–458.

Lösel, F., & Schmucker, M. (2005). The effectiveness of treatment for sexual offenders: A comprehensive meta-analysis. *Journal of Experimental Criminology, 1*(1), 117–146.

Marshall, W. L. (2000). Revisiting the use of pornography by sexual offenders: Implications for theory and practice. *Journal of Sexual Aggression, 6*(1–2), 67–77.

Taylor, M., & Quayle, E. (2003). *Child pornography: An internet crime.* Psychology Press.

Truesdell, J. (2021, June 30). *Cosby survivor Andrea Constand 'disappointed' by his overturned sexual assault conviction.* People. https://people.com/crime/cosby-survivor-andrea-constand-speaks-out-after-sexual-assault-conviction-overturned/

Ullman, S. E., & Peter-Hagene, L. (2014). Social reactions to sexual assault disclosure, coping, perceived control, and PTSD symptoms in sexual assault victims. *Journal of Community Psychology, 42*(4), 495–508.

VirPed. (n.d.). *Welcome to virtuous pedophiles.* VirPed. https://www.virped.org

Wolak, J., Finkelhor, D., & Mitchell, K. (2012). *Trends in arrests for child pornography production: The Third National Juvenile Online Victimization Study (NJOV-3).* Durham, NH: Crimes against Children Research Center.

Index

Note: **bold** page numbers refer to tables; *italic* page numbers refer to figures.

AASI-3 *see* ABEL Assessment for Sexual Interest-3™ (AASI-3)
Abel, G. G. 85, 194, 195: Assessment for Sexual Interest-3™ (AASI-3) 269–270, 281, 290; child protection screening instrument, development of 194–195
abused–abuser hypothesis 82, 105
academic performance, of juvenile sex offenders 143
accusatorial method (of suspect interviewing) 246, 257
ACEs *see* Adverse Childhood Experiences (ACEs)
ACLU *see* American Civil Liberties Union (ACLU)
actuarial assessments 271, **274**, 291
Adam Walsh Act 294, 300–303, *304*, 305, 308, 319
ADD/ADHD *see* attention deficit (hyperactivity) disorder (ADD/ADHD)
adjudicated 174
adult(s): in detention centers, jails, and prisons 193; pornography 62; survivors, CSA allegations by 219–220; victims, disclosure by 213
Adverse Childhood Experiences (ACEs) 142, 174, 282, 291
affective dyscontrol 33–34
Against Our Will: Men, Women, and Rape (Brownmiller) 57–58
ageism 54
aggressive sexual beliefs, and rape 61–62
alcohol- and drug-facilitated rape 247–249, 257
alcohol myopia 63, 77
alcohol use and abuse: in rapists 63
Amelung, T. 83
American Civil Liberties Union (ACLU) 116, 277
American Psychiatric Association 3, 120; on conduct disorder 144; on paraphilias 237–238; on personality disorders 30

America's Most Wanted 301
Androgen Deprivation Therapy 83
anxious-ambivalent attachment style 31
approach-automatic pathway 30
approach-explicit pathway 30
appropriate (or productive interview) questions 241, 257
Argentina: sex-offender registration and notification laws **296**
asexual, definition of 20
Ashcroft v. Free Speech Coalition (2002) 116, 117
assessment(s): *actuarial* 265; criminogenic needs in 264, 291; dynamic factors in 265; empirically-based approaches to 262–264, *263*; goals of 265–266, **266**; nonactuarial 265, 291; overview of 264–266; psychopathy and 273–275, **275**; purpose of 265–266; risk factors of 266; sex-offender assessment tools 266–273, **267–268**, **272–273**; of sex offenders, myths about 328; tools and treatment issues 261–284
Association for the Treatment of Sexual Abusers (ATSA) 3, 277; creation of 10–11; growth of 10–11
athletic organizations: institutional abuse in 188–191, *188*, *189*
ATSA *see* Association for the Treatment of Sexual Abusers (ATSA)
attachment 35, 46
attachment theory 25–27, 31, 46
attention deficit (hyperactivity) disorder (ADD/ADHD): definition of 174; in juvenile sex offenders 144
attitudes and belief systems 53
attitudinal rape myths 54, 77
Australia: SANE programs in 240; sex-offender registration and notification laws **296**

autoerotic asphyxiation 257
autonomy, removal of 56
aversion therapy 278, 291
avoidant-active pathway 30
avoidant attachment style 31
avoidant-passive pathway 30

Barbaree, H. E. 34
battered child syndrome 86, 105
Beckinsale, K. 221
#BeenRapedNeverReported 222
behavioral evidence: in child sexual abuse 99
behavioral therapy 291
behaviorism 27
belief 35, 46
Bera, W. 146, **147**
Bermuda: sex-offender registration and notification laws **296**
Big Brothers Big Sisters 184
Biles, S. 188, *189*
biological theories 23–25
bisexual, definition of 20
BJS *see* Bureau of Justice Statistics (BJS)
Blanchard, R. 120
Blanchett, C. 221
blitz attack 77
Blue Lagoon, The 113
Bourke, M. L. 122
Bowlby, J.: attachment theory 25–27, 31
Boyle, P. 184
Boy Scouts of America 184
brain structural differences 24
brain tumor: and pedophilia 24
Breiding, M. J. 207
Brownmiller, S. 57–58, 206
Bryant, K. 190
Buck, C. 160
Bumby RAPE Scale 54, **55–56**, 207
Bureau of Justice Statistics (BJS) 128
Burke, T. 12, 221
Bush, G. W. 116
Bussière, M. T. 37

Caffey, J. 86
callousness 29, 46
Campus Sex Crimes Prevention Act of 2000 303, 319
Campus Sexual Assault Victims' Bill of Rights (1992) 185, 201

Campus Sexual Violence Elimination Act of 2013 185, 201
Canada: Canadian Strategy for Ethical Conduct in Sport 190; institutional abuse 189–190; SANE programs in 240; sex crimes in 2, 12; sex-offender registration and notification laws **296**
Cantor, D. **186**
CAPTA *see* Child Abuse Prevention and Treatment Act of 1974 (CAPTA)
case adjudication: in rape cases 70
case attrition 66, *67*, 77
castration **276**, 277, 291; anxiety 26, 46
Causes and Context of Sexual Abuse of Minors by the Catholic Priests in the United States: 1950–2010, The (John Jay College of Criminal Justice) 179
Causeway, J. T. 309
CDC *see* Centers for Disease Control and Prevention (CDC)
Center for Sex Offender Management 151, 294, 308
Centers for Disease Control and Prevention (CDC) 9; on child sexual abuse 81
CGT *see* Criminal Geographic Targeting (CGT)
Child Abuse and Neglect 11
Child Abuse Prevention and Treatment Act of 1974 (CAPTA) 86, 105
child exploitation: growing awareness of 113–115
child molestation 176, 180, 184–185; by law enforcement officials 191–193, **191**; myths about 323
child pornography 107–128; behavior, typology of 118, **119**; child sexual abuse vs **118**; combination trader-traveller 121, 138; to commit contact child sexual abuse crimes, using 121–122; computer forensics in 124; criminal justice response to 123–128, *125*; definition of 110–111, 138; distributors 122–123; in Federal Sentencing Guidelines 126, 127; impulsive child pornography offenders 118–119; Internet and 115–117; investigating 123–124; law, history of 111–117, *112*; myths about 15, 108–109, 323–325; neutralization in cases of 125; offenders 117–123; pedophilia *vs.* 109, 120–121; perpetrators, myths and realities on *114*; producers 122–123; profiteers 122–123; prosecuting 124–126; as victimless crime 108–109

child pornography offenders: penalties for 126–128; sentencing of 126–128
Child Pornography Protection Act of 1996 (CPPA) 116
Child Protection Act of 1984 115
child protection screening instrument, development of 194–195
Child Protective Services (CPS) 95
child sexual abuse (CSA) 80–100; allegations by adult survivors 219–220; allegations during custody disputes 220; behavioral evidence in 99; child pornography vs **118**; children's recollections, accuracy of 218–219; criminal justice response to 94–99; definition of 80, 106; factors affecting criminal trial proceedings in 98–99; false accusations in 84–85; false allegations of 218–220; family infiltrators in 93, 106; in Finkelhor's precondition theory 31–33; fixated abusers in 88, **90**, 106; Freud on 10; "getting tough on crime" 87; grooming of 92–94; historical trends in 85–88; joint investigations of 95, 106; materials 110, 138; medical evidence in 98–99; "monsters" as perpetrators of 85; myths about 15, 81–85; in National Child Abuse and Neglect Data System 9–10; pedophilia and 83, **84**; prosecutorial issues in 95–96; protective factors in 82–83, 106; regressed abusers in 88–89, 106; reporting 95; testimony, role of 95–96; typologies 88–92, **90–91**; very young victims 96–98; victimization, risk factors for 206; see also child pornography; institutional abuse; pedophilia/pedophile
child sexual abuse accommodation syndrome 233
child sexual abuse offences 81
child sexual abuse victims: befriending of, by perpetrators 93; desensitization of 94; grooming of 92–94; medical examinations 241–243, **242**; myths about 323
child victims, disclosure by 213–214
Choi, G. Y. 217
chronic health issues 214–215
civic organizations, institutional abuse in 184–185
civil commitment laws: for sex offenders 310–313, *313*; in United States 312, *313*
classical conditioning 27, *28*, 46
classic experimental design 11, *11*; definition of 20
classic rape 68, 77

classism 54
clearance rates: in rape cases 68, 77
Code of Hammurabi 57
coercion-based model 60, 77
cognitive-based theories 27, 29
cognitive-behavioral therapy 280–282, 291
cognitive-behavioral treatment 143, 152, 174, 276
cognitive biases 29, 46, 250–251, 257
cognitive distortions 27, 32, 46, 174, 276, 281, 291
cognitive processes 278
cognitive restructuring 278, 281, 291
cognitive schemas 27, 46
Cohen, L. E. 206
Cohen, S. 1
colonialism 53
Combating Paedophile Information Networks in Europe (COPINE) scale 110, **111**
combination trader–travellers 121, 138
commercial sexual exploitation (CSE) 128
commitment 35, 46
community sanctions, myths about 328–329
computer forensics, in child pornography 124, 138
conditioning 277; classical 27, *28*, 46; operant 27, *28*, 47
conduct disorders: definition of 174; in juvenile sex offenders 144
confirmation bias 250–251, 257
consent 77
consent-based model 60, 77
Constand, A. 327
co-offenders 156, **158**, 174
COPINE see COmbating Paedophile Information Networks in Europe (COPINE) scale
cortisol 212, 233
Cortoni, F. 161, 163
Cosby, B. 1
Costa Rica: sexual violence rates in *4*
CPPA see Child Pornography Protection Act of 1996 (CPPA)
CPS see Child Protective Services (CPS)
Crawford v. Washington (2004) 96
Crews, T. 207
Crime Data Explorer *7, 8*; definition of 20
crime scene: basics 235–237; disorganized 236; mixed 236; organized 236; profiling 235–237
Criminal Geographic Targeting (CGT) 237, 257
Criminal Justice and Behavior 11

criminal justice response: to child pornography 123–128, *125*; to child sexual abuse 94–99; to rape 66–70
criminogenic needs 264, 291
criminological theories 34–39
crossover 36, 46
CSA *see* child sexual abuse (CSA)
CSE *see* commercial sexual exploitation (CSE)
custody disputes, CSA allegations during 220
cybercrime 124, 138
cycle of child sexual abuse 82, 106

Dark Web/Darknet 115, 138
Davin, P. A. 161
Defense Cascade Model 211–212, *212*, 233
De Francis, V. 87
depression: definition of 174; juvenile sex offenders 144
Descriptive Model of Female Sexual Offending 161, 174
detention centers, juveniles and adults in: 193
deterministic cause 46
developmental disabilities 25
deviant sexual behavior 291
disabilities, victims with 209
disclosure: by adult victims 213; by child victims 213–214
disorganized crime scene 258
disorganized offender, characteristics of **236**
Doe v. Big Brothers Big Sisters of America (2005) 184
dominant (suspect) interviews 246, 258
downward departures 127, 138
drinking *see* alcohol use and abuse
Dru Sjodin National Sex Offender Public Registry 319
DSM- 5 (Diagnostic and Statistical Manual of Mental Disorders 5th ed.) 138; on child sexual abuse 83; on child pornography 120; on conduct disorder 144; on pedophilia 179; on secondary traumatic stress 215
dual offenders 121, 138
Duong, Cammy 68
dynamic factors 265, 291

emotional congruence 32
emotional health outcomes 215
emotional intelligence 143, 174
empathy 31; deficits 281

empirically-based approaches 291; to assessment and treatment of sex crime victims 262–264, *263*
ERASOR *see* Estimate of Risk of Adolescent Sexual Offender Recidivism (ERASOR)
Erin's Law 313–314, *314*, 319
errors in probabilities 251–252
Estimate of Risk of Adolescent Sexual Offender Recidivism (ERASOR) 149, **150**
Estrich, S. 206
ethnicity *see* race
executive functioning, in juvenile sex offenders 143
exhibitionism 49
exhibitionist disorder 238, 258
experiential learning 29, 46
experimentation, juvenile sex offenders and 146, 148

false allegations: of child sexual abuse 218–220; rape 51; of sexual violence 217–220
false memory syndrome 219, 233
family dysfunction, with juvenile sex offenders 142–143
family infiltrators 93, 106
fantasies 237–239
Farmer v. Brennan (1994) 193
FBI *see* Federal Bureau of Investigation (FBI)
Federal Bureau of Investigation (FBI) 300; child sexual abuse typology 88–89, **90–91**, 106; Crime Data Explorer 7, *8*; on juvenile sex offenders 140–141; National Incident-Based Reporting System of 7; on organization traps 251; on rape 2–3; Uniform Crime Reports of 5–7, *5*, *6*; Violent Criminal Apprehension Program (ViCAP) 64, 78
Federal Sentencing Guidelines 138; child pornography in 126, 127
Feldman, C. 207
Fells Acres Day School 245
Felson, M. 37, 39, 206
female sex offenders: co-offenders with 156, 158; nurturer 156
fetishistic disorder 238, 258
fight or flight response to threat 211, 233
Finkelhor, D. 87; precondition theory 31–33, *32*
Firmin, H. R. 70
first responders 239–240
Fisher, B. S. **186**
fixated abusers 88, **90**, 106, 182, 201
fixation 47

Florida American Civil Liberties Union 309
forced-choice questions 243, 244, 258
forcible sex offenses: in National Incident-Based Reporting System 7
Foward, S. 160
France: sex-offender registration and notification laws **296**
Freud, S.: on child sexual abuse 10; psychoanalytical theory 26, 30; theory of infantile sexuality 86, 106
frotteuristic disorder 238, 258
functional family therapy 151, 174

Gannon, T. 161, 163
gay: definition of 20
genetics 25
geographical mapping 258
geographical profiling 237, 258
Germany: sex-offender registration and notification laws **296**
girls: number of sex crimes committed by 140–141
good-looking effect 70, 77
Gottfredson, M. R. 35–36
Graham, H. 221
Great Depression 86
grooming 47, 88, 156; in child sexual abuse 30, 82, 92–94; definition of 106, 175; in institutional abuse 189; maintenance 94; online 94; target, befriending 93; target selection 92–93
Groth, A. N. 64, 114
Groth's Typology 64, **65**, 77, 89, **90**, 106
groupthink 251, 258
"gut instinct" 250

Hale, Sir M. 51
Hall, G. C. N. 33, 34
Hannah, D. 221
Hanson, R. K. 37, 283
Hare Psychopathy Checklist Revised (PCL-R) 273–274, 292
Harlow, N. 85
Hazelwood's Typology 64, **65**, 77
Health Research Funding Research Organization 26
Hendricks, L. 310
Hernandez, A. E. 122
heterosexism 54
heterosexual 10

higher-education institutions: sexual assault in 185–187, **186**
Hirschi, T. 35–36
Hirschman, R. 33, 34
historical trauma 209, 233
Holder, E. 59
Holtzclaw, D. 322
homophobia 53, 54
homosexual 10
hormonal response **276**
hormones 23–24, 47
hostile masculinity syndrome 61, 78
Howitt, D. 121
Hudson, S. M. 30
humane (suspect) interviews 241, 258
hunters 237, 258

IACP see International Association of Chiefs of Police (IACP)
ICMEC see International Centre for Missing & Exploited Children (ICMEC)
id 26, 47
impersonal sex, sexual aggression and 62
impulsive child pornography offenders 118–119
impulsivity 29, 47
inappropriate questions 241, 258
Indigenous victims, sexual violence of 209–210
information gathering 246–247, 258
injury 214–215
institutional abuse 176–195; in athletic organizations 188–191, **188**, *189*; barriers to reporting 179; in Boy Scouts of America 184; causes of 180; characteristics of 177–185; child molestation 184–185; in civic organizations 184–185; concealment of 178; definition of 201; fixated abusers in 182; K–12 schools 181–183; by law enforcement officials 191–193, **191**; maintenance in 178; manipulation in 177; myths about 16, 326; opportunistic offenders in 182; "passing the trash" in 183, 201; religious institutions 179–181; sexual assault 185–188; strategies to combat **194**; suggestions for policies and procedures to respond to 193–
integrated theory 34
intelligence deficits 25
International Association of Chiefs of Police (IACP) 217

International Centre for Missing & Exploited
    Children (ICMEC) 108
Internet: and child pornography 115–117
intersexual, definition of 20
interviewing: accusatorial method of suspect 246;
    rapport-building method of 247, 259; suspects
    245–247; victims 244
intimacy effect 70, 78
investigation: abuse, myths about 327–328; in
    alcohol-facilitated rape 247–249; cognitive
    bias in 250–251; common failures in 250–
    252; confirmation bias in 250–251; crime
    scene basics in 235–237; in drug-facilitated
    rape 247–249; errors in probabilities 251–
    252; groupthink in 251; medical examinations
    in 240–243; organizational traps in 251;
    profiling in 235–237; tunnel vision in 250;
    unique obstacles in 247–249; see also crime
    scene
investigation relevant information (IRI) 241,
    258–259
involvement 35, 47
IRI see investigation relevant information (IRI)

Jacobsson, D. 210
Jacob Wetterling Crimes Against Children and
    Sexually Violent Offender Registration Act (the
    Wetterling Act) 293, 299, 303, 319
jails, juveniles and adults in 193
Jamaica: sex-offender registration and notification
    laws **297**
Jarsey: sex-offender registration and notification
    laws **297**
Jeanne Clery Disclosure of Campus Security Policy
    and Campus Crime Statistics Act of 1988
    185, 201
Jeffrey Epstein: Filthy Rich 158
Jenkins, P. 2
Jenney, A. 143
John Jay College of Criminal Justice 179
joint investigations: of child sexual abuse 95, 106
Journal of Child Sexual Abuse 11
Journal of Interpersonal Violence 11
J-SOAP-II *see* Juvenile Sex Offender Assessment
    Protocol-II (J-SOAP-II)
JSORRAT-II *see* Juvenile Sex crime Recidivism Risk
    Assessment Tool-II (JSORRAT-II)
just world hypothesis 50, 78

Juvenile Sex crime Recidivism Risk Assessment Tool-II
    (JSORRAT-II) 149, **150**
Juvenile Sex Offender Assessment Protocol-II
    (J-SOAP-II) 149, **150**
juvenile sex offenders 140–165; academic
    performance and 143; assessment of 149,
    150; attention deficit hyperactivity disorder
    in 144; common characteristics of 141–145;
    conduct disorders in 144; depression in
    144; in detention centers, jails, and prisons
    193; distinctions 145–146; effectiveness
    of treatment for 152; emotional intelligence
    in 143; executive functioning in 143;
    experimentation and 146, 148; explanations
    of 146, 148; exposure to pornography 148;
    family dysfunction and 142–143; learning
    disorders in 143; mental illness among 143;
    myths about 15, 325–326; number of sex
    crimes committed by 140–141, *141*, *142*;
    recidivism among 152–153; sexual-abuse
    cycle 148; trauma exposure 142–143;
    treatment for 149–152; typologies 145–146,
    147; victim characteristics 145; vs. juvenile
    nonsexual offenders 145

Kansas Sexually Violent Predator Act 310–312
Kansas v. Hendricks (1997) 294, 311
Kennedy v. Louisiana (2008) 88
Kenya: sex-offender registration and notification
    laws **297**
Kercher, G. **157**
Kilpatrick, D. G. **186**
Kinsey, A.: on sexual behavior 10
Koss, M. P. **186**
Krone, T. 118, **119**, 120, 121, 123
K-12 schools, abuse in 181–183

lack of empathy 29, 47
Lalumière, M. L. 145
Lane, K. J. 39
Larsen, R. R. 273
Lateef, R. 143
Law Enforcement Assistance Administration
    68–69, 221
law enforcement officials, child molestation/sexual
    assault by 191–193, **191**
learning: experiential 29, 46; vicarious 29, 48
learning disorders, in juvenile sex offenders 143

lesbian: definition of 20
Letourneau, M. K. 156
Levenson, J. S. 142
Levenson Self-Report Scale of Psychopathy 274, 291
LGBTQIA+: definition of 20
longitudinal studies 146, 175
Lösel, F. 283
low base-rate problem 263, 291

Maldives: sex-offender registration and notification laws **297**
Male Athletes Against Rape 191
male rape myths **208**
male sex offenders: women sex offenders vs 155
male victims, sexual violence of 207–209
Malta: sex-offender registration and notification laws **297**
Marshall, W. L. 34
Massachusetts Treatment Center: Child Molester Typology, Version 3 (MTC:CM3) 89, 92
Massachusetts Treatment Center Rapist Typology, Version 3 (MTC: R3) 64, **65**, 78, 79
Masters, W. H. **157**
Mathews, R. 157–158, **157**
Maxfield, M. G. 82
Maxwell, G. 159
Maxwell, S. 158
Mayer, A. **157**
McCarty, L. M. *157*
McGirt v. Oklahoma (2020) 305
McGowen, R. 221
McMartin Pre-School Case 245
McMartin Preschool Trial 87
medical evidence: in child sexual abuse 98–99
medical examinations: of child victims 241–243, **242**; of rape victims 240–241
Megan's Law 293, 299–300, 319
Mendelsohn, B. 204
mens rea 138
mental health outcomes 215
mental illness, in juvenile sex offenders 143
Merryn, E. 313
meta-analysis: definition of 20, 175
#MeToo movement 203, 221–222
military, sexual assault in 187–188
Miller Test 113, 114, 138
Miller v. California (1973) 113

Minnesota Sex Offender Screening Tool- 3.1 (MnSOST-3.1) 291
minor, definition of 111
misogyny 53
mixed crime scene 259
MnSOST-3.1 *see* Minnesota Sex Offender Screening Tool- 3.1 (MnSOST-3.1)
modus operandi (MO) 88–89, 235–237, 259
monsters 2
monsters, child sexual abusers as 85
MOPS 249
moral panic 1, 2, 81, 87, 319; definition of 20
Moral Panic: Changing Concepts of the Child Molester in Modern America (Jenkins) 2
Morry, M. M. 54
MO *see* modus operandi (MO)
multisystemic therapy 151–152, 175
myths: about appropriate responses to persons who have committed a sex crime 16; about assessment and treatment sex offenders 16, 328; about child molestation 323 about community sanctions 328–329; about child pornograpy 15, 108–109, 323–325; about child sexual abuse 15, 81–85, 323; about child victims 323; about institutional abuse 16, 326; about investigating abuse 327–328; about investigations of sex crimes 16; about juvenile sex offenders 15, 325–326; about rape 15, 33, 47, 50–52, **50**, 54, **208**, 322; about rape victims 15, 322; about rapists 322; about sex-crime 1, 14–16, 321–322; about sex crime victims 326–327; about sex-offenders 329; about sex trafficking 15, 323–325; about victims of sex victims 16; about women sex offenders 325–326; male rape **208**

narcissism 29, 47
Nassar, L. 189
National Academy of Sciences 278
National Adolescent Perpetrator Network 151
National Alliance of the Mentally Ill 152
National Center for Missing & Exploited Children: CyberTipline 108
National Child Abuse and Neglect Data System (NCANDS) 9, 20
National College Women Sexual Victimization Survey (NCWSV) 187

National Commission on Pornography and Obscenity 86–87
National Crime Victimization Survey 205
National Crime Victimization Survey (NCVS) 7–9, 9, 20
National Human Trafficking Hotline 128
National Incident-Based Reporting System (NIBRS) 7, 20, 156
National Intimate Partner and Sexual Violence Survey (NIPSVS) 9–10, 20, 207, 214
National Juvenile Online Victimization (N-JOV) Prosecutor Study 124, 126
National Review Board 179
National Sex Offender Public Registry 304–305
National Sex Offender Registry 300, 319
National Society for the Prevention of Cruelty to Children 190
National Task Force on Juvenile Sexual Offending 149
Nature and Scope of Sexual Abuse of Minors by Catholic Priests and Deacons: 1950–2002 (John Jay College of Criminal Justice) 179
NCANDS *see* National Child Abuse and Neglect Data System (NCANDS)
NCVS *see* National Crime Victimization Survey (NCVS)
NCWSV *see* National College Women Sexual Victimization Survey (NCWSV)
neurotransmitters 24, 47
neutralization: in child pornography cases 125; techniques of 139
New York v. Ferber (1982) 114
NIBRS *see* National Incident-Based Reporting System (NIBRS)
NIPSVS *see* National Intimate Partner and Sexual Violence Survey (NIPSVS)
N-JOV *see* National Juvenile Online Victimization (N-JOV) Prosecutor Study
nonactuarial assessments 265, 291
non-forcible sex offenses: in National Incident-Based Reporting System 7
normalization of violence 54
nurturer 156, 175

O'Brien, M. 146, **147**
obscene offenses: in National Incident-Based Reporting System 7
obscenity: definition of 138; history of 112–113

O'Connell, R. 94
Office of Sex Offending Sentencing, Monitoring, Apprehending, Registering, and Tracking (SMART) 303–304, 319
Office of Victims of Crime 240
officer shuffle 193
online grooming 94
open questions 243, 259
operant conditioning 27, *28*, 47; model 277
opportunistic approach 259; in alcohol-facilitated rape 248
opportunistic offender 182, 201
opportunistic rapists (type 1 and 2) 78
organizational traps: in investigations 251
organized crime scene 259
organized offender, characteristics of **236**
Osborne v. Ohio (1990) 115
other specified paraphilic disorder 259
Otto, K. E. 190

Palmer, C. T. 25
Pam Lychner Sex Offender Tracking and Identification Act 294, 300, 319
paraphilias 237–239, 259
paraphilic disorder 238, 259
parental alienation syndrome 233
"passing the trash" 183, 201
pattern-prone offense 192, 201
Pavlov, I. 25; behaviorism 27
PCL-R *see* Hare Psychopathy Checklist Revised (PCL-R)
Pedneault, A. 37
pedophilia/pedophile 179, 324; brain tumor and 24; characteristics of **84**; child pornography offenders and 109, 120–121; child sexual abuse and 83; definition of 106, 138; diagnostic criteria 83; *see also* child sexual abuse (CSA)
pedophilic disorder 259
Pelo, J. 192
penis envy 26, 47
People v. Sharp (2005) 96
Perry's Typology 65, **66**, 78
personality development 29–30
personality pathology 30, 47
pervasively angry rapists (type 3) 78
plethysmograph 291
Pflugradt, D. M. 163

phallometric assessment 120, 138
phased approach 243, 259
physical trauma 214–215
Pitcairn Islands: sex-offender registration and notification laws **297**
Pitts v. State (2005) 96
plea bargain, in rape cases 69, 78
poachers 237, 259
police: reporting and response to rape 67–69
polygraph 278–279, **279**, 291
polyvictimization 213, 233
pornography 33; child *see* child pornography; exposure to 148; in National Incident-Based Reporting System 7
post-traumatic stress disorder (PTSD) 262, 329
PREA *see* Prison Rape Elimination Act of 2003 (PREA)
precondition theory 31–33, *32*
Prendergast, W. E. 82–83
Pretty Baby 113
Preventive Health and Health Services Block Grant 221
primary prevention strategies 313, 319
Prison Rape Elimination Act of 2003 (PREA) 193, 201
prisons, juveniles and adults in 193
proactive approach 259; in alcohol-facilitated rape 248
probabilistic cause 47, 78
Progressive Era (1890–1920) 86
prosecutorial decision-making 69–70, *69*
Prosecutorial Remedies and Other Tools to End the Exploitation of Children Today (PROTECT) Act of 2003 116–117, 120, 127
prospective study 175
Protection of Children Against Sexual Exploitation Act of 1977 115
PROTECT *see* Prosecutorial Remedies and Other Tools to End the Exploitation of Children Today (PROTECT) Act of 2003
prurient interests 138
pseudo child pornography 139
psychoanalytical theory 26, 30
psychological theories 25–30
psychological well-being 281
psychopathy 273–275, **275**, 292
psychosexual development 26, 47

PTSD *see* post-traumatic stress disorder (PTSD)
punishment 27

quadripartite theory 33–34
queer 13; definition of 20
questioning, definition of 20

racism 53, 54
Radar, D. 239
rape 49–71; aggressive sexual beliefs among 61–62; case adjudication with 70; classic 68, 77; clearance rates in cases of 68, 77; criminal justice response to 66–70; definition of 59, 78; false allegations of 51, 217–218; FBI on 2–3; by mentally ill or psychotic 51–52; men/women and 52; myths about 15, 33, 47, 50–52, **50**, 54, **208**, 322; in National Crime Victimization Survey 8; police reporting and response 67–69; prosecutorial decision-making 69–70, *69*; reasons for 60–63; statutory 59, 79; typologies 63–65, **65–66**; in Uniform Crime Reports 5, 5–7, *6*; in Uniform Crime Reports 57, 59; in unsafe, unmonitored places 52; victimization, risk factors for 205; victims, medical examinations of 240–241; and women as property 57
rape culture 52–57, 78; attitudes and belief systems 53; autonomy, removal of 56; definition of 53; normalization of violence 54; peak of the pyramid 56–57
rape law: today 58–60; in United States 57–60, 61
rape reform movement 57–58
rape shield laws 78
rape victims: as "bad" people 50–51; myths about 15, 322; secondary victimization in 66–67, 78
Rapid Risk Assessment of Sex Offender Recidivism (RRASOR) 292
rapists: alcohol use and abuse in 63; Groth's typology of 64, **65**, 77; history of violence in 62–63; hostile masculinity in 61, 78; myths about 322; physical aggression of 62; plea bargain for 69; psychological aggression of 62
rapport-building method of interviewing 247, 259
recidivism 14, 149, 264, 283; definition of 20; in juvenile sex offenders 152–153; of women sex offenders 163, **164**

recovered-memory therapy 233
red herrings 259
regressed abusers 88–89, 106
regression 47
reinforcement 27
relapse prevention 281, 282, 292
religious institutions, abuse in 179–181
religious intolerance 54
Republic of Ireland: sex-offender registration and notification laws **296**
residence restrictions 309–310
retrospective studies 148, 175
risk, need, and responsivity (RNR) Model 264, 292
Risk Matrix 2000/S (RM2000/S) 292
RM2000/S see Risk Matrix 2000/S (RM2000/S)
RNR see risk, need, and responsivity (RNR) Model
Robinson-Keilig, R. A. 217
"Romeo and Juliet" clause 303, 319
Rossmo, D. K. 251
Routine Activities Theory 206, 233
routine activity theory 37–38, 47
RRASOR see Rapid Risk Assessment of Sex Offender Recidivism (RRASOR)
Rumney, P. N. 51

SACJ-Min see Structured Anchored Clinical Judgment (SACJ-Min)
sadism 29, 47
Salter, A. 160
Sandusky, J. 188
SANE see Sexual Assault Nurse Examiner (SANE)
Sarrel, P. M. **157**
Schmucker, M. 283
Sciorra, A. 221
Scorsese, M. 114
Scout's Honor: Sexual Abuse in Americas Most Trusted Institutions (Boyle) 184
Sebold, A. 330
secondary traumatic stress (STS) 216–217, 233
secondary victimization, in rape victims 66–67, 78
secondary victims: definition of 233; of sexual violence 215–217
seduction theory of childhood sexuality 10
self-control theory 35–37, 47
self-regulation model of relapse in sexual offenders 30–31, 47

Sentencing Guidelines Manual 127–128
Seto, M. C. 120, 132, 145
sex chromosome abnormalities 25
sex crime(s): assessment tools and treatment issues related to 261–284; brief history of research on 10; definition of 2–3; effects of 329; failure to report 235; investigations, myths about 16; investigations of 234–253; limitations with nonexperimental research on 11–12, *11*; myths about 1, 14–16, 321–322; research and diversity 12–13; sources and numbers of 3–10; state of current research on 10–13; theories about 21–40; with unique investigations obstacles 247–249; victims, myths about 16, 326–327
sex-crime-specific theories 30–34
sexist humor 54
sex offences, perceptions of 294–295, 320–321
sex-offender assessment tools 266–273, **267–268**, **272–273**; ABEL Assessment for Sexual Interest-3™, 269–270; effectiveness of 273; with objective measures but without cutoff scores 269; Sexual Violence Risk-20, 270–271; Static-99R assessment tool 271, **272–273**; Static-2002 assessment tool 271
Sex Offender Registration and Notification Act (SORNA) see Adam Walsh Act
sex-offender registration and notification laws 295, **296–298**, 305–306; additional requirements for 308–310; assumptions of 306–307; effects of 307–308; residence restrictions 309–310
Sex Offender Risk Appraisal Guide (SORAG) 292
sex offenders 13–14; *versus* person who committed a sex crime 3; sources and numbers of 3–10
sex offenses: in National Incident-Based Reporting System 7
sexting 110, 139
sex trafficking 107, 128–133; definition of 138; laws 128–130, *129*; method of 128–129; myths about 15, 323–325; victims of 131–133, *132*
Sexual Abuse: A Journal of Research and Treatment 10–11
sexual-abuse cycle 148
sexual arousal 32; physiological 33

sexual assault: definition of 78; in higher-education institutions 185–187, **186**; within institutions 185–188; by law enforcement officials 191–193, **191**; in military 187–188; in National Crime Victimization Survey 9; in unsafe, unmonitored places 52; victimization, risk factors for 205; *see also* rape
Sexual Assault Nurse Examiner (SANE) 240–241, 259
Sexual Behavior in the Human Female (Kinsey) 10
Sexual Behaviour in the Human Male (Kinsey) 10
sexual burglary 37–38
sexual gratification 160
sexual gratification rapists (type 4, 5, 6, and 7) 78–79
sexual harassment 49
sexually offending: common causes of 39; theories of 22
sexually transmitted disease (STD) 214
sexual masochism disorder 238, 259
sexual misconduct 181, 202
sexual sadism disorder 238, 259
sexual trauma, neurobiology of 211–213
sexual violence: definition of 202, 233; effects on victims **216**; of elderly victims 206–207; false allegations of 217–220; of Indigenous victims 209–210; of male victims 207–209; pyramid 53; secondary victims of 215–217; victim advocacy 220–222; victimology of 203–222; victim responses to 210–217; victims with disabilities 209
Sexual Violence Risk-20 (SVR-20) 270–271, 292
Shakeshaft, C. 181, 182
signature 260
Skinner, B. F. 25; behaviorism 27; operant-conditioning model 277
Smallbone, S. W. 38
Smith, K. 262, *263*
social control ("bonding") theory 35, 48
social learning theory 39–40
Society for the Prevention of Cruelty to Children 85
sophisticated rape track 92, 106
SORAG *see* Sex Offender Risk Appraisal Guide (SORAG)
SORNA *see* Sex Offender Registration and Notification Act (SORNA)

South Africa: sex-offender registration and notification laws **297**
South Korea: sex-offender registration and notification laws **298**
specific questions 243, 260
Sport England 190
Spotlight 179
Stanko, E. 56
Stanley v. Georgia (1969) 115
State Department of Corrections 311
Static-99R assessment tool 271, **272–273**, 292
Static-2002 assessment tool 271, 292
static factors 292
statutory rape 59, 79
STD *see* sexually transmitted disease (STD)
Steiker, C. S. 128
Structured Anchored Clinical Judgment (SACJ-Min) 292
STS *see* secondary traumatic stress (STS)
Student Right-to-Know and Campus Security Act of 1990 185, 202
Sulkowicz, Emma 66
superego 26, 48
suspects, interviewing 245–247
SVR-20 *see* Sexual Violence Risk-20 (SVR-20)
Sweden: sexual violence rates in 4
Syed, F. **157**

Taiwan: sex-offender registration and notification laws **298**
Taxi Driver 113, 114
techniques of neutralization 139
tertiary prevention strategies 295, 319
testimonial competence 97, 106
testimonial hearsay 96, 106
Texas Senate Criminal Justice Commission 304
theory(ies) 21–40; biological 23–25; criminological 34–39; definition of 22; essential components of 21–23; probabilistic nature of 23; psychological 25–30; sex-crime-specific 30–34; of sexually offending 22
theory of infantile sexuality 86, 106
Thornhill, R. 25
Three-Prong Obscenity Test 113
Thurman, U. 221
Title IX 185, 202

tonic immobility 212, 233
Trafficking Victims Protection Act of 2000 128
transsexual: definition of 20
transvestic fetishism 238, 260
trappers 237, 260
Trauma, Violence and Abuse 11
trauma exposure, in juvenile sex offenders 142–143
trauma-informed care 282, 292
treatment: effectiveness 282–283; history of developments **276**, 276–277; for sex crime victims, obstacles in assessing 261–262; of sex offenders, myths about 328
Trinitad and Tobago: sex-offender registration and notification laws **298**
trollers 237, 260
trophy 237, 260
tunnel vision 250, 260
typologies: child pornography 118, **119**; child sexual abuse 88–92, **90–91**; definition of 79, 139; juvenile sex offenders 145–146, **147**; rape 63–65, **65–66**; women sex offenders 155–160, **157**

UCR *see* Uniform Crime Reports (UCR)
U.K. *see* United Kingdom (U.K.)
unfound 79
Uniform Crime Reports (UCR) 5–7, *5*, *6*, 20; rape in 57, 59
United Kingdom (U.K.): Child Protection Sport Unit 190; sex-offender registration and notification laws **298**
United Nations Office on Drugs and Crime (UNODC) 3–5, **4**, 20
United States: child sexual abuse in 81; civil commitment laws 312, *313*; First Amendment of the Constitution 107, 113, 117; minimum age of consent in 60; rape law in 57–60, *61*; SANE programs in 240; sex crimes and sex offender management policy in 56–57; sex crimes in 2, 12, 22; sex-offender registration and notification laws **298**; 13th Amendment of the U.S. Constitution 128
United States Conference of Catholic Bishops (USCCB): Charter for the Protection of Children and Young People 179
United States v. Tucker (2002) 126
United States v. Williams (2008) 117
UNODC *see* United Nations Office on Drugs and Crime (UNODC)
unsubstantiated 106
USCCB *see* United States Conference of Catholic Bishops (USCCB)
U.S. Civil War (1865–1877) 85
USSC *see* U.S. Sentencing Commission (USSC)
U.S. Sentencing Commission (USSC) 127
U.S. v. Comstock (2009) 312

Vandiver, D. M. **157**
VAWA *see* Violence Against Women Act of 1994 (VAWA)
vicarious learning 29, 48
victimization, early theories of 204
victimology: definition of 233; of sexual violence 203–222
victim precipitation 204, 233
Victims of Crime Act of 1984 221
vigilantism 308
vindictive rapists (type 8 and 9) 79
violence: history of 62–63; normalization of 54; sexual 202
Violence Against Women Act of 1994 (VAWA) 58, 221
Violence and Aggression 11
Violence and Victims 11
Violence Risk Appraisal Guide (VRAG) 292
virtual child pornography 110, 139
Virtuous Pedophiles 323
voyeurism 49
voyeuristic disorder 238, 260
VRAG *see* Violence Risk Appraisal Guide (VRAG)
Vrij, A. 70
vulnerable victim 241, 260

Walker, J. 215
Walsh, J. 301
Ward, T. 30, 31
Webb, L. 117
Wee Care Nursery School 245
Widom, C. S. 39, 82
Williams, J. 235
Williams, L. S. 68
Williams, M. 117
Williams, S. **157**
Williams, W. 207
Winkler, E. 54

Wolak, J. 121
Wolfgang, M. 204
women: number of sex crimes committed by 140–141, *141*; as property 57; Violence Against Women Act 58
women sex offenders 153; assessment of 161–162; characteristics of 153–155; distinctions 155–160; explanations of 160–161; male sex offenders vs 155; myths about 325–326; offense and victim characteristics 153–155; recidivism of 163, **164**; treatment for 162–163; typologies 155–160, **157**
Wortley, R. K. 38
wraparound services 151, 175

xenophobia 53

Zimring, F. E. 37

Made in the USA
San Bernardino, CA
31 August 2017

Kibbles for the Soul

My Other Essays and Books You Might Enjoy

On my ancient and unkempt website you can find these two **free essays**. Go to www.martinkimeldorf.org and then click on the Soul Work page for these two items:

Cosmic Coding

Light and Shadow

Recent **books in print and eBook** formats include:

Writing An Obituary Worth Reading
A Guide to Writing a Fulfilling Life-Review

My Mixology
Cocktails, Funny Tales & Literary Sleight of Hand

How To Stay In Love, Forever
...Forty-plus Years of Love Poems, Letters, and PhotoArt

Sipping From The Rubáiyát's Chalice
My Journey with The Rubáiyát of Omar Khayyám

Kibbles for the Soul

Artwork and Acknowledgements

Martin Kimeldorf created or developed most of the artwork and photomontages from front to back covers. This includes interpreting and collaging images found in the cosmology images found in the public domain at the NASA web site, pictures restored from old family albums and *Kibble Soul Brothers* shot by his brother Lloyd.

The cartoons and photos are reprinted here with permission. This includes Pooch Café cartoons by Paul Gilligan; the picture of *Hugo the Dog* by Marko Savkovich; Irine Parini's two images *Cat-a-Tonic Stare* and *Darkness, My Old Friend*; and Julie Wagner's spider web in *Some Glimpse Beyond The Glass*.

Editorial contributions and encouragements from my wife Judy and brother Howard helped get this work off and running. Reassuring comments from FitzOmar experts Bill Martin, Sandra Mason, and Bob Richardson paved the way for completing this project. This was followed by positive and helpful feedback from Lois Talotta, Jacque Hudlow, Karen Upton. Then there was Alison Keithley; she was my pivotal reviewer in the beginning and finisher at the end. Thank you all for keeping me company on this journey.

Kibbles for the Soul

LXXVI

**Blissfully cooking a gourmet meal one more time,
my life spent searching for fate's plan and rhyme.
Drained the cup; turned it over without regret…
recalling friends and drink, in love entwined.**

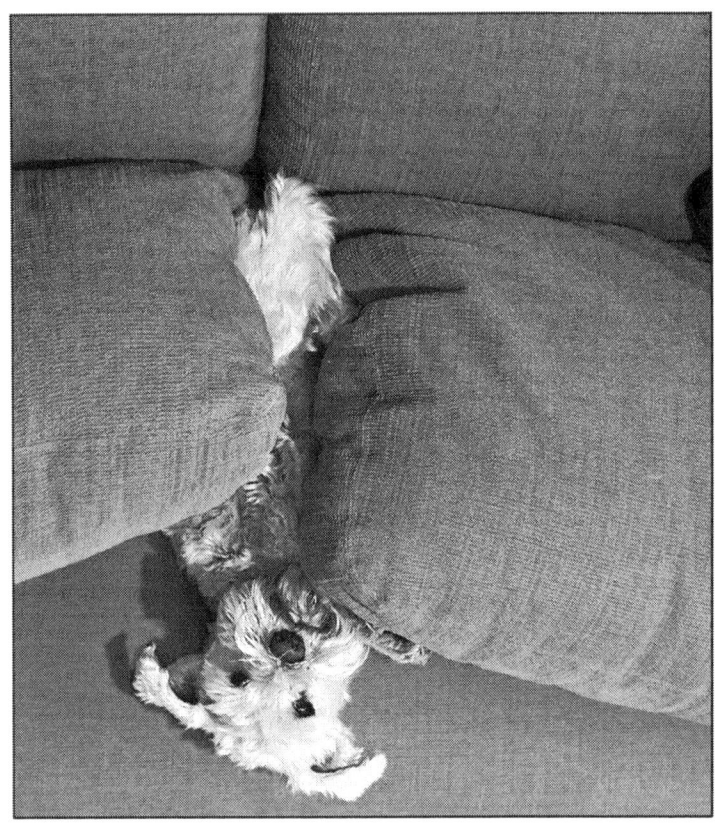

Drain the Cup and Think of Me

Clouded Time

CVI

**Let's speak of the once that was yesterday...
Stories recalled from the gold leaf dossier.
Ignore tomorrow's beckoning finger,
the ringing phone, ticking clock—we disobey**

Some Glimpse Beyond The Glass

CXI

Flitting like bugs in an alien's jar,
not understanding who we really are.
Some glimpse beyond the glass, most remain blind...
The pest persists—a trivial commissar.

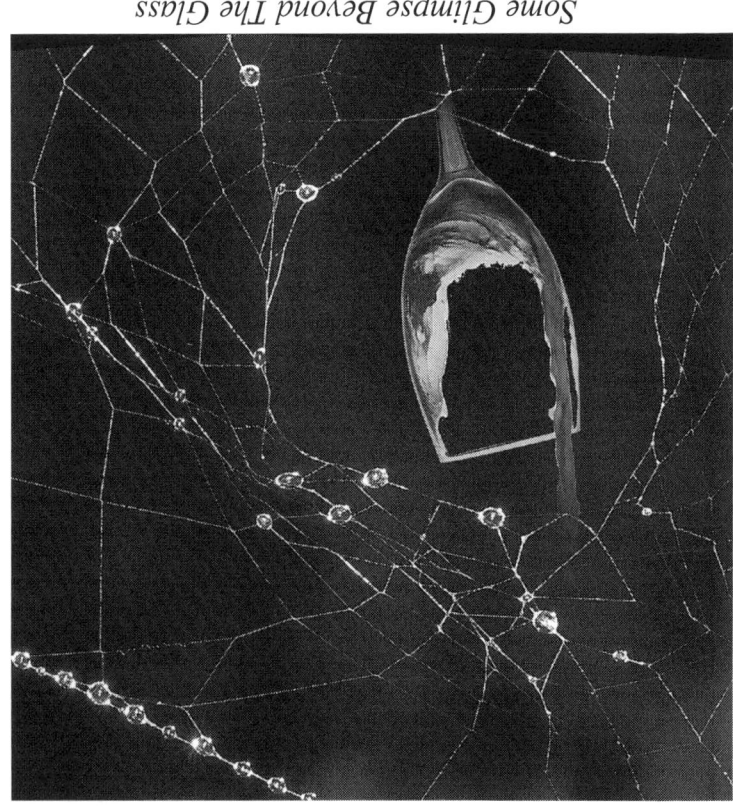

Kibbles for the Soul

Franky Sails Across The Checkerboard

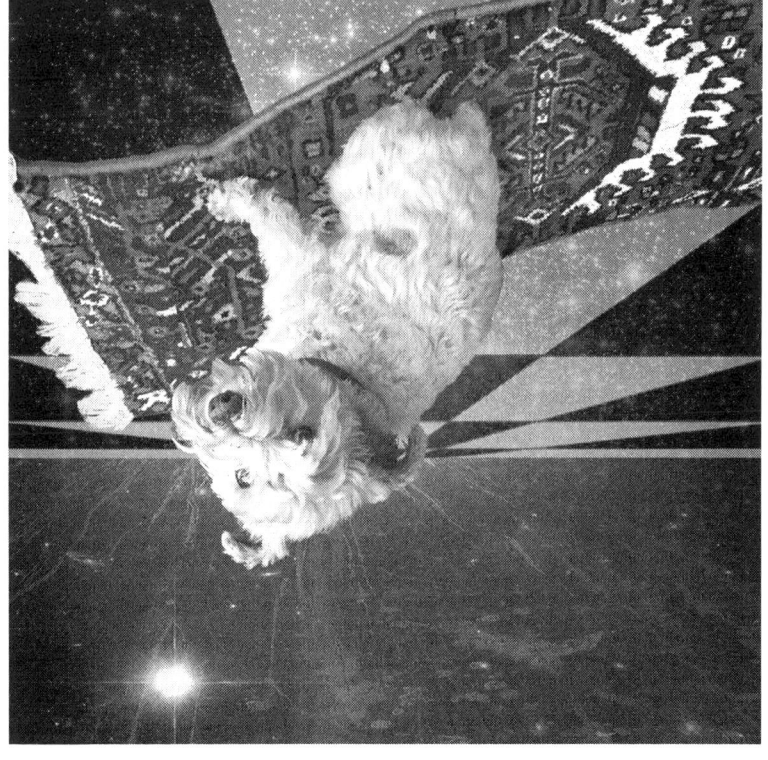

CVII

Firmly make your move within the flow.
The edge of the board comes quickly... you know.
The checkerboard has no in-between grays—
We come, travel quickly... then must go.

Kibbles for the Soul

Kibbles for the Soul

LXXIII

Why does the word Mortality
rhyme so easily with Fatality?
Skipping and dancing with Duality...
In the end whispering Finality.

LXXIV

My Meter is not always kept the same.
I write in the spirit of play and game.
Don't mine my poems like hard lumps of coal, Instead
let verse stir ashes back into flame.

LXXV

Writing hands sum up my journey in this book.
Age, arthritis bequeath a tempered outlook.
Come sip from the Rubáiyát's Chalice,
and reflect upon gourmet meals left to cook.

DRAINING THE CUP

*The Kibble Soul Brothers
Bid Good-Bye*

CII

**April third in I turned GodDamn 70.
But my genetics said this would not be,
My expiration date was 65…
I guess the cosmic joke was played on me!**

Kibbles for the Soul

LXXXII

**The moon—our tranquil and silent partner,
We howl at it and often wonder…**
No matter our complaint or boast
Luna remains a patient listener.

LXXII

**Our tale unwinds oddly and briefly.
No one knows our final destiny—**
Returning to the larger cosmic code,
no longer bound by our mortality…

Kibbles for the Soul

LXXI

**Will our species endure its self-inflicted folly,
to rub noses with the Eskimo finale?
Or did we only crawl from dinosaur swamps,
to be consumed by silent melancholy?**

Franky Wonders About His Destiny

Kibbles for the Soul

remnant light of this now-gone nebula remind one of an Eskimo's face surrounded by a winter parka hood.

His reflections are entitled *Out of Time*. It was one of the most poetic and thoughtful cosmological essays I have ever read. Dan's musings inspired these quatrains. The original post can be found on his blog if you type *https://danspace77.com* into your Google search box.

LXIX

Hubble Telescope sends us across time and space revealing an ancient supernova face.
Did they temper instincts in order to survive?
Will others look back at our Milky Way with grace?

LXX

Eskimo Star-dwellers flew on astral sails.
hesitant to follow stardusty trails…
What choices were made back in deep space? Or were they just shadows in a cosmic folktale?

113

Kibbles for the Soul

THE STAR DUSTY SKY

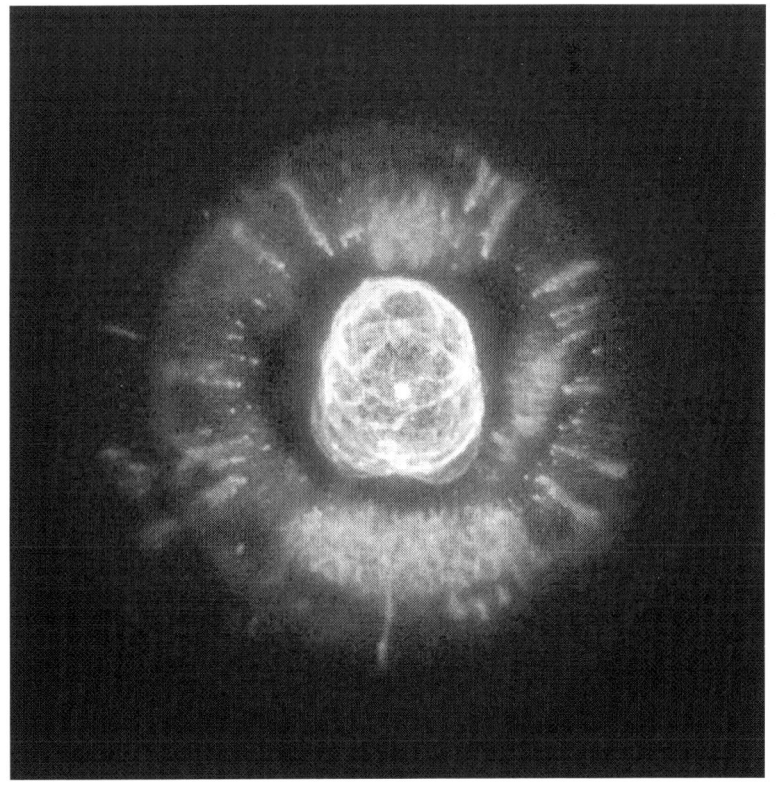

Eskimo Nebula

Credit NASA/Andrew Fruchter (STScI)

On my birthday in 2017, the Danspace Instagram feed contained a reposting of his Eskimo Nebula blog. The nebula (known as NGC 2392) was originally found by Frederick William Herschel on January 17, 1787. The

Kibbles for the Soul

XCII

Asleep we soared on bright butterfly wings.
Was I dramatizing her insect schemes
or she naïvely performing in mine?
Does birth or death awake us from the dream?

Franky Dreaming Eyes Open

XCIII

When we fall into the endless sleep
are we only restored when others weep,
or do we awake in another form?
Is it the fragments or the whole we keep?

111